Developers the world over talk about
Programming Ruby and the Ruby language...

"Ruby is a wonderfully powerful and useful language, and whenever I'm working with it, this book is at my side."

▶ **Martin Fowler**, Chief Scientist, ThoughtWorks

"If your world revolves around Java, as mine did, then you need this outstanding book to learn all the wonderful things you're missing. There's just one catch: you'll be spoiled from then on. Indeed, after reading just a few pages of *Programming Ruby*, programming in any language other than Ruby will feel like you're pushing rope."

▶ **Mike Clark**, Author and Consultant

"Ruby is smart, elegant, and fun, and it deserves a book that's smart, elegant, and fun. The first edition of *Programming Ruby* was such a book; the second edition is even better."

▶ **James Britt**, Administrator, `http://ruby-doc.org`

"The best reason to learn a new programming language is to learn to think differently. The best way to learn to think the Ruby way is to read *Programming Ruby*. Several years ago, with the first edition of this book, I did just that. Since then, I've had a constant stream of *enjoyable* Ruby programming experiences. This is due in no insignificant part to the quality of the source from which I learned the language. I'm not the only person I've heard say that every language should have a book like this."

▶ **Chad Fowler**, Codirector, Ruby Central, Inc.

"The PickAxe got me started on Ruby. It is still the first book I turn to."

▶ **Ryan Davis**, Founder, Seattle.rb

"This book changed my life. Sounds rather clichéd, but it's the truth. After six years and 300,000 lines of Java code, I needed a change. That change occurred upon reading the first edition of this book. With the support of a solid community and ever-growing foundation of superb libraries, I founded a company that largely profits from applying Ruby to solve real-world problems. Ruby is ready for prime time, and this new version of the PickAxe will show a waiting world what a gem Ruby really is."

▶ **Rich Kilmer**, President and CEO, InfoEther LLC

"The first edition of PickAxe has been a desk-side companion for years. The second edition will be an eagerly awaited replacement."

▶ **Tom Enebo**, JRuby Developer

Programming Ruby

Programming Ruby

The Pragmatic Programmers' Guide

Second Edition

Dave Thomas

with Chad Fowler
and Andy Hunt

The Pragmatic Bookshelf
Raleigh, North Carolina   Dallas, Texas

This book is a heavily revised version of the book *Programming Ruby*, originally published by Addison Wesley. This book is printed with their permission.

Our Pragmatic courses, workshops, and other products can help you and your team create better software and have more fun. For more information, as well as the latest Pragmatic titles, please visit us at

http://www.pragmaticprogrammer.com

ISBN 0-9745140-5-5

Text printed on acid-free paper.

Ninth Printing, May 2006

Version: 2006-5-4

Contents

FOREWORD TO THE FIRST EDITION   xxi

FOREWORD TO THE SECOND EDITION   xxiii

PREFACE   xxv

ROAD MAP   xxxi

PART I—FACETS OF RUBY

1 GETTING STARTED   **3**

Installing Ruby 3

Running Ruby 5

Ruby Documentation: RDoc and ri 8

2 RUBY.NEW   **11**

Ruby Is an Object-Oriented Language 11

Some Basic Ruby 13

Arrays and Hashes 16

Control Structures 18

Regular Expressions 19

Blocks and Iterators 21

Reading and 'Riting 23

Onward and Upward 24

3 CLASSES, OBJECTS, AND VARIABLES   **25**

Inheritance and Messages 27

Objects and Attributes 29

Class Variables and Class Methods 33

Access Control 37

Variables 39

4 CONTAINERS, BLOCKS, AND ITERATORS   **43**
Containers 43
Blocks and Iterators 49
Containers Everywhere 57

5 STANDARD TYPES   **59**
Numbers 59
Strings 61
Ranges 66
Regular Expressions 68

6 MORE ABOUT METHODS   **79**
Defining a Method 79
Calling a Method 81

7 EXPRESSIONS   **87**
Operator Expressions 88
Miscellaneous Expressions 89
Assignment 90
Conditional Execution 93
Case Expressions 98
Loops 100
Variable Scope, Loops, and Blocks 105

8 EXCEPTIONS, CATCH, AND THROW   **107**
The Exception Class 107
Handling Exceptions 108
Raising Exceptions 112
Catch and Throw 114

9 MODULES   **117**
Namespaces 117
Mixins 118
Iterators and the Enumerable Module 120
Composing Modules 120
Including Other Files 123

10 BASIC INPUT AND OUTPUT   **127**
What Is an IO Object? 127
Opening and Closing Files 128
Reading and Writing Files 129
Talking to Networks 133

11 THREADS AND PROCESSES   **135**
Multithreading 135
Controlling the Thread Scheduler 140
Mutual Exclusion 141
Running Multiple Processes 147

12 UNIT TESTING   **151**
Test::Unit Framework 152
Structuring Tests 156
Organizing and Running Tests 159

13 WHEN TROUBLE STRIKES   **163**
Ruby Debugger 163
Interactive Ruby 164
Editor Support 165
But It Doesn't Work! 167
But It's Too Slow! 170

PART II—RUBY IN ITS SETTING

14 RUBY AND ITS WORLD   **177**
Command-Line Arguments 177
Program Termination 180
Environment Variables 181
Where Ruby Finds Its Modules 182
Build Environment 183

15 INTERACTIVE RUBY SHELL   **185**
Command Line 185
Configuration 190
Commands 194
Restrictions 196
rtags and xmp 196

16 DOCUMENTING RUBY   **199**
Adding RDoc to Ruby Code 199
Adding RDoc to C Extensions 207
Running RDoc 211
Displaying Program Usage 212

17 PACKAGE MANAGEMENT WITH RUBYGEMS   **215**

Installing RubyGems 216
Installing Application Gems 216
Installing and Using Gem Libraries 218
Creating Your Own Gems 223

18 RUBY AND THE WEB   **235**

Writing CGI Scripts 235
Cookies 244
Improving Performance 247
Choice of Web Servers 247
SOAP and Web Services 249
More Information 253

19 RUBY TK   **255**

Simple Tk Application 255
Widgets 256
Binding Events 260
Canvas 261
Scrolling 263
Translating from Perl/Tk Documentation 265

20 RUBY AND MICROSOFT WINDOWS   **267**

Getting Ruby for Windows 267
Running Ruby Under Windows 268
Win32API 268
Windows Automation 269

21 EXTENDING RUBY   **275**

Your First Extension 275
Ruby Objects in C 278
The Jukebox Extension 284
Memory Allocation 293
Ruby Type System 294
Creating an Extension 296
Embedding a Ruby Interpreter 301
Bridging Ruby to Other Languages 304
Ruby C Language API 305

PART III—RUBY CRYSTALLIZED

22 THE RUBY LANGUAGE   **317**

Source Layout 317
The Basic Types 319
Names 328
Variables and Constants 330
     Predefined Variables 333
Expressions 338
     Boolean Expressions 341
     `if` and `unless` Expressions 343
     `case` Expressions 343
     Loop Constructs 344
Method Definition 345
Invoking a Method 348
Aliasing 351
Class Definition 352
Module Definitions 354
Access Control 356
Blocks, Closures, and Proc Objects 356
Exceptions 360
Catch and Throw 362

23 DUCK TYPING   **365**

Classes Aren't Types 366
Coding like a Duck 370
Standard Protocols and Coercions 371
Walk the Walk, Talk the Talk 377

24 CLASSES AND OBJECTS   **379**

How Classes and Objects Interact 379
Class and Module Definitions 387
Top-Level Execution Environment 393
Inheritance and Visibility 393
Freezing Objects 394

25 LOCKING RUBY IN THE SAFE   **397**

Safe Levels 398
Tainted Objects 399

26 REFLECTION, OBJECTSPACE, AND DISTRIBUTED RUBY   **403**

Looking at Objects 404
Looking at Classes 405
Calling Methods Dynamically 407
System Hooks 410
Tracing Your Program's Execution 412
Marshaling and Distributed Ruby 414
Compile Time? Runtime? Anytime! 419

PART IV—RUBY LIBRARY REFERENCE

27 BUILT-IN CLASSES AND MODULES   **423**

Alphabetical Listing 424
Array 427
Bignum 441
Binding 444
Class 445
Comparable 447
Continuation 448
Dir 449
Enumerable 454
Errno 460
Exception 461
FalseClass 464
File 465
File::Stat 477
FileTest 483
Fixnum 484
Float 487
GC 491
Hash 492
Integer 501
IO 503
Kernel 516
Marshal 535
MatchData 537
Math 540
Method 543
Module 545
NilClass 561
Numeric 562

Object 567
ObjectSpace 578
Proc 580
Process 583
Process::GID 589
Process::Status 591
Process::Sys 594
Process::UID 596
Range 597
Regexp 600
Signal 604
String 606
Struct 626
Struct::Tms 630
Symbol 631
Thread 633
ThreadGroup 640
Time 642
TrueClass 650
UnboundMethod 651

28 Standard Library 653

Abbrev 655
Base64 656
Benchmark 657
BigDecimal 658
CGI 659
CGI::Session 661
Complex 662
CSV 663
Curses 664
Date/DateTime 665
DBM 666
Delegator 667
Digest 668
DL 669
dRuby 670
English 671
Enumerator 672
erb 673
Etc 675
expect 676
Fcntl 677

FileUtils 678
Find 679
Forwardable 680
ftools 681
GDBM 682
Generator 683
GetoptLong 684
GServer 685
Iconv 686
IO/Wait 687
IPAddr 688
jcode 689
Logger 690
Mail 691
mathn 692
Matrix 694
Monitor 695
Mutex 696
Mutex_m 697
Net::FTP 698
Net::HTTP 699
Net::IMAP 701
Net::POP 702
Net::SMTP 703
Net::Telnet 704
NKF 705
Observable 706
open-uri 707
Open3 708
OpenSSL 709
OpenStruct 710
OptionParser 711
ParseDate 713
Pathname 714
PP 715
PrettyPrint 716
Profile 717
Profiler__ 718
PStore 719
PTY 720
Rational 721
readbytes 722
Readline 723

Resolv 724
REXML 725
Rinda 727
RSS 728
Scanf 729
SDBM 730
Set 731
Shellwords 732
Singleton 733
SOAP 734
Socket 735
StringIO 736
StringScanner 737
Sync 738
Syslog 740
Tempfile 741
Test::Unit 742
thread 743
ThreadsWait 744
Time 745
Timeout 746
Tk 747
tmpdir 748
Tracer 749
TSort 750
un 751
URI 752
WeakRef 753
WEBrick 754
Win32API 755
WIN32OLE 756
XMLRPC 757
YAML 758
Zlib 759

PART V—APPENDIXES

A SOCKET LIBRARY   **763**
   BasicSocket 764
   Socket 766
   IPSocket 770
   TCPSocket 771
   SOCKSSocket 772
   TCPServer 773
   UDPSocket 774
   UNIXSocket 776
   UNIXServer 777

B MKMF REFERENCE   **779**
   mkmf 779

C SUPPORT   **783**
   Web Sites 783
   Download Sites 784
   Usenet Newsgroup 784
   Mailing Lists 784

D BIBLIOGRAPHY   **787**

INDEX   **789**

SUMMARY TABLES   **824**

List of Tables

2.1	Example variable and class names	17
5.1	Character class abbreviations	72
7.1	Common comparison operators	95
11.1	Two threads in a race condition	143
13.1	Debugger commands	173
14.1	Environment variables used by Ruby	182
15.1	irb command-line options	186
17.1	Version operators	218
18.1	Command-line options for erb	243
21.1	C/Ruby data type conversion functions and macros	280
22.1	General delimited input	319
22.2	Substitutions in double-quoted strings	321
22.3	Reserved words	329
22.4	Ruby operators (high to low precedence)	339
25.1	Definition of the safe levels	401
27.1	Class Array: pack directives	435
27.2	Class File: match-mode constants	468
27.3	Class File: path separators	470
27.4	Class File: open-mode constants	472
27.5	Class File: lock-mode constants	476
27.6	Class IO: mode strings	504
27.7	Module Kernel: sprintf flag characters	531
27.8	Module Kernel: sprintf field types	532
27.9	Module Kernel: file tests with a single argument	533
27.10	Module Kernel: file tests with two arguments	533
27.11	Class Numeric: methods and subclasses	564
27.12	Class Numeric: divmod, modulo, and remainder	565
27.13	Class String: backslash sequences in substitution strings	614
27.14	Class String: unpack directives	624
27.15	Class Time: strftime directives	648
28.1	Class ERB: inline directives	674
28.2	Class OptionParser: option definitions	712

List of Figures

3.1	Variables hold object references.	41
4.1	How arrays are indexed	45
8.1	Ruby exception hierarchy	109
12.1	Roman numerals generation (with bugs)	153
12.2	Test::Unit assertions	162
13.1	Sample irb session	166
13.2	Comparing variable access costs using benchmark	171
16.1	Browse RDoc output for class counter	200
16.2	Browse RDoc output when source has comments	201
16.3	Using ri to read documentation	202
16.4	Document for class Proc generated by RDoc/ri	203
16.5	Ruby source file documented with RDoc	208
16.6	C source file documented with RDoc	210
16.7	Sample program using RDoc::usage	213
16.8	Help generated by sample program	214
17.1	MomLog package structure	232
18.1	Sample CGI Form	238
18.2	Erb processing a file with loops	245
19.1	Drawing on a Tk Canvas	262
21.1	Wrapping objects around C data types	286
21.2	Building an extension	297
22.1	State transitions for boolean range	342
24.1	A basic object, with its class and superclass	380
24.2	Adding a metaclass to Guitar	381
24.3	Adding a virtual class to an object	384
24.4	An included module and its proxy class	386
27.1	Standard exception hierarchy	462
27.2	Method#arity in action	544

Foreword to the First Edition

Man is driven to create; I know I really love to create things. And while I'm not good at painting, drawing, or music, I can write software.

Shortly after I was introduced to computers, I became interested in programming languages. I believed that an ideal programming language must be attainable, and I wanted to be the designer of it. Later, after gaining some experience, I realized that this kind of ideal, all-purpose language might be more difficult than I had thought. But I was still hoping to design a language that would work for most of the jobs I did everyday. That was my dream as a student.

Years later I talked with colleagues about scripting languages, their power and possibility. As an object-oriented fan for more than fifteen years, it seemed to me that OO programming was very suitable for scripting too. I did some research on the 'net for a while, but the candidates I found, Perl and Python, were not exactly what I was looking for. I wanted a language more powerful than Perl and more object-oriented than Python.

Then, I remembered my old dream and decided to design my own language. At first I was just toying around with it at work. But gradually it grew to be a tool good enough to replace Perl. I named it *Ruby*—after the precious red stone—and released it to the public in 1995.

Since then a lot of people have become interested in Ruby. Believe it or not, Ruby is actually more popular than Python in Japan right now. I hope that eventually it will be just as well received all over the world.

I believe that the purpose of life is, at least in part, to be happy. Based on this belief, Ruby is designed to make programming not only easy but also fun. It allows you to concentrate on the creative side of programming, with less stress. If you don't believe me, read this book and try Ruby. I'm sure you'll find out for yourself.

I'm very thankful to the people who have joined the Ruby community; they have helped me a lot. I almost feel like Ruby is one of my children, but in fact, it is the result of the combined efforts of many people. Without their help, Ruby could never have become what it is.

I am especially thankful to the authors of this book, Dave Thomas and Andy Hunt. Ruby has never been a well-documented language. Because I have always preferred writing programs over writing documents, the Ruby manuals tend to be less thorough than they should be. You had to read the source to know the exact behavior of the language. But now Dave and Andy have done the work for you.

They became interested in a lesser-known language from the Far East. They researched it, read thousands of lines of source code, wrote uncountable test scripts and e-mails, clarified the ambiguous behavior of the language, found bugs (and even fixed some of them), and finally compiled this great book. Ruby is certainly well documented now!

Their work on this book has not been trivial. While they were writing it, I was modifying the language itself. But we worked together on the updates, and this book is as accurate as possible.

It is my hope that both Ruby and this book will serve to make your programming easy and enjoyable. Have fun!

Yukihiro Matsumoto, a.k.a. *"Matz"*
まつもと ゆきひろ
Japan, October 2000

Foreword to the
Second Edition

No one in 1993 would have believed that an object-oriented language created by a Japanese amateur language designer would end up being used worldwide and that the language would become almost as popular as Perl. It was insane. I admit that. I didn't believe it either.

But it happened, far exceeding my expectations. It was caused—at least in part—by the first edition of this book. The famous Pragmatic Programmers chose a dynamic language that was virtually unknown to anyone outside of Japan and wrote a good book about it. It was just like a miracle.

That's now history. The future starts now. We have the second edition of *Programming Ruby*, which is better than the first one. It's no longer a miracle. This time, the grown-up Ruby community helped to develop the book. I just needed to sit and watch the community working together.

I really appreciate the Pragmatic Programmers, Dave Thomas and Andy Hunt, and other people from the community who helped with this book (guys, sorry for not naming you personally). I love the friendliness of the Ruby community. It's the best software community I have ever seen. I also appreciate every programmer in the world who uses Ruby.

The stone has started rolling. It will become a great mountain and fill the whole earth.

Yukihiro Matsumoto, a.k.a. *"Matz"*
まつもと ゆきひろ
Japan, August 2004

Preface

This book is the second edition of the PickAxe, as *Programming Ruby* is known to Rubyists. It is a tutorial and reference for the Ruby programming language. If you have the first edition, you'll find that this version is a significant rewrite.

When Andy and I wrote the first edition, we had to explain the background and appeal of Ruby. Among other things, we wrote "When we discovered Ruby, we realized that we'd found what we'd been looking for. More than any other language with which we have worked, Ruby *stays out of your way*. You can concentrate on solving the problem at hand, instead of struggling with compiler and language issues. That's how it can help you become a better programmer: by giving you the chance to spend your time creating solutions for your users, not for the compiler."

That belief is even stronger today. Four years later. Ruby is still our language of choice: I use it for client applications, I use it to run our publishing business, and I use it for all those little programming jobs I do just to get things running smoothly.

In those four years, Ruby has progressed nicely. A large number of methods have been added to the built-in classes and modules, and the size of the standard library (those libraries included in the Ruby distribution) has grown tremendously. The community now has a standard documentation system (RDoc), and RubyGems may well become the system of choice for packaging Ruby code for distribution.

This change has been wonderful, but it left the original PickAxe looking a tad dated. This book remedies that: like its predecessor, it is written for the very latest version of Ruby.

Ruby Versions

This version of the PickAxe documents Ruby 1.8 (and in particular covers changes incorporated into Ruby 1.8.2).[1]

---

1.   Ruby version numbering follows the same scheme used for many other open-source projects. Releases with even subversion numbers—1.6, 1.8, and so on—are stable, public releases. These are the releases that are prepackaged and made available on the various Ruby Web sites. Development versions of the software

Exactly what version of Ruby did I use to write this book? Let's ask Ruby.

```
% ruby -v
ruby 1.8.2 (2004-12-30) [powerpc-darwin7.7.0]
```

This illustrates an important point. Most of the code samples you see in this book are actually executed each time I format the book. When you see some output from a program, that output was produced by running the code and inserting the results back into the book.

Changes in the Book

Apart from the updates to support Ruby 1.8, you'll find that the book has changed somewhat from the original edition.

In the first half of the book, I've added six new chapters. *Getting Started* is a more complete introduction to getting up-and-running with Ruby than we had in the first book. The second new chapter, *Unit Testing*, reflects a growing emphasis on using testing among Rubyists. Three new chapters cover tools for the Ruby programmer: *irb* for experimenting with Ruby, *RDoc* for documenting your code, and *RubyGems* for packing code for distribution. Finally, a new chapter covers *duck typing*, that slightly slippery philosophy of programming that fits in so well with the ideas behind Ruby.

That's not all that's new. You'll also find that the chapter on threads has been extended significantly with a discussion on synchronization and that the chapter on writing Ruby extensions has been largely rewritten. The chapter on Web programming now discusses alternative templating systems and has a section on SOAP. The language reference chapter has been significantly extended (particularly when dealing with the new rules for blocks, procs, breaks, and returns).

The next quarter of the book, which documents the built-in classes and modules, has more than 250 significant changes. Many of them are new methods, some are deprecated old methods, and some are methods with significant new behavior. You'll also find a number of new modules and classes documented.

Finally, the book includes a section on the standard library. The library has grown extensively since Ruby 1.6 and is now so big that I couldn't document it to any level of detail without making the book thousands of pages long. At the same time, the Ruby Documentation project has been busy adding RDoc documentation to the library source itself. (I explain RDoc in Chapter 16 on page 199.) This means that you will increasingly be able to get accurate, up-to-date documentation on a library module

---

have odd subversion numbers, such as 1.7 and 1.9. These you'll have to download and build for yourself, as described on page 4.

using the ri utility that comes with your Ruby distribution. As a consequence of all this, I decided to change the style of the library documentation—it is now a road map to available libraries, showing code samples and describing the overall use. I'll leave the lower-level details to RDoc.

1.8 Throughout the book I've tried to mark changes between 1.6 and 1.8 using a small symbol in the margin, like the one here. One change I didn't make: I decided to continue to use the word *we* when talking about the authors in the body of the book. Many of the words there come from the first edition, and I certainly don't want to claim any credit for Andy's work on that book.

In all, this book is a significant overhaul of the first version. I hope you find it useful.

Resources

Visit the Ruby Web site http://www.ruby-lang.org to see what's new. Chat with other Ruby users on the newsgroup or mailing lists (see Appendix C).

And I'd certainly appreciate hearing from you. Comments, suggestions, errors in the text, and problems in the examples are all welcome. E-mail us at

   rubybook@pragmaticprogrammer.com

If you tell us about errors in the book, I'll add them to the errata list at

   http://www.pragmaticprogrammer.com/titles/ruby/errata.html

You'll find links to the source code for almost all the book's example code at

   http://www.pragmaticprogrammer.com/titles/ruby

Acknowledgments

For the second edition of the PickAxe, I asked on the Ruby mailing list if anyone would consider helping review the text. I was overwhelmed with the response: almost one hundred people volunteered. To keep it manageable, I had to restrict the list on a first-come basis. Even so, my wonderful reviewers produced more than 1.5Mb of review text. These folks picked on everything, from misplaced commas to missing methods. I couldn't have gotten better help. So a big "thank you" to Richard Amacker, David A. Black, Tony Bowden, James Britt, Warren Brown, Mike Clark, Ryan Davis (thanks for the Japanese PDF!), Guy Decoux, Friedrich Dominicus, Thomas Enebo, Chad Fowler, Hal Fulton, Ben Giddings, Johan Holmberg, Andrew Johnson, Rich Kilmer, Robert Klemme, Yukihiro Matsumoto, Marcel Molina Jr., Roeland Moors, Michael Neumann,

Paul Rogers, Sean Russell, Hugh Sasse, Gavin Sinclair, Tanaka Akira, Juliet Thomas, Glenn Vanderburg, Koen Vervloesem, and Austin Ziegler.

Chad Fowler wrote the chapter on RubyGems. In fact, he wrote it twice. The first time, he was on vacation in Europe. On his way home, his Powerbook was stolen, and he lost all his work. So, when he got back, he cheerfully sat down and did it all again. I can't thank him enough.

Kim Wimpsett had the unenviable job of copyediting the book. She did a tremendous job (and in record time), which was made even more amazing by both the volume of jargon in the book and by my inability to string together more than two words without breaking one or more rules of grammar. Ed Giddens did a great job creating the cover, which nicely blends the old with the new. Thanks to you both!

Finally, I'm still deeply indebted to Yukihiro "Matz" Matsumoto, the creator of Ruby. Throughout this period of growth and change, he has remained helpful, cheery, and dedicated to polishing this gem of a language. The friendly and open spirit of the Ruby community is a direct reflection of the person at its center.

Thank you all. Domo arigato gozaimasu.

Dave Thomas
THE PRAGMATIC PROGRAMMERS
http://www.pragmaticprogrammer.com

Notation Conventions

Throughout this book, we use the following typographic notations.

Literal code examples are shown using a typewriter-like font.

```
class SampleCode
  def run
    #...
  end
end
```

Within the text, Fred#do_something is a reference to an instance method (in this case do_something) of class Fred, Fred.new[2] is a class method, and Fred::EOF is a class constant. The decision to use a hash character to indicate instance methods was a tough one: it isn't valid Ruby syntax, but we thought that it was important to differentiate between the instance and class methods of a particular class. When you see us write File.read, you know we're talking about the class method read. When instead we write File#read, we're referring to the instance method read.

The book contains many snippets of Ruby code. Where possible, we've tried to show what happens when they run. In simple cases, we show the value of expressions on the same line as the expression. For example:

```
a = 1
b = 2
a + b   →   3
```

Here, you can see that the result of evaluating a + b is the value 3, shown to the right of the arrow. Note that if you simply run this program, you wouldn't see the value 3 output—you'd need to use a method such as puts to write it out.

At times, we're also interested in the values of assignment statements, in which case we'll show them.

```
a = 1   →   1
b = 2   →   2
a + b   →   3
```

If the program produces more complex output, we show it below the program code.

```
3.times { puts "Hello!" }
```

produces:

```
Hello!
Hello!
Hello!
```

---

2.   In some other Ruby documentation, you may see class methods written as Fred::new. This is perfectly valid Ruby syntax; we just happen to think that Fred.new is less distracting to read.

In some of the library documentation, we wanted to show where spaces appear in the output. You'll see these spaces as " ␣ " characters.

Command-line invocations are shown with literal text in a Roman font, and parameters you supply are shown in an *italic* font. Optional elements are shown in large square brackets.

```
ruby [ flags ... ] [ progname ] [ arguments ... ]
```

Road Map

The main text of this book has four separate parts, each with its own personality, and each addressing different aspects of the Ruby language.

In Part I, *Facets of Ruby*, you'll find a Ruby tutorial. It starts with some notes on getting Ruby running on your system followed by a short chapter on some of the terminology and concepts that are unique to Ruby. This chapter also includes enough basic syntax so that the other chapters will make sense. The rest of the tutorial is a top-down look at the language. There we talk about classes and objects, types, expressions, and all the other things that make up the language. We end with chapters on unit testing and digging yourself out when trouble strikes.

One of the great things about Ruby is how well it integrates with its environment. Part II, *Ruby in Its Setting*, investigates this. Here you'll find practical information on using Ruby: using the interpreter options, using irb, documenting your Ruby code, and packaging your Ruby gems so that others can enjoy them. You'll also find tutorials on some common Ruby tasks: using Ruby with the Web, creating GUI applications using Tk, and using Ruby in a Microsoft Windows environment (including wonderful things such as native API calls, COM integration, and Windows Automation). And you'll discover just how easy it is to extend Ruby and to embed Ruby within your own code.

Part III, *Ruby Crystallized*, contains more advanced material. Here you'll find all the gory details about the language, the concept of *duck typing*, the metaclass model, tainting, reflection, and marshaling. You could probably speed-read this the first time through, but we think you'll come back to it as you start to use Ruby in earnest.

The *Ruby Library Reference* is Part IV. It's big. We document more than 950 methods in more than 48 built-in classes and modules (up from 800 methods in 40 classes and modules in the previous edition). On top of that, we now document the library modules that are included in the standard Ruby distribution (98 of them).

So, how should you read this book? Well, depending on your level of expertise with programming in general, and OO in particular, you may initially want to read just a few portions of the book. Here are our recommendations.

If you're a beginner, you may want to start with the tutorial material in Part I. Keep the library reference close at hand as you start to write programs. Get familiar with the basic classes such as `Array`, `Hash`, and `String`. As you become more comfortable in the environment, you may want to investigate some of the more advanced topics in Part III.

If you're already comfortable with Perl, Python, Java, or Smalltalk, then we suggest reading Chapter 1 on page 3, which talks about installing and running Ruby, followed by the introduction in Chapter 2. From there, you may want to take the slower approach and keep going with the tutorial that follows, or you can skip ahead to the gritty details starting in Part III, followed by the library reference in Part IV.

Experts, gurus, and "I-don't-need-no-stinking-tutorial" types can dive straight into the language reference in Chapter 22, which begins on page 317, skim the library reference, then use the book as a (rather attractive) coffee coaster.

Of course, nothing is wrong with just starting at the beginning and working your way through page by page.

And don't forget, if you run into a problem that you can't figure out, help is available. See Appendix C, beginning on page 783, for more information.

Part I

Facets of Ruby

Chapter 1

Getting Started

Before we start talking about the Ruby language, it'd be useful if we helped you get Ruby running on your computer. That way you can try sample code and experiment on your own as you read along. We'll also show you some different ways to run Ruby.

Installing Ruby

Quite often, you won't even need to download Ruby. It now comes preinstalled on many Linux distributions, and Mac OS X includes Ruby (although the version of Ruby preinstalled on OS X is normally several minor releases behind the current Ruby version). Try typing **ruby -v** at a command prompt—you may be pleasantly surprised.

If you don't already have Ruby on your system, or if you'd like to upgrade to a newer version, you can install it pretty simply. But first, you have a choice to make: go for a binary distribution, or build Ruby from source?

Binary Distributions

A binary distribution of Ruby simply works out of the box. You install it, and it runs. Binary distributions are prebuilt for a particular operating environment and are convenient if you don't want to mess around with building Ruby from source. The downside of a binary distribution is that you have to take it as given: it may be a minor release or two behind the leading edge, and it may not have the optional libraries that you might want. If you can live with that, you'll need to find a binary distribution for your operating system and machine architecture.

For RPM-based Linux systems, you can search on http://www.rpmfind.net for a suitable Ruby RPM. Enter **ruby** as a search term, and select from the listed version numbers, architectures, and distributions. For example, ruby-1.8.2.i386 is a binary distribution of Ruby 1.8.2 for Intel x86 architectures.

◄ 3 ►

For Debian dpkg-based Linux systems, you can use the `apt-get` system to find and install Ruby. You can use the `apt-cache` command to search for Ruby packages.

```
# apt-cache search ruby interpreter
libapache-mod-ruby - Embedding Ruby in the Apache web server
liberb-ruby1.6 - Tiny eRuby for Ruby 1.6
liberb-ruby1.8 - Tiny eRuby
ruby - An interpreter of object-oriented scripting language Ruby
ruby1.7 - Interpreter of object-oriented scripting language Ruby
ruby1.8 - Interpreter of object-oriented scripting language Ruby
```

You can install any of these packages using `apt-get`.

```
# apt-get install ruby1.8
Reading Package Lists... Done
Building Dependency Tree... Done
The following extra packages will be installed:
  libruby1.8
Suggested packages:
  ruby1.8-examples
The following NEW packages will be installed:
  libruby1.8 ruby1.8
        :      :   :
```

Note that you have to have superuser access to install global packages on a Unix or Linux box, which is why we show the prompt as a #.

If you're running on Microsoft Windows, you'll find the home page of the One-Click Installer at `http://rubyinstaller.rubyforge.org`.

Building Ruby from Source

Because Ruby is an open-source project, you can download the source code to the interpreter and build it on your own system. Compared to using a binary distribution, this gives you a lot more control over where things go, and you can keep your installation totally up-to-date. The downside is that you're taking on the responsibility of managing the build and installation process. This isn't onerous, but it can be scary if you've never installed an open-source application from source.

The first thing to do is to download the source. This comes in three flavors, all from `http://www.ruby-lang.org`.

1. The stable release in *tarball* format. A tarball is an archive file, much like a *zip* file. Click the *Download Ruby* link, and then click the *stable release* link.

2. The *stable snapshot*. This is a tarball, created nightly, of the latest source code in Ruby's stable development branch. The stable branch is intended for production code and in general will be reliable. However, because the snapshot is taken daily, new features may not have received thorough testing yet—the stable tarball in item (1) will be generally more reliable.

3. The *nightly development snapshot*. This is again a tarball, created nightly. Unlike the stable code in (1) and (2), this code is leading edge, as it is taken from the head of the development branch. Expect things to be broken in here.

If you plan on downloading either of the nightly snapshots regularly, it may be easier to subscribe to the source repository directly. The sidebar on the next page gives more details.

Once you've loaded a tarball, you'll have to expand the archive into its constituent files. Use the `tar` command for this (if you don't have `tar` installed, you can try using another archiving utility, as many now support tar-format files).

```
% tar xzf snapshot.tar.gz
ruby/
ruby/bcc32/
ruby/bcc32/Makefile.sub
ruby/bcc32/README.bcc32
     :     :     :
```

This installs the Ruby source tree in the subdirectory ruby/. In that directory you'll find a file named README, which explains the installation procedure in detail. To summarize, you build Ruby on POSIX-based systems using the same four commands you use for most other open-source applications: `./configure`, `make`, `make test`, and `make install`. You can build Ruby under other environments (including Windows) by using a POSIX emulation environment such as cygwin[1] or by using native compilers—see README.win32 in the distribution's win32 subdirectory as a starting point.

Source Code from This Book

We've made the source code from this book available for download from `http://pragmaticprogrammer.com/titles/ruby/code`. Sometimes, the listings of code in the book correspond to a complete source file. Other times, the book contains just a part of the source in a file—the program file may contain additional scaffolding to make the code run.

Running Ruby

Now that Ruby is installed, you'd probably like to run some programs. Unlike compiled languages, you have two ways to run Ruby—you can type in code interactively, or you can create program files and run them. Typing in code interactively is a great way to experiment with the language, but for code that's more complex, or that you will want to run more than once, you'll need to create program files and run them.

---

1. See `http://www.cygwin.com` for details.

The Very Latest Ruby

For those who just have to be on the very latest, hot-off-the-press and *untested* cutting edge (as we were while writing this book), you can get development versions straight from the developers' working repository.

The Ruby developers use CVS (Concurrent Version System, freely available from `https://www.cvshome.org`) as their revision control system. You can check files out as an anonymous user from their archive by executing the following CVS commands:

```
% cvs -z4 -d :pserver:anonymous@cvs.ruby-lang.org:/src ↩
    login
(Logging in to anonymous@cvs.ruby-lang.org)
CVS password: ENTER
% cvs -z4 -d :pserver:anonymous@cvs.ruby-lang.org:/src ↩
    checkout ruby
```

The complete source code tree, just as the developers last left it, will now be copied to a `ruby` subdirectory on your machine.

This command will check out the head of the development tree. If you want the Ruby 1.8 branch, add `-r ruby_1_8` after the word `checkout` in the second command.

If you use the CVSup mirroring utility (conveniently available from `http://www.cvsup.org`), you can find Ruby supfiles on the `ruby-lang` site at `http://cvs.ruby-lang.org/cvsup/`.

Interactive Ruby

One way to run Ruby interactively is simply to type **ruby** at the shell prompt. Here we typed in the single `puts` expression and an end-of-file character (which is Ctrl+D on our system). This process works, but it's painful if you make a typo, and you can't really see what's going on as you type.

```
% ruby
puts "Hello, world!"
^D
Hello, world!
```

For most folks, *irb*—Interactive Ruby—is the tool of choice for executing Ruby interactively. irb is a Ruby Shell, complete with command-line history, line-editing capabilities, and job control. (In fact, it has its own chapter beginning on page 185.) You run irb from the command line. Once it starts, just type in Ruby code. It will show you the value of each expression as it evaluates it.

```
% irb
irb(main):001:0> def sum(n1, n2)
irb(main):002:1>   n1 + n2
irb(main):003:1> end
=> nil
irb(main):004:0> sum(3, 4)
=> 7
irb(main):005:0> sum("cat", "dog")
=> "catdog"
```

We recommend that you get familiar with irb so you can try some of our examples interactively.

There's a trick when you want to use irb to try our example code that's already in a file. Say, for example, you wanted to try the Fibonacci module listed on page 208. You can do this from within irb by loading in the program file and then calling the methods it contains. In this case, the program file is in code/rdoc/fib_example.rb.

```
% irb
irb(main):001:0> load "code/rdoc/fib_example.rb"
=> true
irb(main):002:0> Fibonacci.upto(20)
=> [1, 1, 2, 3, 5, 8, 13]
```

Ruby Programs

You can run a Ruby program from a file as you would any other shell script, Perl program, or Python program. Simply run the Ruby interpreter, giving it the script name as an argument.

```
% ruby myprog.rb
```

You can also use the Unix "shebang" notation as the first line of the program file.[2]

```
#!/usr/local/bin/ruby -w
puts "Hello, world!"
```

If you make this source file executable (using, for instance, chmod +x myprog.rb), Unix lets you run the file as a program.

```
% ./myprog.rb
Hello, world!
```

You can do something similar under Microsoft Windows using file associations, and you can run Ruby GUI applications by double-clicking their names in Explorer.

---

2. If your system supports it, you can avoid hard-coding the path to Ruby in the "shebang" line by using #!/usr/bin/env ruby, which will search your path for ruby and then execute it.

Ruby Documentation: RDoc and ri

As the volume of the Ruby libraries has grown, it has become impossible to document them all in one book; the standard library that comes with Ruby now contains more than 9,000 methods. Fortunately, an alternative to paper documentation exists for these methods (and classes and modules). Many are now documented internally using a system called *RDoc*.

If a source file is documented using RDoc, its documentation can be extracted and converted into HTML and ri formats.

Several sites on the Web contain a complete set of the RDoc documentation for Ruby, but http://www.ruby-doc.org is probably the best known. Browse on over, and you should be able to find at least some form of documentation for any Ruby library. They're adding new documentation all the time.

The ri tool is a local, command-line viewer for this same documentation. Most Ruby distributions now also install the resources used by the ri program.

To find the documentation for a class, type **ri *ClassName***. For example, the following lists the summary information for the GC class. (For a list of classes with ri documentation, type **ri -c**.)

```
% ri GC
---------------------------------------------------------------- Class: GC
     The GC module provides an interface to Ruby's mark and sweep
     garbage collection mechanism. Some of the underlying methods are
     also available via the ObjectSpace module.
------------------------------------------------------------------------

Class methods:
     disable, enable, start

Instance methods:
     garbage_collect
```

For information on a particular method, give its name as a parameter.

```
% ri enable
------------------------------------------------------------- GC::enable
     GC.enable     => true or false
------------------------------------------------------------------------
     Enables garbage collection, returning true if garbage collection
     was previously disabled.

        GC.disable     #=> false
        GC.enable      #=> true
        GC.enable      #=> false
```

If the method you pass to ri occurs in more than one class or module, ri will list all of the alternatives. Reissue the command, prefixing the method name with the name of the class and a dot.

```
% ri start
More than one method matched your request. You can refine
your search by asking for information on one of:

        Date#new_start, Date#start, GC::start, Logger::Application#start,
        Thread::start

% ri GC.start
-------------------------------------------------------------- GC::start
        GC.start                            => nil
        gc.garbage_collect                  => nil
        ObjectSpace.garbage_collect => nil
------------------------------------------------------------------------
        Initiates garbage collection, unless manually disabled.
```

For general help on using ri, type "ri --help". In particular you might want to experiment with the "--format" option, which tells ri how to render decorated text (such as section headings). If your terminal program supports ANSI escape sequences, using "--format ansi" will generate a nice, colorful display. Once you find a set of options you like, you can set them into the RI environment variable. Using my shell (zsh), this would be done using:

```
% export RI="--format ansi --width 70"
```

If a class or module isn't yet documented in RDoc format, ask the friendly folks over at suggestions@ruby-doc.org to consider adding it.

All this command-line hacking may seem a tad off-putting if you're not a regular visitor to the shell prompt. But, in reality, it isn't that difficult, and the power you get from being able to string together commands this way is often surprising. Stick with it, and you'll be well on your way to mastering both Ruby and your computer.

## Chapter 2

Ruby.new

When we originally designed this book, we had a grand plan (we were younger then).
We wanted to document the language from the top down, starting with classes and
objects and ending with the nitty-gritty syntax details. It seemed like a good idea at the
time. After all, most everything in Ruby is an object, so it made sense to talk about
objects first.

Or so we thought.

Unfortunately, it turns out to be difficult to describe a language that way. If you haven't
covered strings, if statements, assignments, and other details, it's difficult to write
examples of classes. Throughout our top-down description, we kept coming across
low-level details we needed to cover so that the example code would make sense.

So, we came up with another grand plan (they don't call us pragmatic for nothing).
We'd still describe Ruby starting at the top. But before we did that, we'd add a short
chapter that described all the common language features used in the examples along
with the special vocabulary used in Ruby, a kind of minitutorial to bootstrap us into the
rest of the book.

Ruby Is an Object-Oriented Language

Let's say it again. Ruby is a genuine object-oriented language. Everything you manipulate is an object, and the results of those manipulations are themselves objects. However, many languages make the same claim, and their users often have a different interpretation of what *object-oriented* means and a different terminology for the concepts
they employ.

So, before we get too far into the details, let's briefly look at the terms and notation that
we'll be using.

When you write object-oriented code, you're normally looking to model concepts from the real world in your code. Typically during this modeling process you'll discover categories of things that need to be represented in code. In a jukebox, the concept of a "song" could be such a category. In Ruby, you'd define a *class* to represent each of these entities. A class is a combination of state (for example, the name of the song) and methods that use that state (perhaps a method to play the song).

Once you have these classes, you'll typically want to create a number of *instances* of each. For the jukebox system containing a class called Song, you'd have separate instances for popular hits such as "Ruby Tuesday," "Enveloped in Python," "String of Pearls," "Small Talk," and so on. The word *object* is used interchangeably with *class instance* (and being lazy typists, we'll probably be using the word *object* more frequently).

In Ruby, these objects are created by calling a *constructor,* a special method associated with a class. The standard constructor is called new.

```
song1 = Song.new("Ruby Tuesday")
song2 = Song.new("Enveloped in Python")
# and so on
```

These instances are both derived from the same class, but they have unique characteristics. First, every object has a unique *object identifier* (abbreviated as *object ID*). Second, you can define *instance variables*, variables with values that are unique to each instance. These instance variables hold an object's state. Each of our songs, for example, will probably have an instance variable that holds the song title.

Within each class, you can define *instance methods*. Each method is a chunk of functionality that may be called from within the class and (depending on accessibility constraints) from outside the class. These instance methods in turn have access to the object's instance variables and hence to the object's state.

Methods are invoked by sending a message to an object. The message contains the method's name, along with any parameters the method may need.[1] When an object receives a message, it looks into its own class for a corresponding method. If found, that method is executed. If the method *isn't* found... well, we'll get to that later.

This business of methods and messages may sound complicated, but in practice it is very natural. Let's look at some method calls.

```
"gin joint".length   →   9
"Rick".index("c")    →   2
-1942.abs            →   1942
sam.play(song)       →   "duh dum, da dum de dum ..."
```

---

1.   This idea of expressing method calls in the form of messages comes from Smalltalk.

(Remember, in the code examples in this book, the arrows show the value of an expression. The result of executing -1942.abs is 1942. If you just typed this code into a file and ran it using Ruby, you'd see no output, because we didn't tell Ruby to display anything. If you're using irb, you'd see the values we show in the book.)

Here, the thing before the period is called the *receiver*, and the name after the period is the method to be invoked. The first example asks a string for its length, and the second asks a different string to find the index of the letter *c*. The third line has a number calculate its absolute value. Finally, we ask Sam to play us a song.

It's worth noting here a major difference between Ruby and most other languages. In (say) Java, you'd find the absolute value of some number by calling a separate function and passing in that number. You could write

```
number = Math.abs(number)      // Java code
```

In Ruby, the ability to determine an absolute value is built into numbers—they take care of the details internally. You simply send the message abs to a number object and let it do the work.

```
number = number.abs
```

The same applies to all Ruby objects: in C you'd write strlen(name), but in Ruby it's name.length, and so on. This is part of what we mean when we say that Ruby is a genuine object-oriented language.

Some Basic Ruby

Not many people like to read heaps of boring syntax rules when they're picking up a new language, so we're going to cheat. In this section we'll hit some of the highlights— the stuff you'll just *have* to know if you're going to write Ruby programs. Later, in Chapter 22, which begins on page 317, we'll go into all the gory details.

Let's start with a simple Ruby program. We'll write a method that returns a cheery, personalized greeting. We'll then invoke that method a couple of times.

```
def say_goodnight(name)
  result = "Good night, " + name
  return result
end
# Time for bed...
puts say_goodnight("John-Boy")
puts say_goodnight("Mary-Ellen")
```

As the example shows, Ruby syntax is clean. You don't need semicolons at the ends of statements as long as you put each statement on a separate line. Ruby comments start with a # character and run to the end of the line. Code layout is pretty much up to you; indentation is not significant (but using two-character indentation will make you friends in the community if you plan on distributing your code).

Methods are defined with the keyword def, followed by the method name (in this case, say_goodnight) and the method's parameters between parentheses. (In fact, the parentheses are optional, but we like to use them.) Ruby doesn't use braces to delimit the bodies of compound statements and definitions. Instead, you simply finish the body with the keyword end. Our method's body is pretty simple. The first line concatenates the literal string "Good night,␣" and the parameter name and assigns the result to the local variable result. The next line returns that result to the caller. Note that we didn't have to declare the variable result; it sprang into existence when we assigned to it.

Having defined the method, we call it twice. In both cases we pass the result to the method puts, which simply outputs its argument followed by a newline (moving on to the next line of output).

```
Good night, John-Boy
Good night, Mary-Ellen
```

The line puts say_goodnight("John-Boy") contains two method calls, one to the method say_goodnight and the other to the method puts. Why does one call have its arguments in parentheses while the other doesn't? In this case it's purely a matter of taste. The following lines are both equivalent.

```
puts say_goodnight("John-Boy")
puts(say_goodnight("John-Boy"))
```

However, life isn't always that simple, and precedence rules can make it difficult to know which argument goes with which method invocation, so we recommend using parentheses in all but the simplest cases.

This example also shows some Ruby string objects. You have many ways to create a string object, but probably the most common is to use string literals: sequences of characters between single or double quotation marks. The difference between the two forms is the amount of processing Ruby does on the string while constructing the literal. In the single-quoted case, Ruby does very little. With a few exceptions, what you type into the string literal becomes the string's value.

In the double-quoted case, Ruby does more work. First, it looks for substitutions— sequences that start with a backslash character—and replaces them with some binary value. The most common of these is \n, which is replaced with a newline character. When a string containing a newline is output, the \n forces a line break.

```
puts "And good night,\nGrandma"
```

produces:

```
And good night,
Grandma
```

The second thing that Ruby does with double-quoted strings is expression interpolation. Within the string, the sequence #{*expression*} is replaced by the value of *expression*. We could use this to rewrite our previous method.

```
def say_goodnight(name)
  result = "Good night, #{name}"
  return result
end
puts say_goodnight('Pa')
```

produces:

```
Good night, Pa
```

When Ruby constructs this string object, it looks at the current value of name and substitutes it into the string. Arbitrarily complex expressions are allowed in the #{...} construct. Here we invoke the capitalize method, defined for all strings, to output our parameter with a leading uppercase letter.

```
def say_goodnight(name)
  result = "Good night, #{name.capitalize}"
  return result
end
puts say_goodnight('uncle')
```

produces:

```
Good night, Uncle
```

As a shortcut, you don't need to supply the braces when the expression is simply a global, instance, or class variable (which we'll talk about shortly).

```
$greeting = "Hello"       # $greeting is a global variable
@name     = "Prudence"    # @name is an instance variable
puts "#$greeting, #@name"
```

produces:

```
Hello, Prudence
```

For more information on strings, as well as on the other Ruby standard types, see Chapter 5, which begins on page 59.

Finally, we could simplify this method some more. The value returned by a Ruby method is the value of the last expression evaluated, so we can get rid of the temporary variable and the return statement altogether.

```
def say_goodnight(name)
  "Good night, #{name}"
end
puts say_goodnight('Ma')
```

produces:

```
Good night, Ma
```

We promised that this section would be brief. We've got just one more topic to cover: Ruby names. For brevity, we'll be using some terms (such as *class variable*) that we aren't going to define here. However, by talking about the rules now, you'll be ahead of the game when we actually come to discuss class variables and the like later.

Ruby uses a convention to help it distinguish the usage of a name: the first characters of a name indicate how the name is used. Local variables, method parameters, and method names should all start with a lowercase letter or with an underscore. Global variables are prefixed with a dollar sign ($), and instance variables begin with an "at" sign (@). Class variables start with two "at" signs (@@). Finally, class names, module names, and constants must start with an uppercase letter. Samples of different names are given in Table 2.1 on the next page.

Following this initial character, a name can be any combination of letters, digits, and underscores (with the proviso that the character following an @ sign may not be a digit). However, by convention multiword instance variables are written with underscores between the words, and multiword class names are written in MixedCase (with each word capitalized). Method names may end with the characters ?, !, and =.

Arrays and Hashes

Ruby's arrays and hashes are indexed collections. Both store collections of objects, accessible using a key. With arrays, the key is an integer, whereas hashes support any object as a key. Both arrays and hashes grow as needed to hold new elements. It's more efficient to access array elements, but hashes provide more flexibility. Any particular array or hash can hold objects of differing types; you can have an array containing an integer, a string, and a floating-point number, as we'll see in a minute.

You can create and initialize a new array object using an *array literal*—a set of elements between square brackets. Given an array object, you can access individual elements by supplying an index between square brackets, as the next example shows. Note that Ruby array indices start at zero.

```
a = [ 1, 'cat', 3.14 ]   # array with three elements
# access the first element
a[0]   →   1
# set the third element
a[2] = nil
# dump out the array
a      →   [1, "cat", nil]
```

You may have noticed that we used the special value nil in this example. In many languages, the concept of *nil* (or *null*) means "no object." In Ruby, that's not the case; nil is an object, just like any other, that happens to represent nothing. Anyway, back to arrays and hashes.

Table 2.1. Example variable and class names

| Local | Variables | | | Constants and Class Names |
	Global	Instance	Class	
name	$debug	@name	@@total	PI
fish_and_chips	$CUSTOMER	@point_1	@@symtab	FeetPerMile
x_axis	$_	@X	@@N	String
thx1138	$plan9	@_	@@x_pos	MyClass
_26	$Global	@plan9	@@SINGLE	JazzSong

Sometimes creating arrays of words can be a pain, what with all the quotes and commas. Fortunately, Ruby has a shortcut: %w does just what we want.

```
a = [ 'ant', 'bee', 'cat', 'dog', 'elk' ]
a[0]   →   "ant"
a[3]   →   "dog"
# this is the same:
a = %w{ ant bee cat dog elk }
a[0]   →   "ant"
a[3]   →   "dog"
```

Ruby hashes are similar to arrays. A hash literal uses braces rather than square brackets. The literal must supply two objects for every entry: one for the key, the other for the value.

For example, you may want to map musical instruments to their orchestral sections. You could do this with a hash.

```
inst_section = {
  'cello'    => 'string',
  'clarinet' => 'woodwind',
  'drum'     => 'percussion',
  'oboe'     => 'woodwind',
  'trumpet'  => 'brass',
  'violin'   => 'string'
}
```

The thing to the left of the => is the key, and that on the right is the corresponding value. Keys in a particular hash must be unique—you can't have two entries for "drum." The keys and values in a hash can be arbitrary objects—you can have hashes where the values are arrays, other hashes, and so on.

Hashes are indexed using the same square bracket notation as arrays.

```
inst_section['oboe']     →   "woodwind"
inst_section['cello']    →   "string"
inst_section['bassoon']  →   nil
```

As the last example shows, a hash by default returns `nil` when indexed by a key it doesn't contain. Normally this is convenient, as `nil` means false when used in conditional expressions. Sometimes you'll want to change this default. For example, if you're using a hash to count the number of times each key occurs, it's convenient to have the default value be zero. This is easily done by specifying a default value when you create a new, empty hash.

```
histogram = Hash.new(0)
histogram['key1']   →   0
histogram['key1'] = histogram['key1'] + 1
histogram['key1']   →   1
```

Array and hash objects have lots of useful methods: see the discussion starting on page 43, and the reference sections starting on pages 427 and 492, for details.

Control Structures

Ruby has all the usual control structures, such as `if` statements and `while` loops. Java, C, and Perl programmers may well get caught by the lack of braces around the bodies of these statements. Instead, Ruby uses the keyword `end` to signify the end of a body.

```
if count > 10
   puts "Try again"
elsif tries == 3
   puts "You lose"
else
   puts "Enter a number"
end
```

Similarly, `while` statements are terminated with `end`.

```
while weight < 100 and num_pallets <= 30
   pallet = next_pallet()
   weight += pallet.weight
   num_pallets += 1
end
```

Most statements in Ruby return a value, which means you can use them as conditions. For example, the method `gets` returns the next line from the standard input stream or `nil` when end of file is reached. Because Ruby treats `nil` as a false value in conditions, you could write the following to process the lines in a file.

```
while line = gets
   puts line.downcase
end
```

Here, the assignment statement sets the variable `line` to either the next line of text or `nil`, and then the `while` statement tests the value of the assignment, terminating the loop when it is `nil`.

Ruby *statement modifiers* are a useful shortcut if the body of an `if` or `while` statement is just a single expression. Simply write the expression, followed by `if` or `while` and the condition. For example, here's a simple `if` statement.

```
if radiation > 3000
  puts "Danger, Will Robinson"
end
```

Here it is again, rewritten using a statement modifier.

```
puts "Danger, Will Robinson" if radiation > 3000
```

Similarly, a `while` loop such as

```
square = 2
while square < 1000
   square = square*square
end
```

becomes the more concise

```
square = 2
square = square*square  while square < 1000
```

These statement modifiers should seem familiar to Perl programmers.

Regular Expressions

Most of Ruby's built-in types will be familiar to all programmers. A majority of languages have strings, integers, floats, arrays, and so on. However, regular expression support is typically built into only scripting languages, such as Ruby, Perl, and awk. This is a shame: regular expressions, although cryptic, are a powerful tool for working with text. And having them built in, rather than tacked on through a library interface, makes a big difference.

Entire books have been written about regular expressions (for example, *Mastering Regular Expressions* [Fri02]), so we won't try to cover everything in this short section. Instead, we'll look at just a few examples of regular expressions in action. You'll find full coverage of regular expressions starting on page 68.

A regular expression is simply a way of specifying a *pattern* of characters to be matched in a string. In Ruby, you typically create a regular expression by writing a pattern between slash characters (*/pattern/*). And, Ruby being Ruby, regular expressions are objects and can be manipulated as such.

For example, you could write a pattern that matches a string containing the text *Perl* or the text *Python* using the following regular expression.

```
/Perl|Python/
```

The forward slashes delimit the pattern, which consists of the two things we're matching, separated by a pipe character (|). This pipe character means "either the thing on the right or the thing on the left," in this case either *Perl* or *Python*. You can use parentheses within patterns, just as you can in arithmetic expressions, so you could also have written this pattern as

```
/P(erl|ython)/
```

You can also specify *repetition* within patterns. /ab+c/ matches a string containing an *a* followed by one or more *b*'s, followed by a *c*. Change the plus to an asterisk, and /ab*c/ creates a regular expression that matches one *a*, zero or more *b*'s, and one *c*.

You can also match one of a group of characters within a pattern. Some common examples are *character classes* such as \s, which matches a whitespace character (space, tab, newline, and so on); \d, which matches any digit; and \w, which matches any character that may appear in a typical word. A dot (.) matches (almost) any character. A table of these character classes appears on page 72.

We can put all this together to produce some useful regular expressions.

```
/\d\d:\d\d:\d\d/      # a time such as 12:34:56
/Perl.*Python/        # Perl, zero or more other chars, then Python
/Perl Python/         # Perl, a space, and Python
/Perl *Python/        # Perl, zero or more spaces, and Python
/Perl +Python/        # Perl, one or more spaces, and Python
/Perl\s+Python/       # Perl, whitespace characters, then Python
/Ruby (Perl|Python)/ # Ruby, a space, and either Perl or Python
```

Once you have created a pattern, it seems a shame not to use it. The match operator =~ can be used to match a string against a regular expression. If the pattern is found in the string, =~ returns its starting position, otherwise it returns nil. This means you can use regular expressions as the condition in if and while statements. For example, the following code fragment writes a message if a string contains the text *Perl* or *Python*.

```
if line =~ /Perl|Python/
  puts "Scripting language mentioned: #{line}"
end
```

The part of a string matched by a regular expression can be replaced with different text using one of Ruby's substitution methods.

```
line.sub(/Perl/, 'Ruby')    # replace first 'Perl' with 'Ruby'
line.gsub(/Python/, 'Ruby') # replace every 'Python' with 'Ruby'
```

You can replace every occurrence of *Perl* and *Python* with *Ruby* using

```
line.gsub(/Perl|Python/, 'Ruby')
```

We'll have a lot more to say about regular expressions as we go through the book.

Blocks and Iterators

This section briefly describes one of Ruby's particular strengths. We're about to look at code blocks: chunks of code you can associate with method invocations, almost as if they were parameters. This is an incredibly powerful feature. One of our reviewers commented at this point: "This is pretty interesting and important, and so if you weren't paying attention before, you should probably start now." We'd have to agree.

You can use code blocks to implement callbacks (but they're simpler than Java's anonymous inner classes), to pass around chunks of code (but they're more flexible than C's function pointers), and to implement iterators.

Code blocks are just chunks of code between braces or between do... end.

```
{ puts "Hello" }        # this is a block
do                      ###
  club.enroll(person)   # and so is this
  person.socialize      #
end                     ###
```

Why are there two kinds of delimiter? It's partly because sometimes one feels more natural to write than another. It's partly too because they have different precedences: the braces bind more tightly than the do/end pairs. In this book, we try to follow what is becoming a Ruby standard and use braces for single-line blocks and do/end for multiline blocks.

Once you've created a block, you can associate it with a call to a method. You do this by putting the start of the block at the end of the source line containing the method call. For example, in the following code, the block containing puts "Hi" is associated with the call to the method greet.

```
greet  { puts "Hi" }
```

If the method has parameters, they appear before the block.

```
verbose_greet("Dave", "loyal customer")  { puts "Hi" }
```

A method can then invoke an associated block one or more times using the Ruby yield statement. You can think of yield as being something like a method call that calls out to the block associated with the method containing the yield.

The following example shows this in action. We define a method that calls yield twice. We then call this method, putting a block on the same line, after the call (and after any arguments to the method).[2]

---

2. Some people like to think of the association of a block with a method as a kind of parameter passing. This works on one level, but it isn't really the whole story. You may be better off thinking of the block and the method as coroutines, which transfer control back and forth between themselves.

```
def call_block
  puts "Start of method"
  yield
  yield
  puts "End of method"
end

call_block { puts "In the block" }
```

produces:

```
Start of method
In the block
In the block
End of method
```

See how the code in the block (`puts "In the block"`) is executed twice, once for each call to `yield`.

You can provide parameters to the call to `yield`: these will be passed to the block. Within the block, you list the names of the arguments to receive these parameters between vertical bars (`|`).

```
def call_block
  yield("hello", 99)
end            \      \

call_block {|str, num| ... }
```

Code blocks are used throughout the Ruby library to implement iterators: methods that return successive elements from some kind of collection, such as an array.

```
animals = %w( ant bee cat dog elk )    # create an array
animals.each {|animal| puts animal }   # iterate over the contents
```

produces:

```
ant
bee
cat
dog
elk
```

Let's look at how we could implement the Array class's each iterator that we used in the previous example. The each iterator loops through every element in the array, calling `yield` for each one. In pseudo-code, this may look like

```
# within class Array...
def each
  for each element     # <-- not valid Ruby
    yield(element)
  end
end
```

Many of the looping constructs that are built into languages such as C and Java are simply method calls in Ruby, with the methods invoking the associated block zero or more times.

```
[ 'cat', 'dog', 'horse' ].each {|name| print name, " " }
5.times {  print "*" }
3.upto(6) {|i|  print i }
('a'..'e').each {|char| print char }
```

produces:

```
cat dog horse *****3456abcde
```

Here we ask the object 5 to call a block five times and then ask the object 3 to call a block, passing in successive values until it reaches 6. Finally, the range of characters from *a* to *e* invokes a block using the method each.

Reading and 'Riting

Ruby comes with a comprehensive I/O library. However, in most of the examples in this book we'll stick to a few simple methods. We've already come across two methods that do output. puts writes its arguments, adding a newline after each. print also writes its arguments, but with no newline. Both can be used to write to any I/O object, but by default they write to standard output.

Another output method we use a lot is printf, which prints its arguments under the control of a format string (just like printf in C or Perl).

```
printf("Number: %5.2f,\nString: %s\n", 1.23, "hello")
```

produces:

```
Number:  1.23,
String: hello
```

In this example, the format string "Number: %5.2f,\nString: %s\n" tells printf to substitute in a floating-point number (allowing five characters in total, with two after the decimal point) and a string. Notice the newlines (\n) embedded in the string; each moves the output onto the next line.

You have many ways to read input into your program. Probably the most traditional is to use the routine gets, which returns the next line from your program's standard input stream.

```
line = gets
print line
```

Ruby Escapes Its Past

In the old days Ruby borrowed a lot from the Perl language. One of these features is a certain "magic" when it comes to global variables, and probably no global is more magical than $_. For example, the `gets` method has a side effect: as well as returning the line just read, it also stores it into $_. If you call `print` with no argument, it prints the contents of $_. If you write an `if` or `while` statement with just a regular expression as the condition, that expression is matched against $_. As a result of all this magic, you could write the following program to look for all lines in a file containing the text *Ruby*.

```
while gets
  if /Ruby/
    print
  end
end
```

However, this style of Ruby programming is rapidly falling out of fashion with purists. As one of these purists happens to be Matz, you'll now find that Ruby issues warnings for many of these special uses: expect to see these features go away in the future.

That doesn't mean you have to write more verbose programs. The "Ruby way" to write this would be to use an iterator and the predefined object `ARGF`, which represents the program's input files.

```
ARGF.each {|line|  print line  if line =~ /Ruby/ }
```

You could write it even more concisely.

```
print ARGF.grep(/Ruby/)
```

In general, there's a move away from some of the Perlisms in the Ruby community. If you run your programs with the -w flag to enable warnings (you *do* run with warnings enabled, don't you?), you'll find the Ruby interpreter catches most of them.

Onward and Upward

That's it. We've finished our lightning-fast tour of some of the basic features of Ruby. We've had a look at objects, methods, strings, containers, and regular expressions, seen some simple control structures, and looked at some rather nifty iterators. We hope this chapter has given you enough ammunition to be able to attack the rest of this book.

Time to move on, and up—up to a higher level. Next, we'll be looking at classes and objects, things that are at the same time both the highest-level constructs in Ruby and the essential underpinnings of the entire language.

## Chapter 3

Classes, Objects, and Variables

From the examples we've shown so far, you may be wondering about our earlier assertion that Ruby is an object-oriented language. Well, this chapter is where we justify that claim. We're going to be looking at how you create classes and objects in Ruby and at some of the ways in which Ruby is more powerful than most object-oriented languages. Along the way, we'll be implementing part of our next billion-dollar product, the Internet Enabled Jazz and Bluegrass jukebox.

After months of work, our highly paid Research and Development folks have determined that our jukebox needs *songs*. So it seems like a good idea to start by setting up a Ruby class that represents things that are songs. We know that a real song has a name, an artist, and a duration, so we'll want to make sure that the song objects in our program do, too.

We'll start by creating the basic class Song,[1] which contains just a single method, initialize.

```
class Song
  def initialize(name, artist, duration)
    @name     = name
    @artist   = artist
    @duration = duration
  end
end
```

initialize is a special method in Ruby programs. When you call Song.new to create a new Song object, Ruby allocates some memory to hold an uninitialized object and

---

1. As we mentioned on page 16, class names start with an uppercase letter, and method names normally start with a lowercase letter.

then calls that object's `initialize` method, passing in any parameters that were passed to new. This gives you a chance to write code that sets up your object's state.

For class Song, the `initialize` method takes three parameters. These parameters act just like local variables within the method, so they follow the local variable naming convention of starting with a lowercase letter.

Each object represents its own song, so we need each of our Song objects to carry around its own song name, artist, and duration. This means we need to store these values as *instance variables* within the object. Instance variables are accessible to all the methods in an object, and each object has its own copy of its instance variables.

In Ruby, an instance variable is simply a name preceded by an "at" sign (@). In our example, the parameter name is assigned to the instance variable @name, artist is assigned to @artist, and duration (the length of the song in seconds) is assigned to @duration.

Let's test our spiffy new class.

```
song = Song.new("Bicyclops", "Fleck", 260)
song.inspect   →   #<Song:0x1c8ac8 @duration=260, @artist="Fleck",
                   @name="Bicyclops">
```

Well, it seems to work. By default, the `inspect` message, which can be sent to any object, formats the object's ID and instance variables. It looks as though we have them set up correctly.

Our experience tells us that during development we'll be printing out the contents of a Song object many times, and `inspect`'s default formatting leaves something to be desired. Fortunately, Ruby has a standard message, `to_s`, that it sends to any object it wants to render as a string. Let's try it on our song.

```
song = Song.new("Bicylops", "Fleck", 260)
song.to_s   →   "#<Song:0x1c8ce4>"
```

That wasn't too useful—it just reported the object ID. So, let's override `to_s` in our class. As we do this, we should also take a moment to talk about how we're showing the class definitions in this book.

In Ruby, classes are never closed: you can always add methods to an existing class. This applies to the classes you write as well as the standard, built-in classes. Just open a class definition for an existing class, and the new contents you specify will be added to whatever's there.

This is great for our purposes. As we go through this chapter, adding features to our classes, we'll show just the class definitions for the new methods; the old ones will still be there. It saves us having to repeat redundant stuff in each example. Obviously, though, if you were creating this code from scratch, you'd probably just throw all the methods into a single class definition.

Enough detail! Let's get back to adding a to_s method to our Song class. We'll use the # character in the string to interpolate the value of the three instance variables.

```
class Song
  def to_s
    "Song: #@name--#@artist (#@duration)"
  end
end
song = Song.new("Bicyclops", "Fleck", 260)
song.to_s   →   "Song: Bicyclops--Fleck (260)"
```

Excellent, we're making progress. However, we've slipped something subtle into the mix. We said that Ruby supports to_s for all objects, but we didn't say how. The answer has to do with inheritance, subclassing, and how Ruby determines what method to run when you send a message to an object. This is a subject for a new section, so....

Inheritance and Messages

Inheritance allows you to create a class that is a refinement or specialization of another class. For example, our jukebox has the concept of songs, which we encapsulate in class Song. Then marketing comes along and tells us that we need to provide karaoke support. A karaoke song is just like any other (it doesn't have a vocal track, but that doesn't concern us). However, it also has an associated set of lyrics, along with timing information. When our jukebox plays a karaoke song, the lyrics should flow across the screen on the front of the jukebox in time with the music.

An approach to this problem is to define a new class, KaraokeSong, that is just like Song but with a lyric track.

```
class KaraokeSong < Song
  def initialize(name, artist, duration, lyrics)
    super(name, artist, duration)
    @lyrics = lyrics
  end
end
```

The "< Song" on the class definition line tells Ruby that a KaraokeSong is a *subclass* of Song. (Not surprisingly, this means that Song is a *superclass* of KaraokeSong. People also talk about parent-child relationships, so KaraokeSong's parent would be Song.) For now, don't worry too much about the initialize method; we'll talk about that super call later.

Let's create a KaraokeSong and check that our code worked. (In the final system, the lyrics will be held in an object that includes the text and timing information.) To test our class, though, we'll just use a string. This is another benefit of dynamically typed languages—we don't have to define everything before we start running code.

```
song = KaraokeSong.new("My Way", "Sinatra", 225, "And now, the...")
song.to_s   →   "Song: My Way--Sinatra (225)"
```

Well, it ran. But why doesn't the to_s method show the lyric?

The answer has to do with the way Ruby determines which method should be called when you send a message to an object. During the initial parsing of the program source, when Ruby comes across the method invocation song.to_s, it doesn't actually know where to find the method to_s. Instead, it defers the decision until the program is run. At that time, it looks at the class of song. If that class implements a method with the same name as the message, that method is run. Otherwise, Ruby looks for a method in the parent class, and then in the grandparent, and so on up the ancestor chain. If it runs out of ancestors without finding the appropriate method, it takes a special action that normally results in an error being raised.[2]

Back to our example. We sent the message to_s to song, an object of class Karaoke-Song. Ruby looks in KaraokeSong for a method called to_s but doesn't find it. The interpreter then looks in KaraokeSong's parent, class Song, and there it finds the to_s method that we defined on page 26. That's why it prints out the song details but not the lyrics—class Song doesn't know anything about lyrics.

Let's fix this by implementing KaraokeSong#to_s. You have a number of ways to do this. Let's start with a bad way. We'll copy the to_s method from Song and add on the lyric.

```
class KaraokeSong
  # ...
  def to_s
    "KS: #@name--#@artist (#@duration) [#@lyrics]"
  end
end
song = KaraokeSong.new("My Way", "Sinatra", 225, "And now, the...")
song.to_s   →   "KS: My Way--Sinatra (225) [And now, the...]"
```

We're correctly displaying the value of the @lyrics instance variable. To do this, the subclass directly accesses the instance variables of its ancestors. So why is this a bad way to implement to_s?

The answer has to do with good programming style (and something called *decoupling*). By poking around inside our parent's internal structure, and explicitly examining its instance variables, we're tying ourselves tightly to its implementation. Say we decided to change Song to store the duration in milliseconds. Suddenly, KaraokeSong would start reporting ridiculous values. The idea of a karaoke version of "My Way" that lasts for 3,750 minutes is just too frightening to consider.

---

2.   In fact, you can intercept this error, which allows you to fake out methods at runtime. This is described under Object#method_missing on page 572.

We get around this problem by having each class handle its own implementation details. When KaraokeSong#to_s is called, we'll have it call its parent's to_s method to get the song details. It will then append to this the lyric information and return the result. The trick here is the Ruby keyword super. When you invoke super with no arguments, Ruby sends a message to the parent of the current object, asking it to invoke a method of the same name as the method invoking super. It passes this method the parameters that were passed to the originally invoked method. Now we can implement our new and improved to_s.

```
class KaraokeSong < Song
  # Format ourselves as a string by appending
  # our lyrics to our parent's #to_s value.
  def to_s
    super + " [#@lyrics]"
  end
end
song = KaraokeSong.new("My Way", "Sinatra", 225, "And now, the...")
song.to_s    →    "Song: My Way--Sinatra (225) [And now, the...]"
```

We explicitly told Ruby that KaraokeSong was a subclass of Song, but we didn't specify a parent class for Song itself. If you don't specify a parent when defining a class, Ruby supplies class Object as a default. This means that all objects have Object as an ancestor and that Object's instance methods are available to every object in Ruby. Back on page 26 we said that to_s is available to all objects. Now we know why; to_s is one of more than 35 instance methods in class Object. The complete list begins on page 567.

So far in this chapter we've been looking at classes and their methods. Now it's time to move on to the objects, such as the instances of class Song.

Objects and Attributes

The Song objects we've created so far have an internal state (such as the song title and artist). That state is private to those objects—no other object can access an object's instance variables. In general, this is a Good Thing. It means that the object is solely responsible for maintaining its own consistency.

However, an object that is totally secretive is pretty useless—you can create it, but then you can't do anything with it. You'll normally define methods that let you access and manipulate the state of an object, allowing the outside world to interact with the object. These externally visible facets of an object are called its *attributes*.

For our Song objects, the first thing we may need is the ability to find out the title and artist (so we can display them while the song is playing) and the duration (so we can display some kind of progress bar).

Inheritance and Mixins

Some object-oriented languages (such as C++) support multiple inheritance, where a class can have more than one immediate parent, inheriting functionality from each. Although powerful, this technique can be dangerous, as the inheritance hierarchy can become ambiguous.

Other languages, such as Java and C#, support single inheritance. Here, a class can have only one immediate parent. Although cleaner (and easier to implement), single inheritance also has drawbacks—in the real world objects often inherit attributes from multiple sources (a ball is both a *bouncing thing* and a *spherical thing*, for example).

Ruby offers an interesting and powerful compromise, giving you the simplicity of single inheritance and the power of multiple inheritance. A Ruby class has only one direct parent, so Ruby is a single-inheritance language. However, Ruby classes can include the functionality of any number of *mixins* (a mixin is like a partial class definition). This provides a controlled multiple-inheritance-like capability with none of the drawbacks. We'll explore mixins more beginning on page 118.

```
class Song
  def name
    @name
  end
  def artist
    @artist
  end
  def duration
    @duration·
  end
end
song = Song.new("Bicyclops", "Fleck", 260)
song.artist    →    "Fleck"
song.name      →    "Bicyclops"
song.duration  →    260
```

Here we've defined three accessor methods to return the values of the three instance variables. The method name(), for example, returns the value of the instance variable @name. Because this is such a common idiom, Ruby provides a convenient shortcut: attr_reader creates these accessor methods for you.

```
class Song
  attr_reader :name, :artist, :duration
end
```

```
song = Song.new("Bicyclops", "Fleck", 260)
song.artist    →    "Fleck"
song.name      →    "Bicyclops"
song.duration  →    260
```

This example has introduced something new. The construct :artist is an expression that returns a Symbol object corresponding to artist. You can think of :artist as meaning the *name* of the variable artist, and plain artist as meaning the *value* of the variable. In this example, we named the accessor methods name, artist, and duration. The corresponding instance variables, @name, @artist, and @duration, will be created automatically. These accessor methods are identical to the ones we wrote by hand earlier.

Writable Attributes

Sometimes you need to be able to set an attribute from outside the object. For example, let's assume that the duration that is initially associated with a song is an estimate (perhaps gathered from information on a CD or in the MP3 data). The first time we play the song, we get to find out how long it actually is, and we store this new value back in the Song object.

In languages such as C++ and Java, you'd do this with *setter functions*.

```
class JavaSong {                        // Java code
  private Duration _duration;
  public void setDuration(Duration newDuration) {
    _duration = newDuration;
  }
}
s = new JavaSong(....);
s.setDuration(length);
```

In Ruby, the attributes of an object can be accessed as if they were any other variable. We've seen this above with phrases such as song.name. So, it seems natural to be able to assign to these variables when you want to set the value of an attribute. In Ruby you do that by creating a method whose name ends with an equals sign. These methods can be used as the target of assignments.

```
class Song
  def duration=(new_duration)
    @duration = new_duration
  end
end
song = Song.new("Bicyclops", "Fleck", 260)
song.duration  →    260
song.duration = 257   # set attribute with updated value
song.duration  →    257
```

The assignment song.duration = 257 invokes the method duration= in the song object, passing it 257 as an argument. In fact, defining a method name ending in an equals sign makes that name eligible to appear on the left side of an assignment.

Again, Ruby provides a shortcut for creating these simple attribute-setting methods.

```
class Song
  attr_writer :duration
end
song = Song.new("Bicyclops", "Fleck", 260)
song.duration = 257
```

Virtual Attributes

These attribute-accessing methods do not have to be just simple wrappers around an object's instance variables. For example, you may want to access the duration in minutes and fractions of a minute, rather than in seconds as we've been doing.

```
class Song
  def duration_in_minutes
    @duration/60.0   # force floating point
  end
  def duration_in_minutes=(new_duration)
    @duration = (new_duration*60).to_i
  end
end
song = Song.new("Bicyclops", "Fleck", 260)
song.duration_in_minutes   →   4.33333333333333
song.duration_in_minutes = 4.2
song.duration              →   252
```

Here we've used attribute methods to create a virtual instance variable. To the outside world, duration_in_minutes seems to be an attribute like any other. Internally, though, it has no corresponding instance variable.

This is more than a curiosity. In his landmark book *Object-Oriented Software Construction* [Mey97], Bertrand Meyer calls this the *Uniform Access Principle*. By hiding the difference between instance variables and calculated values, you are shielding the rest of the world from the implementation of your class. You're free to change how things work in the future without impacting the millions of lines of code that use your class. This is a big win.

Attributes, Instance Variables, and Methods

This description of attributes may leave you thinking that they're nothing more than methods—why'd we need to invent a fancy name for them? In a way, that's absolutely right. An attribute *is* just a method. Sometimes an attribute simply returns the value of an instance variable. Sometimes an attribute returns the result of a calculation. And sometimes those funky methods with equals signs at the end of their names are used to update the state of an object. So the question is, where do attributes stop and regular methods begin? What makes something an attribute, and not just a plain old method? Ultimately, that's one of those "angels on a pinhead" questions. Here's a personal take.

When you design a class, you decide what internal state it has and also decide how that state is to appear on the outside (to users of your class). The internal state is held in instance variables. The external state is exposed through methods we're calling *attributes*. And the other actions your class can perform are just regular methods. It really isn't a crucially important distinction, but by calling the external state of an object its *attributes*, you're helping clue people in to how they should view the class you've written.

Class Variables and Class Methods

So far, all the classes we've created have contained instance variables and instance methods: variables that are associated with a particular instance of the class, and methods that work on those variables. Sometimes classes themselves need to have their own states. This is where class variables come in.

Class Variables

A class variable is shared among all objects of a class, and it is also accessible to the class methods that we'll describe later. Only one copy of a particular class variable exists for a given class. Class variable names start with two "at" signs, such as @@count. Unlike global and instance variables, class variables must be initialized before they are used. Often this initialization is just a simple assignment in the body of the class definition.

For example, our jukebox may want to record how many times each song has been played. This count would probably be an instance variable of the Song object. When a song is played, the value in the instance is incremented. But say we also want to know how many songs have been played in total. We could do this by searching for all the Song objects and adding their counts, or we could risk excommunication from the Church of Good Design and use a global variable. Instead, we'll use a class variable.

```
class Song
  @@plays = 0
  def initialize(name, artist, duration)
    @name     = name
    @artist   = artist
    @duration = duration
    @plays    = 0
  end
```

```
    def play
      @plays  += 1   # same as @plays = @plays + 1
      @@plays += 1
      "This  song: #@plays plays. Total #@@plays plays."
    end
  end
```

For debugging purposes, we've arranged for Song#play to return a string containing the number of times this song has been played, along with the total number of plays for all songs. We can test this easily.

```
  s1 = Song.new("Song1", "Artist1", 234)  # test songs..
  s2 = Song.new("Song2", "Artist2", 345)
  s1.play  →   "This  song: 1 plays. Total 1 plays."
  s2.play  →   "This  song: 1 plays. Total 2 plays."
  s1.play  →   "This  song: 2 plays. Total 3 plays."
  s1.play  →   "This  song: 3 plays. Total 4 plays."
```

Class variables are private to a class and its instances. If you want to make them accessible to the outside world, you'll need to write an accessor method. This method could be either an instance method or, leading us neatly to the next section, a class method.

Class Methods

Sometimes a class needs to provide methods that work without being tied to any particular object. We've already come across one such method. The new method creates a new Song object but is not itself associated with a particular song.

```
  song = Song.new(....)
```

You'll find class methods sprinkled throughout the Ruby libraries. For example, objects of class File represent open files in the underlying file system. However, class File also provides several class methods for manipulating files that aren't open and therefore don't have a File object. If you want to delete a file, you call the class method File.delete, passing in the name.

```
  File.delete("doomed.txt")
```

Class methods are distinguished from instance methods by their definition; class methods are defined by placing the class name and a period in front of the method name (but also see the sidebar on page 36).

```
  class Example
    def instance_method          # instance method
    end
    def Example.class_method      # class method
    end
  end
```

Jukeboxes charge money for each song played, not by the minute. That makes short songs more profitable than long ones. We may want to prevent songs that take too long from being available on the SongList. We could define a class method in SongList that checked to see if a particular song exceeded the limit. We'll set this limit using a class constant, which is simply a constant (remember constants? They start with an uppercase letter) that is initialized in the class body.

```
class SongList
  MAX_TIME = 5*60              #  5 minutes

  def SongList.is_too_long(song)
    return song.duration > MAX_TIME
  end
end
song1 = Song.new("Bicyclops", "Fleck", 260)
SongList.is_too_long(song1)   →   false
song2 = Song.new("The Calling", "Santana", 468)
SongList.is_too_long(song2)   →   true
```

Singletons and Other Constructors

Sometimes you want to override the default way in which Ruby creates objects. As an example, let's look at our jukebox. Because we'll have many jukeboxes, spread all over the country, we want to make maintenance as easy as possible. Part of the requirement is to log everything that happens to a jukebox: the songs played, the money received, the strange fluids poured into it, and so on. Because we want to reserve the network bandwidth for music, we'll store these log files locally. This means we'll need a class that handles logging. However, we want only one logging object per jukebox, and we want that object to be shared among all the other objects that use it.

Enter the Singleton pattern, documented in *Design Patterns* [GHJV95]. We'll arrange things so that the only way to create a logging object is to call MyLogger.create, and we'll ensure that only one logging object is ever created.

```
class MyLogger
  private_class_method :new
  @@logger = nil
  def MyLogger.create
    @@logger = new unless @@logger
    @@logger
  end
end
```

By making MyLogger's new method private, we prevent anyone from creating a logging object using the conventional constructor. Instead, we provide a class method, MyLogger.create. This method uses the class variable @@logger to keep a reference

Class Method Definitions

Back on page 34 we said that class methods are defined by putting the class name and a period in front of the method name. That was actually a simplification (but one that works all the time).

In fact, you can define class methods in a number of ways, but understanding *why* those ways work will have to wait until Chapter 24. For now, we'll just show you the idioms that people use, in case you come across them in Ruby code.

The following all define class methods within class Demo.

```
class Demo
  def Demo.meth1
    # ...
  end
  def self.meth2
    # ...
  end
  class <<self
    def meth3
      # ...
    end
  end
end
```

to a single instance of the logger, returning that instance every time it is called.[3] We can check this by looking at the object identifiers the method returns.

```
MyLogger.create.object_id   →   946790
MyLogger.create.object_id   →   946790
```

Using class methods as pseudo-constructors can also make life easier for users of your class. As a trivial example, let's look at a class Shape that represents a regular polygon. Instances of Shape are created by giving the constructor the required number of sides and the total perimeter.

```
class Shape
  def initialize(num_sides, perimeter)
    # ...
  end
end
```

---

3. The implementation of singletons that we present here is not thread-safe; if multiple threads were running, it would be possible to create multiple logger objects. Rather than add thread safety ourselves, however, we'd probably use the Singleton mixin supplied with Ruby, which is described on page 733.

However, a couple of years later, this class is used in a different application, where the programmers are used to creating shapes by name and by specifying the length of one side, not the perimeter. Simply add some class methods to Shape.

```ruby
class Shape
  def Shape.triangle(side_length)
    Shape.new(3, side_length*3)
  end
  def Shape.square(side_length)
    Shape.new(4, side_length*4)
  end
end
```

Class methods have many interesting and powerful uses, but exploring them won't get our jukebox finished any sooner, so let's move on.

Access Control

When designing a class interface, it's important to consider just how much access to your class you'll be exposing to the outside world. Allow too much access into your class, and you risk increasing the coupling in your application—users of your class will be tempted to rely on details of your class's implementation, rather than on its logical interface. The good news is that the only easy way to change an object's state in Ruby is by calling one of its methods. Control access to the methods, and you've controlled access to the object. A good rule of thumb is never to expose methods that could leave an object in an invalid state. Ruby gives you three levels of protection.

- **Public methods** can be called by anyone—no access control is enforced. Methods are public by default (except for `initialize`, which is always private).

- **Protected methods** can be invoked only by objects of the defining class and its subclasses. Access is kept within the family.

- **Private methods** cannot be called with an explicit receiver—the receiver is always *self*. This means that private methods can be called only in the context of the current object; you can't invoke another object's private methods.

The difference between "protected" and "private" is fairly subtle and is different in Ruby than most common OO languages. If a method is protected, it may be called by *any* instance of the defining class or its subclasses. If a method is private, it may be called only within the context of the calling object—it is never possible to access another object's private methods directly, even if the object is of the same class as the caller.

Ruby differs from other OO languages in another important way. Access control is determined dynamically, as the program runs, not statically. You will get an access violation only when the code attempts to execute the restricted method.

Specifying Access Control

You specify access levels to methods within class or module definitions using one or more of the three functions public, protected, and private. You can use each function in two different ways.

If used with no arguments, the three functions set the default access control of subsequently defined methods. This is probably familiar behavior if you're a C++ or Java programmer, where you'd use keywords such as public to achieve the same effect.

```
class MyClass
    def method1      # default is 'public'
      #...
    end
  protected          # subsequent methods will be 'protected'
    def method2      # will be 'protected'
      #...
    end
  private            # subsequent methods will be 'private'
    def method3      # will be 'private'
      #...
    end
  public             # subsequent methods will be 'public'
    def method4      # and this will be 'public'
      #...
    end
end
```

Alternatively, you can set access levels of named methods by listing them as arguments to the access control functions.

```
class MyClass
  def method1
  end
  # ... and so on
  public    :method1, :method4
  protected :method2
  private   :method3
end
```

It's time for some examples. Perhaps we're modeling an accounting system where every debit has a corresponding credit. Because we want to ensure that no one can break this rule, we'll make the methods that do the debits and credits private, and we'll define our external interface in terms of transactions.

```ruby
class Accounts
    def initialize(checking, savings)
      @checking = checking
      @savings  = savings
    end
  private
    def debit(account, amount)
      account.balance -= amount
    end
    def credit(account, amount)
      account.balance += amount
    end
  public
    #...
    def transfer_to_savings(amount)
      debit(@checking, amount)
      credit(@savings, amount)
    end
    #...
  end
```

Protected access is used when objects need to access the internal state of other objects of the same class. For example, we may want to allow individual Account objects to compare their cleared balances but may want to hide those balances from the rest of the world (perhaps because we present them in a different form).

```ruby
class Account
  attr_reader :cleared_balance  # accessor method 'cleared_balance'
  protected :cleared_balance     # and make it protected
  def greater_balance_than(other)
    return @cleared_balance > other.cleared_balance
  end
end
```

Because cleared_balance is protected, it's available only within Account objects.

Variables

Now that we've gone to the trouble to create all these objects, let's make sure we don't lose them. Variables are used to keep track of objects; each variable holds a reference to an object.

Let's confirm this with some code.

```ruby
person = "Tim"
person.object_id   →   938678
person.class       →   String
person             →   "Tim"
```

On the first line, Ruby creates a new `String` object with the value "Tim." A reference to this object is placed in the local variable `person`. A quick check shows that the variable has indeed taken on the personality of a string, with an object ID, a class, and a value.

So, is a variable an object? In Ruby, the answer is "no." A variable is simply a reference to an object. Objects float around in a big pool somewhere (the heap, most of the time) and are pointed to by variables.

Let's make the example slightly more complicated.

```
person1 = "Tim"
person2 = person1

person1[0] = 'J'

person1    →    "Jim"
person2    →    "Jim"
```

What happened here? We changed the first character of `person1`, but both `person1` and `person2` changed from "Tim" to "Jim."

It all comes back to the fact that variables hold references to objects, not the objects themselves. The assignment of `person1` to `person2` doesn't create any new objects; it simply copies `person1`'s object reference to `person2` so that both `person1` and `person2` refer to the same object. We show this in Figure 3.1 on the facing page.

Assignment *aliases* objects, potentially giving you multiple variables that reference the same object. But can't this cause problems in your code? It can, but not as often as you'd think (objects in Java, for example, work exactly the same way). For instance, in the example in Figure 3.1, you could avoid aliasing by using the `dup` method of `String`, which creates a new `String` object with identical contents.

```
person1 = "Tim"
person2 = person1.dup
person1[0] = "J"
person1    →    "Jim"
person2    →    "Tim"
```

You can also prevent anyone from changing a particular object by freezing it (we talk more about freezing objects on page 394). Attempt to alter a frozen object, and Ruby will raise a `TypeError` exception.

```
person1 = "Tim"
person2 = person1
person1.freeze       # prevent modifications to the object
person2[0] = "J"
```

produces:

```
prog.rb:4:in `[]=': can't modify frozen string (TypeError)
        from prog.rb:4
```

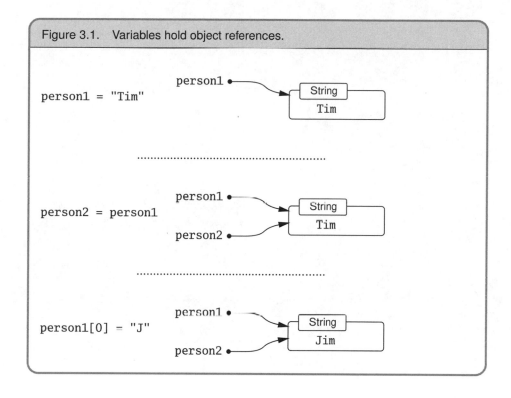

Figure 3.1. Variables hold object references.

That concludes our look at classes and objects in Ruby. This material is important; everything you manipulate in Ruby is an object. And one of the most common things we do with objects is create collections of them. But that's the subject of our next chapter.

## Chapter 4

Containers, Blocks, and Iterators

A jukebox with one song is unlikely to be popular (except perhaps in some very, very scary bars), so pretty soon we'll have to start thinking about producing a catalog of available songs and a playlist of songs waiting to be played. Both of these are *containers:* objects that hold references to one or more other objects.

Both the catalog and the playlist need a similar set of methods: add a song, remove a song, return a list of songs, and so on. The playlist may perform additional tasks, such as inserting advertising every so often or keeping track of cumulative play time, but we'll worry about these things later. In the meantime, it seems like a good idea to develop some kind of generic SongList class, which we can specialize into catalogs and playlists.

Containers

Before we start implementing, we'll need to work out how to store the list of songs inside a SongList object. We have three obvious choices. We could use the Ruby Array type, use the Ruby Hash type, or create our own list structure. Being lazy, for now we'll look at arrays and hashes and choose one of these for our class.

Arrays

The class Array holds a collection of object references. Each object reference occupies a position in the array, identified by a non-negative integer index.

You can create arrays by using literals or by explicitly creating an Array object. A literal array is simply a list of objects between square brackets.

```
a = [ 3.14159, "pie", 99 ]
a.class    →    Array
a.length   →    3
a[0]       →    3.14159
a[1]       →    "pie"
a[2]       →    99
a[3]       →    nil

b = Array.new
b.class    →    Array
b.length   →    0
b[0] = "second"
b[1] = "array"
b          →    ["second", "array"]
```

Arrays are indexed using the [ ] operator. As with most Ruby operators, this is actually a method (an instance method of class Array) and hence can be overridden in subclasses. As the example shows, array indices start at zero. Index an array with a non-negative integer, and it returns the object at that position or returns nil if nothing is there. Index an array with a negative integer, and it counts from the end.

```
a = [ 1, 3, 5, 7, 9 ]
a[-1]     →    9
a[-2]     →    7
a[-99]    →    nil
```

This indexing scheme is illustrated in more detail in Figure 4.1 on the facing page.

You can also index arrays with a pair of numbers, [start, count]. This returns a new array consisting of references to count objects starting at position start.

```
a = [ 1, 3, 5, 7, 9 ]
a[1, 3]    →    [3, 5, 7]
a[3, 1]    →    [7]
a[-3, 2]   →    [5, 7]
```

Finally, you can index arrays using ranges, in which start and end positions are separated by two or three periods. The two-period form includes the end position, and the three-period form does not.

```
a = [ 1, 3, 5, 7, 9 ]
a[1..3]    →    [3, 5, 7]
a[1...3]   →    [3, 5]
a[3..3]    →    [7]
a[-3..-1]  →    [5, 7, 9]
```

The [ ] operator has a corresponding [ ]= operator, which lets you set elements in the array. If used with a single integer index, the element at that position is replaced by whatever is on the right side of the assignment. Any gaps that result will be filled with nil.

```
┌─────────────────────────────────────────────────────────────────────┐
│  Figure 4.1.  How arrays are indexed                                  │
├─────────────────────────────────────────────────────────────────────┤
```

Figure 4.1. How arrays are indexed

Positive →   0   1   2   3   4   5   6   Negative
indices   −7   −6   −5   −4   −3   −2   −1   ← indices
    a = ["ant" | "bat" | "cat" | "dog" | "elk" | "fly" | "gnu"]

a[2] →   ["cat"]

a[-3] →   ["elk"]

a[1..3] →   ["bat" | "cat" | "dog"]

a[-3..-1] →   ["elk" | "fly" | "gnu"]

a[4..-2] →   ["elk" | "fly"]

```
a = [ 1, 3, 5, 7, 9 ]    →    [1, 3, 5, 7, 9]
a[1] = 'bat'             →    [1, "bat", 5, 7, 9]
a[-3] = 'cat'           →    [1, "bat", "cat", 7, 9]
a[3] = [ 9, 8 ]         →    [1, "bat", "cat", [9, 8], 9]
a[6] = 99               →    [1, "bat", "cat", [9, 8], 9, nil, 99]
```

If the index to [ ]= is two numbers (a start and a length) or a range, then those elements in the original array are replaced by whatever is on the right side of the assignment. If the length is zero, the right side is inserted into the array before the start position; no elements are removed. If the right side is itself an array, its elements are used in the replacement. The array size is automatically adjusted if the index selects a different number of elements than are available on the right side of the assignment.

```
a = [ 1, 3, 5, 7, 9 ]    →    [1, 3, 5, 7, 9]
a[2, 2] = 'cat'         →    [1, 3, "cat", 9]
a[2, 0] = 'dog'         →    [1, 3, "dog", "cat", 9]
a[1, 1] = [ 9, 8, 7 ]   →    [1, 9, 8, 7, "dog", "cat", 9]
a[0..3] = []            →    ["dog", "cat", 9]
a[5..6] = 99, 98        →    ["dog", "cat", 9, nil, nil, 99, 98]
```

Arrays have a large number of other useful methods. Using these, you can treat arrays as stacks, sets, queues, dequeues, and fifos. A complete list of array methods starts on page 427.

Hashes

Hashes (sometimes known as *associative arrays*, *maps*, or *dictionaries*) are similar to arrays in that they are indexed collections of object references. However, while you index arrays with integers, you can index a hash with objects of any type: strings, regular expressions, and so on. When you store a value in a hash, you actually supply two objects—the index, normally called the *key*, and the value. You can subsequently retrieve the value by indexing the hash with the same key. The values in a hash can be objects of any type.

The example that follows uses hash literals: a list of *key* => *value* pairs between braces.

```
h = { 'dog' => 'canine', 'cat' => 'feline', 'donkey' => 'asinine' }

h.length    →    3
h['dog']    →    "canine"
h['cow']    = 'bovine'
h[12]       = 'dodecine'
h['cat']    = 99
h           →    {"cow"=>"bovine", "cat"=>99, 12=>"dodecine",
                  "donkey"=>"asinine", "dog"=>"canine"}
```

Compared with arrays, hashes have one significant advantage: they can use any object as an index. However, they also have a significant disadvantage: their elements are not ordered, so you cannot easily use a hash as a stack or a queue.

You'll find that hashes are one of the most commonly used data structures in Ruby. A full list of the methods implemented by class Hash starts on page 492.

Implementing a SongList Container

After that little diversion into arrays and hashes, we're now ready to implement the jukebox's SongList. Let's invent a basic list of methods we need in our SongList. We'll want to add to it as we go along, but this will do for now.

append(song) → list
> Append the given song to the list.

delete_first() → song
> Remove the first song from the list, returning that song.

delete_last() → song
> Remove the last song from the list, returning that song.

[index] → song
> Return the song at the integer *index*.

with_title(title) → song
> Return the song with the given title.

This list gives us a clue to the implementation. The ability to append songs at the end, and remove them from both the front and end, suggests a *dequeue*—a double-ended queue—which we know we can implement using an Array. Similarly, the ability to return a song at an integer position in the list is supported by arrays.

However, you also need to be able to retrieve songs by title, which may suggest using a hash, with the title as a key and the song as a value. Unfortunately, hashes aren't useful in this context. First, a hash is unordered, so we'd probably need to use an ancillary array to keep track of the list. A second, bigger problem is that a hash does not support multiple entries where the keys have the same value. That would be a problem for our playlist, where the same song may be queued for playing multiple times. So, for now we'll stick with an array of songs, searching it for titles when needed. If this becomes a performance bottleneck, we can always add some kind of hash-based lookup later.

We'll start our class with a basic `initialize` method, which creates the `Array` we'll use to hold the songs and stores a reference to it in the instance variable @songs.

```
class SongList
  def initialize
    @songs = Array.new
  end
end
```

The SongList#append method adds the given song to the end of the @songs array. It also returns *self*, a reference to the current SongList object. This is a useful convention, as it lets us chain together multiple calls to append. We'll see an example of this later.

```
class SongList
  def append(song)
    @songs.push(song)
    self
  end
end
```

Then we'll add the `delete_first` and `delete_last` methods, trivially implemented using `Array#shift` and `Array#pop`, respectively.

```
class SongList
  def delete_first
    @songs.shift
  end
  def delete_last
    @songs.pop
  end
end
```

So far, so good. Our next method is [ ], which accesses elements by index. These kind of simple delegating methods occur frequently in Ruby code: don't worry if your code ends up containing a bunch of one- or two-line methods—it's a sign that you're designing things correctly.

```
class SongList
  def [](index)
    @songs[index]
  end
end
```

At this point, a quick test may be in order. To do this, we're going to use a testing framework called TestUnit that comes with the standard Ruby distributions. We won't describe it fully yet (we do that in the *Unit Testing* chapter starting on page 151). For now, we'll just say that the method `assert_equal` checks that its two parameters are equal, complaining bitterly if they aren't. Similarly, the method `assert_nil` complains unless its parameter is `nil`. We're using these assertions to verify that the correct songs are deleted from the list.

The test contains some initial housekeeping, necessary to tell Ruby to use the TestUnit framework and to tell the framework that we're writing some test code. Then we create a SongList and four songs and append the songs to the list. (Just to show off, we use the fact that append returns the SongList object to chain together these method calls.) We can then test our [ ] method, verifying that it returns the correct song (or `nil`) for a set of indices. Finally, we delete songs from the start and end of the list, checking that the correct songs are returned.

```ruby
require 'test/unit'
class TestSongList < Test::Unit::TestCase
  def test_delete
    list = SongList.new
    s1 = Song.new('title1', 'artist1', 1)
    s2 = Song.new('title2', 'artist2', 2)
    s3 = Song.new('title3', 'artist3', 3)
    s4 = Song.new('title4', 'artist4', 4)

    list.append(s1).append(s2).append(s3).append(s4)

    assert_equal(s1, list[0])
    assert_equal(s3, list[2])
    assert_nil(list[9])

    assert_equal(s1, list.delete_first)
    assert_equal(s2, list.delete_first)
    assert_equal(s4, list.delete_last)
    assert_equal(s3, list.delete_last)
    assert_nil(list.delete_last)
  end
end
```

produces:

```
Loaded suite -
Started
.
Finished in 0.002314 seconds.

1 tests, 8 assertions, 0 failures, 0 errors
```

The running test confirms that eight assertions were executed in one test method, and they all passed. We're on our way to a working jukebox!

Now we need to add the facility that lets us look up a song by title. This is going to involve scanning through the songs in the list, checking the title of each. To do this, we first need to spend a couple of pages looking at one of Ruby's neatest features: iterators.

Blocks and Iterators

Our next problem with SongList is to implement the method with_title that takes a string and searches for a song with that title. This seems straightforward: we have an array of songs, so we'll go through it one element at a time, looking for a match.

```
class SongList
  def with_title(title)
    for i in 0...@songs.length
      return @songs[i] if title == @songs[i].name
    end
    return nil
  end
end
```

This works, and it looks comfortingly familiar: a for loop iterating over an array. What could be more natural?

It turns out there *is* something more natural. In a way, our for loop is somewhat too intimate with the array; it asks for a length, and it then retrieves values in turn until it finds a match. Why not just ask the array to apply a test to each of its members? That's just what the find method in Array does.

```
class SongList
  def with_title(title)
    @songs.find {|song| title == song.name }
  end
end
```

The method find is an *iterator*—a method that invokes a block of code repeatedly. Iterators and code blocks are among the more interesting features of Ruby, so let's spend a while looking into them (and in the process we'll find out exactly what that line of code in our with_title method actually does).

Implementing Iterators

A Ruby iterator is simply a method that can invoke a block of code. At first sight, a block in Ruby looks just like a block in C, Java, C#, or Perl. Unfortunately, in this case looks are deceiving—a Ruby block *is* a way of grouping statements, but not in the conventional way.

First, a block may appear only in the source adjacent to a method call; the block is written starting on the same line as the method call's last parameter (or the closing parenthesis of the parameter list). Second, the code in the block is not executed at the time it is encountered. Instead, Ruby remembers the context in which the block appears (the local variables, the current object, and so on) and then enters the method. This is where the magic starts.

Within the method, the block may be invoked, almost as if it were a method itself, using the `yield` statement. Whenever a `yield` is executed, it invokes the code in the block. When the block exits, control picks back up immediately after the `yield`.[1] Let's start with a trivial example.

```
def three_times
  yield
  yield
  yield
end
three_times { puts "Hello" }
```

produces:

```
Hello
Hello
Hello
```

The block (the code between the braces) is associated with the call to the method `three_times`. Within this method, `yield` is called three times in a row. Each time, it invokes the code in the block, and a cheery greeting is printed. What makes blocks interesting, however, is that you can pass parameters to them and receive values from them. For example, we could write a simple function that returns members of the Fibonacci series up to a certain value.[2]

```
def fib_up_to(max)
  i1, i2 = 1, 1        # parallel assignment (i1 = 1 and i2 = 1)
  while i1 <= max
    yield i1
    i1, i2 = i2, i1+i2
  end
end
fib_up_to(1000) {|f| print f, " " }
```

produces:

```
1 1 2 3 5 8 13 21 34 55 89 144 233 377 610 987
```

---

1.   Programming-language buffs will be pleased to know that the keyword `yield` was chosen to echo the `yield` function in Liskov's language CLU, a language that is more than 20 years old and yet contains features that still haven't been widely exploited by the CLU-less.

2.   The basic Fibonacci series is a sequence of integers, starting with two 1s, in which each subsequent term is the sum of the two preceding terms. The series is sometimes used in sorting algorithms and in analyzing natural phenomena.

In this example, the `yield` statement has a parameter. This value is passed to the associated block. In the definition of the block, the argument list appears between vertical bars. In this instance, the variable f receives the value passed to the `yield`, so the block prints successive members of the series. (This example also shows parallel assignment in action. We'll come back to this on page 91.) Although it is common to pass just one value to a block, this is not a requirement; a block may have any number of arguments.

If the parameters to a block are existing local variables, those variables will be used as the block parameters, and their values may be changed by the block's execution. The same thing applies to variables inside the block: if they appear for the first time in the block, they're local to the block. If instead they first appeared outside the block, the variables will be shared between the block and the surrounding environment.[3]

In this (contrived) example, we see that the block inherits the variables a and b from the surrounding scope, but c is local to the block (the method `defined?` returns `nil` if its argument is not defined).

```
a = [1, 2]
b = 'cat'
a.each {|b| c = b * a[1] }
a                  →    [1, 2]
b                  →    2
defined?(c)        →    nil
```

A block may also return a value to the method. The value of the last expression evaluated in the block is passed back to the method as the value of the `yield`. This is how the `find` method used by class `Array` works.[4] Its implementation would look something like the following.

```
class Array
  def find
    for i in 0...size
      value = self[i]
      return value if yield(value)
    end
    return nil
  end
end

[1, 3, 5, 7, 9].find {|v| v*v > 30 }   →   7
```

This passes successive elements of the array to the associated block. If the block returns `true`, the method returns the corresponding element. If no element matches, the method returns `nil`. The example shows the benefit of this approach to iterators. The `Array`

---

3. Although extremely useful at times, this feature may lead to unexpected behavior and is hotly debated in the Ruby community. It is possible that Ruby 2.0 will change the way blocks inherit local variables.

4. The `find` method is actually defined in module `Enumerable`, which is mixed into class `Array`.

class does what it does best, accessing array elements, leaving the application code to concentrate on its particular requirement (in this case, finding an entry that meets some mathematical criteria).

Some iterators are common to many types of Ruby collections. We've looked at `find` already. Two others are `each` and `collect`. `each` is probably the simplest iterator—all it does is yield successive elements of its collection.

```
[ 1, 3, 5, 7, 9 ].each {|i| puts i }
```

produces:

```
1
3
5
7
9
```

The each iterator has a special place in Ruby; on page 103 we'll describe how it's used as the basis of the language's `for` loop, and starting on page 120 we'll see how defining an each method can add a whole lot more functionality to your class for free.

Another common iterator is `collect`, which takes each element from the collection and passes it to the block. The results returned by the block are used to construct a new array. For instance:

```
["H", "A", "L"].collect {|x| x.succ }   →   ["I", "B", "M"]
```

Iterators are not limited to accessing existing data in arrays and hashes. As we saw in the Fibonacci example, an iterator can return derived values. This capability is used by Ruby input/output classes, which implement an iterator interface that returns successive lines (or bytes) in an I/O stream. (This example uses do...end to define a block. The only difference between this notation and using braces to define blocks is precedence: do...end binds lower than {...}. We discuss the impact of this on page 356.)

```
f = File.open("testfile")
f.each do |line|
  puts line
end
f.close
```

produces:

```
This is line one
This is line two
This is line three
And so on...
```

Let's look at just one more useful iterator. The (somewhat obscurely named) `inject` method (defined in the module `Enumerable`) lets you accumulate a value across the

1.8

members of a collection. For example, you can sum all the elements in an array, and find their product, using code such as

```
[1,3,5,7].inject(0) {|sum, element| sum+element}      →  16
[1,3,5,7].inject(1) {|product, element| product*element}  →  105
```

`inject` works like this: the first time the associated block is called, `sum` is set to `inject`'s parameter and `element` is set to the first element in the collection. The second and subsequent times the block is called, `sum` is set to the value returned by the block on the previous call. The final value of `inject` is the value returned by the block the last time it was called. There's one final wrinkle: if `inject` is called with no parameter, it uses the first element of the collection as the initial value and starts the iteration with the second value. This means that we could have written the previous examples as

```
[1,3,5,7].inject {|sum, element| sum+element}       →  16
[1,3,5,7].inject {|product, element| product*element}  →  105
```

Internal and External Iterators

It's worth spending a paragraph comparing Ruby's approach to iterators to that of languages such as C++ and Java. In the Ruby approach, the iterator is internal to the collection—it's simply a method, identical to any other, that happens to call `yield` whenever it generates a new value. The thing that uses the iterator is just a block of code associated with this method.

In other languages, collections don't contain their own iterators. Instead, they generate external helper objects (for example, those based on Java's `Iterator` interface) that carry the iterator state. In this, as in many other ways, Ruby is a transparent language. When you write a Ruby program, you concentrate on getting the job done, not on building scaffolding to support the language itself.

It's probably also worth spending a paragraph looking at why Ruby's internal iterators aren't always the best solution. One area where they fall down badly is where you need to treat an iterator as an object in its own right (for example, passing the iterator into a method that needs to access each of the values returned by that iterator). It's also difficult to iterate over two collections in parallel using Ruby's internal iterator scheme. Fortunately, Ruby 1.8 comes with the `Generator` library (described on page 683), which implements external iterators in Ruby for just such occasions.

1.8

Blocks for Transactions

Although blocks are often the target of an iterator, they also have other uses. Let's look at a few.

You can use blocks to define a chunk of code that must be run under some kind of transactional control. For example, you'll often open a file, do something with its contents, and then want to ensure that the file is closed when you finish. Although you can do this using conventional code, an argument exists for making the file responsible for closing itself. We can do this with blocks. A naive implementation (ignoring error handling) could look something like the following.

```
class File
  def File.open_and_process(*args)
    f = File.open(*args)
    yield f
    f.close()
  end
end


File.open_and_process("testfile", "r") do |file|
  while line = file.gets
    puts line
  end
end
```

produces:

```
This is line one
This is line two
This is line three
And so on...
```

open_and_process is a *class method*—it may be called independently of any particular file object. We want it to take the same arguments as the conventional File.open method, but we don't really care what those arguments are. To do this, we specified the arguments as *args, meaning "collect the actual parameters passed to the method into an array named args." We then call File.open, passing it *args as a parameter. This expands the array back into individual parameters. The net result is that open_and_process transparently passes whatever parameters it received to File.open.

Once the file has been opened, open_and_process calls yield, passing the open file object to the block. When the block returns, the file is closed. In this way, the responsibility for closing an open file has been passed from the user of file objects back to the files themselves.

The technique of having files manage their own life cycle is so useful that the class File supplied with Ruby supports it directly. If File.open has an associated block, then that block will be invoked with a file object, and the file will be closed when the block terminates. This is interesting, as it means that File.open has two different behaviors: when called with a block, it executes the block and closes the file. When called without a block, it returns the file object. This is made possible by the method Kernel.block_given?, which returns true if a block is associated with the current method. Using this method, you could implement something similar to the standard File.open (again, ignoring error handling) using the following.

```
class File
  def File.my_open(*args)
    result = file = File.new(*args)
    # If there's a block, pass in the file and close
    # the file when it returns
    if block_given?
      result = yield file
      file.close
    end

    return result
  end
end
```

This has one last twist: in the previous examples of using blocks to control resources, we haven't addressed error handling. If we wanted to implement these methods properly, we'd need to ensure that we closed files even if the code processing that file somehow aborted. We do this using exception handling, which we talk about later (starting on page 107).

Blocks Can Be Closures

Let's get back to our jukebox for a moment (remember the jukebox?). At some point we'll be working on the code that handles the user interface—the buttons that people press to select songs and control the jukebox. We'll need to associate actions with those buttons: press START and the music starts. It turns out that Ruby's blocks are a convenient way to do this. Let's start by assuming that the people who made the hardware implemented a Ruby extension that gives us a basic button class. (We talk about extending Ruby beginning on page 275.)

```
start_button = Button.new("Start")
pause_button = Button.new("Pause")
# ...
```

What happens when the user presses one of our buttons? In the Button class, the hardware folks rigged things so that a callback method, button_pressed, will be invoked. The obvious way of adding functionality to these buttons is to create subclasses of Button and have each subclass implement its own button_pressed method.

```
class StartButton < Button
  def initialize
    super("Start")      # invoke Button's initialize
  end
  def button_pressed
    # do start actions...
  end
end

start_button = StartButton.new
```

This has two problems. First, this will lead to a large number of subclasses. If the interface to Button changes, this could involve us in a lot of maintenance. Second, the actions performed when a button is pressed are expressed at the wrong level; they are not a feature of the button but are a feature of the jukebox that uses the buttons. We can fix both of these problems using blocks.

```ruby
songlist = SongList.new

class JukeboxButton < Button

  def initialize(label, &action)
    super(label)
    @action = action
  end

  def button_pressed
    @action.call(self)
  end

end

start_button = JukeboxButton.new("Start") { songlist.start }
pause_button = JukeboxButton.new("Pause") { songlist.pause }
```

The key to all this is the second parameter to JukeboxButton#initialize. If the last parameter in a method definition is prefixed with an ampersand (such as &action), Ruby looks for a code block whenever that method is called. That code block is converted to an object of class Proc and assigned to the parameter. You can then treat the parameter as any other variable. In our example, we assigned it to the instance variable @action. When the callback method button_pressed is invoked, we use the Proc#call method on that object to invoke the block.

So what exactly do we have when we create a Proc object? The interesting thing is that it's more than just a chunk of code. Associated with a block (and hence a Proc object) is all the context in which the block was *defined*: the value of self and the methods, variables, and constants in scope. Part of the magic of Ruby is that the block can still use all this original scope information even if the environment in which it was defined would otherwise have disappeared. In other languages, this facility is called a *closure*.

Let's look at a contrived example. This example uses the method lambda, which converts a block to a Proc object.

```ruby
def n_times(thing)
  return lambda {|n| thing * n }
end

p1 = n_times(23)
p1.call(3)    →    69
p1.call(4)    →    92
p2 = n_times("Hello ")
p2.call(3)    →    "Hello Hello Hello "
```

The method n_times returns a Proc object that references the method's parameter, thing. Even though that parameter is out of scope by the time the block is called, the parameter remains accessible to the block.

Containers Everywhere

Containers, blocks, and iterators are core concepts in Ruby. The more you write in Ruby, the more you'll find yourself moving away from conventional looping constructs. Instead, you'll write classes that support iteration over their contents. And you'll find that this code is compact, easy to read, and a joy to maintain.

## Chapter 5

Standard Types

So far we've been having fun implementing pieces of our jukebox code, but we've been negligent. We've looked at arrays, hashes, and procs, but we haven't really covered the other basic types in Ruby: numbers, strings, ranges, and regular expressions. Let's spend a few pages on these basic building blocks now.

Numbers

Ruby supports integers and floating-point numbers. Integers can be any length (up to a maximum determined by the amount of free memory on your system). Integers within a certain range (normally -2^{30} to $2^{30}-1$ or -2^{62} to $2^{62}-1$) are held internally in binary form and are objects of class `Fixnum`. Integers outside this range are stored in objects of class `Bignum` (currently implemented as a variable-length set of short integers). This process is transparent, and Ruby automatically manages the conversion back and forth.

```
num = 81
6.times do
  puts "#{num.class}: #{num}"
  num *= num
end
```

produces:

```
Fixnum: 81
Fixnum: 6561
Fixnum: 43046721
Bignum: 1853020188851841
Bignum: 3433683820292512484657849089281
Bignum: 11790184577738583171520872861412518665678211592275841109096961
```

You write integers using an optional leading sign, an optional base indicator (0 for octal, 0d for decimal [the default], 0x for hex, or 0b for binary), followed by a string of digits in the appropriate base. Underscore characters are ignored in the digit string (some folks use them in place of commas in larger numbers).

```
123456                      => 123456    # Fixnum
0d123456                    => 123456    # Fixnum
123_456                     => 123456    # Fixnum - underscore ignored
-543                        => -543      # Fixnum - negative number
0xaabb                      => 43707     # Fixnum - hexadecimal
0377                        => 255       # Fixnum - octal
-0b10_1010                  => -42       # Fixnum - binary (negated)
123_456_789_123_456_789     => 123456789123456789 # Bignum
```

The integer values of control characters can be generated using ?\C-*x* and ?\c*x* (the control version of x is x&0x9f). Metacharacters (x | 0x80) can be generated using ?\M-*x*. The combination of meta and control is generated using and ?\M-\C-*x*. You can get the integer value of a backslash character using the sequence ?\\.

```
?a            => 97    # ASCII character
?\n           => 10    # code for a newline (0x0a)
?\C-a         => 1     # control a = ?A & 0x9f = 0x01
?\M-a         => 225   # meta sets bit 7
?\M-\C-a      => 129   # meta and control a
?\C-?         => 127   # delete character
```

1.8 A numeric literal with a decimal point and/or an exponent is turned into a Float object, corresponding to the native architecture's double data type. You must both precede and follow the decimal point with a digit (if you write 1.0e3 as 1.e3, Ruby will try to invoke the method e3 in class Fixnum).

All numbers are objects and respond to a variety of messages (listed in full starting on pages 441, 484, 487, 501, and 562). So, unlike (say) C++, you find the absolute value of a number by writing num.abs, not abs(num).

Integers also support several useful iterators. We've seen one already: 6.times in the code example on the preceding page. Others include upto and downto, for iterating up and down between two integers. Class Numeric also provides the more general method step, which is more like a traditional for loop.

```
3.times       { print "X " }
1.upto(5)     {|i| print i, " " }
99.downto(95) {|i| print i, " " }
50.step(80, 5) {|i| print i, " " }
```

produces:

```
X X X 1 2 3 4 5 99 98 97 96 95 50 55 60 65 70 75 80
```

Finally, we'll offer a warning for Perl users. Strings that contain just digits are *not* automatically converted into numbers when used in expressions. This tends to bite most often when reading numbers from a file. For example, we may want to find the sum of the two numbers on each line for a file such as

```
3 4
5 6
7 8
```

The following code doesn't work.

```
some_file.each do |line|
  v1, v2 = line.split    # split line on spaces
  print v1 + v2, " "
end
```

produces:

```
34 56 78
```

The problem is that the input was read as strings, not numbers. The plus operator concatenates strings, so that's what we see in the output. To fix this, use the `Integer` method to convert the string to an integer.

```
some_file.each do |line|
  v1, v2 = line.split
  print Integer(v1) + Integer(v2), " "
end
```

produces:

```
7 11 15
```

Strings

Ruby strings are simply sequences of 8-bit bytes. They normally hold printable characters, but that is not a requirement; a string can also hold binary data. Strings are objects of class `String`.

Strings are often created using string literals—sequences of characters between delimiters. Because binary data is otherwise difficult to represent within program source, you can place various escape sequences in a string literal. Each is replaced with the corresponding binary value as the program is compiled. The type of string delimiter determines the degree of substitution performed. Within single-quoted strings, two consecutive backslashes are replaced by a single backslash, and a backslash followed by a single quote becomes a single quote.

```
'escape using "\\"'     →    escape using "\"
'That\'s right'         →    That's right
```

Double-quoted strings support a boatload more escape sequences. The most common is probably \n, the newline character. Table 22.2 on page 321 gives the complete list. In addition, you can substitute the value of any Ruby code into a string using the sequence #{ *expr* }. If the code is just a global variable, a class variable, or an instance variable, you can omit the braces.

```
"Seconds/day: #{24*60*60}"      →    Seconds/day: 86400
"#{'Ho! '*3}Merry Christmas!"   →    Ho! Ho! Ho! Merry Christmas!
"This is line #$."              →    This is line 3
```

1.8 The interpolated code can be one or more statements, not just an expression.

```
puts  "now is #{ def the(a)
                   'the ' + a
                 end
                 the('time')
              } for all good coders..."
```

produces:

```
now is the time for all good coders...
```

You have three more ways to construct string literals: %q, %Q, and *here documents*.

%q and %Q start delimited single- and double-quoted strings (you can think of %q as a thin quote ', and %Q as a thick quote ").

```
%q/general single-quoted string/    →    general single-quoted string
%Q!general double-quoted string!    →    general double-quoted string
%Q{Seconds/day: #{24*60*60}}        →    Seconds/day: 86400
```

The character following the *q* or *Q* is the delimiter. If it is an opening bracket "[", brace "{", parenthesis "(", or less-than sign "<", the string is read until the matching close symbol is found. Otherwise the string is read until the next occurrence of the same 1.8 delimiter. The delimiter can be any nonalphanumeric or nonmultibyte character.

Finally, you can construct a string using a *here document*.

```
string = <<END_OF_STRING
    The body of the string
    is the input lines up to
    one ending with the same
    text that followed the '<<'
END_OF_STRING
```

A here document consists of lines in the source up to, but not including, the terminating string that you specify after the << characters. Normally, this terminator must start in the first column. However, if you put a minus sign after the << characters, you can indent the terminator.

```
print <<-STRING1, <<-STRING2
    Concat
    STRING1
       enate
       STRING2
```

produces:

```
        Concat
            enate
```

Note that Ruby does not strip leading spaces off the contents of the strings in these cases.

Working with Strings

`String` is probably the largest built-in Ruby class, with more than 75 standard methods. We won't go through them all here; the library reference has a complete list. Instead, we'll look at some common string idioms—things that are likely to pop up during day-to-day programming.

Let's get back to our jukebox. Although it's designed to be connected to the Internet, it also holds copies of some popular songs on a local hard drive. That way, if a squirrel chews through our 'net connection, we'll still be able to entertain the customers.

For historical reasons (are there any other kind?), the list of songs is stored as rows in a flat file. Each row holds the name of the file containing the song, the song's duration, the artist, and the title, all in vertical bar–separated fields. A typical file may start

```
/jazz/j00132.mp3  | 3:45 | Fats     Waller       | Ain't Misbehavin'
/jazz/j00319.mp3  | 2:58 | Louis    Armstrong    | Wonderful World
/bgrass/bg0732.mp3| 4:09 | Strength in Numbers  | Texas Red
        :                      :              :                    :
```

Looking at the data, it's clear that we'll be using some of class `String`'s many methods to extract and clean up the fields before we create Song objects based on them. At a minimum, we'll need to

- break each line into fields,
- convert the running times from mm:ss to seconds, and
- remove those extra spaces from the artists' names.

Our first task is to split each line into fields, and `String#split` will do the job nicely. In this case, we'll pass `split` a regular expression, `/\s*\|\s*/`, that splits the line into tokens wherever `split` finds a vertical bar, optionally surrounded by spaces. And, because the line read from the file has a trailing newline, we'll use `String#chomp` to strip it off just before we apply the split.

```
File.open("songdata") do |song_file|
  songs = SongList.new
  song_file.each do |line|
    file, length, name, title = line.chomp.split(/\s*\|\s*/)
    songs.append(Song.new(title, name, length))
  end
  puts songs[1]
end
```

produces:

```
Song: Wonderful World--Louis    Armstrong (2:58)
```

Unfortunately, whoever created the original file entered the artists' names in columns, so some of them contain extra spaces. These will look ugly on our high-tech, super-twist, flat-panel, Day-Glo display, so we'd better remove these extra spaces before we go much further. We have many ways of doing this, but probably the simplest is String#squeeze, which trims runs of repeated characters. We'll use the squeeze! form of the method, which alters the string in place.

```
File.open("songdata") do |song_file|
  songs = SongList.new
  song_file.each do |line|
    file, length, name, title = line.chomp.split(/\s*\|\s*/)
    name.squeeze!(" ")
    songs.append(Song.new(title, name, length))
  end
  puts songs[1]
end
```

produces:

```
Song: Wonderful World--Louis Armstrong (2:58)
```

Finally, we have the minor matter of the time format: the file says 2:58, and we want the number of seconds, 178. We could use split again, this time splitting the time field around the colon character.

```
mins, secs = length.split(/:/)
```

Instead, we'll use a related method. String#scan is similar to split in that it breaks a string into chunks based on a pattern. However, unlike split, with scan you specify the pattern that you want the chunks to match. In this case, we want to match one or more digits for both the minutes and seconds component. The pattern for one or more digits is /\d+/.

```
File.open("songdata") do |song_file|
  songs = SongList.new
  song_file.each do |line|
    file, length, name, title = line.chomp.split(/\s*\|\s*/)
    name.squeeze!(" ")
    mins, secs = length.scan(/\d+/)
    songs.append(Song.new(title, name, mins.to_i*60+secs.to_i))
  end
  puts songs[1]
end
```

produces:

```
Song: Wonderful World--Louis Armstrong (178)
```

Our jukebox has a keyword search capability. Given a word from a song title or an artist's name, it will list all matching tracks. Type in **fats**, and it may come back with songs by Fats Domino, Fats Navarro, and Fats Waller, for example. We'll implement this by creating an indexing class. Feed it an object and some strings, and it will index that object under every word (of two or more characters) that occurs in those strings. This will illustrate a few more of class String's many methods.

```
class WordIndex
  def initialize
    @index = {}
  end
  def add_to_index(obj, *phrases)
    phrases.each do |phrase|
      phrase.scan(/\w[-\w']+/) do |word|    # extract each word
        word.downcase!
        @index[word] = [] if @index[word].nil?
        @index[word].push(obj)
      end
    end
  end
  def lookup(word)
    @index[word.downcase]
  end
end
```

The String#scan method extracts elements from a string that match a regular expression. In this case, the pattern \w[-\w']+ matches any character that can appear in a word, followed by one or more of the things specified in the brackets (a hyphen, another word character, or a single quote). We'll talk more about regular expressions beginning on page 68. To make our searches case insensitive, we map both the words we extract and the words used as keys during the lookup to lowercase. Note the exclamation mark at the end of the first downcase! method name. As with the squeeze! method we used previously, this is an indication that the method will modify the receiver in place, in this case converting the string to lowercase.[1]

We'll extend our SongList class to index songs as they're added and add a method to look up a song given a word.

```
class SongList
  def initialize
    @songs = Array.new
    @index = WordIndex.new
  end
  def append(song)
    @songs.push(song)
    @index.add_to_index(song, song.name, song.artist)
    self
  end
  def lookup(word)
    @index.lookup(word)
  end
end
```

---

1. This code sample contains a minor bug: the song "Gone, Gone, Gone" would get indexed three times. Can you come up with a fix?

Finally, we'll test it all.

```
songs = SongList.new
song_file.each do |line|
  file, length, name, title = line.chomp.split(/\s*\|\s*/)
  name.squeeze!(" ")
  mins, secs = length.scan(/\d+/)
  songs.append(Song.new(title, name, mins.to_i*60+secs.to_i))
end
puts songs.lookup("Fats")
puts songs.lookup("ain't")
puts songs.lookup("RED")
puts songs.lookup("WoRlD")
```

produces:

```
Song: Ain't Misbehavin'--Fats Waller (225)
Song: Ain't Misbehavin'--Fats Waller (225)
Song: Texas Red--Strength in Numbers (249)
Song: Wonderful World--Louis Armstrong (178)
```

In the preceding code, the lookup method returns an array of matches. When we pass an array to puts, it simply writes each element in turn, separated by a newline.

We could spend the next 50 pages looking at all the methods in class String. However, let's move on instead to look at a simpler data type: the range.

Ranges

Ranges occur everywhere: January to December, 0 to 9, rare to well-done, lines 50 through 67, and so on. If Ruby is to help us model reality, it seems natural for it to support these ranges. In fact, Ruby goes one better: it actually uses ranges to implement three separate features: sequences, conditions, and intervals.

Ranges as Sequences

The first and perhaps most natural use of ranges is to express a sequence. Sequences have a start point, an end point, and a way to produce successive values in the sequence. In Ruby, these sequences are created using the "`..`" and "`...`" range operators. The two-dot form creates an inclusive range, and the three-dot form creates a range that excludes the specified high value.

```
1..10
'a'..'z'
my_array = [ 1, 2, 3 ]
0...my_array.length
```

In Ruby, unlike in some earlier versions of Perl, ranges are not represented internally as lists: the sequence 1..100000 is held as a Range object containing references to two Fixnum objects. If you need to, you can convert a range to a list using the to_a method.

```
(1..10).to_a          →   [1, 2, 3, 4, 5, 6, 7, 8, 9, 10]
('bar'..'bat').to_a   →   ["bar", "bas", "bat"]
```

Ranges implement methods that let you iterate over them and test their contents in a variety of ways.

```
digits = 0..9
digits.include?(5)               →    true
digits.min                       →    0
digits.max                       →    9
digits.reject {|i| i < 5 }       →    [5, 6, 7, 8, 9]
digits.each {|digit| dial(digit) }  →  0..9
```

So far we've shown ranges of numbers and strings. However, as you'd expect from an object-oriented language, Ruby can create ranges based on objects that you define. The only constraints are that the objects must respond to succ by returning the next object in sequence and the objects must be comparable using <=>. Sometimes called the *spaceship operator*, <=> compares two values, returning -1, 0, or $+1$ depending on whether the first is less than, equal to, or greater than the second.

Here's a simple class that represents rows of # signs. We may want to use it as a text-based version of the jukebox volume control.

```
class VU
  include Comparable
  attr :volume
  def initialize(volume)  # 0..9
    @volume = volume
  end
  def inspect
    '#' * @volume
  end
  # Support for ranges
  def <=>(other)
    self.volume <=> other.volume
  end
  def succ
    raise(IndexError, "Volume too big") if @volume >= 9
    VU.new(@volume.succ)
  end
end
```

Because our VU class implements succ and <=>, it can participate in ranges.

```
medium_volume = VU.new(4)..VU.new(7)
medium_volume.to_a                    →   [####, #####, ######, #######]
medium_volume.include?(VU.new(3))  →   false
```

Ranges as Conditions

As well as representing sequences, ranges may also be used as conditional expressions. Here, they act as a kind of toggle switch—they turn on when the condition in the first part of the range becomes true, and they turn off when the condition in the second part becomes true. For example, the following code fragment prints sets of lines from standard input, where the first line in each set contains the word *start* and the last line contains the word *end*.

```
while line = gets
  puts line if line =~ /start/ .. line =~ /end/
end
```

Behind the scenes, the range keeps track of the state of each of the tests. We'll show some examples of this in the description of loops that starts on page 100 and in the language section on page 342.

In older versions of Ruby, bare ranges could be used as conditions in `if`, `while`, and similar statements. You could, for example, have written the previous code fragment as

```
while gets
  print if /start/../end/
end
```

This is no longer supported. Unfortunately, no error is raised; the test will simply succeed each time.

Ranges as Intervals

A final use of the versatile range is as an interval test: seeing if some value falls within the interval represented by the range. We do this using ===, the case equality operator.

```
(1..10)    === 5        →   true
(1..10)    === 15       →   false
(1..10)    === 3.14159  →   true
('a'..'j') === 'c'      →   true
('a'..'j') === 'z'      →   false
```

The example of a case expression on page 98 shows this test in action, determining a jazz style given a year.

Regular Expressions

Back on page 63 when we were creating a song list from a file, we used a regular expression to match the field delimiter in the input file. We claimed that the expression `line.split(/\s*\|\s*/)` matched a vertical bar surrounded by optional whitespace. Let's explore regular expressions in more detail to see why this claim is true.

Regular expressions are used to match patterns against strings. Ruby provides built-in support that makes pattern matching and substitution convenient and concise. In this section we'll work through all the main features of regular expressions. We won't cover some details here: have a look at page 324 for more information.

Regular expressions are objects of type Regexp. They can be created by calling the constructor explicitly or by using the literal forms /*pattern*/ and %r{*pattern*}.

```
a = Regexp.new('^\s*[a-z]')   →   /^\s*[a-z]/
b = /^\s*[a-z]/               →   /^\s*[a-z]/
c = %r{^\s*[a-z]}             →   /^\s*[a-z]/
```

Once you have a regular expression object, you can match it against a string using Regexp#match(*string*) or the match operators =~ (positive match) and !~ (negative match). The match operators are defined for both String and Regexp objects. At least one operand of the match operator must be a regular expression. (In previous versions of Ruby, both could be strings, in which case the second operand was converted into a regular expression behind the scenes.)

```
name = "Fats Waller"
name =~ /a/    →   1
name =~ /z/    →   nil
/a/ =~ name    →   1
```

The match operators return the character position at which the match occurred. They also have the side effect of setting a whole load of Ruby variables. $& receives the part of the string that was matched by the pattern, $` receives the part of the string that preceded the match, and $' receives the string after the match. We can use this to write a method, show_regexp, that illustrates where a particular pattern matches.

```
def show_regexp(a, re)
  if a =~ re
    "#{$`}<<#{$&}>>#{$'}"
  else
    "no match"
  end
end

show_regexp('very interesting', /t/)   →   very in<<t>>eresting
show_regexp('Fats Waller', /a/)        →   F<<a>>ts Waller
show_regexp('Fats Waller', /ll/)       →   Fats Wa<<ll>>er
show_regexp('Fats Waller', /z/)        →   no match
```

The match also sets the thread-local variables $~ and $1 through $9. The variable $~ is a MatchData object (described beginning on page 537) that holds everything you may want to know about the match. $1, and so on, hold the values of parts of the match. We'll talk about these later. And for people who cringe when they see these Perl-like variable names, stay tuned. There's good news at the end of the chapter.

Patterns

Every regular expression contains a pattern, which is used to match the regular expression against a string.

Within a pattern, all characters except ., |, (,), [,], {, }, +, \, ^, $, *, and ? match themselves.

```
show_regexp('kangaroo', /angar/)    →    k<<angar>>oo
show_regexp('!@%&-_=+', /%&/)       →    !@<<%&>>-_=+
```

If you want to match one of these special characters literally, precede it with a back-slash. This explains part of the pattern we used to split the song line, /\s*\|\s*/. The \| means "match a vertical bar." Without the backslash, the | would have meant *alternation* (which we'll describe later).

```
show_regexp('yes | no', /\|/)       →    yes <<|>> no
show_regexp('yes (no)', /\(no\)/)   →    yes <<(no)>>
show_regexp('are you sure?', /e\?/) →    are you sur<<e?>>
```

A backslash followed by an alphanumeric character is used to introduce a special match construct, which we'll cover later. In addition, a regular expression may contain #{ ... } expression substitutions.

Anchors

By default, a regular expression will try to find the first match for the pattern in a string. Match /iss/ against the string "Mississippi," and it will find the substring "iss" starting at position one. But what if you want to force a pattern to match only at the start or end of a string?

The patterns ^ and $ match the beginning and end of a line, respectively. These are often used to *anchor* a pattern match: for example, /^option/ matches the word *option* only if it appears at the start of a line. The sequence \A matches the beginning of a string, and \z and \Z match the end of a string. (Actually, \Z matches the end of a string *unless* the string ends with a \n, it which case it matches just before the \n.)

```
show_regexp("this is\nthe time", /^the/)   →    this is\n<<the>> time
show_regexp("this is\nthe time", /is$/)    →    this <<is>>\nthe time
show_regexp("this is\nthe time", /\Athis/) →    <<this>> is\nthe time
show_regexp("this is\nthe time", /\Athe/)  →    no match
```

Similarly, the patterns \b and \B match word boundaries and nonword boundaries, respectively. Word characters are letters, numbers, and underscores.

```
show_regexp("this is\nthe time", /\bis/)   →    this <<is>>\nthe time
show_regexp("this is\nthe time", /\Bis/)   →    th<<is>> is\nthe time
```

Character Classes

A *character class* is a set of characters between brackets: [*characters*] matches any single character between the brackets. [aeiou] will match a vowel, [,.:;!?] matches punctuation, and so on. The significance of the special regular expression characters— .|()[{+^$*?—is turned off inside the brackets. However, normal string substitution still occurs, so (for example) \b represents a backspace character and \n a newline (see Table 22.2 on page 321). In addition, you can use the abbreviations shown in Table 5.1 on the following page so that (for example) \s matches any whitespace character, not just a literal space. The POSIX character classes in the second half of the table correspond to the ctype(3) macros of the same names.

```
show_regexp('Price $12.', /[aeiou]/)       →   Pr<<i>>ce $12.
show_regexp('Price $12.', /[\s]/)          →   Price<< >>$12.
show_regexp('Price $12.', /[[:digit:]]/)   →   Price $<<1>>2.
show_regexp('Price $12.', /[[:space:]]/)   →   Price<< >>$12.
show_regexp('Price $12.', /[[:punct:]aeiou]/)  →   Pr<<i>>ce $12.
```

Within the brackets, the sequence c_1-c_2 represents all the characters between c_1 and c_2, inclusive.

```
a = 'see [Design Patterns-page 123]'
show_regexp(a, /[A-F]/)      →   see [<<D>>esign Patterns-page 123]
show regexp(a, /[A-Fa-f]/)   →   s<<e>>e [Design Patterns-page 123]
show_regexp(a, /[0-9]/)      →   see [Design Patterns-page <<1>>23]
show_regexp(a, /[0-9][0-9]/) →   see [Design Patterns-page <<12>>3]
```

If you want to include the literal characters] and – within a character class, they must appear at the start. Put a ^ immediately after the opening bracket to negate a character class: [^a-z] matches any character that isn't a lowercase alphabetic.

```
a = 'see [Design Patterns-page 123]'
show_regexp(a, /[]]/)        →   see [Design Patterns-page 123<<]>>
show_regexp(a, /[-]/)        →   see [Design Patterns<<->>page 123]
show_regexp(a, /[^a-z]/)     →   see<< >>[Design Patterns-page 123]
show_regexp(a, /[^a-z\s]/)   →   see <<[>>Design Patterns-page 123]
```

Some character classes are used so frequently that Ruby provides abbreviations for them. These abbreviations are listed in Table 5.1 on the next page—they may be used both within brackets and in the body of a pattern.

```
show_regexp('It costs $12.', /\s/)   →   It<< >>costs $12.
show_regexp('It costs $12.', /\d/)   →   It costs $<<1>>2.
```

Finally, a period (.) appearing outside brackets represents any character except a newline (though in multiline mode it matches a newline, too).

```
a = 'It costs $12.'
show_regexp(a, /c.s/)   →   It <<cos>>ts $12.
show_regexp(a, /./)     →   <<I>>t costs $12.
show_regexp(a, /\./)    →   It costs $12<<.>>
```

Table 5.1. Character class abbreviations

Sequence	As [...]	Meaning
\d	[0-9]	Digit character
\D	[^0-9]	Any character except a digit
\s	[\t\r\n\f]	Whitespace character
\S	[^ \t\r\n\f]	Any character except whitespace
\w	[A-Za-z0-9_]	Word character
\W	[^A-Za-z0-9_]	Any character except a word character
POSIX Character Classes		
[:alnum:]		Alphanumeric
[:alpha:]		Uppercase or lowercase letter
[:blank:]		Blank and tab
[:cntrl:]		Control characters (at least 0x00–0x1f, 0x7f)
[:digit:]		Digit
[:graph:]		Printable character excluding space
[:lower:]		Lowercase letter
[:print:]		Any printable character (including space)
[:punct:]		Printable character excluding space and alphanumeric
[:space:]		Whitespace (same as \s)
[:upper:]		Uppercase letter
[:xdigit:]		Hex digit (0–9, a–f, A–F)

Repetition

When we specified the pattern that split the song list line, /\s*\|\s*/, we said we wanted to match a vertical bar surrounded by an arbitrary amount of whitespace. We now know that the \s sequences match a single whitespace character, so it seems likely that the asterisks somehow mean "an arbitrary amount." In fact, the asterisk is one of a number of modifiers that allow you to match multiple occurrences of a pattern.

If *r* stands for the immediately preceding regular expression within a pattern, then

r∗	matches zero or more occurrences of *r*.
r+	matches one or more occurrences of *r*.
r?	matches zero or one occurrence of *r*.
r{m,n}	matches at least "m" and at most "n" occurrences of *r*.
r{m,}	matches at least "m" occurrences of *r*.
r{m}	matches exactly "m" occurrences of *r*.

These repetition constructs have a high precedence—they bind only to the immediately preceding regular expression in the pattern. /ab+/ matches an *a* followed by one or more *b*'s, not a sequence of *ab*'s. You have to be careful with the * construct too—the pattern /a*/ will match any string; every string has zero or more *a*'s.

These patterns are called *greedy*, because by default they will match as much of the string as they can. You can alter this behavior, and have them match the minimum, by adding a question mark suffix.

```
a = "The moon is made of cheese"
show_regexp(a, /\w+/)              →    <<The>> moon is made of cheese
show_regexp(a, /\s.*\s/)           →    The<< moon is made of >>cheese
show_regexp(a, /\s.*?\s/)          →    The<< moon >>is made of cheese
show_regexp(a, /[aeiou]{2,99}/)    →    The m<<oo>>n is made of cheese
show_regexp(a, /mo?o/)             →    The <<moo>>n is made of cheese
```

Alternation

We know that the vertical bar is special, because our line-splitting pattern had to escape it with a backslash. That's because an unescaped vertical bar (|) matches either the regular expression that precedes it or the regular expression that follows it.

```
a = "red ball blue sky"
show_regexp(a, /d|e/)                 →    r<<e>>d ball blue sky
show_regexp(a, /al|lu/)               →    red b<<al>>l blue sky
show_regexp(a, /red ball|angry sky/)  →    <<red ball>> blue sky
```

There's a trap for the unwary here, as | has a very low precedence. The last example above matches *red ball* or *angry sky*, not *red ball sky* or *red angry sky*. To match *red ball sky* or *red angry sky*, you'd need to override the default precedence using grouping.

Grouping

You can use parentheses to group terms within a regular expression. Everything within the group is treated as a single regular expression.

```
show_regexp('banana', /an*/)     →    b<<an>>ana
show_regexp('banana', /(an)*/)   →    <<>>banana
show_regexp('banana', /(an)+/)   →    b<<anan>>a

a = 'red ball blue sky'
show_regexp(a, /blue|red/)          →    <<red>> ball blue sky
show_regexp(a, /(blue|red) \w+/)    →    <<red ball>> blue sky
show_regexp(a, /(red|blue) \w+/)    →    <<red ball>> blue sky
show_regexp(a, /red|blue \w+/)      →    <<red>> ball blue sky

show_regexp(a, /red (ball|angry) sky/)  →    no match
a = 'the red angry sky'
show_regexp(a, /red (ball|angry) sky/)  →    the <<red angry sky>>
```

Parentheses also collect the results of pattern matching. Ruby counts opening parentheses, and for each stores the result of the partial match between it and the corresponding closing parenthesis. You can use this partial match both within the rest of the pattern and in your Ruby program. Within the pattern, the sequence \1 refers to the match of the first group, \2 the second group, and so on. Outside the pattern, the special variables $1, $2, and so on, serve the same purpose.

```
"12:50am" =~ /(\d\d):(\d\d)(..)/        →    0
"Hour is #$1, minute #$2"               →    "Hour is 12, minute 50"
"12:50am" =~ /((\d\d):(\d\d))(..)/      →    0
"Time is #$1"                           →    "Time is 12:50"
"Hour is #$2, minute #$3"               →    "Hour is 12, minute 50"
"AM/PM is #$4"                          →    "AM/PM is am"
```

The ability to use part of the current match later in that match allows you to look for various forms of repetition.

```
# match duplicated letter
show_regexp('He said "Hello"', /(\w)\1/)    →    He said "He<<ll>>o"
# match duplicated substrings
show_regexp('Mississippi', /(\w+)\1/)       →    M<<ississ>>ippi
```

You can also use back references to match delimiters.

```
show_regexp('He said "Hello"', /(["']).*?\1/)    →    He said
                                                       <<"Hello">>
show_regexp("He said 'Hello'", /(["']).*?\1/)    →    He said
                                                       <<'Hello'>>
```

Pattern-Based Substitution

Sometimes finding a pattern in a string is good enough. If a friend challenges you to find a word that contains the letters *a*, *b*, *c*, *d*, and *e* in order, you could search a word list with the pattern /a.*b.*c.*d.*e/ and find *abjectedness*, *absconded*, *ambuscade*, and *carbacidometer*, among others. That has to be worth something.

However, sometimes you need to change things based on a pattern match. Let's go back to our song list file. Whoever created it entered all the artists' names in lowercase. When we display them on our jukebox's screen, they'd look better in mixed case. How can we change the first character of each word to uppercase?

The methods String#sub and String#gsub look for a portion of a string matching their first argument and replace it with their second argument. String#sub performs one replacement, and String#gsub replaces every occurrence of the match. Both routines return a new copy of the String containing the substitutions. Mutator versions String#sub! and String#gsub! modify the original string.

```
a = "the quick brown fox"
a.sub(/[aeiou]/, '*')    →    "th* quick brown fox"
a.gsub(/[aeiou]/, '*')   →    "th* q**ck br*wn f*x"
a.sub(/\s\S+/, '')       →    "the brown fox"
a.gsub(/\s\S+/, '')      →    "the"
```

The second argument to both functions can be either a `String` or a block. If a block is used, it is passed the matching substring, and the block's value is substituted into the original string.

```
a = "the quick brown fox"
a.sub(/^./) {|match| match.upcase }          →    "The quick brown fox"
a.gsub(/[aeiou]/) {|vowel| vowel.upcase }     →    "thE qUIck brOwn fOx"
```

So, this looks like the answer to converting our artists' names. The pattern that matches the first character of a word is \b\w—look for a word boundary followed by a word character. Combine this with `gsub`, and we can hack the artists' names.

```
def mixed_case(name)
  name.gsub(/\b\w/) {|first| first.upcase }
end
```

```
mixed_case("fats waller")           →    "Fats Waller"
mixed_case("louis armstrong")       →    "Louis Armstrong"
mixed_case("strength in numbers")   →    "Strength In Numbers"
```

Backslash Sequences in the Substitution

Earlier we noted that the sequences \1, \2, and so on, are available in the pattern, standing for the *n*th group matched so far. The same sequences are available in the second argument of sub and gsub.

```
"fred:smith".sub(/(\w+):(\w+)/, '\2, \1')   →    "smith, fred"
"nercpyitno".gsub(/(.)(.)/, '\2\1')          →    "encryption"
```

Additional backslash sequences work in substitution strings: \& (last match), \+ (last matched group), \` (string prior to match), \' (string after match), and \\ (a literal backslash).

It gets confusing if you want to include a literal backslash in a substitution. The obvious thing is to write

```
str.gsub(/\\/, '\\\\')
```

Clearly, this code is trying to replace each backslash in str with two. The programmer doubled up the backslashes in the replacement text, knowing that they'd be converted to \\ in syntax analysis. However, when the substitution occurs, the regular expression engine performs another pass through the string, converting \\ to \, so the net effect is to replace each single backslash with another single backslash. You need to write gsub(/\\/, '\\\\\\\\')!

```
str = 'a\b\c'                        →    "a\b\c"
str.gsub(/\\/, '\\\\\\\\')   →    "a\\b\\c"
```

However, using the fact that \& is replaced by the matched string, you could also write

```
str = 'a\b\c'                →    "a\b\c"
str.gsub(/\\/, '\&\&')   →    "a\\b\\c"
```

If you use the block form of gsub, the string for substitution is analyzed only once (during the syntax pass) and the result is what you intended.

```
str = 'a\b\c'                     →    "a\b\c"
str.gsub(/\\/) { '\\\\' }   →    "a\\b\\c"
```

Finally, as an example of the wonderful expressiveness of combining regular expressions with code blocks, consider the following code fragment from the CGI library module, written by Wakou Aoyama. The code takes a string containing HTML escape sequences and converts it into normal ASCII. Because it was written for a Japanese audience, it uses the n modifier on the regular expressions, which turns off wide-character processing. It also illustrates Ruby's case expression, which we discuss starting on page 98.

```
def unescapeHTML(string)
  str = string.dup
  str.gsub!(/&(.*?);/n) {
    match = $1.dup
    case match
    when /\Aamp\z/ni            then '&'
    when /\Aquot\z/ni           then '"'
    when /\Agt\z/ni             then '>'
    when /\Alt\z/ni             then '<'
    when /\A#(\d+)\z/n          then Integer($1).chr
    when /\A#x([0-9a-f]+)\z/ni  then $1.hex.chr
    end
  }
  str
end
puts unescapeHTML("1&lt;2 &amp;&amp; 4&gt;3")
puts unescapeHTML("&quot;A&quot; = &#65; = &#x41;")
```

produces:

```
1<2 && 4>3
"A" = A = A
```

Object-Oriented Regular Expressions

We have to admit that while all these weird variables are very convenient to use, they aren't very object oriented, and they're certainly cryptic. And didn't we say that everything in Ruby was an object? What has gone wrong here?

Nothing, really. It's just that when Matz designed Ruby, he produced a fully object-oriented regular expression handling system. He then made it look familiar to Perl programmers by wrapping all these $-variables on top of it all. The objects and classes are still there, underneath the surface. So let's spend a while digging them out.

We've already come across one class: regular expression literals create instances of class Regexp (documented beginning on page 600).

```
re = /cat/
re.class    →    Regexp
```

The method `Regexp#match` matches a regular expression against a string. If unsuccessful, the method returns `nil`. On success, it returns an instance of class `MatchData`, documented beginning on page 537. And that `MatchData` object gives you access to all available information about the match. All that good stuff that you can get from the $-variables is bundled in a handy little object.

```
re = /(\d+):(\d+)/     # match a time hh:mm
md = re.match("Time: 12:34am")
md.class                    →    MatchData
md[0]          # == $&    →    "12:34"
md[1]          # == $1    →    "12"
md[2]          # == $2    →    "34"
md.pre_match   # == $`    →    "Time: "
md.post_match  # == $'    →    "am"
```

Because the match data is stored in its own object, you can keep the results of two or more pattern matches available at the same time, something you can't do using the $-variables. In the next example, we're matching the same `Regexp` object against two strings. Each match returns a unique `MatchData` object, which we verify by examining the two subpattern fields.

```
re = /(\d+):(\d+)/      # match a time hh:mm
md1 = re.match("Time: 12:34am")
md2 = re.match("Time: 10:30pm")
md1[1, 2]    →    ["12", "34"]
md2[1, 2]    →    ["10", "30"]
```

So how do the $-variables fit in? Well, after every pattern match, Ruby stores a reference to the result (`nil` or a `MatchData` object) in a thread-local variable (accessible using $~). All the other regular expression variables are then derived from this object. Although we can't really think of a use for the following code, it demonstrates that all the other `MatchData`-related $-variables are indeed slaved off the value in $~.

```
re = /(\d+):(\d+)/
md1 = re.match("Time: 12:34am")
md2 = re.match("Time: 10:30pm")
[ $1, $2 ]   # last successful match       →    ["10", "30"]
$~ = md1
[ $1, $2 ]   # previous successful match   →    ["12", "34"]
```

Having said all this, we have to 'fess up. We normally use the $-variables rather than worrying about `MatchData` objects. For everyday use, they just end up being more convenient. Sometimes we just can't help being pragmatic.

## Chapter 6

More about Methods

So far in this book, we've been defining and using methods without much thought. Now it's time to get into the details.

Defining a Method

As we've seen, a method is defined using the keyword def. Method names should begin with a lowercase letter.[1] Methods that act as queries are often named with a trailing ?, such as instance of?. Methods that are "dangerous," or modify the receiver, may be named with a trailing !. For instance, String provides both a chop and a chop!. The first one returns a modified string; the second modifies the receiver in place. And methods that can be assigned to (a feature we discussed on page 31) end with an equals sign (=). ?, !, and = are the only "weird" characters allowed as method name suffixes.

Now that we've specified a name for our new method, we may need to declare some parameters. These are simply a list of local variable names in parentheses. (The parentheses are optional around a method's arguments; our convention is to use them when a method has arguments and omit them when it doesn't.)

```
def my_new_method(arg1, arg2, arg3)      # 3 arguments
  # Code for the method would go here
end
def my_other_new_method                  # No arguments
  # Code for the method would go here
end
```

Ruby lets you specify default values for a method's arguments—values that will be used if the caller doesn't pass them explicitly. You do this using the assignment operator.

---

1. You won't get an immediate error if you use an uppercase letter, but when Ruby sees you calling the method, it will first guess that it is a constant, not a method invocation, and as a result it may parse the call incorrectly.

```
def cool_dude(arg1="Miles", arg2="Coltrane", arg3="Roach")
  "#{arg1}, #{arg2}, #{arg3}."
end
```

```
cool_dude                            →    "Miles, Coltrane, Roach."
cool_dude("Bart")                    →    "Bart, Coltrane, Roach."
cool_dude("Bart", "Elwood")          →    "Bart, Elwood, Roach."
cool_dude("Bart", "Elwood", "Linus") →    "Bart, Elwood, Linus."
```

The body of a method contains normal Ruby expressions, except that you may not define a nonsingleton class or module within a method. If you define a method inside another method, the inner method gets defined when the outer method executes. The return value of a method is the value of the last expression executed or the result of an explicit `return` expression.

Variable-Length Argument Lists

But what if you want to pass in a variable number of arguments or want to capture multiple arguments into a single parameter? Placing an asterisk before the name of the parameter after the "normal" parameters does just that.

```
def varargs(arg1, *rest)
  "Got #{arg1} and #{rest.join(', ')}"
end
```

```
varargs("one")                  →    "Got one and "
varargs("one", "two")           →    "Got one and two"
varargs "one", "two", "three"   →    "Got one and two, three"
```

In this example, the first argument is assigned to the first method parameter as usual. However, the next parameter is prefixed with an asterisk, so all the remaining arguments are bundled into a new `Array`, which is then assigned to that parameter.

Methods and Blocks

As we discussed in the section on blocks and iterators beginning on page 49, when a method is called, it may be associated with a block. Normally, you simply call the block from within the method using `yield`.

```
def take_block(p1)
  if block_given?
    yield(p1)
  else
    p1
  end
end
```

```
take_block("no block")                             →   "no block"
take_block("no block") {|s| s.sub(/no /, '') }     →   "block"
```

However, if the last parameter in a method definition is prefixed with an ampersand, any associated block is converted to a `Proc` object, and that object is assigned to the parameter.

```
class TaxCalculator
  def initialize(name, &block)
    @name, @block = name, block
  end
  def get_tax(amount)
    "#@name on #{amount} = #{ @block.call(amount) }"
  end
end

tc = TaxCalculator.new("Sales tax") {|amt| amt * 0.075 }

tc.get_tax(100)  →  "Sales tax on 100 = 7.5"
tc.get_tax(250)  →  "Sales tax on 250 = 18.75"
```

Calling a Method

You call a method by specifying a receiver, the name of the method, and optionally some parameters and an optional block.

```
connection.download_MP3("jitterbug") {|p| show_progress(p) }
```

In this example, the object `connection` is the receiver, `download_MP3` is the name of the method, `"jitterbug"` is the parameter, and the stuff between the braces is the associated block.

For class and module methods, the receiver will be the class or module name.

```
File.size("testfile")  →  66
Math.sin(Math::PI/4)   →  0.707106781186548
```

If you omit the receiver, it defaults to `self`, the current object.

```
self.class      →  Object
self.frozen?    →  false
frozen?         →  false
self.object_id  →  978140
object_id       →  978140
```

This defaulting mechanism is how Ruby implements private methods. Private methods may *not* be called with a receiver, so they must be methods available in the current object.

Also, in the previous example we called `self.class`, but we could not call the method `class` without a receiver. This is because `class` is also a keyword in Ruby (it introduces class definitions), so its stand-alone use would generate a syntax error.

The optional parameters follow the method name. If no ambiguity exists, you can omit the parentheses around the argument list when calling a method.[2] However, except in the simplest cases we don't recommend this—some subtle problems can trip you up.[3] Our rule is simple: if you have any doubt, use parentheses.

```
a = obj.hash      # Same as
a = obj.hash()    # this.

obj.some_method "Arg1", arg2, arg3    # Same thing as
obj.some_method("Arg1", arg2, arg3)   # with parentheses.
```

Older Ruby versions compounded the problem by allowing you to put spaces between the method name and the opening parenthesis. This made it hard to parse: is the parenthesis the start of the parameters or the start of an expression? As of Ruby 1.8 you get a warning if you put a space between a method name and an open parenthesis.

Method Return Values

Every called method returns a value (although no rule says you have to use that value). The value of a method is the value of the last statement executed during the method's execution. Ruby has a `return` statement, which exits from the currently executing method. The value of a `return` is the value of its argument(s). It is idiomatic Ruby to omit the `return` if it isn't needed.

```
def meth_one
  "one"
end
meth_one   →   "one"

def meth_two(arg)
  case
  when arg > 0
    "positive"
  when arg < 0
    "negative"
  else
    "zero"
  end
end

meth_two(23)   →   "positive"
meth_two(0)    →   "zero"
```

---

2.   Other Ruby documentation sometimes calls these method calls without parentheses *commands*.

3.   In particular, you *must* use parentheses on a method call that is itself a parameter to another method call (unless it is the last parameter).

```
def meth_three
  100.times do |num|
    square = num*num
    return num, square if square > 1000
  end
end
meth_three   →   [32, 1024]
```

As the last case illustrates, if you give `return` multiple parameters, the method returns them in an array. You can use parallel assignment to collect this return value.

```
num, square = meth_three
num       →   32
square    →   1024
```

Expanding Arrays in Method Calls

Earlier we saw that if you put an asterisk in front of a formal parameter in a method definition, multiple arguments in the call to the method will be bundled into an array. Well, the same thing works in reverse.

When you call a method, you can explode an array, so that each of its members is taken as a separate parameter. Do this by prefixing the array argument (which must follow all the regular arguments) with an asterisk.

```
def five(a, b, c, d, e)
  "I was passed #{a} #{b} #{c} #{d} #{e}"
end

five(1, 2, 3, 4, 5 )        →   "I was passed 1 2 3 4 5"
five(1, 2, 3, *['a', 'b'])  →   "I was passed 1 2 3 a b"
five(*(10..14).to_a)        →   "I was passed 10 11 12 13 14"
```

Making Blocks More Dynamic

We've already seen how to associate a block with a method call.

```
list_bones("aardvark") do |bone|
  # ...
end
```

Normally, this is perfectly good enough—you associate a fixed block of code with a method in the same way you'd have a chunk of code after an `if` or `while` statement.

Sometimes, however, you'd like to be more flexible. For example, we may be teaching math skills.[4] The student could ask for an *n*-plus table or an *n*-times table. If the student

---

4.   Of course, Andy and Dave would have to *learn* math skills first. Conrad Schneiker reminded us that there are three kinds of people: those who can count and those who can't.

asked for a 2-times table, we'd output 2, 4, 6, 8, and so on. (This code does not check its inputs for errors.)

```
print "(t)imes or (p)lus: "
times = gets
print "number: "
number = Integer(gets)

if times =~ /^t/
  puts((1..10).collect {|n| n*number }.join(", "))
else
  puts((1..10).collect {|n| n+number }.join(", "))
end
```

produces:

```
(t)imes or (p)lus: t
number: 2
2, 4, 6, 8, 10, 12, 14, 16, 18, 20
```

This works, but it's ugly, with virtually identical code on each branch of the `if` statement. It would be nice if we could factor out the block that does the calculation.

```
print "(t)imes or (p)lus: "
times = gets
print "number: "
number = Integer(gets)

if times =~ /^t/
  calc = lambda {|n| n*number }
else
  calc = lambda {|n| n+number }
end
puts((1..10).collect(&calc).join(", "))
```

produces:

```
(t)imes or (p)lus: t
number: 2
2, 4, 6, 8, 10, 12, 14, 16, 18, 20
```

If the last argument to a method is preceded by an ampersand, Ruby assumes that it is a `Proc` object. It removes it from the parameter list, converts the `Proc` object into a block, and associates it with the method.

Collecting Hash Arguments

Some languages feature *keyword arguments*—that is, instead of passing arguments in a given order and quantity, you pass the name of the argument with its value, in any order. Ruby 1.8 does not have keyword arguments (making us liars, because in the previous version of this book we said it would have. Perhaps in Ruby 2.0). In the meantime, people are using hashes as a way of achieving the same effect. For example, we could consider adding a more powerful named-search facility to our `SongList`.

```
class SongList
  def create_search(name, params)
    # ...
  end
end
list.create_search("short jazz songs",
                  {
                    'genre'              => "jazz",
                    'duration_less_than' => 270
                  })
```

The first parameter is the search name, and the second is a hash literal containing search parameters. The use of a hash means we can simulate keywords: look for songs with a genre of "jazz" and a duration less than $4\frac{1}{2}$ minutes. However, this approach is slightly clunky, and that set of braces could easily be mistaken for a block associated with the method. So, Ruby has a shortcut. You can place *key* => *value* pairs in an argument list, as long as they follow any normal arguments and precede any array and block arguments. All these pairs will be collected into a single hash and passed as one argument to the method. No braces are needed.

```
list.create_search('short jazz songs',
                  'genre'              => 'jazz',
                  'duration_less_than' => 270)
```

Finally, in idiomatic Ruby you'd probably use symbols rather than strings, as symbols make it clearer that you're referring to the name of something.

```
list.create_search('short jazz songs',
                  :genre               => :jazz,
                  :duration_less_than -> 270)
```

A well-written Ruby program will typically contain many methods, each quite small, so it's worth getting familiar with the options available when defining and using Ruby methods.

## Chapter 7

Expressions

So far we've been fairly cavalier in our use of expressions in Ruby. After all, a = b + c is pretty standard stuff. You could write a whole heap of Ruby code without reading any of this chapter.

But it wouldn't be as much fun ;-).

One of the first differences with Ruby is that anything that can reasonably return a value does: just about everything is an expression. What does this mean in practice?

Some obvious things include the ability to chain statements together.

```
a = b = c = 0              →    0
[ 3, 1, 7, 0 ].sort.reverse   →    [7, 3, 1, 0]
```

Perhaps less obvious, things that are normally statements in C or Java are expressions in Ruby. For example, the `if` and `case` statements both return the value of the last expression executed.

```
song_type = if song.mp3_type == MP3::Jazz
              if song.written < Date.new(1935, 1, 1)
                Song::TradJazz
              else
                Song::Jazz
              end
            else
              Song::Other
            end

rating = case votes_cast
         when 0...10    then Rating::SkipThisOne
         when 10...50   then Rating::CouldDoBetter
         else                Rating::Rave
         end
```

We'll talk more about `if` and `case` starting on page 96.

Operator Expressions

Ruby has the basic set of operators (+, -, *, /, and so on) as well as a few surprises. A complete list of the operators, and their precedences, is given in Table 22.4 on page 339.

In Ruby, many operators are actually implemented as method calls. For example, when you write a*b + c you're actually asking the object referenced by a to execute the method *, passing in the parameter b. You then ask the object that results from that calculation to execute the + method, passing c as a parameter. This is equivalent to writing

```
(a.*(b)).+(c)
```

Because everything is an object, and because you can redefine instance methods, you can always redefine basic arithmetic if you don't like the answers you're getting.

```
class Fixnum
  alias old_plus +    # we can reference the original '+' as 'old_plus'

  # Redefine addition of Fixnums. This
  # is a BAD IDEA!
  def +(other)
    old_plus(other).succ
  end
end

1 + 2       →   4
a = 3
a += 4      →   8
a + a + a   →   26
```

More useful is that classes you write can participate in operator expressions just as if they were built-in objects. For example, we may want to be able to extract a number of seconds of music from the middle of a song. We could do this using the indexing operator [ ] to specify the music to be extracted.

```
class Song
  def [](from_time, to_time)
    result = Song.new(self.title + " [extract]",
                      self.artist,
                      to_time - from_time)
    result.set_start_time(from_time)
    result
  end
end
```

This code fragment extends class Song with the method [ ], which takes two parameters (a start time and an end time). It returns a new song, with the music clipped to the given interval. We could then play the introduction to a song with code such as

```
song[0, 15].play
```

Miscellaneous Expressions

As well as the obvious operator expressions and method calls, and the (perhaps) less obvious statement expressions (such as if and case), Ruby has a few more things that you can use in expressions.

Command Expansion

If you enclose a string in backquotes (sometimes called backticks), or use the delimited form prefixed by %x, it will (by default) be executed as a command by your underlying operating system. The value of the expression is the standard output of that command. Newlines will not be stripped, so it is likely that the value you get back will have a trailing return or linefeed character.

```
`date`                    →    "Thu Aug 26 22:36:31 CDT 2004\n"
`ls`.split[34]            →    "book.out"
%x{echo "Hello there"}    →    "Hello there\n"
```

You can use expression expansion and all the usual escape sequences in the command string.

```
for i in 0..3
  status = `dbmanager status id=#{i}`
  # ...
end
```

The exit status of the command is available in the global variable $?.

Redefining Backquotes

In the description of the command output expression, we said that the string in back-quotes would "by default" be executed as a command. In fact, the string is passed to the method called Kernel.` (a single backquote). If you want, you can override this.

```
alias old_backquote `
def `(cmd)
  result = old_backquote(cmd)
  if $? != 0
    fail "Command #{cmd} failed: #$?"
  end
  result
end
print `date`
print `data`
```

produces:

```
Thu Aug 26 22:36:31 CDT 2004
prog.rb:10: command not found: data
prog.rb:5:in ``': Command data failed: 32512 (RuntimeError)
from prog.rb:10
```

Assignment

Just about every example we've given so far in this book has featured assignment. Perhaps it's about time we said something about it.

An assignment statement sets the variable or attribute on its left side (the *lvalue*) to refer to the value on the right (the *rvalue*). It then returns that value as the result of the assignment expression. This means you can chain assignments, and you can perform assignments in some unexpected places.

```
a = b = 1 + 2 + 3
a   →   6
b   →   6
a = (b = 1 + 2) + 3
a   →   6
b   →   3
File.open(name = gets.chomp)
```

Ruby has two basic forms of assignment. The first assigns an object reference to a variable or constant. This form of assignment is hardwired into the language.

```
instrument = "piano"
MIDDLE_A   = 440
```

The second form of assignment involves having an object attribute or element reference on the left side.

```
song.duration     = 234
instrument["ano"] = "ccolo"
```

These forms are special, because they are implemented by calling methods in the lvalues, which means you can override them.

We've already seen how to define a writable object attribute. Simply define a method name ending in an equals sign. This method receives as its parameter the assignment's rvalue.

```
class Song
  def duration=(new_duration)
    @duration = new_duration
  end
end
```

These attribute-setting methods don't have to correspond with internal instance variables, and you don't need an attribute reader for every attribute writer (or vice versa).

```
class Amplifier
  def volume=(new_volume)
    self.left_channel = self.right_channel = new_volume
  end
end
```

1.8 In older Ruby versions, the result of the assignment was the value returned by the attribute-setting method. In Ruby 1.8, the value of the assignment is *always* the value of the parameter; the return value of the method is discarded.

```
class Test
  def val=(val)
    @val = val
    return 99
  end
end

t = Test.new
a = t.val = 2
a    →   2
```

In older versions of Ruby, a would be set to 99 by the assignment, and in Ruby 1.8 it will be set to 2.

Parallel Assignment

During your first week in a programming course (or the second semester if it was a party school), you may have had to write code to swap the values in two variables.

```
int a - 1;
int b = 2;
int temp;

temp = a;
a = b;
b = temp;
```

You can do this much more cleanly in Ruby.

```
a, b = b, a
```

Ruby assignments are effectively performed in parallel, so the values assigned are not affected by the assignment itself. The values on the right side are evaluated in the order in which they appear before any assignment is made to variables or attributes on the left. A somewhat contrived example illustrates this. The second line assigns to the variables a, b, and c the values of the expressions x, x += 1, and x += 1, respectively.

```
x = 0                             →   0
a, b, c  =  x, (x += 1), (x += 1)  →   [0, 1, 2]
```

When an assignment has more than one lvalue, the assignment expression returns an array of the rvalues. If an assignment contains more lvalues than rvalues, the excess lvalues are set to nil. If a multiple assignment contains more rvalues than lvalues, the extra rvalues are ignored. If an assignment has just one lvalue and multiple rvalues, the rvalues are converted to an array and assigned to the lvalue.

Using Accessors within a Class

Why did we write `self.left_channel` in the example on page 90? Well, writable attributes have a hidden gotcha. Normally, methods within a class can invoke other methods in the same class and its superclasses in functional form (that is, with an implicit receiver of `self`). However, this doesn't work with attribute writers. Ruby sees the assignment and decides that the name on the left must be a local variable, not a method call to an attribute writer.

```
class BrokenAmplifier
  attr_accessor :left_channel, :right_channel
  def volume=(vol)
    left_channel = self.right_channel = vol
  end
end

ba = BrokenAmplifier.new
ba.left_channel = ba.right_channel = 99
ba.volume = 5
ba.left_channel    →    99
ba.right_channel   →    5
```

We forgot to put "`self.`" in front of the assignment to `left_channel`, so Ruby stored the new value in a local variable of method `volume=`; the object's attribute never got updated. This can be a tricky bug to track down.

You can collapse and expand arrays using Ruby's parallel assignment operator. If the last lvalue is preceded by an asterisk, all the remaining rvalues will be collected and assigned to that lvalue as an array. Similarly, if the last rvalue is an array, you can prefix it with an asterisk, which effectively expands it into its constituent values in place. (This is not necessary if the rvalue is the only thing on the right side—the array will be expanded automatically.)

```
a = [1, 2, 3, 4]
b, c = a          →    b == 1,    c == 2
b, *c = a         →    b == 1,    c == [2, 3, 4]
b, c = 99, a      →    b == 99,   c == [1, 2, 3, 4]
b, *c = 99, a     →    b == 99,   c == [[1, 2, 3, 4]]
b, c = 99, *a     →    b == 99,   c == 1
b, *c = 99, *a    →    b == 99,   c == [1, 2, 3, 4]
```

Nested Assignments

Parallel assignments have one more feature worth mentioning. The left side of an assignment may contain a parenthesized list of terms. Ruby treats these terms as if they were a nested assignment statement. It extracts the corresponding rvalue, assigning it to the parenthesized terms, before continuing with the higher-level assignment.

```
b, (c, d), e = 1,2,3,4        →    b == 1, c == 2, d == nil,    e == 3
b, (c, d), e = [1,2,3,4]      →    b == 1, c == 2, d == nil,    e == 3
b, (c, d), e = 1,[2,3],4      →    b == 1, c == 2, d == 3,      e == 4
b, (c, d), e = 1,[2,3,4],5    →    b == 1, c == 2, d == 3,      e == 5
b, (c,*d), e = 1,[2,3,4],5    →    b == 1, c == 2, d == [3, 4], e == 5
```

Other Forms of Assignment

In common with many other languages, Ruby has a syntactic shortcut: a = a + 2 may be written as a += 2.

The second form is converted internally to the first. This means that operators you have defined as methods in your own classes work as you'd expect.

```
class Bowdlerize
  def initialize(string)
    @value = string.gsub(/[aeiou]/, '*')
  end
  def +(other)
    Bowdlerize.new(self.to_s + other.to_s)
  end
  def to_s
    @value
  end
end

a = Bowdlerize.new("damn ")    →    d*mn
a += "shame"                   →    d*mn sh*m*
```

Something you won't find in Ruby are the autoincrement (++) and autodecrement ( ) operators of C and Java. Use the += and-= forms instead.

Conditional Execution

Ruby has several different mechanisms for conditional execution of code; most of them should feel familiar, and many have some neat twists. Before we get into them, though, we need to spend a short time looking at boolean expressions.

Boolean Expressions

Ruby has a simple definition of truth. Any value that is not nil or the constant false is true. You'll find that the library routines use this fact consistently. For example, IO#gets, which returns the next line from a file, returns nil at end of file, enabling you to write loops such as

```
while line = gets
  # process line
end
```

However, C, C++, and Perl programmers sometimes fall into a trap. The number zero is *not* interpreted as a false value. Neither is a zero-length string. This can be a tough habit to break.

Defined?, And, Or, and Not

Ruby supports all the standard boolean operators and introduces the new operator defined?.

Both and and && evaluate to true only if both operands are true. They evaluate the second operand only if the first is true (this is sometimes known as *shortcircuit* evaluation). The only difference in the two forms is precedence (and binds lower than &&).

Similarly, both or and || evaluate to true if either operand is true. They evaluate their second operand only if the first is false. As with and, the only difference between or and || is their precedence.

Just to make life interesting, and and or have the same precedence, and && has a higher precedence than ||.

not and ! return the opposite of their operand (false if the operand is true, and true if the operand is false). And, yes, not and ! differ only in precedence.

All these precedence rules are summarized in Table 22.4 on page 339.

The defined? operator returns nil if its argument (which can be an arbitrary expression) is not defined; otherwise it returns a description of that argument. If the argument is yield, defined? returns the string "yield" if a code block is associated with the current context.

```
defined? 1          →    "expression"
defined? dummy      →    nil
defined? printf     →    "method"
defined? String     →    "constant"
defined? $_         →    "global-variable"
defined? Math::PI   →    "constant"
defined? a = 1      →    "assignment"
defined? 42.abs     →    "method"
```

In addition to the boolean operators, Ruby objects support comparison using the methods ==, ===, <=>, =~, eql?, and equal? (see Table 7.1 on the next page). All but <=> are defined in class Object but are often overridden by descendents to provide appropriate semantics. For example, class Array redefines == so that two array objects are equal if they have the same number of elements and corresponding elements are equal.

Table 7.1. Common comparison operators

Operator	Meaning
==	Test for equal value.
===	Used to compare each of the items with the target in the when clause of a case statement.
<=>	General comparison operator. Returns −1, 0, or +1, depending on whether its receiver is less than, equal to, or greater than its argument.
<, <=, >=, >	Comparison operators for less than, less than or equal, greater than or equal, and greater than.
=~	Regular expression pattern match.
eql?	True if the receiver and argument have both the same type and equal values. 1 == 1.0 returns true, but 1.eql?(1.0) is false.
equal?	True if the receiver and argument have the same object ID.

Both == and =~ have negated forms, != and !~. However, these are converted by Ruby when your program is read. a != b is equivalent to !(a == b), and a !~ b is the same as !(a =~ b). This means that if you write a class that overrides == or =~ you get a working != and !~ for free. But on the flip side, this also means that you cannot define != and !~ independent of == and =~, respectively.

You can use a Ruby range as a boolean expression. A range such as exp1..exp2 will evaluate as false until exp1 becomes true. The range will then evaluate as true until exp2 becomes true. Once this happens, the range resets, ready to fire again. We show some examples of this on page 100.

1.8 Prior to Ruby 1.8, you could use a bare regular expression as a boolean expression. This is now deprecated. You can still use the ~ operator (described on page 601) to match $_ against a pattern.

The Value of Logical Expressions

In the text, we said things such as "and evaluates to true if both operands are true." But it's actually slightly more subtle than that. The operators and, or, && and || actually return the first of their arguments that determine the truth or falsity of the condition. Sounds grand. What does it mean?

Take the expression "val1 and val2". If val1 is either false or nil, then we know the expression cannot be true. In this case, the value of val1 determines the overall value of the expression, so it is the value returned. If val1 has some other value, then the overall value of the expression depends on val2, so its value is returned.

```
nil    and  true    →   nil
false  and  true    →   false
99     and  false   →   false
99     and  nil     →   nil
99     and  "cat"   →   "cat"
```

Note that despite all this magic, the overall truth value of the expression is correct.

The same evaluation takes place for or (except an or expression's value is known early if val1 is not false).

```
false  or  nil     →   nil
nil    or  false   →   false
99     or  false   →   99
```

A common Ruby idiom makes use of this.

```
words[key] ||= []
words[key] << word
```

The first line is equivalent to words[key] = words[key] || []. If the entry in the hash words for key is unset (nil), the value of || will be the second operand, a new, empty array. Thus, this line of code will assign an array to a hash element that doesn't already have a value, leaving it untouched otherwise. You'll sometimes see this written on one line:

```
(words[key] ||= []) << word
```

If and Unless Expressions

An if expression in Ruby is pretty similar to "if" statements in other languages.

```
if song.artist == "Gillespie" then
  handle = "Dizzy"
elsif song.artist == "Parker" then
  handle = "Bird"
else
  handle = "unknown"
end
```

If you lay out your if statements on multiple lines, you can leave off the then keyword.

```
if song.artist == "Gillespie"
  handle = "Dizzy"
elsif song.artist == "Parker"
  handle = "Bird"
else
  handle = "unknown"
end
```

However, if you want to lay out your code more tightly, you can separate the boolean expression from the following statements with the then keyword.

```
if song.artist == "Gillespie" then  handle = "Dizzy"
elsif song.artist == "Parker" then  handle = "Bird"
else  handle = "unknown"
end
```

1.8/ You can get even terser and use a colon (:) in place of the then.

```
if song.artist == "Gillespie":  handle = "Dizzy"
elsif song.artist == "Parker":  handle = "Bird"
else  handle = "unknown"
end
```

You can have zero or more elsif clauses and an optional else clause.

As we've said before, if is an expression, not a statement—it returns a value. You don't have to use the value of an if expression, but it can come in handy.

```
handle = if song.artist == "Gillespie" then
           "Dizzy"
         elsif song.artist == "Parker" then
           "Bird"
         else
           "unknown"
         end
```

Ruby also has a negated form of the if statement.

```
unless song.duration > 180
  cost = 0.25
else
  cost = 0.35
end
```

Finally, for the C fans out there, Ruby also supports the C-style conditional expression.

```
cost = song.duration > 180 ? 0.35 : 0.25
```

A conditional expression returns the value of either the expression before or the expression after the colon, depending on whether the boolean expression before the question mark evaluates to true or false. In this case, if the song duration is greater than three minutes, the expression returns 0.35. For shorter songs, it returns 0.25. Whatever the result, it is then assigned to cost.

If and Unless Modifiers

Ruby shares a neat feature with Perl. Statement modifiers let you tack conditional statements onto the end of a normal statement.

```
mon, day, year = $1, $2, $3 if date =~ /(\d\d)-(\d\d)-(\d\d)/
puts "a = #{a}" if debug
print total unless total.zero?
```

For an `if` modifier, the preceding expression will be evaluated only if the condition is true. `unless` works the other way around.

```
File.foreach("/etc/fstab") do |line|
  next if line =~ /^#/          # Skip comments
  parse(line) unless line =~ /^$/  # Don't parse empty lines
end
```

Because `if` itself is an expression, you can get really obscure with statements such as

```
if artist == "John Coltrane"
  artist = "'Trane"
end unless use_nicknames == "no"
```

This path leads to the gates of madness.

Case Expressions

The Ruby `case` expression is a powerful beast: a multiway `if` on steroids. And just to make it even more powerful, it comes in two flavors.

The first form is fairly close to a series of `if` statements: it lets you list a series of conditions and execute a statement corresponding to the first one that's true. For example, leap years must be divisible by 400, or divisible by 4 and not by 100.

```
leap = case
       when year % 400 == 0: true
       when year % 100 == 0: false
       else year % 4   == 0
       end
```

The second form of the `case` statement is probably more common. You specify a target at the top of the `case` statement, and each `when` clause lists one or more comparisons.

```
case input_line
when "debug"
  dump_debug_info
  dump_symbols
when /p\s+(\w+)/
  dump_variable($1)
when "quit", "exit"
  exit
else
  print "Illegal command: #{input_line}"
end
```

As with `if`, `case` returns the value of the last expression executed, and you can use a `then` keyword if the expression is on the same line as the condition.

```
kind = case year
       when 1850..1889 then "Blues"
       when 1890..1909 then "Ragtime"
       when 1910..1929 then "New Orleans Jazz"
       when 1930..1939 then "Swing"
       when 1940..1950 then "Bebop"
       else                "Jazz"
       end
```

1.8 As with if statements, you can use a colon (:) in place of the then.

```
kind = case year
       when 1850..1889: "Blues"
       when 1890..1909: "Ragtime"
       when 1910..1929: "New Orleans Jazz"
       when 1930..1939: "Swing"
       when 1940..1950: "Bebop"
       else                "Jazz"
       end
```

case operates by comparing the target (the expression after the keyword case) with each of the comparison expressions after the when keywords. This test is done using *comparison === target*. As long as a class defines meaningful semantics for === (and all the built-in classes do), objects of that class can be used in case expressions.

For example, regular expressions define === as a simple pattern match.

```
case line
when /title=(.*)/
  puts "Title is #$1"
when /track=(.*)/
  puts "Track is #$1"
when /artist=(.*)/
  puts "Artist is #$1"
end
```

Ruby classes are instances of class Class, which defines === to test if the argument is an instance of the class or one of its superclasses. So (abandoning the benefits of polymorphism and bringing the gods of refactoring down around your ears), you can test the class of objects.

```
case shape
when Square, Rectangle
  # ...
when Circle
  # ...
when Triangle
  # ...
else
  # ...
end
```

Loops

Don't tell anyone, but Ruby has pretty primitive built-in looping constructs.

The while loop executes its body zero or more times as long as its condition is true. For example, this common idiom reads until the input is exhausted.

```
while line = gets
  # ...
end
```

The until loop is the opposite; it executes the body *until* the condition becomes true.

```
until play_list.duration > 60
  play_list.add(song_list.pop)
end
```

As with if and unless, you can use both of the loops as statement modifiers.

```
a = 1
a *= 2  while a < 100
a -= 10 until a < 100
a   →   98
```

On page 95 in the section on boolean expressions, we said that a range can be used as a kind of flip-flop, returning true when some event happens and then staying true until a second event occurs. This facility is normally used within loops. In the example that follows, we read a text file containing the first ten ordinal numbers ("first," "second," and so on) but print only the lines starting with the one that matches "third" and ending with the one that matches "fifth."

```
file = File.open("ordinal")
while line = file.gets
  puts(line)  if line =~ /third/ .. line =~ /fifth/
end
```

produces:

```
third
fourth
fifth
```

You may find folks who come from Perl writing the previous example slightly differently.

```
file = File.open("ordinal")
while file.gets
  print  if ~/third/ .. ~/fifth/
end
```

produces:

```
third
fourth
fifth
```

This uses some behind-the-scenes magic behavior: `gets` assigns the last line read to the global variable `$_`, the `~` operator does a regular expression match against `$_`, and `print` with no arguments prints `$_`. This kind of code is falling out of fashion in the Ruby community.

The start and end of a range used in a boolean expression can themselves be expressions. These are evaluated each time the overall boolean expression is evaluated. For example, the following code uses the fact that the variable `$.` contains the current input line number to display line numbers one through three and those between a match of `/eig/` and `/nin/`.

```
File.foreach("ordinal") do |line|
  if (($. == 1) || line =~ /eig/) .. (($. == 3) || line =~ /nin/)
    print line
  end
end
```

produces:

```
first
second
third
eighth
ninth
```

You'll come across a wrinkle when you use `while` and `until` as statement modifiers. If the statement they are modifying is a begin/end block, the code in the block will always execute at least one time, regardless of the value of the boolean expression.

```
print "Hello\n" while false
begin
  print "Goodbye\n"
end while false
```

produces:

```
Goodbye
```

Iterators

If you read the beginning of the previous section, you may have been discouraged. "Ruby has pretty primitive built-in looping constructs," it said. Don't despair, gentle reader, for we have good news. Ruby doesn't need any sophisticated built-in loops, because all the fun stuff is implemented using Ruby iterators.

For example, Ruby doesn't have a "for" loop—at least not the kind you'd find in C, C++, and Java. Instead, Ruby uses methods defined in various built-in classes to provide equivalent, but less error-prone, functionality.

Let's look at some examples.

```
3.times do
  print "Ho! "
end
```

produces:

```
Ho! Ho! Ho!
```

It's easy to avoid fence-post and off-by-one errors; this loop will execute three times, period. In addition to `times`, integers can loop over specific ranges by calling `downto` and `upto`, and all numbers can loop using `step`. For instance, a traditional "for" loop that runs from 0 to 9 (something like `i=0; i < 10; i++`) is written as follows.

```
0.upto(9) do |x|
  print x, " "
end
```

produces:

```
0 1 2 3 4 5 6 7 8 9
```

A loop from 0 to 12 by 3 can be written as follows.

```
0.step(12, 3) {|x| print x, " " }
```

produces:

```
0 3 6 9 12
```

Similarly, iterating over arrays and other containers is made easy using their each method.

```
[ 1, 1, 2, 3, 5 ].each {|val| print val, " " }
```

produces:

```
1 1 2 3 5
```

And once a class supports `each`, the additional methods in the `Enumerable` module (documented beginning on page 454 and summarized on pages 120–120) become available. For example, the `File` class provides an `each` method, which returns each line of a file in turn. Using the `grep` method in `Enumerable`, we could iterate over only those lines that meet a certain condition.

```
File.open("ordinal").grep(/d$/) do |line|
  puts line
end
```

produces:

```
second
third
```

Last, and probably least, is the most basic loop of all. Ruby provides a built-in iterator called `loop`.

```
loop do
  # block ...
end
```

The `loop` iterator calls the associated block forever (or at least until you break out of the loop, but you'll have to read ahead to find out how to do that).

For ... In

Earlier we said that the only built-in Ruby looping primitives were `while` and `until`. What's this `for` thing, then? Well, `for` is almost a lump of syntactic sugar. When you write

```
for song in songlist
  song.play
end
```

Ruby translates it into something like

```
songlist.each do |song|
  song.play
end
```

The only difference between the `for` loop and the `each` form is the scope of local variables that are defined in the body. This is discussed on page 105.

You can use `for` to iterate over any object that responds to the method `each`, such as an `Array` or a `Range`.

```
for i in ['fee', 'fi', 'fo', 'fum']
  print i, " "
end
for i in 1..3
  print i, " "
end
for i in File.open("ordinal").find_all {|line| line =~ /d$/}
  print i.chomp, " "
end
```

produces:

```
fee fi fo fum 1 2 3 second third
```

As long as your class defines a sensible `each` method, you can use a `for` loop to traverse its objects.

```
class Periods
  def each
    yield "Classical"
    yield "Jazz"
    yield "Rock"
  end
end
```

```
periods = Periods.new
for genre in periods
  print genre, " "
end
```

produces:

```
Classical Jazz Rock
```

Break, Redo, and Next

The loop control constructs break, redo, and next let you alter the normal flow through a loop or iterator.

break terminates the immediately enclosing loop; control resumes at the statement following the block. redo repeats the loop from the start, but without reevaluating the condition or fetching the next element (in an iterator). next skips to the end of the loop, effectively starting the next iteration.

```
while line = gets
  next if line =~ /^\s*#/    # skip comments
  break if line =~ /^END/    # stop at end
                             # substitute stuff in backticks and try again
  redo if line.gsub!(/`(.*?)`/) { eval($1) }
  # process line ...
end
```

These keywords can also be used with any of the iterator-based looping mechanisms.

```
i=0
loop do
  i += 1
  next if i < 3
  print i
  break if i > 4
end
```

produces:

```
345
```

1.8 As of Ruby 1.8, a value may be passed to break and next. When used in conventional loops, it probably makes sense only to do this with break, where it sets the value returned by the loop. (Any value given to next is effectively lost.) If a conventional loop doesn't execute a break, its value is nil.

```
result = while line = gets
           break(line) if line =~ /answer/
         end
process_answer(result) if result
```

If you want the nitty-gritty detail of how break and next work with blocks and procs, have a look at the reference description starting on page 358. If you are looking for a way of exiting from nested blocks or loops, have a look at `Kernel.catch`, described on pages 362 and 519.

Retry

The `redo` statement causes a loop to repeat the current iteration. Sometimes, though, you need to wind the loop right back to the very beginning. The `retry` statement is just the ticket. `retry` restarts any kind of iterator loop.

```
for i in 1..100
  print "Now at #{i}. Restart? "
  retry if gets =~ /^y/i
end
```

Running this interactively, you may see

```
Now at 1. Restart? n
Now at 2. Restart? y
Now at 1. Restart? n
  . . .
```

`retry` will reevaluate any arguments to the iterator before restarting it. Here's an example of a do-it-yourself `until` loop.

```
def do_until(cond)
  break if cond
  yield
  retry
end
i = 0
do_until(i > 10) do
  print i, " "
  i += 1
end
```

produces:

```
0 1 2 3 4 5 6 7 8 9 10
```

Variable Scope, Loops, and Blocks

The `while`, `until`, and `for` loops are built into the language and do not introduce new scope; previously existing locals can be used in the loop, and any new locals created will be available afterward.

The blocks used by iterators (such as `loop` and `each`) are a little different. Normally, the local variables created in these blocks are not accessible outside the block.

```
[ 1, 2, 3 ].each do |x|
  y = x + 1
end
[ x, y ]
```

produces:

```
prog.rb:4: undefined local variable or method `x' for
 main:Object (NameError)
```

However, if at the time the block executes a local variable already exists with the same name as that of a variable in the block, the existing local variable will be used in the block. Its value will therefore be available after the block finishes. As the following example shows, this applies both to normal variables in the block and to the block's parameters.

```
x = nil
y = nil
[ 1, 2, 3 ].each do |x|
  y = x + 1
end
[ x, y ]   →   [3, 4]
```

Note that the variable need not have been given a value in the outer scope: the Ruby interpreter just needs to have seen it.

```
if false
  a = 1
end
3.times {|i| a = i }

a   →   2
```

The whole issue with variable scope and blocks is one that generates considerable discussion in the Ruby community. The current scheme has definite problems (particularly when variables are unexpectedly aliased inside blocks), but at the same time no one has managed to come up with something that's both better and acceptable to the wider community. Matz is promising changes in Ruby 2.0, but in the meantime, we have a couple of suggestions to minimize the problems with local and block variables interfering.

- Keep your methods and blocks short. The fewer variables, the smaller the chance that they'll clobber each other. It's also easier to eyeball the code and check that you don't have conflicting names.

- Use different naming schemes for local variables and block parameters. For example, you probably don't want a local variable called "i," but that might be perfectly acceptable as a block parameter.

In reality, this problem doesn't arise in practice as often as you may think.

## Chapter 8

Exceptions, Catch, and Throw

So far we've been developing code in Pleasantville, a wonderful place where nothing ever, ever goes wrong. Every library call succeeds, users never enter incorrect data, and resources are plentiful and cheap. Well, that's about to change. Welcome to the real world!

In the real world, errors happen. Good programs (and programmers) anticipate them and arrange to handle them gracefully. This isn't always as easy as it may sound. Often the code that detects an error does not have the context to know what to do about it. For example, attempting to open a file that doesn't exist is acceptable in some circumstances and is a fatal error at other times. What's your file-handling module to do?

The traditional approach is to use return codes. The open method returns some specific value to say it failed. This value is then propagated back through the layers of calling routines until someone wants to take responsibility for it.

The problem with this approach is that managing all these error codes can be a pain. If a function calls open, then read, and finally close, and each can return an error indication, how can the function distinguish these error codes in the value it returns to *its* caller?

To a large extent, exceptions solve this problem. Exceptions let you package information about an error into an object. That exception object is then propagated back up the calling stack automatically until the runtime system finds code that explicitly declares that it knows how to handle that type of exception.

The Exception Class

The package that contains the information about an exception is an object of class Exception or one of class Exception's children. Ruby predefines a tidy hierarchy of exceptions, shown in Figure 8.1 on the next page. As we'll see later, this hierarchy makes handling exceptions considerably easier.

When you need to raise an exception, you can use one of the built-in Exception classes, or you can create one of your own. If you create your own, you may want to make it a subclass of StandardError or one of its children. If you don't, your exception won't be caught by default.

Every Exception has associated with it a message string and a stack backtrace. If you define your own exceptions, you can add additional information.

Handling Exceptions

Our jukebox downloads songs from the Internet using a TCP socket. The basic code is simple (assuming that the filename and the socket are already set up).

```
op_file = File.open(opfile_name, "w")
while data = socket.read(512)
  op_file.write(data)
end
```

What happens if we get a fatal error halfway through the download? We certainly don't want to store an incomplete song in the song list. "I Did It My *click*."

Let's add some exception-handling code and see how it helps. To do exception handling, we enclose the code that could raise an exception in a begin/end block and use one or more rescue clauses to tell Ruby the types of exceptions we want to handle. In this particular case we're interested in trapping SystemCallError exceptions (and, by implication, any exceptions that are subclasses of SystemCallError), so that's what appears on the rescue line. In the error-handling block, we report the error, close and delete the output file, and then reraise the exception.

```
op_file = File.open(opfile_name, "w")
begin
  # Exceptions raised by this code will
  # be caught by the following rescue clause
  while data = socket.read(512)
    op_file.write(data)
  end
rescue SystemCallError
  $stderr.print "IO failed: " + $!
  op_file.close
  File.delete(opfile_name)
  raise
end
```

When an exception is raised, and independent of any subsequent exception handling, Ruby places a reference to the associated Exception object into the global variable $!

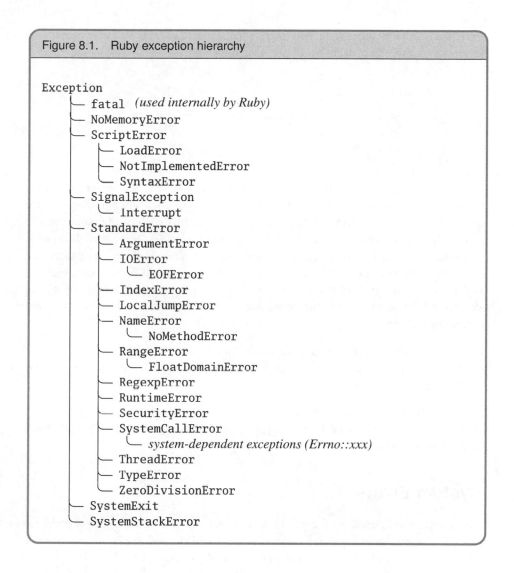

Figure 8.1.   Ruby exception hierarchy

```
Exception
    └── fatal  (used internally by Ruby)
    ├── NoMemoryError
    ├── ScriptError
    │    ├── LoadError
    │    ├── NotImplementedError
    │    └── SyntaxError
    ├── SignalException
    │    └── Interrupt
    ├── StandardError
    │    ├── ArgumentError
    │    ├── IOError
    │    │    └── EOFError
    │    ├── IndexError
    │    ├── LocalJumpError
    │    ├── NameError
    │    │    └── NoMethodError
    │    ├── RangeError
    │    │    └── FloatDomainError
    │    ├── RegexpError
    │    ├── RuntimeError
    │    ├── SecurityError
    │    ├── SystemCallError
    │    │    └── system-dependent exceptions (Errno::xxx)
    │    ├── ThreadError
    │    ├── TypeError
    │    └── ZeroDivisionError
    ├── SystemExit
    └── SystemStackError
```

(the exclamation point presumably mirroring our surprise that any of *our* code could cause errors). In the previous example, we used the $! variable to format our error message.

After closing and deleting the file, we call `raise` with no parameters, which reraises the exception in $!. This is a useful technique, as it allows you to write code that filters exceptions, passing on those you can't handle to higher levels. It's almost like implementing an inheritance hierarchy for error processing.

You can have multiple `rescue` clauses in a `begin` block, and each `rescue` clause can specify multiple exceptions to catch. At the end of each `rescue` clause you can give

Ruby the name of a local variable to receive the matched exception. Many people find this more readable than using $! all over the place.

```
begin
  eval string
rescue SyntaxError, NameError => boom
  print "String doesn't compile: " + boom
rescue StandardError => bang
  print "Error running script: " + bang
end
```

How does Ruby decide which rescue clause to execute? It turns out that the processing is pretty similar to that used by the case statement. For each rescue clause in the begin block, Ruby compares the raised exception against each of the parameters in turn. If the raised exception matches a parameter, Ruby executes the body of the rescue and stops looking. The match is made using *parameter*===$!. For most exceptions, this means that the match will succeed if the exception named in the rescue clause is the same as the type of the currently thrown exception, or is a superclass of that exception.[1] If you write a rescue clause with no parameter list, the parameter defaults to StandardError.

If no rescue clause matches, or if an exception is raised outside a begin/end block, Ruby moves up the stack and looks for an exception handler in the caller, then in the caller's caller, and so on.

Although the parameters to the rescue clause are typically the names of Exception classes, they can actually be arbitrary expressions (including method calls) that return an Exception class.

System Errors

System errors are raised when a call to the operating system returns an error code. On POSIX systems, these errors have names such as EAGAIN and EPERM. (If you're on a Unix box, you could type **man errno** to get a list of these errors.)

Ruby takes these errors and wraps them each in a specific exception object. Each is a subclass of SystemCallError, and each is defined in a module called Errno. This means you'll find exceptions with class names such as Errno::EAGAIN, Errno::EIO, and Errno::EPERM. If you want to get to the underlying system error code, Errno exception objects each have a class constant called (somewhat confusingly) Errno that contains the value.

---

1.   This comparison happens because exceptions are classes, and classes in turn are kinds of Module. The === method is defined for modules, returning true if the class of the operand is the same as or is a descendent of the receiver.

```
Errno::EAGAIN::Errno        →    35
Errno::EPERM::Errno         →    1
Errno::EIO::Errno           →    5
Errno::EWOULDBLOCK::Errno   →    35
```

Note that EWOULDBLOCK and EAGAIN have the same error number. This is a feature of the operating system of the computer used to produce this book—the two constants map to the same error number. To deal with this, Ruby arranges things so that Errno::EAGAIN and Errno::EWOULDBLOCK are treated identically in a rescue clause. If you ask to rescue one, you'll rescue either. It does this by redefining SystemCallError#=== so that if two subclasses of SystemCallError are compared, the comparison is done on their error number and not on their position in the hierarchy.

Tidying Up

Sometimes you need to guarantee that some processing is done at the end of a block of code, regardless of whether an exception was raised. For example, you may have a file open on entry to the block, and you need to make sure it gets closed as the block exits.

The ensure clause does just this. ensure goes after the last rescue clause and contains a chunk of code that will always be executed as the block terminates. It doesn't matter if the block exits normally, if it raises and rescues an exception, or if it is terminated by an uncaught exception—the ensure block will get run.

```
f = File.open("testfile")
begin
  # .. process
rescue
  # .. handle error
ensure
  f.close unless f.nil?
end
```

The else clause is a similar, although less useful, construct. If present, it goes after the rescue clauses and before any ensure. The body of an else clause is executed only if no exceptions are raised by the main body of code.

```
f = File.open("testfile")
begin
  # .. process
rescue
  # .. handle error
else
  puts "Congratulations-- no errors!"
ensure
  f.close unless f.nil?
end
```

Play It Again

Sometimes you may be able to correct the cause of an exception. In those cases, you can use the `retry` statement within a `rescue` clause to repeat the entire `begin/end` block. Clearly, tremendous scope exists for infinite loops here, so this is a feature to use with caution (and with a finger resting lightly on the interrupt key).

As an example of code that retries on exceptions, have a look at the following, adapted from Minero Aoki's `net/smtp.rb` library.

```
@esmtp = true

begin
  # First try an extended login. If it fails because the
  # server doesn't support it, fall back to a normal login

  if @esmtp then
    @command.ehlo(helodom)
  else
    @command.helo(helodom)
  end
rescue ProtocolError
  if @esmtp then
    @esmtp = false
    retry
  else
    raise
  end
end
```

This code tries first to connect to an SMTP server using the EHLO command, which is not universally supported. If the connection attempt fails, the code sets the `@esmtp` variable to `false` and retries the connection. If this fails a second time, the exception is raised up to the caller.

Raising Exceptions

So far we've been on the defensive, handling exceptions raised by others. It's time to turn the tables and go on the offensive. (Some say your gentle authors are always offensive, but that's a different book.)

You can raise exceptions in your code with the `Kernel.raise` method (or its somewhat judgmental synonym, `Kernel.fail`).

```
raise
raise "bad mp3 encoding"
raise InterfaceException, "Keyboard failure", caller
```

The first form simply reraises the current exception (or a `RuntimeError` if there is no current exception). This is used in exception handlers that need to intercept an exception before passing it on.

The second form creates a new `RuntimeError` exception, setting its message to the given string. This exception is then raised up the call stack.

The third form uses the first argument to create an exception and then sets the associated message to the second argument and the stack trace to the third argument. Typically the first argument will be either the name of a class in the `Exception` hierarchy or a reference to an object instance of one of these classes.[2] The stack trace is normally produced using the `Kernel.caller` method.

Here are some typical examples of `raise` in action.

```
raise

raise "Missing name" if name.nil?

if i >= names.size
  raise IndexError, "#{i} >= size (#{names.size})"
end

raise ArgumentError, "Name too big", caller
```

In the last example, we remove the current routine from the stack backtrace, which is often useful in library modules. We can take this further: the following code removes two routines from the backtrace by passing only a subset of the call stack to the new exception.

```
raise ArgumentError, "Name too big", caller[1..-1]
```

Adding Information to Exceptions

You can define your own exceptions to hold any information that you need to pass out from the site of an error. For example, certain types of network errors may be transient depending on the circumstances. If such an error occurs, and the circumstances are right, you could set a flag in the exception to tell the handler that it may be worth retrying the operation.

```
class RetryException < RuntimeError
  attr :ok_to_retry
  def initialize(ok_to_retry)
    @ok_to_retry = ok_to_retry
  end
end
```

---

2. Technically, this argument can be any object that responds to the message `exception` by returning an object such that `object.kind_of?(Exception)` is true.

Somewhere down in the depths of the code, a transient error occurs.

```
def read_data(socket)
  data = socket.read(512)
  if data.nil?
    raise RetryException.new(true), "transient read error"
  end
  # .. normal processing
end
```

Higher up the call stack, we handle the exception.

```
begin
  stuff = read_data(socket)
  # .. process stuff
rescue RetryException => detail
  retry if detail.ok_to_retry
  raise
end
```

Catch and Throw

While the exception mechanism of `raise` and `rescue` is great for abandoning execution when things go wrong, it's sometimes nice to be able to jump out of some deeply nested construct during normal processing. This is where `catch` and `throw` come in handy.

```
catch (:done)  do
  while line = gets
    throw :done unless fields = line.split(/\t/)
    songlist.add(Song.new(*fields))
  end
  songlist.play
end
```

`catch` defines a block that is labeled with the given name (which may be a `Symbol` or a `String`). The block is executed normally until a `throw` is encountered.

When Ruby encounters a `throw`, it zips back up the call stack looking for a `catch` block with a matching symbol. When it finds it, Ruby unwinds the stack to that point and terminates the block. So, in the previous example, if the input does not contain correctly formatted lines, the `throw` will skip to the end of the corresponding `catch`, not only terminating the `while` loop but also skipping the playing of the song list. If the `throw` is called with the optional second parameter, that value is returned as the value of the `catch`.

The following example uses a `throw` to terminate interaction with the user if ! is typed in response to any prompt.

```
def prompt_and_get(prompt)
  print prompt
  res = readline.chomp
  throw :quit_requested if res == "!"
  res
end
catch :quit_requested do
  name = prompt_and_get("Name: ")
  age  = prompt_and_get("Age:  ")
  sex  = prompt_and_get("Sex:  ")
  # ..
  # process information
end
```

As this example illustrates, the throw does not have to appear within the static scope of the catch.

## Chapter 9

Modules

Modules are a way of grouping together methods, classes, and constants. Modules give you two major benefits.

1. Modules provide a namespace and prevent name clashes.

2. Modules implement the mixin facility.

Namespaces

As you start to write bigger and bigger Ruby programs, you'll naturally find yourself producing chunks of reusable code—libraries of related routines that are generally applicable. You'll want to break this code into separate files so the contents can be shared among different Ruby programs.

Often this code will be organized into classes, so you'll probably stick a class (or a set of interrelated classes) into a file.

However, there are times when you want to group things together that don't naturally form a class.

An initial approach may be to put all these things into a file and simply load that file into any program that needs it. This is the way the C language works. However, this approach has a problem. Say you write a set of the trigonometry functions `sin`, `cos`, and so on. You stuff them all into a file, `trig.rb`, for future generations to enjoy. Meanwhile, Sally is working on a simulation of good and evil, and she codes a set of her own useful routines, including `be_good` and `sin`, and sticks them into `moral.rb`. Joe, who wants to write a program to find out how many angels can dance on the head of a pin, needs to load both `trig.rb` and `moral.rb` into his program. But both define a method called `sin`. Bad news.

The answer is the module mechanism. Modules define a *namespace*, a sandbox in which your methods and constants can play without having to worry about being stepped on by other methods and constants. The trig functions can go into one module

```
module Trig
  PI = 3.141592654
  def Trig.sin(x)
   # ..
  end
  def Trig.cos(x)
   # ..
  end
end
```

and the good and bad "moral" methods can go into another.

```
module Moral
  VERY_BAD = 0
  BAD      = 1
  def Moral.sin(badness)
    # ...
  end
end
```

Module constants are named just like class constants, with an initial uppercase letter. The method definitions look similar, too: these module methods are defined just like class methods.

If a third program wants to use these modules, it can simply load the two files (using the Ruby `require` statement, which we discuss on page 123) and reference the qualified names.

```
require 'trig'
require 'moral'
y = Trig.sin(Trig::PI/4)
wrongdoing = Moral.sin(Moral::VERY_BAD)
```

As with class methods, you call a module method by preceding its name with the module's name and a period, and you reference a constant using the module name and two colons.

Mixins

Modules have another, wonderful use. At a stroke, they pretty much eliminate the need for multiple inheritance, providing a facility called a *mixin*.

In the previous section's examples, we defined module methods, methods whose names were prefixed by the module name. If this made you think of class methods, your next thought may well be "what happens if I define instance methods within a module?"

Good question. A module can't have instances, because a module isn't a class. However, you can *include* a module within a class definition. When this happens, all the module's instance methods are suddenly available as methods in the class as well. They get *mixed in*. In fact, mixed-in modules effectively behave as superclasses.

```ruby
module Debug
  def who_am_i?
    "#{self.class.name} (\##{self.object_id}): #{self.to_s}"
  end
end
class Phonograph
  include Debug
  # ...
end
class EightTrack
  include Debug
  # ...
end
ph = Phonograph.new("West End Blues")
et = EightTrack.new("Surrealistic Pillow")

ph.who_am_i?   →   "Phonograph (#945760): West End Blues"
et.who_am_i?   →   "EightTrack (#945740): Surrealistic Pillow"
```

By including the Debug module, both Phonograph and EightTrack gain access to the who_am_i? instance method.

We'll make a couple of points about the include statement before we go on. First, it has nothing to do with files. C programmers use a preprocessor directive called #include to insert the contents of one file into another during compilation. The Ruby include statement simply makes a reference to a named module. If that module is in a separate file, you must use require (or its less commonly used cousin, load) to drag that file in before using include. Second, a Ruby include does not simply copy the module's instance methods into the class. Instead, it makes a reference from the class to the included module. If multiple classes include that module, they'll all point to the same thing. If you change the definition of a method within a module, even while your program is running, all classes that include that module will exhibit the new behavior.[1]

Mixins give you a wonderfully controlled way of adding functionality to classes. However, their true power comes out when the code in the mixin starts to interact with code in the class that uses it. Let's take the standard Ruby mixin Comparable as an example. You can use the Comparable mixin to add the comparison operators (<, <=, ==, >=, and >), as well as the method between?, to a class. For this to work, Comparable assumes that any class that uses it defines the operator <=>. So, as a class writer, you define one method, <=>, include Comparable, and get six comparison functions for free. Let's

---

1. Of course, we're speaking only of methods here. Instance variables are always per object, for example.

try this with our Song class, by making the songs comparable based on their duration. All we have to do is include the Comparable module and implement the comparison operator <=>.

```ruby
class Song
  include Comparable
  def initialize(name, artist, duration)
    @name     = name
    @artist   = artist
    @duration = duration
  end
  def <=>(other)
    self.duration <=> other.duration
  end
end
```

We can check that the results are sensible with a few test songs.

```ruby
song1 = Song.new("My Way",   "Sinatra", 225)
song2 = Song.new("Bicyclops", "Fleck",   260)

song1 <=> song2   →   -1
song1  <  song2   →   true
song1 ==  song1   →   true
song1  >  song2   →   false
```

Iterators and the Enumerable Module

You've probably noticed that the Ruby collection classes support a large number of operations that do various things with the collection: traverse it, sort it, and so on. You may be thinking, "Gee, it'd sure be nice if *my* class could support all these neat-o features, too!" (If you actually thought that, it's probably time to stop watching reruns of 1960s television shows.)

Well, your classes *can* support all these neat-o features, thanks to the magic of mixins and module Enumerable. All you have to do is write an iterator called each, which returns the elements of your collection in turn. Mix in Enumerable, and suddenly your class supports things such as map, include?, and find_all?. If the objects in your collection implement meaningful ordering semantics using the <=> method, you'll also get methods such as min, max, and sort.

Composing Modules

Back on page 52 we discussed the inject method of Enumerable. Enumerable is another standard mixin, implementing a bunch of methods in terms of the host class's each method. Because of this, we can use `inject` in any class that includes the Enumerable module and defines the method each. Many built-in classes do this.

```
[ 1, 2, 3, 4, 5 ].inject {|v,n| v+n }   →   15
( 'a'..'m').inject {|v,n| v+n }         →   "abcdefghijklm"
```

We could also define our own class that mixes in Enumerable and hence gets `inject` support.

```
class VowelFinder
  include Enumerable

  def initialize(string)
    @string = string
  end

  def each
    @string.scan(/[aeiou]/) do |vowel|
      yield vowel
    end
  end
end

vf = VowelFinder.new("the quick brown fox jumped")

vf.inject {|v,n| v+n }   →   "euiooue"
```

Notice that we've used the same pattern in the call to `inject` in these examples — we're using it to perform a summation. When applied to numbers, it returns the arithmetic sum, when applied to strings it concatenates them. We can use a module to encapsulate this functionality too.

```
module Summable
  def sum
    inject {|v,n| v+n }
  end
end

class Array
  include Summable
end

class Range
  include Summable
end

class VowelFinder
  include Summable
end

[ 1, 2, 3, 4, 5 ].sum   →   15
( 'a'..'m').sum         →   "abcdefghijklm"

vf = VowelFinder.new("the quick brown fox jumped")
vf.sum                  →   "euiooue"
```

Instance Variables in Mixins

People coming to Ruby from C++ often ask us, "What happens to instance variables in a mixin? In C++, I have to jump through some hoops to control how variables are shared in a multiple-inheritance hierarchy. How does Ruby handle this?"

Well, for starters, it's not really a fair question, we tell them. Remember how instance variables work in Ruby: the first mention of an @-prefixed variable creates the instance variable *in the current object,* self.

For a mixin, this means that the module you mix into your client class (the *mixee?*) may create instance variables in the client object and may use attr_reader and friends to define accessors for these instance variables. For instance, the Observable module in the following example adds an instance variable @observer_list to any class that includes it.

```ruby
module Observable
  def observers
    @observer_list ||= []
  end
  def add_observer(obj)
    observers << obj
  end
  def notify_observers
    observers.each {|o| o.update }
  end
end
```

However, this behavior exposes us to a risk. A mixin's instance variables can clash with those of the host class or with those of other mixins. The example that follows shows a class that uses our Observer module but that unluckily also uses an instance variable called @observer_list. At runtime, this program will go wrong in some hard-to-diagnose ways.

```ruby
class TelescopeScheduler
  # other classes can register to get notifications
  # when the schedule changes
  include Observable
  def initialize
    @observer_list = []  # folks with telescope time
  end
  def add_viewer(viewer)
    @observer_list << viewer
  end
  # ...
end
```

For the most part, mixin modules don't try to carry their own instance data around—they use accessors to retrieve data from the client object. But if you need to create a mixin that has to have its own state, ensure that the instance variables have unique names to distinguish them from any other mixins in the system (perhaps by using the module's name as part of the variable name). Alternatively, the module could use a module-level hash, indexed by the current object ID, to store instance-specific data without using Ruby instance variables.

```ruby
module Test
  State = {}
  def state=(value)
    State[object_id] = value
  end
  def state
    State[object_id]
  end
end

class Client
  include Test
end

c1 = Client.new
c2 = Client.new
c1.state = 'cat'
c2.state = 'dog'

c1.state   →   "cat"
c2.state   →   "dog"
```

Resolving Ambiguous Method Names

One of the other questions folks ask about mixins is, how is method lookup handled? In particular, what happens if methods with the same name are defined in a class, in that class's parent class, and in a mixin included into the class?

The answer is that Ruby looks first in the immediate class of an object, then in the mixins included into that class, and then in superclasses and their mixins. If a class has multiple modules mixed in, the last one included is searched first.

Including Other Files

Because Ruby makes it easy to write good, modular code, you'll often find yourself producing small files containing some chunk of self-contained functionality—an interface to *x*, an algorithm to do *y*, and so on. Typically, you'll organize these files as class or module libraries.

Having produced these files, you'll want to incorporate them into your new programs. Ruby has two statements that do this. The `load` method includes the named Ruby source file every time the method is executed.

```
load 'filename.rb'
```

The more commonly used `require` method loads any given file only once.[2]

```
require 'filename'
```

Local variables in a loaded or required file are not propagated to the scope that loads or requires them. For example, here's a file called `included.rb`.

```
a = 1
def b
  2
end
```

And here's what happens when we include it into another file.

```
a = "cat"
b = "dog"
require 'included'
a     →   "cat"
b     →   "dog"
b()   →   2
```

`require` has additional functionality: it can load shared binary libraries. Both routines accept relative and absolute paths. If given a relative path (or just a plain name), they'll search every directory in the current load path (`$:`, discussed on page 183) for the file.

Files loaded using `load` or `require` can, of course, include other files, which include other files, and so on. What may *not* be obvious is that `require` is an executable statement—it may be inside an `if` statement, or it may include a string that was just built. The search path can be altered at runtime as well. Just add the directory you want to the array `$:`.

Since `load` will include the source unconditionally, you can use it to reload a source file that may have changed since the program began. The example that follows is (very) contrived.

---

2. This is not strictly true. Ruby keeps a list of the files loaded by `require` in the array `$"`. However, this list contains just the names of files as given to `require`. It's possible to fake Ruby out and get the same file loaded twice.

```
require '/usr/lib/ruby/1.9/English.rb'
require '/usr/lib/ruby/1.9/rdoc/../English.rb'

$"   →   ["/usr/lib/ruby/1.9/English.rb", "/usr/lib/ruby/1.9/rdoc/../English.rb"]
```

In this case, both `require` statements ended up pointing at the same file but used different paths to load it. Some consider this a bug, and this behavior may well change in later releases.

```
5.times do |i|
  File.open("temp.rb","w") do |f|
    f.puts "module Temp"
    f.puts "  def Temp.var"
    f.puts "    #{i}"
    f.puts "  end"
    f.puts "end"
  end
  load "temp.rb"
  puts Temp.var
end
```

produces:

```
0
1
2
3
4
```

For a less contrived use of this facility, consider a Web application that reloads components while running. This allows it to update itself on the fly; it needn't be restarted for new version of the software to be integrated. This is one of the many benefits of using a dynamic language such as Ruby.

Basic Input and Output

Ruby provides what at first sight looks like two separate sets of I/O routines. The first is the simple interface—we've been using it pretty much exclusively so far.

```
print "Enter your name: "
name = gets
```

A whole set of I/O-related methods is implemented in the Kernel module—gets, open, print, printf, putc, puts, readline, readlines, and test—that makes it simple and convenient to write straightforward Ruby programs. These methods typically do I/O to standard input and standard output, which makes them useful for writing filters. You'll find them documented starting on page 516.

The second way, which gives you a lot more control, is to use IO objects.

What Is an IO Object?

Ruby defines a single base class, IO, to handle input and output. This base class is subclassed by classes File and BasicSocket to provide more specialized behavior, but the principles are the same. An IO object is a bidirectional channel between a Ruby program and some external resource.[1] An IO object may have more to it than meets the eye, but in the end you still simply write to it and read from it.

In this chapter, we'll be concentrating on class IO and its most commonly used subclass, class File. For more details on using the socket classes for networking, see the section beginning on page 763.

---

1.   For those who just have to know the implementation details, this means that a single IO object can sometimes be managing more than one operating system file descriptor. For example, if you open a pair of pipes, a single IO object contains both a read pipe and a write pipe.

Opening and Closing Files

As you may expect, you can create a new file object using `File.new`.

```
file = File.new("testfile", "r")
# ... process the file
file.close
```

You can create a `File` object that is open for reading, writing, or both, according to the mode string. (Here we opened `testfile` for reading with an `"r"`. We could also have used `"w"` for write or `"r+"` for read-write. The full list of allowed modes appears on page 504.) You can also optionally specify file permissions when creating a file; see the description of `File.new` on page 470 for details. After opening the file, we can work with it, writing and/or reading data as needed. Finally, as responsible software citizens, we close the file, ensuring that all buffered data is written and that all related resources are freed.

But here Ruby can make life a little bit easier for you. The method `File.open` also opens a file. In regular use, it behaves just like `File.new`. However, if a block is associated with the call, open behaves differently. Instead of returning a new `File` object, it invokes the block, passing the newly opened `File` as a parameter. When the block exits, the file is automatically closed.

```
File.open("testfile", "r") do |file|
  # ... process the file
end
```

This second approach has an added benefit. In the earlier case, if an exception is raised while processing the file, the call to `file.close` may not happen. Once the file variable goes out of scope, then garbage collection will eventually close it, but this may not happen for a while. Meanwhile, resources are being held open.

This doesn't happen with the block form of `File.open`. If an exception is raised inside the block, the file is closed before the exception is propagated on to the caller. It's as if the open method looks like the following.

```
class File
  def File.open(*args)
    result = f = File.new(*args)
    if block_given?
      begin
        result = yield f
      ensure
        f.close
      end
    end
    return result
  end
end
```

Reading and Writing Files

The same methods that we've been using for "simple" I/O are available for all file objects. So, gets reads a line from standard input (or from any files specified on the command line when the script was invoked), and file.gets reads a line from the file object *file*.

For example, we could create a program called copy.rb.

```
while line = gets
  puts line
end
```

If we run this program with no arguments, it will read lines from the console and copy them back to the console. Note that each line is echoed once the return key is pressed. (In this and later examples, we show user input in a bold font.)

```
% ruby copy.rb
These are lines
These are lines
that I am typing
that I am typing
^D
```

We can also pass in one or more filenames on the command line, in which case gets will read from each in turn.

```
% ruby copy.rb testfile
This is line one
This is line two
This is line three
And so on...
```

Finally, we can explicitly open the file and read from it.

```
File.open("testfile") do |file|
  while line = file.gets
    puts line
  end
end
```

produces:

```
This is line one
This is line two
This is line three
And so on...
```

As well as gets, I/O objects enjoy an additional set of access methods, all intended to make our lives easier.

Iterators for Reading

As well as using the usual loops to read data from an IO stream, you can also use various Ruby iterators. IO#each_byte invokes a block with the next 8-bit byte from the IO object (in this case, an object of type File).

```
File.open("testfile") do |file|
  file.each_byte {|ch| putc ch; print "." }
end
```

produces:

```
T.h.i.s. .i.s. .l.i.n.e. .o.n.e.
.T.h.i.s. .i.s. .l.i.n.e. .t.w.o.
.T.h.i.s. .i.s. .l.i.n.e. .t.h.r.e.e.
.A.n.d. .s.o. .o.n.......
.
```

IO#each_line calls the block with each line from the file. In the next example, we'll make the original newlines visible using String#dump, so you can see that we're not cheating.

```
File.open("testfile") do |file|
  file.each_line {|line| puts "Got #{line.dump}" }
end
```

produces:

```
Got "This is line one\n"
Got "This is line two\n"
Got "This is line three\n"
Got "And so on...\n"
```

You can pass each_line any sequence of characters as a line separator, and it will break up the input accordingly, returning the line ending at the end of each line of data. That's why you see the \n characters in the output of the previous example. In the next example, we'll use the character e as the line separator.

```
File.open("testfile") do |file|
  file.each_line("e") {|line|  puts "Got #{ line.dump }" }
end
```

produces:

```
Got "This is line"
Got " one"
Got "\nThis is line"
Got " two\nThis is line"
Got " thre"
Got "e"
Got "\nAnd so on...\n"
```

If you combine the idea of an iterator with the autoclosing block feature, you get
IO.foreach. This method takes the name of an I/O source, opens it for reading, calls
the iterator once for every line in the file, and then closes the file automatically.

```
IO.foreach("testfile") {|line| puts line }
```

produces:

```
This is line one
This is line two
This is line three
And so on...
```

Or, if you prefer, you can retrieve an entire file into a string or into an array of lines.

```
# read into string
str = IO.read("testfile")
str.length    →   66
str[0, 30]    →   "This is line one\nThis is line "

# read into an array
arr = IO.readlines("testfile")
arr.length    →   4
arr[0]        →   "This is line one\n"
```

Don't forget that I/O is never certain in an uncertain world—exceptions will be raised
on most errors, and you should be ready to rescue them and take appropriate action.

Writing to Files

So far, we've been merrily calling puts and print, passing in any old object and
trusting that Ruby will do the right thing (which, of course, it does). But what exactly
is it doing?

The answer is pretty simple. With a couple of exceptions, every object you pass to puts
and print is converted to a string by calling that object's to_s method. If for some
reason the to_s method doesn't return a valid string, a string is created containing the
object's class name and ID, something like #<ClassName:0x123456>.

The exceptions are simple, too. The nil object will print as the string "nil," and an array
passed to puts will be written as if each of its elements in turn were passed separately
to puts.

What if you want to write binary data and don't want Ruby messing with it? Well,
normally you can simply use IO#print and pass in a string containing the bytes to be
written. However, you can get at the low-level input and output routines if you really
want—look at the documentation for IO#sysread and IO#syswrite on page 514.

And how do you get the binary data into a string in the first place? The three common
ways are to use a literal, poke it in byte by byte, or use Array#pack.

```
str1 = "\001\002\003"      →     "\001\002\003"
str2 = ""
str2 << 1 << 2 << 3        →     "\001\002\003"
[ 1, 2, 3 ].pack("c*")     →     "\001\002\003"
```

But I Miss My C++ iostream

Sometimes there's just no accounting for taste.... However, just as you can append an object to an Array using the << operator, you can also append an object to an output IO stream.

```
endl = "\n"
STDOUT << 99 << " red balloons" << endl
```

produces:

```
99 red balloons
```

Again, the << method uses to_s to convert its arguments to strings before sending them on their merry way.

Although we started off disparaging the poor << operator, there are actually some good reasons for using it. Because other classes (such as String and Array) also implement a << operator with similar semantics, you can quite often write code that appends to something using << without caring whether it is added to an array, a file, or a string. This kind of flexibility also makes unit testing easy. We discuss this idea in greater detail in the chapter on duck typing, starting on page 365.

Doing I/O with Strings

There are often times where you need to work with code that assumes it's reading from or writing to one or more files. But you have a problem: the data isn't in files. Perhaps it's available instead via a SOAP service, or it has been passed to you as command-line parameters. Or maybe you're running unit tests, and you don't want to alter the real file system.

Enter StringIO objects. They behave just like other I/O objects, but they read and write strings, not files. If you open a StringIO object for reading, you supply it with a string. All read operations on the StringIO object then read from this string. Similarly, when you want to write to a StringIO object, you pass it a string to be filled.

```
require 'stringio'

ip = StringIO.new("now is\nthe time\nto learn\nRuby!")
op = StringIO.new("", "w")

ip.each_line do |line|
  op.puts line.reverse
end
op.string   →   "\nsi won\n\nemit eht\n\nnrael ot\n!ybuR\n"
```

Talking to Networks

Ruby is fluent in most of the Internet's protocols, both low-level and high-level.

For those who enjoy groveling around at the network level, Ruby comes with a set of classes in the socket library (documented starting on page 763). These classes give you access to TCP, UDP, SOCKS, and Unix domain sockets, as well as any additional socket types supported on your architecture. The library also provides helper classes to make writing servers easier. Here's a simple program that gets information about the "mysql" user on our local machine using the finger protocol.

```
require 'socket'

client = TCPSocket.open('127.0.0.1', 'finger')
client.send("mysql\n", 0)    # 0 means standard packet
puts client.readlines
client.close
```

produces:

```
Login: mysql           Name: MySQL Server
Directory: /var/empty              Shell: /usr/bin/false
Never logged in.
No Mail.
No Plan.
```

At a higher level, the lib/net set of library modules provides handlers for a set of application-level protocols (currently FTP, HTTP, POP, SMTP, and telnet). These are documented starting on page 698. For example, the following program lists the images that are displayed on the Pragmatic Programmer home page.

```
require 'net/http'

h = Net::HTTP.new('www.pragmaticprogrammer.com', 80)

response = h.get('/index.html', nil)

if response.message == "OK"
  puts response.body.scan(/<img src="(.*?)"/m).uniq
end
```

produces:

```
images/title_main.gif
images/dot.gif
/images/Bookshelf_1.5_in_green.png
images/sk_all_small.jpg
images/new.jpg
```

Although attractively simple, this example could be improved significantly. In particular, it doesn't do much in the way of error handling. It should really report "Not Found" errors (the infamous 404), and should handle redirects (which happen when a web server gives the client an alternative address for the requested page).

We can take this to a higher level still. By bringing the open-uri library into a program, the Kernel.open method suddenly recognizes http:// and ftp:// URLs in the filename. Not just that: it also handles redirects automatically.

```
require 'open-uri'
open('http://www.pragmaticprogrammer.com') do |f|
  puts f.read.scan(/<img src="(.*?)"/m).uniq
end
```

produces:

```
images/title_main.gif
images/dot.gif
/images/Bookshelf_1.5_in_green.png
images/sk_all_small.jpg
images/new.jpg
```

Have a look at Chapter 18 on page 235 for more information on using Ruby on the Internet.

## Chapter 11

Threads and Processes

Ruby gives you two basic ways to organize your program so that you can run different parts of it "at the same time." You can split up cooperating tasks *within* the program, using multiple threads, or you can split up tasks between different programs, using multiple processes. Let's look at each in turn.

Multithreading

Often the simplest way to do two things at once is by using *Ruby threads*. These are totally in-process, implemented within the Ruby interpreter. That makes the Ruby threads completely portable—they don't rely on the operating system. At the same time, you don't get certain benefits from having native threads. What does this mean?

You may experience thread starvation (that's where a low-priority thread doesn't get a chance to run). If you manage to get your threads deadlocked, the whole process may grind to a halt. And if some thread happens to make a call to the operating system that takes a long time to complete, all threads will hang until the interpreter gets control back. Finally, if your machine has more than one processor, Ruby threads won't take advantage of that fact—because they run in one process, and in a single native thread, they are constrained to run on one processor at a time.

All this sounds scary. In practice, though, in many circumstances the benefits of using threads far outweigh any potential problems that may occur. Ruby threads are an efficient and lightweight way to achieve parallelism in your code. You just need to understand the underlying implementation issues and design accordingly.

Creating Ruby Threads

Creating a new thread is pretty straightforward. The code that follows is a simple example. It downloads a set of Web pages in parallel. For each URL that it is asked to download, the code creates a separate thread that handles the HTTP transaction.

```
require 'net/http'
pages = %w( www.rubycentral.com slashdot.org www.google.com )
threads = []
for page_to_fetch in pages
  threads << Thread.new(page_to_fetch) do |url|
    h = Net::HTTP.new(url, 80)
    puts "Fetching: #{url}"
    resp = h.get('/', nil )
    puts "Got #{url}:  #{resp.message}"
  end
end
threads.each {|thr|  thr.join }
```

produces:

```
Fetching: www.rubycentral.com
Fetching: slashdot.org
Fetching: www.google.com
Got www.google.com:  OK
Got www.rubycentral.com:  OK
Got slashdot.org:  OK
```

Let's look at this code in more detail, as a few subtle things are happening.

New threads are created with the `Thread.new` call. It is given a block that contains the code to be run in a new thread. In our case, the block uses the `net/http` library to fetch the top page from each of our nominated sites. Our tracing clearly shows that these fetches are going on in parallel.

When we create the thread, we pass the required URL as a parameter. This parameter is passed to the block as `url`. Why do we do this, rather than simply using the value of the variable `page_to_fetch` within the block?

A thread shares all global, instance, and local variables that are in existence at the time the thread starts. As anyone with a kid brother can tell you, sharing isn't always a good thing. In this case, all three threads would share the variable `page_to_fetch`. The first thread gets started, and `page_to_fetch` is set to "www.rubycentral.com". In the meantime, the loop creating the threads is still running. The second time around, `page_to_fetch` gets set to "slashdot.org". If the first thread has not yet finished using the `page_to_fetch` variable, it will suddenly start using this new value. These kinds of bugs are difficult to track down.

However, local variables created within a thread's block are truly local to that thread— each thread will have its own copy of these variables. In our case, the variable `url` will be set at the time the thread is created, and each thread will have its own copy of the page address. You can pass any number of arguments into the block via `Thread.new`.

Manipulating Threads

Another subtlety occurs on the last line in our download program. Why do we call join on each of the threads we created?

When a Ruby program terminates, all threads are killed, regardless of their states. However, you can wait for a particular thread to finish by calling that thread's Thread#join method. The calling thread will block until the given thread is finished. By calling join on each of the requestor threads, you can make sure that all three requests have completed before you terminate the main program. If you don't want to block forever, you can give join a timeout parameter—if the timeout expires before the thread terminates, the join call returns nil. Another variant of join, the method Thread#value, returns the value of the last statement executed by the thread.

In addition to join, a few other handy routines are used to manipulate threads. The current thread is always accessible using Thread.current. You can obtain a list of all threads using Thread.list, which returns a list of all Thread objects that are runnable or stopped. To determine the status of a particular thread, you can use Thread#status and Thread#alive?.

In addition, you can adjust the priority of a thread using Thread#priority=. Higher-priority threads will run before lower-priority threads. We'll talk more about thread scheduling, and stopping and starting threads, in just a bit.

Thread Variables

A thread can normally access any variables that are in scope when the thread is created. Variables local to the block containing the thread code are local to the thread and are not shared.

But what if you need per-thread variables that can be accessed by other threads—including the main thread? Class Thread features a special facility that allows thread-local variables to be created and accessed by name. You simply treat the thread object as if it were a Hash, writing to elements using [ ]= and reading them back using [ ]. In the example that follows, each thread records the current value of the variable count in a thread-local variable with the key mycount. To do this, the code uses the string "mycount" when indexing thread objects. (A *race condition*[1] exists in this code, but we haven't talked about synchronization yet, so we'll just quietly ignore it for now.)

---

1. A race condition occurs when two or more pieces of code (or hardware) both try to access some shared resource, and where the outcome changes depending on the order in which they do so. In the example here, it is possible for one thread to set the value of its mycount variable to count, but before it gets a chance to increment count, the thread gets descheduled and another thread reuses the same value of count. These issues are fixed by synchronizing the access to shared resources (such as the count variable).

```
count = 0
threads = []
10.times do |i|
  threads[i] = Thread.new do
    sleep(rand(0.1))
    Thread.current["mycount"] = count
    count += 1
  end
end
threads.each {|t| t.join; print t["mycount"], ", " }
puts "count = #{count}"
```

produces:

```
4, 1, 0, 8, 7, 9, 5, 6, 3, 2, count = 10
```

The main thread waits for the subthreads to finish and then prints out the value of count captured by each. Just to make it more interesting, we have each thread wait a random time before recording the value.

Threads and Exceptions

What happens if a thread raises an unhandled exception? It depends on the setting of the abort_on_exception flag (documented on pages 633 and 636) and on the setting of the interpreter's *debug* flag (described on page 178).

If abort_on_exception is false and the debug flag is not enabled (the default condition), an unhandled exception simply kills the current thread—all the rest continue to run. In fact, you don't even hear about the exception until you issue a join on the thread that raised it.

In the following example, thread 2 blows up and fails to produce any output. However, you can still see the trace from the other threads.

```
threads = []
4.times do |number|
  threads << Thread.new(number) do |i|
    raise "Boom!" if i == 2
    print "#{i}\n"
  end
end
threads.each {|t| t.join }
```

produces:

```
0
1
3
prog.rb:4: Boom! (RuntimeError)
        from prog.rb:8:in `join'
        from prog.rb:8
        from prog.rb:8:in `each'
        from prog.rb:8
```

We can rescue the exception at the time the threads are joined.

```
threads = []
4.times do |number|
  threads << Thread.new(number) do |i|
    raise "Boom!" if i == 2
    print "#{i}\n"
  end
end
threads.each do |t|
  begin
    t.join
  rescue RuntimeError => e
    puts "Failed: #{e.message}"
  end
end
```

produces:

```
0
1
3
Failed: Boom!
```

However, set `abort_on_exception` to `true`, or use –d to turn on the debug flag, and an unhandled exception kills all running threads. Once thread 2 dies, no more output is produced.

```
Thread.abort_on_exception = true
threads = []
4.times do |number|
  threads << Thread.new(number) do |i|
    raise "Boom!" if i == 2
    print "#{i}\n"
  end
end
threads.each {|t| t.join }
```

produces:

```
0
1
prog.rb:5: Boom! (RuntimeError)
from prog.rb:4:in `initialize'
from prog.rb:4:in `new'
from prog.rb:4
from prog.rb:3:in `times'
from prog.rb:3
```

This code also illustrates a gotcha. Inside the loop, the threads use `print` to write out the number, rather than `puts`. Why? Because behind the scenes, `puts` splits its work into two chunks: it writes its argument, and then it writes a newline. Between these two, a thread could get scheduled, and the output would be interleaved. Calling `print` with a single string that already contains the newline gets around the problem.

Controlling the Thread Scheduler

In a well-designed application, you'll normally just let threads do their thing; building timing dependencies into a multithreaded application is generally considered to be bad form, as it makes the code far more complex and also prevents the thread scheduler from optimizing the execution of your program.

However, sometimes you need to control threads explicitly. Perhaps the jukebox has a thread that displays a light show. We may need to stop it temporarily when the music stops. You may have two threads in a classic producer-consumer relationship, where the consumer has to pause if the producer gets backlogged.

Class `Thread` provides a number of methods to control the thread scheduler. Invoking `Thread.stop` stops the current thread, and invoking `Thread#run` arranges for a particular thread to be run. `Thread.pass` deschedules the current thread, allowing others to run, and `Thread#join` and `Thread#value` suspend the calling thread until a given thread finishes.

We can demonstrate these features in the following, totally pointless program. It creates two child threads, t1 and t2, each of which runs an instance of class `Chaser`. The `chase` method increments a count but doesn't let it get more than two higher than the count in the other thread. To stop it getting higher, the method issues a `Thread.pass`, which allows the `chase` in the other thread to catch up. To make it interesting (for some minor definition of *interesting*), we have the threads suspend themselves initially and then start a random one first.

```ruby
class Chaser
  attr_reader :count
  def initialize(name)
    @name = name
    @count = 0
  end
  def chase(other)
    while @count < 5
      while @count - other.count > 1
        Thread.pass
      end
      @count += 1
      print "#@name: #{count}\n"
    end
  end
end
c1 = Chaser.new("A")
c2 = Chaser.new("B")
threads = [
  Thread.new { Thread.stop; c1.chase(c2) },
  Thread.new { Thread.stop; c2.chase(c1) }
]
```

```
start_index = rand(2)
threads[start_index].run
threads[1 - start_index].run
threads.each {|t| t.join }
```

produces:

```
A: 1
A: 2
B: 1
B: 2
B: 3
B: 4
A: 3
A: 4
A: 5
B: 5
```

However, using these primitives to achieve synchronization in real-life code is not easy—race conditions will always be waiting to bite you. And when you're working with shared data, race conditions pretty much guarantee long and frustrating debugging sessions. In fact, the previous example includes just such a bug; it is possible for count to be incremented in one thread, but before that count can be output, the second thread gets scheduled and outputs its count. The resulting output will be out of sequence.

Fortunately, threads have one additional facility—the idea of *mutual exclusion*. Using this, we can build a number of secure synchronization schemes.

Mutual Exclusion

The lowest-level method of blocking other threads from running uses a global *thread-critical* condition. When the condition is set to true (using the Thread.critical= method), the scheduler will not schedule any existing thread to run. However, this does not block new threads from being created and run. Certain thread operations (such as stopping or killing a thread, sleeping in the current thread, and raising an exception) may cause a thread to be scheduled even when in a critical section.

Using Thread.critical= directly is certainly possible, but it isn't terribly convenient. In fact, we strongly recommend you don't use it unless you have a black belt in multithreading (and a penchant for long debugging sessions). Fortunately, Ruby comes packaged with several alternatives. Right now we'll look at one of these, the Monitor library. You may also want to look at the Sync library (on page 738), the Mutex_m library (beginning on page 697), and the Queue class implemented in the thread library (on page 743).

Monitors

While the threading primitives provide basic synchronization, they can be tricky to use. Over the years, various folks have come up with higher-level alternatives. One that works well, particularly in the context of object-oriented systems, is the concept of a *monitor*.

Monitors wrap an object containing some kind of resource with synchronization functions. To see them in action, let's look at a simple counter that is accessed from two threads.

```
class Counter
  attr_reader :count
  def initialize
    @count = 0
  end
  def tick
    @count += 1
  end
end

c = Counter.new

t1 = Thread.new { 100_000.times {  c.tick } }
t2 = Thread.new { 100_000.times {  c.tick } }

t1.join
t2.join

c.count    →    130082
```

Perhaps surprisingly, the count doesn't equal 200,000. The reason is a single line of code.

```
@count += 1
```

This line is actually more complex than it first appears. Within the Ruby interpreter, it might break down into

```
val = fetch_current(@count)
add 1 to val
store val back into @count
```

Now imagine two threads executing this code at the same time. Table 11.1 on the facing page shows the thread number (*t1* and *t2*), the code being executed, and the value of the counter (which we initialize to 0).

Even though our basic set of load/add/store instructions executed five times, we ended up with a count of three. Because thread 1 interrupted the execution of thread 2 in the middle of a sequence, when thread 2 resumed it stored a stale value back into @count.

Table 11.1. Two threads in a race condition

Thread	Executes...	Result
t1:	val = fetch_current(@count)	@count = 0
t1:	add 1 to val	0
t1:	store val back into @count	@count = 1
t2:	val = fetch_current(@count)	1
t2:	add 1 to val	1
t2:	store val back into @count	@count = 2
t1:	val = fetch_current(@count)	2
t2:	val = fetch_current(@count)	2
t1:	add 1 to val	2
t1:	store val back into @count	@count = 3
t1:	val = fetch_current(@count)	3
t1:	add 1 to val	3
t1:	store val back into @count	@count = 4
t2:	add 1 to val	4
t2:	store val back into @count	@count = 3

The solution is to arrange things so that only one thread can execute the `tick` method's increment at any one time. This is easy using monitors.

```ruby
require 'monitor'
class Counter < Monitor
  attr_reader :count
  def initialize,
    @count = 0
    super
  end
  def tick
    synchronize do
      @count += 1
    end
  end
end

c = Counter.new
t1 = Thread.new { 100_000.times {  c.tick } }
t2 = Thread.new { 100_000.times {  c.tick } }

t1.join; t2.join
c.count   →   200000
```

By making our counter a monitor, it gains access to the `synchronize` method. Only one thread can be executing code within a synchronize block for a particular monitor object at any one time, so we no longer have two threads caching intermediate results at the same time, and our count has its expected value.

We don't have to make our class a subclass of `Monitor` to gain these benefits. We could also mix in a variant, `MonitorMixin`.

```ruby
require 'monitor'
class Counter
  include MonitorMixin
  . . .
end
```

The previous example put the synchronization inside the resource being synchronized. This is appropriate when all accesses to all objects of the class require synchronization. But if you want to control access to objects that require synchronization only in some circumstances, or if the synchronization is spread across a group of objects, then it may be better to use an external monitor.

```ruby
require 'monitor'

class Counter
  attr_reader :count
  def initialize
    @count = 0
  end
  def tick
    @count += 1
  end
end

c = Counter.new
lock = Monitor.new

t1 = Thread.new { 100_000.times { lock.synchronize { c.tick } } }
t2 = Thread.new { 100_000.times { lock.synchronize { c.tick } } }
t1.join; t2.join

c.count    →    200000
```

We can even make specific objects into monitors.

```ruby
require 'monitor'

class Counter
  # as before...
end

c = Counter.new
c.extend(MonitorMixin)

t1 = Thread.new { 100_000.times {  c.synchronize { c.tick } } }
t2 = Thread.new { 100_000.times {  c.synchronize { c.tick } } }

t1.join; t2.join
c.count    →    200000
```

Here, because class `Counter` doesn't know it is a monitor at the time it's defined, we have to perform the synchronization externally (in this case by wrapping the calls to `c.tick`). This is clearly a tad dangerous: if some other code calls `tick` but doesn't realize that synchronization is required, we're back in the same mess we started with.

Queues

Most of the examples in this chapter use the `Monitor` class for synchronization. However, another technique is useful, particularly when you need to synchronize work between producers and consumers. The `Queue` class, located in the `thread` library, implements a thread-safe queuing mechanism. Multiple threads can add and remove objects from the queue, and each addition and removal is guaranteed to be atomic. For an example of this, see the description of the `thread` library on page 743.

Condition Variables

Monitors give us half of what we need, but there's a problem. Say we have two threads accessing a shared queue. One needs to add entries, and the other needs to read them (perhaps the list represents songs waiting to be played on our jukebox: it gets added to when customers make selections, and gets emptied as records get played).

We know we need to synchronize access, so we try something like

```
require 'monitor'
playlist = []
playlist.extend(MonitorMixin)
# Player thread
Thread.new do
  record = nil
  loop do
    playlist.synchronize do        # < < BUG!!!
      sleep 0.1 while playlist.empty?
      record = playlist.shift
    end
    play(record)
  end
end
# Customer request thread
Thread.new do
  loop do
    req = get_customer_request
    playlist.synchronize do
      playlist << req
    end
  end
end
```

But this code has a problem. Inside the player thread, we gain access to the monitor and then loop waiting for something to be added to the playlist. But because we own the monitor, the customer thread will never be able to enter its synchronized block, and will never add something to the playlist. We're stuck. What we need is to be able to signal that the playlist has something in it and to provide synchronization between threads based on this condition, all while staying within the safety of a monitor. More generally, we need to be able to give up temporarily the exclusive use of the critical region and simultaneously tell people that we're waiting for a resource. When the resource becomes available, we need to be able to grab it *and* reobtain the lock on the critical region, all in one step.

That's where *condition variables* come in. A condition variable is a controlled way of communicating an event (or a condition) between two threads. One thread can wait on the condition, and the other can signal it. For example, we could rewrite our jukebox using condition variables. (For the purposes of this code we'll write stub methods for receiving customer requests and playing records. We also have to add a flag to tell the player that it's OK to shut down; normally it would run forever.)

```
require 'monitor'
SONGS = [
  'Blue Suede Shoes',
  'Take Five',
  'Bye Bye Love',
  'Rock Around The Clock',
  'Ruby Tuesday'
]
START_TIME = Time.now
def timestamp
  (Time.now - START_TIME).to_i
end

# Wait for up to two minutes between customer requests
def get_customer_request
  sleep(120 * rand)
  song = SONGS.shift
  puts "#{timestamp}: Requesting #{song}" if song
  song
end

# Songs take between two and three minutes
def play(song)
  puts "#{timestamp}: Playing #{song}"
  sleep(120 + 60*rand)
end
ok_to_shutdown = false
# and here's our original code
playlist = []
playlist.extend(MonitorMixin)
```

```
      plays_pending = playlist.new_cond
      # Customer request thread
      customer = Thread.new do
        loop do
          req = get_customer_request
          break unless req
          playlist.synchronize do
            playlist << req
            plays_pending.signal
          end
        end
      end

      # Player thread
      player = Thread.new do
        loop do
          song = nil
          playlist.synchronize do
            break if ok_to_shutdown && playlist.empty?
            plays_pending.wait_while { playlist.empty? }
            song = playlist.shift
          end
          break unless song
          play(song)
        end
      end

      customer.join
      ok_to_shutdown = true
      player.join
```

produces:

```
      25: Requesting Blue Suede Shoes
      26: Playing Blue Suede Shoes
      70: Requesting Take Five
      195: Requesting Bye Bye Love
      205: Playing Take Five
      294: Requesting Rock Around The Clock
      305: Requesting Ruby Tuesday
      385: Playing Bye Bye Love
      551: Playing Rock Around The Clock
      694: Playing Ruby Tuesday
```

Running Multiple Processes

Sometimes you may want to split a task into several process-sized chunks—or perhaps you need to run a separate process that was not written in Ruby. Not a problem: Ruby has a number of methods by which you may spawn and manage separate processes.

Spawning New Processes

You have several ways to spawn a separate process; the easiest is to run some command and wait for it to complete. You may find yourself doing this to run some separate command or retrieve data from the host system. Ruby does this for you with the `system` and backquote (or backtick) methods.

```
system("tar xzf test.tgz")   →   true
result = `date`
result                       →   "Wed May  3 16:56:19 CDT 2006\n"
```

The method `Kernel.system` executes the given command in a subprocess; it returns `true` if the command was found and executed properly and `false` otherwise. In case of failure, you'll find the subprocess's exit code in the global variable $?.

One problem with `system` is that the command's output will simply go to the same destination as your program's output, which may not be what you want. To capture the standard output of a subprocess, you can use the backquote characters, as with `date` in the previous example. Remember that you may need to use `String#chomp` to remove the line-ending characters from the result.

OK, this is fine for simple cases—we can run some other process and get the return status. But many times we need a bit more control than that. We'd like to carry on a conversation with the subprocess, possibly sending it data and possibly getting some back. The method `IO.popen` does just this. The popen method runs a command as a subprocess and connects that subprocess's standard input and standard output to a Ruby `IO` object. Write to the `IO` object, and the subprocess can read it on standard input. Whatever the subprocess writes is available in the Ruby program by reading from the `IO` object.

For example, on our systems one of the more useful utilities is `pig`, a program that reads words from standard input and prints them in pig latin (or igpay atinlay). We can use this when our Ruby programs need to send us output that our five-year-olds shouldn't be able to understand.

```
pig = IO.popen("/usr/local/bin/pig", "w+")
pig.puts "ice cream after they go to bed"
pig.close_write
puts pig.gets
```

produces:

```
iceway eamcray afterway eythay ogay otay edbay
```

This example illustrates both the apparent simplicity and the real-world complexities involved in driving subprocesses through pipes. The code certainly looks simple enough: open the pipe, write a phrase, and read back the response. But it turns out that the `pig` program doesn't flush the output it writes. Our original attempt at this example, which had a `pig.puts` followed by a `pig.gets`, hung forever. The `pig` program processed our input, but its response was never written to the pipe. We had to insert the `pig.close_write` line. This sends an end-of-file to `pig`'s standard input, and the output we're looking for gets flushed as `pig` terminates.

`popen` has one more twist. If the command you pass it is a single minus sign (−), `popen` will fork a new Ruby interpreter. Both this and the original interpreter will continue running by returning from the `popen`. The original process will receive an IO object back, and the child will receive `nil`. This works only on operating systems that support the `fork(2)` call (and for now this excludes Windows).

```
pipe = IO.popen("-","w+")
if pipe
  pipe.puts "Get a job!"
  STDERR.puts "Child says '#{pipe.gets.chomp}'"
else
  STDERR.puts "Dad says '#{gets.chomp}'"
  puts "OK"
end
```

produces:

```
Dad says 'Get a job!'
Child says 'OK'
```

In addition to the `popen` method, some platforms support the methods `Kernel.fork`, `Kernel.exec`, and `IO.pipe`. The file-naming convention of many IO methods and `Kernel.open` will also spawn subprocesses if you put a | as the first character of the filename (see the introduction to class IO on page 503 for details). Note that you *cannot* create pipes using `File.new`; it's just for files.

Independent Children

Sometimes we don't need to be quite so hands-on: we'd like to give the subprocess its assignment and then go on about our business. Sometime later, we'll check to see if it has finished. For instance, we may want to kick off a long-running external sort.

```
exec("sort testfile > output.txt") if fork.nil?
# The sort is now running in a child process
# carry on processing in the main program

# ... dum di dum ...

# then wait for the sort to finish
Process.wait
```

The call to `Kernel.fork` returns a process ID in the parent, and `nil` in the child, so the child process will perform the `Kernel.exec` call and run sort. Sometime later, we issue a `Process.wait` call, which waits for the sort to complete (and returns its process ID).

If you'd rather be notified when a child exits (instead of just waiting around), you can
set up a signal handler using `Kernel.trap` (described on page 534). Here we set up a
trap on `SIGCLD`, which is the signal sent on "death of child process."

```
trap("CLD") do
  pid = Process.wait
  puts "Child pid #{pid}: terminated"
end
exec("sort testfile > output.txt") if fork.nil?
# do other stuff...
```

produces:

```
Child pid 25816: terminated
```

For more information on using and controlling external processes, see the documentation for `Kernel.open`, `IO.popen`, and the section on the `Process` module on page 583.

Blocks and Subprocesses

`IO.popen` works with a block in pretty much the same way as `File.open` does. If you
pass it a command, such as `date`, the block will be passed an `IO` object as a parameter.

```
IO.popen("date") {|f| puts "Date is #{f.gets}" }
```

produces:

```
Date is Thu Aug 26 22:36:55 CDT 2004
```

The `IO` object will be closed automatically when the code block exits, just as it is with
`File.open`.

If you associate a block with `Kernel.fork`, the code in the block will be run in a Ruby
subprocess, and the parent will continue after the block.

```
fork do
  puts "In child, pid = #$$"
  exit 99
end
pid = Process.wait
puts "Child terminated, pid = #{pid}, status = #{$?.exitstatus}"
```

produces:

```
In child, pid = 25823
Child terminated, pid = 25823, status = 99
```

`$?` is a global variable that contains information on the termination of a subprocess.
See the section on `Process::Status` beginning on page 591 for more information.

Chapter 12

Unit Testing

Unit testing (described in the sidebar on the next page) is a technique that helps developers write better code. It helps before the code is actually written, as thinking about testing leads you naturally to create better, more decoupled designs. It helps as you're writing the code, as it gives you instant feedback on how accurate your code is. And it helps after you've written code, both because it gives you the ability to check that the code still works and because it helps others understand how to use your code.

Unit testing is a Good Thing.

But why have a chapter on unit testing in the middle of a book on Ruby? Because unit testing and languages such as Ruby seem to go hand in hand. The flexibility of Ruby makes writing tests easy, and the tests make it easier to verify that your code is working. Once you get into the swing of it, you'll find yourself writing a little code, writing a test or two, verifying that everything is copacetic, and then writing some more code.

Unit testing is also pretty trivial—run a program that calls part of your application's code, get back some results, and then check the results are what you expected.

Let's say we're testing a Roman number class. So far the code is pretty simple: it just lets us create an object representing a certain number and display that object in Roman numerals. Figure 12.1 on page 153 shows our first stab at an implementation.

We could test this code by writing another program, like this.

```
require 'roman'
r = Roman.new(1)
fail "'i' expected" unless r.to_s == "i"
r = Roman.new(9)
fail "'ix' expected" unless r.to_s == "ix"
```

However, as the number of tests in a project grows, this kind of ad-hoc approach can start to get complicated to manage. Over the years, various unit testing frameworks have emerged to help structure the testing process. Ruby comes with one preinstalled, Nathaniel Talbott's Test::Unit framework.

> ### What is Unit Testing?
>
> Unit testing focuses on small chunks (units) of code, typically individual methods or lines within methods. This is in contrast to most other forms of testing, which consider the system as a whole.
>
> Why focus in so tightly? Because ultimately all software is constructed in layers: code on one layer relies on the correct operation of the code in the layers below. If this underlying code turns out to contain bugs, then all higher layers are potentially affected. This is a big problem. Fred may write the code with a bug one week, and then you may end up calling it, indirectly, two months later. When your code generates incorrect results, it will take you a while to track down the problem in Fred's method. And when you ask Fred why he wrote it that way, the likely answer will be "I don't remember. That was months ago."
>
> If instead Fred had unit tested his code when he wrote it, two things would have happened. First, he'd have found the bug while the code was still fresh in his mind. Second, because the unit test was only looking at the code he'd just written, when the bug *did* appear, he'd only have to look through a handful of lines of code to find it, rather than doing archaeology on the rest of the code base.

Test::Unit Framework

The Test::Unit framework is basically three facilities wrapped into a neat package.

1. It gives you a way of expressing individual tests.
2. It provides a framework for structuring the tests.
3. It gives you flexible ways of invoking the tests.

Assertions == Expected Results

Rather than have you write series of individual `if` statements in your tests, Test::Unit provides a series of assertions that achieve the same thing. Although a number of different styles of assertion exist, they all follow basically the same pattern. Each assertion gives you a way of specifying a desired result or outcome and a way of passing in the actual outcome. If the actual doesn't equal the expected, the assertion outputs a nice message and records the fact as a failure.

For example, we could rewrite our previous test of the Roman class in Test::Unit. For now, ignore the scaffolding code at the start and end, and just look at the `assert_equal` methods.

Figure 12.1.   Roman numerals generation (with bugs)

```
class Roman
  MAX_ROMAN = 4999

  def initialize(value)
    if value <= 0 || value > MAX_ROMAN
      fail "Roman values must be > 0 and <= #{MAX_ROMAN}"
    end
    @value = value
  end
  FACTORS = [["m", 1000], ["cm", 900], ["d",  500], ["cd", 400],
             ["c",  100], ["xc",  90], ["l",   50], ["xl",  40],
             ["x",   10], ["ix",   9], ["v",    5], ["iv",   4],
             ["i",    1]]

  def to_s
    value = @value
    roman = ""
    for code, factor in FACTORS
      count, value = value.divmod(factor)
      roman << code unless count.zero?
    end
    roman
  end
end
```

```
require 'roman'
require 'test/unit'
class TestRoman < Test::Unit::TestCase
  def test_simple
    assert_equal("i", Roman.new(1).to_s)
    assert_equal("ix", Roman.new(9).to_s)
  end
end
```

produces:

```
Loaded suite -
Started
.
Finished in 0.003655 seconds.

1 tests, 2 assertions, 0 failures, 0 errors
```

The first assertion says that we're expecting the Roman number string representation of 1 to be "i", and the second test says we expect 9 to be "ix". Luckily for us, both expectations are met, and the tracing reports that our tests pass.

Let's add a few more tests.

```ruby
require 'roman'
require 'test/unit'
class TestRoman < Test::Unit::TestCase
  def test_simple
    assert_equal("i",   Roman.new(1).to_s)
    assert_equal("ii",  Roman.new(2).to_s)
    assert_equal("iii", Roman.new(3).to_s)
    assert_equal("iv",  Roman.new(4).to_s)
    assert_equal("ix",  Roman.new(9).to_s)
  end
end
```

produces:

```
Loaded suite -
Started
F
Finished in 0.021877 seconds.

  1) Failure:
<"ii"> expected but was
<"i">.

1 tests, 2 assertions, 1 failures, 0 errors
test_simple(TestRoman) [prog.rb:6]:
```

Uh oh! The second assertion failed. See how the error message uses the fact that the assert knows both the expected and actual values: it expected to get "ii" but instead got "i". Looking at our code, you can see a clear bug in to_s. If the count after dividing by the factor is greater than zero, then we should output that many Roman digits. The existing code outputs just one. The fix is easy.

```ruby
def to_s
  value = @value
  roman = ""
  for code, factor in FACTORS
    count, value = value.divmod(factor)
    roman << (code * count)
  end
  roman
end
```

Now let's run our tests again.

```
Loaded suite -
Started
.
Finished in 0.002161 seconds.

1 tests, 5 assertions, 0 failures, 0 errors
```

Looking good. We can now go a step further and remove some of that duplication.

```
require 'roman'
require 'test/unit'
class TestRoman < Test::Unit::TestCase
  NUMBERS = [
    [ 1, "i" ],  [ 2, "ii" ],  [ 3, "iii" ],
    [ 4, "iv"],  [ 5, "v"  ],  [ 9, "ix"  ]
  ]
  def test_simple
    NUMBERS.each do |arabic, roman|
      r = Roman.new(arabic)
      assert_equal(roman, r.to_s)
    end
  end
end
```

produces:

```
Loaded suite -
Started
.
Finished in 0.001179 seconds.

1 tests, 6 assertions, 0 failures, 0 errors
```

What else can we test? Well, the constructor checks that the number we pass in can be represented as a Roman number, throwing an exception if it can't. Let's test the exception.

```
require 'roman'
require 'test/unit'
class TestRoman < Test::Unit::TestCase
  def test_range
    assert_raise(RuntimeError) { Roman.new(0) }
    assert_nothing_raised()    { Roman.new(1) }
    assert_nothing_raised()    { Roman.new(4999) }
    assert_raise(RuntimeError) { Roman.new(5000) }
  end
end
```

produces:

```
Loaded suite -
Started
.
Finished in 0.00125 seconds.

1 tests, 4 assertions, 0 failures, 0 errors
```

We could do a lot more testing on our Roman class, but let's move on to bigger and better things. Before we go, though, we should say that we've only scratched the surface of the set of assertions available inside Test::Unit. Figure 12.2 on page 162 gives a full list. The final parameter to every assertion is a message, which is output before any failure message. This normally isn't needed, as Test::Unit's messages are normally pretty reasonable. The one exception is the test `assert_not_nil`, where the message "<nil> expected to not be nil" doesn't help much. In that case, you may want to add some annotation of your own.

```
require 'test/unit'
class TestsWhichFail < Test::Unit::TestCase
  def test_reading
    assert_not_nil(ARGF.read, "Read next line of input")
  end
end
```

produces:

```
Loaded suite -
Started
F
Finished in 0.033581 seconds.

  1) Failure:
Read next line of input.
<nil> expected to not be nil.

1 tests, 1 assertions, 1 failures, 0 errors
test_reading(TestsWhichFail) [prog.rb:4]:
```

Structuring Tests

Earlier we asked you to ignore the scaffolding around our tests. Now it's time to look at it.

You include Test::Unit facilities in your unit test with the following line.

```
require 'test/unit'
```

Unit tests seem to fall quite naturally into high-level groupings, called *test cases*, and lower level groupings, the test methods themselves. The test cases generally contain all the tests relating to a particular facility or feature. Our Roman number class is fairly simple, so all the tests for it will probably be in a single test case. Within the test case, you'll probably want to organize your assertions into a number of test methods, where each method contains the assertions for one type of test: one method could check regular number conversions, another could test error handling, and so on.

The classes that represent test cases must be subclasses of Test::Unit::TestCase. The methods that hold the assertions must have names that start with `test`. This is important: Test::Unit uses reflection to find tests to run, and only methods whose names start with `test` are eligible.

Quite often you'll find all of the test methods within a test case setting up a particular scenario. Each test method then probes some aspect of that scenario. Finally, each method may then tidy up after itself. For example, we could be testing a class that extracts jukebox playlists from a database.

```ruby
require 'test/unit'
require 'playlist_builder'
require 'dbi'

class TestPlaylistBuilder < Test::Unit::TestCase
  def test_empty_playlist
    db = DBI.connect('DBI:mysql:playlists')
    pb = PlaylistBuilder.new(db)
    assert_equal([], pb.playlist())
    db.disconnect
  end

  def test_artist_playlist
    db = DBI.connect('DBI:mysql:playlists')
    pb = PlaylistBuilder.new(db)
    pb.include_artist("krauss")
    assert(pb.playlist.size > 0, "Playlist shouldn't be empty")
    pb.playlist.each do |entry|
      assert_match(/krauss/i, entry.artist)
    end
    db.disconnect
  end

  def test_title_playlist
    db = DBI.connect('DBI:mysql:playlists')
    pb = PlaylistBuilder.new(db)
    pb.include_title("midnight")
    assert(pb.playlist.size > 0, "Playlist shouldn't be empty")
    pb.playlist.each do |entry|
      assert_match(/midnight/i, entry.title)
    end
    db.disconnect
  end

  # ...
end
```

produces:

```
Loaded suite -
Started
...
Finished in 0.004809 seconds.

3 tests, 23 assertions, 0 failures, 0 errors
```

Each test starts by connecting to the database and creating a new playlist builder. Each test ends by disconnecting from the database. (The idea of using a real database in unit

tests is questionable, as unit tests are supposed to be fast running, context independent, and easy to set up, but it illustrates a point.)

We can extract all this common code into *setup* and *teardown* methods. Within a TestCase class, a method called `setup` will be run before each and every test method, and a method called `teardown` will be run after each test method finishes. Let's emphasize that: the `setup` and `teardown` methods bracket each test, rather than being run once per test case.

Our test would then become

```
require 'test/unit'
require 'playlist_builder'
require 'dbi'
class TestPlaylistBuilder < Test::Unit::TestCase
  def setup
    @db = DBI.connect('DBI:mysql:playlists')
    @pb = PlaylistBuilder.new(@db)
  end
  def teardown
    @db.disconnect
  end
  def test_empty_playlist
    assert_equal([], @pb.playlist())
  end
  def test_artist_playlist
    @pb.include_artist("krauss")
    assert(@pb.playlist.size > 0, "Playlist shouldn't be empty")
    @pb.playlist.each do |entry|
      assert_match(/krauss/i, entry.artist)
    end
  end
  def test_title_playlist
    @pb.include_title("midnight")
    assert(@pb.playlist.size > 0, "Playlist shouldn't be empty")
    @pb.playlist.each do |entry|
      assert_match(/midnight/i, entry.title)
    end
  end
  # ...
end
```

produces:

```
Loaded suite -
Started
...
Finished in 0.00691 seconds.

3 tests, 23 assertions, 0 failures, 0 errors
```

Organizing and Running Tests

The test cases we've shown so far are all runnable Test::Unit programs. If, for example, the test case for the Roman class was in a file called `test_roman.rb`, we could run the tests from the command line using

```
% ruby test_roman.rb
Loaded suite test_roman
Started
..
Finished in 0.039257 seconds.

2 tests, 9 assertions, 0 failures, 0 errors
```

Test::Unit is clever enough to notice that there's no main program, so it collects up all the test case classes and runs each in turn.

If we want, we can ask it to run just a particular test method.

```
% ruby test_roman.rb --name test range
Loaded suite test_roman
Started
.
Finished in 0.006445 seconds.

1 tests, 4 assertions, 0 failures, 0 errors
```

Where to Put Tests

Once you get into unit testing, you may well find yourself generating almost as much test code as production code. All of those tests have to live somewhere. The problem is that if you put them alongside your regular production code source files, your directories start to get bloated—effectively you end up with two files for every production source file.

A common solution is to have a `test/` directory where you place all your test source files. This directory is then placed parallel to the directory containing the code you're developing. For example, for our Roman numeral class, we may have

```
roman
    ├── lib/
    │     ├── roman.rb
    │     └── other files...
    ├── test/
    │     ├── test_roman.rb
    │     └── other tests...
    └── other stuff
```

This works well as a way of organizing files but leaves you with a small problem: how do you tell Ruby where to find the library files to test? For example, if our TestRoman test code was in a `test/` subdirectory, how does Ruby know where to find the `roman.rb` source file, the thing we're trying to test?

An option that *doesn't* work reliably is to build the path into `require` statements in the test and run the tests from the `test/` subdirectory.

```
require 'test/unit'
require '../lib/roman'
class TestRoman < Test::Unit::TestCase
  # ...
end
```

Why doesn't it work? Because our `roman.rb` file may itself require other source files in the library we're writing. It'll load them using `require` (without the leading "../lib/"), and because they aren't in Ruby's $LOAD_PATH, they won't be found. Our test just won't run. A second, less immediate problem is that we won't be able to use these same tests to test our classes once installed on a target system, as then they'll be referenced simply using `require 'roman'`.

A better solution is to run the tests from the directory containing the library being tested. Because the current directory is in the load path, the test code will be able to find it.

```
% ruby ../test/test_roman.rb
```

However, this approach breaks down if you want to be able to run the tests from somewhere else on your system. Perhaps your scheduled build process runs tests for all the software in the application by simply looking for files called `test_xxx` and executing them. In this case, you need a little load path magic. At the front of your test code (for example in `test_roman.rb`), add the following line:

```
$:.unshift File.join(File.dirname(__FILE__), "..", "lib")
require ...
```

This magic works because the test code is in a known location relative to the code being tested. It starts by working out the name of the directory from which the test file is run and then constructing the path to the files under test. This directory is then prepended to the load path (the variable $:). From then on, code such as `require 'roman'` will search the library being tested first.

Test Suites

After a while, you'll grow a decent collection of test cases for your application. You may well find that these tend to cluster: one group of cases tests a particular set of functions, and another group tests a different set of functions. If so, you can group those test cases together into *test suites*, letting you run them all as a group.

This is easy to do in Test::Unit. All you have to do is create a Ruby file that requires `test/unit`, and then requires each of the files holding the test cases you want to group. This way, you build yourself a hierarchy of test material.

- You can run individual tests by name.
- You can run all the tests in a file by running that file.
- You can group a number of files into a test suite and run them as a unit.
- You can group test suites into other test suites.

This gives you the ability to run your unit tests at a level of granularity that you control, testing just one method or testing the entire application.

At this point, it's worthwhile thinking about naming conventions. Nathaniel Talbott, the author of Test::Unit, uses the convention that test cases are in files named `tc_xxx` and test suites are in files named `ts_xxx`.

```
# file ts_dbaccess.rb
require 'test/unit'
require 'tc_connect'
require 'tc_query'
require 'tc_update'
require 'tc_delete'
```

Now, if you run Ruby on the file `ts_dbaccess.rb`, you execute the test cases in the four files you've required.

Is that all there is to it? No, you can make it more complicated if you want. You can manually create and populate `TestSuite` objects, but there doesn't seem to be much point in practice. If you want to find more information, `ri Test::Unit` should help.

Test::Unit comes with a number of fancy GUI test runners. As *real* programmers use the command line, however, these aren't described here. Again, see the documentation for details.

Figure 12.2.   Test::Unit assertions

---

assert(*boolean*, [*message*])
>   Fails if *boolean* is `false` or `nil`.

assert_nil(*obj*, [*message*])
assert_not_nil(*obj*, [*message*])
>   Expects *obj* to be (not) `nil`.

assert_equal(*expected*, *actual*, [*message*])
assert_not_equal(*expected*, *actual*, [*message*])
>   Expects *actual* to equal/not equal *expected*, using `==`.

assert_in_delta(*expected_float*, *actual_float*, *delta*, [*message*])
>   Expects that the actual floating-point value is within *delta* of the expected value.

assert_raise(*Exception*, ...) { *block* }
assert_nothing_raised(*Exception*, ...) { *block* }
>   Expects the block to (not) raise one of the listed exceptions.

assert_instance_of(*klass*, *obj*, [*message*])
assert_kind_of(*klass*, *obj*, [*message*])
>   Expects *obj* to be a kind/instance of *klass*.

assert_respond_to(*obj*, *message*, [*message*])
>   Expects *obj* to respond to *message* (a symbol).

assert_match(*regexp*, *string*, [*message*])
assert_no_match(*regexp*, *string*, [*message*])
>   Expects *string* to (not) match *regexp*.

assert_same(*expected*, *actual*, [*message*])
assert_not_same(*expected*, *actual*, [*message*])
>   Expects *expected*`.equal?(`*actual*`)`.

assert_operator(*obj1*, *operator*, *obj2*, [*message*])
>   Expects the result of sending the message *operator* to *obj1* with parameter *obj2* to be true.

assert_throws(*expected_symbol*, [*message*]) { *block* }
>   Expects the block to throw the given symbol.

assert_send(*send_array*, [*message*])
>   Sends the message in *send_array[1]* to the receiver in *send_array[0]*, passing the rest of *send_array* as arguments. Expects the return value to be true.

flunk(*message*="Flunked")
>   Always fail.

## Chapter 13

When Trouble Strikes

Sad to say, it is possible to write buggy programs using Ruby. Sorry about that.

But not to worry! Ruby has several features that will help debug your programs. We'll look at these features, and then we'll show some common mistakes you can make in Ruby and how to fix them.

Ruby Debugger

Ruby comes with a debugger, which is conveniently built into the base system. You can run the debugger by invoking the interpreter with the -r debug option, along with any other Ruby options and the name of your script.

```
ruby -r debug [ debug-options ] [ programfile ] [ program-arguments ]
```

The debugger supports the usual range of features you'd expect, including the ability to set breakpoints, to step into and step over method calls, and to display stack frames and variables. It can also list the instance methods defined for a particular object or class, and it allows you to list and control separate threads within Ruby. Table 13.1 on page 173 lists all the commands that are available under the debugger.

If your Ruby installation has readline support enabled, you can use cursor keys to move back and forth in command history and use line-editing commands to amend previous input.

To give you an idea of what the Ruby debugger is like, here is a sample session (with user input in bold face type).

```
% ruby -r debug t.rb
Debug.rb
Emacs support available.
t.rb:1:def fact(n)
(rdb:1) list 1-9
[1, 10] in t.rb
```

```
=> 1  def fact(n)
   2    if n <= 0
   3      1
   4    else
   5      n * fact(n-1)
   6    end
   7  end
   8
   9  p fact(5)
(rdb:1) b 2
Set breakpoint 1 at t.rb:2
(rdb:1) c
breakpoint 1, fact at t.rb:2
t.rb:2:  if n <= 0
(rdb:1) disp n
  1: n = 5
(rdb:1) del 1
(rdb:1) watch n==1
Set watchpoint 2
(rdb:1) c
watchpoint 2, fact at t.rb:fact
t.rb:1:def fact(n)
1: n = 1
(rdb:1) where
--> #1  t.rb:1:in `fact'
    #2  t.rb:5:in `fact'
    #3  t.rb:5:in `fact'
    #4  t.rb:5:in `fact'
    #5  t.rb:5:in `fact'
    #6  t.rb:9
(rdb:1) del 2
(rdb:1) c
120
```

Interactive Ruby

If you want to play with Ruby, we recommend Interactive Ruby—irb, for short. irb is essentially a Ruby "shell" similar in concept to an operating system shell (complete with job control). It provides an environment where you can "play around" with the language in real time. You launch irb at the command prompt.

```
irb [ irb-options ] [ ruby_script ] [ program-arguments ]
```

irb will display the value of each expression as you complete it. For instance:

```
% irb
irb(main):001:0> a = 1 +
irb(main):002:0* 2 * 3 /
irb(main):003:0* 4 % 5
```

```
=> 2
irb(main):004:0> 2+2
=> 4
irb(main):005:0> def test
irb(main):006:1> puts "Hello, world!"
irb(main):007:1> end
=> nil
irb(main):008:0> test
Hello, world!
=> nil
irb(main):009:0>
```

irb also allows you to create subsessions, each one of which may have its own context. For example, you can create a subsession with the same (top-level) context as the original session or create a subsession in the context of a particular class or instance. The sample session shown in Figure 13.1 on the next page is a bit longer but shows how you can create subsessions and switch between them.

For a full description of all the commands that irb supports, see the reference beginning on page 185.

As with the debugger, if your version of Ruby was built with GNU readline support, you can use arrow keys (as with Emacs) or vi-style key bindings to edit individual lines or to go back and reexecute or edit a previous line—just like a command shell.

irb is a great learning tool: it's very handy if you want to try an idea quickly and see if it works.

Editor Support

The Ruby interpreter is designed to read a program in one pass; this means you can pipe an entire program to the interpreter's standard input, and it will work just fine.

We can take advantage of this feature to run Ruby code from inside an editor. In Emacs, for instance, you can select a region of Ruby text and use the command Meta-| to execute Ruby. The Ruby interpreter will use the selected region as standard input, and output will go to a buffer named *Shell Command Output*. This feature has come in quite handy for us while writing this book—just select a few lines of Ruby in the middle of a paragraph and try it!

You can do something similar in the vi editor using :%!ruby which *replaces* the program text with its output, or :w_!ruby, which displays the output without affecting the buffer. Other editors have similar features.

While we are on the subject, this would probably be a good place to mention that a Ruby mode for Emacs is included in the Ruby source distribution as ruby-mode.el in the misc/ subdirectory. You can also find syntax-highlighting modules for vim

Figure 13.1. Sample irb session

```
% irb
irb(main):001:0> irb
irb#1(main):001:0> jobs
#0->irb on main (#<Thread:0x401bd654>: stop)
#1->irb#1 on main (#<Thread:0x401d5a28>: running)
irb#1(main):002:0> fg 0
#<IRB::Irb:@scanner=#<RubyLex:0x401ca7>,@signal_status=:IN_EVAL,
        @context=#<IRB::Context:0x401ca86c>>
irb(main):002:0> class VolumeKnob
irb(main):003:1> end
=> nil
irb(main):004:0> irb VolumeKnob
irb#2(VolumeKnob):001:0> def initialize
irb#2(VolumeKnob):002:1> @vol=50
irb#2(VolumeKnob):003:1> end
=> nil
irb#2(VolumeKnob):004:0> def up
irb#2(VolumeKnob):005:1> @vol += 10
irb#2(VolumeKnob):006:1> end
=> nil
irb#2(VolumeKnob):007:0> fg 0
#<IRB::Irb:@scanner=#<RubyLex:0x401ca7>,@signal_status=:IN_EVAL,
        @context=#<IRB::Context:0x401ca86c>>
irb(main):005:0> jobs
#0->irb on main (#<Thread:0x401bd654>: running)
#1->irb#1 on main (#<Thread:0x401d5a28>: stop)
#2->irb#2 on VolumeKnob (#<Thread:0x401c400c>: stop)
irb(main):006:0> VolumeKnob.instance_methods
=> ["up"]
irb(main):007:0> v = VolumeKnob.new
#<VolumeKnob: @vol=50>
irb(main):008:0> irb v
irb#3(#<VolumeKnob:0x401e7d40>):001:0> up
=> 60
irb#3(#<VolumeKnob:0x401e7d40>):002:0> up
=> 70
irb#3(#<VolumeKnob:0x401e7d40>):003:0> up
=> 80
irb#3(VolumeKnob):004:0> fg 0
#<IRB::Irb:@scanner=#<RubyLex:0x401ca7>,@signal_status=:IN_EVAL,
        @context=#<IRB::Context:0x401ca86c>>
irb(main):009:0> kill 1,2,3
=> [1, 2, 3]
irb(main):010:0> jobs
#0->irb on main (#<Thread:0x401bd654>: running)
irb(main):011:0> exit
```

> In this same irb session, we'll create a new subsession in the context of class VolumeKnob.

> We can use fg 0 to switch back to the main session, take at look at all current jobs, and see what instance methods VolumeKnob defines.

> Make a new VolumeKnob object, and create a new subsession with that object as the context.

> Switch back to the main session, kill the subsessions, and exit.

(an enhanced version of the vi editor), jed, and other editors on the 'net. Check the Ruby FAQ (`http://www.rubygarden.org/iowa/faqtotum`) for an up-to-date list and pointers to resources.

But It Doesn't Work!

So you've read through enough of the book, you start to write your very own Ruby program, and it doesn't work. Here's a list of common gotchas and other tips.

- First and foremost, run your scripts with warnings enabled (the −w command-line option).

- If you happen to forget a "," in an argument list—especially to print—you can produce some very odd error messages.

- A parse error at the last line of the source often indicates a missing end keyword, sometimes quite a bit earlier.

- An attribute setter is not being called. Within a class definition, Ruby will parse `setter=` as an assignment to a local variable, not as a method call. Use the form `self.setter=` to indicate the method call.

```
class Incorrect
  attr_accessor :one, :two
  def initialize
    one = 1          # incorrect - sets local variable
    self.two = 2
  end
end

obj = Incorrect.new
obj.one   →   nil
obj.two   →   2
```

- Objects that don't appear to be properly set up may have been victims of an incorrectly spelled initialize method.

```
class Incorrect
  attr_reader :answer
  def initialise        # < < < spelling error
    @answer = 42
  end
end

ultimate = Incorrect.new
ultimate.answer   →   nil
```

The same kind of thing can happen if you misspell the instance variable name.

```
class Incorrect
  attr_reader :answer
  def initialize
    @anwser = 42         #<« spelling error
  end
end

ultimate = Incorrect.new
ultimate.answer   →   nil
```

- Block parameters are in the same scope as local variables. If an existing local variable with the same name as a block parameter exists when the block executes, that variable will be modified by the call to the block. This may or may not be a Good Thing.

```
c = "carbon"
i = "iodine"
elements = [ c, i ]
elements.each_with_index do |element, i|
  # do some chemistry
end
c   →   "carbon"
i   →   1
```

- Watch out for precedence issues, especially when using {} instead of do/end.

```
def one(arg)
  if block_given?
    "block given to 'one' returns #{yield}"
  else
    arg
  end
end

def two
  if block_given?
    "block given to 'two' returns #{yield}"
  end
end
result1 = one two {
  "three"
}
result2 = one two do
  "three"
end
puts "With braces, result = #{result1}"
puts "With do/end, result = #{result2}"
```

produces:

```
With braces, result = block given to 'two' returns three
With do/end, result = block given to 'one' returns three
```

- Output written to a terminal may be buffered. This means you may not see a message you write immediately. In addition, if you write messages to both `$stdout` and `$stderr`, the output may not appear in the order you were expecting. Always use nonbuffered I/O (set sync=true) for debug messages.

- If numbers don't come out right, perhaps they're strings. Text read from a file will be a `String` and will not be automatically converted to a number by Ruby. A call to `Integer` will work wonders (and will throw an exception if the input isn't a well-formed integer). A common mistake Perl programmers make is

```
while line = gets
  num1, num2 = line.split(/,/)
  # ...
end
```

You can rewrite this as

```
while line = gets
  num1, num2 = line.split(/,/)
  num1 = Integer(num1)
  num2 = Integer(num2)
  # ...
end
```

Or, you could convert all the strings using `map`.

```
while line = gets
  num1, num2 = line.split(/,/).map {|val| Integer(val) }
  # ...
end
```

- Unintended aliasing—if you are using an object as the key of a hash, make sure it doesn't change its hash value (or arrange to call Hash#rehash if it does).

```
arr = [1, 2]
hash = { arr => "value" }
hash[arr]      →   "value"
arr[0] = 99
hash[arr]      →   nil
hash.rehash    →   {[99, 2]=>"value"}
hash[arr]      →   "value"
```

- Make sure the class of the object you are using is what you think it is. If in doubt, use `puts my_obj.class`.

- Make sure your method names start with a lowercase letter and class and constant names start with an uppercase letter.

- If method calls aren't doing what you'd expect, make sure you've put parentheses around the arguments.

- Make sure the open parenthesis of a method's parameter list butts up against the end of the method name with no intervening spaces.

- Use irb and the debugger.

- Use Object#freeze. If you suspect that some unknown portion of code is setting a variable to a bogus value, try freezing the variable. The culprit will then be caught during the attempt to modify the variable.

One major technique makes writing Ruby code both easier and more fun. *Develop your applications incrementally.* Write a few lines of code, and then run them. Perhaps use Test::Unit to write some tests. Write a few more lines of code, and then exercise them. One of the major benefits of a dynamically typed language is that things don't have to be complete before you use them.

But It's Too Slow!

Ruby is an interpreted, high-level language, and as such it may not perform as fast as a lower-level language such as C. In the following sections, we'll list some basic things you can do to improve performance; also have a look in the index under *Performance* for other pointers.

Typically, slow-running programs have one or two performance graveyards, places where execution time goes to die. Find and improve these, and suddenly your whole program springs back to life. The trick is finding them. The Benchmark module and the Ruby profilers can help.

Benchmark

You can use the Benchmark module, also described on page 657, to time sections of code. For example, we may wonder which is faster: a large loop using variables local to the loop's block or using variables from the surrounding scope. Figure 13.2 on the facing page shows how to use Benchmark to find out.

You have to be careful when benchmarking, because oftentimes Ruby programs can run slowly because of the overhead of garbage collection. Because this garbage collection can happen any time during your program's execution, you may find that benchmarking gives misleading results, showing a section of code running slowly when in fact the slowdown was caused because garbage collection happened to trigger while that code was executing. The Benchmark module has the bmbm method that runs the tests twice, once as a rehearsal and once to measure performance, in an attempt to minimize the distortion introduced by garbage collection. The benchmarking process itself is relatively well mannered—it doesn't slow down your program much.

Figure 13.2. Comparing variable access costs using benchmark

```ruby
require 'benchmark'
include Benchmark

LOOP_COUNT = 1_000_000

bm(12) do |test|
  test.report("normal:")    do
    LOOP_COUNT.times do |x|
      y = x + 1
    end
  end
  test.report("predefine:") do
    x = y = 0
    LOOP_COUNT.times do |x|
      y = x + 1
    end
  end
end
```
produces:
```
                  user     system      total         real
normal:        3.110000   0.000000   3.110000 (   4.954929)
predefine:     2.560000   0.000000   2.560000 (   3.009354)
```

The Profiler

Ruby comes with a code profiler (documentation begins on page 717). The profiler shows you the number of times each method in the program is called and the average and cumulative time that Ruby spends in those methods.

You can add profiling to your code using the command-line option -r profile or from within the code using require 'profile'. For example:

```ruby
require 'profile'
count = 0
words = File.open("/usr/share/dict/words")
while word = words.gets
  word = word.chomp!
  if word.length == 12
    count += 1
  end
end
puts "#{count} twelve-character words"
```

The first time we ran this (without profiling) against a dictionary of almost 235,000 words, it takes several seconds to complete. This seems excessive, so we added the -r profile command-line option and tried again. Eventually we saw output that looked like the following.

```
20460 twelve-character words
  %    cumulative   self              self    total
 time   seconds    seconds   calls  ms/call  ms/call  name
 7.76    12.01      12.01   234937    0.05     0.05    String#chomp!
 7.75    24.00      11.99   234938    0.05     0.05    IO#gets
 7.71    35.94      11.94   234937    0.05     0.05    String#length
 7.62    47.74      11.80   234937    0.05     0.05    Fixnum#==
 0.59    48.66       0.92    20460    0.04     0.04    Fixnum#+
 0.01    48.68       0.02        1   20.00    20.00    Profiler__.start_profile
 0.00    48.68       0.00        1    0.00     0.00    File#initialize
 0.00    48.68       0.00        1    0.00     0.00    Fixnum#to_s
 0.00    48.68       0.00        1    0.00     0.00    File#open
 0.00    48.68       0.00        1    0.00     0.00    Kernel.puts
 0.00    48.68       0.00        2    0.00     0.00    IO#write
 0.00    48.68       0.00        1    0.00 154800.00    #toplevel
```

The first thing to notice is that the timings shown are a lot slower than when the program runs without the profiler. Profiling has a serious overhead, but the assumption is that it applies across the board, and therefore the relative numbers are still meaningful. This particular program clearly spends a lot of time in the loop, which executes almost 235,000 times. We could probably improve performance if we could either make the stuff in the loop less expensive or eliminate the loop altogether. One way of doing the latter is to read the word list into one long string, then use a pattern to match and extract all twelve character words.

```ruby
require 'profile'
words = File.read("/usr/share/dict/words")
count = words.scan(PATT= /^............\n/).size
puts "#{count} twelve-character words"
```

Our profile numbers are now a lot better (and the program runs more than five times faster when we take the profiling back out).

```
20460 twelve-character words
  %    cumulative   self              self    total
 time   seconds    seconds   calls  ms/call  ms/call  name
96.67     0.29       0.29        1  290.00   290.00    String#scan
 6.67     0.31       0.02        1   20.00    20.00    Profiler__.start_profile
 0.00     0.31       0.00        1    0.00     0.00    Array#size
 0.00     0.31       0.00        1    0.00     0.00    Kernel.puts
 0.00     0.31       0.00        2    0.00     0.00    IO#write
 0.00     0.31       0.00        1    0.00     0.00    Fixnum#to_s
 0.00     0.31       0.00        1    0.00   300.00    #toplevel
 0.00     0.31       0.00        1    0.00     0.00    File#read
```

Remember to check the code without the profiler afterward, though—sometimes the slowdown the profiler introduces can mask other problems.

Ruby is a wonderfully transparent and expressive language, but it does not relieve the programmer of the need to apply common sense: creating unnecessary objects, performing unneeded work, and creating bloated code will slow down your programs regardless of the language.

Table 13.1. Debugger commands

b [reak] [file|class:]line	Set breakpoint at given line in *file* (default current file) or *class*.
b [reak] [file|class:]name	Set breakpoint at *method* in *file* or *class*.
b [reak]	Display breakpoints and watchpoints.
wat [ch] expr	Break when expression becomes true.
del [ete] [nnn]	Delete breakpoint *nnn* (default all).
cat [ch] exception	Stop when *exception* is raised.
cat [ch]	List current catches.
tr [ace] (on|off) [all]	Toggle execution trace of current or all threads.
disp [lay] expr	Display value of *nnn* every time debugger gets control.
disp [lay]	Show current displays.
undisp [lay] [nnn]	Remove display (default all).
c [ont]	Continue execution.
s [tep] nnn=1	Execute next *nnn* lines, stepping into methods.
n [ext] nnn=1	Execute next *nnn* lines, stepping over methods.
fin [ish]	Finish execution of the current function.
q [uit]	Exit the debugger.
w [here]	Display current stack frame.
f [rame]	Synonym for where.
l [ist] [start–end]	List source lines from start to end.
up nnn=1	Move up *nnn* levels in the stack frame.
down nnn=1	Move down *nnn* levels in the stack frame.
v [ar] g [lobal]	Display global variables.
v [ar] l [ocal]	Display local variables.
v [ar] i [stance] *obj*	Display instance variables of *obj*.
v [ar] c [onst] Name	Display constants in class or module name.
m [ethod] i [nstance] *obj*	Display instance methods of *obj*.
m [ethod] Name	Display instance methods of the class or module name.
th [read] l [ist]	List all threads.
th [read] [c[ur[rent]]]	Display status of current thread.
th [read] [c[ur[rent]]] nnn	Make thread *nnn* current, and stop it.
th [read] stop nnn	Make thread *nnn* current, and stop it.
th [read] resume nnn	Resume thread *nnn*.
th [read] [sw[itch]] nnn	Switch thread context to nnn.
[p] expr	Evaluate *expr* in the current context. *expr* may include assignment to variables and method invocations.
h[elp]	Show summary of commands.
empty	A null command repeats the last command.

Part II

Ruby in Its Setting

Ruby and Its World

It's an unfortunate fact of life that our applications have to deal with the big, bad world. In this chapter, we'll look at how Ruby interacts with its environment. Microsoft Windows users will probably also want to look at platform-specific information beginning on page 267.

Command-Line Arguments

"In the beginning was the command line."[1] Regardless of the system in which Ruby is deployed, whether it be a super high-end scientific graphics workstation or an embedded PDA device, you've got to start the Ruby interpreter somehow, and that gives us the opportunity to pass in command-line arguments.

A Ruby command line consists of three parts: options to the Ruby interpreter, optionally the name of a program to run, and optionally a set of arguments for that program.

```
ruby [ options ] [ -- ] [ programfile ] [ arguments ]
```

The Ruby options are terminated by the first word on the command line that doesn't start with a hyphen, or by the special flag -- (two hyphens).

If no filename is present on the command line, or if the filename is a single hyphen (-), Ruby reads the program source from standard input.

Arguments for the program itself follow the program name. For example:

```
% ruby -w - "Hello World"
```

will enable warnings, read a program from standard input, and pass it the quoted string "Hello World" as an argument.

---

1.   This is the title of a marvelous essay by Neal Stephenson (available online at http://www.spack. org/index.cgi/InTheBeginningWasTheCommandLine).

Command-Line Options

-0[*octal*]

    The 0 flag (the digit zero) specifies the record separator character (\0, if no digit follows). -00 indicates paragraph mode: records are separated by two successive default record separator characters. -0777 reads the entire file at once (as it is an illegal character). Sets $/.

-a   Autosplit mode when used with -n or -p; equivalent to executing $F = $_.split at the top of each loop iteration.

-C *directory*

    Changes working directory to *directory* before executing.

-c   Checks syntax only; does not execute the program.

--copyright

    Prints the copyright notice and exits.

-d, --debug

    Sets $DEBUG and $VERBOSE to true. This can be used by your programs to enable additional tracing.

-e '*command*'

    Executes *command* as one line of Ruby source. Several -e's are allowed, and the commands are treated as multiple lines in the same program. If *programfile* is omitted when -e is present, execution stops after the -e commands have been run. Programs run using -e have access to the old behavior of ranges and regular expressions in conditions—ranges of integers compare against the current input line number, and regular expressions match against $_.

-F *pattern*

    Specifies the input field separator ($;) used as the default for split() (affects the -a option).

-h, --help

    Displays a short help screen.

-I *directories*

    Specifies directories to be prepended to $LOAD_PATH ($:). Multiple -I options may be present. Multiple directories may appear following each -I, separated by a colon (:) on Unix-like systems and by a semicolon (;) on DOS/Windows systems.

-i [*extension*]

    Edits ARGV files in place. For each file named in ARGV, anything you write to standard output will be saved back as the contents of that file. A backup copy of the file will be made if *extension* is supplied.

```
% ruby -pi.bak -e "gsub(/Perl/, 'Ruby')" *.txt
```

-K *kcode*

Specifies the code set to be used. This option is useful mainly when Ruby is used for Japanese-language processing. *kcode* may be one of: e, E for EUC; s, S for SJIS; u, U for UTF-8; or a, A, n, N for ASCII.

-l Enables automatic line-ending processing; sets $\ to the value of $/ and chops every input line automatically.

-n Assumes a while gets; ...; end loop around your program. For example, a simple grep command could be implemented as

```
% ruby -n -e "print if /wombat/" *.txt
```

-p Places your program code within the loop while gets; ...; print; end.

```
% ruby -p -e "$_.downcase!" *.txt
```

-r *library*

requires the named library before executing.

-S Looks for the program file using RUBYPATH or PATH environment variable.

-s Any command-line switches found after the program filename, but before any filename arguments or before a --, are removed from ARGV and set to a global variable named for the switch. In the following example, the effect of this would be to set the variable $opt to "electric".

```
% ruby -s prog -opt=electric ./mydata
```

-T[*level*]

Sets the safe level, which among other things enables tainting checks (see page 397). Sets $SAFE.

-v, --verbose

Sets $VERBOSE to true, which enables verbose mode. Also prints the version number. In verbose mode, compilation warnings are printed. If no program filename appears on the command line, Ruby exits.

--version

Displays the Ruby version number and exits.

-w Enables verbose mode. Unlike -v, reads program from standard input if no program files are present on the command line. We recommend running your Ruby programs with -w.

-W *level*

Sets the level of warnings issued. With a *level* or two (or with no level specified), equivalent to -w—additional warnings are given. If *level* is 1, runs at the standard (default) warning level. With -W0 absolutely no warnings are given (including those issued using Kernel.warn).

-X *directory*

    Changes working directory to *directory* before executing. Same as –C *directory*.

-x [*directory*]

    Strips off text before #!ruby line and changes working directory to *directory* if given.

-y, --yydebug

    Enables yacc debugging in the parser *(waaay too much information)*.

ARGV

Any command-line arguments after the program filename are available to your Ruby program in the global array ARGV. For instance, assume test.rb contains the following program:

```
ARGV.each {|arg| p arg }
```

Invoke it with the following command line:

```
% ruby -w test.rb "Hello World" a1 1.6180
```

It'll generate the following output:

```
"Hello World"
"a1"
"1.6180"
```

There's a gotcha here for all you C programmers—ARGV[0] is the first argument to the program, not the program name. The name of the current program is available in the global variable $0. Notice that all the values in ARGV are strings.

If your program attempts to read from standard input (or uses the special file ARGF, described on page 336), the program arguments in ARGV will be taken to be filenames, and Ruby will read from these files. If your program takes a mixture of arguments and filenames, make sure you empty the nonfilename arguments from the ARGV array before reading from the files.

Program Termination

The method Kernel#exit terminates your program, returning a status value to the operating system. However, unlike some languages, exit doesn't terminate the program immediately. Kernel#exit first raises a SystemExit exception, which you may catch, and then performs a number of cleanup actions, including running any registered at_exit methods and object finalizers. See the reference for Kernel#exit beginning on page 521 for details.

Environment Variables

You can access operating system environment variables using the predefined variable ENV. It responds to the same methods as Hash.[2]

```
ENV['SHELL']      →   "/bin/sh"
ENV['HOME']       →   "/Users/dave"
ENV['USER']       →   "dave"
ENV.keys.size     →   32
ENV.keys[0, 7]    →   ["MANPATH", "TERM_PROGRAM", "TERM", "SHELL",
                       "SAVEHIST", "HISTSIZE", "MAKEFLAGS"]
```

The values of some environment variables are read by Ruby when it first starts. These variables modify the behavior of the interpreter, as shown in Table 14.1 on the next page.

Writing to Environment Variables

A Ruby program may write to the ENV object. On most systems this changes the values of the corresponding environment variables. However, this change is local to the process that makes it and to any subsequently spawned child processes. This inheritance of environment variables is illustrated in the code that follows. A subprocess changes an environment variable, and this change is inherited by a process that it then starts. However, the change is not visible to the original parent. (This just goes to prove that parents never really know what their children are doing.)

```
puts "In parent, term = #{ENV['TERM']}"
fork do
  puts "Start of child 1, term = #{ENV['TERM']}"
  ENV['TERM'] = "ansi"
  fork do
    puts "Start of child 2, term = #{ENV['TERM']}"
  end
  Process.wait
  puts "End of child 1, term = #{ENV['TERM']}"
end
Process.wait
puts "Back in parent, term = #{ENV['TERM']}"
```

produces:

```
In parent, term = xterm-color
Start of child 1, term = xterm-color
Start of child 2, term = ansi
End of child 1, term = ansi
Back in parent, term = xterm-color
```

---

2.   ENV is not actually a hash, but if you need to, you can convert it into a Hash using ENV#to_hash.

Table 14.1. Environment variables used by Ruby

Variable Name	Description
DLN_LIBRARY_PATH	Search path for dynamically loaded modules.
HOME	Points to user's home directory. Used when expanding ~ in file and directory names.
LOGDIR	Fallback pointer to the user's home directory if $HOME is not set. Used only by Dir.chdir.
OPENSSL_CONF	Specify location of OpenSSL configuration file.
RUBYLIB	Additional search path for Ruby programs ($SAFE must be 0).
RUBYLIB_PREFIX	(Windows only) Mangle the RUBYLIB search path by adding this prefix to each component.
RUBYOPT	Additional command-line options to Ruby; examined after real command-line options are parsed ($SAFE must be 0).
RUBYPATH	With -S option, search path for Ruby programs (defaults to PATH).
RUBYSHELL	Shell to use when spawning a process under Windows; if not set, will also check SHELL or COMSPEC.
RUBY_TCL_DLL	Override default name for TCL shared library or DLL.
RUBY_TK_DLL	Override default name for Tk shared library or DLL. Both this and RUBY_TCL_DLL must be set for either to be used.

1.8 (OPENSSL_CONF)

Where Ruby Finds Its Modules

You use require or load to bring a library module into your Ruby program. Some of these modules are supplied with Ruby, some you may have installed off the Ruby Application Archive, and some you may have written yourself. How does Ruby find them?

When Ruby is built for your particular machine, it predefines a set of standard directories to hold library stuff. Where these are depends on the machine in question. You can determine this from the command line with something like

```
% ruby -e 'puts $:'
```

On a typical Linux box, you'll probably find something such as the following. Note that as of Ruby 1.8, the order of these directories has changed—architecture-specific directories now follow their machine-independent counterparts.

```
/usr/local/lib/ruby/site_ruby/1.8
/usr/local/lib/ruby/site_ruby/1.8/i686-linux
/usr/local/lib/ruby/site_ruby
/usr/local/lib/ruby/1.8
/usr/local/lib/ruby/1.8/i686-linux
.
```

The site_ruby directories are intended to hold modules and extensions that you've added. The architecture-dependent directories (i686-linux in this case) hold executables and other things specific to this particular machine. All these directories are automatically included in Ruby's search for modules.

Sometimes this isn't enough. Perhaps you're working on a large project written in Ruby, and you and your colleagues have built a substantial library of Ruby code. You want everyone on the team to have access to all this code. You have a couple of options to accomplish this. If your program runs at a safe level of zero (see Chapter 25 beginning on page 397), you can set the environment variable RUBYLIB to a list of one or more directories to be searched.[3] If your program is not *setuid*, you can use the command-line parameter -I to do the same thing.

The Ruby variable $: is an array of places to search for loaded files. As we've seen, this variable is initialized to the list of standard directories, plus any additional ones you specified using RUBYLIB and -I. You can always add additional directories to this array from within your running program.

Just to make things more interesting, a new way of organizing libraries came along just in time to make it into this book. Chapter 17 on page 215 describes RubyGems, a network-enabled package management system.

Build Environment

When Ruby is compiled for a particular architecture, all the relevant settings used to build it (including the architecture of the machine on which it was compiled, compiler options, source code directory, and so on) are written to the module Config within the library file rbconfig.rb. After installation, any Ruby program can use this module to get details on how Ruby was compiled.

```
require 'rbconfig'
include Config
CONFIG["host"]    →   "powerpc-apple-darwin7.7.0"
CONFIG["libdir"]  →   "/Users/dave/ruby1.8/lib"
```

Extension libraries use this configuration file in order to compile and link properly on any given architecture. See Chapter 21 beginning on page 275 and the reference for mkmf beginning on page 779 for details.

---

3.   The separator between entries depends on your platform. For Windows, it's a semicolon; for Unix, it's a colon.

## Chapter 15

Interactive Ruby Shell

Back on page 164 we introduced irb, a Ruby module that lets you enter Ruby programs interactively and see the results immediately. This chapter goes into more detail on using and customizing irb.

Command Line

irb is run from the command line.

irb *[irb-options] [ruby_script] [program arguments]*

The command-line options for irb are listed in Table 15.1 on the next page. Typically, you'll run irb with no options, but if you want to run a script and watch the blow-by-blow description as it runs, you can provide the name of the Ruby script and any options for that script.

Once started, irb displays a prompt and waits for input. In the examples that follow, we'll use irb's default prompt, which shows the current binding, the indent (nesting) level, and the line number.

At a prompt, you can type Ruby code. irb includes a Ruby parser, so it knows when statements are incomplete. When this happens, the prompt will end with an asterisk. You can leave irb by typing **exit** or **quit**, or by entering an end-of-file character (unless IGNORE_EOF mode is set).

```
% irb
irb(main):001:0> 1 + 2
=> 3
irb(main):002:0> 3 +
irb(main):003:0* 4
=> 7
irb(main):004:0> quit
%
```

Table 15.1. irb command-line options

Option	Description
`--back-trace-limit` n	Display backtrace information using the top n and last n entries. The default value is 16.
`-d`	Set `$DEBUG` to true (same as `ruby -d`).
`-f`	Suppress reading `~/.irbrc`.
`-I` *path*	specify the `$LOAD_PATH` directory.
`--inf-ruby-mode`	Set up irb to run in `inf-ruby-mode` under Emacs. Change the prompt and suppress `--readline`.
`--inspect`	Use `Object#inspect` to format output (the default, unless in math mode).
`--irb_debug` n	Set internal debug level to n (only useful for irb development).
`-m`	Math mode (fraction and matrix support is available).
`--noinspect`	Do not use inspect for output.
`--noprompt`	Do not display a prompt.
`--noreadline`	Do not use `Readline` extension module.
`--prompt` *prompt-mode*	Switch prompt. Predefined prompt modes are `null`, `default`, `classic`, `simple`, `xmp`, and `inf-ruby`.
`--prompt-mode` *prompt-mode*	Same as `--prompt`.
`-r` *load-module*	Same as `ruby -r`.
`--readline`	Use `readline` extension module.
`--simple-prompt`	Use simple prompts.
`--tracer`	Display trace for execution of commands.
`-v, --version`	Print the version of irb.

During an irb session, the work you do is accumulated in irb's workspace. Variables you set, methods you define, and classes you create are all remembered and may be used subsequently.

```
irb(main):001:0> def fib_up_to(n)
irb(main):002:1>   f1, f2 = 1, 1
irb(main):003:1>   while f1 <= n
irb(main):004:2>     puts f1
irb(main):005:2>     f1, f2 = f2, f1+f2
irb(main):006:2>   end
irb(main):007:1> end
=> nil
irb(main):008:0> fib_up_to(4)
1
1
2
3
=> nil
```

Notice the nil return values. These are the results of defining the method and then running it. The method output the Fibonacci numbers but then returned nil.

A great use of irb is experimenting with code you've already written. Perhaps you want to track down a bug, or maybe you just want to play. If you load your program into irb, you can then create instances of the classes it defines and invoke its methods. For example, the file code/fib_up_to.rb contains the following method definition.

```
def fib_up_to(max)
  i1, i2 = 1, 1
  while i1 <= max
    yield i1
    i1, i2 = i2, i1+i2
  end
end
```

We can load this into irb and play with the method.

```
% irb
irb(main):001:0> load 'code/fib_up_to.rb'
=> true
irb(main):002:0> result = []
=> []
irb(main):003:0> fib_up_to(20) {|val| result << val}
=> nil
irb(main):004:0> result
=> [1, 1, 2, 3, 5, 8, 13]
```

In this example, we use load, rather than require, to include the file in our session. We do this as a matter of practice: load allows us to load the same file multiple times, so if we find a bug and edit the file, we could reload it into our irb session.

Tab Completion

If your Ruby installation has readline support, then you can use irb's completion facility. Once loaded (and we'll get to how to load it shortly), completion changes the meaning of the [TAB] key when typing expressions at the irb prompt. When you press [TAB] partway through a word, irb will look for possible completions that make sense at that point. If there is only one, irb will fill it in automatically. If there's more than one valid option, irb initially does nothing. However, if you hit [TAB] again, it will display the list of valid completions at that point.

For example, you may be in the middle of an irb session, having just assigned a string object to the variable a.

```
irb(main):002:0> a = "cat"
=> "cat"
```

You now want to try the method String#reverse on this object. You start by typing a.re and then hit [TAB] twice.

```
irb(main):003:0> a.re TAB  TAB
a.reject        a.replace       a.respond_to?  a.reverse      a.reverse!
```

irb lists all the methods supported by the object in a whose names start with "re." We see the one we want, reverse, and enter the next character of its name, *v*, followed by the TAB key.

```
irb(main):003:0> a.rev TAB
irb(main):003:0> a.reverse
=> "tac"
irb(main):004:0>
```

irb responds to the TAB key by expanding the name as far as it can go, in this case completing the word reverse. If we keyed TAB twice at this point, it would show us the current options, reverse and reverse!. However, as reverse is the one we want, we instead hit ENTER, and the line of code is executed.

Tab completion isn't limited to built-in names. If we define a class in irb, then tab completion works when we try to invoke one of its methods.

```
irb(main):004:0> class Test
irb(main):005:1>   def my_method
irb(main):006:2>   end
irb(main):007:1> end
=> nil
irb(main):008:0> t = Test.new
=> #<Test:0x35b724>
irb(main):009:0> t.my TAB
irb(main):009:0> t.my_method
```

Tab completion is implemented as an extension library, irb/completion. You can load it when you invoke irb from the command line.

```
% irb -r irb/completion
```

You can also load the completion library when irb is running.

```
irb(main):001:0> require 'irb/completion'
=> true
```

If you use tab completion all the time, it's probably most convenient to put the require command into your .irbrc file.

```
require 'irb/completion'
```

Subsessions

irb supports multiple, concurrent sessions. One is always current; the others lie dormant until activated. Entering the command irb within irb creates a subsession, entering the jobs command lists all sessions, and entering fg activates a particular dormant session.

This example also illustrates the -r command-line option, which loads in the given file before irb starts.

```
% irb -r code/fib_up_to.rb
irb(main):001:0> result = []
=> []
irb(main):002:0> fib_up_to(10) {|val| result << val }
=> nil
irb(main):003:0> result
=> [1, 1, 2, 3, 5, 8]
irb(main):004:0> #  Create a nested irb session
irb(main):005:0* irb
irb#1(main):001:0> result = %w{ cat dog horse }
=> ["cat", "dog", "horse"]
irb#1(main):002:0> result.map {|val| val.upcase }
=> ["CAT", "DOG", "HORSE"]
irb#1(main):003:0> jobs
=> #0->irb on main (#<Thread:0x331740>: stop)
#1->irb#1 on main (#<Thread:0x341694>: running)
irb#1(main):004:0> fg 0
irb(main):006:0> result
=> [1, 1, 2, 3, 5, 8]
irb(main):007:0> fg 1
irb#1(main):005:0> result
=> ["cat", "dog", "horse"]
```

Subsessions and Bindings

If you specify an object when you create a subsession, that object becomes the value of *self* in that binding. This is a convenient way to experiment with objects. In the following example, we create a subsession with the string "wombat" as the default object. Methods with no receiver will be executed by that object.

```
% irb
irb(main):001:0> self
=> main
irb(main):002:0> irb "wombat"
irb#1(wombat):001:0> self
=> "wombat"
irb#1(wombat):002:0> upcase
=> "WOMBAT"
irb#1(wombat):003:0> size
=> 6
irb#1(wombat):004:0> gsub(/[aeiou]/, '*')
=> "w*mb*t"
irb#1(wombat):005:0> irb_exit
irb(main):003:0> self
=> main
irb(main):004:0> upcase
NameError: undefined local variable or method `upcase' for main:Object
```

Configuration

irb is remarkably configurable. You can set configuration options with command-line options, from within an initialization file, and while you're inside irb itself.

Initialization File

irb uses an initialization file in which you can set commonly used options or execute any required Ruby statements. When irb is run, it will try to load an initialization file from one of the following sources in order: `~/.irbrc`, `.irbrc`, `irb.rc`, `_irbrc`, and `$irbrc`.

Within the initialization file you may run any arbitrary Ruby code. You can also set configuration values. The list of configuration variables is given starting on page 192—the values that can be used in an initialization file are the symbols (starting with a colon). You use these symbols to set values into the `IRB.conf` hash. For example, to make `SIMPLE` the default prompt for all your irb sessions, you could have the following in your initialization file.

```
IRB.conf[:PROMPT_MODE] = :SIMPLE
```

As an interesting twist on configuring irb, you can set `IRB.conf[:IRB_RC]` to a `Proc` object. This proc will be invoked whenever the irb context is changed and will receive the configuration for that context as a parameter. You can use this facility to change the configuration dynamically based on the context. For example, the following `.irbrc` file sets the prompt so that only the main prompt shows the irb level, but continuation prompts and the result still line up.

```
IRB.conf[:IRB_RC] = proc do |conf|
  leader = " " * conf.irb_name.length
  conf.prompt_i = "#{conf.irb_name} --> "
  conf.prompt_s = leader + ' \-" '
  conf.prompt_c = leader + ' \-+ '
  conf.return_format   = leader + " ==> %s\n\n"
  puts "Welcome!"
end
```

An irb session using this `.irbrc` file looks like the following.

```
% irb
Welcome!
irb --> 1 + 2
    ==> 3

irb --> 2 +
    \-+ 6
    ==> 8
```

Extending irb

Because the things you type to irb are interpreted as Ruby code, you can effectively extend irb by defining new top-level methods. For example, you may want to be able to look up the documentation for a class or method while in irb. If you add the following to your .irbrc file, you'll add a method called ri, which invokes the external ri command on its arguments. (You'll need to use ri.bat under Windows.)

```
def ri(*names)
  system(%{ri #{names.map {|name| name.to_s}.join(" ")}})
end
```

The next time you start irb, you'll be able to use this method to get documentation.

```
irb(main):001:0> ri Proc
--------------------------------------------------------- Class: Proc
     Proc objects are blocks of code that have been bound to a set of
     local variables. Once bound, the code may be called in different
     contexts and still access those variables.
     and so on...
irb(main):002:0> ri :strftime
--------------------------------------------------------- Time#strftime
     time.strftime( string ) => string
-----------------------------------------------------------------
     Formats time according to the directives in the given format
     string. Any text not listed as a directive will be passed through
     to the output string.

     Format meaning:
       %a - The abbreviated weekday name (``Sun'')
       %A - The  full  weekday  name (``Sunday'')
       %b - The abbreviated month name (``Jan'')
       %B - The  full  month  name (``January'')
       %c - The preferred local date and time representation
       %d - Day of the month (01..31)
     and so on...
irb(main):003:0> ri "String.each"
--------------------------------------------------------- String#each
     str.each(separator=$/) |substr| block       => str
     str.each_line(separator=$/) |substr| block  => str
-----------------------------------------------------------------
     Splits str using the supplied parameter as the record separator
     ($/ by default), passing each substring in turn to the supplied
     block. If a zero-length record separator is supplied, the string
     is split on \n characters, except that multiple successive
     newlines are appended together.

     print "Example one\n"
     "hello\nworld".each |s| p s
     and so on...
```

Interactive Configuration

Most configuration values are also available while you're running irb. The list starting on the current page shows these values as conf.*xxx*. For example, to change your prompt back to DEFAULT, you could use the following.

```
irb(main):001:0> 1 +
irb(main):002:0* 2
=> 3
irb(main):003:0> conf.prompt_mode = :SIMPLE
=> :SIMPLE
>> 1 +
?> 2
=> 3
```

irb Configuration Options

In the descriptions that follow, a label of the form :XXX signifies a key used in the IRB.conf hash in an initialization file, and conf.xxx signifies a value that can be set interactively. The value in square brackets at the end of the description is the option's default.

:AUTO_INDENT / conf.auto_indent_mode

> If true, irb will indent nested structures as you type them. [false]

:BACK_TRACE_LIMIT / conf.back_trace_limit

> Displays lines n initial and n final lines of backtrace. [16]

:CONTEXT_MODE

> What binding to use for new workspaces: $0 \rightarrow$ proc at the top level, $1 \rightarrow$ binding in a loaded, anonymous file, $2 \rightarrow$ per thread binding in a loaded file, $3 \rightarrow$ binding in a top-level function. [3]

:DEBUG_LEVEL / conf.debug_level

> Sets the internal debug level to n. Useful if you're debugging irb's lexer. [0]

:IGNORE_EOF / conf.ignore_eof

> Specifies the behavior of an end of file received on input. If true, it will be ignored; otherwise, irb will quit. [false]

:IGNORE_SIGINT / conf.ignore_sigint

> If false, ^C (Ctrl+c) will quit irb. If true, ^C during input will cancel input and return to the top level; during execution, ^C will abort the current operation. [true]

:INSPECT_MODE / conf.inspect_mode

> Specifies how values will be displayed: true means use inspect, false uses to_s, and nil uses inspect in nonmath mode and to_s in math mode. [nil]

:IRB_RC

Can be set to a proc object that will be called when an irb session (or subsession) is started. [nil]

conf.last_value

The last value output by irb. [...]

:LOAD_MODULES / conf.load_modules

A list of modules loaded via the –r command-line option. [[]]

:MATH_MODE / conf.math_mode

If true, irb runs with the mathn library loaded (see page 692). [false]

conf.prompt_c

The prompt for a continuing statement (for example, immediately after an "if"). [depends]

conf.prompt_i

The standard, top-level prompt. [depends]

:PROMPT_MODE / conf.prompt_mode

The style of prompt to display. [:DEFAULT]

conf.prompt_s

The prompt for a continuing string. [depends]

:PROMPT

See *Configuring the Prompt* on page 195. [{ ... }]

:RC / conf.rc

If false, do not load an initialization file. [true]

conf.return_format

The format used to display the results of expressions entered interactively. [depends]

:SINGLE_IRB

If true, nested irb sessions will all share the same binding; otherwise a new binding will be created according to the value of :CONTEXT_MODE. [nil]

conf.thread

A read-only reference to the currently executing Thread object. [current thread]

:USE_LOADER / conf.use_loader

Specifies whether irb's own file reader method is used with load/require. [false]

:USE_READLINE / conf.use_readline

irb will use the readline library if available (see page 723) unless this option is set to false, in which case readline will never be used, or nil, in which case readline will not be used in inf-ruby-mode. [depends]

:USE_TRACER / conf.use_tracer

> If true, traces the execution of statements. [false]

:VERBOSE / conf.verbose

> In theory switches on additional tracing when true; in practice almost no extra tracing results. [true]

Commands

At the irb prompt, you can enter any valid Ruby expression and see the results. You can also use any of the following commands to control the irb session.

exit, quit, irb_exit, irb_quit

> Quits this irb session or subsession. If you've used cb to change bindings (see below), exits from this binding mode.

conf, context, irb_context

> Displays current configuration. Modifying the configuration is achieved by invoking methods of conf. The list starting on page 192 shows the available conf settings. For example, to set the default prompt to something subservient, you could use

```
irb(main):001:0> conf.prompt_i = "Yes, Master? "
=> "Yes, Master? "
Yes, Master? 1 + 2
```

cb, irb_change_binding ⟨ *obj* ⟩

> Creates and enters a new binding that has its own scope for local variables. If *obj* is given, it will be used as self in the new binding.

irb ⟨ *obj* ⟩

> Starts an irb subsession. If *obj* is given, it will be used as self.

jobs, irb_jobs

> Lists irb subsessions.

fg *n*, **irb_fg** *n*

> Switches into the specified irb subsession. *n* may be any of: an irb subsession number, a thread ID, an irb object, or the object that was the value of *self* when a subsession was launched.

kill *n*, **irb_kill** *n*

> Kills an irb subsession. *n* may be any of the values as described for irb_fg.

Configuring the Prompt

You have a lot of flexibility in configuring the prompts that irb uses. Sets of prompts are stored in the prompt hash, `IRB.conf[:PROMPT]`.

For example, to establish a new prompt mode called "MY_PROMPT", you could enter the following (either directly at an irb prompt or in the `.irbrc` file).

```
IRB.conf[:PROMPT][:MY_PROMPT] = { # name of prompt mode
  :PROMPT_I => '-->',             # normal prompt
  :PROMPT_S => '--"',             # prompt for continuing strings
  :PROMPT_C => '--+',             # prompt for continuing statement
  :RETURN => "    ==>%s\n"        # format to return value
}
```

Once you've defined a prompt, you have to tell irb to use it. From the command line, you can use the `--prompt` option. (Notice how the name of the prompt mode is automatically converted to uppercase, with hyphens changing to underscores.)

```
% irb --prompt my-prompt
```

If you want to use this prompt in all your future irb sessions, you can set it as a configuration value in your `.irbrc` file.

```
IRB.conf[:PROMPT_MODE] = :MY_PROMPT
```

The symbols `PROMPT_I`, `PROMPT_S`, and `PROMPT_C` specify the format for each of the prompt strings. In a format string, certain "%" sequences are expanded.

Flag	Description
%N	Current command.
%m	to_s of the main object (self).
%M	inspect of the main object (self).
%l	Delimiter type. In strings that are continued across a line break, %l will display the type of delimiter used to begin the string, so you'll know how to end it. The delimiter will be one of ", ', /,], or `.
%ni	Indent level. The optional number n is used as a width specification to printf, as `printf("%$n$d")`.
%nn	Current line number (n used as with the indent level).
%%	A literal percent sign.

For instance, the default prompt mode is defined as follows.

```
IRB.conf[:PROMPT_MODE][:DEFAULT] = {
    :PROMPT_I => "%N(%m):%03n:%i> ",
    :PROMPT_S => "%N(%m):%03n:%i%l ",
    :PROMPT_C => "%N(%m):%03n:%i* ",
    :RETURN => "%s\n"
}
```

Restrictions

Because of the way irb works, it is slightly incompatible with the standard Ruby interpreter. The problem lies in the determination of local variables.

Normally, Ruby looks for an assignment statement to determine if something is a variable—if a name hasn't been assigned to, then Ruby assumes that name is a method call.

```
eval "var = 0"
var
```

produces:

```
prog.rb:2: undefined local variable or method `var'
 for main:Object (NameError)
```

In this case, the assignment is there, but it's within a string, so Ruby doesn't take it into account.

irb, on the other hand, executes statements as they are entered.

```
irb(main):001:0> eval "var = 0"
0
irb(main):002:0> var
0
```

In irb, the assignment was executed before the second line was encountered, so var is correctly identified as a local variable.

If you need to match the Ruby behavior more closely, you can place these statements within a begin/end pair.

```
irb(main):001:0> begin
irb(main):002:1*   eval "var = 0"
irb(main):003:1>   var
irb(main):004:1> end
NameError: undefined local variable or method `var'
(irb):3:in `irb_binding'
```

rtags and xmp

Just in case irb wasn't already complex enough, let's add a few more wrinkles. Along with the main irb program, the irb suite includes some extra goodies. In the next sections we'll look at two: rtags and xmp.

rtags

rtags is a command used to create a TAGS file for use with either the Emacs or vi editor.

```
rtags [ -vi ] [ files ]...
```

By default, rtags makes a TAGS file suitable for Emacs (see `etags.el`). The `-vi` option makes a TAGS file for use with vi.

`rtags` needs to be installed in the same manner as irb (that is, you need to install irb in the library path and make a link from `irb/rtags.rb` to `bin/rtags`).

xmp

irb's `xmp` is an "example printer"—that is, a pretty-printer that shows the value of each expression as it is run (much like the script we wrote to format the examples in this book). There is also another stand-alone `xmp` in the archives.

`xmp` can be used as follows.

```
require 'irb/xmp'
xmp <<END
artist = "Doc Severinsen"
artist.upcase
END
```

produces:

```
artist = "Doc Severinsen"
    ==> "Doc Severinsen"
artist.upcase
    ==> "DOC SEVERINSEN"
```

Or, `xmp` can be used as an object instance. Used in this fashion, the object maintains context between invocations.

```
require 'irb/xmp'
x = XMP.new
x.puts 'artist = "Louis Prima"'
x.puts 'artist.upcase'
```

produces:

```
artist = "Louis Prima"
    ==> "Louis Prima"
artist.upcase
    ==> "LOUIS PRIMA"
```

You can explicitly provide a binding with either form; otherwise, `xmp` uses the caller's environment.

```
xmp code_string, abinding
XMP.new(abinding)
```

Note that `xmp` does not work with multithreading.

## Chapter 16

Documenting Ruby

1.8

As of version 1.8, Ruby comes bundled with RDoc, a tool that extracts and formats documentation that's embedded in Ruby source code files. This tool is used to document the built-in Ruby classes and modules. An increasing number of libraries and extensions are also documented this way.

RDoc does two jobs. First, it analyzes Ruby and C source files, looking for information to document.[1] Second, it takes this information and converts it into something readable. Out of the box, RDoc produces two kinds of output: HTML and ri. Figure 16.1 on the following page shows some HTML-format RDoc output in a browser window. This is the result of feeding RDoc a Ruby source file with no additional documentation—RDoc does a credible job of producing something meaningful. If our source code contains comments, RDoc can use them to spice up the documentation it produces. Typically, the comment before an element is used to document that element, as shown in Figure 16.2 on page 201.

RDoc can also be used to produce documentation that can be read by the ri command-line utility. For example, if we ask RDoc to document the code in Figure 16.2 this way, we can then access the documentation using ri, as shown in Figure 16.3 on page 202. New Ruby distributions have the built-in classes and modules (and some libraries) documented this way. Figure 16.4 on page 203 shows the output produced if you type **ri Proc**.

Adding RDoc to Ruby Code

RDoc parses Ruby source files to extract the major elements (classes, modules, methods, attributes, and so on). You can choose to associate additional documentation with these by simply adding a comment block before the element in the file.

---

1.   RDoc can also document Fortran 77 programs.

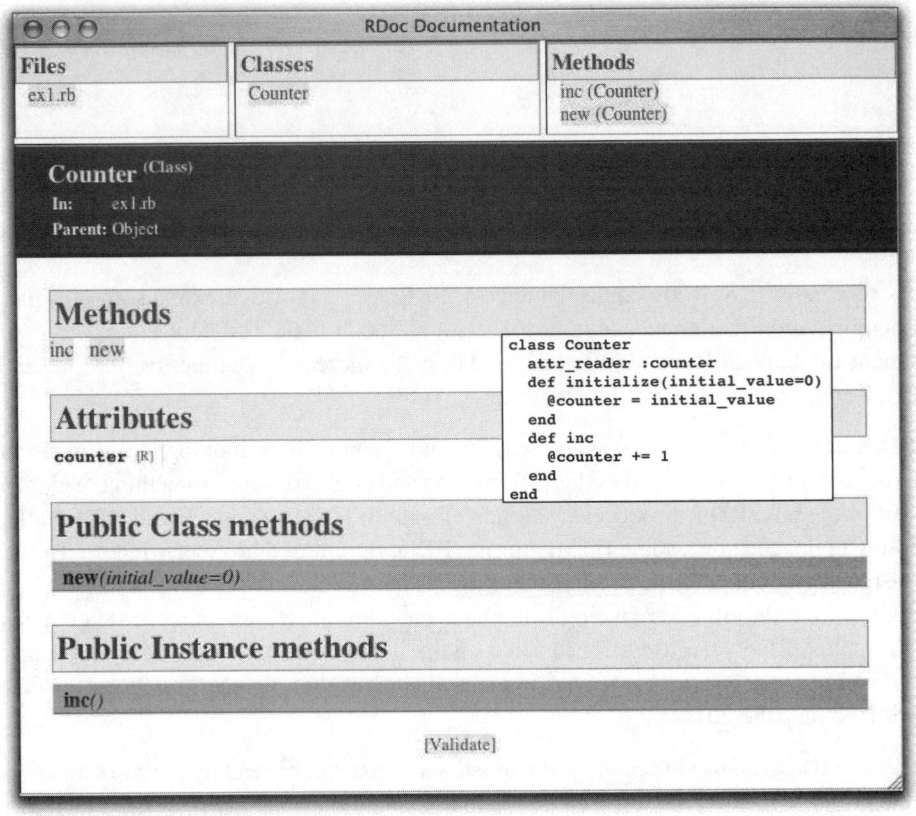

Files	Classes	Methods
ex1.rb	Counter	inc (Counter)
		new (Counter)

Counter (Class)

In: ex1.rb
Parent: Object

Methods

inc new

```
class Counter
  attr_reader :counter
  def initialize(initial_value=0)
    @counter = initial_value
  end
  def inc
    @counter += 1
  end
end
```

Attributes

counter [R]

Public Class methods

new(*initial_value=0*)

Public Instance methods

inc()

[Validate]

This figure shows some RDoc output in a browser window. The overlaid box shows the source program from which this output was generated. Even though the source contains no internal documentation, RDoc still manages to extract interesting information from it. We have three panes at the top of the screen showing the files, classes, and methods for which we have documentation. For class Counter, RDoc shows us the attributes and methods (including the method signatures). And if we clicked a method signature, RDoc would pop up a window containing the source code for the corresponding method.

Figure 16.1. Browse RDoc output for class counter

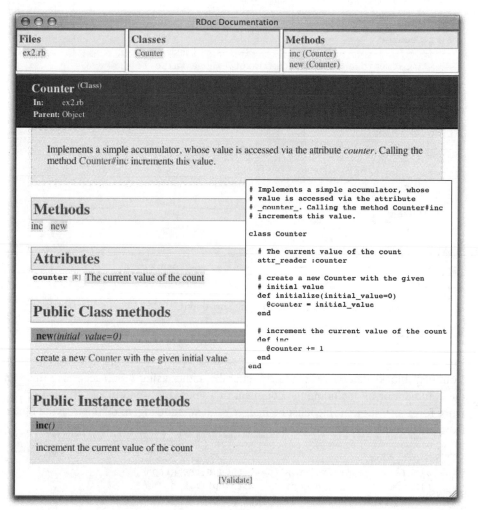

Notice how the comments before each element now appear in the RDoc output, reformatted into HTML. Less obvious is that RDoc has detected hyperlink opportunities in our comments: in the class-level comment, the reference to Counter#inc is a hyperlink to the method description, and in the command for the new method, the reference to class Counter hyperlinks back to the class documentation. This is a key feature of RDoc: it is designed to be unintrusive in the Ruby source files and to make up for this by trying to be clever when producing output.

Figure 16.2. Browse RDoc output when source has comments

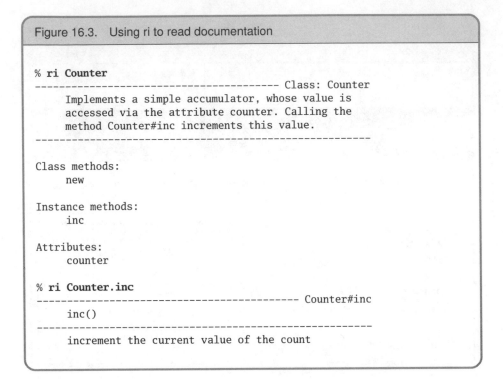

Figure 16.3. Using ri to read documentation

```
% ri Counter
------------------------------------- Class: Counter
     Implements a simple accumulator, whose value is
     accessed via the attribute counter. Calling the
     method Counter#inc increments this value.
-------------------------------------------------

Class methods:
     new

Instance methods:
     inc

Attributes:
     counter

% ri Counter.inc
------------------------------------------- Counter#inc
     inc()
-------------------------------------------------
     increment the current value of the count
```

Comment blocks can be written fairly naturally, either using # on successive lines of the comment or by including the comment in a =begin...=end block. If you use the latter form, the =begin line must be flagged with an rdoc tag, to distinguish the block from other styles of documentation.

```
=begin rdoc
Calculate the minimal-cost path though the graph
using Debrinkski's algorithm, with optimized
inverse pruning of isolated leaf nodes.
=end
def calculate_path
  . . .
end
```

Within a documentation comment, paragraphs are lines that share the left margin. Text indented past this margin is formatted verbatim.

Nonverbatim text can be marked up. To set individual words in italic, bold, or typewriter fonts, you can use _word_, *word*, and +word+ respectively. If you want to do this to multiple words, or text containing non-word characters, you can use multiple words, more words, and <tt>yet more words</tt>. Putting a backslash before inline markup stops it being interpreted.

```
Figure 16.4.   Document for class Proc generated by RDoc/ri

% ri Proc
---------------------------------------- Class: Proc
     Proc objects are blocks of code that have been
     bound to a set of local variables. Once bound,
     the code may be called in different contexts and
     still access those variables.

         def gen_times(factor)
           return Proc.new |n| n*factor
         end

         times3 = gen_times(3)
         times5 = gen_times(5)

         times3.call(12)              #=> 36
         times5.call(5)               #=> 25
         times3.call(times5.call(4))  #=> 60


------------------------------------------------------

Class methods:
     new

Instance methods:
     ==, [], arity, binding, call, clone, eql?, hash,
     to_proc, to_s
```

RDoc stops processing comments if it finds a comment line starting #--. This can be used to separate external from internal comments or to stop a comment being associated with a method, class, or module. Documenting can be turned back on by starting a line with #++.

```
# Extract the age and calculate the
# date of birth.
#--
# FIXME: fails if the birthday falls on
# February 29th, or if the person
# was born before epoch and the installed
# Ruby doesn't support negative time_t
#++
# The DOB is returned as a Time object.
#--
# But should probably change to use Date.

def get_dob(person)
         ...
    end
```

Hyperlinks

Names of classes, source files, and any method names containing an underscore or preceded by a hash character are automatically hyperlinked from comment text to their description.

Hyperlinks to the 'net starting `http:`, `mailto:`, `ftp:`, and `www:` are recognized. An HTTP URL that references an external image file is converted into an inline <IMG...> tag. Hyperlinks starting `link:` are assumed to refer to local files whose paths are relative to the `--op` directory, where output files are stored.

Hyperlinks can also be of the form `label[url]`, in which case the label is used in the displayed text and `url` is used as the target. If the label contains multiple words, surround it in braces: `{two words}[url]`.

Lists

Lists are typed as indented paragraphs with

- a * or - (for bullet lists),

- a digit followed by a period for numbered lists,

- an uppercase or lowercase letter followed by a period for alpha lists.

For example, you could produce something like the previous text with

```
#  Lists are typed as indented paragraphs with
#  * a * or - (for bullet lists),
#  * a digit followed by a period for
#    numbered lists,
#  * an upper or lower case letter followed
#    by a period for alpha lists.
```

Note how subsequent lines in a list item are indented to line up with the text in the element's first line.

Labeled lists (sometimes called *description lists*) are typed using square brackets for the label.

```
#  [cat]    small domestic animal
#  [+cat+]  command to copy standard input
#           to standard output
```

Labeled lists may also be produced by putting a double colon after the label. This sets the result in tabular form, so the descriptions all line up.

```
#  cat::   small domestic animal
#  +cat+:: command to copy standard input
#          to standard output
```

For both kinds of labeled lists, if the body text starts on the same line as the label, then the start of that text determines the block indent for the rest of the body. The text may also start on the line following the label, indented from the start of the label. This is often preferable if the label is long. Both the following are valid labeled list entries

```
#   <tt>--output</tt> <i>name [, name]</i>::
#       specify the name of one or more output files. If multiple
#       files are present, the first is used as the index.
#
#   <tt>--quiet:</tt>:: do not output the names, sizes, byte counts,
#                       index areas, or bit ratios of units as
#                       they are processed.
```

Headings

Headings are entered on lines starting with equals signs. The more equals signs, the higher the level of heading.

```
#   = Level One Heading
#   == Level Two Heading
#   and so on...
```

Rules (horizontal lines) are entered using three or more hyphens.

```
#   and so it goes...
#   ----
#   The next section...
```

Documentation Modifiers

Method parameter lists are extracted and displayed with the method description. If a method calls `yield`, then the parameters passed to yield will also be displayed. For example, consider the following code.

```
def fred
  ...
  yield line, address
```

This will get documented as:

```
fred() {|line, address| ... }
```

You can override this using a comment containing `:yields:` ... on the same line as the method definition.

```
def fred      # :yields: index, position
  ...
  yield line, address
```

which will get documented as

```
fred() {|index, position| ... }
```

:yields: is an example of a documentation modifier. These appear immediately after the start of the document element they are modifying.

Other modifiers include

:nodoc: *[all]*

> Don't include this element in the documentation. For classes and modules, the methods, aliases, constants, and attributes directly within the affected class or module will also be omitted from the documentation. By default, though, modules and classes within that class or module will be documented. This is turned off by adding the all modifier. For example, in the following code, only class SM::Input will be documented.

```
module SM  #:nodoc:
  class Input
  end
end
module Markup #:nodoc: all
  class Output
  end
end
```

:doc:

> Force a method or attribute to be documented even if it wouldn't otherwise be. Useful if, for example, you want to include documentation of a particular private method.

:notnew:

> (Only applicable to the initialize instance method.) Normally RDoc assumes that the documentation and parameters for #initialize are actually for the corresponding class's new method and so fakes out a new method for the class. The :notnew: modifier stops this. Remember that #initialize is protected, so you won't see the documentation unless you use the -a command-line option.

Other Directives

Comment blocks can contain other directives.

:call-seq: *lines...*

> Text up to the next blank comment line is used as the calling sequence when generating documentation (overriding the parsing of the method parameter list). A line is considered blank even if it starts with a #. For this one directive, the leading colon is optional.

:include: *filename*

> Include the contents of the named file at this point. The file will be searched for in the directories listed by the --include option or in the current directory by

default. The contents of the file will be shifted to have the same indentation as the
: at the start of the :include: directive.

:title: *text*

Sets the title for the document. Equivalent to the --title command-line parameter. (The command-line parameter overrides any :title: directive in the source.)

:main: *name*

Equivalent to the --main command-line parameter, setting the initial page displayed for this documentation.

:stopdoc: / :startdoc:

Stop and start adding new documentation elements to the current container. For
example, if a class has a number of constants that you don't want to document, put
a :stopdoc: before the first and a :startdoc: after the last. If you don't specify
a :startdoc: by the end of the container, disables documentation for the entire
class or module.

:enddoc:

Document nothing further at the current lexical level.

Figure 16.5 on the following page shows a more complete example of a source file
documented using RDoc.

Adding RDoc to C Extensions

RDoc also understands many of the conventions used when writing extensions to Ruby
in C.

Most C extensions have an Init_*Classname* function. RDoc takes this as the class
definition—any C comment before the Init_ method will be used as the class's documentation.

The Init_ function is normally used to associate C functions with Ruby method names.
For example, a Cipher extension may define a Ruby method salt=, implemented by
the C function salt_set using a call such as

```
rb_define_method(cCipher, "salt=", salt_set, 1);
```

RDoc parses this call, adding the salt= method to the class documentation. RDoc then
searches the C source for the C function salt_set. If this function is preceded by a
comment block, RDoc uses this for the method's documentation.

This basic scheme works with no effort on your part beyond writing the normal documentation in the comments for functions. However, RDoc cannot discern the calling
sequence for the corresponding Ruby method. In this example, the RDoc output will

Figure 16.5. Ruby source file documented with RDoc

```ruby
# This module encapsulates functionality related to the
# generation of Fibonacci sequences.
#--
# Copyright (c) 2004 Dave Thomas, The Pragmatic Programmers, LLC.
# Licensed under the same terms as Ruby. No warranty is provided.
module Fibonacci

  # Calculate the first _count_ Fibonacci numbers, starting with 1,1.
  #
  # :call-seq:
  #   Fibonacci.sequence(count)                -> array
  #   Fibonacci.sequence(count) {|val| ... }   -> nil
  #
  # If a block is given, supply successive values to the block and
  # return +nil+, otherwise return all values as an array.
  def Fibonacci.sequence(count, &block)
    result, block = setup_optional_block(block)
    generate do |val|
      break if count <= 0
      count -= 1
      block[val]
    end
    result
  end

  # Calculate the Fibonacci numbers up to and including _max_.
  #
  # :call-seq:
  #   Fibonacci.upto(count)                -> array
  #   Fibonacci.upto(count) {|val ... }    -> nil
  #
  # If a block is given, supply successive values to the
  # block and return +nil+, otherwise return all values as an array.
  def Fibonacci.upto(max, &block)
    result, block = setup_optional_block(block)
    generate do |val|
      break if val > max
      block[val]
    end
    result
  end

  private

  # Yield a sequence of Fibonacci numbers to a block.
  def Fibonacci.generate
    f1, f2 = 1, 1
    loop do
      yield f1
      f1, f2 = f2, f1+f2
    end
  end

  # If a block parameter is given, use it, otherwise accumulate into an
  # array. Return the result value and the block to use.
  def Fibonacci.setup_optional_block(block)
    if block.nil?
      [ result = [], lambda {|val| result << val } ]
    else
      [ nil, block ]
    end
  end
end
```

show a single argument with the (somewhat meaningless) name "arg1." You can override this using the call-seq directive in the function's comment. The lines following call-seq (up to a blank line) are used to document the calling sequence of the method.

```
/*
 * call-seq:
 *   cipher.salt = number
 *   cipher.salt = "string"
 *
 * Sets the salt of this cipher to either a binary +number+ or
 * bits in +string+.
 */
static VALUE
salt_set(cipher, salt)
...
```

If a method returns a meaningful value, it should be documented in the call-seq following the characters ->.

```
/*
 * call-seq:
 *   cipher.keylen   -> Fixnum or nil
 */
```

Although RDoc heuristics work well for finding the class and method comments for simple extensions, it doesn't always work for more complex implementations. In these cases, you can use the directives Document-class: and Document-method: to indicate that a C comment relates to a given class or method, respectively. The modifiers take the name of the Ruby class or method that's being documented.

```
/*
 * Document-method: reset
 *
 * Clear the current buffer and prepare to add new
 * cipher text. Any accumulated output cipher text
 * is also cleared.
 */
```

Finally, it is possible in the Init_ method to associate a Ruby method with a C function in a different C source file. RDoc would not find this function without your help: you add a reference to the file containing the function definition by adding a special comment to the rb_define_method call. The following example tells RDoc to look in the file md5.c for the function (and related comment) corresponding to the md5 method.

```
rb_define_method(cCipher, "md5", gen_md5, -1); /* in md5.c */
```

Figure 16.6 on the next page shows a C source file documented using RDoc. Note that the bodies of several internal methods have been elided to save space.

Figure 16.6. C source file documented with RDoc

```
#include "ruby.h"
#include "cdjukebox.h"

static VALUE cCDPlayer;
static void cd_free(void *p) { ... }
static VALUE cd_alloc(VALUE klass) { ... }
static void progress(CDJukebox *rec, int percent) { ... }

/* call-seq:
 *    CDPlayer.new(unit)  -> new_cd_player
 *
 * Assign the newly created CDPlayer to a particular unit
 */
static VALUE cd_initialize(VALUE self, VALUE unit) {
  int unit_id;
  CDJukebox *jb;

  Data_Get_Struct(self, CDJukebox, jb);

  unit_id = NUM2INT(unit);
  assign_jukebox(jb, unit_id);

  return self;
}

/* call-seq:
 *   player.seek(int_disc, int_track)  -> nil
 *   player.seek(int_disc, int_track) {|percent| } -> nil
 *
 * Seek to a given part of the track, invoking the block
 * with the percent complete as we go.
 */
static VALUE
cd_seek(VALUE self, VALUE disc, VALUE track) {
  CDJukebox *jb;
  Data_Get_Struct(self, CDJukebox, jb);

  jukebox_seek(jb, NUM2INT(disc), NUM2INT(track), progress);
  return Qnil;
}

/* call-seq:
 *   player.seek_time -> Float
 *
 * Return the average seek time for this unit (in seconds)
 */
static VALUE
cd_seek_time(VALUE self)
{
  double tm;
  CDJukebox *jb;
  Data_Get_Struct(self, CDJukebox, jb);
  tm = get_avg_seek_time(jb);
  return rb_float_new(tm);
}

/* Interface to the Spinzalot[http://spinzalot.cd]
 * CD Player library.
 */

void Init_CDPlayer() {
  cCDPlayer = rb_define_class("CDPlayer", rb_cObject);
  rb_define_alloc_func(cCDPlayer, cd_alloc);
  rb_define_method(cCDPlayer, "initialize", cd_initialize, 1);
  rb_define_method(cCDPlayer, "seek", cd_seek, 2);
  rb_define_method(cCDPlayer, "seek_time", cd_seek_time, 0);
}
```

Running RDoc

You run RDoc from the command line.

```
% rdoc [options]  [filenames...]
```

Type **rdoc --help** for an up-to-date option summary.

Files are parsed, and the information they contain collected, before any output is produced. This allows cross-references between all files to be resolved. If a name is a directory, it is traversed. If no names are specified, all Ruby files in the current directory (and subdirectories) are processed.

A typical use may be to generate documentation for a package of Ruby source (such as RDoc itself).

```
% rdoc
```

This command generates HTML documentation for all the Ruby and C source files in and below the current directory. These will be stored in a documentation tree starting in the subdirectory doc/.

RDoc uses file extensions to determine how to process each file. Filenames ending .rb and .rbw are assumed to be Ruby source. Files ending .c are parsed as C files. All other files are assumed to contain just markup (with or without leading # comment markers). If directory names are passed to RDoc, they are scanned recursively for C and Ruby source files only. To include nonsource files such as READMEs in the documentation process, their names must be given explicitly on the command line.

When writing a Ruby library, you often have some source files that implement the public interface, but the majority are internal and of no interest to the readers of your documentation. In these cases, construct a .document file in each of your project's directories. If RDoc enters a directory containing a .document file, it will process only the files in that directory whose names match one of the lines in that file. Each line in the file can be a filename, a directory name, or a wildcard (a file system "glob" pattern). For example, to include all Ruby files whose names start main, along with the file constants.rb, you could use a .document file containing

```
main*.rb
constants.rb
```

Some project standards ask for documentation in a top-level README file. You may find it convenient to write this file in RDoc format, and then use the :include: directive to incorporate this document into that for the main class.

Create Documentation for ri

RDoc is also used to create documentation which will be later displayed using ri.

When you run ri, it by default looks for documentation in three places:[2]

1. the *system* documentation directory, which holds the documentation distributed with Ruby, and which is created by the Ruby install process,

2. the *site* directory, which contains sitewide documentation added locally, and

3. the *user* documentation directory, stored under the user's own home directory.

You can find these three directories in the following locations.

- `$datadir/ri/<ver>/system/...`
- `$datadir/ri/<ver>/site/...`
- `~/.rdoc/....`

The variable `$datadir` is the configured data directory for the installed Ruby. Find your local *datadir* using

```
ruby -r rbconfig -e 'p Config::CONFIG["datadir"]'
```

To add documentation to ri, you need to tell RDoc which output directory to use. For your own use, it's easiest to use the `--ri` option.

```
% rdoc --ri  file1.rb file2.rb
```

If you want to install sitewide documentation, use the `--ri-site` option.

```
% rdoc --ri-site  file1.rb file2.rb
```

The `--ri-system` option is normally used only to install documentation for Ruby's built-in classes and standard libraries. You can regenerate this documentation from the Ruby source distribution (not from the installed libraries themselves).

```
% cd <ruby source base>/lib
% rdoc --ri-system
```

Displaying Program Usage

Most command line programs have some kind of facility to describe their correct usage; give them invalid parameters and they'll report a short error message followed by a synopsis of their actual options. And, if you're using RDoc, you'll probably have described

---

2.   You can override the directory location using the `--op` option to RDoc, and subsequently using the `--doc-dir` option with ri.

Figure 16.7.　Sample program using RDoc::usage

```
# == Synopsis
#
# Display the current date and time, optionally honoring
# a format string.
#
# == Usage
#
#    ruby showtime.rb  [ -h | --help ] [ -f | --fmt fmtstring ]
#
# fmtstring::
#    A +strftime+ format string controlling the
#    display of the date and time. If omitted,
#    use <em>"%Y-%m-%d %H:%M"</em>
#
# == Author
# Dave Thomas, The Pragmatic Programmers, LLC
#
# == Copyright
# Copyright (c) 2004 The Pragmatic Programmers.
# Licensed under the same terms as Ruby.

require 'optparse'
require 'rdoc/usage'

fmt = "%Y-%m-%d %H:%M"
opts = OptionParser.new
opts.on("-h", "--help") { RDoc::usage }
opts.on("-f", "--fmt FMTSTRING") {|str| fmt = str }
opts.parse(ARGV) rescue RDoc::usage('usage')

puts Time.now.strftime(fmt)
```

how the program should be used in a RDoc comment at the start of the main program. Rather than duplicate all this information in a puts somewhere, you can use RDoc::usage to extract it straight from the command and write it to the user.

You can pass RDoc::usage a number of string parameters. If present, it extracts from the comment block only those sections named by parameters (where a section starts with a heading equal to the parameter, ignoring case). With no string parameters, RDoc::usage displays the entire comment. In addition, RDoc::usage exits the program after displaying the usage message. If the first parameter in the call is an integer, it is used as the program's exit code (otherwise RDoc::usage exits with a zero error code). If you don't want to exit the program after displaying a usage message, call RDoc::usage_no_exit.

Figure 16.7 shows a trivial program that displays the time. It uses RDoc::usage to display the complete comment block if the user asks for help, and to display just the

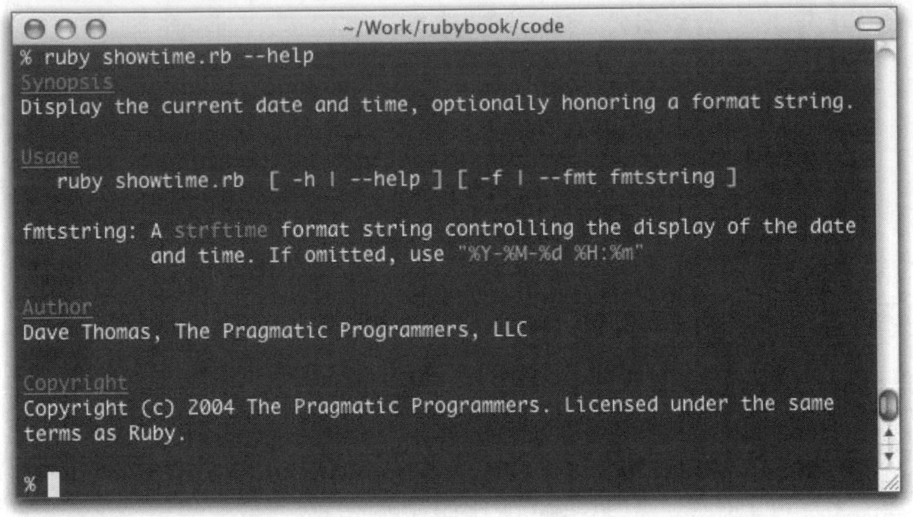

```
● ● ●                          ~/Work/rubybook/code                              ⬭
% ruby showtime.rb --help
Synopsis
Display the current date and time, optionally honoring a format string.

Usage
    ruby showtime.rb  [ -h | --help ] [ -f | --fmt fmtstring ]

fmtstring: A strftime format string controlling the display of the date
           and time. If omitted, use "%Y-%M-%d %H:%m"

Author
Dave Thomas, The Pragmatic Programmers, LLC

Copyright
Copyright (c) 2004 The Pragmatic Programmers. Licensed under the same
terms as Ruby.

%
```

Figure 16.8. Help generated by sample program

usage section if the user gives an invalid option. Figure 16.8 shows the output generated in response to a --help option.

RDoc::usage honors the RI environment variable, which can be used to set the display width and output style. The output in Figure 16.8 was generated with the RI option set to "-f ansi." Although not too apparent if you're looking at this figure in the black-and-white book, the section headings, code font, and emphasized font are shown in different colors using ANSI escape sequences.

Chad Fowler *is a leading figure in the Ruby community. He's on the board of Ruby Central, Inc. He's one of the organizers of RubyConf. And he's one of the writers of RubyGems. All this makes him uniquely qualified to write this chapter.*

Chapter 17

Package Management with RubyGems

RubyGems is a standardized packaging and installation framework for libraries and applications, making it easy to locate, install, upgrade, and uninstall Ruby packages. It provides users and developers with four main facilities.

1. A standardized package format,

2. A central repository for hosting packages in this format,

3. Installation and management of multiple, simultaneously installed versions of the same library,

4. End-user tools for querying, installing, uninstalling, and otherwise manipulating these packages.

Before RubyGems came along, installing a new library involved searching the Web, downloading a package, and attempting to install it—only to find that its dependencies haven't been met. If the library you want is packaged using RubyGems, however, you can now simply ask RubyGems to install it (and all its dependencies). Everything is done for you.

In the RubyGems world, developers bundle their applications and libraries into single files called *gems*. These files conform to a standardized format, and the RubyGems system provides a command-line tool, appropriately named *gem*, for manipulating these gem files.

In this chapter, we'll see how to

1. Install RubyGems on your computer.
2. Use RubyGems to install other applications and libraries.
3. Write your own gems.

Installing RubyGems

To use RubyGems, you'll first need to download and install the RubyGems system from the project's home page at `http://rubygems.rubyforge.org`. After downloading and unpacking the distribution, you can install it using the included installation script.

```
% cd rubygems-0.7.0
% ruby install.rb
```

Depending on your operating system, you may need suitable privileges to write files into Ruby's `site_ruby/` and `bin/` directories.

The best way to test that RubyGems was installed successfully also happens to be the most important command you'll learn.

```
% gem help
RubyGems is a sophisticated package manager for Ruby.  This is
a basic help message containing pointers to more information.

  Usage:
    gem -h/--help
    gem -v/--version
    gem command [arguments...] [options...]

  Examples:
    gem install rake
    gem list --local
    gem build package.gemspec
    gem help install

  Further help:
    gem help commands          list all 'gem' commands
    gem help examples          show some examples of usage
    gem help <COMMAND>         show help on COMMAND
                                 (e.g. 'gem help install')

  Further information:
    http://rubygems.rubyforge.org
```

Because RubyGems' help is quite comprehensive, we won't go into detail about each of the available RubyGems commands and options in this chapter.

Installing Application Gems

Let's start by using RubyGems to install an application that is written in Ruby. Jim Weirich's Rake (`http://rake.rubyforge.org`) holds the distinction of being the first application that was available as a gem. Not only that, but it's generally a great tool to have around, as it is a build tool similar to Make and Ant. In fact, you can even use Rake to build gems!

Locating and installing Rake with RubyGems is simple.

```
% gem install -r rake
Attempting remote installation of 'Rake'
Successfully installed rake, version 0.4.3
% rake --version
rake, version 0.4.3
```

RubyGems downloads the Rake package and installs it. Because Rake is an application, RubyGems downloads both the Rake libraries and the command-line program `rake`.

You control the gem program using subcommands, each of which has its own options and help screen. In this example, we used the `install` subcommand with the `-r` option, which tells it to operate remotely. (Many RubyGems operations can be performed either locally or remotely. For example, you can use the `query` command either to display all the gems that are available remotely for installation or to display a list of gems you already have installed. For this reason, subcommands accept the options `-r` and `-l`, specifying whether an operation is meant to be carried out remotely or locally.)

If for some reason—perhaps because of a potential compatibility issue—you wanted an older version of Rake, you could use RubyGems' version requirement operators to specify criteria by which a version would be selected.

```
% gem install -r rake -v "< 0.4.3"
Attempting remote installation of 'rake'
Successfully installed rake, version 0.4.2
% rake --version
rake, version 0.4.2
```

Table 17.1 on the following page lists the version requirement operators. The `-v` argument in our previous example asks for the highest version lower than 0.4.3.

There's a subtlety when it comes to installing different versions of the same application with RubyGems. Even though RubyGems keeps separate versions of the application's library files, it does not version the actual command you use to run the application. As a result, each install of an application effectively overwrites the previous one.

During installation, you can also add the `-t` option to the RubyGems `install` command, causing RubyGems to run the gem's test suite (if one has been created). If the tests fail, the installer will prompt you to either keep or discard the gem. This is a good way to gain a little more confidence that the gem you've just downloaded works on your system the way the author intended.

```
% gem install SomePoorlyTestedProgram -t
Attempting local installation of 'SomePoorlyTestedProgram-1.0.1'
Successfully installed SomePoorlyTestedProgram, version 1.0.1
23 tests, 22 assertions, 0 failures, 1 errors...keep Gem? [Y/n] n
Successfully uninstalled SomePoorlyTestedProgram version 1.0.1
```

Had we chosen the default and kept the gem installed, we could have inspected the gem to try to determine the cause of the failing test.

Table 17.1. Version operators

Both the require_gem method and the add_dependency attribute in a Gem::Specification accept an argument that specifies a version dependency. RubyGems version dependencies are of the form operator major.minor.patch_level. Listed below is a table of all the possible version operators.

Operator	Description
=	Exact version match. Major, minor, and patch level must be identical.
!=	Any version that is not the one specified.
>	Any version that is greater (even at the patch level) than the one specified.
<	Any version that is less than the one specified.
>=	Any version greater than or equal to the specified version.
<=	Any version less than or equal to the specified version.
~>	"Boxed" version operator. Version must be greater than or equal to the specified version *and* less than the specified version after having its minor version number increased by one. This is to avoid API incompatibilities between minor version releases.

Installing and Using Gem Libraries

Using RubyGems to install a complete application was a good way to get your feet wet and to start to learn your way around the gem command. However, in most cases, you'll use RubyGems to install Ruby libraries for use in your own programs. Since RubyGems enables you to install and manage multiple versions of the same library, you'll also need to do some new, RubyGems-specific things when you require those libraries in your code.

Perhaps you've been asked by your mother to create a program to help her maintain and publish a diary. You have decided that you would like to publish the diary in HTML format, but you are worried that your mother may not understand all of the ins and outs of HTML markup. For this reason, you've opted to use one of the many excellent templating packages available for Ruby. After some research, you've decided on Michael Granger's BlueCloth, based on its reputation for being very simple to use.

You first need to find and install the BlueCloth gem.

```
% gem query -rn Blue
*** REMOTE GEMS ***
BlueCloth (0.0.4, 0.0.3, 0.0.2)
    BlueCloth is a Ruby implementation of Markdown, a text-to-HTML
    conversion tool for web writers. Markdown allows you to write using
    an easy-to-read, easy-to-write plain text format, then convert it
    to structurally valid XHTML (or HTML).
```

This invocation of the query command uses the −n option to search the central gem repository for any gem whose name matches the regular expression /Blue/. The results show that three available versions of BlueCloth exist (0.0.4, 0.0.3, and 0.0.2). Because you want to install the most recent one, you don't have to state an explicit version on the install command; the latest is downloaded by default.

```
% gem install -r BlueCloth
Attempting remote installation of 'BlueCloth'
Successfully installed BlueCloth, version 0.0.4
```

Generating API Documentation

Being that this is your first time using BlueCloth, you're not exactly sure how to use it. You need some API documentation to get started. Fortunately, with the addition of the −−rdoc option to the install command, RubyGems will generate RDoc documentation for the gem it is installing. For more information on RDoc, see Chapter 16 on page 199.

```
% gem install -r BlueCloth --rdoc
Attempting remote installation of 'BlueCloth'
Successfully installed BlueCloth, version 0.0.4
Installing RDoc documentation for BlueCloth-0.0.4...
WARNING: Generating RDoc on .gem that may not have RDoc.
        bluecloth.rb: cc.............................
Generating HTML...
```

Having generated all this useful HTML documentation, how can you view it? You have at least two options. The hard way (though it really isn't that hard) is to open RubyGems' documentation directory and browse the documentation directly. As with most things in RubyGems, the documentation for each gem is stored in a central, protected, RubyGems-specific place. This will vary by system and by where you may explicitly choose to install your gems. The most reliable way to find the documents is to ask the gem command where your RubyGems main directory is located. For example:

```
% gem environment gemdir
/usr/local/lib/ruby/gems/1.8
```

RubyGems stores generated documentation in the doc/ subdirectory of this directory, in this case /usr/local/lib/ruby/gems/1.8/doc. You can open the file index.html and view the documentation. If you find yourself using this path often, you can create a shortcut. Here's one way to do that on Mac OS X boxes.

```
% gemdoc=`gem environment gemdir`/doc
% ls $gemdoc
BlueCloth-0.0.4
% open $gemdoc/BlueCloth-0.0.4/rdoc/index.html
```

To save time, you could declare $gemdoc in your login shell's profile or rc file.

The second (and easier) way to view gems' RDoc documentation is to use RubyGems' included gem_server utility. To start gem_server, simply type

```
% gem_server
[2004-07-18 11:28:51] INFO  WEBrick 1.3.1
[2004-07-18 11:28:51] INFO  ruby 1.8.2 (2004-06-29) [i386-mswin32]
[2004-07-18 11:28:51] INFO  WEBrick::HTTPServer#start: port=8808
```

gem_server starts a Web server running on whatever computer you run it on. By default, it will start on port 8808 and will serve gems and their documentation from the default RubyGems installation directory. Both the port and the gem directory are overridable via command-line options, using the -p and -d options, respectively.

Once you've started the gem_server program, if you are running it on your local computer, you can access the documentation for your installed gems by pointing your Web browser to http://localhost:8808. There, you will see a list of the gems you have installed with their descriptions and links to their RDoc documentation.

Let's Code!

Now you've got BlueCloth installed and you know how to use it, you're ready to write some code. Having used RubyGems to download the library, we can now also use it to load the library components into our application. Prior to RubyGems, we'd say something like

```
require 'bluecloth'
```

With RubyGems, though, we can take advantage of its packaging and versioning support. To do this, we use require_gem in place of require.

```
require 'rubygems'
require_gem 'BlueCloth', ">= 0.0.4"
doc = BlueCloth::new <<MARKUP
 This is some sample [text][1].  Just learning to use [BlueCloth][1].
 Just a simple test.
 [1]: http://ruby-lang.org
MARKUP
puts doc.to_html
```

produces:

```
<p>This is some sample <a href="http://ruby-lang.org">text</a>.  Just
 learning to use <a href="http://ruby-lang.org">BlueCloth</a>.
 Just a simple test.</p>
```

The first two lines are the RubyGems-specific code. The first line loads the RubyGems core libraries that we'll need in order to work with installed gems.

```
require 'rubygems'
```

The second line is where most of the magic happens.

```
require_gem 'BlueCloth', '>= 0.0.4'
```

This line adds the BlueCloth gem to Ruby's $LOAD_PATH and uses `require` to load any libraries that the gem's creator specified to be autoloaded. Let's say that again a slightly different way.

Each gem is considered to be a bundle of resources. It may contain one library file or one hundred. In an old-fashioned, non-RubyGems library, all these files would be copied into some shared location in the Ruby library tree, a location that was in Ruby's predefined load path.

RubyGems doesn't work this way. Instead, it keeps each version of each gem in its own self-contained directory tree. The gems are not injected into the standard Ruby library directories. As a result, RubyGems needs to do some fancy footwork so that you can get to these files. It does this by adding the gem's directory tree to Ruby's load path. From inside a running program, the effect is the same: `require` just works. From the outside, though, RubyGems gives you far better control over what's loaded into your Ruby programs.

In the case of BlueCloth, the templating code is distributed as one file, `bluecloth.rb`; that's the file that `require_gem` will load. `require_gem` has an optional second argument, which specifies a version requirement. In this example, you've specified that BlueCloth version 0.0.4 or greater be installed to use this code. If you had required version 0.0.5 or greater, this program would fail, because the version you've just installed is too low to meet the requirement of the program.

```
require 'rubygems'
require_gem 'BlueCloth', '>= 0.0.5'
```

produces:

```
/usr/local/lib/ruby/site_ruby/rubygems.rb:30:
         in `require_gem': (LoadError)
RubyGem version error: BlueCloth(0.0.4 not >= 0.0.5)
from prog.rb:2
```

As we said earlier, the version requirement argument is optional, and this example is obviously contrived. But, it's easy to imagine how this feature can be useful as different projects begin to depend on multiple, potentially incompatible, versions of the same library.

Dependent on RubyGems?

Astute readers (that's all of you) will have noticed that the code we've created so far is dependent on the RubyGems package being installed. In the long term, that'll be a fairly safe bet (we're guessing that RubyGems will make its way into the Ruby core distribution). For now, though, RubyGems is not part of the standard Ruby distribution,

---

The Code Behind the Curtain

So just what does happen behind the scenes when you call the magic `require_gem` method?

First, the gems library modifies your `$LOAD_PATH`, including any directories you have added to the gemspec's `require_paths`. Second, it calls Ruby's `require` method on any files specified in the gemspec's `autorequires` attribute (described on page 224). It's this `$LOAD_PATH`-modifying behavior that enables RubyGems to manage multiple installed versions of the same library.

---

so users of your software may not have RubyGems installed on their computers. If we distribute code that has `require 'rubygems'` in it, that code will fail.

You can use at least two techniques to get around this issue. First, you can wrap the RubyGems-specific code in a block and use Ruby's exception handling to rescue the resultant `LoadError` should RubyGems not be found during the `require`.

```
begin
  require 'rubygems'
  require_gem 'BlueCloth', ">= 0.0.4"
rescue LoadError
  require 'bluecloth'
end
```

This code first tries to require in the RubyGems library. If this fails, the `rescue` stanza is invoked, and your program will try to load BlueCloth using a conventional `require`. This latter require will fail if BlueCloth isn't installed, which is the same behavior users see now if they're not using RubyGems.

As of RubyGems 0.8.0, requiring `rubygems.rb` will install an overloaded version of Ruby's `require` method. Having loaded the RubyGems framework, you could say

```
require 'bluecloth'
```

Although this looks like conventional code, behind the scenes RubyGems will load `bluecloth.rb` from the first match it finds in its list of currently installed gems.

The overloaded `require` method *almost* allows you to free your applications from any RubyGems-specific code. The one exception is that the RubyGems library must be loaded before any calls to require gem-installed libraries.

To avoid RubyGems dependencies, the Ruby interpreter can be called with the -r switch

```
ruby -rubygems myprogram.rb
```

This will cause the interpreter to load the RubyGems framework, thereby installing RubyGems' overloaded version of the `require` method. To globally cause RubyGems to load with each invocation of the Ruby interpreter on a given system, you can set the `RUBYOPT` environment variable

```
% export RUBYOPT=rubygems
```

You can then run the ruby interpreter without explicitly loading the RubyGems framework, and gem-installed libraries will be available to the applications that need them.

The biggest disadvantage of using the overloaded `require` method is that you lose the ability to manage multiple installed versions of the same library. If you need a specific version of a library, it's better to use the `LoadError` method described previously.

Creating Your Own Gems

By now, you've seen how easy RubyGems makes things for the users of an application or library and are probably ready to make a gem of your own. If you're creating code to be shared with the open-source community, RubyGems are an ideal way for end-users to discover, install, and uninstall your code. They also provide a powerful way to manage internal, company projects, or even personal projects, since they make upgrades and rollbacks so simple. Ultimately, the availability of more gems makes the Ruby community stronger. These gems have to come from somewhere; we're going to show you how they can start coming from you.

Let's say you've finally gotten your mother's online diary application, MomLog, finished, and you have decided to release it under an open-source license. After all, other programmers have mothers, too. Naturally, you want to release MomLog as a gem (moms love it when you give them gems).

Package Layout

The first task in creating a gem is organizing your code into a directory structure that makes sense. The same rules that you would use in creating a typical tar or zip archive apply in package organization. Some general conventions follow.

- Put all of your Ruby source files under a subdirectory called `lib/`. Later, we'll show you how to ensure that this directory will be added to Ruby's `$LOAD_PATH` when users load this gem.

- If it's appropriate for your project, include a file under `lib/yourproject.rb` that performs the necessary `require` commands to load the bulk of the project's functionality. Before RubyGems' autorequire feature, this made things easier for others to use a library. Even with RubyGems, it makes it easier for others to explore your code if you give them an obvious starting point.

- Always include a README file including a project summary, author contact information, and pointers for getting started. Use RDoc format for this file so you can add it to the documentation that will be generated during gem installation. Remember to include a copyright and license in the README file, as many commercial users won't use a package unless the license terms are clear.

- Tests should go in a directory called `test/`. Many developers use a library's unit tests as a usage guide. It's nice to put them somewhere predictable, making them easy for others to find.

- Any executable scripts should go in a subdirectory called `bin/`.

- Source code for Ruby extensions should go in `ext/`.

- If you've got a great deal of documentation to include with your gem, it's good to keep it in its own subdirectory called `docs/`. If your README file is in the top level of your package, be sure to refer readers to this location.

This directory layout is illustrated in Figure 17.1 on page 232.

The Gem Specification

Now that you've got your files laid out as you want them, it's time to get to the heart of gem creation: the gem specification, or *gemspec*. A gemspec is a collection of metadata in Ruby or YAML (see page 758) that provides key information about your gem. The gemspec is used as input to the gem-building process. You can use several different mechanisms to create a gem, but they're all conceptually the same. Here's your first, basic MomLog gem.

```
require 'rubygems'
SPEC = Gem::Specification.new do |s|
  s.name     = "MomLog"
  s.version  = "1.0.0"
  s.author   = "Jo Programmer"
  s.email    = "jo@joshost.com"
  s.homepage = "http://www.joshost.com/MomLog"
  s.platform = Gem::Platform::RUBY
  s.summary  = "An online Diary for families"
  candidates = Dir.glob("{bin,docs,lib,test}/**/*")
  s.files    = candidates.delete_if do |item|
                 item.include?("CVS") || item.include?("rdoc")
               end
  s.require_path    = "lib"
  s.autorequire     = "momlog"
  s.test_file       = "test/ts_momlog.rb"
  s.has_rdoc        = true
  s.extra_rdoc_files = ["README"]
  s.add_dependency("BlueCloth", ">= 0.0.4")
end
```

Let's quickly walk through this example. A gem's metadata is held in an object of class Gem::Specification. The gemspec can be expressed in either YAML or Ruby code. Here we'll show the Ruby version, as it's generally easier to construct and more flexible in use. The first five attributes in the specification give basic information such as the gem's name, the version, and the author's name, e-mail, and home page.

In this example, the next attribute is the platform on which this gem can run. In this case, the gem is a pure Ruby library with no operating system–specific requirements, so we've set the platform to RUBY. If this gem were written for Windows only, for example, the platform would be listed as WIN32. For now, this field is only informational, but in the future it will be used by the gem system for intelligent selection of precompiled native extension gems.

The gem's summary is the short description that will appear when you run a gem query (as in our previous BlueCloth example).

The files attribute is an array of pathnames to files that will be included when the gem is built. In this example, we've used Dir.glob to generate the list and filtered out CVS and RDoc files.

Runtime Magic

The next two attributes, require_path and autorequire, let you specify the directories that will be added to the $LOAD_PATH when require_gem loads the gem, as well as any files that will automatically be loaded using require. In this example, lib refers to a relative path under the MomLog gem directory, and the autorequire will cause lib/momlog.rb to be required when require_gem "MomLog" is called. RubyGems also provides require_paths, a plural version of require_path. This takes an array, allowing you to specify a number of directories to include in $LOAD_PATH.

Adding Tests and Documentation

The test_file attribute holds the relative pathname to a single Ruby file included in the gem that should be loaded as a Test::Unit test suite. (You can use the plural form, test_files, to reference an array of files containing tests.) For details on how to create a test suite, see Chapter 12 on page 151 on unit testing.

Finishing up this example, we have two attributes controlling the production of local documentation of the gem. The has_rdoc attribute specifies that you have added RDoc comments to your code. It's possible to run RDoc on totally uncommented code, providing a browsable view of its interfaces, but obviously this is a lot less valuable than running RDoc on well-commented code. has_rdoc is a way for you to tell the world, "Yes. It's worth generating the documentation for this gem."

RDoc has the convenience of being very readable in both source and rendered form, making it an excellent choice for an included README file with a package. The rdoc command normally runs only on source code files. The extra_rdoc_files attribute takes an array of paths to non-source files in your gem that you would like to be included in the generation of RDoc documentation.

Adding Dependencies

For your gem to work properly, users are going to need to have BlueCloth installed.

We saw earlier how to set a load-time version dependency for a library. Now we need to tell our gemspec about that dependency, so the installer will ensure that it is present while installing MomLog. We do that with the addition of a single method call to our Gem::Specification object.

```
s.add_dependency("BlueCloth", ">= 0.0.4")
```

The arguments to our add_dependency method are identical to those of require_gem, which we explained earlier.

After generating this gem, attempting to install it on a clean system would look something like this.

```
% gem install pkg/MomLog-1.0.0.gem
Attempting local installation of 'pkg/MomLog-1.0.0.gem'
/usr/local/lib/ruby/site_ruby/1.8/rubygems.rb:50:in `require_gem':
    (LoadError)
Could not find RubyGem BlueCloth (>= 0.0.4)
```

Because you are performing a local installation from a file, RubyGems won't attempt to resolve the dependency for you. Instead, it fails noisily, telling you that it needs Blue-Cloth to complete the installation. You could then install BlueCloth as we did before, and things would go smoothly the next time you attempted to install the MomLog gem.

If you had uploaded MomLog to the central RubyGems repository and then tried to install it on a clean system, you would be prompted to automatically install BlueCloth as part of the MomLog installation.

```
% gem install -r MomLog
Attempting remote installation of 'MomLog'
Install required dependency BlueCloth? [Yn]   y
Successfully installed MomLog, version 1.0.0
```

Now you've got both BlueCloth and MomLog installed, and your mother can start happily publishing her diary. Had you chosen not to install BlueCloth, the installation would have failed as it did during the local installation attempt.

As you add more features to MomLog, you may find yourself pulling in additional external gems to support those features. The add_dependency method can be called multiple times in a single gemspec, supporting as many dependencies as you need it to support.

Ruby Extension Gems

So far, all of the examples we've looked at have been pure Ruby code. However, many Ruby libraries arc created as native extensions (see Chapter 21 on page 275). You have two ways to package and distribute this kind of library as a gem. You can distribute the gem in source format and have the installer compile the code at installation time. Alternatively, you can precompile the extensions and distribute one gem for each separate platform you want to support.

For source gems, RubyGems provides an additional `Gem::Specification` attribute called `extensions`. This attribute is an array of paths to Ruby files that will generate Makefiles. The most typical way to create one of these programs is to use Ruby's `mkmf` library (see Chapter 21 on page 275 and the appendix about `mkmf` on page 779). These files are conventionally named `extconf.rb`, though any name will do.

Your mom has a computerized recipe database that is near and dear to her heart. She has been storing her recipes in it for years, and you would like to give her the ability to publish these recipes on the Web for her friends and family. You discover that the recipe program, MenuBuilder, has a fairly nice native API and decide to write a Ruby extension to wrap it. Since the extension may be useful to others who aren't necessarily using MomLog, you decide to package it as a separate gem and add it as an additional dependency for MomLog.

Here's the gemspec.

```
require 'rubygems'
spec = Gem::Specification.new do |s|
  s.name = "MenuBuilder"
  s.version = "1.0.0"
  s.author = "Jo Programmer"
  s.email = "jo@joshost.com"
  s.homepage = "http://www.joshost.com/projects/MenuBuilder"
  s.platform = Gem::Platform::RUBY
  s.summary = "A Ruby wrapper for the MenuBuilder recipe database."
  s.files = ["ext/main.c", "ext/extconf.rb"]
  s.require_path = "."
  s.autorequire = "MenuBuilder"
  s.extensions = ["ext/extconf.rb"]
end
if $0 == __FILE__
  Gem::manage_gems
  Gem::Builder.new(spec).build
end
```

Note that you have to include source files in the specification's `files` list so they'll be included in the gem package for distribution.

When a source gem is installed, RubyGems runs each of its `extensions` programs and then executes the resultant Makefile.

```
% gem install MenuBuilder-1.0.0.gem
Attempting local installation of 'MenuBuilder-1.0.0.gem'
ruby extconf.rb inst MenuBuilder-1.0.0.gem
creating Makefile
make
gcc -fPIC -g -O2  -I. -I/usr/local/lib/ruby/1.8/i686-linux \
    -I/usr/local/lib/ruby/1.8/i686-linux -I.   -c main.c
gcc -shared  -L"/usr/local/lib" -o MenuBuilder.so main.o  \
    -ldl -lcrypt -lm   -lc
make install
install -c -p -m 0755 MenuBuilder.so \
    /usr/local/lib/ruby/gems/1.8/gems/MenuBuilder-1.0.0/.
Successfully installed MenuBuilder, version 1.0.0
```

RubyGems does not have the capability to detect system library dependencies that source gems may have. Should your source gems depend on a system library that is not installed, the gem installation will fail, and any error output from the make command will be displayed.

Distributing source gems obviously requires that the consumer of the gem have a working set of development tools. At a minimum, they'll need some kind of make program and a compiler. Particularly for Windows users, these tools may not be present. You can get around this limitation by distributing precompiled gems.

Creation of precompiled gems is simple—add the compiled shared object files (DLLs on Windows) to the gemspec's `files` list, and make sure these files are in one of the gem's `require_path` attributes. As with pure Ruby gems, the `require_gem` command will modify Ruby's `$LOAD_PATH`, and the shared object will be accessible via `require`.

Since these gems will be platform specific, you can also use the `platform` attribute (remember this from the first gemspec example?) to specify the target platform for the gem. The `Gem::Specification` class defines constants for Windows, Intel Linux, Macintosh, and pure Ruby. For platforms not included in this list, you can use the value of the `RUBY_PLATFORM` variable. This attribute is purely informational for now, but it's a good habit to acquire. Future RubyGems releases will use the `platform` attribute to intelligently select precompiled gems for the platform on which the installer is running.

Building the Gem File

The MomLog gemspec we just created is runnable as a Ruby program. Invoking it will create a gem file, MomLog-0.5.0.gem.

```
% ruby momlog.gemspec
Attempting to build gem spec 'momlog.gemspec'
Successfully built RubyGem
Name: MomLog
Version: 0.5.0
File: MomLog-0.5.0.gem
```

Alternatively, you can use the gem build command to generate the gem file.

```
% gem build momlog.gemspec
Attempting to build gem spec 'momlog.gemspec'
Successfully built RubyGem
Name: MomLog
Version: 0.5.0
File: MomLog-0.5.0.gem
```

Now that you've got a gem file, you can distribute it like any other package. You can put it on an FTP server or a Web site for download or e-mail it to your friends. Once your friends have got this file on their local computers (downloading from your FTP server if necessary), they can install the gem (assuming they have RubyGems installed too) by calling

```
% gem install MomLog-0.5.0.gem
Attempting local installation of 'MomLog-0.5.0.gem'
Successfully installed MomLog, version 0.5.0
```

If you would like to release your gem to the Ruby community, the easiest way is to use RubyForge (http://rubyforge.org). RubyForge is an open-source project management Web site. It also hosts the central gem repository. Any gem files released using RubyForge's file release feature will be automatically picked up and added to the central gem repository several times each day. The advantage to potential users of your software is that it will be available via RubyGems' remote query and installation operations, making installation even easier.

Building with Rake

Last but certainly not least, we can use Rake to build gems (remember Rake, the pure-Ruby build tool we mentioned back on page 216). Rake uses a command file called a Rakefile to control the build. This defines (in Ruby syntax!) a set of *rules* and *tasks*. The intersection of make's rule-driven concepts and Ruby's power make for a build and release automator's dream environment. And, what release of a Ruby project would be complete without the generation of a gem?

For details on how to use Rake, see the project Web page at http://rake.rubyforge. org. Its documents are comprehensive and always up-to-date. Here, we'll focus on just enough Rake to build a gem. From the Rake documentation:

Tasks are the main unit of work in a Rakefile. Tasks have a name (usually given as a symbol or a string), a list of prerequisites (more symbols or strings), and a list of actions (given as a block).

Normally, you can use Rake's built-in task method to define your own named tasks in your Rakefile. For special cases, it makes sense to provide helper code to automate some of the repetitive work you would have to do otherwise. Gem creation is one of these special cases. Rake comes with a special *TaskLib*, called GemPackageTask, that helps integrate gem creation into the rest of your automated build and release process.

To use GemPackageTask in your Rakefile, create the gemspec exactly as we did previously, but this time place it into your Rakefile. We then feed this specification to GemPackageTask.

```
require 'rubygems'
Gem::manage_gems
require 'rake/gempackagetask'

spec = Gem::Specification.new do |s|
  s.name      = "MomLog"
  s.version   = "0.5.0"
  s.author    = "Jo Programmer"
  s.email     = "jo@joshost.com"
  s.homepage  = "http://www.joshost.com/MomLog"
  s.platform  = Gem::Platform::RUBY
  s.summary   = "An online Diary for families"
  s.files = FileList["{bin,tests,lib,docs}/**/*"].exclude("rdoc").to_a
  s.require_path     = "lib"
  s.autorequire      = "momlog"
  s.test_file        = "tests/ts_momlog.rb"
  s.has_rdoc         = true
  s.extra_rdoc_files = ["README"]
  s.add_dependency("BlueCloth", ">= 0.0.4")
  s.add_dependency("MenuBuilder", ">= 1.0.0")
end

Rake::GemPackageTask.new(spec) do |pkg|
    pkg.need_tar = true
end
```

Note that you'll have to require the rubygems package into your Rakefile. You'll also notice that we've used Rake's FileList class instead of Dir.glob to build the list of files. FileList is smarter than Dir.glob for this purpose in that it automatically ignores commonly unused files (such as the CVS directory that the CVS version control tool leaves lying around).

Internally, the GemPackageTask generates a Rake target with the identifier

    package_directory/gemname-gemversion.gem

In our case, this identifier will be pkg/MomLog-0.5.0.gem. You can invoke this task from the same directory where you've put the Rakefile.

```
% rake pkg/MomLog-0.5.0.gem
(in /home/chad/download/gembook/code/MomLog)
  Successfully built RubyGem
  Name: MomLog
  Version: 0.5.0
  File: MomLog-0.5.0.gem
```

Now that you've got a task, you can use it like any other Rake task, adding dependencies to it or adding it to the dependency list of another task, such as deployment or release packaging.

Maintaining Your Gem (and One Last Look at MomLog)

You've released MomLog, and it's attracting new, adoring users every week. You have taken great care to package it cleanly and are using Rake to build your gem.

Your gem being "in the wild" with your contact information attached to it, you know that it's only a matter of time before you start receiving feature requests (and fan mail!) from your users. But, your first request comes via a phone call from none other than dear old Mom. She has just gotten back from a vacation in Florida and asks you how she can include her vacation pictures in her diary. You don't think an explanation of command-line FTP would be time well spent, and being the ever-devoted son or daughter, you spend your evening coding a nice photo album module for MomLog.

Since you have added functionality to the application (as opposed to just fixing a bug), you decide to increase MomLog's version number from 1.0.0 to 1.1.0. You also add a set of tests for the new functionality and a document about how to set up the photo upload functionality.

Figure 17.1 on the next page shows the complete directory structure of your final MomLog 1.1.0 package. The final gem specification (extracted from the Rakefile) looks like this.

```
spec = Gem::Specification.new do |s|
  s.name     = "MomLog"
  s.version  = "1.1.0"
  s.author   = "Jo Programmer"
  s.email    = "jo@joshost.com"
  s.homepage = "http://www.joshost.com/MomLog"
  s.platform = Gem::Platform::RUBY
  s.summary  = "An online diary, recipe publisher, " +
               "and photo album for families."
  s.files = FileList["{bin,tests,lib,docs}/**/*"].exclude("rdoc").to_a
  s.require_path    = "lib"
  s.autorequire     = "momlog"
  s.test_file       = "tests/ts_momlog.rb"
  s.has_rdoc        = true
  s.extra_rdoc_files = ["README", "docs/DatabaseConfiguration.rdoc",
               "docs/Installing.rdoc", "docs/PhotoAlbumSetup.rdoc"]
  s.add_dependency("BlueCloth", ">= 0.0.4")
  s.add_dependency("MenuBuilder", ">= 1.0.0")
end
```

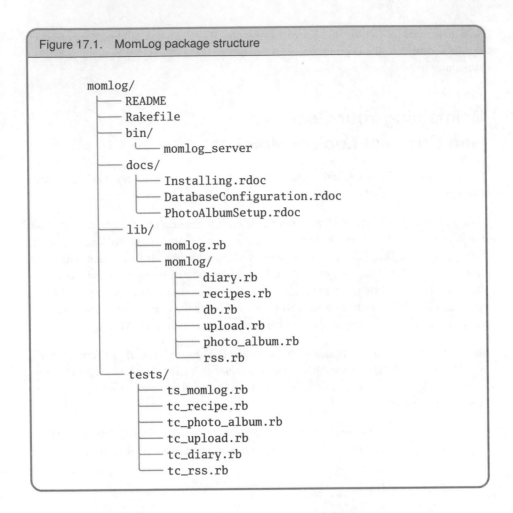

Figure 17.1.   MomLog package structure

```
momlog/
    ├── README
    ├── Rakefile
    ├── bin/
    │   └── momlog_server
    ├── docs/
    │   ├── Installing.rdoc
    │   ├── DatabaseConfiguration.rdoc
    │   └── PhotoAlbumSetup.rdoc
    ├── lib/
    │   ├── momlog.rb
    │   └── momlog/
    │       ├── diary.rb
    │       ├── recipes.rb
    │       ├── db.rb
    │       ├── upload.rb
    │       ├── photo_album.rb
    │       └── rss.rb
    └── tests/
        ├── ts_momlog.rb
        ├── tc_recipe.rb
        ├── tc_photo_album.rb
        ├── tc_upload.rb
        ├── tc_diary.rb
        └── tc_rss.rb
```

You run Rake over your Rakefile, generating the updated MomLog gem, and you're ready to release the new version. You log into your RubyForge account, and upload your gem to the "Files" section of your project. While you wait for RubyGems' automated process to release the gem into the central gem repository, you type a release announcement to post to your RubyForge project.

Within about an hour, you log in to your mother's Web server to install the new software for her. RubyGems makes things easy, but we have to take special care of Mom.

```
% gem query -rn MomLog

*** REMOTE GEMS ***

MomLog (1.1.0, 1.0.0)
    An online diary, recipe publisher, and photo album for families.
```

Great! The query indicates that there are two versions of MomLog available now. You type the `install` command without specifying a version argument, because you know that the default is to install the most recent version.

```
% gem install -r MomLog
Attempting remote installation of 'MomLog'
Successfully installed MomLog, version 1.1.0
```

You haven't changed any of the dependencies for MomLog, so your existing BlueCloth and MenuBuilder installations meet the requirements for MomLog 1.1.0.

Now that Mom's happy, it's time to go try some of her recently posted recipes.

Chapter 18

Ruby and the Web

Ruby is no stranger to the Internet. Not only can you write your own SMTP server, FTP daemon, or Web server in Ruby, but you can also use Ruby for more usual tasks such as CGI programming or as a replacement for PHP.

Many options are available for using Ruby to implement Web applications, and a single chapter can't do them all justice. Instead, we'll try to touch some of the highlights and point you toward libraries and resources that can help.

Let's start with some simple stuff: running Ruby programs as Common Gateway Interface (CGI) programs.

Writing CGI Scripts

You can use Ruby to write CGI scripts quite easily. To have a Ruby script generate HTML output, all you need is something like

```
#!/usr/bin/ruby
print "Content-type: text/html\r\n\r\n"
print "<html><body>Hello World! It's #{Time.now}</body></html>\r\n"
```

Put this script in a CGI directory, mark it as executable, and you'll be able to access it via your browser. (If your Web server doesn't automatically add headers, you'll need to add the response header yourself.)

```
#!/usr/bin/ruby
print "HTTP/1.0 200 OK\r\n"
print "Content-type: text/html\r\n\r\n"
print "<html><body>Hello World! It's #{Time.now}</body></html>\r\n"
```

However, that's hacking around at a pretty low level. You'd need to write your own request parsing, session management, cookie manipulation, output escaping, and so on. Fortunately, options are available to make this easier.

Using cgi.rb

Class CGI provides support for writing CGI scripts. With it, you can manipulate forms, cookies, and the environment; maintain stateful sessions; and so on. It's a fairly large class, but we'll take a quick look at its capabilities here.

Quoting

When dealing with URLs and HTML code, you must be careful to quote certain characters. For instance, a slash character (/) has special meaning in a URL, so it must be "escaped" if it's not part of the pathname. That is, any / in the query portion of the URL will be translated to the string %2F and must be translated back to a / for you to use it. Space and ampersand are also special characters. To handle this, CGI provides the routines CGI.escape and CGI.unescape.

```
require 'cgi'
puts CGI.escape("Nicholas Payton/Trumpet & Flugel Horn")
```

produces:

```
Nicholas+Payton%2FTrumpet+%26+Flugel+Horn
```

More frequently, you may want to escape HTML special characters.

```
require 'cgi'
puts CGI.escapeHTML("a < 100 && b > 200")
```

produces:

```
a &lt; 100 &amp;&amp; b &gt; 200
```

To get really fancy, you can decide to escape only certain HTML elements within a string.

```
require 'cgi'
puts CGI.escapeElement('<hr><a href="/mp3">Click Here</a><br>','A')
```

produces:

```
<hr>&lt;a href=&quot;/mp3&quot;&gt;Click Here&lt;/a&gt;<br>
```

Here only the A element is escaped; other elements are left alone. Each of these methods has an "un-" version to restore the original string.

```
require 'cgi'
puts CGI.unescapeHTML("a &lt; 100 &amp;&amp; b &gt; 200")
```

produces:

```
a < 100 && b > 200
```

Query Parameters

HTTP requests from the browser to your application may contain parameters, either passed as part of the URL or passed as data embedded in the body of the request.

Processing of these parameters is complicated by the fact that a value with a given name may be returned multiple times in the same request. For example, say we're writing a survey to find out why folks like Ruby. The HTML for our form looks like this.

```
<html>
  <head><title>Test Form</title></head>
  <body>
    I like Ruby because:

    <form target="cgi-bin/survey.rb">
      <input type="checkbox" name="reason" value="flexible" />
        It's flexible<br />
      <input type="checkbox" name="reason" value="transparent" />
        It's transparent<br />
      <input type="checkbox" name="reason" value="perlish" />
        It's like Perl<br />
      <input type="checkbox" name="reason" value="fun" />
        It's fun

      <p>
        Your name: <input type="text" name="name">
      </p>

      <input type="submit"/>

    </form>

  </body>
</html>
```

When someone fills in this form, they might check multiple reasons for liking Ruby (as shown in Figure 18.1 on the following page). In this case, the form data corresponding to the name `reason` will have three values, corresponding to the three checked boxes.

Class `CGI` gives you access to form data in a couple of ways. First, we can just treat the CGI object as a hash, indexing it with field names and getting back field values.

```
require 'cgi'
cgi = CGI.new
cgi['name']     →    "Dave Thomas"
cgi['reason']   →    "flexible"
```

However, this doesn't work well with the `reason` field: we see only one of the three values. We can ask to see them all by using the `CGI#params` method. The value returned by `params` acts like a hash containing the request parameters. You can both read and write this hash (the latter allows you to modify the data associated with a request). Note that each of the values in the hash is actually an array.

1.8

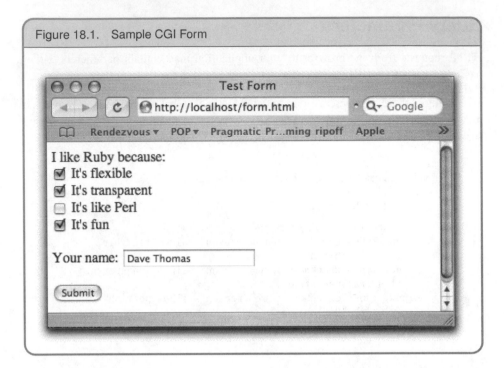

Figure 18.1. Sample CGI Form

```
require 'cgi'
cgi = CGI.new
cgi.params                →    {"name"=>["Dave Thomas"],
                               "reason"=>["flexible", "transparent",
                               "fun"]}
cgi.params['name']        →    ["Dave Thomas"]
cgi.params['reason']      →    ["flexible", "transparent", "fun"]
cgi.params['name'] = [ cgi['name'].upcase ]
cgi.params                →    {"name"=>["DAVE THOMAS"],
                               "reason"=>["flexible", "transparent",
                               "fun"]}
```

You can determine if a particular parameter is present in a request using CGI#has_key?.

```
require 'cgi'
cgi = CGI.new
cgi.has_key?('name')   →    true
cgi.has_key?('age')    →    false
```

Generating HTML

CGI contains a huge number of methods that can be used to create HTML—one method per element. To enable these methods, you must create a CGI object by calling CGI.new, passing in the required level of HTML. In these examples, we'll use html3.

To make element nesting easier, these methods take their content as code blocks. The code blocks should return a String, which will be used as the content for the element. For this example, we've added some gratuitous newlines to make the output fit on the page.

```
require 'cgi'
cgi = CGI.new("html3")  # add HTML generation methods
cgi.out {
  cgi.html {
    cgi.head { "\n"+cgi.title{"This Is a Test"} } +
    cgi.body { "\n"+
      cgi.form {"\n"+
        cgi.hr +
        cgi.h1 { "A Form: " } + "\n"+
        cgi.textarea("get_text") +"\n"+
        cgi.br +
        cgi.submit
      }
    }
  }
}
```

produces:

```
Content-Type: text/html
Content-Length: 302

<!DOCTYPE HTML PUBLIC "-//W3C//DTD HTML 3.2 Final//EN"><HTML><HEAD>
<TITLE>This Is a Test</TITLE></HEAD><BODY>
<FORM METHOD="post" ENCTYPE="application/x-www-form-urlencoded">
<HR><H1>A Form: </H1>
<TEXTAREA NAME="get_text" ROWS="10" COLS="70"></TEXTAREA>
<BR><INPUT TYPE="submit"></FORM></BODY></HTML>
```

This code will produce an HTML form titled "This Is a Test," followed by a horizontal rule, a level-one header, a text input area, and finally a submit button. When the submit comes back, you'll have a CGI parameter named get_text containing the text the user entered.

Although quite interesting, this method of generating HTML is fairly laborious and probably isn't used much in practice. Most people seem to write the HTML directly, use a templating system, or use an application framework, such as Iowa. Unfortunately, we don't have space here to discuss Iowa—have a look at the online documentation at http://enigo.com/projects/iowa, or look at Chapter 6 of *The Ruby Developer's Guide* [FJN02]—but we can look at templating.

Templating Systems

Templating systems let you separate the presentation and logic of your application. It seems that just about everyone who writes a Web application using Ruby at some point also writes a templating system: the RubyGarden wiki lists quite a few,[1] and even this list isn't complete. For now, let's just look at three: RDoc templates, Amrita, and erb/eruby.

RDoc Templates

The RDoc documentation system (described in Chapter 16 on page 199) includes a very simple templating system that it uses to generate all its XML and HTML output. Because RDoc is distributed as part of standard Ruby, the templating system is available wherever Ruby 1.8.2 or later is installed. However, the templating system does not use conventional HTML or XML markup (as it is intended to be used to generate output in many different formats), so files marked up with RDoc templates may not be easy to edit using conventional HTML editing tools.

```
require 'rdoc/template'
HTML = %{Hello, %name%.
<p>
The reasons you gave were:
<ul>
START:reasons
    <li>%reason_name% (%rank%)
END:reasons
</ul>
}
data = {
  'name' => 'Dave Thomas',
  'reasons' => [
    { 'reason_name' => 'flexible',    'rank' => '87' },
    { 'reason_name' => 'transparent', 'rank' => '76' },
    { 'reason_name' => 'fun',         'rank' => '94' },
  ]
}


t = TemplatePage.new(HTML)
t.write_html_on(STDOUT, data)
```

produces:

```
Hello, Dave Thomas.
<p>
The reasons you gave were:
<ul>
    <li>flexible (87)
    <li>transparent (76)
    <li>fun (94)
</ul>
```

---

1. http://www.rubygarden.org/ruby?HtmlTemplates

The constructor is passed a string containing the template to be used. The method `write_html_on` is then passed a hash containing names and values. If the template contains the sequence %xxxx%, the hash is consulted, and the value corresponding to the name xxx is substituted in. If the template contains START:yyy, the hash value corresponding to yyy is assumed to be an array of hashes. The template lines between START:yyy and END:yyy are repeated for each element in that array. The templates also support conditions: lines between IF:zzz and ENDIF:zzz are included in the output only if the hash has a key zzz.

Amrita

Amrita[2] is a library that generates HTML documents from a template that is itself valid HTML. This makes Amrita easy to use with existing HTML editors. It also means that Amrita templates display correctly as freestanding HTML pages.

Amrita uses the `id` tags in HTML elements to determine the values to be substituted. If the value corresponding to a given name is `nil` or `false`, the HTML element won't be included in the resulting output. If the value is an array, it iterates the corresponding HTML element.

```
require 'amrita/template'
include Amrita

HTML = %{<p id="greeting" />
<p>The reasons you gave were:</p>
<ul>
    <li id="reasons"><span id="reason_name"></span>,
                     <span id="rank"></span>
</ul>
}
data = {
  :greeting => 'Hello, Dave Thomas',
  :reasons  => [
    { :reason_name => 'flexible',    :rank => '87' },
    { :reason_name => 'transparent', :rank => '76' },
    { :reason_name => 'fun',         :rank => '94' },
  ]
}
t = TemplateText.new(HTML)
t.prettyprint = true
t.expand(STDOUT, data)
```

produces:

```
<p>Hello, Dave Thomas</p>
<p>The reasons you gave were:</p>
```

---

2.   http://www.brain-tokyo.jp/research/amrita/rdocs/

```
<ul>
  <li>flexible, 87 </li>
  <li>transparent, 76 </li>
  <li>fun, 94 </li>
</ul>
```

erb and eruby

So far we've looked at using Ruby to create HTML output, but we can turn the problem inside out; we can actually embed Ruby in an HTML document.

A number of packages allow you to embed Ruby statements in some other sort of a document, especially in an HTML page. Generically, this is known as "eRuby." Specifically, several different implementations of eRuby exist, including eruby and erb. eruby, written by Shugo Maeda, is available for download from the Ruby Application Archive. erb, its little cousin, is written in pure Ruby and is included with the standard distribution. We'll look at erb here.

Embedding Ruby in HTML is a very powerful concept—it basically gives us the equivalent of a tool such as ASP, JSP, or PHP, but with the full power of Ruby.

Using erb

erb is normally used as a filter. Text within the input file is passed through untouched, with the following exceptions

Expression	Description
<% ruby code %>	Execute the Ruby code between the delimiters.
<%= ruby expression %>	Evaluate the Ruby expression, and replace the sequence with the expression's value.
<%# ruby code %>	The Ruby code between the delimiters is ignored (useful for testing).
% line of ruby code	A line that starts with a percent is assumed to contain just Ruby code.

You invoke erb as

    erb *[options] [document]*

If the *document* is omitted, eruby will read from standard input. The command-line options for erb are shown in Table 18.1 on the facing page.

Let's look at some simple examples. We'll run the erb executable on the following input.

```
% a = 99
<%= a %> bottles of beer...
```

Table 18.1. Command-line options for erb

Option	Description
-d	Sets $DEBUG to true.
-K*kcode*	Specifies an alternate encoding system (see page 179).
-n	Display resulting Ruby script (with line numbers).
-r *library*	Loads the named *library*.
-P	Doesn't do erb processing on lines starting %.
-S *level*	Sets the *safe level*.
-T *mode*	Sets the *trim mode*.
-v	Enables verbose mode.
-x	Displays resulting Ruby script.

The line starting with the percent sign simply executes the given Ruby statement. The next line contains the sequence <%= a %>, which substitutes in the value of a.

```
erb f1.erb
```

produces:

```
99 bottles of beer...
```

erb works by rewriting its input as a Ruby script and then executing that script. You can see the Ruby that erb generates using the -n or -x option.

```
erb -x f1.erb
```

produces:

```
_erbout = '';  a = 99
_erbout.concat(( a ).to_s); _erbout.concat " bottles of beer...\n"
_erbout
```

Notice how erb builds a string, _erbout, containing both the static strings from the template and the results of executing expressions (in this case the value of a).

Of course, you can embed Ruby within a more complex document type, such as HTML. Figure 18.2 on page 245 shows a couple of loops in an HTML document.

Installing eruby in Apache

If you want to use erb-like page generation for a Web site that gets a reasonable amount of traffic, you'll probably want to switch across to using eruby, which has better performance. You can then configure the Apache Web server to automatically parse Ruby-embedded documents using eRuby, much in the same way that PHP does. You create Ruby-embedded files with an .rhtml suffix and configure the Web server to run the eruby executable on these documents to produce the desired HTML output.

To use eruby with the Apache Web server, you need to perform the following steps.

1. Copy the eruby binary to the cgi-bin directory.

2. Add the following two lines to httpd.conf.

```
AddType application/x-httpd-eruby .rhtml
Action application/x-httpd-eruby /cgi-bin/eruby
```

3. If desired, you can also add or replace the DirectoryIndex directive such that it includes index.rhtml. This lets you use Ruby to create directory listings for directories that do not contain an index.html. For instance, the following directive would cause the embedded Ruby script index.rhtml to be searched for and served if neither index.html nor index.shtml existed in a directory.

```
DirectoryIndex index.html index.shtml index.rhtml
```

Of course, you could also simply use a sitewide Ruby script as well.

```
DirectoryIndex index.html index.shtml /cgi-bin/index.rb
```

Cookies

Cookies are a way of letting Web applications store their state on the user's machine. Frowned upon by some, cookies are still a convenient (if unreliable) way of remembering session information.

The Ruby CGI class handles the loading and saving of cookies for you. You can access the cookies associated with the current request using the CGI#cookies method, and you can set cookies back into the browser by setting the cookies parameter of CGI#out to reference either a single cookie or an array of cookies.

```
#!/usr/bin/ruby
COOKIE_NAME = 'chocolate chip'
require 'cgi'
cgi = CGI.new
values = cgi.cookies[COOKIE_NAME]
if values.empty?
  msg = "It looks as if you haven't visited recently"
else
  msg = "You last visited #{values[0]}"
end
cookie = CGI::Cookie.new(COOKIE_NAME, Time.now.to_s)
cookie.expires = Time.now + 30*24*3600 # 30 days
cgi.out("cookie" => cookie ) { msg }
```

Figure 18.2. Erb processing a file with loops

```
<!DOCTYPE HTML PUBLIC "-//W3C//DTD HTML 4.01//EN">
<html>
<head>
<title>eruby example</title>
</head>
<body>
<h1>Enumeration</h1>
<ul>
%5.times do |i|
  <li>number <%=i%></li>
%end
</ul>
<h1>"Environment variables starting with "T"</h1>
<table>
%ENV.keys.grep(/^T/).each do |key|
  <tr><td><%=key%></td><td><%=ENV[key]%></td></tr>
%end
</table>
</body>
</html>
```

produces:

```
<!DOCTYPE HTML PUBLIC "-//W3C//DTD HTML 4.01//EN">
<html>
<head>
<title>eruby example</title>
</head>
<body>
<h1>Enumeration</h1>
<ul>
  <li>number 0</li>
  <li>number 1</li>
  <li>number 2</li>
  <li>number 3</li>
  <li>number 4</li>
</ul>
<h1>"Environment variables starting with "T"</h1>
<table>
  <tr><td>TERM_PROGRAM</td><td>iTerm.app</td></tr>
  <tr><td>TERM</td><td>xterm-color</td></tr>
</table>
</body>
</html>
```

Sessions

Cookies by themselves still need a bit of work to be useful. We really want *session:* information that persists between requests from a particular Web browser. Sessions are handled by class CGI::Session, which uses cookies but provides a higher-level abstraction.

As with cookies, sessions emulate a hashlike behavior, letting you associate values with keys. Unlike cookies, sessions store the majority of their data on the server, using the browser-resident cookie simply as a way of uniquely identifying the server-side data. Sessions also give you a choice of storage techniques for this data: it can be held in regular files, in a PStore (see the description on page 719), in memory, or even in your own customized store.

Sessions should be closed after use, as this ensures that their data is written out to the store. When you've permanently finished with a session, you should delete it.

```ruby
require 'cgi'
require 'cgi/session'

cgi = CGI.new("html3")
sess = CGI::Session.new(cgi,
                        "session_key" => "rubyweb",
                        "prefix" => "web-session."
                        )
if sess['lastaccess']
  msg = "You were last here #{sess['lastaccess']}."
else
  msg = "Looks like you haven't been here for a while"
end
count = (sess["accesscount"] || 0).to_i
count += 1
msg << "<p>Number of visits: #{count}"

sess["accesscount"] = count
sess["lastaccess"]  = Time.now.to_s
sess.close

cgi.out {
  cgi.html {
    cgi.body {
      msg
    }
  }
}
```

The code in the previous example used the default storage mechanism for sessions: persistent data was stored in files in your default temporary directory (see Dir.tmpdir). The filenames will all start web-session. and will end with a hashed version of the session number. See ri CGI::Session for more information.

Improving Performance

You can use Ruby to write CGI programs for the Web, but, as with most CGI programs, the default configuration has to start a new copy of Ruby with every cgi-bin page access. That's expensive in terms of machine utilization and can be painfully slow for Web surfers. The Apache Web server solves this problem by supporting loadable *modules*.

Typically, these modules are dynamically loaded and become part of the running Web server process—you have no need to spawn another interpreter over and over again to service requests; the Web server *is* the interpreter.

And so we come to mod_ruby (available from the archives), an Apache module that links a full Ruby interpreter into the Apache Web server itself. The README file included with mod_ruby provides details on how to compile and install it.

Once installed and configured, you can run Ruby scripts pretty much as you could without mod_ruby, except that now they will come up much faster. You can also take advantage of the extra facilities that mod_ruby provides (such as tight integration into Apache's request handling).

You have some things to watch, however. Because the interpreter remains in memory between requests, it may end up handling requests from multiple applications. It's possible for libraries in these applications to clash (particularly if different libraries contain classes with the same name). You also cannot assume that the same interpreter will handle the series of requests from one browser's session—Apache will allocate handler processes using its internal algorithms.

Some of these issues are resolved using the FastCGI protocol. This is an interesting hack, available to all CGI-style programs, not just Ruby. It uses a very small proxy program, typically running as an Apache module. When requests are received, this proxy then forwards them to a particular long-running process that acts like a normal CGI script. The results are fed back to the proxy, and then back to the browser. FastCGI has the same advantages as running mod_ruby, as the interpreter is always running in the background. It also gives you more control over how requests are allocated to interpreters. You'll find more information at http://www.fastcgi.com.

Choice of Web Servers

So far, we've been running Ruby scripts under the control of the Apache Web server. However, Ruby 1.8 and later comes bundled with WEBrick, a flexible, pure-Ruby HTTP server toolkit. Basically, it's an extensible plug in–based framework that lets you write servers to handle HTTP requests and responses. Here's a basic HTTP server that serves documents and directory indexes.

1.8

```
#!/usr/bin/ruby
require 'webrick'
include WEBrick

s = HTTPServer.new(
  :Port         => 2000,
  :DocumentRoot => File.join(Dir.pwd, "/html")
)

trap("INT") { s.shutdown }

s.start
```

The HTTPServer constructor creates a new Web server on port 2000. The code sets the document root to be the html/ subdirectory of the current directory. It then uses Kernel.trap to arrange to shut down tidily on interrupts before starting the server running. If you point your browser at http://localhost:2000, you should see a listing of your html subdirectory.

WEBrick can do far more that serve static content. You can use it just like a Java servlet container. The following code mounts a simple servlet at the location /hello. As requests arrive, the do_GET method is invoked. It uses the response object to display the user agent information and parameters from the request.

```
#!/usr/bin/ruby

require 'webrick'
include WEBrick

s = HTTPServer.new( :Port => 2000 )

class HelloServlet < HTTPServlet::AbstractServlet
  def do_GET(req, res)
    res['Content-Type'] = "text/html"
    res.body = %{
      <html><body>
        Hello. You're calling from a #{req['User-Agent']}
       <p>
        I see parameters: #{req.query.keys.join(', ')}
      </body></html>
    }
  end
end

s.mount("/hello", HelloServlet)

trap("INT"){ s.shutdown }

s.start
```

More information on WEBrick is available from http:///www.webrick.org. There you'll find links to a set of useful servlets, including one that lets you write SOAP servers in Ruby.

SOAP and Web Services

<u>1.8</u> Speaking of SOAP, Ruby now comes with an implementation of SOAP.[3] This lets you write both servers and clients using Web services. By their nature, these applications can operate both locally and remotely across a network. SOAP applications are also unaware of the implementation language of their network peers, so SOAP is a convenient way of interconnecting Ruby applications with those written in languages such as Java, Visual Basic, or C++.

SOAP is basically a marshaling mechanism which uses XML to send data between two nodes in a network. It is typically used to implement remote procedure calls, RPCs, between distributed processes. A SOAP server publishes one or more interfaces. These interfaces are defined in terms of data types and methods that use those types. SOAP clients then create local proxies that SOAP connects to interfaces on the server. A call to a method on the proxy is then passed to the corresponding interface on the server. Return values generated by the method on the server are passed back to the client via the proxy.

Let's start with a trivial SOAP service. We'll write an object that does interest calculations. Initially, it offers a single method, compound, that determines compound interest given a principal, an interest rate, the number of times interested is compounded per year, and the number of years. For management purposes, we'll also keep track of how many times this method was called and make that count available via an accessor. Note that this class is just regular Ruby code—it doesn't know that it's running in a SOAP environment.

```ruby
class InterestCalculator
  attr_reader :call_count
  def initialize
    @call_count = 0
  end
  def compound(principal, rate, freq, years)
    @call_count += 1
    principal*(1.0 + rate/freq)**(freq*years)
  end
end
```

Now we'll make an object of this class available via a SOAP server. This will enable client applications to call the object's methods over the network. We're using the stand-alone server here, which is convenient when testing, as we can run it from the command line. You can also run Ruby SOAP servers as CGI scripts or under mod_ruby.

---

3. SOAP once stood for Simple Object Access Protocol. When folks could no longer stand the irony, the acronym was dropped, and now SOAP is just a name.

```
require 'soap/rpc/standaloneServer'
require 'interestcalc'
NS = 'http://pragprog.com/InterestCalc'
class Server2 < SOAP::RPC::StandaloneServer
  def on_init
    calc = InterestCalculator.new
    add_method(calc, 'compound', 'principal', 'rate', 'freq', 'years')
    add_method(calc, 'call_count')
  end
end
svr = Server2.new('Calc', NS, '0.0.0.0', 12321)
trap('INT') { svr.shutdown }
svr.start
```

This code defines a class which implements a standalone SOAP server. When it is initialized, the class creates a `InterestCalculator` object (an instance of the class we just wrote). It then uses `add_method` to add the two methods implemented by this class, `compound` and `call_count`. Finally, the code creates and runs an instance of this server class. The parameters to the constructor are the name of the application, the default namespace, the address of the interface to use, and the port.

We then need to write some client code to access this server. The client creates a local proxy for the `InterestCalculator` service on the server, adds the methods it wants to use, and then calls them.

```
require 'soap/rpc/driver'
proxy = SOAP::RPC::Driver.new("http://localhost:12321",
                              "http://pragprog.com/InterestCalc")
proxy.add_method('compound', 'principal', 'rate', 'freq', 'years')
proxy.add_method('call_count')
puts "Call count: #{proxy.call_count}"
puts "5 years, compound annually: #{proxy.compound(100, 0.06, 1, 5)}"
puts "5 years, compound monthly:  #{proxy.compound(100, 0.06, 12, 5)}"
puts "Call count: #{proxy.call_count}"
```

To test this, we can run the server in one console window (the output here has been reformated slightly to fit the width of this page).

```
% ruby server.rb
I, [2004-07-26T10:55:51.629451 #12327]  INFO
        -- Calc: Start of Calc.
I, [2004-07-26T10:55:51.633755 #12327]  INFO
        -- Calc: WEBrick 1.3.1
I, [2004-07-26T10:55:51.635146 #12327]  INFO
        -- Calc: ruby 1.8.2 (2004-07-26) [powerpc-darwin]
I, [2004-07-26T10:55:51.639347 #12327]  INFO
        -- Calc: WEBrick::HTTPServer#start: pid=12327 port=12321
```

We then run the client in another window.

```
% ruby client.rb
Call count: 0
5 years, compound annually: 133.82255776
5 years, compound monthly:  134.885015254931
Call count: 2
```

Looking good! Flush with success, we call all our friends over and run it again.

```
% ruby client.rb
Call count: 2
5 years, compound annually: 133.82255776
5 years, compound monthly:  134.885015254931
Call count: 4
```

Notice how the call count now starts at two the second time we run the client. The server creates a single `InterestCalculator` object to service incoming requests, and this object is reused for each request.

SOAP and Google

Obviously the real benefit of SOAP is the way it lets you interoperate with other services on the Web. As an example, let's write some Ruby code to send queries to Google's Web API.

Before sending queries to Google, you need a developer key. Go to `http://www.google.com/apis` and follow the instructions in step 2, *Create a Google Account*. After you fill in your e-mail address and supply a password, Google will send you a developer key. In the following examples, we'll assume that you've stored this key in the file `.google_key` in your home directory.

Let's start at the most basic level. Looking at the documentation for the Google API method `doGoogleSearch`, we discover it has ten (!) parameters.

key	The developer key
q	The query string
start	The index of the first required result
maxResults	The maximum number of results to return per query
filter	If enabled, compresses results so that similar pages and pages from the same domain are only shown once
restrict	Restricts the search to a subset of the Google Web index
safeSearch	If enabled, removes possible adult content from the results
lr	Restricts the search to documents in a given set of languages
ie	Ignored (was input encoding)
oe	Ignored (was output encoding)

We can use the `add_method` call to construct a SOAP proxy for the `doGoogleSearch` method. The following example does just that, printing out the first entry returned if you search Google for the term *pragmatic*.

```
require 'soap/rpc/driver'
require 'cgi'
endpoint = 'http://api.google.com/search/beta2'
namespace = 'urn:GoogleSearch'
soap = SOAP::RPC::Driver.new(endpoint, namespace)
soap.add_method('doGoogleSearch', 'key', 'q', 'start',
                              'maxResults', 'filter', 'restrict',
                              'safeSearch', 'lr', 'ie', 'oe')
query = 'pragmatic'
key = File.read(File.join(ENV['HOME'], ".google_key")).chomp
result = soap.doGoogleSearch(key, query, 0, 1, false, nil,
                              false, nil, nil, nil)
printf "Estimated number of results is %d.\n",
       result.estimatedTotalResultsCount
printf "Your query took %6f seconds.\n", result.searchTime
first = result.resultElements[0]
puts first.title
puts first.URL
puts CGI.unescapeHTML(first.snippet)
```

Run this, and you'll see something such as the following (notice how the query term has been highlighted by Google).

```
Estimated number of results is 550000.
Your query took 0.123762 seconds.
The <b>Pragmatic</b> Programmers, LLC
http://www.pragmaticprogrammer.com/
Home of Andrew Hunt and David Thomas's best-selling book 'The
<b>Pragmatic</b> Programmer'<br> and The '<b>Pragmatic</b> Starter Kit
(tm)' series. <b>...</b> The <b>Pragmatic</b> Bookshelf TM. <b>...</b>
```

However, SOAP allows for the dynamic discovery of the interface of objects on the server. This is done using WSDL, the Web Services Description Language. A WSDL file is an XML document that describes the types, methods, and access mechanisms for a Web services interface. SOAP clients can read WSDL files to create the interfaces to a server automatically.

Google publishes the WSDL describing its interface at `http://api.google.com/ GoogleSearch.wsdl`. We can alter our search application to read this WSDL, which removes the need to add the doGoogleSearch method explicitly.

```
require 'soap/wsdlDriver'
require 'cgi'
WSDL_URL = "http://api.google.com/GoogleSearch.wsdl"
soap = SOAP::WSDLDriverFactory.new(WSDL_URL).createDriver
query = 'pragmatic'
key = File.read(File.join(ENV['HOME'], ".google_key")).chomp
result = soap.doGoogleSearch(key, query, 0, 1, false,
                              nil, false, nil, nil, nil)
```

```
printf "Estimated number of results is %d.\n",
       result.estimatedTotalResultsCount
printf "Your query took %6f seconds.\n", result.searchTime
first = result.resultElements[0]
puts first.title
puts first.URL
puts CGI.unescapeHTML(first.snippet)
```

Finally, we can take this a step further using Ian Macdonald's Google library (available in the RAA). It encapsulates the Web services API behind a nice interface (nice if for no other reason than it eliminates the need for all those extra parameters). The library also has methods to construct the date ranges and other restrictions on a Google query and provides interfaces to the Google cache and the spell-checking facility. The following code is our "pragmatic" search using Ian's library.

```
require 'google'
require 'cgi'

key = File.read(File.join(ENV['HOME'], ".google_key")).chomp

google = Google::Search.new(key)
result = google.search('pragmatic')

printf "Estimated number of results is %d.\n",
       result.estimatedTotalResultsCount

printf "Your query took %6f seconds.\n", result.searchTime
first = result.resultElements[0]
puts first.title
puts first.url
puts CGI.unescapeHTML(first.snippet)
```

More Information

Ruby Web programming is a big topic. To dig deeper, you may want to look at Chapter 9 in *The Ruby Way* [Ful01], where you'll find many examples of network and Web programming, and Chapter 6 of *The Ruby Developer's Guide* [FJN02], where you'll find some good examples of structuring CGI applications, along with some example Iowa code.

If SOAP strikes you being complex, you may want to look at using XML-RPC, which is described briefly on page 757.

A number of other Ruby Web development frameworks are available on the 'net. This is a dynamic area: new contenders appear constantly, and it is hard for a printed book to be definitive. However, two frameworks that are currently attracting mindshare in the Ruby community are

- Rails (http://www.rubyonrails.org), and
- CGIKit (http://www.spice-of-life.net/cgikit/index_en.html).

## Chapter 19

Ruby Tk

The Ruby Application Archive contains several extensions that provide Ruby with a graphical user interface (GUI), including extensions for Fox, GTK, and others.

The Tk extension is bundled in the main distribution and works on both Unix and Windows systems. To use it, you need to have Tk installed on your system. Tk is a large system, and entire books have been written about it, so we won't waste time or resources by delving too deeply into Tk itself but instead concentrate on how to access Tk features from Ruby. You'll need one of these reference books in order to use Tk with Ruby effectively. The binding we use is closest to the Perl binding, so you probably want to get a copy of *Learning Perl/Tk* [Wal99] or *Perl/Tk Pocket Reference* [Lid98].

Tk works along a composition model—that is, you start by creating a container (such as a TkFrame or TkRoot) and then create the widgets (another name for GUI components) that populate it, such as buttons or labels. When you are ready to start the GUI, you invoke Tk.mainloop. The Tk engine then takes control of the program, displaying widgets and calling your code in response to GUI events.

Simple Tk Application

A simple Tk application in Ruby may look something like this.

```
require 'tk'
root = TkRoot.new { title "Ex1" }
TkLabel.new(root) do
  text  'Hello, World!'
  pack('padx' => 15, 'pady' => 15, 'side' => 'left')
end
Tk.mainloop
```

Let's look at the code a little more closely. After loading the tk extension module, we create a root-level frame using TkRoot.new. We then make a TkLabel widget as a child of the root frame, setting several options for the label. Finally, we pack the root frame and enter the main GUI event loop.

It's a good habit to specify the root explicitly, but you could leave it out—along with the extra options—and boil this down to a three-liner.

```
require 'tk'
TkLabel.new { text 'Hello, World!'; pack }
Tk.mainloop
```

That's all there is to it! Armed with one of the Perl/Tk books we reference at the start of this chapter, you can now produce all the sophisticated GUIs you need. But then again, if you'd like to stick around for some more details, here they come.

Widgets

Creating widgets is easy. Take the name of the widget as given in the Tk documentation and add a Tk to the front of it. For instance, the widgets Label, Button, and Entry become the classes TkLabel, TkButton, and TkEntry. You create an instance of a widget using new, just as you would any other object. If you don't specify a parent for a given widget, it will default to the root-level frame. We usually want to specify the parent of a given widget, along with many other options—color, size, and so on. We also need to be able to get information back from our widgets while our program is running by setting up *callbacks* (routines invoked when certain events happen) and sharing data.

Setting Widget Options

If you look at a Tk reference manual (the one written for Perl/Tk, for example), you'll notice that options for widgets are usually listed with a hyphen—as a command-line option would be. In Perl/Tk, options are passed to a widget in a Hash. You can do that in Ruby as well, but you can also pass options using a code block; the name of the option is used as a method name within the block and arguments to the option appear as arguments to the method call. Widgets take a parent as the first argument, followed by an optional hash of options or the code block of options. Thus, the following two forms are equivalent.

```
TkLabel.new(parent_widget) do
  text    'Hello, World!'
  pack('padx'  => 5,
       'pady'  => 5,
       'side'  => 'left')
end
# or
TkLabel.new(parent_widget, 'text' => 'Hello, World!').pack(...)
```

One small caution when using the code block form: the scope of variables is not what you think it is. The block is actually evaluated in the context of the widget's object, not the caller's. This means that the caller's instance variables will not be available in the block, but local variables from the enclosing scope and globals will be (not that you use global variables, of course.) We'll show option passing using both methods in the examples that follow.

Distances (as in the padx and pady options in these examples) are assumed to be in pixels but may be specified in different units using one of the suffixes c (centimeter), i (inch), m (millimeter), or p (point). "12p", for example, is twelve points.

Getting Widget Data

We can get information back from widgets by using callbacks and by binding variables.

Callbacks are very easy to set up. The command option (shown in the TkButton call in the example that follows) takes a Proc object, which will be called when the callback fires. Here we pass the proc in as a block associated with the method call, but we could also have used Kernel.lambda to generate an explicit Proc object.

```
require 'tk'
TkButton.new do
  text "EXIT"
  command { exit }
  pack('side'=>'left', 'padx'=>10, 'pady'=>10)
end
Tk.mainloop
```

We can also bind a Ruby variable to a Tk widget's value using a TkVariable proxy. This arranges things so that whenever the widget's value changes, the Ruby variable will automatically be updated, and whenever the variable is changed, the widget will reflect the new value.

We show this in the following example. Notice how the TkCheckButton is set up; the documentation says that the variable option takes a *var reference* as an argument. For this, we create a Tk variable reference using TkVariable.new. Accessing mycheck.value will return the string "0" or "1" depending on whether the checkbox is checked. You can use the same mechanism for anything that supports a var reference, such as radio buttons and text fields.

```
require 'tk'
packing = { 'padx'=>5, 'pady'=>5, 'side' => 'left' }
checked = TkVariable.new
def checked.status
  value == "1" ? "Yes" : "No"
end
```

```
status = TkLabel.new do
  text checked.status
  pack(packing)
end

TkCheckButton.new  do
  variable checked
  pack(packing)
end

TkButton.new do
  text "Show status"
  command { status.text(checked.status) }
  pack(packing)
end

Tk.mainloop
```

Setting/Getting Options Dynamically

In addition to setting a widget's options when it's created, you can reconfigure a widget while it's running. Every widget supports the `configure` method, which takes a `Hash` or a code block in the same manner as new. We can modify the first example to change the label text in response to a button click.

```
require 'tk'
root = TkRoot.new { title "Ex3" }

top = TkFrame.new(root) { relief 'raised'; border 5 }

lbl = TkLabel.new(top) do
  justify 'center'
  text    'Hello, World!'
  pack('padx'=>5, 'pady'=>5, 'side' => 'top')
end

TkButton.new(top) do
  text "Ok"
  command { exit }
  pack('side'=>'left', 'padx'=>10, 'pady'=>10)
end

TkButton.new(top) do
  text "Cancel"
  command { lbl.configure('text'=>"Goodbye, Cruel World!") }
  pack('side'=>'right', 'padx'=>10, 'pady'=>10)
end
top.pack('fill'=>'both', 'side' =>'top')
Tk.mainloop
```

Now when the `Cancel` button is clicked, the text in the label will change immediately from "Hello, World!" to "Goodbye, Cruel World!"

You can also query widgets for particular option values using `cget`.

```
require 'tk'
b = TkButton.new do
  text    "OK"
  justify "left"
  border  5
end
b.cget('text')     →   "OK"
b.cget('justify')  →   "left"
b.cget('border')   →   5
```

Sample Application

Here's a slightly longer example, showing a genuine application—a pig latin generator. Type in the phrase such as **Ruby rules**, and the Pig It button will instantly translate it into pig latin.

```
require 'tk'
class PigBox
  def pig(word)
    leading_cap = word =~ /^[A-Z]/
    word.downcase!
    res = case word
      when /^[aeiouy]/
        word+"way"
      when /^([^aeiouy]+)(.*)/
        $2+$1+"ay"
      else
        word
    end
    leading_cap ? res.capitalize : res
  end
  def show_pig
    @text.value = @text.value.split.collect{|w| pig(w)}.join(" ")
  end
  def initialize
    ph = { 'padx' => 10, 'pady' => 10 }      # common options
    root = TkRoot.new { title "Pig" }
    top = TkFrame.new(root) { background "white" }
    TkLabel.new(top) {text 'Enter Text:' ; pack(ph) }
    @text = TkVariable.new
    TkEntry.new(top, 'textvariable' =>  @text).pack(ph)
    pig_b = TkButton.new(top) { text 'Pig It'; pack ph}
    pig_b.command { show_pig }
    exit_b = TkButton.new(top) {text 'Exit'; pack ph}
    exit_b.command { exit }
    top.pack('fill'=>'both', 'side' =>'top')
  end
end
PigBox.new
Tk.mainloop
```

Geometry Management

In the example code in this chapter, you'll see references to the widget method `pack`. That's a very important call, as it turns out—leave it off and you'll never see the widget. `pack` is a command that tells the geometry manager to place the widget according to constraints that we specify. Geometry managers recognize three commands.

Command	Placement Specification
pack	Flexible, constraint-based placement
place	Absolute position
grid	Tabular (row/column) position

As `pack` is the most commonly used command, we'll use it in our examples.

Binding Events

Our widgets are exposed to the real world; they get clicked, the mouse moves over them, the user tabs into them; all these things, and more, generate *events* that we can capture. You can create a *binding* from an event on a particular widget to a block of code, using the widget's `bind` method.

For instance, suppose we've created a button widget that displays an image. We'd like the image to change when the user's mouse is over the button.

```ruby
require 'tk'
image1 = TkPhotoImage.new { file "img1.gif" }
image2 = TkPhotoImage.new { file "img2.gif" }
b = TkButton.new(@root) do
  image    image1
  command  { exit }
  pack
end
b.bind("Enter") { b.configure('image'=>image2) }
b.bind("Leave") { b.configure('image'=>image1) }

Tk.mainloop
```

First, we create two GIF image objects from files on disk, using TkPhotoImage. Next we create a button (very cleverly named "b"), which displays the image image1. We then bind the Enter event so that it dynamically changes the image displayed by the button to image2 when the mouse is over the button, and the Leave event to revert back to image1 when the mouse leaves the button.

This example shows the simple events Enter and Leave. But the named event given as an argument to bind can be composed of several substrings, separated with dashes, in the order *modifier-modifier-type-detail*. Modifiers are listed in the Tk reference and include Button1, Control, Alt, Shift, and so on. *Type* is the name of the event (taken from the X11 naming conventions) and includes events such as ButtonPress, KeyPress, and Expose. *Detail* is either a number from 1 to 5 for buttons or a keysym for keyboard input. For instance, a binding that will trigger on mouse release of button 1 while the control key is pressed could be specified as

```
Control-Button1-ButtonRelease
```
or
```
Control-ButtonRelease-1
```

The event itself can contain certain fields such as the time of the event and the x and y positions. bind can pass these items to the callback, using *event field codes*. These are used like printf specifications. For instance, to get the x and y coordinates on a mouse move, you'd specify the call to bind with three parameters. The second parameter is the Proc for the callback, and the third parameter is the event field string.

```
canvas.bind("Motion", lambda {|x, y| do_motion (x, y)}, "%x %y")
```

Canvas

Tk provides a Canvas widget with which you can draw and produce PostScript output. Figure 19.1 on the following page shows a simple bit of code (adapted from the distribution) that will draw straight lines. Clicking and holding button 1 will start a line, which will be "rubber-banded" as you move the mouse around. When you release button 1, the line will be drawn in that position.

A few mouse clicks, and you've got an instant masterpiece.

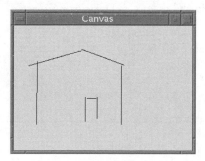

As they say, "We couldn't find the artist, so we had to hang the picture...."

Figure 19.1.   Drawing on a Tk Canvas

```ruby
require 'tk'

class Draw
  def do_press(x, y)
    @start_x = x
    @start_y = y
    @current_line = TkcLine.new(@canvas, x, y, x, y)
  end

  def do_motion(x, y)
    if @current_line
      @current_line.coords @start_x, @start_y, x, y
    end
  end

  def do_release(x, y)
    if @current_line
      @current_line.coords @start_x, @start_y, x, y
      @current_line.fill 'black'
      @current_line = nil
    end
  end

  def initialize(parent)
    @canvas = TkCanvas.new(parent)
    @canvas.pack
    @start_x = @start_y = 0
    @canvas.bind("1", lambda {|e| do_press(e.x, e.y)})
    @canvas.bind("B1-Motion",
                 lambda {|x, y| do_motion(x, y)}, "%x %y")
    @canvas.bind("ButtonRelease-1",
                 lambda {|x, y| do_release(x, y)},
                 "%x %y")
  end
end

root = TkRoot.new { title 'Canvas' }
Draw.new(root)
Tk.mainloop
```

Scrolling

Unless you plan on drawing very small pictures, the previous example may not be all that useful. TkCanvas, TkListbox, and TkText can be set up to use scrollbars, so you can work on a smaller subset of the "big picture."

Communication between a scrollbar and a widget is bidirectional. Moving the scrollbar means that the widget's view has to change; but when the widget's view is changed by some other means, the scrollbar has to change as well to reflect the new position.

Since we haven't done much with lists yet, our scrolling example will use a scrolling list of text. In the following code fragment, we'll start by creating a plain old TkListbox and an associated TkScrollbar. The scrollbar's callback (set with command) will call the list widget's yview method, which will change the value of the visible portion of the list in the y direction.

After that callback is set up, we make the inverse association: when the list feels the need to scroll, we'll set the appropriate range in the scrollbar using TkScrollbar#set. We'll use this same fragment in a fully functional program in the next section.

```
list_w = TkListbox.new(frame) do
  selectmode 'single'
  pack 'side' => 'left'
end
list_w.bind("ButtonRelease-1") do
  busy do
    filename = list_w.get(*list_w.curselection)
    tmp_img = TkPhotoImage.new { file filename }
    scale   = tmp_img.height / 100
    scale   = 1 if scale < 1
    image_w.copy(tmp_img, 'subsample' => [scale, scale])
    image_w.pack
  end
end
scroll_bar = TkScrollbar.new(frame) do
  command {|*args| list_w.yview *args }
  pack    'side' => 'left', 'fill' => 'y'
end
list_w.yscrollcommand  {|first,last| scroll_bar.set(first,last) }
```

Just One More Thing

We could go on about Tk for another few hundred pages, but that's another book. The following program is our final Tk example—a simple GIF image viewer. You can select a GIF filename from the scrolling list, and a thumb nail version of the image will be displayed. We'll point out just a *few* more things.

Have you ever used an application that creates a "busy cursor" and then forgets to reset it to normal? A neat trick in Ruby will prevent this from happening. Remember how `File.new` uses a block to ensure that the file is closed after it is used? We can do a similar thing with the method busy, as shown in the next example.

This program also demonstrates some simple `TkListbox` manipulations—adding elements to the list, setting up a callback on a mouse button release,[1] and retrieving the current selection.

So far, we've used `TkPhotoImage` to display images directly, but you can also zoom, subsample, and show portions of images as well. Here we use the subsample feature to scale down the image for viewing.

```ruby
require 'tk'
class GifViewer
  def initialize(filelist)
    setup_viewer(filelist)
  end
  def run
    Tk.mainloop
  end
  def setup_viewer(filelist)
    @root = TkRoot.new {title 'Scroll List'}
    frame = TkFrame.new(@root)

    image_w = TkPhotoImage.new
    TkLabel.new(frame) do
      image image_w
      pack 'side'=>'right'
    end

    list_w = TkListbox.new(frame) do
      selectmode 'single'
      pack 'side' => 'left'
    end
    list_w.bind("ButtonRelease-1") do
      busy do
        filename = list_w.get(*list_w.curselection)
        tmp_img = TkPhotoImage.new { file filename }
        scale   = tmp_img.height / 100
        scale   = 1 if scale < 1
        image_w.copy(tmp_img, 'subsample' => [scale, scale])
        image_w.pack
      end
    end
```

---

1.   You probably want the button release, not the press, as the widget gets selected on the button press.

```
      filelist.each do |name|
        list_w.insert('end', name) # Insert each file name into the list
      end

      scroll_bar = TkScrollbar.new(frame) do
        command {|*args| list_w.yview *args }
        pack     'side' => 'left', 'fill' => 'y'
      end

      list_w.yscrollcommand  {|first,last| scroll_bar.set(first,last) }
      frame.pack
    end

    # Run a block with a 'wait' cursor
    def busy
      @root.cursor "watch" # Set a watch cursor
      yield
    ensure
      @root.cursor "" # Back to original
  end

  end

  viewer = GifViewer.new(Dir["screenshots/gifs/*.gif"])
  viewer.run
```

Translating from Perl/Tk Documentation

That's it, you're on your own now. For the most part, you can easily translate the documentation given for Perl/Tk to Ruby. There are a few exceptions; some methods are not implemented, and some extra functionality is undocumented. Until a Ruby/Tk book comes out, your best bet is to ask on the newsgroup or read the source code.

But in general, it's pretty easy to see what's happening. Remember that options may be given as a hash, or in code block style, and the scope of the code block is within the TkWidget being used, not your class instance.

Object Creation

In the Perl/Tk mapping, parents are responsible for creating their child widgets. In Ruby, the parent is passed as the first parameter to the widget's constructor.

```
Perl/Tk:  $widget = $parent->Widget( [ option => value ] )
Ruby:     widget = TkWidget.new(parent, option-hash)
          widget = TkWidget.new(parent) { code block }
```

You may not need to save the returned value of the newly created widget, but it's there if you do. Don't forget to pack a widget (or use one of the other geometry calls), or it won't be displayed.

Options

```
Perl/Tk:  -background => color
Ruby:     'background' => color
          { background color }
```

Remember that the code block scope is different.

Variable References

```
Perl/Tk:  -textvariable => \$variable
          -textvariable => varRef
Ruby:     ref = TkVariable.new
          'textvariable' => ref
          { textvariable ref }
```

Use TkVariable to attach a Ruby variable to a widget's value. You can then use the value accessors in TkVariable (TkVariable#value and TkVariable#value=) to affect the contents of the widget directly.

## Chapter 20

Ruby and Microsoft Windows

Ruby runs in a number of different environments. Some of these are Unix-based, and others are based on the various flavors of Microsoft Windows. Ruby came from people who were Unix-centric, but over the years it has also developed a whole lot of useful features in the Windows world, too. In this chapter, we'll look at these features and share some secrets to using Ruby effectively under Windows.

Getting Ruby for Windows

Two flavors of Ruby are available for the Windows environment.

The first is a version of Ruby that runs natively—that is, it is just another Windows application. The easiest way to get this distribution is to use the One-Click Installer, which loads a ready-made binary distribution onto your box. Follow the links from `http://rubyinstaller.rubyforge.org/` to get the latest version.

If you're feeling more adventurous, or if you need to compile in libraries that aren't supplied with the binary distribution, then you can build Ruby from source. You'll need the Microsoft VC++ compiler and associated tools to do this. Download the source of Ruby from `http://www.ruby-lang.org`, or use CVS to check out the latest development version. Then read the file `win32\README.win32` for instructions.

A second alternative uses an emulation layer called Cygwin. This provides a Unix-like environment on top of Windows. The Cygwin version of Ruby is the closest to Ruby running on Unix platforms, but running it means you must also install Cygwin. If you want to take this route, you can download the Cygwin version of Ruby from `http://ftp.ruby-lang.org/pub/ruby/binaries/cygwin/`. You'll also need Cygwin itself. The download link has a pointer to the required dynamic link library (DLL), or you can go to `http://www.cygwin.com` and download the full package (but be careful: you need to make sure the version you get is compatible with the Ruby you downloaded).

Which version to choose? When the first edition of this book was produced, the Cygwin version of Ruby was the distribution of choice. That situation has changed: the native build has become more and more functional over time, to the point where this is now our preferred Windows build of Ruby.

Running Ruby Under Windows

You'll find two executables in the Ruby Windows distribution.

ruby.exe is meant to be used at a command prompt (a DOS shell), just as in the Unix version. For applications that read and write to the standard input and output, this is fine. But this also means that anytime you run ruby.exe, you'll get a DOS shell even if you don't want one—Windows will create a new command prompt window and display it while Ruby is running. This may not be appropriate behavior if, for example, you double-click a Ruby script that uses a graphical interface (such as Tk), or if you are running a Ruby script as a background task or from inside another program.

In these cases, you'll want to use rubyw.exe. It is the same as ruby.exe except that it does not provide standard in, standard out, or standard error and does not launch a DOS shell when run.

The installer (by default) sets file associations so that files with the extension .rb will automatically use rubyw.exe. By doing this, you can double-click Ruby scripts, and they will simply run without popping up a DOS shell.

Win32API

If you plan on doing Ruby programming that needs to access some Windows 32 API functions directly, or that needs to use the entry points in some other DLLs, we've got good news for you—the Win32API library.

As an example, here's some code that's part of a larger Windows application used by our book fulfillment system to download and print invoices and receipts. A Web application generates a PDF file, which the Ruby script running on Windows downloads into a local file. The script then uses the print shell command under Windows to print this file.

```
arg   = "ids=#{resp.intl_orders.join(",")}"
fname = "/temp/invoices.pdf"

site = Net::HTTP.new(HOST, PORT)
site.use_ssl = true
http_resp, = site.get2("/fulfill/receipt.cgi?" + arg,
                       'Authorization' => 'Basic ' +
                       ["name:passwd"].pack('m').strip )
```

```
File.open(fname, "wb") {|f| f.puts(http_resp.body) }
shell = Win32API.new("shell32","ShellExecute",
                     ['L','P','P','P','P','L'], 'L' )
shell.Call(0, "print", fname, 0,0, SW_SHOWNORMAL)
```

You create a `Win32API` object that represents a call to a particular DLL entry point by specifying the name of the function, the name of the DLL that contains the function, and the function signature (argument types and return type). In the previous example, the variable `shell` wraps the Windows function `ShellExecute` in the `shell32` DLL. It takes six parameters (a number, four string pointers, and a number) and returns a number. (These parameter types are described on page 755.) The resulting object can then be used to make the call to print the file that we downloaded.

Many of the arguments to DLL functions are binary structures of some form. `Win32API` handles this by using Ruby `String` objects to pass the binary data back and forth. You will need to pack and unpack these strings as necessary (see the example on page 755).

Windows Automation

If groveling around in the low-level Windows API doesn't interest you, Windows Automation may—you can use Ruby as a client for Windows Automation thanks to a Ruby extension called WIN32OLE, written by Masaki Suketa. Win32OLE is part of the standard Ruby distribution.

1.8

Windows Automation allows an automation controller (a client) to issue commands and queries against an automation server, such as Microsoft Excel, Word, PowerPoint, and so on.

You can execute a method of an automation server by calling a method of the same name from a `WIN32OLE` object. For instance, you can create a new `WIN32OLE` client that launches a fresh copy of Internet Explorer and commands it to visit its home page.

```
ie = WIN32OLE.new('InternetExplorer.Application')
ie.visible = true
ie.gohome
```

You could also make it navigate to a particular page.

```
ie = WIN32OLE.new('InternetExplorer.Application')
ie.visible = true
ie.navigate("http://www.pragmaticprogrammer.com")
```

Methods that aren't known to `WIN32OLE` (such as `visible`, `gohome`, or `navigate`) are passed on to the `WIN32OLE#invoke` method, which sends the proper commands to the server.

Getting and Setting Properties

You can set and get *properties* from the server using normal Ruby hash notation. For example, to set the `Rotation` property in an Excel chart, you could write

```
excel = WIN32OLE.new("excel.application")
excelchart = excel.Charts.Add()
...
excelchart['Rotation'] = 45
puts excelchart['Rotation']
```

An OLE object's parameters are automatically set up as attributes of the `WIN32OLE` object. This means you can set a parameter by assigning to an object attribute.

```
excelchart.rotation = 45
r = excelchart.rotation
```

The following example is a modified version of the sample file `excel2.rb` (found in the `ext/win32/samples` directory). It starts Excel, creates a chart, and then rotates it on the screen. Watch out, Pixar!

```
require 'win32ole'
#    -4100 is the value for the Excel constant xl3DColumn.
ChartTypeVal = -4100;

excel = WIN32OLE.new("excel.application")
# Create and rotate the chart
excel['Visible'] = TRUE

excel.Workbooks.Add()
excel.Range("a1")['Value'] = 3
excel.Range("a2")['Value'] = 2
excel.Range("a3")['Value'] = 1

excel.Range("a1:a3").Select()

excelchart = excel.Charts.Add()
excelchart['Type'] = ChartTypeVal

30.step(180, 5) do |rot|
  excelchart.rotation = rot
  sleep(0.1)
end

excel.ActiveWorkbook.Close(0)
excel.Quit()
```

Named Arguments

Other automation client languages such as Visual Basic have the concept of *named arguments*. Suppose you had a Visual Basic routine with the signature

```
Song(artist, title, length):    rem Visual Basic
```

Instead of calling it with all three arguments in the order specified, you could use named arguments.

```
Song title := 'Get It On':      rem Visual Basic
```

This is equivalent to the call Song(nil, 'Get It On', nil).

In Ruby, you can use this feature by passing a hash with the named arguments.

```
Song.new('title' => 'Get It On')
```

for each

Where Visual Basic has a "for each" statement to iterate over a collection of items in a server, a WIN32OLE object has an each method (which takes a block) to accomplish the same thing.

```
require 'win32ole'
excel = WIN32OLE.new("excel.application")
excel.Workbooks.Add
excel.Range("a1").Value = 10
excel.Range("a2").Value = 20
excel.Range("a3").Value = "=a1+a2"
excel.Range("a1:a3").each do |cell|
  p cell.Value
end
```

Events

Your automation client written in Ruby can register itself to receive events from other programs. This is done using the WIN32OLE_EVENT class. This example (based on code from the Win32OLE 0.1.1 distribution) shows the use of an event sink that logs the URLs that a user browses to when using Internet Explorer.

```
require 'win32ole'
$urls = []
def navigate(url)
  $urls << url
end
def stop_msg_loop
  puts "IE has exited..."
  throw :done
end
def default_handler(event, *args)
  case event
  when "BeforeNavigate"
    puts "Now Navigating to #{args[0]}..."
  end
end
```

```ruby
ie = WIN32OLE.new('InternetExplorer.Application')
ie.visible = TRUE
ie.gohome
ev = WIN32OLE_EVENT.new(ie, 'DWebBrowserEvents')

ev.on_event {|*args| default_handler(*args)}
ev.on_event("NavigateComplete") {|url| navigate(url)}
ev.on_event("Quit") {|*args| stop_msg_loop}

catch(:done) do
  loop do
    WIN32OLE_EVENT.message_loop
  end
end

puts "You Navigated to the following URLs: "
$urls.each_with_index do |url, i|
  puts "(#{i+1}) #{url}"
end
```

Optimizing

As with most (if not all) high-level languages, it can be all too easy to churn out code that is unbearably slow, but that can be easily fixed with a little thought.

With WIN32OLE, you need to be careful with unnecessary dynamic lookups. Where possible, it is better to assign a WIN32OLE object to a variable and then reference elements from it, rather than creating a long chain of "." expressions.

For example, instead of writing

```ruby
workbook.Worksheets(1).Range("A1").value = 1
workbook.Worksheets(1).Range("A2").value = 2
workbook.Worksheets(1).Range("A3").value = 4
workbook.Worksheets(1).Range("A4").value = 8
```

we can eliminate the common subexpressions by saving the first part of the expression to a temporary variable and then make calls from that variable.

```ruby
worksheet = workbook.Worksheets(1)

worksheet.Range("A1").value = 1
worksheet.Range("A2").value = 2
worksheet.Range("A3").value = 4
worksheet.Range("A4").value = 8
```

You can also create Ruby stubs for a particular Windows type library. These stubs wrap the OLE object in a Ruby class with one method per entry point. Internally, the stub uses the entry point's number, not name, which speeds access.

Generate the wrapper class using the olegen.rb script in the ext\win32ole\samples directory, giving it the name of the type library to reflect on.

```
C:\> ruby olegen.rb 'NetMeeting 1.1 Type Library' >netmeeting.rb
```

The external methods and events of the type library are written as Ruby methods to the given file. You can then include it in your programs and call the methods directly. Let's try some timings.

```
require 'netmeeting'
require 'benchmark'
include Benchmark

bmbm(10) do |test|

  test.report("Dynamic") do
    nm = WIN32OLE.new('NetMeeting.App.1')
    10000.times { nm.Version }
  end

  test.report("Via proxy") do
    nm = NetMeeting_App_1.new
    10000.times { nm.Version }
  end
end
```

produces:

```
Rehearsal  -----------------------------------
Dynamic    0.600000   0.200000   0.800000 (  1.623000)
Via proxy  0.361000   0.140000   0.501000 (  0.961000)
----------------------------------- total: 1.301000sec

               user     system     total       real
Dynamic    0.471000   0.110000   0.581000 (  1.522000)
Via proxy  0.470000   0.130000   0.600000 (  0.952000)
```

The proxy version is more than 40 percent faster than the code that does the dynamic lookup.

More Help

If you need to interface Ruby to Windows NT, 2000, or XP, you may want to have a look at Daniel Berger's Win32Utils project (http://rubyforge.org/projects/win32utils/). There you'll find modules for interfacing to the Windows' clipboard, event log, scheduler, and so on.

Also, the DL library (described briefly on page 669) allows Ruby programs to invoke methods in dynamically loaded shared objects. On Windows, this means that your Ruby code can load and invoke entry points in a Windows DLL. For example, the following code, taken from the DL source code in the standard Ruby distribution, pops up a message box on a Windows machine, and determines which button the user clicked.

```
require 'dl'
User32 = DL.dlopen("user32")
MB_OKCANCEL = 1
```

```
message_box = User32['MessageBoxA', 'ILSSI']
r, rs = message_box.call(0, 'OK?', 'Please Confirm', MB_OKCANCEL)
case r
when 1
  print("OK!\n")
when 2
  print("Cancel!\n")
end
```

This code opens the User32 DLL. It then creates a Ruby object, message_box, that wraps the MessageBoxA entry point. The second paramater, "ILSSI", declares that the method returns an Integer, and takes a Long, two Strings, and an Integer as parameters.

The wrapper object is then used to call the message box entry point in the DLL. The return values are the result (in this case, the identifier of the button pressed by the user) and an array of the parameters passed in (which we ignore).

## Chapter 21

Extending Ruby

It is easy to extend Ruby with new features by writing code in Ruby. But every now and then you need to interface to things at a lower level. Once you start adding in low-level code written in C, the possibilities are endless. Having said this, the stuff in this chapter is pretty advanced and should probably be skipped the first time through the book.

Extending Ruby with C is pretty easy. For instance, suppose we are building a custom Internet-ready jukebox for the Sunset Diner and Grill. It will play MP3 audio files from a hard disk or audio CDs from a CD jukebox. We want to be able to control the jukebox hardware from a Ruby program. The hardware vendor gave us a C header file and a binary library to use; our job is to construct a Ruby object that makes the appropriate C function calls.

Much of the information in this chapter is taken from the README.EXT file that is included in the distribution. If you are planning on writing a Ruby extension, you may want to refer to that file for more details as well as the latest changes.

Your First Extension

Just to introduce extension writing, let's write one. This extension is purely a test of the process—it does nothing that you couldn't do in pure Ruby. We'll also present some stuff without too much explanation—all the messy details will be given later.

The extension we write will have the same functionality as the following Ruby class.

```
class MyTest
  def initialize
    @arr = Array.new
  end
  def add(obj)
    @arr.push(obj)
  end
end
```

That is, we'll be writing an extension in C that is plug-compatible with that Ruby class. The equivalent code in C should look somewhat familiar.

```c
#include "ruby.h"
static int id_push;
static VALUE t_init(VALUE self)
{
  VALUE arr;

  arr = rb_ary_new();
  rb_iv_set(self, "@arr", arr);
  return self;
}
static VALUE t_add(VALUE self, VALUE obj)
{
  VALUE arr;

  arr = rb_iv_get(self, "@arr");
  rb_funcall(arr, id_push, 1, obj);
  return arr;
}
VALUE cTest;

void Init_my_test() {
  cTest = rb_define_class("MyTest", rb_cObject);
  rb_define_method(cTest, "initialize", t_init, 0);
  rb_define_method(cTest, "add", t_add, 1);
  id_push = rb_intern("push");
}
```

Let's go through this example in detail, as it illustrates many of the important concepts in this chapter. First, we need to include the header file ruby.h to obtain the necessary Ruby definitions.

Now look at the last function, Init_my_test. Every extension defines a C global function named Init_*name*. This function will be called when the interpreter first loads the extension *name* (or on startup for statically linked extensions). It is used to initialize the extension and to insinuate it into the Ruby environment. (Exactly how Ruby knows that an extension is called *name* we'll cover later.) In this case, we define a new class named MyTest, which is a subclass of Object (represented by the external symbol rb_cObject; see ruby.h for others).

Next we set up add and initialize as two instance methods for class MyTest. The calls to rb_define_method establish a binding between the Ruby method name and the C function that will implement it. If Ruby code calls the add method on one of our objects, the interpreter will in turn call the C function t_add with one argument.

Similarly, when new is called for this class, Ruby will construct a basic object and then call initialize, which we have defined here to call the C function t_init with no (Ruby) arguments.

Now go back and look at the definition of `t_init`. Even though we said it took no arguments, it has a parameter here! In addition to any Ruby arguments, every method is passed an initial VALUE argument that contains the receiver for this method (the equivalent of `self` in Ruby code).

The first thing we'll do in `t_init` is create a Ruby array and set the instance variable `@arr` to point to it. Just as you would expect if you were writing Ruby source, referencing an instance variable that doesn't exist creates it. We then return a pointer to ourselves.

WARNING: Every C function that is callable from Ruby *must* return a VALUE, even if it's just `Qnil`. Otherwise, a core dump (or GPF) will be the likely result.

Finally, the function `t_add` gets the instance variable `@arr` from the current object and calls `Array#push` to push the passed value onto that array. When accessing instance variables in this way, the @ prefix is mandatory—otherwise the variable is created but cannot be referenced from Ruby.

Despite the extra, clunky syntax that C imposes, you're still writing in Ruby—you can manipulate objects using all the method calls you've come to know and love, with the added advantage of being able to craft tight, fast code when needed.

Building Our Extension

We'll have a lot more to say about building extensions later. For now, though, all we have to do is follow these steps.

1. Create a file called `extconf.rb` in the same directory as our `my_test.c` C source file. The file `extconf.rb` should contain the following two lines.

   ```
   require 'mkmf'
   create_makefile("my_test")
   ```

2. Run `extconf.rb`. This will generate a Makefile.

   ```
   % ruby extconf.rb
   creating Makefile
   ```

3. Use make to build the extension. This is what happens on an OS X system.

   ```
   % make
   gcc -fno-common -g -O2 -pipe -fno-common  -I.
       -I/usr/lib/ruby/1.9/powerpc-darwin7.4.0
       -I/usr/lib/ruby/1.9/powerpc-darwin7.4.0 -I.   -c my_test.c
   cc -dynamic -bundle -undefined suppress -flat_namespace
       -L'/usr/lib' -o my_test.bundle my_test.o  -ldl -lobjc
   ```

The result of all this is the extension, all nicely bundled up in a shared object (a `.so`, `.dll`, or [on OS X] a `.bundle`).

Running Our Extension

We can use our extension from Ruby simply by `require`-ing it dynamically at runtime (on most platforms). We can wrap this up in a test to verify that things are working as we expect.

```
require 'my_test'
require 'test/unit'

class TestTest < Test::Unit::TestCase

  def test_test
    t = MyTest.new
    assert_equal(Object, MyTest.superclass)
    assert_equal(MyTest, t.class)

    t.add(1)
    t.add(2)

    assert_equal([1,2], t.instance_eval("@arr"))
  end
end
```

produces:

```
Finished in 0.012271 seconds.
1 tests, 3 assertions, 0 failures, 0 errors
```

Once we're happy that our extension works, we can then install it globally by running `make install`.

Ruby Objects in C

When we wrote our first extension, we cheated, because it didn't really do anything with the Ruby objects—it didn't do calculations based on Ruby numbers, for example. Before we can do this, we need to find out how to represent and access Ruby data types from within C.

Everything in Ruby is an object, and all variables are references to objects. When we're looking at Ruby objects from within C code, the situation is pretty much the same. Most Ruby objects are represented as C pointers to an area in memory that contains the object's data and other implementation details. In C code, all these references are via variables of type VALUE, so when you pass Ruby objects around, you'll do it by passing VALUEs.

This has one exception. For performance reasons, Ruby implements Fixnums, Symbols, true, false, and nil as so-called *immediate values*. These are still stored in variables of type VALUE, but they aren't pointers. Instead, their value is stored directly in the variable.

So sometimes VALUEs are pointers, and sometimes they're immediate values. How does the interpreter pull off this magic? It relies on the fact that all pointers point to areas of memory aligned on 4- or 8-byte boundaries. This means that it can guarantee that the low 2 bits in a pointer will always be zero. When it wants to store an immediate value, it arranges to have at least one of these bits set, allowing the rest of the interpreter code to distinguish immediate values from pointers. Although this sounds tricky, it's actually easy to use in practice, largely because the interpreter comes with a number of macros and methods that simplify working with the type system.

This is how Ruby implements object-oriented code in C: A Ruby object is an allocated structure in memory that contains a table of instance variables and information about the class. The class itself is another object (an allocated structure in memory) that contains a table of the methods defined for that class. Ruby is built upon this foundation.

Working With Immediate Objects

As we said above, immediate values are not pointers: Fixnum, Symbol, true, false, and nil are stored directly in VALUE.

Fixnum values are stored as 31-bit numbers[1] that are formed by shifting the original number left 1 bit and then setting the LSB, or least significant bit (bit 0), to 1. When VALUE is used as a pointer to a specific Ruby structure, it is guaranteed always to have an LSB of zero; the other immediate values also have LSBs of zero. Thus, a simple bit test can tell you whether you have a Fixnum. This test is wrapped in a macro, FIXNUM_P. Similar tests let you check for other immediate values.

```
FIXNUM_P(value)  → nonzero if value is a Fixnum
SYMBOL_P(value)  → nonzero if value is a Symbol
NIL_P(value)     → nonzero if value is nil
RTEST(value)     → nonzero if value is neither nil nor false
```

Several useful conversion macros for numbers as well as other standard data types are shown in Table 21.1 on the next page.

The other immediate values (true, false, and nil) are represented in C as the constants Qtrue, Qfalse, and Qnil, respectively. You can test VALUE variables against these constants directly or use the conversion macros (which perform the proper casting).

Working with Strings

In C, we're used to working with null-terminated strings. Ruby strings, however, are more general and may well include embedded nulls. The safest way to work with Ruby

---

1.   Or 63-bit on wider CPU architectures.

Table 21.1. C/Ruby data type conversion functions and macros

C Data Types to Ruby Objects:

	INT2NUM(*int*)	→ *Fixnum* or *Bignum*
	INT2FIX(*int*)	→ *Fixnum* (faster)
	LONG2NUM(*long*	→ *Fixnum* or *Bignum*
	LONG2FIX(*int*)	→ *Fixnum* (faster)
	LL2NUM(*long long*)	→ *Fixnum* or *Bignum* (if native system supports *long long* type)
	ULL2NUM(*long long*)	→ *Fixnum* or *Bignum* (if native system supports *long long* type)
	CHR2FIX(*char*)	→ *Fixnum*
	rb_str_new2(*char* *)	→ *String*
	rb_float_new(*double*)	→ *Float*

Ruby Objects to C Data Types:

int	NUM2INT(*Numeric*)	(Includes type check)
int	FIX2INT(*Fixnum*)	(Faster)
unsigned int	NUM2UINT(*Numeric*)	(Includes type check)
unsigned int	FIX2UINT(*Fixnum*)	(Includes type check)
long	NUM2LONG(*Numeric*)	(Includes type check)
long	FIX2LONG(*Fixnum*)	(Faster)
unsigned long	NUM2ULONG(*Numeric*)	(Includes type check)
char	NUM2CHR(*Numeric* or *String*)	(Includes type check)
double	NUM2DBL(*Numeric*)	
	see text for strings...	

strings, therefore, is to do what the interpreter does and use both a pointer and a length. In fact, Ruby `String` objects are actually references to an `RString` structure, and the `RString` structure contains both a length and a pointer field. You can access the structure via the RSTRING macro.

```
VALUE str;
RSTRING(str)->len → length of the Ruby string
RSTRING(str)->ptr → pointer to string storage
```

However, life is slightly more complicated than that. Rather than using the VALUE object directly when you need a string value, you probably want to call the method `StringValue`, passing it the original value. It'll return an object that you can use RSTRING on or throw an exception if it can't derive a string from the original. This is all part of Ruby 1.8's duck typing initiative, described in more detail on pages 294 and 365. The `StringValue` method checks to see if its operand is a `String`. If not, it tries to invoke `to_str` on the object, throwing a `TypeError` exception if it can't.

So, if you want to write some code that iterates over all the characters in a `String` object, you may write:

```
static VALUE iterate_over(VALUE original_str) {
  int i;
  char *p;
  VALUE str = StringValue(original_str);
  p = RSTRING(str)->ptr;    // may be null
  for (i = 0; i < RSTRING(str)->len; i++, p++) {
    // process *p
  }
  return str;
}
```

If you want to bypass the length, and just access the underlying string pointer, you can use the convenience method `StringValuePtr`, which both resolves the string reference and then returns the C pointer to the contents.

If you plan to use a string to access or control some external resource, you probably want to hook into Ruby's tainting mechanism. In this case you'll use the method `SafeStringValue`, which works like `StringValue` but throws an exception if its argument is tainted and the safe level is greater than zero.

Working with Other Objects

When VALUEs are not immediate, they are pointers to one of the defined Ruby object structures—you can't have a VALUE that points to an arbitrary area of memory. The structures for the basic built-in classes are defined in `ruby.h` and are named R*Classname*: RArray, RBignum, RClass, RData, RFile, RFloat, RHash, RObject, RRegexp, RString, and RStruct.

You can check to see what type of structure is used for a particular VALUE in a number of ways. The macro TYPE(*obj*) will return a constant representing the C type of the given object: T_OBJECT, T_STRING, and so on. Constants for the built-in classes are defined in `ruby.h`. Note that the *type* we are referring to here is an implementation detail—it is not the same as the class of an object.

If you want to ensure that a VALUE pointer points to a particular structure, you can use the macro Check_Type, which will raise a TypeError exception if *value* is not of the expected *type* (which is one of the constants T_STRING, T_FLOAT, and so on).

```
Check_Type(VALUE value, int type)
```

Again, note that we are talking about "type" as the C structure that represents a particular built-in type. The class of an object is a different beast entirely. The class objects for the built-in classes are stored in C global variables named rb_c*Classname* (for instance, rb_cObject); modules are named rb_m*Modulename*.

Pre 1.8 String Access

Prior to Ruby 1.8, if a VALUE was supposed to contain a string, you'd access the RSTRING fields directly, and that would be it. In 1.8, however, the gradual introduction of duck typing, along with various optimizations, mean that this approach probably won't work the way you'd like. In particular, the ptr field of a STRING object might be null for zero-length strings. If you use the 1.8 StringValue method, it handles this case, resetting null pointers to reference instead a single, shared, empty string.

So, how do you write an extension that will work with both Ruby 1.6 and 1.8? Carefully, and with macros. Perhaps something such as this.

```
#if !defined(StringValue)
#  define StringValue(x) (x)
#endif
#if !defined(StringValuePtr)
#  define StringValuePtr(x) ((STR2CSTR(x)))
#endif
```

This code defines the 1.8 StringValue and StringValuePtr macros in terms of the older 1.6 counterparts. If you then write code in terms of these macros, it should compile and run on both older and newer interpreters.

If you want your code to have 1.8 duck-typing behavior, even when running under 1.6, you may want to define StringValue slightly differently. The difference between this and the previous implementation is described on page 294.

```
#if !defined(StringValue)
#  define StringValue(x) do {                          \
       if (TYPE(x) != T_STRING) x = rb_str_to_str(x);  \
     } while (0)
#endif
```

It isn't advisable to alter the data in these C structures directly, however—you may look, but don't touch. Instead, you'll normally use the supplied C functions to manipulate Ruby data (we'll talk more about this in just a moment).

However, in the interests of efficiency you may need to dig into these structures to obtain data. To dereference members of these C structures, you have to cast the generic VALUE to the proper structure type. ruby.h contains a number of macros that perform the proper casting for you, allowing you to dereference structure members easily. These macros are named RCLASSNAME, as in RSTRING or RARRAY. We've already seen the use of RSTRING when working with strings. You can do the same with arrays.

```
VALUE arr;
RARRAY(arr)->len   →  length of the Ruby array
RARRAY(arr)->capa  →  capacity of the Ruby array
RARRAY(arr)->ptr   →  pointer to array storage
```

There are similar accessors for hashes (RHASH), files (RFILE), and so on. Having said all this, you need to be careful about building too much dependence on checking types into your extension code. We have more to say about extensions and the Ruby type system on page 294.

Global Variables

Most of the time, your extensions will implement classes, and the Ruby code uses those classes. The data you share between the Ruby code and the C code will be wrapped tidily inside objects of the class. This is how it should be.

Sometimes, though, you may need to implement a global variable, accessible by both your C extension and by Ruby code.

The easiest way to do this is to have the variable be a VALUE (that is, a Ruby object). You then bind the address of this C variable to the name of a Ruby variable. In this case, the $ prefix is optional, but it helps clarify that this is a global variable. And remember: making a stack-based variable a Ruby global is not going to work (for long).

```
static  VALUE hardware_list;
static VALUE Init_SysInfo() {
  rb_define_class(....);

  hardware_list = rb_ary_new();
  rb_define_variable("$hardware", &hardware_list);
  ...
  rb_ary_push(hardware_list, rb_str_new2("DVD"));
  rb_ary_push(hardware_list, rb_str_new2("CDPlayer1"));
  rb_ary_push(hardware_list, rb_str_new2("CDPlayer2"));
}
```

The Ruby side can then access the C variable hardware_list as $hardware.

```
$hardware   →   ["DVD", "CDPlayer1", "CDPlayer2"]
```

Sometimes, though, life is more complicated. Perhaps you want to define a global variable whose value must be calculated when it is accessed. You do this by defining *hooked* and *virtual* variables. A hooked variable is a real variable that is initialized by a named function when the corresponding Ruby variable is accessed. Virtual variables are similar but are never stored: their value purely comes from evaluating the hook function. See the API section that begins on page 308 for details.

If you create a Ruby object from C and store it in a C global variable *without* exporting it to Ruby, you must at least tell the garbage collector about it, lest ye be reaped inadvertently.

```
static VALUE obj;
// ...
obj = rb_ary_new();
rb_global_variable(obj);
```

The Jukebox Extension

We've covered enough of the basics now to return to our jukebox example—interfacing C code with Ruby and sharing data and behavior between the two worlds.

Wrapping C Structures

We've got the vendor's library that controls the audio CD jukebox units, and we're ready to wire it into Ruby. The vendor's header file looks like this.

```
typedef struct _cdjb {
  int    statusf;
  int    request;
  void *data;
  char   pending;
  int    unit_id;
  void *stats;
} CDJukebox;
// Allocate a new CDJukebox structure
CDJukebox *new_jukebox(void);

// Assign the Jukebox to a player
void assign_jukebox(CDJukebox *jb, int unit_id);

// Deallocate when done (and take offline)
void free_jukebox(CDJukebox *jb);

// Seek to a disc, track and notify progress
void jukebox_seek(CDJukebox *jb,
                  int disc,
                  int track,
                  void (*done)(CDJukebox *jb, int percent));
// ... others...

// Report a statistic
double get_avg_seek_time(CDJukebox *jb);
```

This vendor has its act together; while they might not admit it, the code is written with an object-oriented flavor. We don't know what all those fields mean within the CDJukeBox structure, but that's OK—we can treat it as an opaque pile of bits. The vendor's code knows what to do with it; we just have to carry it around.

Anytime you have a C-only structure that you would like to handle as a Ruby object, you should wrap it in a special, internal Ruby class called DATA (type T_DATA). Two macros do this wrapping, and one macro retrieves your structure back out again.

API: C Data Type Wrapping

VALUE **Data_Wrap_Struct**(VALUE class, void (*mark)(),
                    void (*free)(), void *ptr)

> Wraps the given C data type *ptr*, registers the two garbage collection routines (see below), and returns a VALUE pointer to a genuine Ruby object. The C type of the resulting object is T_DATA, and its Ruby class is *class*.

VALUE **Data_Make_Struct**(VALUE class, *c-type*, void (*mark)(),
                    void (*free)(), *c-type* *)

> Allocates and sets to zero a structure of the indicated type first and then proceeds as Data_Wrap_Struct. *c-type* is the name of the C data type that you're wrapping, not a variable of that type.

Data_Get_Struct(VALUE obj, *c-type*, *c-type* *)

> Returns the original pointer. This macro is a type-safe wrapper around the macro DATA_PTR(obj), which evaluates the pointer.

The object created by Data_Wrap_Struct is a normal Ruby object, except that it has an additional C data type that can't be accessed from Ruby. As you can see in Figure 21.1 on the following page, this C data type is separate from any instance variables that the object contains. But since it's a separate thing, how do you get rid of it when the garbage collector claims this object? What if you have to release some resource (close some file, clean up some lock or IPC mechanism, and so on)?

Ruby uses a mark and sweep garbage collection scheme. During the mark phase, Ruby looks for pointers to areas of memory. It marks these areas as "in use" (because something is pointing to them). If those areas themselves contain more pointers, the memory these pointers reference is also marked, and so on. At the end of the mark phase, all memory that is referenced will have been marked, and any orphaned areas will not have a mark. At this point the sweep phase starts, freeing off memory that isn't marked.

To participate in Ruby's mark-and-sweep garbage collection process, you must define a routine to free your structure and possibly a routine to mark any references from your structure to other structures. Both routines take a void pointer, a reference to your structure. The *mark* routine will be called by the garbage collector during its "mark" phase. If your structure references other Ruby objects, then your mark function needs to identify these objects using rb_gc_mark(*value*). If the structure doesn't reference other Ruby objects, you can simply pass 0 as a function pointer.

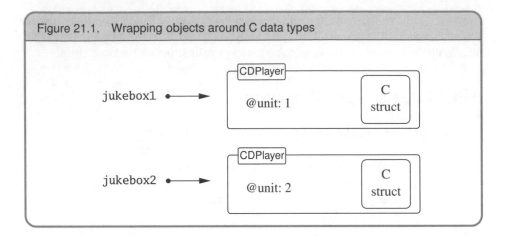

Figure 21.1. Wrapping objects around C data types

When the object needs to be disposed of, the garbage collector will call the *free* routine to free it. If you have allocated any memory yourself (for instance, by using Data_Make_Struct), you'll need to pass a free function—even if it's just the standard C library's free routine. For complex structures that you have allocated, your free function may need to traverse the structure to free all the allocated memory.

Let's look at our CD player interface. The vendor library passes the information around between its various functions in a CDJukebox structure. This structure represents the state of the jukebox and therefore is a good candidate for wrapping within our Ruby class. You create new instances of this structure by calling the library's CDPlayerNew method. You'd then want to wrap that created structure inside a new CDPlayer Ruby object. A fragment of code to do this may look like the following. (We'll talk about that magic *klass* parameter in a minute.)

```
CDJukebox *jukebox;
VALUE obj;

// Vendor library creates the Jukebox
jukebox = new_jukebox();

// then we wrap it inside a Ruby CDPlayer object
obj = Data_Wrap_Struct(klass, 0, cd_free, jukebox);
```

Once this code had executed, *obj* would hold a reference to a newly allocated CDPlayer Ruby object, wrapping a new CDJukebox C structure. Of course, to get this code to compile, we'd need to do some more work. We'd have to define the CDPlayer class and store a reference to it in the variable cCDPlayer. We'd also have to define the function to free off our object, cdplayer_free. That's easy: it just calls the vendor library dispose method.

```
static void cd_free(void *p) {
  free_jukebox(p);
}
```

However, code fragments do not a program make. We need to package all this stuff in a way that integrates it into the interpreter. And to do that, we need to look at some of the conventions the interpreter uses.

Object Creation

1.8

Ruby 1.8 has rationalized the creation and initialization of objects. Although the old ways still work, the new way, using allocation functions, is much tidier (and is less likely to be deprecated in the future).

The basic idea is simple. Let's say you're creating an object of class CDPlayer in your Ruby program.

```
cd = CDPlayer.new
```

Underneath the covers, the interpreter calls the class method new for CDPlayer. As CDPlayer hasn't defined a method new, Ruby looks into its parent, class Class.

The implementation of new in class Class is fairly simple: it allocates memory for the new object and then calls the object's initialize method to initialize that memory.

So, if our CDPlayer extension is to be a good Ruby citizen, it should work within this framework. This means that we'll need to implement an allocation function and an initialize method.

Allocation Functions

The allocation function is responsible for creating the memory used by your object. If the object you're implementing doesn't use any data other than Ruby instance variables, then you don't need to write an allocation function—Ruby's default allocator will work just fine. But if your class wraps a C structure, you'll need to allocate space for that structure in the allocation function. The allocation function gets passed the class of the object being allocated. In our case it will in all likelihood be a cCDPlayer, but we'll use the parameter as given, as this means that we'll work correctly if subclassed.

```
static VALUE cd_alloc(VALUE klass) {
  CDJukebox *jukebox;
  VALUE obj;

  // Vendor library creates the Jukebox
  jukebox = new_jukebox();

  // then we wrap it inside a Ruby CDPlayer object
  obj = Data_Wrap_Struct(klass, 0, cd_free, jukebox);

  return obj;
}
```

You then need to register your allocation function in your class's initialization code.

```
void Init_CDPlayer() {
  cCDPlayer = rb_define_class("CDPlayer", rb_cObject);
  rb_define_alloc_func(cCDPlayer, cd_alloc);
  // ...
}
```

Most objects probably need to define an initializer too. The allocation function creates an empty, uninitialized object, and we'll need to fill in specific values. In the case of the CD player, the constructor is called with the unit number of the player to be associated with this object.

```
static VALUE cd_initialize(VALUE self, VALUE unit) {
  int unit_id;
  CDJukebox *jb;

  Data_Get_Struct(self, CDJukebox, jb);

  unit_id = NUM2INT(unit);
  assign_jukebox(jb, unit_id);

  return self;
}
```

One of the reasons for this multistep object creation protocol is that it lets the interpreter handle situations where objects have to be created by "back-door means." One example is when objects are being deserialized from their marshaled form. Here, the interpreter needs to create an empty object (by calling the allocator), but it cannot call the initializer (as it has no knowledge of the parameters to use). Another common situation is when objects are duplicated or cloned.

One further issue lurks here. Because users can choose to bypass the constructor, you need to ensure that your allocation code leaves the returned object in a valid state. It may not contain all the information it would have had, had it been set up by #initialize, but it at least needs to be usable.

Cloning Objects

All Ruby objects can be copied using one of two methods, dup and clone. The two methods are similar: Both produce a new instance of their receiver's class by calling the allocation function. Then they copy across any instance variables from the original. clone then goes a bit further and copies the original's singleton class (if it has one) and flags (such as the flag that indicates that an object is frozen). You can think of dup as being a copy of the contents and clone as being a copy of the full object.

However, the Ruby interpreter doesn't know how to handle copying the internal state of objects that you write as C extensions. For example, if your object wraps a C structure that contains an open file descriptor, it's up to the semantics of your implementation whether that descriptor should simply be copied to the new object or whether a new file descriptor should be opened.

Pre-1.8 Object Allocation

1.8

Prior to Ruby 1.8, if you wanted to allocate additional space in an object, either you had to put that code in the `initialize` method, or you had to define a `new` method for your class. Guy Decoux recommends the following hybrid approach for maximizing compatibility between 1.6 and 1.8 extensions.

```
static VALUE cd_alloc(VALUE klass) {
  // same as before
}
static VALUE cd_new(int argc, VALUE *argv, VALUE klass) {
  VALUE obj = rb_funcall2(klass,
                          rb_intern("allocate"), 0, 0);
  rb_obj_call_init(obj, argc, argv);
  return obj;
}

void init_CDPlayer() {

  // ...

#if HAVE_RB_DEFINE_ALLOC_FUNC
  // 1.8 allocation
  rb_define_alloc_func(cCDPlayer, cd_alloc);
#else
  // define manual allocation function for 1.6
  rb_define_singleton_method(cCDPlayer, "allocate",
                             cd_alloc, 0);
#endif
  rb_define_singleton_method(cCDPlayer, "new", cd_new, -1);

  // ...
}
```

If you're writing code that should run on both recent and old versions of Ruby, you'll need to take an approach similar to this. However, you'll probably also need to handle cloning and duplication, and you'll need to consider what happens when your object gets marshaled.

To handle this, the interpreter delegates to your code the responsibility of copying the internal state of objects that you implement. After copying the object's instance variables, the interpreter invokes the new object's `initialize_copy` method, passing in a reference to the original object. It's up to you to implement meaningful semantics in this method.

For our `CDPlayer` class we'll take a fairly simple approach to the cloning issue: we'll simply copy across the `CDJukebox` structure from the original object.

There's a wee chunk of strange code in this example. To test that the original object is indeed something we can clone the new one from, the code checks to see that the original

1. has a TYPE of T_DATA (which means that it's a noncore object), and

2. has a free function with the same address as our free function.

This is a relatively high-performance way of verifying that the original object is compatible with our own (as long as you don't share free functions between classes). An alternative, which is slower, would be to use rb_obj_is_kind_of and do a direct test on the class.

```
static VALUE cd_init_copy(VALUE copy, VALUE orig) {
  CDJukebox *orig_jb;
  CDJukebox *copy_jb;

  if (copy == orig)
    return copy;
  // we can initialize the copy from other CDPlayers
  // or their subclasses only
  if (TYPE(orig) != T_DATA ||
      RDATA(orig)->dfree != (RUBY_DATA_FUNC)cd_free) {
    rb_raise(rb_eTypeError, "wrong argument type");
  }
  // copy all the fields from the original
  // object's CDJukebox structure to the
  // new object
  Data_Get_Struct(orig, CDJukebox, orig_jb);
  Data_Get_Struct(copy, CDJukebox, copy_jb);
  MEMCPY(copy_jb, orig_jb, CDJukebox, 1);

  return copy;
}
```

Our copy method does not have to allocate a wrapped structure to receive the original objects CDJukebox structure: the cd_alloc method has already taken care of that.

Note that in this case it's correct to do type checking based on classes: we need the original object to have a wrapped CDJukebox structure, and the only objects that have one of these are derived from class CDPlayer.

Putting It All Together

OK, finally we're ready to write all the code for our CDPlayer class.

```
#include "ruby.h"
#include "cdjukebox.h"

static VALUE cCDPlayer;
```

```c
// Helper function to free a vendor CDJukebox
static void cd_free(void *p) {
  free_jukebox(p);
}
// Allocate a new CDPlayer object, wrapping
// the vendor's CDJukebox structure
static VALUE cd_alloc(VALUE klass) {
  CDJukebox *jukebox;
  VALUE obj;

  // Vendor library creates the Jukebox
  jukebox = new_jukebox();

  // then we wrap it inside a Ruby CDPlayer object
  obj = Data_Wrap_Struct(klass, 0, cd_free, jukebox);

  return obj;
}
// Assign the newly created CDPLayer to a
// particular unit
static VALUE cd_initialize(VALUE self, VALUE unit) {
  int unit_id;
  CDJukebox *jb;

  Data_Get_Struct(self, CDJukebox, jb);

  unit_id = NUM2INT(unit);
  assign_jukebox(jb, unit_id);

  return self;
}
// Copy across state (used by clone and dup).  For jukeboxes, we
// actually create a new vendor object and set its unit number from
// the old
static VALUE cd_init_copy(VALUE copy, VALUE orig) {
  CDJukebox *orig_jb;
  CDJukebox *copy_jb;

  if (copy == orig)
    return copy;

  // we can initialize the copy from other CDPlayers or their
  // subclasses only
  if (TYPE(orig) != T_DATA ||
      RDATA(orig)->dfree != (RUBY_DATA_FUNC)cd_free) {
    rb_raise(rb_eTypeError, "wrong argument type");
  }

  // copy all the fields from the original object's CDJukebox
  // structure to the new object
  Data_Get_Struct(orig, CDJukebox, orig_jb);
  Data_Get_Struct(copy, CDJukebox, copy_jb);
  MEMCPY(copy_jb, orig_jb, CDJukebox, 1);

  return copy;
}
```

```c
// The progress callback yields to the caller the percent complete
static void progress(CDJukebox *rec, int percent) {
  if (rb_block_given_p()) {
    if (percent > 100) percent = 100;
    if (percent < 0) percent = 0;
    rb_yield(INT2FIX(percent));
  }
}
// Seek to a given part of the track, invoking the progress callback
// as we go
static VALUE
cd_seek(VALUE self, VALUE disc, VALUE track) {
  CDJukebox *jb;
  Data_Get_Struct(self, CDJukebox, jb);

  jukebox_seek(jb,
               NUM2INT(disc),
               NUM2INT(track),
               progress);
  return Qnil;
}
// Return the average seek time for this unit
static VALUE
cd_seek_time(VALUE self)
{
  double tm;
  CDJukebox *jb;
  Data_Get_Struct(self, CDJukebox, jb);
  tm = get_avg_seek_time(jb);
  return rb_float_new(tm);
}
// Return this player's unit number
static VALUE
cd_unit(VALUE self) {
  CDJukebox *jb;
  Data_Get_Struct(self, CDJukebox, jb);

  return INT2NUM(jb->unit_id);
}

void Init_CDPlayer() {
  cCDPlayer = rb_define_class("CDPlayer", rb_cObject);
  rb_define_alloc_func(cCDPlayer, cd_alloc);

  rb_define_method(cCDPlayer, "initialize", cd_initialize, 1);
  rb_define_method(cCDPlayer, "initialize_copy", cd_init_copy, 1);

  rb_define_method(cCDPlayer, "seek", cd_seek, 2);
  rb_define_method(cCDPlayer, "seek_time", cd_seek_time, 0);
  rb_define_method(cCDPlayer, "unit", cd_unit, 0);
}
```

Now we can control our jukebox from Ruby in a nice, object-oriented way.

```
require 'CDPlayer'
p = CDPlayer.new(13)
puts "Unit is #{p.unit}"
p.seek(3, 16) {|x| puts "#{x}% done" }
puts "Avg. time was #{p.seek_time} seconds"
p1 = p.dup
puts "Cloned unit = #{p1.unit}"
```

produces:

```
Unit is 13
26% done
79% done
100% done
Avg. time was 1.2 seconds
Cloned unit = 13
```

This example demonstrates most of what we've talked about so far, with one additional neat feature. The vendor's library provided a callback routine—a function pointer that is called every so often while the hardware is grinding its way to the next disc. We've set that up here to run a code block passed as an argument to seek. In the progress function, we check to see if there is an iterator in the current context and, if there is, run it with the current percent done as an argument.

Memory Allocation

You may sometimes need to allocate memory in an extension that won't be used for object storage—perhaps you've got a giant bitmap for a Bloom filter, an image, or a whole bunch of little structures that Ruby doesn't use directly.

To work correctly with the garbage collector, you should use the following memory allocation routines. These routines do a little bit more work than the standard malloc. For instance, if ALLOC_N determines that it cannot allocate the desired amount of memory, it will invoke the garbage collector to try to reclaim some space. It will raise a NoMemError if it can't or if the requested amount of memory is invalid.

API: Memory Allocation

type * **ALLOC_N(** *c-type*, n **)**

Allocates *n c-type* objects, where *c-type* is the literal name of the C type, not a variable of that type.

type * **ALLOC(** *c-type* **)**

Allocates a *c-type* and casts the result to a pointer of that type.

REALLOC_N(*var*, *c-type*, n)

> Reallocates *n* *c-type*s and assigns the result to *var*, a pointer to a variable of type *c-type*.

type * ALLOCA_N(*c-type*, n)

> Allocates memory for *n* objects of *c-type* on the stack—this memory will be automatically freed when the function that invokes ALLOCA_N returns.

Ruby Type System

1.8

In Ruby, we rely less on the type (or class) of an object and more on its capabilities. This is called *duck typing*. We describe it in more detail in Chapter 23 on page 365. You'll find many examples of this if you examine the source code for the interpreter itself. For example, the following code implements the Kernel.exec method.

```
VALUE
rb_f_exec(argc, argv)
    int argc;
    VALUE *argv;
{
    VALUE prog = 0;
    VALUE tmp;

    if (argc == 0) {
        rb_raise(rb_eArgError, "wrong number of arguments");
    }

    tmp = rb_check_array_type(argv[0]);
    if (!NIL_P(tmp)) {
        if (RARRAY(tmp)->len != 2) {
            rb_raise(rb_eArgError, "wrong first argument");
        }
        prog = RARRAY(tmp)->ptr[0];
        SafeStringValue(prog);
        argv[0] = RARRAY(tmp)->ptr[1];
    }
    if (argc == 1 && prog == 0) {
        VALUE cmd = argv[0];

        SafeStringValue(cmd);
        rb_proc_exec(RSTRING(cmd)->ptr);
    }
    else {
        proc_exec_n(argc, argv, prog);
    }
    rb_sys_fail(RSTRING(argv[0])->ptr);
    return Qnil;                    /* dummy */
}
```

The first parameter to this method may be a string or an array containing two strings. However, the code doesn't explicitly check the type of the argument. Instead, it first calls `rb_check_array_type`, passing in the argument. What does this method do? Let's see.

```
VALUE
rb_check_array_type(ary)
    VALUE ary;
{
    return rb_check_convert_type(ary, T_ARRAY, "Array", "to_ary");
}
```

The plot thickens. Let's track down `rb_check_convert_type`.

```
VALUE
rb_check_convert_type(val, type, tname, method)
    VALUE val;
    int type;
    const char *tname, *method;
{
    VALUE v;
    /* always convert T_DATA */
    if (TYPE(val) == type && type != T_DATA) return val;
    v = convert_type(val, tname, method, Qfalse);
    if (NIL_P(v)) return Qnil;
    if (TYPE(v) != type) {
        rb_raise(rb_eTypeError, "%s#%s should return %s",
                rb_obj_classname(val), method, tname);
    }
    return v;
}
```

Now we're getting somewhere. If the object is the correct type (T_ARRAY in our example), then the original object is returned. Otherwise, we don't give up quite yet. Instead we call our original object and ask if it can represent itself as an array (we call its `to_ary` method). If it can, we're happy and continue. The code is saying "I don't need an Array, I just need something that can be represented as an array." This means that `Kernel.exec` will accept as an array any parameter that implements a `to_ary` method. We discuss these conversion protocols in more detail (but from the Ruby perspective) starting on page 371.

What does all this mean to you as an extension writer? There are two messages. First, try to avoid checking the types of parameters passed to you. Instead, see if there's a `rb_check_xxx_type` method that will convert the parameter into the type that you need. If not, look for an existing conversion function (such as `rb_Array`, `rb_Float`, or `rb_Integer`) that'll do the trick for you. Second, if you're writing an extension that implements something that may be meaningfully used as a Ruby string or array, consider implementing `to_str` or `to_ary` methods, allowing objects implemented by your extension to be used in string or array contexts.

Creating an Extension

Having written the source code for an extension, we now need to compile it so Ruby can use it. We can either do this as a shared object, which is dynamically loaded at runtime, or statically link the extension into the main Ruby interpreter itself. The basic procedure is the same.

1. Create the C source code file(s) in a given directory.
2. Optionally create any supporting Ruby files in a lib subdirectory.
3. Create extconf.rb.
4. Run extconf.rb to create a Makefile for the C files in this directory.
5. Run make.
6. Run make install.

Creating a Makefile with extconf.rb

Figure 21.2 on the facing page shows the overall workflow when building an extension. The key to the whole process is the extconf.rb program that you, as a developer, create. In extconf.rb, you write a simple program that determines what features are available on the user's system and where those features may be located. Executing extconf.rb builds a customized Makefile, tailored for both your application and the system on which it's being compiled. When you run the make command against this Makefile, your extension is built and (optionally) installed.

The simplest extconf.rb may be just two lines long, and for many extensions this is sufficient.

```
require 'mkmf'
create_makefile("Test")
```

The first line brings in the mkmf library module (described starting on page 779). This contains all the commands we'll be using. The second line creates a Makefile for an extension called "Test." (Note that "Test" is the name of the extension; the makefile will always be called Makefile.) Test will be built from all the C source files in the current directory. When your code is loaded, Ruby will call its Init_Test method.

Let's say that we run this extconf.rb program in a directory containing a single source file, main.c. The result is a makefile that will build our extension. On a Linux box, this executes the following commands.

```
gcc -fPIC -I/usr/local/lib/ruby/1.8/i686-linux -g -O2  \
  -c main.c -o main.o
gcc -shared -o Test.so main.o -lc
```

The result of this compilation is Test.so, which may be dynamically linked into Ruby at runtime with require.

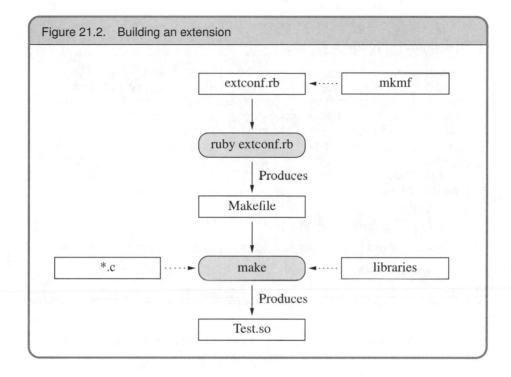

Figure 21.2.   Building an extension

Under Mac OS X, the commands are different, but the result is the same: a shared object (a *bundle* on the Mac) is created.

```
gcc -fno-common -g -O2 -pipe -fno-common \
    -I/usr/lib/ruby/1.8/powerpc-darwin  \
    -I/usr/lib/ruby/1.8/powerpc-darwin -c main.c

cc -dynamic -bundle -undefined suppress -flat_namespace \
    -L'/usr/lib'  -o Test.bundle main.o -ldl -lobjc
```

See how the mkmf commands have automatically located platform-specific libraries and used options specific to the local compiler. Pretty neat, eh?

Although this basic extconf.rb program works for many simple extensions, you may have to do some more work if your extension needs header files or libraries that aren't included in the default compilation environment or if you conditionally compile code based on the presence of libraries or functions.

A common requirement is to specify nonstandard directories where include files and libraries may be found. This is a two-step process. First, your extconf.rb should contain one or more dir_config commands. This specifies a tag for a set of directories. Then, when you run the extconf.rb program, you tell mkmf where the corresponding physical directories are on the current system.

> ### Dividing Up the Namespace
>
> Increasingly, extension writers are being good citizens. Rather than install their work directory into one of Ruby's library directories, they're using subdirectories to group their files together. This is easy with extconf.rb. If the parameter to the create_makefile call contains forward slashes, mkmf assumes that everything before the last slash is a directory name and that the remainder is the extension name. The extension will be installed into the given directory (relative to the Ruby directory tree). In the following example, the extension will still be named Test.
>
> ```
> require 'mkmf'
> create_makefile("wibble/Test")
> ```
>
> However, when you require this class in a Ruby program, you'd write
>
> ```
> require 'wibble/Test'
> ```

If extconf.rb contains the line dir_config(*name*), then you give the location of the corresponding directories with the command-line options

--with-*name*-include=*directory*

    Add *directory*/include to the compile command.

--with-*name*-lib=*directory*

    Add *directory*/lib to the link command.

If (as is common) your include and library directories are subdirectories called include and lib of some other directory, you can take a shortcut.

--with-*name*-dir=*directory*

    Add *directory*/lib and *directory*/include to the link command and compile command, respectively.

As well as specifying all these --with options when you run extconf.rb, you can also use the --with options that were specified when Ruby was built for your machine. This means you can discover and use the locations of libraries that are used by Ruby itself.

To make all this concrete, let's say you need to use the vendor's CDJukebox libraries and include files for the CD player we're developing. Your extconf.rb may contain

```
require 'mkmf'
dir_config('cdjukebox')
# .. more stuff
create_makefile("CDPlayer")
```

You'd then run `extconf.rb` with something like

```
% ruby extconf.rb --with-cdjukebox-dir=/usr/local/cdjb
```

The generated `Makefile` would assume that `/usr/local/cdjb/lib` contained the libraries and `/usr/local/cdjb/include` the include files.

The `dir_config` command adds to the list of places to search for libraries and include files. It does not, however, link the libraries into your application. To do that, you'll need to use one or more `have_library` or `find_library` commands.

`have_library` looks for a given entry point in a named library. If it finds the entry point, it adds the library to the list of libraries to be used when linking your extension. `find_library` is similar but allows you to specify a list of directories to search for the library. Here are the contents of the `extconf.rb` that we use to link our CD player.

```
require 'mkmf'
dir_config("cdjukebox")
have_library("cdjukebox", "new_jukebox")
create_makefile("CDPlayer")
```

A particular library may be in different places depending on the host system. The X Window system, for example, is notorious for living in different directories on different systems. The `find_library` command will search a list of supplied directories to find the right one (this is different from `have library`, which uses only configuration information for the search). For example, to create a `Makefile` that uses X Windows and a JPEG library, `extconf.rb` may contain

```
require 'mkmf'
if have_library("jpeg","jpeg_mem_init") and
   find_library("X11", "XOpenDisplay",
                "/usr/X11/lib",      # list of directories
                "/usr/X11R6/lib",    # to check
                "/usr/openwin/lib")  # for library
then
    create_makefile("XThing")
else
    puts "No X/JPEG support available"
end
```

We've added some additional functionality to this program. All the `mkmf` commands return `false` if they fail. This means we can write an `extconf.rb` that generates a `Makefile` only if everything it needs is present. The Ruby distribution does this so that it will try to compile only those extensions that are supported on your system.

You also may want your extension code to be able to configure the features it uses depending on the target environment. For example, our CD jukebox may be able to use a high-performance MP3 decoder if the end user has one installed. We can check by looking for its header file.

```
require 'mkmf'
dir_config('cdjukebox')
have_library('cdjb', 'CDPlayerNew')
have_header('hp_mp3.h')
create_makefile("CDJukeBox")
```

We can also check to see if the target environment has a particular function in any of the libraries we'll be using. For example, the `setpriority` call would be useful but isn't always available. We can check for it with

```
require 'mkmf'
dir_config('cdjukebox')
have_func('setpriority')
create_makefile("CDJukeBox")
```

Both `have_header` and `have_func` define preprocessor constants if they find their targets. The names are formed by converting the target name to uppercase and prepending HAVE_. Your C code can take advantage of this using constructs such as

```
#if defined(HAVE_HP_MP3_H)
#   include <hp_mp3.h>
#endif

#if defined(HAVE_SETPRIORITY)
   err = setpriority(PRIOR_PROCESS, 0, -10)
#endif
```

If you have special requirements that can't be met with all these `mkmf` commands, your program can directly add to the global variables $CFLAGS and $LFLAGS, which are passed to the compiler and linker, respectively.

Sometimes you'll create an `extconf.rb`, and it just doesn't seem to work. You give it the name of a library, and it swears that no such library has ever existed on the entire planet. You tweak and tweak, but `mkmf` still can't find the library you need. It would be nice if you could find out exactly what it's doing behind the scenes. Well, you can. Each time you run your `extconf.rb` script, `mkmf` generates a log file containing details of what it did. If you look in `mkmf.log`, you'll be able to see what steps the program used to try to find the libraries you requested. Sometimes trying these steps manually will help you track down the problem.

Installation Target

The Makefile produced by your `extconf.rb` will include an "install" target. This will copy your shared library object into the correct place on your (or your users') local file system. The destination is tied to the installation location of the Ruby interpreter you used to run `extconf.rb` in the first place. If you have multiple Ruby interpreters installed on your box, your extension will be installed into the directory tree of the one that ran `extconf.rb`.

In addition to installing the shared library, extconf.rb will check for the presence of a lib/ subdirectory. If it finds one, it will arrange for any Ruby files there to be installed along with your shared object. This is useful if you want to split the work of writing your extension between low-level C code and higher-level Ruby code.

Static Linking

Finally, if your system doesn't support dynamic linking, or if you have an extension module that you want to have statically linked into Ruby itself, edit the file ext/Setup in the distribution and add your directory to the list of extensions in the file. In your extension's directory, create a file named MANIFEST containing a list of all the files in your extension (source, extconf.rb, lib/, and so on). Then rebuild Ruby. The extensions listed in Setup will be statically linked into the Ruby executable. If you want to disable any dynamic linking, and link all extensions statically, edit ext/Setup to contain the following option.

```
option nodynamic
```

A Shortcut

If you are extending an existing library written in C or C++, you may want to investigate SWIG (http://www.swig.org). SWIG is an interface generator: it takes a library definition (typically from a header file) and automatically generates the glue code needed to access that library from another language. SWIG supports Ruby, meaning that it can generate the C source files that wrap external libraries in Ruby classes.

Embedding a Ruby Interpreter

In addition to extending Ruby by adding C code, you can also turn the problem around and embed Ruby itself within your application. You have two ways to do this. The first is to let the interpreter take control by calling ruby_run. This is the easiest approach, but it has one significant drawback—the interpreter never returns from a ruby_run call. Here's an example.

```c
#include "ruby.h"
int main(void) {
  /* ... our own application stuff ... */
  ruby_init();
  ruby_init_loadpath();
  ruby_script("embedded");
  rb_load_file("start.rb");
  ruby_run();
  exit(0);
}
```

To initialize the Ruby interpreter, you need to call ruby_init(). But on some plat-forms, you may need to take special steps before that.

```
#if defined(NT)
  NtInitialize(&argc, &argv);
#endif
#if defined(__MACOS__) && defined(__MWERKS__)
  argc = ccommand(&argv);
#endif
```

See main.c in the Ruby distribution for any other special defines or setup needed for your platform.

You need the Ruby include and library files accessible to compile this embedded code. On my box (Mac OS X) I have the Ruby 1.8 interpreter installed in a private directory, so my Makefile looks like this.

```
WHERE=/Users/dave/ruby1.8/lib/ruby/1.8/powerpc-darwin/
CFLAGS=-I$(WHERE) -g
LDFLAGS=-L$(WHERE) -lruby -ldl -lobjc

embed:  embed.o
        $(CC) -o embed embed.o $(LDFLAGS)
```

The second way of embedding Ruby allows Ruby code and your C code to engage in more of a dialogue: the C code calls some Ruby code, and the Ruby code responds. You do this by initializing the interpreter as normal. Then, rather than entering the interpreter's main loop, you instead invoke specific methods in your Ruby code. When these methods return, your C code gets control back.

There's a wrinkle, though. If the Ruby code raises an exception and it isn't caught, your C program will terminate. To overcome this, you need to do what the interpreter does and protect all calls that could raise an exception. This can get messy. The rb_protect method call wraps the call to another C function. That second function should invoke our Ruby method. However, the method wrapped by rb_protect is defined to take just a single parameter. To pass more involves some ugly C casting.

Let's look at an example. Here's a simple Ruby class that implements a method to return the sum of the numbers from one to *max*.

```
class Summer
  def sum(max)
    raise "Invalid maximum #{max}" if max < 0
    (max*max + max)/2
  end
end
```

Let's write a C program that calls an instance of this class multiple times. To create the instance, we'll get the class object (by looking for a top-level constant whose name is the name of our class). We'll then ask Ruby to create an instance of that class—rb_class_new_instance is actually a call to Class.new. (The two initial 0 parameters are the argument count and a dummy pointer to the arguments themselves.) Once we have that object, we can invoke its sum method using rb_funcall.

```
#include "ruby.h"
static int id_sum;
int Values[] = { 5, 10, 15, -1, 20, 0 };
static VALUE wrap_sum(VALUE args) {
  VALUE *values = (VALUE *)args;
  VALUE  summer = values[0];
  VALUE  max    = values[1];
  return rb_funcall(summer, id_sum, 1, max);
}
static VALUE protected_sum(VALUE summer, VALUE max) {
  int error;
  VALUE args[2];
  VALUE result;

  args[0] = summer;
  args[1] = max;
  result = rb_protect(wrap_sum, (VALUE)args, &error);

  return error ? Qnil : result;
}


int main(void) {
  int value;
  int *next = Values;

  ruby_init();
  ruby_init_loadpath();
  ruby_script("embedded");
  rb_require("sum.rb");

  // get an instance of Summer
  VALUE summer = rb_class_new_instance(0, 0,
                     rb_const_get(rb_cObject, rb_intern("Summer")));

  id_sum = rb_intern("sum");

  while (value = *next++) {
    VALUE  result = protected_sum(summer, INT2NUM(value));
    if (NIL_P(result))
      printf("Sum to %d doesn't compute!\n", value);
    else
      printf("Sum to %d is %d\n", value, NUM2INT(result));
  }
  ruby_finalize();
  exit(0);
}
```

One last thing: the Ruby interpreter was not originally written with embedding in mind. Probably the biggest problem is that it maintains state in global variables, so it isn't thread-safe. You can embed Ruby—just one interpreter per process.

A good resource for embedding Ruby in C++ programs is at http://metaeditor. sourceforge.net/embed/. This page also contains links to other examples of embedding Ruby.

API: Embedded Ruby API

void **ruby_init**( )

> Sets up and initializes the interpreter. This function should be called before any other Ruby-related functions.

void **ruby_init_loadpath**( )

> Initializes the $: (load path) variable; necessary if your code loads any library modules.

void **ruby_options**(int argc, char **argv)

> Gives the Ruby interpreter the command-line options.

void **ruby_script**(char *name)

> Sets the name of the Ruby script (and $0) to *name*.

void **rb_load_file**(char *file)

> Loads the given file into the interpreter.

void **ruby_run**( )

> Runs the interpreter.

void **ruby_finalize**( )

> Shuts down the interpreter.

For another example of embedding a Ruby interpreter within another program, see also eruby, which is described beginning on page 242.

Bridging Ruby to Other Languages

So far, we've discussed extending Ruby by adding routines written in C. However, you can write extensions in just about any language, as long as you can bridge the two languages with C. Almost anything is possible, including awkward marriages of Ruby and C++, Ruby and Java, and so on.

But you may be able to accomplish the same thing without resorting to C code. For example, you could bridge to other languages using middleware such as SOAP or COM. See the section on SOAP (page 249) and the section on Windows Automation beginning on page 269 for more details.

Ruby C Language API

Last, but by no means least, here are some C-level functions that you may find useful when writing an extension.

Some functions require an ID: you can obtain an ID for a string by using `rb_intern` and reconstruct the name from an ID by using `rb_id2name`.

As most of these C functions have Ruby equivalents that are already described in detail elsewhere in this book, the descriptions here will be brief.

The following listing is not complete. Many more functions are available—too many to document them all, as it turns out. If you need a method that you can't find here, check `ruby.h` or `intern.h` for likely candidates. Also, at or near the bottom of each source file is a set of method definitions that describes the binding from Ruby methods to C functions. You may be able to call the C function directly or search for a wrapper function that calls the function you need. The following list, based on the list in `README.EXT`, shows the main source files in the interpreter.

Ruby Language Core
> `class.c, error.c, eval.c, gc.c, object.c, parse.y, variable.c`

Utility Functions
> `dln.c, regex.c, st.c, util.c`

Ruby Interpreter
> `dmyext.c, inits.c, keywords main.c, ruby.c, version.c`

Base Library
> `array.c, bignum.c, compar.c, dir.c, enum.c, file.c, hash.c, io.c, marshal.c, math.c, numeric.c, pack.c, prec.c, process.c, random.c, range.c, re.c, signal.c, sprintf.c, string.c, struct.c, time.c`

API: Defining Classes

> VALUE **rb_define_class**(char *name, VALUE superclass)
>> Defines a new class at the top level with the given *name* and *superclass* (for class Object, use `rb_cObject`).

> VALUE **rb_define_module**(char *name)
>> Defines a new module at the top level with the given *name*.

> VALUE **rb_define_class_under**(VALUE under, char *name,
>>   VALUE superclass)
>> Defines a nested class under the class or module *under*.

VALUE **rb_define_module_under**(VALUE under, char *name)
>> Defines a nested module under the class or module *under*.

void **rb_include_module**(VALUE parent, VALUE module)
>> Includes the given *module* into the class or module *parent*.

void **rb_extend_object**(VALUE obj, VALUE module)
>> Extends *obj* with *module*.

VALUE **rb_require**(const char *name)
>> Equivalent to require *name*. Returns Qtrue or Qfalse.

API: Defining Structures

VALUE **rb_struct_define**(char *name, char *attribute..., NULL)
>> Defines a new structure with the given attributes.

VALUE **rb_struct_new**(VALUE sClass, VALUE args..., NULL)
>> Creates an instance of *sClass* with the given attribute values.

VALUE **rb_struct_aref**(VALUE struct, VALUE idx)
>> Returns the element named or indexed by *idx*.

VALUE **rb_struct_aset**(VALUE struct, VALUE idx, VALUE val)
>> Sets the attribute named or indexed by *idx* to *val*.

API: Defining Methods

In some of the function definitions that follow, the parameter *argc* specifies how many arguments a Ruby method takes. It may have the following values.

argc	**Function Prototype**
0..17	VALUE func(VALUE self, VALUE arg...) The C function will be called with this many actual arguments.
−1	VALUE func(int argc, VALUE *argv, VALUE self) The C function will be given a variable number of arguments passed as a C array.
−2	VALUE func(VALUE self, VALUE args) The C function will be given a variable number of arguments passed as a Ruby array.

In a function that has been given a variable number of arguments, you can use the C function rb_scan_args to sort things out (see below).

void **rb_define_method**(VALUE classmod, char *name,
                          VALUE(*func)(), int argc)

> Defines an instance method in the class or module *classmod* with the given *name*, implemented by the C function *func* and taking *argc* arguments.

void **rb_define_alloc_func**(VALUE classmod, VALUE(*func)())

> Identifies the allocator for *classmod*.

void **rb_define_module_function**(VALUE module, char *name,
                                    VALUE(*func)(), int argc)

> Defines a method in class *module* with the given *name*, implemented by the C function *func* and taking *argc* arguments.

void **rb_define_global_function**(char *name, VALUE(*func)(),
                                    int argc)

> Defines a global function (a private method of Kernel) with the given *name*, implemented by the C function *func* and taking *argc* arguments.

void **rb_define_singleton_method**(VALUE classmod, char *name,
                                     VALUE(*func)(), int argc)

> Defines a singleton method in class *classmod* with the given *name*, implemented by the C function *func* and taking *argc* arguments.

int **rb_scan_args**(int argcount, VALUE *argv, char *fmt, ...)

> Scans the argument list and assigns to variables similar to scanf: *fmt* is a string containing zero, one, or two digits followed by some flag characters. The first digit indicates the count of mandatory arguments; the second is the count of optional arguments. A * means to pack the rest of the arguments into a Ruby array. A & means that an attached code block will be taken and assigned to the given variable (if no code block was given, Qnil will be assigned). After the *fmt* string, pointers to VALUE are given (as with scanf) to which the arguments are assigned.

```
VALUE name, one, two, rest;
rb_scan_args(argc, argv, "12", &name, &one, &two);
rb_scan_args(argc, argv, "1*", &name, &rest);
```

void **rb_undef_method**(VALUE classmod, const char *name)

> Undefines the given method *name* in the given *classmod* class or module.

void **rb_define_alias**(VALUE classmod, const char *newname,
                          const char *oldname)

> Defines an alias for *oldname* in class or module *classmod*.

API: Defining Variables and Constants

void **rb_define_const**(VALUE classmod, char *name, VALUE value)

> Defines a constant in the class or module *classmod*, with the given *name* and *value*.

void **rb_define_global_const**(char *name, VALUE value)

> Defines a global constant with the given *name* and *value*.

void **rb_define_variable**(const char *name, VALUE *object)

> Exports the address of the given *object* that was created in C to the Ruby namespace as *name*. From Ruby, this will be a global variable, so *name* should start with a leading dollar sign. Be sure to honor Ruby's rules for allowed variable names; illegally named variables will not be accessible from Ruby.

void **rb_define_class_variable**(VALUE class, const char *name, VALUE val)

> Defines a class variable *name* (which must be specified with a @@ prefix) in the given *class*, initialized to *value*.

void **rb_define_virtual_variable**(const char *name, VALUE(*getter)(), void(*setter)())

> Exports a virtual variable to a Ruby namespace as the global $*name*. No actual storage exists for the variable; attempts to get and set the value will call the given functions with the prototypes.

```
VALUE getter(ID id, VALUE *data,
        struct global_entry *entry);
void setter(VALUE value, ID id, VALUE *data,
        struct global_entry *entry);
```

> You will likely not need to use the *entry* parameter and can safely omit it from your function declarations.

void **rb_define_hooked_variable**(const char *name, VALUE *variable, VALUE(*getter)(), void(*setter)())

> Defines functions to be called when reading or writing to *variable*. See also rb_define_virtual_variable.

void **rb_define_readonly_variable**(const char *name, VALUE *value)

> Same as rb_define_variable, but read-only from Ruby.

void **rb_define_attr**(VALUE variable, const char *name, int read,
                   int write)

> Creates accessor methods for the given *variable*, with the given *name*. If *read* is nonzero, create a read method; if *write* is nonzero, create a write method.

void **rb_global_variable**(VALUE *obj)

> Registers the given address with the garbage collector.

API: Calling Methods

VALUE **rb_class_new_instance**((int argc, VALUE *argv,
                         VALUE klass))

> Return a new instance of class *klass*. *argv* is a pointer to an array of *argc* parameters.

VALUE **rb_funcall**(VALUE recv, ID id, int argc, ...)

> Invokes the method given by *id* in the object *recv* with the given number of arguments *argc* and the arguments themselves (possibly none).

VALUE **rb_funcall2**(VALUE recv, ID id, int argc, VALUE *args)

> Invokes the method given by *id* in the object *recv* with the given number of arguments *argc* and the arguments themselves given in the C array *args*.

VALUE **rb_funcall3**(VALUE recv, ID id, int argc, VALUE *args)

> Same as rb_funcall2 but will not call private methods.

VALUE **rb_apply**(VALUE recv, ID name, int argc, VALUE args)

> Invokes the method given by *id* in the object *recv* with the given number of arguments *argc* and the arguments themselves given in the Ruby Array *args*.

ID **rb_intern**(char *name)

> Returns an ID for a given *name*. If the name does not exist, a symbol table entry will be created for it.

char * **rb_id2name**(ID id)

> Returns a name for the given *id*.

VALUE **rb_call_super**(int argc, VALUE *args)

> Calls the current method in the superclass of the current object.

API: Exceptions

void **rb_raise**(VALUE exception, const char *fmt, ...)

>Raises an *exception*. The given string *fmt* and remaining arguments are interpreted as with printf.

void **rb_fatal**(const char *fmt, ...)

>Raises a Fatal exception, terminating the process. No rescue blocks are called, but ensure blocks will be called. The given string *fmt* and remaining arguments are interpreted as with printf.

void **rb_bug**(const char *fmt, ...)

>Terminates the process immediately—no handlers of any sort will be called. The given string *fmt* and remaining arguments are interpreted as with printf. You should call this function only if a fatal bug has been exposed. You don't write fatal bugs, do you?

void **rb_sys_fail**(const char *msg)

>Raises a platform-specific exception corresponding to the last known system error, with the given *msg*.

VALUE **rb_rescue**(VALUE (*body)(), VALUE args, VALUE(*rescue)(), VALUE rargs)

>Executes *body* with the given *args*. If a StandardError exception is raised, then execute *rescue* with the given *rargs*.

VALUE **rb_ensure**(VALUE(*body)(), VALUE args, VALUE(*ensure)(), VALUE eargs)

>Executes *body* with the given *args*. Whether or not an exception is raised, execute *ensure* with the given *eargs* after *body* has completed.

VALUE **rb_protect**(VALUE (*body)(), VALUE args, int *result)

>Executes *body* with the given *args* and returns nonzero in *result* if any exception was raised.

void **rb_notimplement**( )

>Raises a NotImpError exception to indicate that the enclosed function is not implemented yet or not available on this platform.

void **rb_exit**(int status)

>Exits Ruby with the given *status*. Raises a SystemExit exception and calls registered exit functions and finalizers.

void **rb_warn**(const char *fmt, ...)

> Unconditionally issues a warning message to standard error. The given string *fmt* and remaining arguments are interpreted as with printf.

void **rb_warning**(const char *fmt, ...)

> Conditionally issues a warning message to standard error if Ruby was invoked with the –w flag. The given string *fmt* and remaining arguments are interpreted as with printf.

API: Iterators

void **rb_iter_break**( )

> Breaks out of the enclosing iterator block.

VALUE **rb_each**(VALUE obj)

> Invokes the each method of the given *obj*.

VALUE **rb_yield**(VALUE arg)

> Transfers execution to the iterator block in the current context, passing *arg* as an argument. Multiple values may be passed in an array.

int **rb_block_given_p**( )

> Returns true if yield would execute a block in the current context— that is, if a code block was passed to the current method and is available to be called.

VALUE **rb_iterate**(VALUE (*method)(), VALUE args,
            VALUE (*block)(), VALUE arg2)

> Invokes *method* with argument *args* and block *block*. A yield from that method will invoke *block* with the argument given to yield and a second argument *arg2*.

VALUE **rb_catch**(const char *tag, VALUE (*proc)(), VALUE value)

> Equivalent to Ruby catch.

void **rb_throw**(const char *tag , VALUE value)

> Equivalent to Ruby throw.

API: Accessing Variables

VALUE **rb_iv_get**(VALUE obj, char *name)

> Returns the instance variable *name* (which must be specified with a @ prefix) from the given *obj*.

VALUE **rb_ivar_get**(VALUE obj, ID name)
>Returns the instance variable *name* from the given *obj*.

VALUE **rb_iv_set**(VALUE obj, char *name, VALUE value)
>Sets the value of the instance variable *name* (which must be specified with a @ prefix) in the given *obj* to *value*. Returns *value*.

VALUE **rb_ivar_set**(VALUE obj, ID name, VALUE value)
>Sets the value of the instance variable *name* in the given *obj* to *value*. Returns *value*.

VALUE **rb_gv_set**(const char *name, VALUE value)
>Sets the global variable *name* (the $ prefix is optional) to *value*. Returns *value*.

VALUE **rb_gv_get**(const char *name)
>Returns the global variable *name* (the $ prefix is optional).

void **rb_cvar_set**(VALUE class, ID name, VALUE val, int unused)
>Sets the class variable *name* in the given *class* to *value*.

VALUE **rb_cvar_get**(VALUE class, ID name)
>Returns the class variable *name* from the given *class*.

int **rb_cvar_defined**(VALUE class, ID name)
>Returns Qtrue if the given class variable *name* has been defined for *class*; otherwise, returns Qfalse.

void **rb_cv_set**(VALUE class, const char *name, VALUE val)
>Sets the class variable *name* (which must be specified with a @@ prefix) in the given *class* to *value*.

VALUE **rb_cv_get**(VALUE class, const char *name)
>Returns the class variable *name* (which must be specified with a @@ prefix) from the given *class*.

API: Object Status

OBJ_TAINT(VALUE obj)
>Marks the given *obj* as tainted.

int **OBJ_TAINTED**(VALUE obj)
>Returns nonzero if the given *obj* is tainted.

OBJ_FREEZE(VALUE obj)
>Marks the given *obj* as frozen.

int **OBJ_FROZEN**(VALUE obj)
> Returns nonzero if the given *obj* is frozen.

SafeStringValue(VALUE str)
> Raises SecurityError if current safe level > 0 and *str* is tainted, or raises a TypeError if *str* is not a T_STRING or if $SAFE >= 4.

int **rb_safe_level**( )
> Returns the current safe level.

void **rb_secure**(int level)
> Raises SecurityError if *level* <= current safe level.

void **rb_set_safe_level**(int newlevel)
> Sets the current safe level to *newlevel*.

API: Commonly Used Methods

VALUE **rb_ary_new**( )
> Returns a new Array with default size.

VALUE **rb_ary_new2**(long length)
> Returns a new Array of the given *length*.

VALUE **rb_ary_new3**(long length, ...)
> Returns a new Array of the given *length* and populated with the remaining arguments.

VALUE **rb_ary_new4**(long length, VALUE *values)
> Returns a new Array of the given *length* and populated with the C array *values*.

void **rb_ary_store**(VALUE self, long index, VALUE value)
> Stores *value* at *index* in array *self*.

VALUE **rb_ary_push**(VALUE self, VALUE value)
> Pushes *value* onto the end of array *self*. Returns *value*.

VALUE **rb_ary_pop**(VALUE self)
> Removes and returns the last element from the array *self*.

VALUE **rb_ary_shift**(VALUE self)
> Removes and returns the first element from the array *self*.

VALUE **rb_ary_unshift**(VALUE self, VALUE value)
> Pushes *value* onto the front of array *self*. Returns *value*.

VALUE **rb_ary_entry**(VALUE self, long index)
> Returns array *self*'s element at *index*.

int **rb_respond_to**(VALUE self, ID method)
> Returns nonzero if *self* responds to *method*.

VALUE **rb_thread_create**(VALUE (*func)(), void *data)
> Runs *func* in a new thread, passing *data* as an argument.

VALUE **rb_hash_new**( )
> Returns a new, empty Hash.

VALUE **rb_hash_aref**(VALUE self, VALUE key)
> Returns the element corresponding to *key* in *self*.

VALUE **rb_hash_aset**(VALUE self, VALUE key, VALUE value)
> Sets the value for *key* to *value* in *self*. Returns *value*.

VALUE **rb_obj_is_instance_of**(VALUE obj, VALUE klass)
> Returns Qtrue if *obj* is an instance of *klass*.

VALUE **rb_obj_is_kind_of**(VALUE obj, VALUE klass)
> Returns Qtrue if *klass* is the class of *obj* or *class* is one of the super-classes of the class of *obj*.

VALUE **rb_str_new**(const char *src, long length)
> Returns a new String initialized with *length* characters from *src*.

VALUE **rb_str_new2**(const char *src)
> Returns a new String initialized with the null-terminated C string *src*.

VALUE **rb_str_dup**(VALUE str)
> Returns a new String object duplicated from *str*.

VALUE **rb_str_cat**(VALUE self, const char *src, long length)
> Concatenates *length* characters from the string *src* onto the String *self*. Returns *self*.

VALUE **rb_str_concat**(VALUE self, VALUE other)
> Concatenates *other* onto the String *self*. Returns *self*.

VALUE **rb_str_split**(VALUE self, const char *delim)
> Returns an array of String objects created by splitting *self* on *delim*.

Part III

Ruby Crystallized

## Chapter 22

The Ruby Language

This chapter is a bottom-up look at the Ruby language. Most of what appears here is the syntax and semantics of the language itself—we mostly ignore the built-in classes and modules (these are covered in depth starting on page 423). However, Ruby sometimes implements features in its libraries that in most languages would be part of the basic syntax. We've included these methods here and have tried to flag them with "Library" in the margin.

The contents of this chapter may look familiar—with good reason. We've covered just about all of this in the earlier tutorial chapters. Consider this chapter to be a self-contained reference to the core Ruby language.

Source Layout

Ruby programs are written in 7-bit ASCII, Kanji (using EUC or SJIS), or UTF-8. If a code set other than 7-bit ASCII is used, the KCODE option must be set appropriately, as shown on page 179.

Ruby is a line-oriented language. Ruby expressions and statements are terminated at the end of a line unless the parser can determine that the statement is incomplete—for example if the last token on a line is an operator or comma. A semicolon can be used to separate multiple expressions on a line. You can also put a backslash at the end of a line to continue it onto the next. Comments start with # and run to the end of the physical line. Comments are ignored during syntax analysis.

```
a = 1
b = 2; c = 3
d = 4 + 5 +
    6 + 7        # no '\' needed
e = 8 + 9   \
    + 10         # '\' needed
```

Physical lines between a line starting with =begin and a line starting with =end are ignored by Ruby and may be used to comment out sections of code or to embed documentation.

Ruby reads its program input in a single pass, so you can pipe programs to the Ruby interpreter's standard input stream.

```
echo 'puts "Hello"' | ruby
```

If Ruby comes across a line anywhere in the source containing just "__END__", with no leading or trailing whitespace, it treats that line as the end of the program—any subsequent lines will not be treated as program code. However, these lines can be read into the running program using the global IO object DATA, described on page 337.

BEGIN and END Blocks

Every Ruby source file can declare blocks of code to be run as the file is being loaded (the BEGIN blocks) and after the program has finished executing (the END blocks).

```
BEGIN {
   begin code
}

END {
   end code
}
```

A program may include multiple BEGIN and END blocks. BEGIN blocks are executed in the order they are encountered. END blocks are executed in reverse order.

General Delimited Input

As well as the normal quoting mechanism, alternative forms of literal strings, arrays, regular expressions, and shell commands are specified using a generalized delimited syntax. All these literals start with a percent character, followed by a single character that identifies the literal's type. These characters are summarized in Table 22.1 on the facing page; the actual literals are described in the corresponding sections later in this chapter.

Following the type character is a delimiter, which can be any nonalphabetic or non-multibyte character. If the delimiter is one of the characters (, [, {, or <, the literal consists of the characters up to the matching closing delimiter, taking account of nested delimiter pairs. For all other delimiters, the literal comprises the characters up to the next occurrence of the delimiter character.

```
%q/this is a string/
%q-string-
%q(a (nested) string)
```

Table 22.1. General delimited input

Type	Meaning	See Page
%q	Single-quoted string	320
%Q, %	Double-quoted string	320
%w, %W	Array of strings	322
%r	Regular expression pattern	324
%x	Shell command	338

Delimited strings may continue over multiple lines; the line endings and all spaces at the start of continuation lines will be included in the string.

```
meth = %q{def fred(a)
          a.each {|i| puts i }
        end}
```

The Basic Types

The basic types in Ruby are numbers, strings, arrays, hashes, ranges, symbols, and regular expressions.

Integer and Floating-Point Numbers

Ruby integers are objects of class Fixnum or Bignum. Fixnum objects hold integers that fit within the native machine word minus 1 bit. Whenever a Fixnum exceeds this range, it is automatically converted to a Bignum object, whose range is effectively limited only by available memory. If an operation with a Bignum result has a final value that will fit in a Fixnum, the result will be returned as a Fixnum.

Integers are written using an optional leading sign, an optional base indicator (0 for octal, 0d for decimal, 0x for hex, or 0b for binary), followed by a string of digits in the appropriate base. Underscore characters are ignored in the digit string.

```
123456                    => 123456    # Fixnum
0d123456                  => 123456    # Fixnum
123_456                   => 123456    # Fixnum - underscore ignored
-543                      => -543      # Fixnum - negative number
0xaabb                    => 43707     # Fixnum - hexadecimal
0377                      => 255       # Fixnum - octal
-0b10_1010                => -42       # Fixnum - binary (negated)
123_456_789_123_456_789   => 123456789123456789 # Bignum
```

You can get the integer value corresponding to an ASCII character by preceding that character with a question mark. Control characters can be generated using ?\C-*x* and

?\c*x* (the control version of *x* is x&0x9f). Meta characters (x | 0x80) can be generated using ?\M-*x*. The combination of meta and control is generated using and ?\M-\C-*x*. You can get the integer value of a backslash character using the sequence ?\\.

```
?a           => 97    # ASCII character
?\n          => 10    # code for a newline (0x0a)
?\C-a        => 1     # control a = ?A & 0x9f = 0x01
?\M-a        => 225   # meta sets bit 7
?\M-\C-a     => 129   # meta and control a
?\C-?        => 127   # delete character
```

A numeric literal with a decimal point and/or an exponent is turned into a Float object, corresponding to the native architecture's double data type. You must follow the decimal point with a digit, as 1.e3 tries to invoke the method e3 in class Fixnum. As of Ruby 1.8 you must also place at least one digit before the decimal point.

1.8

```
12.34        →    12.34
-0.1234e2    →    -12.34
1234e-2      →    12.34
```

Strings

Ruby provides a number of mechanisms for creating literal strings. Each generates objects of type String. The different mechanisms vary in terms of how a string is delimited and how much substitution is done on the literal's content.

Single-quoted string literals ('*stuff*' and %q/*stuff*/) undergo the least substitution. Both convert the sequence \\ into a single backslash, and the form with single quotes converts \' into a single quote. All other backslashes appear literally in the string.

```
'hello'                     →    hello
'a backslash \'\\''         →    a backslash '\'
%q/simple string/           →    simple string
%q(nesting (really) works)  →    nesting (really) works
%q no_blanks_here ;         →    no_blanks_here
```

Double-quoted strings ("*stuff*", %Q/*stuff*/, and %/*stuff*/) undergo additional substitutions, shown in Table 22.2 on the next page.

```
a   = 123
"\123mile"                  →    Smile
"Say \"Hello\""             →    Say "Hello"
%Q!"I said 'nuts'," I said! →    "I said 'nuts'," I said
%Q{Try #{a + 1}, not #{a - 1}} →  Try 124, not 122
%<Try #{a + 1}, not #{a - 1}> →   Try 124, not 122
"Try #{a + 1}, not #{a - 1}" →    Try 124, not 122
%{ #{ a = 1; b = 2; a + b } } →    3
```

Strings can continue across multiple input lines, in which case they will contain newline characters. It is also possible to use here documents to express long string literals. Whenever Ruby parses the sequence <<*identifier* or <<*quoted string*, it replaces it with

Table 22.2. Substitutions in double-quoted strings			
\a	Bell/alert (0x07)	\nnn	Octal *nnn*
\b	Backspace (0x08)	\xnn	Hex *nn*
\e	Escapc (0x1b)	\cx	Control-*x*
\f	Formfeed (0x0c)	\C-x	Control-*x*
\n	Newline (0x0a)	\M-x	Meta-*x*
\r	Return (0x0d)	\M-\C-x	Meta-control-*x*
\s	Space (0x20)	\x	*x*
\t	Tab (0x09)	#{code}	Value of *code*
\v	Vertical tab (0x0b)		

a string literal built from successive logical input lines. It stops building the string when it finds a line that starts with *identifier* or *quoted string*. You can put a minus sign immediately after the << characters, in which case the terminator can be indented from the left margin. If a quoted string was used to specify the terminator, its quoting rules will be applied to the here document; otherwise, double-quoting rules apply.

```
print <<HERE
Double quoted \
here document.
It is #{Time.now}
HERE

print <<-'THERE'
    This is single quoted.
    The above used #{Time.now}
    THERE
```

produces:

```
Double quoted here document.
It is Thu Aug 26 22:37:12 CDT 2004
    This is single quoted.
    The above used #{Time.now}
```

Adjacent single- and double-quoted strings in the input are concatenated to form a single String object.

```
'Con' "cat" 'en' "ate"   →   "Concatenate"
```

Strings are stored as sequences of 8-bit bytes,[1] and each byte may contain any of the 256 8-bit values, including null and newline. The substitution sequences in Table 22.2 allow nonprinting characters to be inserted conveniently and portably.

---

1.   For use in Japan, the jcode library supports a set of operations of strings written with EUC, SJIS, or UTF-8 encoding. The underlying string, however, is still accessed as a series of bytes.

Every time a string literal is used in an assignment or as a parameter, a new `String` object is created.

```
3.times do
  print 'hello'.object_id, " "
end
```

produces:

```
937140 937110 937080
```

The documentation for class `String` starts on page 606.

Ranges

Outside the context of a conditional expression, *expr*..*expr* and *expr*...*expr* construct `Range` objects. The two-dot form is an inclusive range; the one with three dots is a range that excludes its last element. See the description of class `Range` on page 597 for details. Also see the description of conditional expressions on page 342 for other uses of ranges.

Arrays

Literals of class `Array` are created by placing a comma-separated series of object references between square brackets. A trailing comma is ignored.

```
arr = [ fred, 10, 3.14, "This is a string", barney("pebbles"), ]
```

1.8 Arrays of strings can be constructed using the shortcut notations %w and %W. The lowercase form extracts space-separated tokens into successive elements of the array. No substitution is performed on the individual strings. The uppercase version also converts the words to an array, but performs all the normal double-quoted string substitutions on each individual word. A space between words can be escaped with a backslash. This is a form of general delimited input, described on pages 318–319.

```
arr = %w( fred wilma barney betty great\ gazoo )
arr   →   ["fred", "wilma", "barney", "betty", "great gazoo"]
arr = %w( Hey!\tIt is now -#{Time.now}- )
arr   →   ["Hey!\\tIt", "is", "now", "-#{Time.now}-"]
arr = %W( Hey!\tIt is now -#{Time.now}- )
arr   →   ["Hey!\tIt", "is", "now", "-Thu Aug 26 22:37:13 CDT 2004-"]
```

Hashes

A literal Ruby `Hash` is created by placing a list of key/value pairs between braces, with either a comma or the sequence => between the key and the value. A trailing comma is ignored.

```
colors = { "red"   => 0xf00,
           "green" => 0x0f0,
           "blue"  => 0x00f
         }
```

There is no requirement for the keys and/or values in a particular hash to have the same type.

Requirements for a Hash Key

Hash keys must respond to the message hash by returning a hash code, and the hash code for a given key must not change. The keys used in hashes must also be comparable using eql?. If eql? returns true for two keys, then those keys must also have the same hash code. This means that certain classes (such as Array and Hash) can't conveniently be used as keys, because their hash values can change based on their contents.

If you keep an external reference to an object that is used as a key, and use that reference to alter the object, thus changing its hash code, the hash lookup based on that key may not work.

Because strings are the most frequently used keys, and because string contents are often changed, Ruby treats string keys specially. If you use a String object as a hash key, the hash will duplicate the string internally and will use that copy as its key. The copy will be frozen. Any changes made to the original string will not affect the hash.

If you write your own classes and use instances of them as hash keys, you need to make sure that either (a) the hashes of the key objects don't change once the objects have been created or (b) you remember to call the Hash#rehash method to reindex the hash whenever a key hash *is* changed.

Symbols

A Ruby symbol is an identifier corresponding to a string of characters, often a name. You construct the symbol for a name by preceding the name with a colon, and you can construct the symbol for an arbitrary string by preceding a string literal with a colon. Substitution occurs in double-quoted strings. A particular name or string will always generate the same symbol, regardless of how that name is used within the program.

```
:Object
:my_variable
:"Ruby rules"
a = "cat"
:'catsup'    →    :catsup
:"#{a}sup"   →    :catsup
:'#{a}sup'   →    :"\#{a}sup"
```

Other languages call this process *interning,* and call symbols *atoms.*

Regular Expressions

Regular expression literals are objects of type Regexp. They are created explicitly by calling the Regexp.new constructor or implicitly by using the literal forms, */pattern/* and %r{*pattern*}. The %r construct is a form of general delimited input (described on pages 318–319).

```
/pattern/
/pattern/options
%r{pattern}
%r{pattern}options
Regexp.new( 'pattern' [ , options ] )
```

Regular Expression Options

A regular expression may include one or more options that modify the way the pattern matches strings. If you're using literals to create the Regexp object, then the options are one or more characters placed immediately after the terminator. If you're using Regexp.new, the options are constants used as the second parameter of the constructor.

i   *Case Insensitive.* The pattern match will ignore the case of letters in the pattern and string. Setting $= to make matches case insensitive is now deprecated.

o   *Substitute Once.* Any #... substitutions in a particular regular expression literal will be performed just once, the first time it is evaluated. Otherwise, the substitutions will be performed every time the literal generates a Regexp object.

m   *Multiline Mode.* Normally, "." matches any character except a newline. With the /m option, "." matches any character.

x   *Extended Mode.* Complex regular expressions can be difficult to read. The x option allows you to insert spaces, newlines, and comments in the pattern to make it more readable.

Another set of options allows you to set the language encoding of the regular expression. If none of these options is specified, the interpreter's default encoding (set using –K or $KCODE) is used.

n:	no encoding (ASCII)	e:	EUC
s:	SJIS	u:	UTF-8

Regular Expression Patterns

regular characters

All characters except ., |, (,), [, \, ^, {, +, $, *, and ? match themselves. To match one of these characters, precede it with a backslash.

^   Matches the beginning of a line.

$ Matches the end of a line.

\A   Matches the beginning of the string.

\z	Matches the end of the string.
\Z	Matches the end of the string *unless* the string ends with a \n, in which case it matches just before the \n.
\b, \B	Match word boundaries and nonword boundaries respectively.
\G	The position where a previous repetitive search completed (but only in some situations). See the additional information on the following page.
[*characters*]	A bracket expression matches any of a list of characters between the brackets. The characters . | ( ) [{ + ^ $ * ?, which have special meanings elsewhere in patterns, lose their special significance between brackets. The sequences *nnn*, \x*nn*, \c*x*, \C-*x*, \M-*x*, and \M-\C-*x* have the meanings shown in Table 22.2 on page 321. The sequences \d, \D, \s, \S, \w, and \W are abbreviations for groups of characters, as shown in Table 5.1 on page 72. The sequence [:*class*:] matches a POSIX character class, also shown in Table 5.1 on page 72. (Note that the open and close brackets are part of the class, so the pattern /[_[:digit:]]/ would match a digit or an underscore.) The sequence c_1-c_2 represents all the characters between c_1 and c_2, inclusive. Literal] or – characters must appear immediately after the opening bracket. A caret character (^) immediately following the opening bracket negates the sense of the match—the pattern matches any character that isn't in the character class.
\d, \s, \w	Abbreviations for character classes that match digits, whitespace, and word characters, respectively. These abbreviations are summarized in Table 5.1 on page 72.
\D, \S, \W	The negated forms of \d, \s, and \w, matching characters that are not digits, whitespace, or word characters.
. (period)	Appearing outside brackets, matches any character except a newline. (With the /m option, it matches newline, too).
re∗	Matches zero or more occurrences of *re*.
re+	Matches one or more occurrences of *re*.
re{m,n}	Matches at least "m" and at most "n" occurrences of *re*.
re{m,}	Matches at least "m" occurrences of *re*.
re{m}	Matches exactly "m" occurrences of *re*.
re?	Matches zero or one occurrence of *re*. The ∗, +, and {m,n} modifiers are greedy by default. Append a question mark to make them minimal.
re1|*re2*	Matches either *re1* or *re2*. | has a low precedence.

(...) Parentheses are used to group regular expressions. For example, the pattern /abc+/ matches a string containing an *a*, a *b*, and one or more *c*'s. /(abc)+/ matches one or more sequences of *abc*. Parentheses are also used to collect the results of pattern matching. For each opening parenthesis, Ruby stores the result of the partial match between it and the corresponding closing parenthesis as successive groups. Within the same pattern, \1 refers to the match of the first group, \2 the second group, and so on. Outside the pattern, the special variables $1, $2, and so on, serve the same purpose.

1.8 The anchor \G works with the repeating match methods `String#gsub`, `String#gsub!`, `String#index`, and `String#scan`. In a repetitive match, it represents the position in the string where the last match in the iteration ended. \G initially points to the start of the string (or to the character referenced by the second parameter of `String#index`).

```
"a01b23c45 d56".scan(/[a-z]\d+/)    →    ["a01", "b23", "c45", "d56"]
"a01b23c45 d56".scan(/\G[a-z]\d+/)  →    ["a01", "b23", "c45"]
"a01b23c45 d56".scan(/\A[a-z]\d+/)  →    ["a01"]
```

Substitutions

#{...} Performs an expression substitution, as with strings. By default, the substitution is performed each time a regular expression literal is evaluated. With the /o option, it is performed just the first time.

\0, \1, \2, ... \9, \&, \\`, \', \+
Substitutes the value matched by the *n*th grouped subexpression, or by the entire match, pre- or postmatch, or the highest group.

Regular Expression Extensions

In common with Perl and Python, Ruby regular expressions offer some extensions over traditional Unix regular expressions. All the extensions are entered between the characters (? and). The parentheses that bracket these extensions are groups, but they do not generate back references: they do not set the values of \1 and $1 etc.

(?# *comment*)
Inserts a comment into the pattern. The content is ignored during pattern matching.

(?:*re*) Makes *re* into a group without generating backreferences. This is often useful when you need to group a set of constructs but don't want the group to set the value of $1 or whatever. In the example that follows, both patterns match a date with either colons or spaces between the month, day, and year. The first form stores the separator character in $2 and $4, but the second pattern doesn't store the separator in an external variable.

```
date = "12/25/01"
date =~ %r{(\d+)(/|:)(\d+)(/|:)(\d+)}
[$1,$2,$3,$4,$5]   →   ["12", "/", "25", "/", "01"]
date =~ %r{(\d+)(?:/|:)(\d+)(?:/|:)(\d+)}
[$1,$2,$3]         →   ["12", "25", "01"]
```

(?=*re*)   Matches *re* at this point, but does not consume it (also known charmingly as *zero-width positive lookahead*). This lets you look forward for the context of a match without affecting $&. In this example, the scan method matches words followed by a comma, but the commas are not included in the result.

```
str = "red, white, and blue"
str.scan(/[a-z]+(?=,)/)   →   ["red", "white"]
```

(?!*re*)   Matches if *re* does not match at this point. Does not consume the match (zero-width negative lookahead). For example, /hot(?!dog)(\w+)/ matches any word that contains the letters *hot* that aren't followed by *dog*, returning the end of the word in $1.

(?>*re*)   Nests an independent regular expression within the first regular expression.anchored at the current match position. If it consumes characters, these will no longer be available to the higher-level regular expression. This construct therefore inhibits backtracking, which can be a performance enhancement. For example, the pattern /a.*b.*a/ takes exponential time when matched against a string containing an *a* followed by a number of *b*'s, but with no trailing *a*. However, in some cases this can be avoided by using a nested regular expression /a(?>.*b).*a/. In this form, the nested expression consumes all the input string up to the last possible *b* character. When the check for a trailing *a* then fails, there is no need to backtrack, and the pattern match fails promptly. (This pattern has different semantics than the original if the match shouldn't go up to the last *b*.)

```
require 'benchmark'
include Benchmark

str = "a" + ("b" * 5000)

bm(8) do |test|
  test.report("Normal:") { str =~ /^a.*b.*a/ }
  test.report("Nested:") { str =~ /^a(?>.*b).*a/ }
end
```

produces:

```
                user      system      total        real
Normal:      0.460000   0.010000   0.470000 (  0.466996)
Nested:      0.000000   0.000000   0.000000 (  0.000435)
```

(?imx)   Turns on the corresponding i, m, or x option. If used inside a group, the effect is limited to that group.

(?-imx)	Turns off the i, m, or x option.
(?imx:*re*)	Turns on the i, m, or x option for *re*.
(?-imx:*re*)	Turns off the i, m, or x option for *re*.

Names

Ruby names are used to refer to constants, variables, methods, classes, and modules. The first character of a name helps Ruby to distinguish its intended use. Certain names, listed in Table 22.3 on the next page, are reserved words and should not be used as variable, method, class, or module names.

Method names are described in the section beginning on page 345.

In these descriptions, *lowercase letter* means the characters *a* though *z*, as well as _, the underscore. *Uppercase letter* means *A* though *Z*, and *digit* means *0* through *9*. A *name* is an uppercase letter, lowercase letter, or an underscore, followed by *name characters*: any combination of upper- and lowercase letters, underscores, and digits.

A **local variable name** consists of a lowercase letter followed by name characters. It is conventional to use underscores rather than camelCase to write multiword names, but the interpreter does not enforce this.

```
fred  anObject  _x  three_two_one
```

An **instance variable name** starts with an "at" sign (@) followed by a name. It is generally a good idea to use a lowercase letter after the @.

```
@name  @_  @size
```

A **class variable name** starts with two "at" signs (@@) followed by a name.

```
@@name  @@_  @@Size
```

A **constant name** starts with an uppercase letter followed by name characters. Class names and module names are constants and follow the constant naming conventions. By convention, constant object references are normally spelled using uppercase letters and underscores throughout, while class and module names are MixedCase.

```
module Math
  ALMOST_PI = 22.0/7.0
end
class BigBlob
end
```

Global variables, and some special system variables, start with a dollar sign ($) followed by name characters. In addition, Ruby defines a set of two-character global variable names in which the second character is a punctuation character. These predefined

Table 22.3. Reserved words

__FILE__	and	def	end	in	or	self	unless
__LINE__	begin	defined?	ensure	module	redo	super	until
BEGIN	break	do	false	next	rescue	then	when
END	case	else	for	nil	retry	true	while
alias	class	elsif	if	not	return	undef	yield

variables are listed starting on page 333. Finally, a global variable name can be formed using $- followed by a single letter or underscore. These latter variables typically mirror the setting of the corresponding command-line option (see the table starting on page 335 for details).

```
$params  $PROGRAM  $!  $_  $-a  $-K
```

Variable/Method Ambiguity

When Ruby sees a name such as a in an expression, it needs to determine if it is a local variable reference or a call to a method with no parameters. To decide which is the case, Ruby uses a heuristic. As Ruby parses a source file, it keeps track of symbols that have been assigned to. It assumes that these symbols are variables. When it subsequently comes across a symbol that could be a variable or a method call, it checks to see if it has seen a prior assignment to that symbol. If so, it treats the symbol as a variable; otherwise it treats it as a method call. As a somewhat pathological case of this, consider the following code fragment, submitted by Clemens Hintze.

```
def a
  print "Function 'a' called\n"
  99
end
for i in 1..2
  if i == 2
    print "a=", a, "\n"
  else
    a = 1
    print "a=", a, "\n"
  end
end
```

produces:

```
a=1
Function 'a' called
a=99
```

During the parse, Ruby sees the use of a in the first print statement and, as it hasn't yet seen any assignment to a, assumes that it is a method call. By the time it gets to the second print statement, though, it *has* seen an assignment, and so treats a as a variable.

Note that the assignment does not have to be executed—Ruby just has to have seen it. This program does not raise an error.

```
a = 1 if false; a
```

Variables and Constants

Ruby variables and constants hold references to objects. Variables themselves do not have an intrinsic type. Instead, the type of a variable is defined solely by the messages to which the object referenced by the variable responds.[2]

A Ruby *constant* is also a reference to an object. Constants are created when they are first assigned to (normally in a class or module definition). Ruby, unlike less flexible languages, lets you alter the value of a constant, although this will generate a warning message.

```
MY_CONST = 1
MY_CONST = 2    # generates a warning
```

produces:

```
prog.rb:2: warning: already initialized constant MY_CONST
```

Note that although constants should not be changed, you can alter the internal states of the objects they reference.

```
MY_CONST = "Tim"
MY_CONST[0] = "J"    # alter string referenced by constant
MY_CONST    →    "Jim"
```

Assignment potentially *aliases* objects, giving the same object different names.

Scope of Constants and Variables

Constants defined within a class or module may be accessed unadorned anywhere within the class or module. Outside the class or module, they may be accessed using the scope operator, :: prefixed by an expression that returns the appropriate class or module object. Constants defined outside any class or module may be accessed unadorned or by using the scope operator :: with no prefix. Constants may not be defined in methods. Constants may be added to existing classes and modules from the outside by using the class or module name and the scope operator before the constant name.

```
OUTER_CONST = 99
```

---

2.   When we say that a variable is not typed, we mean that any given variable can at different times hold references to objects of many different types.

```
class Const
  def get_const
    CONST
  end
  CONST = OUTER_CONST + 1
end

Const.new.get_const  →   100
Const::CONST         →   100
::OUTER_CONST        →   99
Const::NEW_CONST = 123
```

Global variables are available throughout a program. Every reference to a particular global name returns the same object. Referencing an uninitialized global variable returns nil.

Class variables are available throughout a class or module body. Class variables must be initialized before use. A class variable is shared among all instances of a class and is available within the class itself.

```
class Song
  @@count = 0
  def initialize
    @@count += 1
  end
  def Song.get_count
    @@count
  end
end
```

Class variables belong to the innermost enclosing class or module. Class variables used at the top level are defined in Object and behave like global variables. Class variables defined within singleton methods belong to the top level (although this usage is deprecated and generates a warning). In Ruby 1.9, class variables will be private to the defining class.

1.8

```
class Holder
  @@var = 99
  def Holder.var=(val)
    @@var = val
  end
  def var
    @@var
  end
end
@@var = "top level variable"
a = Holder.new

a.var  →   99

Holder.var = 123
a.var  →   123
```

```
# This references the top-level object
def a.get_var
  @@var
end
a.get_var   →   "top level variable"
```

Class variables are shared by children of the class in which they are first defined.

```
class Top
  @@A = 1
  def dump
    puts values
  end
  def values
    "#{self.class.name}: A = #@@A"
  end
end
class MiddleOne < Top
  @@B = 2
  def values
    super + ", B = #@@B"
  end
end
class MiddleTwo < Top
  @@B = 3
  def values
    super + ", B = #@@B"
  end
end
class BottomOne < MiddleOne; end
class BottomTwo < MiddleTwo; end

Top.new.dump
MiddleOne.new.dump
MiddleTwo.new.dump
BottomOne.new.dump
BottomTwo.new.dump
```

produces:

```
Top: A = 1
MiddleOne: A = 1, B = 2
MiddleTwo: A = 1, B = 3
BottomOne: A = 1, B = 2
BottomTwo: A = 1, B = 3
```

Instance variables are available within instance methods throughout a class body. Referencing an uninitialized instance variable returns nil. Each instance of a class has a unique set of instance variables. Instance variables are not available to class methods (although classes (and modules) also may have instance variables—see page 388).

Local variables are unique in that their scopes are statically determined but their existence is established dynamically.

A local variable is created dynamically when it is first assigned a value during program execution. However, the scope of a local variable is statically determined to be the immediately enclosing block, method definition, class definition, module definition, or top-level program. Referencing a local variable that is in scope but that has not yet been created generates a NameError exception. Local variables with the same name are different variables if they appear in disjoint scopes.

Method parameters are considered to be variables local to that method.

Block parameters are assigned values when the block is invoked.

```
a = [ 1, 2, 3 ]
a.each {|i|  puts i  } # i local to block
a.each {|$i| puts $i } # assigns to global $i
a.each {|@i| puts @i } # assigns to instance variable @i
a.each {|I|  puts I  } # generates warning assigning to constant
a.each {|b.meth| }     # invokes meth= in object b
sum = 0
var = nil
a.each {|var| sum += var } # uses sum and var from enclosing scope
```

If a local variable (including a block parameter) is first assigned in a block, it is local to the block. If instead a variable of the same name is already established at the time the block executes, the block will inherit that variable.

A block takes on the set of local variables in existence at the time that it is created. This forms part of its binding. Note that although the binding of the variables is fixed at this point, the block will have access to the *current* values of these variables when it executes. The binding preserves these variables even if the original enclosing scope is destroyed.

The bodies of while, until, and for loops are part of the scope that contains them; previously existing locals can be used in the loop, and any new locals created will be available outside the bodies afterward.

Predefined Variables

The following variables are predefined in the Ruby interpreter. In these descriptions, the notation [r/o] indicates that the variables are read-only; an error will be raised if a program attempts to modify a read-only variable. After all, you probably don't want to change the meaning of true halfway through your program (except perhaps if you're a politician). Entries marked [thread] are thread local.

Many global variables look something like Snoopy swearing: $_, $!, $&, and so on. This is for "historical" reasons, as most of these variable names come from Perl. If you find memorizing all this punctuation difficult, you may want to have a look at the library file called English, documented on page 671, which gives the commonly used global variables more descriptive names.

In the tables of variables and constants that follow, we show the variable name, the type of the referenced object, and a description.

Exception Information

$!	Exception	The exception object passed to `raise`. [thread]
$@	Array	The stack backtrace generated by the last exception. See `Kernel#caller` on page 518 for details. [thread]

Pattern Matching Variables

These variables (except $=) are set to `nil` after an unsuccessful pattern match.

$&	String	The string matched (following a successful pattern match). This variable is local to the current scope. [r/o, thread]
$+	String	The contents of the highest-numbered group matched following a successful pattern match. Thus, in `"cat" =~/(c|a)(t|z)/`, $+ will be set to "t". This variable is local to the current scope. [r/o, thread]
$`	String	The string preceding the match in a successful pattern match. This variable is local to the current scope. [r/o, thread]
$'	String	The string following the match in a successful pattern match. This variable is local to the current scope. [r/o, thread]
$=	Object	Deprecated. If set to any value apart from `nil` or `false`, all pattern matches will be case insensitive, string comparisons will ignore case, and string hash values will be case insensitive.
$1 to $9	String	The contents of successive groups matched in a successful pattern match. In `"cat" =~/(c|a)(t|z)/`, $1 will be set to "a" and $2 to "t". This variable is local to the current scope. [r/o, thread]
$~	MatchData	An object that encapsulates the results of a successful pattern match. The variables $&, $`, $', and $1 to $9 are all derived from $~. Assigning to $~ changes the values of these derived variables. This variable is local to the current scope. [thread]

1.8 for the $= row.

Input/Output Variables

$/	String	The input record separator (newline by default). This is the value that routines such as `Kernel#gets` use to determine record boundaries. If set to `nil`, `gets` will read the entire file.
$-0	String	Synonym for $/.
$\	String	The string appended to the output of every call to methods such as `Kernel#print` and `IO#write`. The default value is `nil`.
$,	String	The separator string output between the parameters to methods such as `Kernel#print` and `Array#join`. Defaults to `nil`, which adds no text.
$.	Fixnum	The number of the last line read from the current input file.
$;	String	The default separator pattern used by `String#split`. May be set from the command line using the `-F` flag.

	$<	Object	An object that provides access to the concatenation of the contents of all the files given as command-line arguments or $stdin (in the case where there are no arguments). $< supports methods similar to a File object: binmode, close, closed?, each, each_byte, each_line, eof, eof?, file, filename, fileno, getc, gets, lineno, lineno=, path, pos, pos=, read, readchar, readline, readlines, rewind, seek, skip, tell, to_a, to_i, to_io, to_s, along with the methods in Enumerable. The method file returns a File object for the file currently being read. This may change as $< reads through the files on the command line. [r/o]
	$>	IO	The destination of output for Kernel#print and Kernel#printf. The default value is $stdout.
	$_	String	The last line read by Kernel#gets or Kernel#readline. Many string-related functions in the Kernel module operate on $_ by default. The variable is local to the current scope. [thread]
1.8	$defout	IO	Synonym for $>. Obsolete: use $stdout.
1.8	$deferr	IO	Synonym for STDERR. Obsolete: use $stderr.
	$-F	String	Synonym for $;.
	$stderr	IO	The current standard error output.
	$stdin	IO	The current standard input.
1.8	$stdout	IO	The current standard output. Assignment to $stdout is deprecated: use $stdout.reopen instead.

Execution Environment Variables

$0	String	The name of the top-level Ruby program being executed. Typically this will be the program's filename. On some operating systems, assigning to this variable will change the name of the process reported (for example) by the ps(1) command.
$*	Array	An array of strings containing the command-line options from the invocation of the program. Options used by the Ruby interpreter will have been removed. [r/o]
$"	Array	An array containing the filenames of modules loaded by require. [r/o]
$$	Fixnum	The process number of the program being executed. [r/o]
$?	Process::Status	The exit status of the last child process to terminate. [r/o, thread]
$:	Array	An array of strings, where each string specifies a directory to be searched for Ruby scripts and binary extensions used by the load and require methods. The initial value is the value of the arguments passed via the -I command-line option, followed by an installation-defined standard library location, followed by the current directory ("."). This variable may be set from within a program to alter the default search path; typically, programs use $: << dir to append dir to the path. [r/o]
$-a	Object	True if the -a option is specified on the command line. [r/o]

$-d	Object	Synonym for $DEBUG.
$DEBUG	Object	Set to true if the -d command-line option is specified.
__FILE__	String	The name of the current source file. [r/o]
$F	Array	The array that receives the split input line if the -a command-line option is used.
$FILENAME	String	The name of the current input file. Equivalent to $<.filename. [r/o]
$-i	String	If in-place edit mode is enabled (perhaps using the -i command-line option), $-i holds the extension used when creating the backup file. If you set a value into $-i, enables in-place edit mode. See page 178.
$-I	Array	Synonym for $:. [r/o]
$-K	String	Sets the multibyte coding system for strings and regular expressions. Equivalent to the -K command-line option. See page 179.
$-l	Object	Set to true if the -l option (which enables line-end processing) is present on the command line. See page 179. [r/o]
__LINE__	String	The current line number in the source file. [r/o]
$LOAD_PATH	Array	A synonym for $:. [r/o]
$-p	Object	Set to true if the -p option (which puts an implicit while gets ... end loop around your program) is present on the command line. See page 179. [r/o]
$SAFE	Fixnum	The current safe level (see page 398). This variable's value may never be reduced by assignment. [thread]
$VERBOSE	Object	Set to true if the -v, --version, -W, or -w option is specified on the command line. Set to false if no option, or -W1 is given. Set to nil if -W0 was specified. Setting this option to true causes the interpreter and some library routines to report additional information. Setting to nil suppresses all warnings (including the output of Kernel.warn).
$-v	Object	Synonym for $VERBOSE.
$-w	Object	Synonym for $VERBOSE.

1.8

Standard Objects

ARGF	Object	A synonym for $<.
ARGV	Array	A synonym for $*.
ENV	Object	A hash-like object containing the program's environment variables. An instance of class Object, ENV implements the full set of Hash methods. Used to query and set the value of an environment variable, as in ENV["PATH"] and ENV["term"]="ansi".
false	FalseClass	Singleton instance of class FalseClass. [r/o]
nil	NilClass	The singleton instance of class NilClass. The value of uninitialized instance and global variables. [r/o]

| self | Object | The receiver (object) of the current method. [r/o] |
| true | TrueClass | Singleton instance of class TrueClass. [r/o] |

Global Constants

The following constants are defined by the Ruby interpreter.

DATA	IO	If the main program file contains the directive __END__, then the constant DATA will be initialized so that reading from it will return lines following __END__ from the source file.
FALSE	FalseClass	Synonym for false.
NIL	NilClass	Synonym for nil.
RUBY_PLATFORM	String	The identifier of the platform running this program. This string is in the same form as the platform identifier used by the GNU configure utility (which is not a coincidence).
RUBY_RELEASE_DATE	String	The date of this release.
RUBY_VERSION	String	The version number of the interpreter.
STDERR	IO	The actual standard error stream for the program. The initial value of $stderr.
STDIN	IO	The actual standard input stream for the program. The initial value of $stdin.
STDOUT	IO	The actual standard output stream for the program. The initial value of $stdout.
SCRIPT_LINES__	Hash	If a constant SCRIPT_LINES__ is defined and references a Hash, Ruby will store an entry containing the contents of each file it parses, with the file's name as the key and an array of strings as the value. See Kernel.require on page 528 for an example.
TOPLEVEL_BINDING	Binding	A Binding object representing the binding at Ruby's top level— the level where programs are initially executed.
TRUE	TrueClass	Synonym for true.

The constant __FILE__ and the variable $0 are often used together to run code only if it appears in the file run directly by the user. For example, library writers often use this to include tests in their libraries that will be run if the library source is run directly, but not if the source is required into another program.

```
# library code
# ...
if __FILE__ == $0
  # tests...
end
```

Expressions

Single terms in an expression may be any of the following.

- **Literal**. Ruby literals are numbers, strings, arrays, hashes, ranges, symbols, and regular expressions. These are described starting on page 319.

- **Shell command**. A shell command is a string enclosed in backquotes or in a general delimited string (page 318) starting with %x. The value of the string is the standard output of running the command represented by the string under the host operating system's standard shell. The execution also sets the $? variable with the command's exit status.

  ```
  filter = "*.c"
  files = `ls #{filter}`
  files = %x{ls #{filter}}
  ```

- **Symbol generator**. A Symbol object is created by prefixing an operator, string, variable, constant, method, class, module name with a colon. The symbol object will be unique for each different name but does not refer to a particular instance of the name, so the symbol for (say) :fred will be the same regardless of context. A symbol is similar to the concept of atoms in other high-level languages.

- **Variable reference** or **constant reference**. A variable is referenced by citing its name. Depending on scope (see page 330), a constant is referenced either by citing its name or by qualifying the name, using the name of the class or module containing the constant and the scope operator (::).

  ```
  barney    # variable reference
  APP_NAMR  # constant reference
  Math::PI  # qualified constant reference
  ```

- **Method invocation**. The various ways of invoking a method are described starting on page 348.

Operator Expressions

Expressions may be combined using operators. Table 22.4 on the facing page lists the Ruby operators in precedence order. The operators with a ✓ in the Method column are implemented as methods, and may be overridden.

More on Assignment

The assignment operator assigns one or more *rvalues* (the *r* stands for "right," as rvalues tend to appear on the right side of assignments) to one or more *lvalues* ("left" values). What is meant by assignment depends on each individual lvalue.

Table 22.4. Ruby operators (high to low precedence)

Method	Operator	Description
✓	[ ] [ ]=	Element reference, element set
✓	**	Exponentiation
✓	! ~ + -	Not, complement, unary plus and minus (method names for the last two are +@ and -@)
✓	* / %	Multiply, divide, and modulo
✓	+ -	Plus and minus
✓	>> <<	Right and left shift
✓	&	"And" (bitwise for integers)
✓	^ |	Exclusive "or" and regular "or" (bitwise for integers)
✓	<= < > >=	Comparison operators
✓	<=> == === != =~ !~	Equality and pattern match operators (!= and !~ may not be defined as methods)
	&&	Logical "and"
	||	Logical "or"
	.. ...	Range (inclusive and exclusive)
	? :	Ternary if-then-else
	= %= /= -= += |= &=	Assignment
	>>= <<= *= &&= ||= **=	
	defined?	Check if symbol defined
	not	Logical negation
	or and	Logical composition
	if unless while until	Expression modifiers
	begin/end	Block expression

If an lvalue is a variable or constant name, that variable or constant receives a reference to the corresponding rvalue.

```
a = /regexp/
b, c, d = 1, "cat", [ 3, 4, 5 ]
```

If the lvalue is an object attribute, the corresponding attribute setting method will be called in the receiver, passing as a parameter the rvalue.

```
obj = A.new
obj.value = "hello"   # equivalent to obj.value=("hello")
```

If the lvalue is an array element reference, Ruby calls the element assignment operator ([ ]=) in the receiver, passing as parameters any indices that appear between the brackets followed by the rvalue. This is illustrated in the following table.

Element Reference	Actual Method Call
`obj[] = "one"`	`obj.[]=("one")`
`obj[1] = "two"`	`obj.[]=(1, "two")`
`obj["a", /^cat/] = "three"`	`obj.[]=("a", /^cat/, "three")`

1.8 The value of an assignment expression is its rvalue. This is true even if the assignment is to an attribute method that returns something different.

Parallel Assignment

An assignment expression may have one or more lvalues and one or more rvalues. This section explains how Ruby handles assignment with different combinations of arguments.

1. If the last rvalue is prefixed with an asterisk and implements `to_ary`, the rvalue is replaced with the elements of the array, with each element forming its own rvalue.

2. If the assignment contains multiple lvalues and one rvalue, the rvalue is converted into an `Array`, and this array is expanded into a set of rvalues as described in (1).

3. Successive rvalues are assigned to the lvalues. This assignment effectively happens in parallel, so that (for example) `a,b=b,a` swaps the values in `a` and `b`.

4. If there are more lvalues than rvalues, the excess will have `nil` assigned to them.

5. If there are more rvalues than lvalues, the excess will be ignored.

6. These rules are modified slightly if the last lvalue is preceded with an asterisk. This lvalue will always receive an array during the assignment. The array will consist of whatever rvalue would normally have been assigned to this lvalue, followed by the excess rvalues (if any).

7. If an lvalue contains a parenthesized list, the list is treated as a nested assignment statement, and then it is assigned from the corresponding rvalue as described by these rules.

The tutorial has examples starting on page 91.

Block Expressions

```
begin
    body
end
```

Expressions may be grouped between `begin` and `end`. The value of the block expression is the value of the last expression executed.

Block expressions also play a role in exception handling, which is discussed starting on page 360.

Boolean Expressions

Ruby predefines the globals `false` and `nil`. Both of these values are treated as being false in a boolean context. All other values are treated as being true. The constant `true` is available for when you need an explicit "true" value.

And, Or, Not, and Defined?

The `and` and `&&` operators evaluate their first operand. If false, the expression returns the value of the first operand; otherwise, the expression returns the value of the second operand.

```
expr1   and   expr2
expr1   &&    expr2
```

The `or` and `||` operators evaluate their first operand. If true, the expression returns the value of their first operand; otherwise, the expression returns the value of the second operand.

```
expr1   or   expr2
expr1   ||   expr2
```

The `not` and `!` operators evaluate their operand. If true, the expression returns false. If false, the expression returns true. For historical reasons, a string, regexp, or range may not appear as the single argument to `not` or `!`.

The word forms of these operators (`and`, `or`, and `not`) have a lower precedence than the corresponding symbol forms (`&&`, `||`, and `!`). See Table 22.4 on page 339 for details.

The `defined?` operator returns `nil` if its argument, which can be an arbitrary expression, is not defined. Otherwise, it returns a description of that argument. For examples, see page 94 in the tutorial.

Comparison Operators

The Ruby syntax defines the comparison operators `==`, `===`, `<=>`, `<`, `<=`, `>`, `>=`, `=~`. All of these operators are implemented as methods. By convention, the language also uses the standard methods `eql?` and `equal?` (see Table 7.1 on page 95). Although the operators have intuitive meaning, it is up to the classes that implement them to produce meaningful comparison semantics. The library reference starting on page 423 describes the comparison semantics for the built-in classes. The module `Comparable` provides support for implementing the operators `==`, `<`, `<=`, `>`, `>=`, and the method `between?` in terms of `<=>`. The operator `===` is used in `case` expressions, described on page 343.

Both `==` and `=~` have negated forms, `!=` and `!~`. Ruby converts these during syntax analysis: `a != b` is mapped to `!(a == b)`, and `a !~ b` is mapped to `!(a =~ b)`. No methods correspond to `!=` and `!~`.

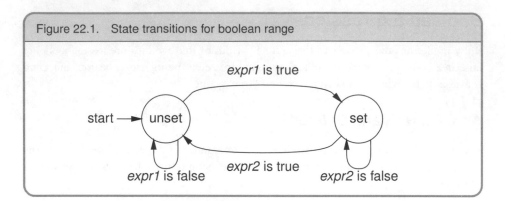

Figure 22.1. State transitions for boolean range

Ranges in Boolean Expressions

```
if   expr1 .. expr2
while expr1 ... expr2
```

A range used in a boolean expression acts as a flip-flop. It has two states, set and unset, and is initially unset. On each call, the range executes a transition in the state machine shown in Figure 22.1. The range expression returns `true` if the state machine is in the set state at the end of the call, and `false` otherwise.

The two-dot form of a range behaves slightly differently than the three-dot form. When the two-dot form first makes the transition from unset to set, it immediately evaluates the end condition and makes the transition accordingly. This means that if *expr1* and *expr2* both evaluate to `true` on the same call, the two-dot form will finish the call in the unset state. However, it still returns `true` for this call.

The three-dot form does not evaluate the end condition immediately upon entering the set state.

The difference is illustrated by the following code.

```
a = (11..20).collect {|i| (i%4 == 0)..(i%3 == 0) ? i : nil}
a  →  [nil, 12, nil, nil, nil, 16, 17, 18, nil, 20]

a = (11..20).collect {|i| (i%4 == 0)...(i%3 == 0) ? i : nil}
a  →  [nil, 12, 13, 14, 15, 16, 17, 18, nil, 20]
```

Regular Expressions in Boolean Expressions

In versions of Ruby prior to 1.8, a single regular expression in boolean expression was matched against the current value of the variable $_. This behavior is now only supported if the condition appears in a command-line –e parameter. In regular code, the use of implicit operands and $_ is being slowly phased out, so it is better to use an explicit match against a variable. If a match against $_ is required, use

```
if ~/re/ ...      or       if $_ =~ /re/ ...
```

`if` and `unless` Expressions

```
if boolean-expression [ then | : ]
  body
[ elsif boolean-expression [ then | : ]
  body , ... ]
[ else
  body ]
end

unless boolean-expression [ then | : ]
  body
[ else
  body ]
end
```

The then keyword (or a colon) separates the body from the condition. It is not required if the body starts on a new line. The value of an `if` or `unless` expression is the value of the last expression evaluated in whichever body is executed.

`if` and `unless` Modifiers

```
expression if      boolean-expression
expression unless  boolean-expression
```

evaluates *expression* only if *boolean-expression* is true (for `if`) or false (for `unless`).

Ternary Operator

```
boolean-expression ? expr1 : expr2
```

returns *expr1* if *boolean expression* is true and *expr2* otherwise.

`case` Expressions

Ruby has two forms of `case` statement. The first allows a series of conditions to be evaluated, executing code corresponding to the first condition that is true.

```
case
when condition [, condition ]... [ then | : ]
    body
when condition [, condition ]... [ then | : ]
    body
  ...
[ else
    body ]
end
```

The second form of a case expression takes a target expression following the `case` keyword. It searches for a match by starting at the first (top left) comparison, performing *comparison === target*.

```
case target
when comparison [, comparison ]... [ then | : ]
    body
when comparison [, comparison ]... [ then | : ]
    body
  ...
[ else
    body  ]
end
```

A comparison can be an array reference preceded by an asterisk, in which case it is expanded into that array's elements before the tests are performed on each. When a comparison returns true, the search stops, and the body associated with the comparison is executed (no break is required). case then returns the value of the last expression executed. If no *comparison* matches: if an else clause is present, its body will be executed; otherwise, case silently returns nil.

The then keyword (or a colon) separates the when comparisons from the bodies and is not needed if the body starts on a new line.

Loops

```
while boolean-expression [ do | : ]
    body
end
```

executes *body* zero or more times as long as *boolean-expression* is true.

```
until boolean-expression [ do | : ]
    body
end
```

executes *body* zero or more times as long as *boolean-expression* is false.

In both forms, the do or colon separates *boolean-expression* from the *body* and can be omitted when the body starts on a new line.

```
for name [, name ]... in expression [ do | : ]
    body
end
```

The for loop is executed as if it were the following each loop, except that local variables defined in the body of the for loop will be available outside the loop, and those defined within an iterator block will not.

```
expression.each do | name [, name ]... |
    body
end
```

Library

loop, which iterates its associated block, is not a language construct—it is a method in module Kernel.

```
loop do
  print "Input: "
  break unless line = gets
  process(line)
end
```

while and until Modifiers

```
expression while boolean-expression
expression until boolean-expression
```

If *expression* is anything other than a begin/end block, executes *expression* zero or more times while *boolean-expression* is true (for while) or false (for until).

If *expression* is a begin/end block, the block will always be executed at least one time.

break, redo, next, and retry

break, redo, next, and retry alter the normal flow through a while, until, for, or iterator controlled loop.

break terminates the immediately enclosing loop—control resumes at the statement following the block. redo repeats the loop from the start, but without reevaluating the condition or fetching the next element (in an iterator). The next keyword skips to the end of the loop, effectively starting the next iteration. retry restarts the loop, reevaluating the condition.

1.8

break and next may optionally take one or more arguments. If used within a block, the given argument(s) are returned as the value of the yield. If used within a while, until, or for loop, the value given to break is returned as the value of the statement, and the value given to next is silently ignored. If break is never called, or if it is called with no value, the loop returns nil.

```
match = while line = gets
          next if line =~ /^#/
          break line if line =~ /ruby/
        end

match = for line in ARGF.readlines
          next if line =~ /^#/
          break line if line =~ /ruby/
        end
```

Method Definition

```
def defname [ ( [ arg [ =val ], ... ] [ ,  *vararg ] [ , &blockarg ] ) ]
  body
end
```

defname is both the name of the method and optionally the context in which it is valid.

```
defname  ←   methodname
             constant.methodname
             (expr).methodname
```

A *methodname* is either a redefinable operator (see Table 22.4 on page 339) or a name. If *methodname* is a name, it should start with a lowercase letter (or underscore) optionally followed by upper- and lowercase letters, underscores, and digits. A *methodname* may optionally end with a question mark (?), exclamation point (!), or equals sign (=). The question mark and exclamation point are simply part of the name. The equals sign is also part of the name but additionally signals that this method may be used as an lvalue (described on page 31).

A method definition using an unadorned method name within a class or module definition creates an instance method. An instance method may be invoked only by sending its name to a receiver that is an instance of the class that defined it (or one of that class's subclasses).

Outside a class or module definition, a definition with an unadorned method name is added as a private method to class `Object`, and hence may be called in any context without an explicit receiver.

A definition using a method name of the form *constant.methodname* or the more general *(expr).methodname* creates a method associated with the object that is the value of the constant or expression; the method will be callable only by supplying the object referenced by the expression as a receiver. This style of definition creates per object or *singleton methods*.

```
class MyClass
  def MyClass.method      # definition
  end
end

MyClass.method            # call

obj = Object.new
def obj.method            # definition
end

obj.method                # call

def (1.class).fred        # receiver may be an expression
end

Fixnum.fred               # call
```

Method definitions may not contain class or module definitions. They may contain nested instance or singleton method definitions. The internal method is defined when the enclosing method is executed. The internal method does *not* act as a closure in the context of the nested method—it is self contained.

```
def toggle
  def toggle
    "subsequent times"
  end
  "first time"
end

toggle   →   "first time"
toggle   →   "subsequent times"
toggle   →   "subsequent times"
```

The body of a method acts as if it were a begin/end block, in that it may contain exception handling statements (rescue, else, and ensure).

Method Arguments

A method definition may have zero or more regular arguments, an optional array argument, and an optional block argument. Arguments are separated by commas, and the argument list may be enclosed in parentheses.

A regular argument is a local variable name, optionally followed by an equals sign and an expression giving a default value. The expression is evaluated at the time the method is called. The expressions are evaluated from left to right. An expression may reference a parameter that precedes it in the argument list.

```
def options(a=99, b=a+1)
  [ a, b ]
end
options           →   [99, 100]
options 1         →   [1, 2]
options 2, 4      →   [2, 4]
```

The optional array argument must follow any regular arguments and may not have a default. When the method is invoked, Ruby sets the array argument to reference a new object of class Array. If the method call specifies any parameters in excess of the regular argument count, all these extra parameters will be collected into this newly created array.

```
def varargs(a, *b)
  [ a, b ]
end
varargs 1         →   [1, []]
varargs 1, 2      →   [1, [2]]
varargs 1, 2, 3   →   [1, [2, 3]]
```

If an array argument follows arguments with default values, parameters will first be used to override the defaults. The remainder will then be used to populate the array.

```
def mixed(a, b=99, *c)
  [ a, b, c]
end
mixed 1            →    [1, 99, []]
mixed 1, 2         →    [1, 2, []]
mixed 1, 2, 3      →    [1, 2, [3]]
mixed 1, 2, 3, 4   →    [1, 2, [3, 4]]
```

The optional block argument must be the last in the list. Whenever the method is called, Ruby checks for an associated block. If a block is present, it is converted to an object of class Proc and assigned to the block argument. If no block is present, the argument is set to nil.

```
def example(&block)
  puts block.inspect
end

example
example { "a block" }
```

produces:

```
nil
#<Proc:0x001c9940@-:6>
```

Invoking a Method

```
[ receiver.  ] name  [  parameters  ] [  block  ]
[ receiver:: ] name  [  parameters  ] [  block  ]

parameters  ←  ( [ param, ... ]  [ , hashlist ] [ *array ] [ &a_proc ] )

   block    ←  { blockbody }
               do blockbody end
```

Initial parameters are assigned to the actual arguments of the method. Following these parameters may be a list of *key* => *value* pairs. These pairs are collected into a single new Hash object and passed as a single parameter.

Following these parameters may be a single parameter prefixed with an asterisk. If this parameter is an array, Ruby replaces it with zero or more parameters corresponding to the elements of the array.

```
def regular(a, b, *c)
  # ..
end
regular 1, 2, 3, 4
regular(1, 2, 3, 4)
regular(1, *[2, 3, 4])
```

A block may be associated with a method call using either a literal block (which must start on the same source line as the last line of the method call) or a parameter containing a reference to a `Proc` or `Method` object prefixed with an ampersand character. Regardless of the presence of a block argument, Ruby arranges for the value of the global function `Kernel.block_given?` to reflect the availability of a block associated with the call.

```ruby
a_proc   = lambda { 99 }
an_array = [ 98, 97, 96 ]
def block
  yield
end
block { }
block do
      end
block(&a_proc)
def all(a, b, c, *d, &e)
  puts "a = #{a.inspect}"
  puts "b - #{b.inspect}"
  puts "c = #{c.inspect}"
  puts "d = #{d.inspect}"
  puts "block = #{yield(e).inspect}"
end
all('test', 1 => 'cat', 2 => 'dog', *an_array, &a_proc)
```

produces:

```
a = "test"
b = {1=>"cat", 2=>"dog"}
c = 98
d - [07, 06]
block = 99
```

A method is called by passing its name to a receiver. If no receiver is specified, `self` is assumed. The receiver checks for the method definition in its own class and then sequentially in its ancestor classes. The instance methods of included modules act as if they were in anonymous superclasses of the class that includes them. If the method is not found, Ruby invokes the method `method_missing` in the receiver. The default behavior defined in `Kernel.method_missing` is to report an error and terminate the program.

Library

When a receiver is explicitly specified in a method invocation, it may be separated from the method name using either a period "." or two colons "::". The only difference between these two forms occurs if the method name starts with an uppercase letter. In this case, Ruby will assume that a `receiver::Thing` method call is actually an attempt to access a constant called `Thing` in the receiver *unless* the method invocation has a parameter list between parentheses.

```
Foo.Bar()       #  method call
Foo.Bar         #  method call
Foo::Bar()      #  method call
Foo::Bar        #  constant access
```

The return value of a method is the value of the last expression executed.

```
return [ expr, ... ]
```

A `return` expression immediately exits a method. The value of a `return` is nil if it is called with no parameters, the value of its parameter if it is called with one parameter, or an array containing all of its parameters if it is called with more than one parameter.

super

```
super  [ ( [ param, ... ] [ *array ] )  ]  [ block ]
```

Within the body of a method, a call to super acts just like a call to that original method, · except that the search for a method body starts in the superclass of the object that was found to contain the original method. If no parameters (and no parentheses) are passed to super, the original method's parameters will be passed; otherwise, the parameters to super will be passed.

Operator Methods

```
expr1 operator
operator expr1
expr1 operator expr2
```

If the operator in an operator expression corresponds to a redefinable method (see the Table 22.4 on page 339), Ruby will execute the operator expression as if it had been written

```
(expr1).operator()        or
(expr1).operator(expr2)
```

Attribute Assignment

```
receiver.attrname = rvalue
```

When the form *receiver.attrname* appears as an lvalue, Ruby invokes a method named *attrname=* in the receiver, passing *rvalue* as a single parameter. The value returned by this assignment is always *rvalue*—the return value of the method *attrname=* is discarded. If you want to access the return value (in the unlikely event that it isn't the *rvalue* anyway), send an explicit message to the method.

1.8

```
class Demo
  attr_reader :attr
  def attr=(val)
    @attr = val
    "return value"
  end
end

d = Demo.new

# In all these cases, @attr is set to 99
d.attr = 99        →    99
d.attr=(99)        →    99
d.send(:attr=, 99) →    "return value"
d.attr             →    99
```

Element Reference Operator

receiver[*expr [, expr]...*]
receiver[*expr [, expr]...*] = *rvalue*

When used as an rvalue, element reference invokes the method [ ] in the receiver, passing as parameters the expressions between the brackets.

When used as an lvalue, element reference invokes the method [ ]= in the receiver, passing as parameters the expressions between the brackets, followed by the *rvalue* being assigned.

Aliasing

alias *new_name old_name*

creates a new name that refers to an existing method, operator, global variable, or regular expression backreference ($&, $`, $', and $+). Local variables, instance variables, class variables, and constants may not be aliased. The parameters to alias may be names or symbols.

```
class Fixnum
  alias plus +
end
1.plus(3)         →    4

alias $prematch $`
"string" =~ /i/   →    3
$prematch         →    "str"

alias :cmd :`
cmd "date"        →    "Thu Aug 26 22:37:16 CDT 2004\n"
```

When a method is aliased, the new name refers to a copy of the original method's body. If the method is subsequently redefined, the aliased name will still invoke the original implementation.

```
def meth
  "original method"
end
alias original meth
def meth
  "new and improved"
end
meth       →   "new and improved"
original   →   "original method"
```

Class Definition

```
class [ scope:: ] classname  [ < superexpr ]
  body
end

class << obj
  body
end
```

A Ruby class definition creates or extends an object of class `Class` by executing the code in *body*. In the first form, a named class is created or extended. The resulting `Class` object is assigned to a constant named *classname* (see below for scoping rules). This name should start with an uppercase letter. In the second form, an anonymous (singleton) class is associated with the specific object.

If present, *superexpr* should be an expression that evaluates to a `Class` object that will be the superclass of the class being defined. If omitted, it defaults to class `Object`.

Within *body*, most Ruby expressions are executed as the definition is read. However:

- Method definitions will register the methods in a table in the class object.

- Nested class and module definitions will be stored in constants within the class, not as global constants. These nested classes and modules can be accessed from outside the defining class using ":::" to qualify their names.

```
module NameSpace
  class Example
    CONST = 123
  end
end
obj = NameSpace::Example.new
a = NameSpace::Example::CONST
```

- The `Module#include` method will add the named modules as anonymous super-classes of the class being defined.

1.8 The *classname* in a class definition may be prefixed by the names of existing classes or modules using the scope operator (::). This syntax inserts the new definition into the namespace of the prefixing module(s) and/or class(es) but does not interpret the definition in the scope of these outer classes. A *classname* with a leading scope operator places that class or module in the top-level scope.

In the following example, class C is inserted into module A's namespace but is not interpreted in the context of A. As a result, the reference to CONST resolves to the top-level constant of that name, not A's version. We also have to fully qualify the singleton method name, as C on its own is not a known constant in the context of A::C.

```
CONST = "outer"

module A
  CONST = "inner"    # This is A::CONST
end

module A
  class B
    def B.get_const
      CONST
    end
  end
end

A::B.get_const    →    "inner"

class A::C
  def (A::C).get_const
    CONST
  end
end

A::C.get_const    →    "outer"
```

It is worth emphasizing that a class definition is executable code. Many of the directives used in class definition (such as attr and include) are actually simply private instance methods of class Module (documented starting on page 554).

Chapter 24, which begins on page 379, describes in more detail how Class objects interact with the rest of the environment.

Creating Objects from Classes

```
obj = classexpr.new [ ( [ args, ... ] ) ]
```

Class Class defines the instance method Class#new, which creates an object of the class of the receiver (*classexpr* in the syntax example). This is done by calling the
1.8 method *classexpr*.allocate. You can override this method, but your implementation must return an object of the correct class. It then invokes initialize in the newly created object, and passes it any arguments originally passed to new.

If a class definition overrides the class method new without calling super, no objects of that class can be created, and calls to new will silently return nil.

Like any other method, initialize should call super if it wants to ensure that parent classes have been properly initialized. This is not necessary when the parent is Object, as class Object does no instance-specific initialization.

Class Attribute Declarations

Library

Class attribute declarations are not part of the Ruby syntax: they are simply methods defined in class Module that create accessor methods automatically.

```
class name
  attr attribute  [ , writable ]
  attr_reader      attribute [, attribute ]...
  attr_writer      attribute [, attribute ]...
  attr_accessor    attribute [, attribute ]...
end
```

Module Definitions

```
module name
  body
end
```

A module is basically a class that cannot be instantiated. Like a class, its body is executed during definition and the resulting Module object is stored in a constant. A module may contain class and instance methods and may define constants and class variables. As with classes, module methods are invoked using the Module object as a receiver, and constants are accessed using the "::" scope resolution operator. The name in a module definition may optionally be preceded by the names of enclosing class(es) and/or module(s).

```
CONST = "outer"
module Mod
  CONST = 1
  def Mod.method1    # module method
    CONST + 1
  end
end
module Mod::Inner
  def (Mod::Inner).method2
    CONST + " scope"
  end
end

Mod::CONST          →    1
Mod.method1         →    2
Mod::Inner::method2 →    "outer scope"
```

Mixins—Including Modules

```
class|module name
  include expr
end
```

A module may be included within the definition of another module or class using the
`include` method. The module or class definition containing the `include` gains access   *Library*
to the constants, class variables, and instance methods of the module it includes.

If a module is included within a class definition, the module's constants, class variables, and instance methods are effectively bundled into an anonymous (and inaccess-
ible) superclass for that class. Objects of the class will respond to messages sent to the
module's instance methods. Calls to methods not defined in the class will be passed to
the module(s) mixed into the class before being passed to any parent class. A module
may choose to define an `initialize` method, which will be called upon the creation
of an object of a class that mixes in the module if either: (a) the class does not define
its own `initialize` method, or (b) the class's `initialize` method invokes `super`.

A module may also be included at the top level, in which case the module's constants,
class variables, and instance methods become available at the top level.

Module Functions

Although `include` is useful for providing mixin functionality, it is also a way of bringing the constants, class variables, and instance methods of a module into another namespace. However, functionality defined in an instance method will not be available as a
module method.

```
module Math
  def sin(x)
    #
  end
end
# Only way to access Math.sin is...
include Math
sin(1)
```

The method `Module#module_function` solves this problem by taking one or more   *Library*
module instance methods and copying their definitions into corresponding module
methods.

```
module Math
  def sin(x)
    #
  end
  module_function :sin
end
Math.sin(1)
include Math
sin(1)
```

The instance method and module method are two different methods: the method definition is copied by `module_function`, not aliased.

Access Control

Ruby defines three levels of protection for module and class constants and methods:

- **Public**. Accessible to anyone.

- **Protected**. Can be invoked only by objects of the defining class and its subclasses.

- **Private**. Can be called only in functional form (that is, with an implicit `self` as the receiver). Private methods therefore can be called only in the defining class and by direct descendents within the same object. See discussion starting on page 37 for examples.

  ```
  private    [ symbol, ... ]
  protected  [ symbol, ... ]
  public     [ symbol, ... ]
  ```

Library

Each function can be used in two different ways.

1. If used with no arguments, the three functions set the default access control of subsequently defined methods.

2. With arguments, the functions set the access control of the named methods and constants.

Access control is enforced when a method is invoked.

Blocks, Closures, and Proc Objects

A code block is a set of Ruby statements and expressions between braces or a do/end pair. The block may start with an argument list between vertical bars. A code block may appear only immediately after a method invocation. The start of the block (the brace or the do) must be on the same logical line as the end of the invocation.

```
invocation  do  | a1, a2, ... |
end

invocation  {   | a1, a2, ... |
}
```

Braces have a high precedence; do has a low precedence. If the method invocation has parameters that are not enclosed in parentheses, the brace form of a block will bind to the last parameter, not to the overall invocation. The do form will bind to the invocation.

Within the body of the invoked method, the code block may be called using the `yield`
keyword. Parameters passed to the `yield` will be assigned to arguments in the block.
A warning will be generated if `yield` passes multiple parameters to a block that takes
just one. The return value of the `yield` is the value of the last expression evaluated in
the block or the value passed to a `next` statement executed in the block.

A block is a *closure*; it remembers the context in which it was defined, and it uses that
context whenever it is called. The context includes the value of *self*, the constants, class
variables, local variables, and any captured block.

```ruby
class Holder
  CONST = 100
  def call_block
    a = 101
    @a = 102
    @@a = 103
    yield
  end
end
class Creator
  CONST = 0
  def create_block
    a = 1
    @a = 2
    @@a = 3
    proc do
      puts "a = #{a}"
      puts "@a = #@a"
      puts "@@a = #@@a"
      puts yield
    end
  end
end
block = Creator.new.create_block { "original" }
Holder.new.call_block(&block)
```

produces:

```
a = 1
@a = 2
@@a = 3
original
```

Proc Objects, break, and next

Ruby's blocks are chunks of code attached to a method that operate in the context in
which they were defined. Blocks are not objects, but they can be converted into objects
of class Proc. There are three ways of converting a block into a Proc object.

1. By passing a block to a method whose last parameter is prefixed with an ampersand. That parameter will receive the block as a `Proc` object.

   ```
   def meth1(p1, p2, &block)
     puts block.inspect
   end
   meth1(1,2) { "a block" }
   meth1(3,4)
   ```

   produces:

   ```
   #<Proc:0x001c9940@-:4>
   nil
   ```

Library

2. By calling `Proc.new`, again associating it with a block.

   ```
   block = Proc.new { "a block" }
   block   →   #<Proc:0x001c9ae4@-:1>
   ```

Library

1.8

3. By calling the method `Kernel.lambda` (or the equivalent, if mildly deprecated,
   method `Kernel.proc`), associating a block with the call.

   ```
   block = lambda { "a block" }
   block   →   #<Proc:0x001c9b0c@-:1>
   ```

The first two styles of `Proc` object are identical in use. We'll call these objects *raw
procs*. The third style, generated by `lambda`, adds some additional functionality to the
Proc object, as we'll see in a minute. We'll call these objects *lambdas*.

Within either kind of block, executing `next` causes the block to exit. The value of the
block is the value (or values) passed to `next`, or it's `nil` if no values are passed.

```
def meth
  res = yield
  "The block returns #{res}"
end

meth { next 99 }   →   "The block returns 99"

pr = Proc.new { next 99 }
pr.call            →   99

pr = lambda { next 99 }
pr.call            →   99
```

Within a raw proc, a `break` terminates the method that invoked the block. The return
value of the method is any parameters passed to the `break`.

Return and Blocks

A `return` from inside a *block* that's still in scope acts as a return from that scope.
A return from a block whose original context is not longer valid raises an exception

(LocalJumpError or ThreadError depending on the context). The following example illustrates the first case.

```
def meth1
  (1..10).each do |val|
    return val          # returns from method
  end
end
meth1   →   1
```

This example shows a return failing because the context of its block no longer exists.

```
def meth2(&b)
  b
end

res = meth2 { return }
res.call
```

produces:

```
prog.rb:5: unexpected return (LocalJumpError)
from prog.rb:5:in `call'
from prog.rb:6
```

And here's a return failing because the block is created in one thread and called in another.

```
def meth3
  yield
end

t = Thread.new do
  meth3 { return }
end

t.join
```

produces:

```
prog.rb:6: return can't jump across threads (ThreadError)
from prog.rb:9:in `join'
from prog.rb:9
```

The situation with Proc objects is slightly more complicated. If you use Proc.new to create a proc from a block, that proc acts like a block, and the previous rules apply.

```
def meth4
  p = Proc.new { return 99 }
  p.call
  puts "Never get here"
end

meth4   →   99
```

If the `Proc` object is created using `Kernel.proc` or `Kernel.lambda`, it behaves more like a free-standing method body: a `return` simply returns from the block to the caller of the block.

```
def meth5
  p = lambda { return 99 }
  res = p.call
  "The block returned #{res}"
end

meth5   →   "The block returned 99"
```

Because of this, if you use `Module#define_method`, you'll probably want to pass it a proc created using `lambda`, not `Proc.new`, as `return` will work as expected in the former and will generate a `LocalJumpError` in the latter.

Exceptions

Ruby exceptions are objects of class `Exception` and its descendents (a full list of the built-in exceptions is given in Figure 27.1 on page 462).

Raising Exceptions

Library

The `Kernel.raise` method raises an exception.

```
raise
raise string
raise thing [ , string [ stack trace ] ]
```

The first form reraises the exception in `$!` or a new `RuntimeError` if `$!` is `nil`.

The second form creates a new `RuntimeError` exception, setting its message to the given string.

The third form creates an exception object by invoking the method `exception` on its first argument. It then sets this exception's message and backtrace to its second and third arguments.

Class `Exception` and objects of class `Exception` contain a factory method called `exception`, so an exception class name or instance can be used as the first parameter to `raise`.

When an exception is raised, Ruby places a reference to the `Exception` object in the global variable `$!`.

Handling Exceptions

Exceptions may be handled

- within the scope of a begin/end block,

```
begin
  code...
  code...
[ rescue  [ parm, ... ] [ => var ] [ then ]
    error handling code... , ... ]
[ else
    no exception code... ]
[ ensure
    always executed code... ]
  end
```

- within the body of a method,

```
def method and args
  code...
  code...
[ rescue  [ parm, ... ] [ => var ] [ then ]
    error handling code... , ... ]
[ else
    no exception code... ]
[ ensure
    always executed code... ]
  end
```

1.8
- and after the execution of a single statement.

```
statement [ rescue statement, ... ]
```

A block or method may have multiple rescue clauses, and each rescue clause may specify zero or more exception parameters. A rescue clause with no parameter is treated as if it had a parameter of StandardError. This means that some lower-level exceptions will not be caught by a parameterless rescue class. If you want to rescue every exception, use

```
rescue Exception => e
```

When an exception is raised, Ruby scans up the call stack until it finds an enclosing begin/end block, method body, or statement with a rescue modifier. For each rescue clause in that block, Ruby compares the raised exception against each of the rescue
1.8
clause's parameters in turn; each parameter is tested using *parameter*===$!. If the raised exception matches a rescue parameter, Ruby executes the body of the rescue and stops looking. If a matching rescue clause ends with => and a variable name, the variable is set to $!.

Although the parameters to the rescue clause are typically the names of Exception classes, they can actually be arbitrary expressions (including method calls) that return an appropriate class.

If no rescue clause matches the raised exception, Ruby moves up the stack looking for a higher-level begin/end block that matches. If an exception propagates to the top level of the main thread without being rescued, the program terminates with a message.

If an else clause is present, its body is executed if no exceptions were raised in *code*. Exceptions raised during the execution of the else clause are not captured by rescue clauses in the same block as the else.

If an ensure clause is present, its body is always executed as the block is exited (even if an uncaught exception is in the process of being propagated).

Within a rescue clause, raise with no parameters will reraise the exception in $!.

Rescue Statement Modifier

A statement may have an optional rescue modifier followed by another statement (and by extension another rescue modifier, and so on). The rescue modifier takes no exception parameter and rescues StandardError and its children.

If an exception is raised to the left of a rescue modifier, the statement on the left is abandoned, and the value of the overall line is the value of the statement on the right.

```
values = [ "1", "2.3", /pattern/ ]

result = values.map {|v| Integer(v) rescue Float(v) rescue String(v) }

result   →   [1, 2.3, "(?-mix:pattern)"]
```

Retrying a Block

The retry statement can be used within a rescue clause to restart the enclosing begin/end block from the beginning.

Catch and Throw

Library

The method Kernel.catch executes its associated block.

```
catch ( symbol | string )  do
  block...
end
```

Library

The method Kernel.throw interrupts the normal processing of statements.

```
throw( symbol | string [ , obj ] )
```

When a throw is executed, Ruby searches up the call stack for the first catch block with a matching symbol or string. If it is found, the search stops, and execution resumes past the end of the catch's block. If the throw was passed a second parameter, that value is returned as the value of the catch. Ruby honors the ensure clauses of any block expressions it traverses while looking for a corresponding catch.

If no catch block matches the throw, Ruby raises a NameError exception at the location of the throw.

## Chapter 23

Duck Typing

You'll have noticed that in Ruby we don't declare the types of variables or methods—everything is just some kind of object.

Now, it seems like folks react to this in two ways. Some like this kind of flexibility and feel comfortable writing code with dynamically typed variables and methods. If you're one of those people, you might want to skip to the section called "Classes Aren't Types" on the following page. Some, though, get nervous when they think about all those objects floating around unconstrained. If you've come to Ruby from a language such as C# or Java, where you're used to giving all your variables and methods a type, you may feel that Ruby is just too sloppy to use to write "real" applications.

It isn't.

We'd like to spend a couple of paragraphs trying to convince you that the lack of static typing is not a problem when it comes to writing reliable applications. We're not trying to criticize other languages here. Instead, we'd just like to contrast approaches.

The reality is that the static type systems in most mainstream languages don't really help that much in terms of program security. If Java's type system were reliable, for example, it wouldn't need to implement ClassCastException. The exception is necessary, though, because there is runtime type uncertainty in Java (as there is in C++, C#, and others). Static typing can be good for optimizing code, and it can help IDEs do clever things with tooltip help, but we haven't seen much evidence that it promotes more reliable code.

On the other hand, once you use Ruby for a while, you realize that dynamically typed variables actually add to your productivity in many ways. You'll also be surprised to discover that your fears about the type chaos were unfounded. Large, long-running, Ruby programs run significant applications and just don't throw any type-related errors. Why is this?

Partly, it's a question of common sense. If you coded in Java (pre Java 1.5), all your containers were effectively untyped: everything in a container was just an Object, and you cast it to the required type when you extracted an element. And yet you probably never saw a `ClassCastException` when you ran these programs. The structure of the code just didn't permit it: you put `Person` objects in, and you later took `Person` objects out. You just don't write programs that would work in another way.

Well, it's the same in Ruby. If you use a variable for some purpose, the chances are very good that you'll be using it for the same purpose when you access it again three lines later. The kind of chaos that *could* happen just doesn't happen.

On top of that, folks who code Ruby a lot tend to adopt a certain style of coding. They write lots of short methods and tend to test as they go along. The short methods mean that the scope of most variables is limited: there just isn't that much time for things to go wrong with their type. And the testing catches the silly errors when they happen: typos and the like just don't get a chance to propagate through the code.

The upshot is that the "safety" in "type safety" is often illusory and that coding in a more dynamic language such as Ruby is both safe and productive. So, if you're nervous about the lack of static typing in Ruby, we suggest you try to put those concerns on the back burner for a little while, and give Ruby a try. We think you'll be surprised at how rarely you see errors because of type issues, and at how much more productive you feel once you start to exploit the power of dynamic typing.

Classes Aren't Types

The issue of types is actually somewhat deeper than an ongoing debate between strong typing advocates and the hippie-freak dynamic typing crowd. The real issue is the question, what is a type in the first place?

If you've been coding in conventional typed languages, you've probably been taught that the *type* of an object is its *class*—all objects are instances of some class, and that class is the object's type. The class defines the operations (methods) that the object can support, along with the state (instance variables) on which those methods operate. Let's look at some Java code.

```
Customer  c;
c = database.findCustomer("dave");    /* Java */
```

This fragment declares the variable c to be of type `Customer` and sets it to reference the customer object for Dave that we've created from some database record. So the type of the object in c is `Customer`, right?

Maybe. However, even in Java, the issue is slightly deeper. Java supports the concept of *interfaces*, which are a kind of emasculated abstract base class. A Java class can be declared as implementing multiple interfaces. Using this facility, you may have defined your classes as follows.

```
public interface Customer {
  long  getID();
  Calendar getDateOfLastContact();
  // ...
}
public class Person
  implements Customer {
  public long getID() { ... }
  public Calendar getDateOfLastContact() { ... }
  // ...
}
```

So even in Java, the class is not always the type—sometimes the type is a subset of the class, and sometimes objects implement multiple types.

In Ruby, the class is never (OK, almost never) the type. Instead, the type of an object is defined more by what that object can do. In Ruby, we call this *duck typing*. If an object walks like a duck and talks like a duck, then the interpreter is happy to treat it as if it were a duck.

Let's look at an example. Perhaps we've written a method to write our customer's name to the end of an open file.

```
class Customer
  def initialize(first_name, last_name)
    @first_name = first_name
    @last_name  = last_name
  end
  def append_name_to_file(file)
    file << @first_name << " " << @last_name
  end
end
```

Being good programmers, we'll write a unit test for this. Be warned, though—it's messy (and we'll improve on it shortly).

```
require 'test/unit'
require 'addcust'
class TestAddCustomer < Test::Unit::TestCase
  def test_add
    c = Customer.new("Ima", "Customer")
    f = File.open("tmpfile", "w") do |f|
      c.append_name_to_file(f)
    end
    f = File.open("tmpfile") do |f|
      assert_equal("Ima Customer", f.gets)
    end
  ensure
    File.delete("tmpfile") if File.exist?("tmpfile")
  end
end
```

produces:

```
Finished in 0.003473 seconds.
1 tests, 1 assertions, 0 failures, 0 errors
```

We have to do all that work to create a file to write to, then reopen it, and read in the contents to verify the correct string was written. We also have to delete the file when we've finished (but only if it exists).

Instead, though, we could rely on duck typing. All we need is something that walks like a file and talks like a file that we can pass in to the method under test. And all that means *in this circumstance* is that we need an object that responds to the << method by appending something. Do we have something that does this? How about a humble String?

```
require 'test/unit'
require 'addcust'
class TestAddCustomer < Test::Unit::TestCase
  def test_add
    c = Customer.new("Ima", "Customer")
    f = ""
    c.append_name_to_file(f)
    assert_equal("Ima Customer", f)
  end
end
```

produces:

```
Finished in 0.001951 seconds.
1 tests, 1 assertions, 0 failures, 0 errors
```

The method under test thinks it's writing to a file, but instead it's just appending to a string. At the end, we can then just test that the content is correct.

We didn't have to use a string—for the object we're testing here, an array would work just as well.

```
require 'test/unit'
require 'addcust'
class TestAddCustomer < Test::Unit::TestCase
  def test_add
    c = Customer.new("Ima", "Customer")
    f = []
    c.append_name_to_file(f)
    assert_equal(["Ima", " ", "Customer"], f)
  end
end
```

produces:

```
Finished in 0.001111 seconds.
1 tests, 1 assertions, 0 failures, 0 errors
```

Indeed, this form may be more convenient if we wanted to check that the correct individual things were inserted.

So duck typing is convenient for testing, but what about in the body of applications themselves? Well, it turns out that the same thing that made the tests easy in the previous example also makes it easy to write flexible application code.

In fact, Dave had an interesting experience where duck typing dug him (and a client) out of a hole. He'd written a large Ruby-based Web application that (among other things) kept a database table full of details of participants in a competition. The system provided a comma-separated value (CSV) download capability, allowing administrators to import this information into their local spreadsheets.

Just before competition time, the phone starts ringing. The download, which had been working fine up to this point, was now taking so long that requests were timing out. The pressure was intense, as the administrators had to use this information to build schedules and send out mailings.

A little experimentation showed that the problem was in the routine that took the results of the database query and generated the CSV download. The code looked something like

```
def csv_from_row(op, row)
  res = ""
  until row.empty?
    entry = row.shift.to_s
    if /[,"]/ =~ entry
      entry = entry.gsub(/"/, '""')
      res << '"' << entry << '"'
    else
      res << entry
    end
    res << "," unless row.empty?
  end
  op << res << CRLF
end
result = ""
query.each_row {|row|  csv_from_row(result, row)}
http.write result
```

When this code ran against moderate-size data sets, it performed fine. But at a certain input size, it suddenly slowed right down. The culprit? Garbage collection. The approach was generating thousands of intermediate strings and building one big result string, one line at a time. As the big string grew, it needed more space, and garbage collection was invoked, which necessitated scanning and removing all the intermediate strings.

The answer was simple and surprisingly effective. Rather than build the result string as it went along, the code was changed to store each CSV row as an element in an array. This meant that the intermediate lines were still referenced and hence were no longer garbage. It also meant that we were no longer building an ever-growing string that forced garbage collection. Thanks to duck typing, the change was trivial.

```ruby
def csv_from_row(op, row)
  # as before
end
result = []
query.each_row {|row|  csv_from_row(result, row)}
http.write result.join
```

All that changed is that we passed an array into the `csv_from_row` method. Because it (implicitly) used duck typing, the method itself was not modified: it continued to append the data it generated to its parameter, not caring what type that parameter was. After the method returned its result, we joined all those individual lines into one big string. This one change reduced the time to run from more than 3 minutes to a few seconds.

Coding like a Duck

If you want to write your programs using the duck typing philosophy, you really only need to remember one thing: an object's type is determined by what it can do, not by its class. (In fact, Ruby 1.8 now deprecates the method `Object#type` in favor of `Object#class` for just this reason: the method returns the class of the receiver, so the name `type` was misleading.)

1.8

What does this mean in practice? At one level, it simply means that there's often little value testing the class of an object.

For example, you may be writing a routine to add song information to a string. If you come from a C# or Java background, you may be tempted to write:

```ruby
def append_song(result, song)
  # test we're given the right parameters
  unless result.kind_of?(String)
    fail TypeError.new("String expected")
  end
  unless song.kind_of?(Song)
    fail TypeError.new("Song expected")
  end

  result << song.title << " (" << song.artist << ")"
end

result = ""
append_song(result, song)   →   "I Got Rhythm (Gene Kelly)"
```

Embrace Ruby's duck typing and you'd write something far simpler.

```
def append_song(result, song)
  result << song.title << " (" << song.artist << ")"
end

result = ""
append_song(result, song)   →   "I Got Rhythm (Gene Kelly)"
```

You don't need to check the type of the arguments. If they support << (in the case of *result*) or `title` and `artist` (in the case of *song*), everything will just work. If they don't, your method will throw an exception anyway (just as it would have done if you'd checked the types). But without the check, your method is suddenly a lot more flexible: you could pass it an array, a string, a file, or any other object that appends using <<, and it would just work.

Now sometimes you may want more than this style of *laissez-faire* programming. You may have good reasons to check that a parameter can do what you need. Will you get thrown out of the duck typing club if you check the parameter against a class? No, you won't.[1] But you may want to consider checking based on the object's capabilities, rather than its class.

```
def append_song(result, song)
  # test we're given the right parameters
  unless result.respond_to?(:<<)
    fail TypeError.new("'result' needs '<<' capability")
  end
  unless song.respond_to?(:artist) && song.respond_to?(:title)
    fail TypeError.new("'song' needs 'artist' and 'title'")
  end

  result << song.title << " (" << song.artist << ")"
end

result = ""
append_song(result, song)   →   "I Got Rhythm (Gene Kelly)"
```

However, before going down this path, make sure you're getting a real benefit—it's a lot of extra code to write and to maintain.

Standard Protocols and Coercions

Although not technically part of the language, the interpreter and standard library use various protocols to handle issues that other languages would deal with using types.

Some objects have more than one natural representation. For example, you may be writing a class to represent Roman numbers (I, II, III, IV, V, and so on). This class

---

1. The duck typing club doesn't check to see if you're a member anyway....

is not necessarily a subclass of `Integer`, because its objects are representations of numbers, not numbers in their own right. At the same time they do have an integer-like quality. It would be nice to be able to use objects of our Roman number class wherever Ruby was expecting to see an integer.

To do this, Ruby has the concept of *conversion protocols*—an object may elect to have itself converted to an object of another class. Ruby has three standard ways of doing this.

We've already come across the first. Methods such as `to_s` and `to_i` convert their receiver into strings and integers. These conversion methods are not particularly strict: if an object has some kind of decent representation as a string, for example, it will probably have a `to_s` method. Our Roman class would probably implement `to_s` in order to return the string representation of a number (VII, for instance).

The second form of conversion function uses methods with names such as `to_str` and `to_int`. These are strict conversion functions: you implement them only if your object can naturally be used every place a string or an integer could be used. For example, our Roman number objects have a clear representation as an integer and so should implement `to_int`. When it comes to stringiness, however, we have to think a bit harder.

Roman numbers clearly have a string representation, but are they strings? Should we be able to use them wherever we can use a string itself? No, probably not. Logically, they're a representation of a number. You can represent them as strings, but they aren't plug-compatible with strings. For this reason, a Roman number won't implement `to_str`—it isn't really a string. Just to drive this home: Roman numerals can be converted to strings using `to_s`, but they aren't inherently strings, so they don't implement `to_str`.

To see how this works in practice, let's look at opening a file. The first parameter to `File.new` can be either an existing file descriptor (represented by an integer) or a file name to open. However, Ruby doesn't simply look at the first parameter and check whether its type is `Fixnum` or `String`. Instead, it gives the object passed in the opportunity to represent itself as a number or a string. If it were written in Ruby, it may look something like

```
class File
  def File.new(file, *args)
    if file.respond_to?(:to_int)
      IO.new(file.to_int, *args)
    else
      name = file.to_str
      # call operating system to open file 'name'
    end
  end
end
```

So let's see what happens if we want to pass a file descriptor integer stored as a Roman number into File.new. Because our class implements to_int, the first respond_to? test will succeed. We'll pass an integer representation of our number to IO.open, and the file descriptor will be returned, all wrapped up in a new IO object.

A small number of strict conversion functions are built into the standard library.

to_ary → Array

Used when interpreter needs to convert a object into an array for parameter passing or multiple assignment.

```
class OneTwo
  def to_ary
    [ 1, 2 ]
  end
end
ot = OneTwo.new
a, b = ot
puts "a = #{a}, b = #{b}"
printf("%d -- %d\n", *ot)
```

produces:

```
a = 1, b = 2
1 -- 2
```

to_hash → Hash

Used when the interpreter expects to see Hash. (The only known use is the second parameter to Hash#replace.)

to_int → Integer

Used when the interpreter expects to see an integer value (such as a file descriptor or as a parameter to Kernel.Integer).

to_io → IO

Used when the interpreter is expecting IO objects (for example, as parameters to IO#reopen or IO.select).

to_proc → Proc

Used to convert an object prefixed with an ampersand in a method call.

```
class OneTwo
  def to_proc
    proc { "one-two" }
  end
end
def silly
  yield
end
ot = OneTwo.new
silly(&ot)   →   "one-two"
```

to_str → **String**

Used pretty much any place the interpreter is looking for a `String` value.

```
class OneTwo
  def to_str
    "one-two"
  end
end

ot = OneTwo.new

puts("count: " + ot)
File.open(ot) rescue puts $!.message
```

produces:

```
count: one-two
No such file or directory - one-two
```

Note, however, that the use of `to_str` is not universal—some methods that want string arguments do not call `to_str`.

```
File.join("/user", ot)    →    "/user/#<OneTwo:0x1c974c>"
```

to_sym → **Symbol**

Express the receiver as a symbol. Not used by the interpreter for conversions and probably not useful in user code.

One last point: classes such as `Integer` and `Fixnum` implement the `to_int` method, and `String` implements `to_str`. That way you can call the strict conversion functions polymorphically:

```
# it doesn't matter if obj is a Fixnum or a
# Roman number, the conversion still succeeds
num = obj.to_int
```

Numeric Coercion

Back on page 372 we said there were three types of conversion performed by the interpreter. We covered loose and strict conversion. The third is numeric coercion.

Here's the problem. When you write "1+2", Ruby knows to call the + on the object 1 (a Fixnum), passing it the Fixnum 2 as a parameter. However, when you write "1+2.3", the same + method now receives a `Float` parameter. How can it know what to do (particularly as checking the classes of your parameters is against the spirit of duck typing)?

The answer lies in Ruby's coercion protocol, based on the method `coerce`. The basic operation of `coerce` is simple. It takes two numbers (one as its receiver, the other as a parameter). It returns a two-element array containing representations of these two numbers (but with the parameter first, followed by the receiver). The `coerce` method guarantees that these two objects will have the same class and therefore that they can be added (or multiplied, or compared, or whatever).

```
1.coerce(2)           →   [2, 1]
1.coerce(2.3)         →   [2.3, 1.0]
(4.5).coerce(2.3)     →   [2.3, 4.5]
(4.5).coerce(2)       →   [2.0, 4.5]
```

The trick is that the receiver calls the coerce method of its parameter to generate this array. This technique, called *double dispatch*, allows a method to change its behavior based not only on its class but also on the class of its parameter. In this case, we're letting the parameter decide exactly *what* classes of objects should get added (or multiplied, divided, and so on).

Let's say that we're writing a new class that's intended to take part in arithmetic. To participate in coercion, we need to implement a coerce method. This takes some other kind of number as a parameter and returns an array containing two objects of the same class, whose values are equivalent to its parameter and itself.

For our Roman number class, it's fairly easy. Internally, each Roman number object holds its real value as a Fixnum in an instance variable, @value. The coerce method checks to see if the class of its parameter is also an Integer. If so, it returns its parameter and its internal value. If not, it first converts both to floating point.

```
class Roman
  def initialize(value)
    @value = value
  end

  def coerce(other)
    if  Integer === other
      [ other, @value ]
    else
      [ Float(other), Float(@value) ]
    end
  end

  # .. other Roman stuff
end

iv = Roman.new(4)
xi = Roman.new(11)

3 * iv    →    12
1.1 * xi  →    12.1
```

Of course, class Roman as implemented doesn't know how to do addition itself: you couldn't have written "xi + 3" in the previous example, as Roman doesn't have a "plus" method. And that's probably as it should be. But let's go wild and implement addition for Roman numbers.

376 ► CHAPTER 23. DUCK TYPING

```ruby
class Roman
  MAX_ROMAN = 4999
  attr_reader :value
  protected :value
  def initialize(value)
    if value <= 0 || value > MAX_ROMAN
      fail "Roman values must be > 0 and <= #{MAX_ROMAN}"
    end
    @value = value
  end
  def coerce(other)
    if  Integer === other
      [ other, @value ]
    else
      [ Float(other), Float(@value) ]
    end
  end
  def +(other)
    if Roman === other
      other = other.value
    end
    if Fixnum === other && (other + @value) < MAX_ROMAN
      Roman.new(@value + other)
    else
      x, y = other.coerce(@value)
      x + y
    end
  end
  FACTORS = [["m", 1000], ["cm", 900], ["d",   500], ["cd", 400],
            ["c",  100], ["xc",  90], ["l",    50], ["xl",  40],
            ["x",   10], ["ix",   9], ["v",     5], ["iv",   4],
            ["i",    1]]
  def to_s
    value = @value
    roman = ""
    for code, factor in FACTORS
      count, value = value.divmod(factor)
      roman << (code * count)
    end
    roman
  end
end
iv = Roman.new(4)
xi = Roman.new(11)

iv + 3          →    vii
iv + 3 + 4      →    xi
iv + 3.14159    →    7.14159
xi + 4900       →    mmmmcmxi
xi + 4990       →    5001
```

Finally, be careful with `coerce`—try always to coerce into a more general type, or you may end up generating coercion loops, where A tries to coerce to B, and B tries to coerce back to A.

Walk the Walk, Talk the Talk

Duck typing can generate controversy. Every now and then a thread flares on the mailing lists, or someone blogs for or against the concept. Many of the contributors to these discussions have some fairly extreme positions.

Ultimately, though, duck typing isn't a set of rules; it's just a style of programming. Design your programs to balance paranoia and flexibility. If you feel the need to constrain the types of objects that the users of a method pass in, ask yourself why. Try to determine what could go wrong if you were expecting a `String` and instead get an `Array`. Sometimes, the difference is crucially important. Often, though, it isn't. Try erring on the more permissive side for a while, and see if bad things happen. If not, perhaps duck typing isn't just for the birds.

## Chapter 24

Classes and Objects

Classes and objects are obviously central to Ruby, but at first sight they can seem a little confusing. There seem to be a lot of concepts: classes, objects, class objects, instance methods, class methods, singleton classes, and virtual classes. In reality, however, Ruby has just a single underlying class and object structure, which we'll discuss in this chapter. In fact, the basic model is so simple, we can describe it in a single paragraph.

A Ruby object has three components: a set of flags, some instance variables, and an associated class. A Ruby class is an object of class `Class`, which contains all the object things plus a list of methods and a reference to a superclass (which is itself another class). All method calls in Ruby nominate a receiver (which is by default `self`, the current object). Ruby finds the method to invoke by looking at the list of methods in the receiver's class. If it doesn't find the method there, it looks in any included modules, then in its superclass, modules in the superclass, and then in the superclass's superclass, and so on. If the method cannot be found in the receiver's class or any of its ancestors, Ruby invokes the method `method_missing` on the original receiver.

And that's it—the entire explanation. On to the next chapter.

"But wait," you cry, "I spent good money on this chapter. What about all this other stuff—virtual classes, class methods, and so on. How do they work?" Good question.

How Classes and Objects Interact

All class/object interactions are explained using the simple model given above: objects reference classes, and classes reference zero or more superclasses. However, the implementation details can get a tad tricky.

We've found that the simplest way of visualizing all this is to draw the actual structures that Ruby implements. So, in the following pages we'll look at all the possible combinations of classes and objects. Note that these are not class diagrams in the UML sense; we're showing structures in memory and pointers between them.

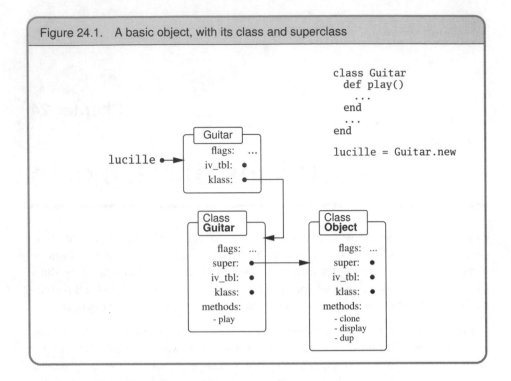

Figure 24.1. A basic object, with its class and superclass

Your Basic, Everyday Object

Let's start by looking at an object created from a simple class. Figure 24.1 shows an object referenced by a variable, `lucille`; the object's class, `Guitar`; and that class's superclass, `Object`. Notice how the object's class reference, `klass`, points to the class object and how the `super` pointer from that class references the parent class.

If we invoke the method `lucille.play()`, Ruby goes to the receiver, `lucille`, and follows the `klass` reference to the class object for `Guitar`. It searches the method table, finds `play`, and invokes it.

If instead we call `lucille.display()`, Ruby starts off the same way but cannot find `display` in the method table in class `Guitar`. It then follows the `super` reference to `Guitar`'s superclass, `Object`, where it finds and executes the method.

What's the Meta?

Astute readers (yup, that's all of you) will have noticed that the `klass` members of `Class` objects point to nothing meaningful in Figure 24.1. We now have all the information we need to work out what they *should* reference.

When you say `lucille.play()`, Ruby follows `lucille`'s `klass` pointer to find a class object in which to search for methods. So what happens when you invoke a

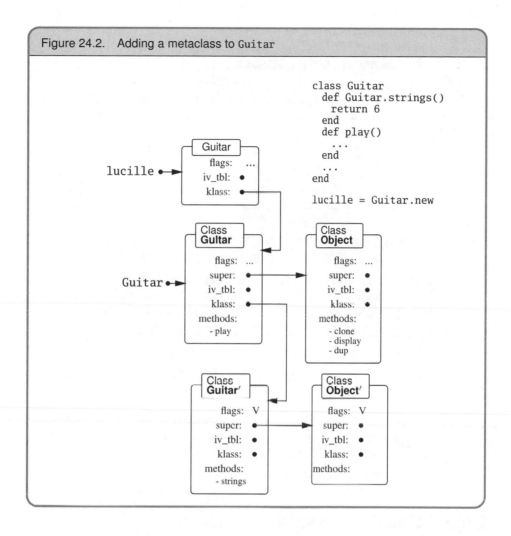

Figure 24.2.   Adding a metaclass to `Guitar`

class method, such as `Guitar.strings(...)`? Here the receiver is the class object itself, `Guitar`. So, to be consistent, we need to stick the methods in some other class, referenced from `Guitar`'s `klass` pointer. This new class will contain all of `Guitar`'s class methods. Although the terminology is slightly dubious, we'll call this a *metaclass* (see the sidebar on the next page). We'll denote the metaclass of `Guitar` as `Guitar'`. But that's not the whole story. Because `Guitar` is a subclass of `Object`, its metaclass `Guitar'` will be a subclass of `Object`'s metaclass, `Object'`. In Figure 24.2, we show these additional metaclasses.

When Ruby executes `Guitar.strings()`, it follows the same process as before: it goes to the receiver, class `Guitar`; follows the `klass` reference to class `Guitar'`; and finds the method.

Finally, note that a *V* has crept into the flags in class `Guitar'`. The classes that Ruby creates automatically are marked internally as *virtual classes*. Virtual classes are treated

---

Metaclasses and Singleton Classes

During the review of this book, the use of the term *metaclass* generated a fair amount of discussion, as Ruby's metaclasses are different from those in languages such as Smalltalk. Eventually, Matz weighed in with the following

You can call it *metaclass* but, unlike Smalltalk, it's not a class of a class; it's a singleton class of a class.

- Every object in Ruby has its own attributes (methods, constants, and so on) that in other languages are held by classes. It's just like each object having its own class.

- To handle per-object attributes, Ruby provides a classlike *something* for each object that is sometimes called a *singleton class*.

- In the current implementation, singleton classes are specially flagged class objects between objects and their class. These can be "virtual" classes if the language implementer chooses.

- Singleton classes for classes behave just like Smalltalk's metaclasses.

---

slightly differently within Ruby. The most obvious difference from the outside is that they are effectively invisible: they will never appear in a list of objects returned from methods such as `Module#ancestors` or `ObjectSpace.each_object`, and you cannot create instances of them using new.

Object-Specific Classes

Ruby allows you to create a class tied to a particular object. In the following example, we create two `String` objects. We then associate an anonymous class with one of them, overriding one of the methods in the object's base class and adding a new method.

```
a = "hello"
b = a.dup

class <<a
  def to_s
    "The value is '#{self}'"
  end
  def two_times
    self + self
  end
end
```

```
a.to_s       →   "The value is 'hello'"
a.two_times  →   "hellohello"
b.to_s       →   "hello"
```

This example uses the `class <<obj` notation, which basically says "build me a new class just for object *obj*." We could also have written it as

```
a = "hello"
b = a.dup
def a.to_s
  "The value is '#{self}'"
end
def a.two_times
  self + self
end
```

```
a.to_s       →   "The value is 'hello'"
a.two_times  →   "hellohello"
b.to_s       →   "hello"
```

The effect is the same in both cases: a class is added to the object a. This gives us a strong hint about the Ruby implementation: a virtual class is created and inserted as a's direct class. a's original class, `String`, is made this virtual class's superclass. The before and after pictures are shown in Figure 24.3 on the next page.

Remember that in Ruby classes are never closed; you can always open a class and add new methods to it. The same applies to virtual classes. If an object's `klass` reference already points to a virtual class, a new one will not be created. This means that the first of the two method definitions in the previous example will create a virtual class, but the second will simply add a method to it.

The `Object#extend` method adds the methods in its parameter to its receiver, so it also creates a virtual class if needed. `obj.extend(Mod)` is basically equivalent to

```
class <<obj
  include Mod
end
```

Mixin Modules

When a class includes a module, that module's instance methods become available as instance methods of the class. It's almost as if the module becomes a superclass of the class that uses it. Not surprisingly, that's about how it works. When you include a module, Ruby creates an anonymous proxy class that references that module and inserts that proxy as the direct superclass of the class that did the including. The proxy class contains references to the instance variables and methods of the module. This is important: the same module may be included in many different classes and will appear in many different inheritance chains. However, thanks to the proxy class, there is still

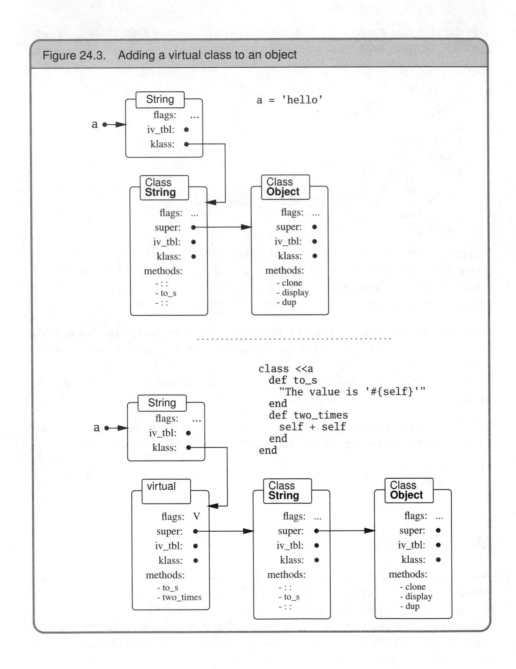

Figure 24.3.   Adding a virtual class to an object

only one underlying module: change a method definition in that module, and it will change in all classes that include that module, both past and future.

```
module SillyModule
  def hello
    "Hello."
  end
end

class SillyClass
  include SillyModule
end

s = SillyClass.new
s.hello   →   "Hello."
module SillyModule
  def hello
    "Hi, there!"
  end
end

s.hello   →   "Hi, there!"
```

The relationship between classes and the mixin modules they include is shown in Figure 24.4 on the following page. If multiple modules are included, they are added to the chain in order.

If a module itself includes other modules, a chain of proxy classes will be added to any class that includes that module, one proxy for each module that is directly or indirectly included.

Extending Objects

Just as you can define an anonymous class for an object using class *<<obj*, you can mix a module into an object using Object#extend. For example:

```
module Humor
  def tickle
    "hee, hee!"
  end
end

a = "Grouchy"
a.extend Humor
a.tickle   →   "hee, hee!"
```

There is an interesting trick with extend. If you use it within a class definition, the module's methods become class methods. This is because calling extend is equivalent to self.extend, so the methods are added to self, which in a class definition is the class itself.

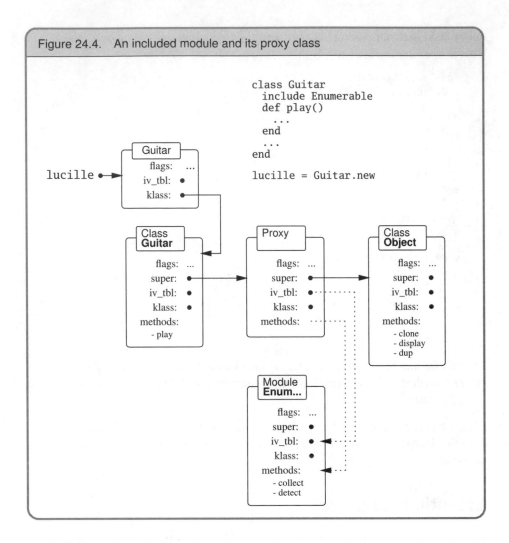

Figure 24.4. An included module and its proxy class

Here's an example of adding a module's methods at the class level.

```
module Humor
  def tickle
    "hee, hee!"
  end
end
class Grouchy
  include Humor
  extend  Humor
end

Grouchy.tickle  →  "hee, hee!"
a = Grouchy.new
a.tickle        →  "hee, hee!"
```

Class and Module Definitions

Having exhausted the combinations of classes and objects, we can (thankfully) get back to programming by looking at the nuts and bolts of class and module definitions.

In languages such as C++ and Java, class definitions are processed at compile time: the compiler creates symbol tables, works out how much storage to allocate, constructs dispatch tables, and does all those other obscure things we'd rather not think too hard about.

Ruby is different. In Ruby, class and module definitions are executable code. Although parsed at compile time, the classes and modules are created at runtime, when the definition is encountered. (The same is also true of method definitions.) This allows you to structure your programs far more dynamically than in most conventional languages. You can make decisions once, when the class is being defined, rather than each time those objects of the class are used. The class in the following example decides as it is being defined what version of a decryption routine to create.

```ruby
module Tracing
  # ...
end

class MediaPlayer
  include Tracing if $DEBUG

  if ::EXPORT_VERSION
    def decrypt(stream)
      raise "Decryption not available"
    end
  else
    def decrypt(stream)
      # ...
    end
  end
end
```

If class definitions are executable code, this implies that they execute in the context of some object: self must reference *something*. Let's find out what it is.

```ruby
class Test
  puts "Class of self = #{self.class}"
  puts "Name of self  = #{self.name}"
end
```

produces:

```
Class of self = Class
Name of self  = Test
```

This means that a class definition is executed with that class as the current object. Referring back to the section about metaclasses on page 380, we can see that this means that methods in the metaclass and its superclasses will be available during the execution of the method definition. We can check this out.

```
class Test
  def Test.say_hello
    puts "Hello from #{name}"
  end
  say_hello
end
```

produces:

```
Hello from Test
```

In this example we define a class method, `Test.say_hello`, and then call it in the body of the class definition. Within `say_hello`, we call `name`, an instance method of class `Module`. Because `Module` is an ancestor of `Class`, its instance methods can be called without an explicit receiver within a class definition.

Class Instance Variables

If a class definition is executed in the context of some object, that implies that a class may have instance variables.

```
class Test
  @cls_var = 123
  def Test.inc
    @cls_var += 1
  end
end

Test.inc   →   124
Test.inc   →   125
```

If classes have their own instance variables, can we use `attr_reader` and friends to access them? We can, but we have to run these methods in the correct place. For regular instance variables, the attribute accessors are defined at the class level. For class instance variables, we have to define the accessors in the metaclass.

```
class Test
  @cls_var = 123
  class <<self
    attr_reader :cls_var
  end
end

Test.cls_var   →   123
```

This leads us to an interesting point. Many of the directives that you use when defining a class or module, things such as `alias_method`, `attr`, and `public`, are simply methods in class `Module`. This creates some intriguing possibilities—you can extend the functionality of class and module definitions by writing Ruby code. Let's look at a couple of examples.

As a first example, let's look at adding a basic documentation facility to modules and classes. This would allow us to associate a string with modules and classes that we write, a string that is accessible as the program is running. We'll choose a simple syntax.

```
class Example
  doc "This is a sample documentation string"
  # .. rest of class
end
```

We need to make doc available to any module or class, so we need to make it an instance method of class Module.

```
class Module
  @@docs = []

  # Invoked during class definitions
  def doc(str)
    @@docs[self.name] = self.name + ":\n" + str.gsub(/^\s+/, '')
  end

  # invoked to get documentation
  def Module::doc(aClass)
    # If we're passed a class or module, convert to string
    # ('<=' for classes checks for same class or subtype)
    aClass = aClass.name if aClass.class <= Module
    @@docs[aClass] || "No documentation for #{aClass}"
  end
end

class Example
  doc "This is a sample documentation string"
  # .. rest of class
end

module Another
  doc <<-edoc
    And this is a documentation string
    in a module
  edoc
  # rest of module
end

puts Module::doc(Example)
puts Module::doc("Another")
```

produces:

```
Example:
This is a sample documentation string
Another:
And this is a documentation string
in a module
```

The second example is a performance enhancement based on Tadayoshi Funaba's `date` module (described beginning on page 665). Say we have a class that represents some underlying quantity (in this case, a date). The class may have many attributes that present the same underlying date in different ways: as a Julian day number, as a string, as a [year, month, day] triple, and so on. Each value represents the same date and may involve a fairly complex calculation to derive. We therefore would like to calculate each attribute only once, when it is first accessed.

The manual way would be to add a test to each accessor.

```
class ExampleDate
  def initialize(day_number)
    @day_number = day_number
  end

  def as_day_number
    @day_number
  end

  def as_string
    unless @string
      # complex calculation
      @string = result
    end
    @string
  end

  def as_YMD
    unless @ymd
      # another calculation
      @ymd = [ y, m, d ]
    end
    @ymd
  end
  # ...
end
```

This is a clunky technique—let's see if we can come up with something sexier.

What we're aiming for is a directive that indicates that the body of a particular method should be invoked only once. The value returned by that first call should be cached. Thereafter, calling that same method should return the cached value without reevaluating the method body again. This is similar to Eiffel's once modifier for routines. We'd like to be able to write something such as

```
class ExampleDate
  def as_day_number
    @day_number
  end

  def as_string
    # complex calculation
  end
```

```
    def as_YMD
      # another calculation
      [ y, m, d ]
    end
    once :as_string, :as_YMD
  end
```

We can use once as a directive by writing it as a class method of ExampleDate, but what should it look like internally? The trick is to have it rewrite the methods whose names it is passed. For each method, it creates an alias for the original code, and then creates a new method with the same name. Here's Tadayoshi Funaba's code, slightly reformatted.

```
  def once(*ids) # :nodoc:
    for id in ids
      module_eval <<-"end;"
        alias_method :__#{id.to_i}__, :#{id.to_s}
        private :__#{id.to_i}__
        def #{id.to_s}(*args, &block)
          (@__#{id.to_i}__ ||= [__#{id.to_i}__(*args, &block)])[0]
        end
      end;
    end
  end
```

This code uses module_eval to execute a block of code in the context of the calling module (or, in this case, the calling class). The original method is renamed __*nnn*__, where the *nnn* part is the integer representation of the method name's symbol ID. The code uses the same name for the caching instance variable. A method with the original name is then defined. If the caching instance variable has a value, that value is returned; otherwise the original method is called, and its return value cached and returned.

Understand this code, and you'll be well on the way to true Ruby mastery.

However, we can take it further. Look in the date module, and you'll see method once written slightly differently.

```
  class Date
    class << self
      def once(*ids)
        # ...
      end
    end
    # ...
  end
```

The interesting thing here is the inner class definition, class << self. This defines a class based on the object self, and self happens to be the class object for Date. The result? Every method within the inner class definition is automatically a class method of Date.

The once feature is generally applicable—it should work for any class. If you took once and made it a private instance method of class Module, it would be available for use in any Ruby class. (And of course you *could* do this, as class Module is open, and you are free to add methods to it.)

Class Names Are Constants

We've said that when you invoke a class method, all you're doing is sending a message to the Class object itself. When you say something such as String.new("gumby"), you're sending the message new to the object that is class String. But how does Ruby know to do this? After all, the receiver of a message should be an object reference, which implies that there must be a constant called *String* somewhere containing a reference to the String object.[1] And in fact, that's exactly what happens. All the built-in classes, along with the classes you define, have a corresponding global constant with the same name as the class. This is both straightforward and subtle. The subtlety comes from the fact that two things are named (for example) String in the system. There's a *constant* that references class String (an object of class Class), and there's the (class) object itself.

The fact that class names are just constants means that you can treat classes just like any other Ruby object: you can copy them, pass them to methods, and use them in expressions.

```
def factory(klass, *args)
  klass.new(*args)
end

factory(String, "Hello")          →    "Hello"
factory(Dir,    ".")              →    #<Dir:0x1c90e4>

flag = true
(flag ? Array : Hash)[1, 2, 3, 4]  →    [1, 2, 3, 4]
flag = false
(flag ? Array : Hash)[1, 2, 3, 4]  →    {1=>2, 3=>4}
```

This has another facet: if a class with no name is assigned to a constant, Ruby gives the class the name of the constant.

```
var = Class.new
var.name   →    ""

Wibble = var
var.name   →    "Wibble"
```

---

1.   It will be a constant, not a variable, because *String* starts with an uppercase letter.

Top-Level Execution Environment

Many times in this book we've claimed that everything in Ruby is an object. However, we've used one thing time and time again that appears to contradict this—the top-level Ruby execution environment.

```
puts "Hello, World"
```

Not an object in sight. We may as well be writing some variant of Fortran or BASIC. But dig deeper, and you'll come across objects and classes lurking in even the simplest code.

We know that the literal "Hello, World" generates a Ruby String, so that's one object. We also know that the bare method call to puts is effectively the same as self.puts. But what is self?

```
self.class    →    Object
```

At the top level, we're executing code in the context of some predefined object. When we define methods, we're actually creating (private) instance methods for class Object. This is fairly subtle; as they are in class Object, these methods are available everywhere. And because we're in the context of Object, we can use all of Object's methods (including those mixed-in from Kernel) in function form. This explains why we can call Kernel methods such as puts at the top level (and indeed throughout Ruby): these methods are part of every object.

Top-level instance variables also belong to this top-level object.

Inheritance and Visibility

The one last wrinkle to class inheritance is fairly obscure.

Within a class definition, you can change the visibility of a method in an ancestor class. For example, you can do something like

```
class Base
  def aMethod
    puts "Got here"
  end
  private :aMethod
end
class Derived1 < Base
  public :aMethod
end
class Derived2 < Base
end
```

In this example, you would be able to invoke aMethod in instances of class Derived1 but not via instances of Base or Derived2.

So how does Ruby pull off this feat of having one method with two different visibilities? Simply put, it cheats.

If a subclass changes the visibility of a method in a parent, Ruby effectively inserts a hidden proxy method in the subclass that invokes the original method using super. It then sets the visibility of that proxy to whatever you requested. This means that the code

```
class Derived1 < Base
  public :aMethod
end
```

is effectively the same as

```
class Derived1 < Base
  def aMethod(*args)
    super
  end
  public :aMethod
end
```

The call to super can access the parent's method regardless of its visibility, so the rewrite allows the subclass to override its parent's visibility rules. Pretty scary, eh?

Freezing Objects

Sometimes you've worked hard to make your object exactly right, and you'll be damned if you'll let anyone just change it. Perhaps you need to pass some kind of opaque object between two of your classes via some third-party object, and you want to make sure it arrives unmodified. Perhaps you want to use an object as a hash key and need to make sure that no one modifies it while it's being used. Perhaps something is corrupting one of your objects, and you'd like Ruby to raise an exception as soon as the change occurs.

Ruby provides a very simple mechanism to help with this. Any object can be *frozen* by invoking Object#freeze. A frozen object may not be modified: you can't change its instance variables (directly or indirectly), you can't associate singleton methods with it, and, if it is a class or module, you can't add, delete, or modify its methods. Once frozen, an object stays frozen: there is no Object#thaw. You can test to see if an object is frozen using Object#frozen?.

What happens when you copy a frozen object? That depends on the method you use. If you call an object's clone method, the entire object state (including whether it is frozen) is copied to the new object. On the other hand, dup typically copies only the object's contents—the new copy will not inherit the frozen status.

```
str1 = "hello"
str1.freeze      →   "hello"
str1.frozen?     →   true
str2 = str1.clone
str2.frozen?     →   true
str3 = str1.dup
str3.frozen?     →   false
```

Although freezing objects may initially seem like a good idea, you may want to hold off doing it until you come across a real need. Freezing is one of those ideas that looks essential on paper but isn't used much in practice.

## Chapter 25

Locking Ruby in the Safe

Walter Webcoder has a great idea for a portal site: the Web Arithmetic Page. Surrounded by all sorts of cool mathematical links and banner ads that will make him rich is a simple Web form containing a text field and a button. Users type an arithmetic expression into the field, click the button, and the answer is displayed. All the world's calculators become obsolete overnight; Walter cashes in and retires to devote his life to his collection of car license plate numbers.

Implementing the calculator is easy, thinks Walter. He accesses the contents of the form field using Ruby's CGI library and uses the eval method to evaluate the string as an expression.

```
require 'cgi'
cgi = CGI.new("html4")
# Fetch the value of the form field "expression"
expr = cgi["expression"].to_s
begin
  result = eval(expr)
rescue Exception => detail
  # handle bad expressions
end
# display result back to user...
```

Roughly seven seconds after Walter puts the application online, a twelve-year-old from Waxahachie with glandular problems and no real life types **system("rm *")** into the form and, like his computer's files, Walter's dreams come tumbling down.

Walter learned an important lesson: *All external data is dangerous. Don't let it close to interfaces that can modify your system.* In this case, the content of the form field was the external data, and the call to eval was the security breach.

Fortunately, Ruby provides support for reducing this risk. All information from the outside world can be marked as *tainted*. When running in a safe mode, potentially dangerous methods will raise a SecurityError if passed a tainted object.

Safe Levels

The variable $SAFE determines Ruby's level of paranoia. Table 25.1 on page 401 gives more details of the checks performed at each safe level.

$SAFE	Constraints
0	No checking of the use of externally supplied (tainted) data is performed. This is Ruby's default mode.
≥ 1	Ruby disallows the use of tainted data by potentially dangerous operations.
≥ 2	Ruby prohibits the loading of program files from globally writable locations.
≥ 3	All newly created objects are considered tainted.
≥ 4	Ruby effectively partitions the running program in two. Nontainted objects may not be modified.

The default value of $SAFE is zero under most circumstances. However, if a Ruby script is run *setuid* or *setgid*,[1] or if it run under mod_ruby, its safe level is automatically set to 1. The safe level may also be set by using the −T command-line option and by assigning to $SAFE within the program. It is not possible to lower the value of $SAFE by assignment.

The current value of $SAFE is inherited when new threads are created. However, within each thread, the value of $SAFE may be changed without affecting the value in other threads. This facility may be used to implement secure "sandboxes," areas where external code may run safely without risk to the rest of your application or system. Do this by wrapping code that you load from a file in its own, anonymous module. This will protect your program's namespace from any unintended alteration.

```
f=open(filename,"w")
f.print ...   # write untrusted program into file.
f.close
Thread.start do
  $SAFE = 4
  load(filename, true)
end
```

With a $SAFE level of 4, you can load *only* wrapped files. See the description of Kernel.load on page 524 for details.

This concept is used by Clemens Wyss on Ruby CHannel (http://www.ruby.ch). On this site, you can run the code from the first edition of this book. You can also type

---

1. A Unix script may be flagged to be run under a different user or group ID than the person running it. This allows the script to have privileges that the user does not have; the script can access resources that the user would otherwise be prohibited from using. These scripts are called *setuid* or *setgid*.

Ruby code into a window and execute it. And yet he doesn't lose sleep at night, as his site runs your code in a sandbox.

You can find a listing of the source of this sandbox at http://www.approximity.com/cgi-bin/rubybuch_wiki/wpage.rb?nd=214.

1.8, The safe level in effect when a Proc object is created is stored with that object. A Proc may not be passed to a method if it is tainted and the current safe level is greater than that in effect when the block was created.

Tainted Objects

Any Ruby object derived from some external source (for example, a string read from a file or an environment variable) is automatically marked as being tainted. If your program uses a tainted object to derive a new object, then that new object will also be tainted, as shown in the code below. Any object with external data somewhere in its past will be tainted. This tainting process is performed regardless of the current safe level. You can see if an object is tainted using Object#tainted?.

```
# internal data                    # external data
# =============                     # =============

x1 = "a string"                     y1 = ENV["HOME"]
x1.tainted?        →    false       y1.tainted?        →    true

x2 = x1[2, 4]                       y2 = y1[2, 4]
x2.tainted?        →    false       y2.tainted?        →    true

x1 =~ /([a-z])/    →    0           y1 =~ /([a-z])/    →    2
$1.tainted?        →    false       $1.tainted?        →    true
```

You can force any object to become tainted by invoking its taint method. If the safe level is less than 3, you can remove the taint from an object by invoking untaint.[2] This is not something to do lightly.

Clearly, Walter should have run his CGI script at a safe level of 1. This would have raised an exception when the program tried to pass form data to eval. Once this had happened, Walter would have had a number of choices. He could have chosen to implement a proper expression parser, bypassing the risks inherent in using eval. However, being lazy, it's more likely he'd have performed some simple sanity check on the form data and untaint it if it looked innocuous.

---

2.   You can also use some devious tricks to do this without using untaint. We'll leave it up to your darker side to find them.

```
require 'cgi';
$SAFE = 1
cgi = CGI.new("html4")
expr = cgi["expression"].to_s
if expr =~ %r{\A[-+*/\d\seE.()]*\z}
  expr.untaint
  result = eval(expr)
  # display result back to user...
else
  # display error message...
end
```

Personally, we think Walter is still taking undue risks. We'd probably prefer to see a real parser here, but implementing one here has nothing to teach us about tainting, so we'll move onto other topics.

Table 25.1. Definition of the safe levels

$SAFE >= 1

- The environment variables RUBYLIB and RUBYOPT are not processed, and the current directory is not added to the path.
- The command-line options -e, -i, -I, -r, -s, -S, and -x are not allowed.
- Can't start processes from $PATH if any directory in it is world-writable.
- Can't manipulate or chroot to a directory whose name is a tainted string.
- Can't glob tainted strings.
- Can't eval tainted strings.
- Can't load or require a file whose name is a tainted string (unless the load is wrapped).
- Can't manipulate or query the status of a file or pipe whose name is a tainted string.
- Can't execute a system command or exec a program from a tainted string.
- Can't pass trap a tainted string.

$SAFE >= 2

- Can't change, make, or remove directories, or use chroot.
- Can't load a file from a world-writable directory.
- Can't load a file from a tainted filename starting with ~.
- Can't use File#chmod, File#chown, File#lstat, File.stat, File#truncate, File.umask, File#flock, IO#ioctl, IO#stat, Kernel#fork, Kernel#syscall, Kernel#trap. Process.setpgid, Process.setsid, Process.setpriority, or Process.egid=.
- Can't handle signals using trap.

$SAFE >= 3

- All objects are tainted when they are created.
- Can't untaint objects.

$SAFE >= 4

- Can't modify a nontainted array, hash, or string.
- Can't modify a global variable.
- Can't access instance variables of nontainted objects.
- Can't change an environment variable.
- Can't close or reopen nontainted files.
- Can't freeze nontainted objects.
- Can't change visibility of methods (private/public/protected).
- Can't make an alias in a nontainted class or module.
- Can't get meta-information (such as method or variable lists).
- Can't define, redefine, remove, or undef a method in a nontainted class or module.
- Can't modify Object.
- Can't remove instance variables or constants from nontainted objects.
- Can't manipulate threads, terminate a thread other than the current thread, or set abort_on_exception.
- Can't have thread local variables.
- Can't raise an exception in a thread with a lower $SAFE value.
- Can't move threads between ThreadGroups.
- Can't invoke exit, exit!, or abort.
- Can load only wrapped files, and can't include modules in untainted classes and modules.
- Can't convert symbol identifiers to object references.
- Can't write to files or pipes.
- Can't use autoload.
- Can't taint objects.

Chapter 26

Reflection, ObjectSpace, and Distributed Ruby

One of the many advantages of dynamic languages such as Ruby is the ability to *introspect*—to examine aspects of the program from within the program itself. Java, for one, calls this feature *reflection* but Ruby's capabilities go beyond Java's.

The word *reflection* conjures up an image of looking at oneself in the mirror—perhaps investigating the relentless spread of that bald spot on the top of one's head. That's a pretty apt analogy: we use reflection to examine parts of our programs that aren't normally visible from where we stand.

In this deeply introspective mood, while we are contemplating our navels and burning incense (being careful not to swap the two tasks), what can we learn about our program? We might discover

- what objects it contains,
- the class hierarchy,
- the attributes and methods of objects, and
- information on methods.

Armed with this information, we can look at particular objects and decide which of their methods to call at runtime—even if the class of the object didn't exist when we first wrote the code. We can also start doing clever things, perhaps modifying the program as it's running.

Sound scary? It needn't be. In fact, these reflection capabilities let us do some very useful things. Later in this chapter we'll look at distributed Ruby and marshaling, two reflection-based technologies that let us send objects around the world and through time.

Looking at Objects

Have you ever craved the ability to traverse *all* the living objects in your program? We have! Ruby lets you perform this trick with `ObjectSpace.each_object`. We can use it to do all sorts of neat tricks.

For example, to iterate over all objects of type `Numeric`, you'd write the following.

```
a = 102.7
b = 95.1
ObjectSpace.each_object(Numeric) {|x| p x }
```

produces:

```
95.1
102.7
2.71828182845905
3.14159265358979
2.22044604925031e-16
1.79769313486232e+308
2.2250738585072e-308
```

Hey, where did all those extra numbers come from? We didn't define them in our program. If you look on pages 487 and 540, you'll see that the `Float` class defines constants for the maximum and minimum float, as well as epsilon, the smallest distinguishable difference between two floats. The `Math` module defines constants for e and π. Since we are examining *all* living objects in the system, these turn up as well.

Let's try the same example with different numbers.

```
a = 102
b = 95
ObjectSpace.each_object(Numeric) {|x| p x }
```

produces:

```
2.71828182845905
3.14159265358979
2.22044604925031e-16
1.79769313486232e+308
2.2250738585072e-308
```

Neither of the `Fixnum` objects we created showed up. That's because `ObjectSpace` doesn't know about objects with immediate values: `Fixnum`, `Symbol`, `true`, `false`, and `nil`.

Looking Inside Objects

Once you've found an interesting object, you may be tempted to find out just what it can do. Unlike static languages, where a variable's type determines its class, and hence the methods it supports, Ruby supports liberated objects. You really cannot tell exactly what an object can do until you look under its hood.[1] We talk about this in the *Duck Typing* chapter starting on page 365.

For instance, we can get a list of all the methods to which an object will respond.

```
r = 1..10 # Create a Range object
list = r.methods
list.length    →   68
list[0..3]     →   ["collect", "to_a", "instance_eval", "all?"]
```

Or, we can check to see if an object supports a particular method.

```
r.respond_to?("frozen?")   →   true
r.respond_to?(:has_key?)   →   false
"me".respond_to?("==")     →   true
```

We can determine our object's class and its unique object ID and test its relationship to other classes.

```
num = 1
num.id                   →   3
num.class                →   Fixnum
num.kind_of? Fixnum      →   true
num.kind_of? Numeric     →   true
num.instance_of? Fixnum  →   true
num.instance_of? Numeric →   false
```

Looking at Classes

Knowing about objects is one part of reflection, but to get the whole picture, you also need to be able to look at classes—the methods and constants that they contain.

Looking at the class hierarchy is easy. You can get the parent of any particular class using Class#superclass. For classes *and* modules, Module#ancestors lists both superclasses and mixed-in modules.

```
klass = Fixnum
begin
  print klass
  klass = klass.superclass
  print " < " if klass
end while klass
puts
p Fixnum.ancestors
```

produces:

```
Fixnum < Integer < Numeric < Object
[Fixnum, Integer, Precision, Numeric, Comparable, Object, Kernel]
```

---

1. Or under its bonnet, for objects created to the east of the Atlantic.

If you want to build a complete class hierarchy, just run that code for every class in the system. We can use `ObjectSpace` to iterate over all `Class` objects.

```
ObjectSpace.each_object(Class) do |klass|
  # ...
end
```

Looking Inside Classes

We can find out a bit more about the methods and constants in a particular object. Instead of just checking to see whether the object responds to a given message, we can ask for methods by access level, and we can ask for just singleton methods. We can also have a look at the object's constants, local, and instance variables.

```
class Demo
  @@var = 99
  CONST = 1.23

  private
    def private_method
    end
  protected
    def protected_method
    end
  public
    def public_method
      @inst = 1
      i = 1
      j = 2
      local_variables
    end

  def Demo.class_method
  end
end
```

```
Demo.private_instance_methods(false)          →   ["private_method"]
Demo.protected_instance_methods(false)        →   ["protected_method"]
Demo.public_instance_methods(false)           →   ["public_method"]
Demo.singleton_methods(false)                 →   ["class_method"]
Demo.class_variables                          →   ["@@var"]
Demo.constants - Demo.superclass.constants    →   ["CONST"]

demo = Demo.new
demo.instance_variables                       →   []
# Get 'public_method' to return its local variables
# and set an instance variable
demo.public_method                            →   ["i", "j"]
demo.instance_variables                       →   ["@inst"]
```

Module.constants returns *all* the constants available via a module, including constants from the module's superclasses. We're not interested in those just at the moment, so we'll subtract them from our list.

You may be wondering what all the false parameters were in the previous code. As of Ruby 1.8, these reflection methods will by default recurse into parent classes, and their parents, and so on up the ancestor chain. Passing in false stops this kind of prying.

Given a list of method names, we may now be tempted to try calling them. Fortunately, that's easy with Ruby.

Calling Methods Dynamically

C and Java programmers often find themselves writing some kind of dispatch table: functions that are invoked based on a command. Think of a typical C idiom where you have to translate a string to a function pointer.

```
typedef struct {
  char *name;
  void (*fptr)();
} Tuple;

Tuple list[]= {
  { "play",   fptr_play },
  { "stop",   fptr_stop },
  { "record", fptr_record },
  { 0, 0 },
};

...

void dispatch(char *cmd) {
  int i = 0;
  for (; list[i].name; i++) {
    if (strncmp(list[i].name,cmd,strlen(cmd)) == 0) {
      list[i].fptr();
      return;
    }
  }
  /* not found */
}
```

In Ruby, you can do all this in one line. Stick all your command functions into a class, create an instance of that class (we called it commands), and ask that object to execute a method called the same name as the command string.

```
commands.send(command_string)
```

Oh, and by the way, it does much more than the C version—it's dynamic. The Ruby version will find new methods added at runtime just as easily.

You don't have to write special command classes for send: it works on any object.

```
"John Coltrane".send(:length)          →   13
"Miles Davis".send("sub", /iles/, '.')  →   "M. Davis"
```

Another way of invoking methods dynamically uses Method objects. A Method object is like a Proc object: it represents a chunk of code and a context in which it executes. In this case, the code is the body of the method, and the context is the object that created the method. Once we have our Method object, we can execute it sometime later by sending it the message call.

```
trane = "John Coltrane".method(:length)
miles = "Miles Davis".method("sub")

trane.call              →   13
miles.call(/iles/, '.')  →   "M. Davis"
```

You can pass the Method object around as you would any other object, and when you invoke Method#call, the method is run just as if you had invoked it on the original object. It's like having a C-style function pointer but in a fully object-oriented style.

You can also use Method objects with iterators.

```
def double(a)
  2*a
end

mObj = method(:double)

[ 1, 3, 5, 7 ].collect(&mObj)   →   [2, 6, 10, 14]
```

Method objects are bound to one particular object. You can create *unbound* methods (of class UnboundMethod) and then subsequently bind them to one or more objects. The binding creates a new Method object. As with aliases, unbound methods are references to the definition of the method at the time they are created.

1.8

```
unbound_length = String.instance_method(:length)
class String
  def length
    99
  end
end
str = "cat"
str.length              →   99
bound_length = unbound_length.bind(str)
bound_length.call   →   3
```

As good things come in threes, here's yet another way to invoke methods dynamically. The eval method (and its variations such as class_eval, module_eval, and instance_eval) will parse and execute an arbitrary string of legal Ruby source code.

```
trane = %q{"John Coltrane".length}
miles = %q{"Miles Davis".sub(/iles/, '.')}}

eval trane   →   13
eval miles   →   "M. Davis"
```

When using eval, it can be helpful to state explicitly the context in which the expression should be evaluated, rather than using the current context. You can obtain a context by calling Kernel#binding at the desired point.

```
def get_a_binding
  val = 123
  binding
end

val = "cat"

the_binding = get_a_binding
eval("val", the_binding)   →   123
eval("val")                →   "cat"
```

The first eval evaluates val in the context of the binding *as it was* as the method get_a_binding was executing. In this binding, the variable val had a value of 123. The second eval evaluates val in the toplevel binding, where it has the value "cat".

Performance Considerations

As we've seen in this section, Ruby gives us several ways to invoke an arbitrary method of some object: Object#send, Method#call, and the various flavors of eval.

You may prefer to use any one of these techniques depending on your needs, but be aware that eval is significantly slower than the others (or, for optimistic readers, send and call are significantly faster than eval).

```
require 'benchmark'
include Benchmark

test = "Stormy Weather"
m = test.method(:length)
n - 100000

bm(12) {|x|
  x.report("call") { n.times { m.call } }
  x.report("send") { n.times { test.send(:length) } }
  x.report("eval") { n.times { eval "test.length" } }
}
```

produces:

	user	system	total	real
call	0.250000	0.000000	0.250000	(0.340967)
send	0.210000	0.000000	0.210000	(0.254237)
eval	1.410000	0.000000	1.410000	(1.656809)

System Hooks

A *hook* is a technique that lets you trap some Ruby event, such as object creation. The simplest hook technique in Ruby is to intercept calls to methods in system classes. Perhaps you want to log all the operating system commands your program executes. Simply rename the method Kernel.system and substitute it with one of your own that both logs the command and calls the original Kernel method.

```
module Kernel
  alias_method :old_system, :system
  def system(*args)
    result = old_system(*args)
    puts "system(#{args.join(', ')}) returned #{result}"
    result
  end
end

system("date")
system("kangaroo", "-hop 10", "skippy")
```

produces:

```
Thu Aug 26 22:37:22 CDT 2004
system(date) returned true
system(kangaroo, -hop 10, skippy) returned false
```

A more powerful hook is catching objects as they are created. If you can be present when every object is born, you can do all sorts of interesting things: you can wrap them, add methods to them, remove methods from them, add them to containers to implement persistence, you name it. We'll show a simple example here: we'll add a time stamp to every object as it's created. First, we'll add a timestamp attribute to every object in the system. We can do this by hacking class Object itself.

```
class Object
  attr_accessor :timestamp
end
```

Then we need to hook object creation to add this time stamp. One way to do this is to do our method renaming trick on Class#new, the method that's called to allocate space for a new object. The technique isn't perfect—some built-in objects, such as literal strings, are constructed without calling new—but it'll work just fine for objects we write.

```
class Class
  alias_method :old_new,  :new
  def new(*args)
    result = old_new(*args)
    result.timestamp = Time.now
    result
  end
end
```

Finally, we can run a test. We'll create a couple of objects a few milliseconds apart and check their time stamps.

```
class Test
end

obj1 = Test.new
sleep(0.002)
obj2 = Test.new

obj1.timestamp.to_f  →  1116425239.97018
obj2.timestamp.to_f  →  1116425239.98023
```

All this method renaming is fine, and it really does work, but be aware that it can cause problems. If a subclass does the same thing, and renames the methods using the same names, you'll end up with an infinite loop. You can avoid this by aliasing your methods to a unique symbol name or by using a consistent naming convention.

There are other, more refined ways to get inside a running program. Ruby provides several callback methods that let you trap certain events in a controlled way.

Runtime Callbacks

You can be notified whenever one of the following events occurs.

Event	Callback Method
Adding an instance method	`Module#method_added`
Removing an instance method	`Module#method_removed`
Undefining an instance method	`Module#method_undefined`
Adding a singleton method	`Kernel.singleton_method_added`
Removing a singleton method	`Kernel.singleton_method_removed`
Undefining a singleton method	`Kernel.singleton_method_undefined`
Subclassing a class	`Class#inherited`
Mixing in a module	`Module#extend_object`

By default, these methods do nothing. If you define the callback method in your class, it'll be invoked automatically. The actual call sequences are illustrated in the library descriptions for each callback method.

Keeping track of method creation and class and module usage lets you build an accurate picture of the dynamic state of your program. This can be important. For example, you may have written code that wraps all the methods in a class, perhaps to add transactional support or to implement some form of delegation. This is only half the job: the dynamic nature of Ruby means that users of this class could add new methods to it at any time. Using these callbacks, you can write code that wraps these new methods as they are created.

Tracing Your Program's Execution

While we're having fun reflecting on all the objects and classes in our programs, let's not forget about the humble statements that make our code actually do things. It turns out that Ruby lets us look at these statements, too.

First, you can watch the interpreter as it executes code. `set_trace_func` executes a `Proc` with all sorts of juicy debugging information whenever a new source line is executed, methods are called, objects are created, and so on. You'll find a full description on page 529, but here's a taste.

```
class Test
  def test
    a = 1
    b = 2
  end
end
set_trace_func proc {|event, file, line, id, binding, classname|
  printf "%8s %s:%-2d %10s %8s\n", event, file, line, id, classname
}
t = Test.new
t.test
```

produces:

```
    line prog.rb:11                    false
  c-call prog.rb:11           new      Class
  c-call prog.rb:11 initialize         Object
c-return prog.rb:11 initialize         Object
c-return prog.rb:11           new      Class
    line prog.rb:12                    false
    call prog.rb:2            test      Test
    line prog.rb:3            test      Test
    line prog.rb:4            test      Test
  return prog.rb:4            test      Test
```

The method `trace_var` (described on page 532) lets you add a hook to a global variable; whenever an assignment is made to the global, your `Proc` object is invoked.

How Did We Get Here?

A fair question, and one we ask ourselves regularly. Mental lapses aside, in Ruby at least you can find out exactly "how you got there" by using the method `caller`, which returns an `Array` of `String` objects representing the current call stack.

```
def cat_a
  puts caller.join("\n")
end
def cat_b
  cat_a
end
```

```
def cat_c
  cat_b
end
cat_c
```

produces:

```
prog.rb:5:in `cat_b'
prog.rb:8:in `cat_c'
prog.rb:10
```

Once you've figured out how you got there, where you go next is up to you.

Source Code

Ruby executes programs from plain old files. You can look at these files to examine the source code that makes up your program using one of a number of techniques.

The special variable __FILE__ contains the name of the current source file. This leads to a fairly short (if cheating) Quine—a program that outputs its own source code.

```
print File.read(__FILE__)
```

The method Kernel.caller returns the call stack—the list of stack frames in existence at the time the method was called. Each entry in this list starts off with a filename, a colon, and a line number in that file. You can parse this information to display source. In the following example, we have a main program, main.rb, that calls a method in a separate file, sub.rb. That method in turns invokes a block, where we traverse the call stack and write out the source lines involved. Notice the use of a hash of file contents, indexed by the filename.

Here's the code that dumps out the call stack, including source information.

```
def dump_call_stack
  file_contents = {}
  puts "File                        Line   Source Line"
  puts "-------------------------+----+-----------"
  caller.each do |position|
    next unless position =~ /\A(.*?):(\d+)/
    file = $1
    line = Integer($2)
    file_contents[file] ||= File.readlines(file)
    printf("%-25s:%3d - %s", file, line,
           file_contents[file][line-1].lstrip)
  end
end
```

The (trivial) file sub.rb contains a single method.

```
def sub_method(v1, v2)
  main_method(v1*3, v2*6)
end
```

And here's the main program, which invokes the stack dumper after being called back by the submethod.

```
require 'sub'
require 'stack_dumper'
def main_method(arg1, arg2)
  dump_call_stack
end
sub_method(123, "cat")
```

produces:

```
File                     Line  Source Line
-------------------------+----+------------
code/caller/main.rb      :  5 - dump_call_stack
./code/caller/sub.rb     :  2 - main_method(v1*3, v2*6)
code/caller/main.rb      :  8 - sub_method(123, "cat")
```

The SCRIPT_LINES__ constant is closely related to this technique. If a program initializes a constant called SCRIPT_LINES__ with a hash, that hash will receive the source code of every file subsequently loaded into the interpreter using require or load. See Kernel.require on page 528 for an example.

Marshaling and Distributed Ruby

Java features the ability to *serialize* objects, letting you store them somewhere and reconstitute them when needed. You can use this facility, for instance, to save a tree of objects that represent some portion of application state—a document, a CAD drawing, a piece of music, and so on.

Ruby calls this kind of serialization *marshaling* (think of railroad marshaling yards where individual cars are assembled in sequence into a complete train, which is then dispatched somewhere). Saving an object and some or all of its components is done using the method Marshal.dump. Typically, you will dump an entire object tree starting with some given object. Later, you can reconstitute the object using Marshal.load.

Here's a short example. We have a class Chord that holds a collection of musical notes. We'd like to save away a particularly wonderful chord so we can e-mail it to a couple of hundred of our closest friends. They can then load it into their copy of Ruby and savor it too. Let's start with the classes for Note and Chord.

```
Note = Struct.new(:value)
class Note
  def to_s
    value.to_s
  end
end
```

```
class Chord
  def initialize(arr)
    @arr = arr
  end
  def play
    @arr.join('-')
  end
end
```

Now we'll create our masterpiece and use `Marshal.dump` to save a serialized version of it to disk.

```
c = Chord.new( [ Note.new("G"),
                 Note.new("Bb"),
                 Note.new("Db"),
                 Note.new("E") ] )
File.open("posterity", "w+") do |f|
  Marshal.dump(c, f)
end
```

Finally, our grandchildren read it in and are transported by our creation's beauty.

```
File.open("posterity") do |f|
  chord = Marshal.load(f)
end

chord.play   →   "G-Bb-Db-E"
```

Custom Serialization Strategy

Not all objects can be dumped: bindings, procedure objects, instances of class IO, and singleton objects cannot be saved outside the running Ruby environment (a TypeError will be raised if you try). Even if your object doesn't contain one of these problematic objects, you may want to take control of object serialization yourself.

Marshal provides the hooks you need. In the objects that require custom serialization, simply implement two instance methods: one called marshal_dump, which writes the object out to a string, and one called marshal_load, which reads a string that you'd previously created and uses it to initialize a newly allocated object. (In earlier Ruby versions you'd use methods called _dump and _load, but the new versions play better with Ruby 1.8's new allocation scheme.) The instance method marshal_dump should return an object representing the state to be dumped. When the object is subsequently reconstituted using Marshal.load, the method marshal_load will be called with this object and will use it to set the state of its receiver—it will be run in the context of an allocated but not initialized object of the class being loaded.

For instance, here is a sample class that defines its own serialization. For whatever reasons, Special doesn't want to save one of its internal data members, @volatile. The author has decided to serialize the two other instance variables in an array.

```ruby
class Special
  def initialize(valuable, volatile, precious)
    @valuable = valuable
    @volatile = volatile
    @precious = precious
  end
  def marshal_dump
    [ @valuable, @precious ]
  end
  def marshal_load(variables)
    @valuable = variables[0]
    @precious = variables[1]
    @volatile = "unknown"
  end
  def to_s
    "#@valuable #@volatile #@precious"
  end
end
obj = Special.new("Hello", "there", "World")
puts "Before: obj = #{obj}"
data = Marshal.dump(obj)
obj = Marshal.load(data)
puts "After: obj = #{obj}"
```

produces:

```
Before: obj = Hello there World
After: obj = Hello unknown World
```

For more details, see the reference section on `Marshal` beginning on page 535.

YAML for Marshaling

The `Marshal` module is built into the interpreter and uses a binary format to store objects externally. While fast, this binary format has one major disadvantage: if the interpreter changes significantly, the marshal binary format may also change, and old dumped files may no longer be loadable.

An alternative is to use a less fussy external format, preferably one using text rather than binary files. One option, supplied as a standard library as of Ruby 1.8, is YAML.[2]

We can adapt our previous marshal example to use YAML. Rather than implement specific loading and dumping methods to control the marshal process, we simply define the method `to_yaml_properties`, which returns a list of instance variables to be saved.

---

2. http://www.yaml.org. YAML stands for YAML Ain't Markup Language, but that hardly seems important.

```ruby
require 'yaml'
class Special
  def initialize(valuable, volatile, precious)
    @valuable = valuable
    @volatile = volatile
    @precious = precious
  end

  def to_yaml_properties
    %w{ @precious @valuable }
  end

  def to_s
    "#@valuable #@volatile #@precious"
  end
end
obj = Special.new("Hello", "there", "World")
puts "Before: obj = #{obj}"
data = YAML.dump(obj)
obj = YAML.load(data)
puts "After: obj = #{obj}"
```

produces:

```
Before: obj = Hello there World
After: obj = Hello  World
```

We can have a look at what YAML creates as the serialized form of the object—it's pretty simple.

```ruby
obj = Special.new("Hello", "there", "World")
puts YAML.dump(obj)
```

produces:

```
--- !ruby/object:Special
precious: World
valuable: Hello
```

Distributed Ruby

Since we can serialize an object or a set of objects into a form suitable for out-of-process storage, we can use this capability for the *transmission* of objects from one process to another. Couple this capability with the power of networking, and *voilà*: you have a distributed object system. To save you the trouble of having to write the code, we suggest using Masatoshi Seki's Distributed Ruby library (drb), which is now available as a standard Ruby library.

1.8

Using drb, a Ruby process may act as a server, as a client, or as both. A drb server acts as a source of objects, while a client is a user of those objects. To the client, it appears that the objects are local, but in reality the code is still being executed remotely.

A server starts a service by associating an object with a given port. Threads are created internally to handle incoming requests on that port, so remember to join the drb thread before exiting your program.

```
require 'drb'
class TestServer
  def add(*args)
    args.inject {|n,v| n + v}
  end
end
server = TestServer.new
DRb.start_service('druby://localhost:9000', server)
DRb.thread.join   # Don't exit just yet!
```

A simple drb client simply creates a local drb object and associates it with the object on the remote server; the local object is a proxy.

```
require 'drb'
DRb.start_service()
obj = DRbObject.new(nil, 'druby://localhost:9000')
# Now use obj
puts "Sum is: #{obj.add(1, 2, 3)}"
```

The client connects to the server and calls the method add, which uses the magic of inject to sum its arguments. It returns the result, which the client prints out.

```
Sum is: 6
```

The initial nil argument to DRbObject indicates that we want to attach to a new distributed object. We could also use an existing object.

Ho hum, you say. This sounds like Java's RMI, or CORBA, or whatever. Yes, it is a functional distributed object mechanism—but it is written in just a few hundred lines of Ruby code. No C, nothing fancy, just plain old Ruby code. Of course, it has no naming service or trader service, or anything like you'd see in CORBA, but it is simple and reasonably fast. On my 2.5GHz Power Mac system, this sample code runs at about 1,300 remote message calls per second.

And, if you like the look of Sun's JavaSpaces, the basis of the JINI architecture, you'll be interested to know that drb is distributed with a short module that does the same kind of thing. JavaSpaces is based on a technology called Linda. To prove that its Japanese author has a sense of humor, Ruby's version of Linda is known as *Rinda*.

If you like your remote messaging fat, dumb, and interoperable, you could also look into the SOAP libraries distributed with Ruby.[3]

1.8

---

3. This is a comment on SOAP, which long-ago abandoned the *Simple* part of its acronym. The Ruby implementation of SOAP is a wonderful piece of work.

Compile Time? Runtime? Anytime!

The important thing to remember about Ruby is that there isn't a big difference between "compile time" and "runtime." It's all the same. You can add code to a running process. You can redefine methods on the fly, change their scope from `public` to `private`, and so on. You can even alter basic types, such as `Class` and `Object`.

Once you get used to this flexibility, it is hard to go back to a static language such as C++ or even to a half-static language such as Java.

But then, why would you want to do that?

Part IV

Ruby Library Reference

Chapter 27

Built-in Classes and Modules

This chapter documents the classes and modules built into the standard Ruby language. They are available to every Ruby program automatically; no `require` is required. This section does not contain the various predefined variables and constants; these are listed starting on page 333.

In the descriptions starting on page 427, we show sample invocations for each method.

new	String.new(*some_string*) → *new_string*

This description shows a class method that is called as `String.new`. The italic parameter indicates that a single string is passed in, and the arrow indicates that another string is returned from the method. Because this return value has a different name than that of the parameter, it represents a different object.

When we illustrate instance methods, we show a sample call with a dummy object name in italics as the receiver.

each	*str*.each(*sep*=$/) {| *record* | *block* } → *str*

The parameter to `String#each` is shown to have a default value; call `each` with no parameter, and the value of `$/` will be used. This method is an iterator, so the call is followed by a block. `String#each` returns its receiver, so the receiver's name (*str* in this case) appears again after the arrow.

Some methods have optional parameters. We show these parameters between angle brackets, ⟨ *xxx* ⟩. (Additionally, we use the notation ⟨ *xxx* ⟩* to indicate zero or more occurrences of *xxx* and use ⟨ *xxx* ⟩+ to indicate one or more occurrences of *xxx*.)

index	*self*.index(*str* ⟨ , *offset* ⟩) → *pos* or `nil`

Finally, for methods that can be called in several different forms, we list each form on a separate line.

Alphabetical Listing

Standard classes are listed alphabetically, followed by the standard modules. Within each, we list the class (or module) methods, followed by its instance methods.

Summary of Built-in Classes

Array (page 427): *Class:* [ ], new. *Instance:* &, *, +, −, <<, <=>, ==, [ ], [ ]=, |, assoc, at, clear, collect!, compact, compact!, concat, delete, delete_at, delete_if, each, each_index, empty?, eql?, fetch, fill, first, flatten, flatten!, include?, index, indexes, indices, insert, join, last, length, map!, nitems, pack, pop, push, rassoc, reject!, replace, reverse, reverse!, reverse_each, rindex, shift, size, slice, slice!, sort, sort!, to_a, to_ary, to_s, transpose, uniq, uniq!, unshift, values_at.

Bignum (page 441): *Instance:* Arithmetic operations, Bit operations, <=>, ==, [ ], abs, div, divmod, eql?, modulo, quo, remainder, size, to_f, to_s.

Binding (page 444)

Class (page 445): *Class:* inherited, new. *Instance:* allocate, new, superclass.

Continuation (page 448): *Instance:* call.

Dir (page 449): *Class:* [ ], chdir, chroot, delete, entries, foreach, getwd, glob, mkdir, new, open, pwd, rmdir, unlink. *Instance:* close, each, path, pos, pos=, read, rewind, seek, tell.

Exception (page 461): *Class:* exception, new. *Instance:* backtrace, exception, message, set_backtrace, status, success?, to_s, to_str.

FalseClass (page 464): *Instance:* &, ^, |.

File (page 465): *Class:* atime, basename, blockdev?, chardev?, chmod, chown, ctime, delete, directory?, dirname, executable?, executable_real?, exist?, exists?, expand_path, extname, file?, fnmatch, fnmatch?, ftype, grpowned?, join, lchmod, lchown, link, lstat, mtime, new, open, owned?, pipe?, readable?, readable_real?, readlink, rename, setgid?, setuid?, size, size?, socket?, split, stat, sticky?, symlink, symlink?, truncate, umask, unlink, utime, writable?, writable_real?, zero?. *Instance:* atime, chmod, chown, ctime, flock, lchmod, lchown, lstat, mtime, path, truncate.

File::Stat (page 477): *Instance:* <=>, atime, blksize, blockdev?, blocks, chardev?, ctime, dev, dev_major, dev_minor, directory?, executable?, executable_real?, file?, ftype, gid, grpowned?, ino, mode, mtime, nlink, owned?, pipe?, rdev, rdev_major, rdev_minor, readable?, readable_real?, setgid?, setuid?, size, size?, socket?, sticky?, symlink?, uid, writable?, writable_real?, zero?.

Fixnum (page 484): *Class:* . *Instance:* Arithmetic operations, Bit operations, <=>, [ ], abs, div, divmod, id2name, modulo, quo, size, to_f, to_s, to_sym, zero?.

Float (page 487): *Instance:* Arithmetic operations, <=>, ==, abs, ceil, divmod, eql?, finite?, floor, infinite?, modulo, nan?, round, to_f, to_i, to_int, to_s, truncate, zero?.

Hash (page 492): *Class:* [ ], new. *Instance:* ==, [ ], [ ]=, clear, default, default=, default_proc, delete, delete_if, each, each_key, each_pair, each_value, empty?, fetch, has_key?, has_value?, include?, index, indexes, indices, invert, key?, keys, length, member?, merge, merge!, rehash, reject, reject!, replace, select, shift, size, sort, store, to_a, to_hash, to_s, update, value?, values, values_at.

Integer (page 501): *Instance:* ceil, chr, downto, floor, integer?, next, round, succ, times, to_i, to_int, truncate, upto.

IO (page 503): *Class:* for_fd, foreach, new, open, pipe, popen, read, readlines, select, sysopen. *Instance:* <<, binmode, clone, close, close_read, close_write, closed?, each, each_byte, each_line, eof, eof?, fcntl, fileno, flush, fsync, getc, gets, ioctl, isatty, lineno, lineno=, pid, pos, pos=, print, printf, putc, puts, read, readchar, readline, readlines, reopen, rewind, seek, stat, sync, sync=, sysread, sysseek, syswrite, tell, to_i, to_io, tty?, ungetc, write.

MatchData (page 537): *Instance:* [ ], begin, captures, end, length, offset, post_match, pre_match, select, size, string, to_a, to_s, values_at.

Method (page 543): *Instance:* [ ], ==, arity, call, eql?, to_proc, unbind.

Module (page 545): *Class:* constants, nesting, new. *Instance:* <, <=, >, >=, <=>, ===, ancestors, autoload, autoload?, class_eval, class_variables, clone, const_defined?, const_get, const_missing, const_set, constants, include?, included_modules, instance_method, instance_methods, method_defined?, module_eval, name, private_class_method, private_instance_methods, private_method_defined?, protected_instance_methods, protected_method_defined?, public_class_method, public_instance_methods, public_method_defined?. *Private:* alias_method, append_features, attr, attr_accessor, attr_reader, attr_writer, define_method, extend_object, extended, include, included, method_added, method_removed, method_undefined, module_function, private, protected, public, remove_class_variable, remove_const, remove_method, undef_method.

NilClass (page 561): *Instance:* &, ^, |, nil?, to_a, to_f, to_i, to_s.

Numeric (page 562): *Instance:* +@, -@, <=>, abs, ceil, coerce, div, divmod, eql?, floor, integer?, modulo, nonzero?, quo, remainder, round, step, to_int, truncate, zero?.

Object (page 567): *Instance:* ==, ===, =~, __id__, __send__, class, clone, display, dup, eql?, equal?, extend, freeze, frozen?, hash, id, initialize_copy, inspect, instance_eval, instance_of?, instance_variable_get, instance_variable_set, instance_variables, is_a?, kind_of?, method, method_missing, methods, nil?, object_id, private_methods, protected_methods, public_methods, respond_to?, send, singleton_methods, taint, tainted?, to_a, to_s, type, untaint. *Private:* initialize, remove_instance_variable, singleton_method_added, singleton_method_removed, singleton_method_undefined.

Proc (page 580): *Class:* new. *Instance:* [ ], ==, arity, binding, call, to_proc, to_s.

Process::Status (page 591): *Instance:* ==, &, >>, coredump?, exited?, exitstatus, pid, signaled?, stopped?, success?, stopsig, termsig, to_i, to_int, to_s.

Range (page 597): *Class:* new. *Instance:* ==, ===, begin, each, end, eql?, exclude_end?, first, include?, last, member?, step.

Regexp (page 600): *Class:* compile, escape, last_match, new, quote. *Instance:* ==, ===, =~, ~, casefold?, inspect, kcode, match, options, source, to_s.

String (page 606): *Class:* new. *Instance:* %, *, +, <<, <=>, ==, ===, =~, [ ], [ ]=, ~, capitalize, capitalize!, casecmp, center, chomp, chomp!, chop, chop!, concat, count, crypt, delete, delete!, downcase, downcase!, dump, each_byte, each_line, empty?, gsub, gsub!, hex, include?, index, insert, intern, length, ljust, lstrip, lstrip!, match, next, next!, oct, replace, reverse, reverse!, rindex, rjust, rstrip, rstrip!, scan, size, slice, slice!, split, squeeze, squeeze!, strip, strip!, sub, sub!, succ, succ!, sum, swapcase, swapcase!, to_f, to_i, to_s, to_str, to_sym, tr, tr!, tr_s, tr_s!, unpack, upcase, upcase!, upto.

Struct (page 626): *Class:* new, new, [ ], members. *Instance:* ==, [ ], [ ]=, each, each_pair, length, members, size, to_a, values, values_at.

Struct::Tms (page 630)

Symbol (page 631): *Class:* all_symbols. *Instance:* id2name, inspect, to_i, to_int, to_s, to_sym.

Thread (page 633): *Class:* abort_on_exception, abort_on_exception=, critical, critical=, current, exit, fork, kill, list, main, new, pass, start, stop. *Instance:* [ ], [ ]=, abort_on_exception, abort_on_exception=, alive?, exit, group, join, keys, key?, kill, priority, priority=, raise, run, safe_level, status, stop?, terminate, value, wakeup.

ThreadGroup (page 640): *Class:* new. *Instance:* add, enclose, enclosed?, freeze, list.

Time (page 642): *Class:* at, gm, local, mktime, new, now, times, utc. *Instance:* +, −, <=>, asctime, ctime, day, dst?, getgm, getlocal, getutc, gmt?, gmtime, gmt_offset, gmtoff, hour, isdst, localtime, mday, min, mon, month, sec, strftime, to_a, to_f, to_i, to_s, tv_sec, tv_usec, usec, utc, utc?, utc_offset, wday, yday, year, zone.

TrueClass (page 650): *Instance:* &, ^, |.

UnboundMethod (page 651): *Instance:* arity, bind.

Summary of Built-in Modules

Comparable (page 447): *Instance:* Comparisons, between?.

Enumerable (page 454): *Instance:* all?, any?, collect, detect, each_with_index, entries, find, find_all, grep, include?, inject, map, max, member?, min, partition, reject, select, sort, sort_by, to_a, zip.

Errno (page 460)

FileTest (page 483)

GC (page 491): *Class:* disable, enable, start. *Instance:* garbage_collect.

Kernel (page 516): *Class:* Array, Float, Integer, String, ` (backquote), abort, at_exit, autoload, autoload?, binding, block_given?, callcc, caller, catch, chomp, chomp!, chop, chop!, eval, exec, exit, exit!, fail, fork, format, gets, global_variables, gsub, gsub!, iterator?, lambda, load, local_variables, loop, open, p, print, printf, proc, putc, puts, raise, rand, readline, readlines, require, scan, select, set_trace_func, sleep, split, sprintf, srand, sub, sub!, syscall, system, test, throw, trace_var, trap, untrace_var, warn.

Marshal (page 535): *Class:* dump, load, restore.

Math (page 540): *Class:* acos, acosh, asin, asinh, atan, atanh, atan2, cos, cosh, erf, erfc, exp, frexp, hypot, ldexp, log, log10, sin, sinh, sqrt, tan, tanh.

ObjectSpace (page 578): *Class:* _id2ref, define_finalizer, each_object, garbage_collect, undefine_finalizer.

Process (page 583): *Class:* abort, detach, egid, egid=, euid, euid=, exit, exit!, fork, getpgid, getpgrp, getpriority, gid, gid=, groups, groups=, initgroups, kill, maxgroups, maxgroups=, pid, ppid, setpgid, setpgrp, setpriority, setsid, times, uid, uid=, wait, waitall, wait2, waitpid, waitpid2.

Process::GID (page 589): *Class:* change_privilege, eid, eid=, grant_privilege, re_exchange, re_exchangeable?, rid, sid_available?, switch.

Process::Sys (page 594): *Class:* getegid, geteuid, getgid, getuid, issetugid, setegid, seteuid, setgid, setregid, setresgid, setresuid, setreuid, setrgid, setruid, setuid.

Process::UID (page 596): *Class:* change_privilege, eid, eid=, grant_privilege, re_exchange, re_exchangeable?, rid, sid_available?, switch.

Signal (page 604): *Class:* list, trap.

| Class | **Array** | < | Object |

Arrays are ordered, integer-indexed collections of any object. Array indexing starts at 0, as in C or Java. A negative index is assumed to be relative to the end of the array; that is, an index of −1 indicates the last element of the array, −2 is the next to last element in the array, and so on.

Mixes in

Enumerable:

> all?, any?, collect, detect, each_with_index, entries, find, find_all, grep, include?, inject, map, max, member?, min, partition, reject, select, sort, sort_by, to_a, zip

Class methods

[ ]   Array[⟨ obj ⟩*] → *an_array*

Returns a new array populated with the given objects. Equivalent to the operator form `Array.[](...)`.

```
Array.[]( 1, 'a', /^A/ )    ›   [1, "a", /^A/]
Array[ 1, 'a', /^A/ ]       →   [1, "a", /^A/]
[ 1, 'a', /^A/ ]            →   [1, "a", /^A/]
```

new
$$\text{Array.new} \rightarrow \textit{an\_array}$$
$$\text{Array.new} (\textit{size=0, obj=}\texttt{nil}) \rightarrow \textit{an\_array}$$
$$\text{Array.new}(\textit{array}) \rightarrow \textit{an\_array}$$
$$\text{Array.new}(\textit{size}) \{ | i | \textit{block} \} \rightarrow \textit{an\_array}$$

Returns a new array. In the first form, the new array is empty. In the second it is created with *size* copies of *obj* (that is, *size* references to the same *obj*). The third form creates a copy of the array passed as a parameter (the array is generated by calling `to_ary` on the parameter). In the last form, an array of the given size is created. Each element in this array is calculated by passing the element's index to the given block and storing the return value.

```
Array.new          →   []
Array.new(2)       →   [nil, nil]
Array.new(5, "A")  →   ["A", "A", "A", "A", "A"]

# only one instance of the default object is created
a = Array.new(2, Hash.new)
a[0]['cat'] = 'feline'
a    →   [{"cat"=>"feline"}, {"cat"=>"feline"}]
a[1]['cat'] = 'Felix'
a    →   [{"cat"=>"Felix"}, {"cat"=>"Felix"}]
```

A rray

```
a = Array.new(2) { Hash.new }  # Multiple instances
a[0]['cat'] = 'feline'
a   →   [{"cat"=>"feline"}, {}]

squares = Array.new(5) {|i| i*i}
squares   →   [0, 1, 4, 9, 16]

copy = Array.new(squares)      # initialized by copying
squares[5] = 25
squares   →   [0, 1, 4, 9, 16, 25]
copy      →   [0, 1, 4, 9, 16]
```

Instance methods

&

                               arr & other_array → an_array

Set Intersection—Returns a new array containing elements common to the two arrays, with no duplicates. The rules for comparing elements are the same as for hash keys. If you need setlike behavior, see the library class Set on page 731.

```
[ 1, 1, 3, 5 ] & [ 1, 2, 3 ]   →   [1, 3]
```

*

                               *arr * int → an_array*
                               *arr * str → a_string*

Repetition—With an argument that responds to to_str, equivalent to *arr*.join(*str*). Otherwise, returns a new array built by concatenating *int* copies of *arr*.

```
[ 1, 2, 3 ] * 3      →   [1, 2, 3, 1, 2, 3, 1, 2, 3]
[ 1, 2, 3 ] * "--"   →   "1--2--3"
```

+

                               arr + other_array → an_array

Concatenation—Returns a new array built by concatenating the two arrays together to produce a third array.

```
[ 1, 2, 3 ] + [ 4, 5 ]   →   [1, 2, 3, 4, 5]
```

−

                               arr - other_array → an_array

Array Difference—Returns a new array that is a copy of the original array, removing any items that also appear in *other_array*. If you need setlike behavior, see the library class Set on page 731.

```
[ 1, 1, 2, 2, 3, 3, 4, 5 ] - [ 1, 2, 4 ]   →   [3, 3, 5]
```

<<

                               arr << obj → arr

Append—Pushes the given object on to the end of this array. This expression returns the array itself, so several appends may be chained together. See also Array#push.

```
[ 1, 2 ] << "c" << "d" << [ 3, 4 ]   →   [1, 2, "c", "d", [3, 4]]
```

A rray

<=>   *arr <=> other_array →* −1, 0, +1

Comparison—Returns an integer −1, 0, or +1 if this array is less than, equal to, or greater than *other_array*. Each object in each array is compared (using <=>). If any value isn't equal, then that inequality is the return value. If all the values found are equal, then the return is based on a comparison of the array lengths. Thus, two arrays are "equal" according to Array#<=> if and only if they have the same length and the value of each element is equal to the value of the corresponding element in the other array.

```
[ "a", "a", "c" ]    <=> [ "a", "b", "c" ]   →   -1
[ 1, 2, 3, 4, 5, 6 ] <=> [ 1, 2 ]            →   1
```

==   *arr == obj →* true or false

Equality—Two arrays are equal if they contain the same number of elements and if each element is equal to (according to Object#==) the corresponding element in the other array. If *obj* is not an array, attempt to convert it using to_ary and return *obj==arr*.

```
[ "a", "c" ]    == [ "a", "c", 7 ]   →   false
[ "a", "c", 7 ] == [ "a", "c", 7 ]   →   true
[ "a", "c", 7 ] == [ "a", "d", "f" ] →   false
```

[ ]   *arr[int] →* obj or nil
                                                   arr[start, length] → an array or nil
                                                   arr[range] → an_array or nil

Element Reference—Returns the element at index *int*, returns a subarray starting at index *start* and continuing for *length* elements, or returns a subarray specified by *range*. Negative indices count backward from the end of the array (−1 is the last element). Returns nil if the index of the first element selected is greater than the array size. If the start index equals the array size and a *length* or *range* parameter is given, an empty array is returned. Equivalent to Array#slice.

1.8

```
a = [ "a", "b", "c", "d", "e" ]
a[2] +  a[0] + a[1]   →   "cab"
a[6]                  →   nil
a[1, 2]               →   ["b", "c"]
a[1..3]               →   ["b", "c", "d"]
a[4..7]               →   ["e"]
a[6..10]              →   nil
a[-3, 3]              →   ["c", "d", "e"]

# special cases
a[5]      →   nil
a[5, 1]   →   []
a[5..10]  →   []
```

[ ]=

$$arr[int] = obj \rightarrow obj$$
$$arr[start, length] = obj \rightarrow obj$$
$$arr[range] = obj \rightarrow obj$$

Element Assignment—Sets the element at index *int*, replaces a subarray starting at index *start* and continuing for *length* elements, or replaces a subarray specified by *range*. If *int* is greater than the current capacity of the array, the array grows automatically. A negative *int* will count backward from the end of the array. Inserts elements if *length* is zero. If *obj* is nil, deletes elements from *arr*. If *obj* is an array, the form with the single index will insert that array into *arr*, and the forms with a length or with a range will replace the given elements in *arr* with the array contents. An IndexError is raised if a negative index points past the beginning of the array. See also Array#push and Array#unshift.

```
a = Array.new              →    []
a[4] = "4";            a   →    [nil, nil, nil, nil, "4"]
a[0] = [ 1, 2, 3 ];    a   →    [[1, 2, 3], nil, nil, nil, "4"]
a[0, 3] = [ 'a', 'b', 'c' ]; a →  ["a", "b", "c", nil, "4"]
a[1..2] = [ 1, 2 ];    a   →    ["a", 1, 2, nil, "4"]
a[0, 2] = "?";         a   →    ["?", 2, nil, "4"]
a[0..2] = "A";         a   →    ["A", "4"]
a[-1]   = "Z";         a   →    ["A", "Z"]
a[1..-1] = nil;        a   →    ["A"]
```

|

$$arr \mid other\_array \rightarrow an\_array$$

Set Union—Returns a new array by joining this array with *other_array*, removing duplicates. The rules for comparing elements are the same as for hash keys. If you need setlike behavior, see the library class Set on page 731.

```
[ "a", "b", "c" ] | [ "c", "d", "a" ]   →   ["a", "b", "c", "d"]
```

assoc

$$arr.assoc(\ obj\ ) \rightarrow an\_array \text{ or } nil$$

Searches through an array whose elements are also arrays comparing *obj* with the first element of each contained array using *obj*.== . Returns the first contained array that matches (that is, the first *assoc*iated array) or nil if no match is found. See also Array#rassoc.

```
s1 = [ "colors", "red", "blue", "green" ]
s2 = [ "letters", "a", "b", "c" ]
s3 = "foo"
a  = [ s1, s2, s3 ]
a.assoc("letters")   →   ["letters", "a", "b", "c"]
a.assoc("foo")       →   nil
```

at

$$arr.at(\ int\ ) \rightarrow obj \text{ or } nil$$

Returns the element at index *int*. A negative index counts from the end of *arr*. Returns nil if the index is out of range. See also `Array#[]`. (`Array#at` is slightly faster than `Array#[]`, as it does not accept ranges, and so on.)

```
a = [ "a", "b", "c", "d", "e" ]
a.at(0)    →   "a"
a.at(-1)   ›   "e"
```

clear
arr.clear → arr

Removes all elements from *arr*.

```
a = [ "a", "b", "c", "d", "e" ]
a.clear   →   []
```

collect!
arr.collect! {| obj | block } → arr

Invokes *block* once for each element of *arr*, replacing the element with the value returned by *block*. See also `Enumerable#collect`.

```
a = [ "a", "b", "c", "d" ]
a.collect! {|x|  x + "!" }   →    ["a!", "b!", "c!", "d!"]
a                            →    ["a!", "b!", "c!", "d!"]
```

compact
arr.compact → an_array

Returns a copy of *arr* with all `nil` elements removed.

```
[ "a", nil, "b", nil, "c", nil ].compact   →   ["a", "b", "c"]
```

compact!
arr.compact! → arr or <code>nil</code>

Removes `nil` elements from *arr*. Returns `nil` if no changes were made.

```
[ "a", nil, "b", nil, "c" ].compact!   →   ["a", "b", "c"]
[ "a", "b", "c" ].compact!             →   nil
```

concat
arr.concat(other_array) → arr

Appends the elements in *other_array* to *arr*.

```
[ "a", "b" ].concat( ["c", "d"] )   →   ["a", "b", "c", "d"]
```

delete
arr.delete(obj) → obj or <code>nil</code>
arr.delete(obj) { block } → obj or <code>nil</code>

Deletes items from *arr* that are equal to *obj*. If the item is not found, returns `nil`. If the optional code block is given, returns the result of *block* if the item is not found.

```
a = [ "a", "b", "b", "b", "c" ]
a.delete("b")                   →    "b"
a                               →    ["a", "c"]
a.delete("z")                   →    nil
a.delete("z") { "not found" }   →    "not found"
```

Array

delete_at

arr.delete_at(*index*) → *obj* or nil

Deletes the element at the specified index, returning that element, or nil if the index is out of range. See also `Array#slice!`.

```
a = %w( ant bat cat dog )
a.delete_at(2)    →   "cat"
a                 →   ["ant", "bat", "dog"]
a.delete_at(99)   →   nil
```

delete_if

arr.delete_if {| *item* | *block* } → *arr*

Deletes every element of *arr* for which *block* evaluates to true.

```
a = [ "a", "b", "c" ]
a.delete_if {|x| x >= "b" }   →   ["a"]
```

each

arr.each {| *item* | *block* } → *arr*

Calls *block* once for each element in *arr*, passing that element as a parameter.

```
a = [ "a", "b", "c" ]
a.each {|x| print x, " -- " }
```

produces:

```
a -- b -- c --
```

each_index

arr.each_index {| *index* | *block* } → *arr*

Same as `Array#each` but passes the index of the element instead of the element itself.

```
a = [ "a", "b", "c" ]
a.each_index {|x| print x, " -- " }
```

produces:

```
0 -- 1 -- 2 --
```

empty?

arr.empty? → true or false

Returns true if *arr* array contains no elements.

```
[].empty?          →   true
[ 1, 2, 3 ].empty?   →   false
```

eql?

arr.eql?(*other*) → true or false

Returns true if *arr* and *other* are the same object or if *other* is an object of class Array with the same length and content as *arr*. Elements in the arrays are compared using `Object#eql?`. See also `Array#<=>`.

```
[ "a", "b", "c" ].eql?(["a", "b", "c"])   →   true
[ "a", "b", "c" ].eql?(["a", "b"])        →   false
[ "a", "b", "c" ].eql?(["b", "c", "d"])   →   false
```

fetch

$$arr.\text{fetch}(\ index\ ) \rightarrow obj$$
$$arr.\text{fetch}(\ index,\ default\ ) \rightarrow obj$$
$$arr.\text{fetch}(\ index\ )\ \{\ |\ i\ |\ block\ \}\ \rightarrow obj$$

1.8

Tries to return the element at position *index*. If the index lies outside the array, the first form throws an `IndexError` exception, the second form returns *default*, and the third form returns the value of invoking the block, passing in the index. Negative values of *index* count from the end of the array.

```
a = [ 11, 22, 33, 44 ]
a.fetch(1)            →   22
a.fetch(-1)           →   44
a.fetch(-1, 'cat')    →   44
a.fetch(4, 'cat')     →   "cat"
a.fetch(4) {|i| i*i } →   16
```

fill

$$arr.\text{fill}(\ obj\ ) \rightarrow arr$$
$$arr.\text{fill}(\ obj,\ start\ \langle\ ,\ length\ \rangle\ ) \rightarrow arr$$
$$arr.\text{fill}(\ obj,\ range\ ) \rightarrow arr$$
$$arr.\text{fill}\ \{\ |\ i\ |\ block\ \}\ \rightarrow arr$$
$$arr.\text{fill}(\ start\ \langle\ ,\ length\ \rangle\ )\ \{\ |\ i\ |\ block\ \}\ \rightarrow arr$$
$$arr.\text{fill}(\ range\ )\ \{\ |\ i\ |\ block\ \}\ \rightarrow arr$$

1.8

The first three forms set the selected elements of *arr* (which may be the entire array) to *obj*. A *start* of `nil` is equivalent to zero. A *length* of `nil` is equivalent to *arr*.length. The last three forms fill the array with the value of the block. The block is passed the absolute index of each element to be filled.

```
a = [ "a", "b", "c", "d" ]
a.fill("x")          →   ["x", "x", "x", "x"]
a.fill("z", 2, 2)    →   ["x", "x", "z", "z"]
a.fill("y", 0..1)    →   ["y", "y", "z", "z"]
a.fill {|i| i*i}     →   [0, 1, 4, 9]
a.fill(-3) {|i| i+100} → [0, 101, 102, 103]
```

first

$$arr.\text{first} \rightarrow obj\ \text{or}\ nil$$
$$arr.\text{first}(\ count\ ) \rightarrow an\_array$$

1.8

Returns the first element, or the first *count* elements, of *arr*. If the array is empty, the first form returns `nil`, and the second returns an empty array.

```
a = [ "q", "r", "s", "t" ]
a.first     →   "q"
a.first(1)  →   ["q"]
a.first(3)  →   ["q", "r", "s"]
```

flatten

$$arr.\text{flatten} \rightarrow an\_array$$

Returns a new array that is a one-dimensional flattening of this array (recursively). That is, for every element that is an array, extract its elements into the new array.

```
s = [ 1, 2, 3 ]            →   [1, 2, 3]
t = [ 4, 5, 6, [7, 8] ]    →   [4, 5, 6, [7, 8]]
a = [ s, t, 9, 10 ]        →   [[1, 2, 3], [4, 5, 6, [7, 8]], 9, 10]
a.flatten                  →   [1, 2, 3, 4, 5, 6, 7, 8, 9, 10]
```

flatten!   *arr*.flatten! → *arr* or nil

Same as `Array#flatten` but modifies the receiver in place. Returns nil if no modifications were made (i.e., *arr* contains no subarrays).

```
a = [ 1, 2, [3, [4, 5] ] ]
a.flatten!   →   [1, 2, 3, 4, 5]
a.flatten!   →   nil
a            →   [1, 2, 3, 4, 5]
```

include?   *arr*.include?(*obj*) → true or false

Returns true if the given object is present in *arr* (that is, if any object == *obj*), false
otherwise.

```
a = [ "a", "b", "c" ]
a.include?("b")   →   true
a.include?("z")   →   false
```

index   *arr*.index(*obj*) → *int* or nil

Returns the index of the first object in *arr* that is == to *obj*. Returns nil if no match is
found.

```
a = [ "a", "b", "c" ]
a.index("b")   →   1
a.index("z")   →   nil
```

indexes   *arr*.indexes(*i1, i2, ... iN*) → *an_array*

1.8, Deprecated; use `Array#values_at`.

indices   *arr*.indices(*i1, i2, ... iN*) → *an_array*

1.8, Deprecated; use `Array#values_at`.

insert   *arr*.insert(*index*, ⟨ *obj* ⟩⁺) → *arr*

1.8, If *index* is not negative, inserts the given values before the element with the given index.
If *index* is −1, appends the values to *arr*. Otherwise inserts the values after the element
with the given index.

```
a = %w{ a b c d }
a.insert(2, 99)        →   ["a", "b", 99, "c", "d"]
a.insert(-2, 1, 2, 3)  →   ["a", "b", 99, "c", 1, 2, 3, "d"]
a.insert(-1, "e")      →   ["a", "b", 99, "c", 1, 2, 3, "d", "e"]
```

Array

Table 27.1. Template characters for `Array#pack`

Directive	Meaning
@	Moves to absolute position
A	ASCII string (space padded, count is width)
a	ASCII string (null padded, count is width)
B	Bit string (descending bit order)
b	Bit string (ascending bit order)
C	Unsigned char
c	Char
D, d	Double-precision float, native format
E	Double-precision float, little-endian byte order
e	Single-precision float, little-endian byte order
F, f	Single-precision float, native format
G	Double-precision float, network (big-endian) byte order
g	Single-precision float, network (big-endian) byte order
H	Hex string (high nibble first)
h	Hex string (low nibble first)
I	Unsigned integer
i	Integer
L	Unsigned long
l	Long
M	Quoted printable, MIME encoding (see RFC2045)
m	Base64 encoded string
N	Long, network (big-endian) byte order
n	Short, network (big-endian) byte order
P	Pointer to a structure (fixed-length string)
p	Pointer to a null-terminated string
Q, q	64-bit number
S	Unsigned short
s	Short
U	UTF-8
u	UU-encoded string
V	Long, little-endian byte order
v	Short, little-endian byte order
w	BER-compressed integer[1]
X	Back up a byte
x	Null byte
Z	Same as A

1.0

1.8

[1] The octets of a BER-compressed integer represent an unsigned integer in base 128, most significant digit first, with as few digits as possible. Bit eight (the high bit) is set on each byte except the last (*Self-Describing Binary Data Representation*, MacLeod)

A rray

join
arr.join($separator=\$,$) → str

Returns a string created by concatenating each element of the array to a string, separating each by *separator*.

```
[ "a", "b", "c" ].join        →    "abc"
[ "a", "b", "c" ].join("-")   →    "a-b-c"
```

last
arr.last → obj or nil

arr.last($count$) → an_array

1.8 Returns the last element, or last *count* elements, of *arr*. If the array is empty, the first form returns nil, the second an empty array.

```
[ "w", "x", "y", "z" ].last       →    "z"
[ "w", "x", "y", "z" ].last(1)    →    ["z"]
[ "w", "x", "y", "z" ].last(3)    →    ["x", "y", "z"]
```

length
arr.length → int

Returns the number of elements in *arr*. See also Array#nitems.

```
[ 1, nil, 3, nil, 5 ].length    →    5
```

map!
arr.map! {| obj | $block$ } → arr

Synonym for Array#collect!.

nitems
arr.nitems → int

Returns the number of non-nil elements in *arr*. See also Array#length.

```
[ 1, nil, 3, nil, 5 ].nitems    →    3
```

pack
arr.pack ($template$) → $binary\_string$

1.8 Packs the contents of *arr* into a binary sequence according to the directives in *template* (see Table 27.1 on the page before). Directives A, a, and Z may be followed by a count, which gives the width of the resulting field. The remaining directives also may take a count, indicating the number of array elements to convert. If the count is an asterisk (∗), all remaining array elements will be converted. Any of the directives "sSiIlL" may be followed by an underscore (_) to use the underlying platform's native size for the specified type; otherwise, they use a platform-independent size. Spaces are ignored
1.8 in the template string. Comments starting with # to the next newline or end of string are also ignored. See also String#unpack on page 623.

```
a = [ "a", "b", "c" ]
n = [ 65, 66, 67 ]
a.pack("A3A3A3")   →    "a␣␣b␣␣c␣␣"
a.pack("a3a3a3")   →    "a\000\000b\000\000c\000\000"
n.pack("ccc")      →    "ABC"
```

A rray

pop

arr.pop → *obj* or nil

Removes the last element from *arr* and returns it or returns nil if the array is empty.

```
a = [ "a", "m", "z" ]
a.pop   →   "z"
a       →   ["a", "m"]
```

push

arr.push(⟨ *obj* ⟩*) → *arr*

Appends the given argument(s) to *arr*.

```
a = [ "a", "b", "c" ]
a.push("d", "e", "f")   →   ["a", "b", "c", "d", "e", "f"]
```

rassoc

arr.rassoc(*key*) → *an_array* or nil

Searches through the array whose elements are also arrays. Compares *key* with the second element of each contained array using ==. Returns the first contained array that matches. See also Array#assoc.

```
a = [ [ 1, "one"], [2, "two"], [3, "three"], ["ii", "two"] ]
a.rassoc("two")    →   [2, "two"]
a.rassoc("four")   →   nil
```

reject!

arr.reject! { *block* } item → *arr* or nil

Equivalent to Array#delete_if, but returns nil if no changes were made. Also see Enumerable#reject.

replace

arr.replace(*other_array*) → *arr*

Replaces the contents of *arr* with the contents of *other_array*, truncating or expanding if necessary.

```
a = [ "a", "b", "c", "d", "e" ]
a.replace([ "x", "y", "z" ])   →   ["x", "y", "z"]
a                              →   ["x", "y", "z"]
```

reverse

arr.reverse → *an_array*

Returns a new array using *arr*'s elements in reverse order.

```
[ "a", "b", "c" ].reverse   →   ["c", "b", "a"]
[ 1 ].reverse               →   [1]
```

reverse!

arr.reverse! → *arr*

1.8 Reverses *arr* in place.

```
a = [ "a", "b", "c" ]
a.reverse!       →   ["c", "b", "a"]
a                →   ["c", "b", "a"]
[ 1 ].reverse!   →   [1]
```

reverse_each

arr.reverse_each { | *item* | *block* } → *arr*

Same as `Array#each`, but traverses *arr* in reverse order.

```
a = [ "a", "b", "c" ]
a.reverse_each {|x| print x, " " }
```

produces:

```
c b a
```

rindex

arr.rindex(*obj*) → *int* or `nil`

Returns the index of the last object in *arr* such that the object == *obj*. Returns `nil` if no match is found.

```
a = [ "a", "b", "b", "b", "c" ]
a.rindex("b")   →   3
a.rindex("z")   →   nil
```

shift

arr.shift → *obj* or `nil`

Returns the first element of *arr* and removes it (shifting all other elements down by one). Returns `nil` if the array is empty.

```
args = [ "-m", "-q", "filename" ]
args.shift   →   "-m"
args         →   ["-q", "filename"]
```

size

arr.size → *int*

Synonym for `Array#length`.

slice

arr.slice(*int*) → *obj*
arr.slice(*start*, *length*) → *an_array*
arr.slice(*range*) → *an_array*

Synonym for `Array#[ ]`.

```
a = [ "a", "b", "c", "d", "e" ]
a.slice(2) + a.slice(0) + a.slice(1)   →   "cab"
a.slice(6)                             →   nil
a.slice(1, 2)                          →   ["b", "c"]
a.slice(1..3)                          →   ["b", "c", "d"]
a.slice(4..7)                          →   ["e"]
a.slice(6..10)                         →   nil
a.slice(-3, 3)                         →   ["c", "d", "e"]
# special cases
a.slice(5)                             →   nil
a.slice(5, 1)                          →   []
a.slice(5..10)                         →   []
```

slice!

arr.slice!(*int*) → *obj* or nil
arr.slice!(*start*, *length*) → *an_array* or nil
arr.slice!(*range*) → *an_array* or nil

Deletes the element(s) given by an index (optionally with a length) or by a range. Returns the deleted object, subarray, or nil if the index is out of range. Equivalent to

```
def slice!(*args)
  result = self[*args]
  self[*args] = nil
  result
end

a = [ "a", "b", "c" ]
a.slice!(1)      →    "b"
a                →    ["a", "c"]
a.slice!(-1)     →    "c"
a                →    ["a"]
a.slice!(100)    →    nil
a                →    ["a"]
```

sort

arr.sort → *an_array*
arr.sort {| *a,b* | *block* } → *an_array*

Returns a new array created by sorting *arr*. Comparisons for the sort will be done using the <=> operator or using an optional code block. The block implements a comparison between *a* and *b*, returning −1, 0, or +1. See also Enumerable#sort_by.

```
a = [ "d", "a", "e", "c", "b" ]
a.sort                  →    ["a", "b", "c", "d", "e"]
a.sort {|x,y| y <=> x } →    ["e", "d", "c", "b", "a"]
```

sort!

arr.sort! → *arr*
arr.sort! {| *a,b* | *block* } → *arr*

Sorts *arr* in place (see Array#sort). *arr* is effectively frozen while a sort is in progress.

```
a = [ "d", "a", "e", "c", "b" ]
a.sort!   →   ["a", "b", "c", "d", "e"]
a         →   ["a", "b", "c", "d", "e"]
```

to_a

arr.to_a → *arr*
array_subclass.to_a → *array*

If *arr* is an array, returns *arr*. If *arr* is a subclass of Array, invokes to_ary, and uses the result to create a new array object.

to_ary

arr.to_ary → *arr*

Returns *arr*.

A rray

to_s
arr.to_s → str

Returns arr.join.

```
[ "a", "e", "i", "o" ].to_s   →   "aeio"
```

transpose
arr.transpose → an_array

1.8 Assumes that arr is an array of arrays and transposes the rows and columns.

```
a = [[1,2], [3,4], [5,6]]
a.transpose   →   [[1, 3, 5], [2, 4, 6]]
```

uniq
arr.uniq → an_array

Returns a new array by removing duplicate values in arr, where duplicates are detected by comparing using eql? and hash.

```
a = [ "a", "a", "b", "b", "c" ]
a.uniq   →   ["a", "b", "c"]
```

uniq!
arr.uniq! → arr or nil

Same as Array#uniq, but modifies the receiver in place. Returns nil if no changes are made (that is, no duplicates are found).

```
a = [ "a", "a", "b", "b", "c" ]
a.uniq!   →   ["a", "b", "c"]
b = [ "a", "b", "c" ]
b.uniq!   →   nil
```

unshift
arr.unshift(⟨ obj ⟩⁺) → arr

Prepends object(s) to arr.

```
a = [ "b", "c", "d" ]
a.unshift("a")   →   ["a", "b", "c", "d"]
a.unshift(1, 2)  →   [1, 2, "a", "b", "c", "d"]
```

values_at
arr.values_at(⟨ $selector$ ⟩*) → an_array

1.8 Returns an array containing the elements in arr corresponding to the given selector(s). The selectors may be either integer indices or ranges.

```
a = %w{ a b c d e f }
a.values_at(1, 3, 5)      →   ["b", "d", "f"]
a.values_at(1, 3, 5, 7)   →   ["b", "d", "f", nil]
a.values_at(-1, -3, -5, -7)  →   ["f", "d", "b", nil]
a.values_at(1..3, 2...5)  →   ["b", "c", "d", "c", "d", "e"]
```

Class **Bignum** < Integer

Bignum objects hold integers outside the range of Fixnum. Bignum objects are created automatically when integer calculations would otherwise overflow a Fixnum. When a calculation involving Bignum objects returns a result that will fit in a Fixnum, the result is automatically converted.

For the purposes of the bitwise operations and [ ], a Bignum is treated as if it were an infinite-length bitstring with 2's complement representation.

While Fixnum values are immediate, Bignum objects are not—assignment and parameter passing work with references to objects, not the objects themselves.

Instance methods

Arithmetic operations

Performs various arithmetic operations on *big*.

big	+	*number*	Addition
big	−	*number*	Subtraction
big	*	*number*	Multiplication
big	/	*number*	Division
big	%	*number*	Modulo
big	**	*number*	Exponentiation
big	-@		Unary minus

Bit operations

Performs various operations on the binary representations of the Bignum.

~ *big*			Invert bits
big	|	*number*	Bitwise OR
big	&	*number*	Bitwise AND
big	^	*number*	Bitwise EXCLUSIVE OR
big	<<	*number*	Left-shift *number* bits
big	>>	*number*	Right-shift *number* bits (with sign extension)

<=>   *big* <=> *number* → −1, 0, +1

Comparison—Returns −1, 0, or +1 depending on whether *big* is less than, equal to, or greater than *number*. This is the basis for the tests in Comparable.

==   *big* == *obj* → true or false

Returns true only if *obj* has the same value as *big*. Contrast this with Bignum#eql?, which requires *obj* to be a Bignum.

```
68719476736 == 68719476736.0   →   true
```

B ignum

[ ]   *big*[*n*] → 0, 1

Bit Reference—Returns the *n*th bit in the (assumed) binary representation of *big*, where *big*[0] is the least significant bit.

```
a = 9**15

50.downto(0) do |n|
  print a[n]
end
```

produces:

000101110110100000111000011110010100111100010111001

abs   *big*.abs → *bignum*

Returns the absolute value of *big*.

```
1234567890987654321.abs    →    1234567890987654321
-1234567890987654321.abs   →    1234567890987654321
```

div   *big*.div(*number*) → *other_number*

1.8 Synonym for Bignum#/.

```
-1234567890987654321.div(13731)        →    -89910996357706
-1234567890987654321.div(13731.0)      →    -89910996357705.5
-1234567890987654321.div(-987654321)   →    1249999989
```

divmod   *big*.divmod(*number*) → *array*

See Numeric#divmod on page 565.

eql?   *big*.eql?(*obj*) → true or false

Returns true only if *obj* is a Bignum with the same value as *big*. Contrast this with Bignum#==, which performs type conversions.

```
68719476736.eql? 68719476736     →    true
68719476736  ==  68719476736     →    true
68719476736.eql? 68719476736.0   →    false
68719476736  ==  68719476736.0   →    true
```

modulo   *big*.modulo(*number*) → *number*

1.8 Synonym for Bignum#%.

quo   *big*.quo(*number*) → *float*

1.8 Returns the floating-point result of dividing *big* by *number*.

```
-1234567890987654321.quo(13731)        →    -89910996357705.5
-1234567890987654321.quo(13731.0)      →    -89910996357705.5
-1234567890987654321.div(-987654321)   →    1249999989
```

Bignum

---

remainder   *big*.remainder(*number*) → *other_number*

1.8,   Returns the remainder after dividing *big* by *number*.

```
-1234567890987654321.remainder(13731)      →   -6966
-1234567890987654321.remainder(13731.24)   →   -9906.22531493148
```

---

size   *big*.size → *integer*

Returns the number of bytes in the machine representation of *big*.

```
(256**10 - 1).size   →   12
(256**20 - 1).size   →   20
(256**40 - 1).size   →   40
```

---

to_f   *big*.to_f → *float*

Converts *big* to a Float. If *big* doesn't fit in a Float, the result is infinity.

---

to_s   *big*.to_s(*base*=10) → *str*

1.8,   Returns a string containing the representation of *big* radix *base* (2 to 36).

```
12345654321.to_s         →   "12345654321"
12345654321.to_s(2)      →   "1011011111110110111011110000110001"
12345654321.to_s(8)      →   "133766736061"
12345654321.to_s(16)     →   "2dfdbbc31"
12345654321.to_s(26)     →   "1dp1pc6d"
78546939656932.to_s(36)  →   "rubyrules"
```

Class

Binding < Object

Objects of class `Binding` encapsulate the execution context at some particular place in the code and retain this context for future use. The variables, methods, value of `self`, and possibly an iterator block that can be accessed in this context are all retained. Binding objects can be created using `Kernel#binding` and are made available to the callback of `Kernel#set_trace_func`.

These binding objects can be passed as the second argument of the `Kernel#eval` method, establishing an environment for the evaluation.

```
class Demo
  def initialize(n)
    @secret = n
  end
  def get_binding
    return binding()
  end
end

k1 = Demo.new(99)
b1 = k1.get_binding
k2 = Demo.new(-3)
b2 = k2.get_binding

eval("@secret", b1)   →   99
eval("@secret", b2)   →   -3
eval("@secret")       →   nil
```

Binding objects have no class-specific methods.

Class < Module

Classes in Ruby are first-class objects—each is an instance of class Class.

When a new class is defined (typically using class *Name* ... end), an object of type Class is created and assigned to a constant (*Name*, in this case). When Name.new is called to create a new object, the new instance method in Class is run by default, which in turn invokes allocate to allocate memory for the object, before finally calling the new object's initialize method.

1.8

Class methods

inherited   *cls*.inherited(*sub_class*)

Invoked by Ruby when a subclass of *cls* is created. The new subclass is passed as a parameter.

```
class Top
  def Top.inherited(sub)
    puts "New subclass: #{sub}"
  end
end
class Middle < Top
end
class Bottom < Middle
end
```

produces:

```
New subclass: Middle
New subclass: Bottom
```

new   Class.new(*super_class*=Object) ⟨ { *block* } ⟩ → *cls*

1.8

Creates a new anonymous (unnamed) class with the given superclass (or Object if no parameter is given). If passed a block, that block is used as the body of the class.

```
p = lambda do
  def hello
    "Hello, Dave"
  end
end

FriendlyClass = Class.new(&p)
f = FriendlyClass.new
f.hello   →   "Hello, Dave"
```

Instance methods

Class 1.8

---
allocate   *cls*.allocate → *obj*

Allocates space for a new object of *cls*'s class. The returned object must be an instance of *cls*. Calling new is basically the same as calling the class method `allocate` to create an object, followed by calling `initialize` on that new object. You cannot override `allocate` in normal programs; Ruby invokes it without going through conventional method dispatch.

```ruby
class MyClass
  def MyClass.another_new(*args)
    o = allocate
    o.send(:initialize, *args)
    o
  end
  def initialize(a, b, c)
    @a, @b, @c = a, b, c
  end
end

mc = MyClass.another_new(4, 5, 6)
mc.inspect    →    "#<MyClass:0x1c9378 @c=6, @b=5, @a=4>"
```

---
new   *cls*.new(⟨ *args* ⟩*) → *obj*

Calls `allocate` to create a new object of *cls*'s class and then invokes the newly created object's `initialize` method, passing it *args*.

---
superclass   *cls*.superclass → *super_class* or `nil`

Returns the superclass of *cls* or returns `nil`.

```ruby
Class.superclass     →     Module
Object.superclass    →     nil
```

Module **Comparable**

Relies on: <=>

The Comparable mixin is used by classes whose objects may be ordered. The class must define the <=> operator, which compares the receiver against another object, returning −1, 0, or +1 depending on whether the receiver is less than, equal to, or greater than the other object. Comparable uses <=> to implement the conventional comparison operators (<, <=, ==, >=, and >) and the method between?.

```
class CompareOnSize
  include Comparable
  attr :str
  def <=>(other)
    str.length <=> other.str.length
  end
  def initialize(str)
    @str = str
  end
end

s1 = CompareOnSize.new("Z")
s2 = CompareOnSize.new([1,2])
s3 = CompareOnSize.new("XXX")

s1 < s2                  →    true
s2.between?(s1, s3)      →    true
s3.between?(s1, s2)      →    false
[ s3, s2, s1 ].sort      →    ["Z", [1, 2], "XXX"]
```

Instance methods

Comparisons

obj < *other_object* → true or false
obj <= *other_object* → true or false
obj == *other_object* → true or false
obj >= *other_object* → true or false
obj > *other_object* → true or false

Compares two objects based on the receiver's <=> method.

between?

obj.between?(*min*, *max*) → true or false

Returns false if *obj* <=> *min* is less than zero or if *obj* <=> *max* is greater than zero, true otherwise.

```
3.between?(1, 5)                 →    true
6.between?(1, 5)                 →    false
'cat'.between?('ant', 'dog')     →    true
'gnu'.between?('ant', 'dog')     →    false
```

Class	**Continuation** < Object

Continuation objects are generated by `Kernel#callcc`. They hold a return address and execution context, allowing a nonlocal return to the end of the `callcc` block from anywhere within a program. Continuations are somewhat analogous to a structured version of C's `setjmp/longjmp` (although they contain more state, so you may consider them closer to threads).

This (somewhat contrived) example allows the inner loop to abandon processing early.

```
callcc do |cont|
  for i in 0..4
    print "\n#{i}: "
    for j in i*5...(i+1)*5
      cont.call() if j == 7
      printf "%3d", j
    end
  end
end
print "\n"
```

produces:

```
0:  0  1  2  3  4
1:  5  6
```

This example shows that the call stack for methods is preserved in continuations.

```
def strange
  callcc {|continuation| return continuation}
  print "Back in method, "
end
print "Before method. "
continuation = strange()
print "After method. "
continuation.call if continuation
```

produces:

Before method. After method. Back in method, After method.

Instance methods

call	*cont*.call(⟨ *args* ⟩*)

Invokes the continuation. The program continues from the end of the `callcc` block. If no arguments are given, the original `callcc` returns `nil`. If one argument is given, `callcc` returns it. Otherwise, an array containing *args* is returned.

```
callcc {|cont|  cont.call }          →   nil
callcc {|cont|  cont.call 1 }        →   1
callcc {|cont|  cont.call 1, 2, 3 }  →   [1, 2, 3]
```

Dir < Object

Objects of class Dir are directory streams representing directories in the underlying filesystem. They provide a variety of ways to list directories and their contents. See also File, page 465.

The directory used in these examples contains the two regular files (config.h and main.rb), the parent directory (..), and the directory itself (.).

Mixes in

Enumerable:

> all?, any?, collect, detect, each_with_index, entries, find, find_all, grep, include?, inject, map, max, member?, min, partition, reject, select, sort, sort_by, to_a, zip

Class methods

[ ]   Dir[*glob_pattern*] → *array*

1.8   Equivalent to calling Dir.glob(*glob_pattern*, 0).

---

chdir   Dir.chdir(⟨ *dir* ⟩) → 0
Dir.chdir(⟨ *dir* ⟩) {| path | *block* } → *obj*

Changes the current working directory of the process to the given string. When called without an argument, changes the directory to the value of the environment variable HOME or LOGDIR. Raises a SystemCallError (probably Errno::ENOENT) if the target directory does not exist.

1.8   If a block is given, it is passed the name of the new current directory, and the block is executed with that as the current directory. The original working directory is restored when the block exits. The return value of chdir is the value of the block. chdir blocks can be nested, but in a multithreaded program an error will be raised if a thread attempts to open a chdir block while another thread has one open. This is because the underlying operating system only understands the concept of a single current working directory at any one time.

```
Dir.chdir("/var/log")
puts Dir.pwd
Dir.chdir("/tmp") do
  puts Dir.pwd
  Dir.chdir("/usr") do
    puts Dir.pwd
  end
  puts Dir.pwd
end
puts Dir.pwd
```

produces:

```
/var/log
/tmp
/usr
/tmp
/var/log
```

chroot Dir.chroot(*dirname*) → 0

Changes this process's idea of the file system root. Only a privileged process may make this call. Not available on all platforms. On Unix systems, see chroot(2) for more information.

```
Dir.chdir("/production/secure/root")
Dir.chroot("/production/secure/root")   → 0
Dir.pwd                                  → "/"
```

delete Dir.delete(*dirname*) → 0

Deletes the named directory. Raises a subclass of SystemCallError if the directory isn't empty.

entries Dir.entries(*dirname*) → *array*

Returns an array containing all of the filenames in the given directory. Will raise a SystemCallError if the named directory doesn't exist.

```
Dir.entries("testdir")   →   [".", "..", "config.h", "main.rb"]
```

foreach Dir.foreach(*dirname*) {| *filename* | *block* } → nil

Calls the block once for each entry in the named directory, passing the filename of each entry as a parameter to the block.

```
Dir.foreach("testdir") {|x| puts "Got #{x}" }
```

produces:

```
Got .
Got ..
Got config.h
Got main.rb
```

getwd Dir.getwd → *dirname*

Returns a string containing the canonical path to the current working directory of this process. Note that on some operating systems this name may not be the name you gave to Dir.chdir. On OS X, for example, /tmp is a symlink.

```
Dir.chdir("/tmp")   →   0
Dir.getwd           →   "/private/tmp"
```

glob   Dir.glob(*glob_pattern*, ⟨ *flags* ⟩) → *array*
                            Dir.glob(*glob_pattern*, ⟨ *flags* ⟩) {| *filename* | *block* } → false

1.8

Returns the filenames found by expanding the pattern given in *glob_pattern*, either as
elements in *array* or as parameters to the block. Note that this pattern is not a regexp
(it's closer to a shell glob). See File.fnmatch on page 468 for the meaning of the
flags parameter. Case sensitivity depends on your system (so File::FNM_CASEFOLD is
ignored). Metacharacters in the pattern are

*   Any sequence of characters in a filename: "*" will match all files, "c*"
will match all files beginning with "c", "*c" will match all files ending
with "c", and "*c*" will match all files that have "c" in their name.

**   Matches zero or more directories (so "**/fred") matches a file named
"fred" in or below the current directory).

?   Matches any one character in a filename.

[*chars*]   Matches any one of *chars*. If the first character in *chars* is ^, matches
any character not in the remaining set.

{*patt*,...}   Matches one of the patterns specified between braces. These patterns
may contain other metacharacters.

\   Removes any special significance in the next character.

```
Dir.chdir("testdir")              →   0
Dir["config.?"]                   →   ["config.h"]
Dir.glob("config.?")              →   ["config.h"]
Dir.glob("*.[a-z][a-z]")          →   ["main.rb"]
Dir.glob("*.[^r]*")               →   ["config.h"]
Dir.glob("*.{rb,h}")              →   ["main.rb", "config.h"]
Dir.glob("*")                     →   ["config.h", "main.rb"]
Dir.glob("*", File::FNM_DOTMATCH) →   [".", "..", "config.h",
                                       "main.rb"]

Dir.chdir("..")                   →   0
Dir.glob("code/**/fib*.rb")       →   ["code/fib_up_to.rb",
                                       "code/rdoc/fib_example.rb"]
Dir.glob("**/rdoc/fib*.rb")       →   ["code/rdoc/fib_example.rb"]
```

mkdir   Dir.mkdir(*dirname* ⟨ , *permissions* ⟩) → 0

Makes a new directory named *dirname*, with permissions specified by the optional
parameter *permissions*. The permissions may be modified by the value of File.umask
and are ignored on Windows. Raises a SystemCallError if the directory cannot be
created. See also the discussion of permissions on page 465.

new   Dir.new(*dirname*) → *dir*

Returns a new directory object for the named directory.

open

Dir.open(*dirname*) → *dir*
Dir.open(*dirname*) {| *dir* | *block* } → *obj*

With no block, open is a synonym for `Dir.new`. If a block is present, it is passed *dir* as a parameter. The directory is closed at the end of the block, and `Dir.open` returns the value of the block.

pwd

Dir.pwd → *dirname*

Synonym for `Dir.getwd`.

rmdir

Dir.rmdir(*dirname*) → 0

Synonym for `Dir.delete`.

unlink

Dir.unlink(*dirname*) → 0

Synonym for `Dir.delete`.

Instance methods

close

dir.close → `nil`

Closes the directory stream. Any further attempts to access *dir* will raise an `IOError`.

```
d = Dir.new("testdir")
d.close   →   nil
```

each

dir.each {| *filename* | *block* } → *dir*

Calls the block once for each entry in this directory, passing the filename of each entry as a parameter to the block.

```
d = Dir.new("testdir")
d.each  {|name| puts "Got #{name}" }
```

produces:

```
Got .
Got ..
Got config.h
Got main.rb
```

path

dir.path → dirname

Returns the path parameter passed to *dir*'s constructor.

```
d = Dir.new("..")
d.path   →   ".."
```

pos

dir.pos → *int*

Synonym for `Dir#tell`.

pos=   *dir*.pos(*int*) → *int*

1.8   Synonym for `Dir#seek`, but returns the position parameter.

```
d = Dir.new("testdir")   →   #<Dir:0x1c9378>
d.read                   →   "."
i = d.pos                →   1
d.read                   →   ".."
d.pos = i                →   1
d.read                   →   ".."
```

read   *dir*.read → *filename* or nil

Reads the next entry from *dir* and returns it as a string. Returns nil at the end of the stream.

```
d = Dir.new("testdir")
d.read   →   "."
d.read   →   ".."
d.read   →   "config.h"
```

rewind   *dir*.rewind → *dir*

Repositions *dir* to the first entry.

```
d = Dir.new("testdir")
d.read     →   "."
d.rewind   →   #<Dir:0x1c96c8>
d.read     →   "."
```

seek   *dir*.seek(*int*) → *dir*

Seeks to a particular location in *dir*. *int* must be a value returned by `Dir#tell` (it is not necessarily a simple index into the entries).

```
d = Dir.new("testdir")   →   #<Dir:0x1c9378>
d.read                   →   "."
i = d.tell               →   1
d.read                   →   ".."
d.seek(i)                →   #<Dir:0x1c9378>
d.read                   →   ".."
```

tell   *dir*.tell → *int*

Returns the current position in *dir*. See also `Dir#seek`.

```
d = Dir.new("testdir")
d.tell   →   1
d.read   →   "."
d.tell   →   2
```

E numerable

Module Enumerable

Relies on: each, <=>

The Enumerable mixin provides collection classes with several traversal and searching methods and with the ability to sort. The class must provide a method each, which yields successive members of the collection. If Enumerable#max, #min, #sort, or #sort_by is used, the objects in the collection must also implement a meaningful <=> operator, as these methods rely on an ordering between members of the collection.

Instance methods

all?

enum.all? ⟨ {| *obj* | *block* } ⟩ → true or false

1.8

Passes each element of the collection to the given block. The method returns true if the block never returns false or nil. If the block is not given, Ruby adds an implicit block of {|obj| obj} (that is all? will return true only if none of the collection members is false or nil.)

```
%w{ ant bear cat}.all? {|word| word.length >= 3}   →   true
%w{ ant bear cat}.all? {|word| word.length >= 4}   →   false
[ nil, true, 99 ].all?                             →   false
```

any?

enum.any? ⟨ {| *obj* | *block* } ⟩ → true or false

1.8

Passes each element of the collection to the given block. The method returns true if the block ever returns a value other than false or nil. If the block is not given, Ruby adds an implicit block of {|obj| obj} (that is, any? will return true if at least one of the collection members is not false or nil).

```
%w{ ant bear cat}.any? {|word| word.length >= 3}   →   true
%w{ ant bear cat}.any? {|word| word.length >= 4}   →   true
[ nil, true, 99 ].any?                             →   true
```

collect

enum.collect {| *obj* | *block* } → *array*

Returns a new array containing the results of running *block* once for every element in *enum*.

```
(1..4).collect {|i| i*i }   →   [1, 4, 9, 16]
(1..4).collect { "cat" }    →   ["cat", "cat", "cat", "cat"]
```

detect

enum.detect(*ifnone* = nil) {| *obj* | *block* } → *obj* or nil

1.8

Passes each entry in *enum* to *block*. Returns the first for which *block* is not false. Returns nil if no object matches unless the proc *ifnone* is given, in which case it is called and its result returned.

```
(1..10).detect  {|i| i % 5 == 0 and i % 7 == 0 }   →   nil
(1..100).detect {|i| i % 5 == 0 and i % 7 == 0 }   →   35
sorry = lambda { "not found" }
(1..10).detect(sorry) {|i| i > 50}                 →   "not found"
```

each_with_index   *enum*.each_with_index {| *obj, i* | *block* } → *enum*

Calls *block* with two arguments, the item and its index, for each item in *enum*.

```
hash = Hash.new
%w(cat dog wombat).each_with_index do |item, index|
  hash[item] = index
end
hash   →   {"cat"=>0, "wombat"=>2, "dog"=>1}
```

entries   *enum*.entries → *array*

Synonym for Enumerable#to_a.

find   *enum*.find(*ifnone* = nil) {| *obj* | *block* } → *obj* or nil

Synonym for Enumerable#detect.

find_all   *enum*.find_all {| *obj* | *block* } → *array*

Returns an array containing all elements of *enum* for which *block* is not false (see also
Enumerable#reject).

```
(1..10).find_all {|i|  i % 3 == 0 }   →   [3, 6, 9]
```

grep   *enum*.grep(*pattern*) → *array*
                              enum.grep(*pattern*) {| *obj* | *block* } → *array*

Returns an array of every element in *enum* for which `pattern === element`. If the
optional *block* is supplied, each matching element is passed to it, and the block's result
is stored in the output array.

```
(1..100).grep 38..44   →   [38, 39, 40, 41, 42, 43, 44]
c = IO.constants
c.grep(/SEEK/)         →   ["SEEK_CUR", "SEEK_SET", "SEEK_END"]
res = c.grep(/SEEK/) {|v| IO.const_get(v) }
res                    →   [1, 0, 2]
```

include?   *enum*.include?(*obj*) → true or false

Returns `true` if any member of *enum* equals *obj*. Equality is tested using `==`.

```
IO.constants.include? "SEEK_SET"         →   true
IO.constants.include? "SEEK_NO_FURTHER"  →   false
```

E numerable

inject
$$enum.\text{inject}(initial) \; \{\,|\,memo, obj\,|\; block \,\} \;\rightarrow\; obj$$
$$enum.\text{inject} \; \{\,|\,memo, obj\,|\; block \,\} \;\rightarrow\; obj$$

1.8

Combines the elements of *enum* by applying the block to an accumulator value (*memo*) and each element in turn. At each step, *memo* is set to the value returned by the block. The first form lets you supply an initial value for *memo*. The second form uses the first element of the collection as the initial value (and skips that element while iterating).

```
# Sum some numbers
(5..10).inject {|sum, n| sum + n }            →    45
# Multiply some numbers
(5..10).inject(1) {|product, n| product * n }  →    151200

# find the longest word
longest = %w{ cat sheep bear }.inject do |memo, word|
   memo.length > word.length ? memo : word
end
longest                                        →    "sheep"

# find the length of the longest word
longest = %w{ cat sheep bear }.inject(0) do |memo, word|
   memo >= word.length ? memo : word.length
end
longest                                        →    5
```

map
$$enum.\text{map} \; \{\,|\,obj\,|\; block \,\} \;\rightarrow\; array$$

Synonym for `Enumerable#collect`.

max
$$enum.\text{max} \;\rightarrow\; obj$$
$$enum.\text{max} \; \{\,|\,a,b\,|\; block \,\} \;\rightarrow\; obj$$

Returns the object in *enum* with the maximum value. The first form assumes all objects implement <=>; the second uses the block to return *a* <=> *b*.

```
a = %w(albatross dog horse)
a.max                                 →    "horse"
a.max {|a,b| a.length <=> b.length }  →    "albatross"
```

member?
$$enum.\text{member?}(\,obj\,) \;\rightarrow\; \text{true or false}$$

Synonym for `Enumerable#include?`.

min
$$enum.\text{min} \;\rightarrow\; obj$$
$$enum.\text{min} \; \{\,|\,a,b\,|\; block \,\} \;\rightarrow\; obj$$

Returns the object in *enum* with the minimum value. The first form assumes all objects implement `Comparable`; the second uses the block to return *a* <=> *b*.

```
a = %w(albatross dog horse)
a.min                                 →    "albatross"
a.min {|a,b| a.length <=> b.length }  →    "dog"
```

partition	*enum*.partition {	*obj*	*block* } → [*true_array, false_array*]

<u>1.8</u> Returns two arrays, the first containing the elements of *enum* for which the block evaluates to true, the second containing the rest.

```
(1..6).partition {|i| (i&1).zero?}   →   [[2, 4, 6], [1, 3, 5]]
```

reject	*enum*.reject {	*obj*	*block* } → *array*

Returns an array containing the elements of *enum* for which *block* is false (see also Enumerable#find_all).

```
(1..10).reject {|i|  i % 3 == 0 }   →   [1, 2, 4, 5, 7, 8, 10]
```

select	*enum*.select {	*obj*	*block* } → *array*

Synonym for Enumerable#find_all.

sort	*enum*.sort → *array*
	enum.sort {	*a, b*	*block* } → *array*

Returns an array containing the items in *enum* sorted, either according to their own <=> method or by using the results of the supplied block. The block should return −1, 0, or +1 depending on the comparison between *a* and *b*. As of Ruby 1.8, the method Enumerable#sort_by implements a built-in Schwartzian Transform, useful when key computation or comparison is expensive.

```
%w(rhea kea flea).sort       →   ["flea", "kea", "rhea"]

(1..10).sort {|a,b| b <=> a}   →   [10, 9, 8, 7, 6, 5, 4, 3, 2, 1]
```

sort_by	*enum*.sort_by {	*obj*	*block* } → *array*

<u>1.8</u> Sorts *enum* using keys generated by mapping the values in *enum* through the given block, using the result of that block for element comparison.

```
sorted = %w{ apple pear fig }.sort_by {|word| word.length}

sorted   →   ["fig", "pear", "apple"]
```

Internally, sort_by generates an array of tuples containing the original collection element and the mapped value. This makes sort_by fairly expensive when the keysets are simple.

```
require 'benchmark'
include Benchmark
a = (1..100000).map {rand(100000)}
bm(10) do |b|
  b.report("Sort")    { a.sort }
  b.report("Sort by") { a.sort_by {|a| a} }
end
```

produces:

```
                user      system      total        real
Sort         0.070000   0.010000   0.080000 (  0.085860)
Sort by      1.580000   0.010000   1.590000 (  1.811626)
```

However, consider the case where comparing the keys is a nontrivial operation. The following code sorts some files on modification time using the basic `sort` method.

```
files = Dir["*"]

sorted = files.sort {|a,b| File.new(a).mtime <=> File.new(b).mtime}

sorted   →   ["mon", "tues", "wed", "thurs"]
```

This sort is inefficient: it generates two new `File` objects during every comparison. A slightly better technique is to use the `Kernel#test` method to generate the modification times directly.

```
files = Dir["*"]

sorted = files.sort do |a,b|
  test(?M, a) <=> test(?M, b)
end

sorted   →   ["mon", "tues", "wed", "thurs"]
```

This still generates many unnecessary `Time` objects. A more efficient technique is to cache the sort keys (modification times in this case) before the sort. Perl users often call this approach a Schwartzian Transform, named after Randal Schwartz. We construct a temporary array, where each element is an array containing our sort key along with the filename. We sort this array and then extract the filename from the result.

```
sorted = Dir["*"].collect {|f|
    [test(?M, f), f]
}.sort.collect {|f| f[1] }

sorted   →   ["mon", "tues", "wed", "thurs"]
```

This is exactly what `sort_by` does internally.

```
sorted = Dir["*"].sort_by {|f| test(?M, f)}

sorted   →   ["mon", "tues", "wed", "thurs"]
```

`sort_by` can also be useful for multilevel sorts. One trick, which relies on the fact that arrays are compared element by element, is to have the block return an array of each of the comparison keys. For example, to sort a list of words first on their length and then alphabetically, you could write.

```
words = %w{ puma cat bass ant aardvark gnu fish }
sorted = words.sort_by {|w| [w.length, w] }
sorted   →   ["ant", "cat", "gnu", "bass", "fish", "puma", "aardvark"]
```

to_a   *enum*.to_a → *array*

Returns an array containing the items in *enum*.

```
(1..7).to_a                      →    [1, 2, 3, 4, 5, 6, 7]
{ 'a'=>1, 'b'=>2, 'c'=>3 }.to_a  →    [["a", 1], ["b", 2], ["c", 3]]
```

zip   *enum*.zip(⟨ *arg* ⟩⁺) → *array*
                                   enum.zip(⟨ *arg* ⟩⁺) {| *arr* | *block* } → nil

1.8   Converts any arguments to arrays and then merges elements of *enum* with corresponding elements from each argument. The result is an array containing the same number
of elements as *enum*. Each element is a *n*-element array, where *n* is one more than the
count of arguments. If the size of any argument is less than the number of elements
in *enum*, nil values are supplied. If a block given, it is invoked for each output array,
otherwise an array of arrays is returned.

```
a = [ 4, 5, 6 ]
b = [ 7, 8, 9 ]

(1..3).zip(a, b)     →    [[1, 4, 7], [2, 5, 8], [3, 6, 9]]
"cat\ndog".zip([1])  →    [["cat\n", 1], ["dog", nil]]
(1..3).zip           →    [[1], [2], [3]]
```

E rrno

Module **Errno**

Ruby exception objects are subclasses of Exception. However, operating systems typically report errors using plain integers. Module Errno is created dynamically to map these operating system errors to Ruby classes, with each error number generating its own subclass of SystemCallError. As the subclass is created in module Errno, its name will start Errno::.

```
Exception
    StandardError
        SystemCallError
            Errno::xxx
```

The names of the Errno:: classes depend on the environment in which Ruby runs. On a typical Unix or Windows platform, you'll find Ruby has Errno classes such as Errno::EACCES, Errno::EAGAIN, Errno::EINTR, and so on.

The integer operating system error number corresponding to a particular error is available as the class constant Errno::*error*::Errno.

```
Errno::EACCES::Errno   →   13
Errno::EAGAIN::Errno   →   35
Errno::EINTR::Errno    →   4
```

The full list of operating system errors on your particular platform is available as the constants of Errno. Any user-defined exceptions in this module (including subclasses of existing exceptions) must also define an Errno constant.

```
Errno.constants   →   E2BIG, EACCES, EADDRINUSE, EADDRNOTAVAIL,
                      EAFNOSUPPORT, EAGAIN, EALREADY, ...
```

1.8   As of Ruby 1.8, exceptions are matched in rescue clauses using Module#===. The === method is overridden for class SystemCallError to compare based on the Errno value. Thus if two distinct Errno classes have the same underlying Errno value, they will be treated as the same exception by a rescue clause.

Class **Exception** < Object

Descendents of class Exception are used to communicate between raise methods and rescue statements in begin/end blocks. Exception objects carry information about the exception—its type (the exception's class name), an optional descriptive string, and optional traceback information.

The standard library defines the exceptions shown in Figure 27.1 on the following page. See also the description of Errno on the preceding page.

Class methods

exception   Exception.exception(⟨ *message* ⟩) → *exc*

Creates and returns a new exception object, optionally setting the message to *message*.

new   Exception.new(⟨ *message* ⟩) → *exc*

Creates and returns a new exception object, optionally setting the message to *message*.

Instance methods

backtrace   *exc*.backtrace → *array*

Returns any backtrace associated with the exception. The backtrace is an array of strings, each containing either *filename:line: in 'method'* or *filename:line*.

```
def a
  raise "boom"
end
def b
  a()
end
begin
  b()
rescue => detail
  print detail.backtrace.join("\n")
end
```

produces:

```
prog.rb:2:in `a'
prog.rb:6:in `b'
prog.rb:10
```

exception   *exc*.exception(⟨ *message* ⟩) → *exc* or *exception*

With no argument, returns the receiver. Otherwise, creates a new exception object of the same class as the receiver but with a different message.

E xception

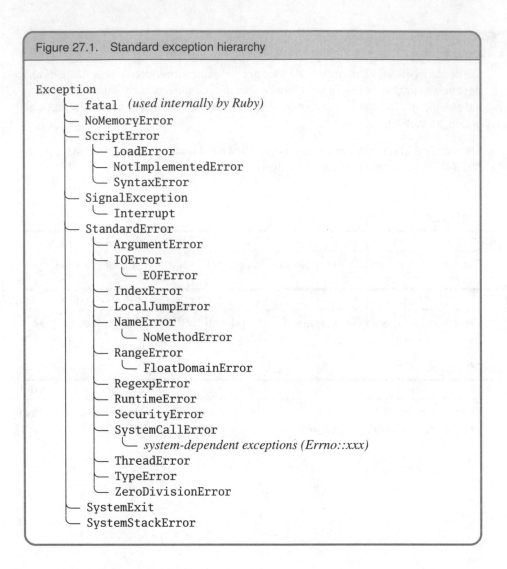

Figure 27.1. Standard exception hierarchy

```
Exception
      └─ fatal  (used internally by Ruby)
      ─ NoMemoryError
      ─ ScriptError
           └─ LoadError
           ─ NotImplementedError
           └─ SyntaxError
      ─ SignalException
           └─ Interrupt
      ─ StandardError
           ─ ArgumentError
           ─ IOError
                └─ EOFError
           ─ IndexError
           ─ LocalJumpError
           ─ NameError
                └─ NoMethodError
           ─ RangeError
                └─ FloatDomainError
           ─ RegexpError
           ─ RuntimeError
           ─ SecurityError
           ─ SystemCallError
                └─ system-dependent exceptions (Errno::xxx)
           ─ ThreadError
           ─ TypeError
           └─ ZeroDivisionError
      ─ SystemExit
      └─ SystemStackError
```

---

message   *exc*.message → *msg*

Returns the message associated with this exception.

---

set_backtrace   *exc*.set_backtrace(*array*) → *array*

Sets the backtrace information associated with *exc*. The argument must be an array of
String objects in the format described in Exception#backtrace.

---

status   *exc*.status → status

1.8 (SystemExit only) Returns the exit status associated with this SystemExit exception.
Normally this status is set using the Kernel#exit.

```
begin
  exit(99)
rescue SystemExit => e
  puts "Exit status is: #{e.status}"
end
```

produces:

```
Exit status is: 99
```

success?

1.8 (SystemExit only) Returns true is the exit status if nil or zero.

```
begin
  exit(99)
rescue SystemExit => e
  print "This program "
  if e.success?
    print "did"
  else
    print "did not"
  end
  puts " succeed"
end
```

produces:

```
This program did not succeed
```

to_s

Returns the message associated with this exception (or the name of the exception if no message is set).

```
begin
  raise "The message"
rescue Exception => e
  puts e.to_s
end
```

produces:

```
The message
```

to_str

Returns the message associated with this exception (or the name of the exception if no message is set). Implementing to_str gives exceptions a stringlike behavior.

Class **FalseClass** < Object

The global value `false` is the only instance of class `FalseClass` and represents a logically false value in boolean expressions. The class provides operators allowing `false` to participate correctly in logical expressions.

Instance methods

&   false & *obj* → false

And—Returns `false`. *obj* is always evaluated as it is the argument to a method call—no short-circuit evaluation is performed in this case. In other words, the following code, which uses &&, will not invoke the lookup method.

```
def lookup(val)
  puts "Looking up #{val}"
  return true
end
false && lookup("cat")
```

However, this code, using &, will:

```
false & lookup("cat")
```

produces:

```
Looking up cat
```

^   false ^ *obj* → true or false

Exclusive Or—If *obj* is `nil` or `false`, returns `false`; otherwise, returns `true`.

| false | *obj* → true or false

Or—Returns `false` if *obj* is `nil` or `false`; `true` otherwise.

| Class | **File** < IO |

A `File` is an abstraction of any file object accessible by the program and is closely associated with class IO, page 503. `File` includes the methods of module `FileTest` as class methods, allowing you to write (for example) `File.exist?("foo")`.

In this section, *permission bits* are a platform-specific set of bits that indicate permissions of a file. On Unix-based systems, permissions are viewed as a set of three octets, for the owner, the group, and the rest of the world. For each of these entities, permissions may be set to read, write, or execute the file.

	Owner			Group			Other	
r	w	x	r	w	x	r	w	x
4	2	1	4	2	1	4	2	1

The permission bits 0644 (in octal) would thus be interpreted as read/write for owner and read-only for group and other. Higher-order bits may also be used to indicate the type of file (plain, directory, pipe, socket, and so on) and various other special features. If the permissions are for a directory, the meaning of the execute bit changes; when set, the directory can be searched.

Each file has three associated times. The *atime* is the time the file was last accessed. The *ctime* is the time that the file status (not necessarily the file contents) were last changed. Finally, the *mtime* is the time the file's data was last modified. In Ruby, all these times are returned as Time objects.

On non-POSIX operating systems, there may be only the ability to make a file read-only or read/write. In this case, the remaining permission bits will be synthesized to resemble typical values. For instance, on Windows the default permission bits are 0644, which means read/write for owner, read-only for all others. The only change that can be made is to make the file read-only, which is reported as 0444.

See also `Pathname` on page 714.

Class methods

atime   File.atime(*filename*) → *time*

Returns a Time object containing the last access time for the named file, or returns epoch if the file has not been accessed.

```
File.atime("testfile")   →   Thu Aug 26 22:36:07 CDT 2004
```

basename   File.basename(*filename* ⟨ , *suffix* ⟩) → *string*

Returns the last component of the filename given in *filename*. If *suffix* is given and present at the end of *filename*, it is removed. Any extension can be removed by giving an extension of ".*".

1.8

```
File.basename("/home/gumby/work/ruby.rb")          →    "ruby.rb"
File.basename("/home/gumby/work/ruby.rb", ".rb")   →    "ruby"
File.basename("/home/gumby/work/ruby.rb", ".*")    →    "ruby"
```

blockdev?   File.blockdev?(*filename*) → true or false

Returns `true` if the named file is a block device, and returns `false` if it isn't or if the operating system doesn't support this feature.

```
File.blockdev?("testfile")   →    false
```

chardev?   File.chardev?(*filename*) → true or false

Returns `true` if the named file is a character device, and returns `false` if it isn't or if the operating system doesn't support this feature.

```
File.chardev?("/dev/tty")   →    true
```

chmod   File.chmod(*permission* ⟨ , *filename* ⟩⁺) → *int*

Changes permission bits on the named file(s) to the bit pattern represented by *permission*. Actual effects are operating system dependent (see the beginning of this section). On Unix systems, see `chmod(2)` for details. Returns the number of files processed.

```
File.chmod(0644, "testfile", "out")   →    2
```

chown   File.chown(*owner*, *group* ⟨ , *filename* ⟩⁺) → *int*

Changes the owner and/or group of the named file(s) to the given numeric owner and group IDs. Only a process with superuser privileges may change the owner of a file. The current owner of a file may change the file's group to any group to which the owner belongs. A `nil` or −1 owner or group ID is ignored. Returns the number of files processed.

```
File.chown(nil, 100, "testfile")
```

ctime   File.ctime(*filename*) → *time*

Returns a Time object containing the time that the file status associated with the named file was changed.

```
File.ctime("testfile")   →    Thu Aug 26 22:37:31 CDT 2004
```

delete   File.delete(⟨ *filename* ⟩⁺) → *int*

Deletes the named file(s). Returns the number of files processed. See also `Dir.rmdir`.

```
File.open("testrm", "w+") {}
File.delete("testrm")   →    1
```

directory? File.directory?(*path*) → true or false

Returns true if the named file is a directory, false otherwise.

```
File.directory?(".")   →   true
```

dirname File.dirname(*filename*) → *filename*

Returns all components of the filename given in *filename* except the last one.

```
File.dirname("/home/gumby/work/ruby.rb")   →   "/home/gumby/work"
File.dirname("ruby.rb")                     →   "."
```

executable? File.executable?(*filename*) → true or false

Returns true if the named file is executable. The tests are made using the effective owner of the process.

```
File.executable?("testfile")   →   false
```

executable_real? File.executable_real?(*filename*) → true or false

Same as File#executable?, but tests using the real owner of the process.

exist? File.exist?(*filename*) → true or false

Returns true if the named file or directory exists.

```
File.exist?("testfile")   →   true
```

exists? File.exists? (*filename*) → true or false

Synonym for File.exist?.

expand_path File.expand_path(*filename* ⟨ , *dirstring* ⟩) → *filename*

Converts a pathname to an absolute pathname. Relative paths are referenced from the current working directory of the process unless *dirstring* is given, in which case it will be used as the starting point. The given pathname may start with a ~, which expands to the process owner's home directory (the environment variable HOME must be set correctly). *~user* expands to the named user's home directory.

```
File.expand_path("~testuser/bin")        →   "/Users/testuser/bin"
File.expand_path("../../bin", "/tmp/x")  →   "/bin"
```

extname File.extname(*path*) → *string*

1.8   Returns the extension (the portion of filename in *path* after the period).

```
File.extname("test.rb")        →   ".rb"
File.extname("a/b/d/test.rb")  →   ".rb"
File.extname("test")           →   ""
```

File

Table 27.2. Match-mode constants

FNM_NOESCAPE	Backslash does not escape special characters in globs, and a backslash in the pattern must match a backslash in the filename.
FNM_PATHNAME	Forward slashes in the filename are treated as separating parts of a path and so must be explicitly matched in the pattern.
FNM_DOTMATCH	If this option is not specified, filenames containing leading periods must be matched by an explicit period in the pattern. A leading period is one at the start of the filename or (if FNM_PATHNAME is specified) following a slash.
FNM_CASEFOLD	Filename matches are case insensitive

---

file?   File.file?(*filename*) → `true` or `false`

Returns `true` if the named file is a regular file (not a device file, directory, pipe, socket, and so on).

```
File.file?("testfile")   →   true
File.file?(".")          →   false
```

---

fnmatch   File.fnmatch(*glob_pattern*, *path*, ⟨ *flags* ⟩) → `true` or `false`

1.8

Returns true if *path* matches against *glob_pattern*. The pattern is not a regular expression; instead it follows rules similar to shell filename globbing. Because fnmatch in implemented by the underlying operating system, it may have different semantics to `Dir.glob`. A *glob_pattern* may contain the following metacharacters.

**	Matches subdirectories recursively.
*	Matches zero or more characters.
?	Matches any single character.
[*charset*]	Matches any character from the given set of characters. A range of characters is written as *from–to*. The set may be negated with an initial caret (^).
\	Escapes any special meaning of the next character.

flags is a bitwise OR of the FNM_xxx parameters listed on the current page. See also `Dir.glob` on page 451.

```
File.fnmatch('cat',       'cat')       →   true
File.fnmatch('cat',       'category')  →   false
File.fnmatch('c{at,ub}s', 'cats')      →   false
File.fnmatch('c{at,ub}s', 'cubs')      →   false
File.fnmatch('c{at,ub}s', 'cat')       →   false
File.fnmatch('c?t',       'cat')       →   true
File.fnmatch('c\?t',      'cat')       →   false
```

```
File.fnmatch('c??t',    'cat')                      →  false
File.fnmatch('c*',      'cats')                     →  true
File.fnmatch('c/**/t', 'c/a/b/c/t')                 →  true
File.fnmatch('c*t',     'cat')                      →  true
File.fnmatch('c\at',    'cat')                      →  true
File.fnmatch('c\at',    'cat', File::FNM_NOESCAPE)  →  false
File.fnmatch('a?b',     'a/b')                      →  true
File.fnmatch('a?b',     'a/b', File::FNM_PATHNAME)  →  false

File.fnmatch('*',    '.profile')                            →  false
File.fnmatch('*',    '.profile', File::FNM_DOTMATCH)        →  true
File.fnmatch('*',    'dave/.profile')                       →  true
File.fnmatch('*',    'dave/.profile', File::FNM_DOTMATCH)   →  true
File.fnmatch('*',    'dave/.profile', File::FNM_PATHNAME)   →  false
File.fnmatch('*/*', 'dave/.profile', File::FNM_PATHNAME)    →  false
STRICT = File::FNM_PATHNAME | File::FNM_DOTMATCH
File.fnmatch('*/*', 'dave/.profile', STRICT)                →  true
```

fnmatch?

File.fnmatch?(*glob_pattern, path,* ⟨ *flags* ⟩) → (true or false)

1.8 Synonym for File#fnmatch.

ftype

File.ftype(*filename*) → *filetype*

Identifies the type of the named file. The return string is one of file, directory, characterSpecial, blockSpecial, fifo, link, socket, or unknown.

```
File.ftype("testfile")    →  "file"
File.ftype("/dev/tty")    →  "characterSpecial"
system("mkfifo wibble")   →  true
File.ftype("wibble")      →  "fifo"
```

grpowned?

File.grpowned?(*filename*) → true or false

Returns true if the effective group ID of the process is the same as the group ID of the named file. On Windows, returns false.

```
File.grpowned?("/etc/passwd")   →   false
```

join

File.join(⟨ *string* ⟩[+]) → *filename*

Returns a new string formed by joining the strings using File::SEPARATOR. The various separators are listed in Table 27.3 on the next page.

```
File.join("usr", "mail", "gumby")   →   "usr/mail/gumby"
```

lchmod

File.lchmod(*permission,* ⟨ *filename* ⟩[+]) → 0

1.8 Equivalent to File.chmod, but does not follow symbolic links (so it will change the permissions associated with the link, not the file referenced by the link). Often not available.

Table 27.3. Path separator constants (platform specific)

`ALT_SEPARATOR`	Alternate path separator.
`PATH_SEPARATOR`	Separator for filenames in a search path (such as : or ;).
`SEPARATOR`	Separator for directory components in a filename (such as \ or /).
`Separator`	Alias for SEPARATOR.

lchown   File.lchown(*owner, group,* ⟨ *filename* ⟩$^+$) → 0

1.8   Equivalent to `File.chown`, but does not follow symbolic links (so it will change the owner associated with the link, not the file referenced by the link). Often not available.

link   File.link(*oldname, newname*) → 0

Creates a new name for an existing file using a hard link. Will not overwrite *newname* if it already exists (in which case `link` raises a subclass of `SystemCallError`). Not available on all platforms.

```
File.link("testfile", "testfile.2")   →   0
f = File.open("testfile.2")
f.gets                                 →   "This is line one\n"
File.delete("testfile.2")
```

lstat   File.lstat(*filename*) → *stat*

Returns status information for *file* as an object of type `File::Stat`. Same as `IO#stat` (see page 513), but does not follow the last symbolic link. Instead, reports on the link itself.

```
File.symlink("testfile", "link2test")  →   0
File.stat("testfile").size             →   66
File.lstat("link2test").size           →   8
File.stat("link2test").size            →   66
```

mtime   File.mtime(*filename*) → *time*

Returns a `Time` object containing the modification time for the named file.

```
File.mtime("testfile")  →   Tue May 17 16:26:41 CDT 2005
File.mtime("/tmp")      →   Wed May 18 09:07:03 CDT 2005
```

new   File.new(*filename, modestring*="r") → *file*
File.new(*filename* ⟨ *, modenum* ⟨ *, permission* ⟩ ⟩) → *file*
File.new(*fd* ⟨ *, modenum* ⟨ *, permission* ⟩ ⟩) → *file*

Opens the file named by *filename* (or associates the already-open file given by *fd*) according to *modestring* (the default is r) and returns a new `File` object. The *modestring* is described in Table 27.6 on page 504. The file mode may optionally be specified as a `Fixnum` by *or*-ing together the flags described in Table 27.4 on page 472. Optional permission bits may be given in *permission*. These mode and permission bits are platform dependent; on Unix systems, see open(2) for details.

```
f = File.new("testfile", "r")
f = File.new("newfile",  "w+")
f = File.new("newfile", File::CREAT|File::TRUNC|File::RDWR, 0644)
```

open

File.open(*filename, modestring*="r") → *file*

File.open(*filename* 〈 , *modenum* 〈 , *permission* 〉 〉) → *file*

File.open(*fd* 〈 , *modenum* 〈 , *permission* 〉 〉) → *file*

File.open(*filename, modestring*="r") {| file | *block* } → *obj*

File.open(*filename* 〈 , *modenum* 〈 , *permission* 〉 〉) {| file | *block* } → *obj*

File.open(*fd* 〈 , *modenum* 〈 , *permission* 〉 〉) {| file | *block* } → *obj*

With no associated block, open is a synonym for File.new. If the optional code block is given, it will be passed *file* as an argument, and the file will automatically be closed when the block terminates. In this instance, File.open returns the value of the block.

owned?

File.owned?(*filename*) → true or false

Returns true if the effective user ID of the process is the same as the owner of the named file.

```
File.owned?("/etc/passwd")   →   false
```

pipe?

File.pipe?(*filename*) → true or false

Returns true if the operating system supports pipes and the named file is a pipe, false otherwise.

```
File.pipe?("testfile")   →   false
```

readable?

File.readable?(*filename*) → true or false

Returns true if the named file is readable by the effective user ID of this process.

```
File.readable?("testfile")   →   true
```

readable_real?

File.readable_real?(*filename*) → true or false

Returns true if the named file is readable by the real user ID of this process.

```
File.readable_real?("testfile")   →   true
```

readlink

File.readlink(*filename*) → *filename*

Returns the given symbolic link as a string. Not available on all platforms.

```
File.symlink("testfile", "link2test")   →   0
File.readlink("link2test")              →   "testfile"
```

Table 27.4. Open-mode constants

APPEND	Open the file in append mode; all writes will occur at end of file.
CREAT	Create the file on open if it does not exist.
EXCL	When used with CREAT, open will fail if the file exists.
NOCTTY	When opening a terminal device (see IO#isatty on page 510), do not allow it to become the controlling terminal.
NONBLOCK	Open the file in nonblocking mode.
RDONLY	Open for reading only.
RDWR	Open for reading and writing.
TRUNC	Open the file and truncate it to zero length if the file exists.
WRONLY	Open for writing only.

rename   File.rename(*oldname*, *newname*) → 0

Renames the given file or directory to the new name. Raises a `SystemCallError` if the file cannot be renamed.

```
File.rename("afile", "afile.bak")   →   0
```

setgid?   File.setgid?(*filename*) → `true` or `false`

Returns `true` if the named file's set-group-id permission bit is set, and returns `false` if it isn't or if the operating system doesn't support this feature.

```
File.setgid?("/usr/sbin/lpc")   →   false
```

setuid?   File.setuid?(*filename*) → `true` or `false`

Returns `true` if the named file's set-user-id permission bit is set, and returns `false` if it isn't or if the operating system doesn't support this feature.

```
File.setuid?("/bin/su")   →   false
```

size   File.size(*filename*) → *int*

Returns the size of the file in bytes.

```
File.size("testfile")   →   66
```

size?   File.size?(*filename*) → *int* or `nil`

Returns `nil` if the named file is of zero length; otherwise, returns the size. Usable as a condition in tests.

```
File.size?("testfile")    →   66
File.size?("/dev/zero")   →   nil
```

socket?

File.socket?(*filename*) → `true` or `false`

Returns `true` if the named file is a socket, and returns `false` if it isn't or if the operating system doesn't support this feature.

split

File.split(*filename*) → *array*

Splits the given string into a directory and a file component and returns them in a two-element array. See also `File.dirname` and `File.basename`.

```
File.split("/home/gumby/.profile")    →    ["/home/gumby", ".profile"]
File.split("ruby.rb")                 →    [".", "ruby.rb"]
```

stat

File.stat(*filename*) → *stat*

Returns a `File::Stat` object for the named file (see `File::Stat`, page 477).

```
stat = File.stat("testfile")
stat.mtime        →    Thu Aug 26 12:33:23 CDT 2004
stat.blockdev?    →    false
stat.ftype        →    "file"
```

sticky?

File.sticky?(*filename*) → `true` or `false`

Returns `true` if the named file has its sticky bit set, and returns `false` if it doesn't or if the operating system doesn't support this feature.

symlink

File.symlink(*oldname*, *newname*) → 0 or `nil`

Creates a symbolic link called *newname* for the file *oldname*. Returns `nil` on all platforms that do not support symbolic links.

```
File.symlink("testfile", "link2test")    →    0
```

symlink?

File.symlink?(*filename*) → `true` or `false`

Returns `true` if the named file is a symbolic link, and returns `false` if it isn't or if the operating system doesn't support this feature.

```
File.symlink("testfile", "link2test")    →    0
File.symlink?("link2test")               →    true
```

truncate

File.truncate(*filename*, *int*) → 0

Truncates the file *filename* to be at most *int* bytes long. Not available on all platforms.

```
f = File.new("out", "w")
f.write("1234567890")       →    10
f.close                     →    nil
File.truncate("out", 5)     →    0
File.size("out")            →    5
```

umask   File.umask(⟨ *int* ⟩) → *int*

Returns the current umask value for this process. If the optional argument is given, set the umask to that value and return the previous value. Umask values are *excluded* from the default permissions; so a umask of 0222 would make a file read-only for everyone. See also the discussion of permissions on page 465.

```
File.umask(0006)    →    18
File.umask          →    6
```

unlink   File.unlink(⟨ *filename* ⟩+) → *int*

Synonym for File.delete. See also Dir.rmdir.

```
File.open("testrm", "w+") {}   →   nil
File.unlink("testrm")          →   1
```

utime   File.utime(*accesstime*, *modtime* ⟨ , *filename* ⟩+) → *int*

Changes the access and modification times on a number of files. The times must be instances of class Time or integers representing the number of seconds since epoch. Returns the number of files processed. Not available on all platforms.

```
File.utime(0, 0, "testfile")          →   1
File.mtime("testfile")                →   Wed Dec 31 18:00:00 CST 1969
File.utime(0, Time.now, "testfile")   →   1
File.mtime("testfile")                →   Thu Aug 26 22:37:33 CDT 2004
```

writable?   File.writable?(*filename*) → true or false

Returns true if the named file is writable by the effective user ID of this process.

```
File.writable?("/etc/passwd")   →   false
File.writable?("testfile")      →   true
```

writable_real?   File.writable_real?(*filename*) → true or false

Returns true if the named file is writable by the real user ID of this process.

zero?   File.zero?(*filename*) → true or false

Returns true if the named file is of zero length, and returns false otherwise.

```
File.zero?("testfile")    →   false
File.open("zerosize", "w") {}
File.zero?("zerosize")    →   true
```

Instance methods

atime
file.atime → time

Returns a Time object containing the last access time for *file*, or returns epoch if the file has not been accessed.

```
File.new("testfile").atime  →   Wed Dec 31 18:00:00 CST 1969
```

chmod
file.chmod(permission) → 0

Changes permission bits on *file* to the bit pattern represented by *permission*. Actual effects are platform dependent; on Unix systems, see chmod(2) for details. Follows symbolic links. See the discussion of permissions on page 465. Also see File#lchmod.

```
f = File.new("out", "w");
f.chmod(0644)   →   0
```

chown
file.chown(owner, group) → 0

Changes the owner and group of *file* to the given numeric owner and group IDs. Only a process with superuser privileges may change the owner of a file. The current owner of a file may change the file's group to any group to which the owner belongs. A nil or −1 owner or group id is ignored. Follows symbolic links. See also File#lchown.

```
File.new("testfile").chown(502, 1000)
```

ctime
file.ctime → time

Returns a Time object containing the time that the file status associated with *file* was changed.

```
File.new("testfile").ctime  →   Thu Aug 26 22:37:33 CDT 2004
```

flock
file.flock (locking_constant) › 0 or false

Locks or unlocks a file according to *locking_constant* (a logical *or* of the values in Table 27.5 on the next page). Returns false if File::LOCK_NB is specified and the operation would otherwise have blocked. Not available on all platforms.

```
File.new("testfile").flock(File::LOCK_UN)  →   0
```

lchmod
file.lchmod(permission) → 0

1.8 Equivalent to File#chmod, but does not follow symbolic links (so it will change the permissions associated with the link, not the file referenced by the link). Often not available.

lchown
file.lchown(owner, group) → 0

1.8 Equivalent to File#chown, but does not follow symbolic links (so it will change the owner associated with the link, not the file referenced by the link). Often not available.

Table 27.5. Lock-mode constants

LOCK_EX	Exclusive lock. Only one process may hold an exclusive lock for a given file at a time.
LOCK_NB	Don't block when locking. May be combined with other lock options using logical *or*.
LOCK_SH	Shared lock. Multiple processes may each hold a shared lock for a given file at the same time.
LOCK_UN	Unlock.

lstat
file.lstat → *stat*

Same as IO#stat, but does not follow the last symbolic link. Instead, reports on the link itself.

```
File.symlink("testfile", "link2test")   →    0
File.stat("testfile").size              →    66
f = File.new("link2test")
f.lstat.size                            →    8
f.stat.size                             →    66
```

mtime
file.mtime → *time*

Returns a Time object containing the modification time for *file*.

```
File.new("testfile").mtime   →   Thu Aug 26 22:37:33 CDT 2004
```

path
file.path → *filename*

Returns the pathname used to create *file* as a string. Does not normalize the name.

```
File.new("testfile").path              →    "testfile"
File.new("/tmp/../tmp/xxx", "w").path  →    "/tmp/../tmp/xxx"
```

truncate
file.truncate(*int*) → 0

Truncates *file* to at most *int* bytes. The file must be opened for writing. Not available on all platforms.

```
f = File.new("out", "w")
f.syswrite("1234567890")   →    10
f.truncate(5)              →    0
f.close()                  →    nil
File.size("out")           →    5
```

Class   File::Stat   <   Object

Objects of class File::Stat encapsulate common status information for File objects. The information is recorded at the moment the File::Stat object is created; changes made to the file after that point will not be reflected. File::Stat objects are returned by IO#stat, File.stat, File#lstat, and File.lstat. Many of these methods may return platform-specific values, and not all values are meaningful on all systems. See also Kernel#test on page 531.

Mixes in

Comparable:

  <, <=, ==, >=, >, between?

Instance methods

<=>   *statfile <=> other_stat → −1, 0, 1*

Compares File::Stat objects by comparing their respective modification times.

```
f1 = File.new("f1", "w")
sleep 1
f2 = File.new("f2", "w")
f1.stat <=> f2.stat    →    -1
# Methods in Comparable are also available
f1.stat > f2.stat      →    false
f1.stat < f2.stat      →    true
```

atime   *statfile.atime → time*

Returns a Time object containing the last access time for *statfile*, or returns epoch if the file has not been accessed.

```
File.stat("testfile").atime       →    Wed Dec 31 18:00:00 CST 1969
File.stat("testfile").atime.to_i  →    0
```

blksize   *statfile.blksize → int*

Returns the native file system's block size. Will return nil on platforms that don't support this information.

```
File.stat("testfile").blksize   →    4096
```

blockdev?   *statfile.blockdev? → true or false*

Returns true if the file is a block device, and returns false if it isn't or if the operating system doesn't support this feature.

```
File.stat("testfile").blockdev?    →    false
File.stat("/dev/disk0").blockdev?  →    true
```

blocks
statfile.blocks → *int*

Returns the number of native file system blocks allocated for this file, or returns nil if the operating system doesn't support this feature.

```
File.stat("testfile").blocks   →   8
```

chardev?
statfile.chardev? → true or false

Returns true if the file is a character device, and returns false if it isn't or if the operating system doesn't support this feature.

```
File.stat("/dev/tty").chardev?   →   true
File.stat("testfile").chardev?   →   false
```

ctime
statfile.ctime → *time*

Returns a Time object containing the time that the file status associated with *statfile* was changed.

```
File.stat("testfile").ctime   →   Thu Aug 26 22:37:33 CDT 2004
```

dev
statfile.dev → *int*

Returns an integer representing the device on which *statfile* resides. The bits in the device integer will often encode major and minor device information.

```
File.stat("testfile").dev          →   234881033
"%x" % File.stat("testfile").dev   →   "e000009"
```

dev_major
statfile.dev_major → *int*

1.8, Returns the major part of File::Stat#dev or nil if the operating system doesn't support this feature.

```
File.stat("testfile").dev_major   →   14
```

dev_minor
statfile.dev_minor → *int*

1.8, Returns the minor part of File::Stat#dev or nil if the operating system doesn't support this feature.

```
File.stat("testfile").dev_minor   →   9
```

directory?
statfile.directory? → true or false

Returns true if *statfile* is a directory, and returns false otherwise.

```
File.stat("testfile").directory?   →   false
File.stat(".").directory?          →   true
```

executable?

statfile.executable? → true or false

Returns true if *statfile* is executable or if the operating system doesn't distinguish executable files from nonexecutable files. The tests are made using the effective owner of the process.

```
File.stat("testfile").executable?   →   false
```

executable_real?

statfile.executable_real? → true or false

Same as executable?, but tests using the real owner of the process.

file?

statfile.file? → true or false

Returns true if *statfile* is a regular file (not a device file, pipe, socket, and so on).

```
File.stat("testfile").file?   →   true
```

ftype

statfile.ftype → type_string

Identifies the type of *statfile*. The return string is one of: file, directory, characterSpecial, blockSpecial, fifo, link, socket, or unknown.

```
File.stat("/dev/tty").ftype   →   "characterSpecial"
```

gid

statfile.gid → int

Returns the numeric group ID of the owner of *statfile*.

```
File.stat("testfile").gid   →   502
```

grpowned?

statfile.grpowned? → true or false

Returns true if the effective group ID of the process is the same as the group ID of *statfile*. On Windows, returns false.

```
File.stat("testfile").grpowned?      →   true
File.stat("/etc/passwd").grpowned?   →   false
```

ino

statfile.ino → int

Returns the inode number for *statfile*.

```
File.stat("testfile").ino   →   422829
```

mode

statfile.mode → int

Returns an integer representing the permission bits of *statfile*. The meaning of the bits is platform dependent; on Unix systems, see stat(2).

```
File.chmod(0644, "testfile")         →   1
File.stat("testfile").mode.to_s(8)   →   "100644"
```

File::Stat

mtime   *statfile*.mtime → *time*

Returns a Time object containing the modification time for *statfile*.

```
File.stat("testfile").mtime  →  Thu Aug 26 22:37:33 CDT 2004
```

nlink   *statfile*.nlink → *int*

Returns the number of hard links to *statfile*.

```
File.stat("testfile").nlink           →   1
File.link("testfile", "testfile.bak") →   0
File.stat("testfile").nlink           →   2
```

owned?   *statfile*.owned? → true or false

Returns true if the effective user ID of the process is the same as the owner of *statfile*.

```
File.stat("testfile").owned?       →   true
File.stat("/etc/passwd").owned?    →   false
```

pipe?   *statfile*.pipe? → true or false

Returns true if the operating system supports pipes and *statfile* is a pipe.

rdev   *statfile*.rdev → *int*

Returns an integer representing the device type on which *statfile* (which should be a special file) resides. Returns nil if the operating system doesn't support this feature.

```
File.stat("/dev/disk0s1").rdev  →   234881025
File.stat("/dev/tty").rdev      →   33554432
```

rdev_major   *statfile*.rdev_major → *int*

1.8 Returns the major part of File::Stat#rdev or nil if the operating system doesn't support this feature.

```
File.stat("/dev/disk0s1").rdev_major  →   14
File.stat("/dev/tty").rdev_major      →   2
```

rdev_minor   *statfile*.rdev_minor → *int*

1.8 Returns the minor part of File::Stat#rdev or nil if the operating system doesn't support this feature.

```
File.stat("/dev/disk0s1").rdev_minor  →   1
File.stat("/dev/tty").rdev_minor      →   0
```

readable?   *statfile*.readable? → true or false

Returns true if *statfile* is readable by the effective user ID of this process.

```
File.stat("testfile").readable?  →   true
```

readable_real? *statfile*.readable_real? → `true` or `false`

Returns `true` if *statfile* is readable by the real user ID of this process.

```
File.stat("testfile").readable_real?     →    true
File.stat("/etc/passwd").readable_real?  →    true
```

setgid? *statfile*.setgid? → `true` or `false`

Returns `true` if *statfile* has the set-group-id permission bit set, and returns `false` if it doesn't or if the operating system doesn't support this feature.

```
File.stat("testfile").setgid?            →    false
File.stat("/usr/sbin/postdrop").setgid?  →    true
```

setuid? *statfile*.setuid? → `true` or `false`

Returns `true` if *statfile* has the set-user-id permission bit set, and returns `false` if it doesn't or if the operating system doesn't support this feature.

```
File.stat("testfile").setuid?     →    false
File.stat("/usr/bin/su").setuid?  →    true
```

size *statfile*.size → *int*

Returns the size of *statfile* in bytes.

```
File.stat("/dev/zero").size  →    0
File.stat("testfile").size   →    66
```

size? *statfile*.size? → *int* or `nil`

Returns `nil` if *statfile* is a zero-length file; otherwise, returns the file size. Usable as a condition in tests.

```
File.stat("/dev/zero").size?  →    nil
File.stat("testfile").size?   →    66
```

socket? *statfile*.socket? → `true` or `false`

Returns `true` if *statfile* is a socket, and returns `false` if it isn't or if the operating system doesn't support this feature.

```
File.stat("testfile").socket?  →    false
```

sticky? *statfile*.sticky? → `true` or `false`

Returns `true` if *statfile* has its sticky bit set, and returns `false` if it doesn't or if the operating system doesn't support this feature.

```
File.stat("testfile").sticky?  →    false
```

File::Stat

symlink?   *statfile*.symlink? → `true` or `false`

Returns `true` if *statfile* is a symbolic link, `false` if it isn't or if the operating system doesn't support this feature. As `File.stat` automatically follows symbolic links, `symlink?` will always be `false` for an object returned by `File.stat`.

```
File.symlink("testfile", "alink")   →   0
File.stat("alink").symlink?         →   false
File.lstat("alink").symlink?        →   true
```

uid   *statfile*.uid → *int*

Returns the numeric user ID of the owner of *statfile*.

```
File.stat("testfile").uid   →   502
```

writable?   *statfile*.writable? → `true` or `false`

Returns true if *statfile* is writable by the effective user ID of this process.

```
File.stat("testfile").writable?   →   true
```

writable_real?   *statfile*.writable_real? → `true` or `false`

Returns true if *statfile* is writable by the real user ID of this process.

```
File.stat("testfile").writable_real?   →   true
```

zero?   *statfile*.zero? → `true` or `false`

Returns `true` if *statfile* is a zero-length file; `false` otherwise.

```
File.stat("testfile").zero?   →   false
```

Module FileTest

FileTest implements file test operations similar to those used in File::Stat. The methods in FileTest are duplicated in class File. Rather than repeat the documentation here, we list the names of the methods and refer you to the documentation for File starting on page 465. FileTest appears to be a somewhat vestigial module.

The FileTest methods are

1.8 blockdev?, chardev?, directory?, executable?, executable_real?, exist?, exists?, file?, grpowned?, owned?, pipe?, readable?, readable_real?, setgid?, setuid?, size, size?, socket?, sticky?, symlink?, world_readable?, world_writable?, writable?, writable_real?, and zero?

F ixnum

Fixnum < Integer

A `Fixnum` holds `Integer` values that can be represented in a native machine word (minus 1 bit). If any operation on a `Fixnum` exceeds this range, the value is automatically converted to a `Bignum`.

`Fixnum` objects have immediate value. This means that when they are assigned or passed as parameters, the actual object is passed, rather than a reference to that object. Assignment does not alias `Fixnum` objects. As there is effectively only one `Fixnum` object instance for any given integer value, you cannot, for example, add a singleton method to a `Fixnum`.

Instance methods

Arithmetic operations

Performs various arithmetic operations on *fix*.

fix	+	*numeric*	Addition
fix	–	*numeric*	Subtraction
fix	*	*numeric*	Multiplication
fix	/	*numeric*	Division
fix	%	*numeric*	Modulo
fix	**	*numeric*	Exponentiation
fix	-@		Unary minus

Bit operations

Performs various operations on the binary representations of the `Fixnum`.

~ *fix*			Invert bits
fix	|	*numeric*	Bitwise OR
fix	&	*numeric*	Bitwise AND
fix	^	*numeric*	Bitwise EXCLUSIVE OR
fix	<<	*numeric*	Left-shift *numeric* bits
fix	>>	*numeric*	Right-shift *numeric* bits (with sign extension)

<=>   *fix* <=> *numeric* → −1, 0, +1

Comparison—Returns −1, 0, or +1 depending on whether *fix* is less than, equal to, or greater than *numeric*. This is the basis for the tests in `Comparable`.

```
42 <=> 13   →   1
13 <=> 42   →   -1
-1 <=> -1   →   0
```

[ ]

$fix[\ n\ ] \rightarrow 0, 1$

Bit Reference—Returns the *n*th bit in the binary representation of *fix*, where *fix*[0] is the least significant bit.

```
a = 0b11001100101010
30.downto(0) {|n| print a[n] }
```

produces:

0000000000000000011001100101010

abs

$fix.abs \rightarrow int$

Returns the absolute value of *fix*.

```
-12345.abs   →   12345
12345.abs    →   12345
```

div

$fix.div(\ numeric\ ) \rightarrow integer$

1.8 Synonym for Fixnum#/. Integer division always yields an integral result.

```
654321.div(13731)      →   47
654321.div(13731.34)   →   47
```

divmod

$fix.divmod(\ numeric\ ) \rightarrow array$

See Numeric#divmod on on page 565.

id2name

$fix.id2name \rightarrow string$ or nil

Returns the name of the object whose symbol ID is *fix*. If there is no symbol in the symbol table with this value, returns nil. id2name has nothing to do with the method Object.object_id. See Fixnum#to_sym, String#intern on page 615, and class Symbol on page 631.

```
symbol = :@inst_var    →   :@inst_var
id     = symbol.to_i   →   9866
id.id2name             →   "@inst_var"
```

modulo

$fix.modulo(\ numeric\ ) \rightarrow numeric$

1.8 Synonym for Fixnum#%.

```
654321.modulo(13731)      →   8964
654321.modulo(13731.24)   →   8952.72000000001
```

quo

$fix.quo(\ numeric\ ) \rightarrow float$

1.8 Returns the floating-point result of dividing *fix* by *numeric*.

```
654321.quo(13731)      →   47.6528293642124
654321.quo(13731.24)   →   47.6519964693647
```

Fixnum

size   *fix*.size → *int*

Returns the number of *bytes* in the machine representation of a Fixnum.

```
1.size            →    4
-1.size           →    4
2147483647.size   →    4
```

to_f   *fix*.to_f → *float*

Converts *fix* to a Float.

to_s   *fix*.to_s(*base*=10) → *string*

1.8   Returns a string containing the representation of *fix* radix *base* (2 to 36).

```
12345.to_s                           →    "12345"
12345.to_s(2)                        →    "11000000111001"
12345.to_s(8)                        →    "30071"
12345.to_s(10)                       →    "12345"
12345.to_s(16)                       →    "3039"
12345.to_s(36)                       →    "9ix"
848237232330358117454971710.to_s(36) →    "anotherrubyhacker"
```

to_sym   *fix*.to_sym → *symbol*

1.8   Returns the symbol whose integer value is *fix*. See also Fixnum#id2name.

```
fred = :fred.to_i
fred.id2name    →    "fred"
fred.to_sym     →    :fred
```

zero?   *fix*.zero? → true or false

Returns true if *fix* is zero.

```
42.zero?   →    false
0.zero?    →    true
```

Class **Float** < Numeric

Float objects represent real numbers using the native architecture's double-precision floating-point representation.

Class constants

DIG	Precision of Float (in decimal digits)
EPSILON	The smallest Float such that $1.0 + \text{EPSILON} \neq 1.0$
MANT_DIG	The number of mantissa digits (base RADIX)
MAX	The largest Float
MAX_10_EXP	The maximum integer x such that 10^x is a finite Float
MAX_EXP	The maximum integer x such that $\text{FLT\_RADIX}^{(x-1)}$ is a finite Float
MTN	The smallest Float
MIN_10_EXP	The minimum integer x such that 10^x is a finite Float
MIN_EXP	The minimum integer x such that $\text{FLT\_RADIX}^{(x-1)}$ is a finite Float
RADIX	The radix of floating-point representations
ROUNDS	The rounding mode for floating-point operations. Possible values include

    -1 if the mode is indeterminate

      0 if rounding is toward zero

      1 if rounding is to nearest representable value

      2 if rounding is toward $+\infty$

      3 if rounding is toward $-\infty$

Instance methods

Arithmetic operations

Performs various arithmetic operations on *flt*.

flt	+	*numeric*	Addition
flt	−	*numeric*	Subtraction
flt	*	*numeric*	Multiplication
flt	/	*numeric*	Division
flt	%	*numeric*	Modulo
flt	**	*numeric*	Exponentiation
flt	-@		Unary minus

<=>   *flt* <=> *numeric* → $-1, 0, +1$

Returns -1, 0, or $+1$ depending on whether *flt* is less than, equal to, or greater than *numeric*. This is the basis for the tests in Comparable.

Float

== $flt == obj \rightarrow$ `true` or `false`

Returns `true` only if *obj* has the same value as *flt*. Contrast this with `Float#eql?`, which requires *obj* to be a `Float`.

```
1.0 == 1.0          →    true
(1.0).eql?(1.0)     →    true
1.0 == 1            →    true
(1.0).eql?(1)       →    false
```

---

abs $flt.abs \rightarrow numeric$

Returns the absolute value of *flt*.

```
(-34.56).abs    →    34.56
-34.56.abs      →    34.56
```

---

ceil $flt.ceil \rightarrow int$

Returns the smallest `Integer` greater than or equal to *flt*.

```
1.2.ceil       →    2
2.0.ceil       →    2
(-1.2).ceil    →    -1
(-2.0).ceil    →    -2
```

---

divmod $flt.divmod(\ numeric\ ) \rightarrow array$

See Numeric#divmod on page 565.

---

eql? $flt.eql?(\ obj\ ) \rightarrow$ `true` or `false`

Returns `true` only if *obj* is a `Float` with the same value as *flt*. Contrast this with `Float#==`, which performs type conversions.

```
1.0.eql?(1)    →    false
1.0 == 1       →    true
```

---

finite? $flt.finite? \rightarrow$ `true` or `false`

Returns `true` if *flt* is a valid IEEE floating-point number (it is not infinite, and nan? is false).

```
(42.0).finite?       →    true
(1.0/0.0).finite?    →    false
```

---

floor $flt.floor \rightarrow int$

Returns the largest integer less than or equal to *flt*.

```
1.2.floor       →    1
2.0.floor       →    2
(-1.2).floor    →    -2
(-2.0).floor    →    -2
```

infinite?

flt.infinite? → nil, −1, +1

Returns nil, −1, or +1 depending on whether *flt* is finite, −∞, or +∞.

```
(0.0).infinite?       →    nil
(-1.0/0.0).infinite?  →    -1
(+1.0/0.0).infinite?  →    1
```

modulo

flt.modulo(numeric) → numeric

1.8   Synonym for Float#%.

```
6543.21.modulo(137)      →    104.21
6543.21.modulo(137.24)   →    92.9299999999996
```

nan?

flt.nan? → true or false

Returns true if *flt* is an invalid IEEE floating-point number.

```
(-1.0).nan?     →    false
(0.0/0.0).nan?  →    true
```

round

flt.round → int

Rounds *flt* to the nearest integer. Equivalent to

```
def round
  case
  when self > 0.0 then (self+0.5).floor
  when self < 0.0 then return (self-0.5).ceil
  else 0
  end
end

1.5.round       →    2
(-1.5).round    →    -2
```

to_f

flt.to_f → flt

Returns *flt*.

to_i

flt.to_i → int

Returns *flt* truncated to an Integer.

```
1.5.to_i     →    1
(-1.5).to_i  →    -1
```

to_int

flt.to_int → int

Synonym for Float#to_i.

to_s   *flt*.to_s → *string*

Returns a string containing a representation of self. As well as a fixed or exponential form of the number, the call may return NaN, Infinity, and -Infinity.

truncate   *flt*.truncate → *int*

1.8 Synonym for Float#to_i.

zero?   *flt*.zero? → true or false

Returns true if *flt* is 0.0.

Module ## GC

The GC module provides an interface to Ruby's mark and sweep garbage collection mechanism. Some of the underlying methods are also available via the ObjectSpace module, described beginning on page 578.

Module methods

disable
GC.disable → true or false

Disables garbage collection, returning true if garbage collection was already disabled.

```
GC.disable   →   false
GC.disable   →   true
```

enable
GC.enable → true or false

Enables garbage collection, returning true if garbage collection was disabled.

```
GC.disable   →   false
GC.enable    →   true
GC.enable    →   false
```

start
GC.start → nil

Initiates garbage collection, unless manually disabled.

```
GC.start   →   nil
```

Instance methods

garbage_collect
garbage_collect → nil

Equivalent to GC.start.

```
include GC
garbage_collect   →   nil
```

Class **Hash** < Object

A Hash is a collection of key/value pairs. It is similar to an Array, except that indexing is done via arbitrary keys of any object type, not an integer index. The order in which keys and/or values are returned by the various iterators over hash contents may seem arbitrary and will generally not be in insertion order.

Hashes have a *default value*. This value is returned when an attempt is made to access keys that do not exist in the hash. By default, this value is nil.

Mixes in

Enumerable:
> all?, any?, collect, detect, each_with_index, entries, find, find_all, grep, include?, inject, map, max, member?, min, partition, reject, select, sort, sort_by, to_a, zip

Class methods

[ ]   Hash[⟨ *key* => *value* ⟩*] → *hsh*

Creates a new hash populated with the given objects. Equivalent to creating a hash using the literal { *key*=>*value*, ... }. Keys and values occur in pairs, so there must be an even number of arguments.

```
Hash["a", 100, "b", 200]      →    {"a"=>100, "b"=>200}
Hash["a" => 100, "b" => 200]  →    {"a"=>100, "b"=>200}
{ "a" => 100, "b" => 200 }    →    {"a"=>100, "b"=>200}
```

new   Hash.new → *hsh*
                                                                  Hash.new(*obj*) → *hsh*
                                                  Hash.new {| *hash, key* | *block* } → *hsh*

1.8 Returns a new, empty hash. If this hash is subsequently accessed by a key that doesn't correspond to a hash entry, the value returned depends on the style of new used to create the hash. In the first form, the access returns nil. If *obj* is specified, this single object will be used for all *default values*. If a block is specified, it will be called with the hash object and the key, and it should return the default value. It is the block's responsibility to store the value in the hash if required.

```
h = Hash.new("Go Fish")
h["a"] = 100
h["b"] = 200
h["a"]             →   100
h["c"]             →   "Go Fish"
# The following alters the single default object
h["c"].upcase!     →   "GO FISH"
h["d"]             →   "GO FISH"
h.keys             →   ["a", "b"]
```

```
# While this creates a new default object each time
h = Hash.new {|hash, key| hash[key] = "Go Fish: #{key}" }
h["c"]            →    "Go Fish: c"
h["c"].upcase!    →    "GO FISH: C"
h["d"]            →    "Go Fish: d"
h.keys            →    ["c", "d"]
```

Instance methods

==   *hsh == obj* → true or false

Equality—Two hashes are equal if they have the same default value, they contain the same number of keys, and the value corresponding to each key in the first hash is equal (using ==) to the value for the same key in the second. If *obj* is not a hash, attempt to convert it using to_hash and return *obj == hsh*.

```
h1 = { "a" => 1, "c" => 2 }
h2 = { 7 => 35, "c" => 2, "a" => 1 }
h3 = { "a" => 1, "c" => 2, 7 => 35 }
h4 = { "a" => 1, "d" => 2, "f" => 35 }
h1 == h2   →    false
h2 == h3   →    true
h3 == h4   →    false
```

[ ]   *hsh[key]* → *value*

Element Reference—Retrieves the *value* stored for *key*. If not found, returns the default value (see Hash.new for details).

```
h = { "a" => 100, "b" => 200 }
h["a"]   →    100
h["c"]   →    nil
```

[ ]=   *hsh[key] = value* → *value*

Element Assignment—Associates the value given by *value* with the key given by *key*. *key* should not have its value changed while it is in use as a key (a String passed as a key will be duplicated and frozen).

```
h = { "a" => 100, "b" => 200 }
h["a"] = 9
h["c"] = 4
h   →    {"a"=>9, "b"=>200, "c"=>4}
```

clear   *hsh*.clear → *hsh*

Removes all key/value pairs from *hsh*.

```
h = { "a" => 100, "b" => 200 }   →    {"a"=>100, "b"=>200}
h.clear                          →    {}
```

H ash

---

default   *hsh*.default(*key*=nil) → *obj*

1.8, Returns the default value, the value that would be returned by *hsh*[*key*] if *key* did not
exist in *hsh*. See also Hash.new and Hash#default=.

```
h = Hash.new                          →    {}
h.default                             →    nil
h.default(2)                          →    nil

h = Hash.new("cat")                   →    {}
h.default                             →    "cat"
h.default(2)                          →    "cat"

h = Hash.new {|h,k| h[k] = k.to_i*10} →    {}
h.default                             →    0
h.default(2)                          →    20
```

---

default=   *hsh*.default = *obj* → *hsh*

Sets the default value, the value returned for a key that does not exist in the hash. It is
not possible to set the a default to a Proc that will be executed on each key lookup.

```
h = { "a" => 100, "b" => 200 }
h.default = "Go fish"
h["a"]      →    100
h["z"]      →    "Go fish"
# This doesn't do what you might hope...
h.default = proc do |hash, key|
  hash[key] = key + key
end
h[2]        →    #<Proc:0x001c94e0@-:6>
h["cat"]    →    #<Proc:0x001c94e0@-:6>
```

---

default_proc   *hsh*.default_proc → *obj* or nil

1.8, If Hash.new was invoked with a block, return that block; otherwise return nil.

```
h = Hash.new {|h,k| h[k] = k*k }  →    {}
p = h.default_proc                →    #<Proc:0x001c997c@-:1>
a = []                            →    []
p.call(a, 2)
a                                 →    [nil, nil, 4]
```

---

delete   *hsh*.delete(*key*) → *value*
                                              hsh.delete(*key*) {| *key* | *block* } → *value*

Deletes from *hsh* the entry whose key is to *key*, returning the corresponding value. If
1.8, the key is not found, returns nil. If the optional code block is given and the key is not
found, pass it the key and return the result of *block*.

```
h = { "a" => 100, "b" => 200 }
h.delete("a")                              →    100
h.delete("z")                              →    nil
h.delete("z") {|el| "#{el} not found" }    →    "z not found"
```

---

delete_if   *hsh*.delete_if {| *key, value* | *block* } → *hsh*

Deletes every key/value pair from *hsh* for which *block* is true.

```
h = { "a" => 100, "b" => 200, "c" => 300 }
h.delete_if {|key, value| key >= "b" }   →   {"a"=>100}
```

---

each   *hsh*.each {| *key, value* | *block* } → *hsh*

Calls *block* once for each key in *hsh*, passing the key and value as parameters.

```
h = { "a" => 100, "b" => 200 }
h.each {|key, value| puts "#{key} is #{value}" }
```

produces:

```
a is 100
b is 200
```

---

each_key   *hsh*.each_key {| *key* | *block* } → *hsh*

Calls *block* once for each key in *hsh*, passing the key as a parameter.

```
h = { "a" => 100, "b" => 200 }
h.each_key {|key| puts key }
```

produces:

```
a
b
```

---

each_pair   *hsh*.each pair {| *key, value* | *block* } → *hsh*

Synonym for Hash#each.

---

each_value   *hsh*.each_value {| *value* | *block* } → *hsh*

Calls *block* once for each key in *hsh*, passing the value as a parameter.

```
h = { "a" -> 100, "b" => 200 }
h.each_value {|value| puts value }
```

produces:

```
100
200
```

---

empty?   *hsh*.empty? → true or false

Returns true if *hsh* contains no key/value pairs.

```
{}.empty?   →   true
```

fetch   *hsh*.fetch(*key* ⟨ , *default* ⟩) → *obj*
                                       hsh.fetch(*key*) { | *key* | *block* } → *obj*

Returns a value from the hash for the given key. If the key can't be found, several
options exist: With no other arguments, it will raise an `IndexError` exception; if
default is given, then that will be returned; if the optional code block is specified, then
that will be run and its result returned. `fetch` does not evaluate any default values
supplied when the hash was created—it only looks for keys in the hash.

```
h = { "a" => 100, "b" => 200 }
h.fetch("a")                              →    100
h.fetch("z", "go fish")                   →    "go fish"
h.fetch("z") {|el| "go fish, #{el}"}      →    "go fish, z"
```

The following example shows that an exception is raised if the key is not found and a
default value is not supplied.

```
h = { "a" => 100, "b" => 200 }
h.fetch("z")
```

produces:

```
prog.rb:2:in `fetch': key not found (IndexError)
from prog.rb:2
```

has_key?   *hsh*.has_key?(*key*) → true or false

Returns `true` if the given key is present in *hsh*.

```
h = { "a" => 100, "b" => 200 }
h.has_key?("a")   →    true
h.has_key?("z")   →    false
```

has_value?   *hsh*.has_value?(*value*) → true or false

Returns `true` if the given value is present for some key in *hsh*.

```
h = { "a" => 100, "b" => 200 }
h.has_value?(100)   →    true
h.has_value?(999)   →    false
```

include?   *hsh*.include?(*key*) → true or false

Synonym for Hash#has_key?.

index   *hsh*.index(*value*) → *key*

Searches the hash for an entry whose value == *value*, returning the corresponding key.
If multiple entries have this value, the key returned will be that on one of the entries. If
not found, returns `nil`.

```
h = { "a" => 100, "b" => 200 }
h.index(200)   →    "b"
h.index(999)   →    nil
```

indexes
hsh.indexes(⟨ key ⟩⁺) → array

1.8   Deprecated in favor of Hash#values_at.

---

indices
hsh.indices(⟨ key ⟩⁺) → array

1.8   Deprecated in favor of Hash#values_at.

---

invert
hsh.invert → other_hash

Returns a new hash created by using *hsh*'s values as keys, and the keys as values. If *hsh* has duplicate values, the result will contain only one of them as a key—which one is not predictable.

```
h = { "n" => 100, "m" => 100, "y" => 300, "d" => 200, "a" => 0 }
h.invert   →   {0=>"a", 100=>"n", 200=>"d", 300=>"y"}
```

---

key?
hsh.key?(key) → true or false

Synonym for Hash#has_key?.

---

keys
hsh.keys → array

Returns a new array populated with the keys from this hash. See also Hash#values.

```
h = { "a" => 100, "b" => 200, "c" => 300, "d" => 400 }
h.keys   →   ["a", "b", "c", "d"]
```

---

length
hsh.length → fixnum

Returns the number of key/value pairs in the hash.

```
h = { "d" => 100, "a" => 200, "v" => 300, "e" => 400 }
h.length       →    4
h.delete("a")  →    200
h.length       →    3
```

---

member?
hsh.member?(key) → true or false

Synonym for Hash#has_key?.

---

merge
hsh.merge(other_hash) → result_hash
hsh.merge(other_hash) {| key, old_val, new_val | block } → result_hash

1.8   Returns a new hash containing the contents of *other_hash* and the contents of *hsh*. With no block parameter, overwrites entries in *hsh* with duplicate keys with those from *other_hash*. If a block is specified, it is called with each duplicate key and the values from the two hashes. The value returned by the block is stored in the new hash.

```
h1 = { "a" => 100, "b" => 200 }
h2 = { "b" => 254, "c" => 300 }
h1.merge(h2)              →     {"a"=>100, "b"=>254, "c"=>300}
h1.merge(h2) {|k,o,n| o}  →     {"a"=>100, "b"=>200, "c"=>300}
h1                        →     {"a"=>100, "b"=>200}
```

---

merge!   *hsh*.merge!(*other_hash*) → *hsh*

hsh.merge!(*other_hash*) {| key, old_val, new_val| *block* } → *hsh*

1.8   Adds the contents of *other_hash* to *hsh*, overwriting entries with duplicate keys with those from *other_hash*.

```
h1 = { "a" => 100, "b" => 200 }
h2 = { "b" => 254, "c" => 300 }
h1.merge!(h2)             →     {"a"=>100, "b"=>254, "c"=>300}
h1 = { "a" => 100, "b" => 200 }
h1.merge!(h2) {|k,o,n| o} →     {"a"=>100, "b"=>200, "c"=>300}
h1                        →     {"a"=>100, "b"=>200, "c"=>300}
```

---

rehash   *hsh*.rehash → *hsh*

Rebuilds the hash based on the current hash values for each key. If values of key objects have changed since they were inserted, this method will reindex *hsh*. If Hash#rehash is called while an iterator is traversing the hash, an IndexError will be raised in the iterator.

```
a = [ "a", "b" ]
c = [ "c", "d" ]
h = { a => 100, c => 300 }
h[a]         →   100
a[0] = "z"
h[a]         →   nil
h.rehash     →   {["z", "b"]=>100, ["c", "d"]=>300}
h[a]         →   100
```

---

reject   *hsh*.reject {| *key, value* | *block* } → *hash*

Same as Hash#delete_if, but works on (and returns) a copy of *hsh*. Equivalent to *hsh*.dup.delete_if.

---

reject!   *hsh*.reject! {| *key, value*| *block* } → *hsh* or nil

Equivalent to Hash#delete_if, but returns nil if no changes were made.

---

replace   *hsh*.replace(*other_hash*) → *hsh*

Replaces the contents of *hsh* with the contents of *other_hash*.

```
h = { "a" => 100, "b" => 200 }
h.replace({ "c" => 300, "d" => 400 })   →   {"c"=>300, "d"=>400}
```

select   *hsh*.select {| *key, value* | *block* } → *array*

Returns a new array consisting of [key, value] pairs for which the block returns true. Also see Hash#values_at.

```
h = { "a" => 100, "b" => 200, "c" => 300 }
h.select {|k,v| k > "a"}    →    [["b", 200], ["c", 300]]
h.select {|k,v| v < 200}    →    [["a", 100]]
```

shift   *hsh*.shift → *array* or nil

1.8

Removes a key/value pair from *hsh* and returns it as the two-item array [*key, value*]. If the hash is empty, returns the default value, calls the default proc (with a key value of nil), or returns nil.

```
h = { 1 => "a", 2 => "b", 3 => "c" }
h.shift    →    [1, "a"]
h          →    {2=>"b", 3=>"c"}
```

size   *hsh*.size → *fixnum*

Synonym for Hash#length.

sort   *hsh*.sort → *array*
           hsh.sort {| *a, b* | *block* } → *array*

Converts *hsh* to a nested array of [*key, value*] arrays and sorts it, using Array#sort.

```
h = { "a" => 20, "b" => 30, "c" => 10  }
h.sort                    →    [["a", 20], ["b", 30], ["c", 10]]
h.sort {|a,b| a[1]<=>b[1]}  →    [["c", 10], ["a", 20], ["b", 30]]
```

store   *hsh*.store(*key, value*) → *value*

Synonym for Element Assignment (Hash#[]=).

to_a   *hsh*.to_a → *array*

Converts *hsh* to a nested array of [*key, value*] arrays.

```
h = { "c" => 300, "a" => 100, "d" => 400, "c" => 300  }
h.to_a    →    [["a", 100], ["c", 300], ["d", 400]]
```

to_hash   *hsh*.to_hash → *hsh*

See page 372.

to_s   *hsh*.to_s → *string*

Converts *hsh* to a string by converting the hash to an array of [*key, value*] pairs and then converting that array to a string using Array#join with the default separator.

```
h = { "c" => 300, "a" => 100, "d" => 400, "c" => 300  }
h.to_s    →    "a100c300d400"
```

update   *hsh*.update(*other_hash*) → *hsh*
                      hsh.update(*other_hash*) {| key, old_val, new_val | *block* } → *hsh*

1.8   Synonym for Hash#merge!.

---

value?   *hsh*.value?(*value*) → true or false

Synonym for Hash#has_value?.

---

values   *hsh*.values → *array*

Returns an array populated with the values from *hsh*. See also Hash#keys.

```
h = { "a" => 100, "b" => 200, "c" => 300 }
h.values   →   [100, 200, 300]
```

---

values_at   *hsh*.values_at(⟨ *key* ⟩⁺) → *array*

1.8   Returns an array consisting of values for the given key(s). Will insert the *default value* for keys that are not found.

```
h = { "a" => 100, "b" => 200, "c" => 300 }
h.values_at("a", "c")        →   [100, 300]
h.values_at("a", "c", "z")   →   [100, 300, nil]
h.default = "cat"
h.values_at("a", "c", "z")   →   [100, 300, "cat"]
```

Class Integer < Numeric

Subclasses: Bignum, Fixnum

Integer is the basis for the two concrete classes that hold whole numbers, Bignum and Fixnum. (If you've come here looking for the iterator step, it's on page 566.)

Instance methods

ceil
$$int.\text{ceil} \rightarrow integer$$

Synonym for Integer#to_i.

chr
$$int.\text{chr} \rightarrow string$$

Returns a string containing the ASCII character represented by the receiver's value.

```
65.chr    →   "A"
?a.chr    →   "a"
230.chr   →   "\346"
```

downto
$$int.\text{downto}(integer) \{| i | block \} \rightarrow int$$

Iterates *block*, passing decreasing values from *int* down to and including *integer*.

```
5.downto(1) {|n| print n, ".. " }
print "  Liftoff!\n"
```

produces:

```
5.. 4.. 3.. 2.. 1..   Liftoff!
```

floor
$$int.\text{floor} \rightarrow integer$$

Returns the largest integer less than or equal to *int*. Equivalent to Integer#to_i.

```
1.floor      →   1
(-1).floor   →   -1
```

integer?
$$int.\text{integer?} \rightarrow \text{true}$$

Always returns true.

next
$$int.\text{next} \rightarrow integer$$

Returns the Integer equal to *int* + 1.

```
1.next     →   2
(-1).next  →   0
```

round
$$int.\text{round} \rightarrow integer$$

Synonym for Integer#to_i.

succ   *int*.succ → *integer*

Synonym for `Integer#next`.

times   *int*.times {| *i* | *block* } → *int*

Iterates block *int* times, passing in values from zero to *int* −1.

```
5.times do |i|
  print i, " "
end
```
produces:
```
0 1 2 3 4
```

to_i   *int*.to_i → *int*

Returns *int*.

to_int   *int*.to_int → *integer*

Synonym for `Integer#to_i`.

truncate   *int*.truncate → *integer*

Synonym for `Integer#to_i`.

upto   *int*.upto(*integer*) {| *i* | *block* } → *int*

Iterates *block*, passing in integer values from *int* up to and including *integer*.

```
5.upto(10) {|i| print i, " " }
```
produces:
```
5 6 7 8 9 10
```

Class **IO** < Object

Subclasses: File

Class IO is the basis for all input and output in Ruby. An I/O stream may be *duplexed* (that is, bidirectional) and so may use more than one native operating system stream.

Many of the examples in this section use class File, the only standard subclass of IO. The two classes are closely associated.

As used in this section, *portname* may take any of the following forms.

- A plain string represents a filename suitable for the underlying operating system.

- A string starting with | indicates a subprocess. The remainder of the string following the | is invoked as a process with appropriate input/output channels connected to it.

- A string equal to | – will create another Ruby instance as a subprocess.

The IO class uses the Unix abstraction of *file descriptors*, small integers that represent open files. Conventionally, standard input has an fd of 0, standard output an fd of 1, and standard error an fd of 2.

Ruby will convert pathnames between different operating system conventions if possible. For instance, on a Windows system the filename /gumby/ruby/test.rb will be opened as \gumby\ruby\test.rb. When specifying a Windows style filename in a double-quoted Ruby string, remember to escape the backslashes.

```
"c:\\gumby\\ruby\\test.rb"
```

Our examples here will use the Unix-style forward slashes; File::SEPARATOR can be used to get the platform-specific separator character.

I/O ports may be opened in any one of several different modes, which are shown in this section as *modestring*. This mode string must be one of the values listed in Table 27.6 on the following page.

Mixes in

Enumerable:
```
all?, any?, collect, detect, each_with_index, entries, find, find_all,
grep, include?, inject, map, max, member?, min, partition, reject,
select, sort, sort_by, to_a, zip
```

Table 27.6. Mode strings

Mode	Meaning
r	Read-only, starts at beginning of file (default mode).
r+	Read/write, starts at beginning of file.
w	Write-only, truncates an existing file to zero length or creates a new file for writing.
w+	Read/write, truncates existing file to zero length or creates a new file for reading and writing.
a	Write-only, starts at end of file if file exists; otherwise creates a new file for writing.
a+	Read/write, starts at end of file if file exists; otherwise creates a new file for reading and writing.
b	(DOS/Windows only) Binary file mode (may appear with any of the key letters listed above).

Class methods

for_fd　　　　　　　　　　　　　　　　　　IO.for_fd(*int, modestring*) → *io*

1.8　　Synonym for IO.new.

foreach　　　　　　　IO.foreach(*portname, separator=$/*) {| *line* | *block* } → nil

Executes the block for every line in the named I/O port, where lines are separated by *separator*.

```
IO.foreach("testfile") {|x| puts "GOT: #{x}" }
```

produces:

```
GOT: This is line one
GOT: This is line two
GOT: This is line three
GOT: And so on...
```

new　　　　　　　　　　　　　　　　　　IO.new(*int, modestring*) → *io*

Returns a new IO object (a stream) for the given integer file descriptor and mode string. See also IO#fileno and IO.for_fd.

```
a = IO.new(2, "w")      # '2' is standard error
STDERR.puts "Hello"
a.puts "World"
```

produces:

```
Hello
World
```

open
IO.open(*int*, *modestring*) → *io*
IO.open(*int*, *modestring*) {| *io* | *block* } → *obj*

With no associated block, open is a synonym for IO.new. If the optional code block is given, it will be passed *io* as an argument, and the IO object will automatically be closed when the block terminates. In this instance, IO.open returns the value of the block.

```
IO.open(1, "w") do |io|
  io.puts "Writing to stdout"
end
```

produces:

```
Writing to stdout
```

pipe
IO.pipe → *array*

Creates a pair of pipe endpoints (connected to each other) and returns them as a two-element array of IO objects: [*read_file*, *write_file*]. *write_file* is automatically placed into sync mode. Not available on all platforms.

In the example below, the two processes close the ends of the pipe that they are not using. This is not just a cosmetic nicety. The read end of a pipe will not generate an end-of-file condition if any writers have the pipe still open. In the case of the parent process, the rd.read will never return if it does not first issue a wr.close.

```
rd, wr = IO.pipe
if fork
  wr.close
  puts "Parent got: <#{rd.read}>"
  rd.close
  Process.wait
else
  rd.close
  puts "Sending message to parent"
  wr.write "Hi Dad"
  wr.close
end
```

produces:

```
Sending message to parent
Parent got: <Hi Dad>
```

popen
IO.popen(*cmd*, *modestring*="r") → *io*
IO.popen(*cmd*, *modestring*="r") {| *io* | *block* } → *obj*

Runs the specified command string as a subprocess; the subprocess's standard input and output will be connected to the returned IO object. The parameter *cmd* may be a string or (in Ruby 1.9) an array of strings. In the latter case, the array is used as the argv parameter for the new process, and no special shell processing is performed on the strings. If *cmd* is a string, it will be subject to shell expansion. If the *cmd* string starts with a minus sign (–), and the operating system supports fork(2), then the current Ruby process is forked. The default mode for the new file object is r, but *modestring* may be set to any of the modes in Table 27.6 on page 504.

If a block is given, Ruby will run the command as a child connected to Ruby with a pipe. Ruby's end of the pipe will be passed as a parameter to the block. In this case IO.popen returns the value of the block.

If a block is given with a *cmd_string* of "–", the block will be run in two separate processes: once in the parent and once in a child. The parent process will be passed the pipe object as a parameter to the block, the child version of the block will be passed nil, and the child's standard in and standard out will be connected to the parent through the pipe. Not available on all platforms. Also see the Open3 library on page 708 and Kernel#exec on page 521.

```
pipe = IO.popen("uname")
p(pipe.readlines)
puts "Parent is #{Process.pid}"
IO.popen("date") {|pipe| puts pipe.gets }
IO.popen("-") {|pipe| STDERR.puts "#{Process.pid} is here, pipe=#{pipe}" }
```

produces:

```
["Darwin\n"]
Parent is 9778
Wed May 18 09:07:29 CDT 2005
9778 is here, pipe=#<IO:0x1ce418>
9781 is here, pipe=
```

read IO.read(*portname*, ⟨ *length*=$/ ⟨ , *offset* ⟩ ⟩) → *string*

Opens the file, optionally seeks to the given offset, and then returns *length* bytes (defaulting to the rest of the file). read ensures the file is closed before returning.

```
IO.read("testfile")        →  "This is line one\nThis is line
                              two\nThis is line three\nAnd so
                              on...\n"
IO.read("testfile", 20)    →  "This is line one\nThi"
IO.read("testfile", 20, 10)  →  "ne one\nThis is line "
```

readlines IO.readlines(*portname*, *separator*=$/) → *array*

Reads the entire file specified by *portname* as individual lines, and returns those lines in an array. Lines are separated by *separator*.

```
a = IO.readlines("testfile")
a[0]   →   "This is line one\n"
```

select	IO.select(*read_array* ⟨ , *write_array* ⟨ , *error_array* ⟨ , *timeout* ⟩ ⟩ ⟩) → *array* or nil

See Kernel#select on page 528.

sysopen	IO.sysopen(*path,* ⟨ *mode* ⟨ , *perm* ⟩ ⟩) → *int*

1.8 Opens the given path, returning the underlying file descriptor as a Fixnum.

```
IO.sysopen("testfile")   →   3
```

Instance methods

<<	*io* << *obj* → *io*

String Output—Writes *obj* to *io*. *obj* will be converted to a string using to_s.

```
STDOUT << "Hello " << "world!\n"
```

produces:

```
Hello world!
```

binmode	*io*.binmode → *io*

Puts *io* into binary mode. This is useful only in MS-DOS/Windows environments. Once a stream is in binary mode, it cannot be reset to nonbinary mode.

clone	*io*.clone → *io*

Creates a new I/O stream, copying all the attributes of *io*. The file position is shared as well, so reading from the clone will alter the file position of the original, and vice versa.

close	*io*.close → nil

Closes *io* and flushes any pending writes to the operating system. The stream is unavailable for any further data operations; an IOError is raised if such an attempt is made. I/O streams are automatically closed when they are claimed by the garbage collector.

close_read	*io*.close_read → nil

Closes the read end of a duplex I/O stream (i.e., one that contains both a read and a write stream, such as a pipe). Will raise an IOError if the stream is not duplexed.

```
f = IO.popen("/bin/sh","r+")
f.close_read
f.readlines
```

produces:

```
prog.rb:3:in `readlines': not opened for reading (IOError)
from prog.rb:3
```

---

close_write   *io*.close_write → nil

Closes the write end of a duplex I/O stream (i.e., one that contains both a read and a write stream, such as a pipe). Will raise an IOError if the stream is not duplexed.

```
f = IO.popen("/bin/sh","r+")
f.close_write
f.print "nowhere"
```

produces:

```
prog.rb:3:in `write': not opened for writing (IOError)
from prog.rb:3:in `print'
from prog.rb:3
```

---

closed?   *io*.closed? → true or false

Returns true if *io* is completely closed (for duplex streams, both reader and writer), and returns false otherwise.

```
f = File.new("testfile")
f.close          →    nil
f.closed?        →    true
f = IO.popen("/bin/sh","r+")
f.close_write    →    nil
f.closed?        →    false
f.close_read     →    nil
f.closed?        →    true
```

---

each   *io*.each(*separator*=$/) {| *line* | *block* } → *io*

Executes the block for every line in *io*, where lines are separated by *separator*. *io* must be opened for reading or an IOerror will be raised.

```
f = File.new("testfile")
f.each {|line| puts "#{f.lineno}: #{line}" }
```

produces:

```
1: This is line one
2: This is line two
3: This is line three
4: And so on...
```

---

each_byte   *io*.each_byte {| *byte* | *block* } → nil

Calls the given block once for each byte (a Fixnum in the range 0 to 255) in *io*, passing the byte as an argument. The stream must be opened for reading or an IOerror will be raised.

```
f = File.new("testfile")
checksum = 0
f.each_byte {|x| checksum ^= x }   →    #<File:testfile>
checksum                            →    12
```

each_line

io.each_line(*separator=$/*) {| *line* | *block* } → *io*

Synonym for IO#each.

eof

io.cof → `true` or `false`

Returns `true` if *io* is at end of file. The stream must be opened for reading or an IOError will be raised.

```
f = File.new("testfile")
dummy = f.readlines
f.eof    →    true
```

eof?

io.eof? → `true` or `false`

Synonym for IO#eof.

fcntl

io.fcntl(*cmd, arg*) → *int*

Provides a mechanism for issuing low-level commands to control or query file-oriented I/O streams. Commands (which are integers), arguments, and the result are platform dependent. If *arg* is a number, its value is passed directly. If it is a string, it is interpreted as a binary sequence of bytes. On Unix platforms, see fcntl(2) for details. The Fcntl module provides symbolic names for the first argument (see page 677). Not implemented on all platforms.

fileno

io.fileno → *int*

Returns an integer representing the numeric file descriptor for *io*.

```
STDIN.fileno    →    0
STDOUT.fileno   →    1
```

flush

io.flush → *io*

Flushes any buffered data within *io* to the underlying operating system (note that this is Ruby internal buffering only; the OS may buffer the data as well).

```
STDOUT.print "no newline"
STDOUT.flush
```

produces:

```
no newline
```

fsync

io.fsync → 0 or `nil`

1.8

Immediately writes all buffered data in *io* to disk. Returns `nil` if the underlying operating system does not support *fsync(2)*. Note that fsync differs from using IO#sync=. The latter ensures that data is flushed from Ruby's buffers but does not guarantee that the underlying operating system actually writes it to disk.

getc   *io*.getc → *int* or nil

Gets the next 8-bit byte (0..255) from *io*. Returns nil if called at end of file.

```
f = File.new("testfile")
f.getc   →   84
f.getc   →   104
```

gets   *io*.gets(*separator*=$/) → *string* or nil

Reads the next "line" from the I/O stream; lines are separated by *separator*. A separator
of nil reads the entire contents, and a zero-length separator reads the input a paragraph
at a time (two successive newlines in the input separate paragraphs). The stream must
be opened for reading or an IOerror will be raised. The line read in will be returned
and also assigned to $_. Returns nil if called at end of file.

```
File.new("testfile").gets   →   "This is line one\n"
$_                          →   "This is line one\n"
```

ioctl   *io*.ioctl(*cmd*, *arg*) → *int*

Provides a mechanism for issuing low-level commands to control or query I/O devices.
The command (which is an integer), arguments, and results are platform dependent. If
arg is a number, its value is passed directly. If it is a string, it is interpreted as a binary
sequence of bytes. On Unix platforms, see ioctl(2) for details. Not implemented on
all platforms.

isatty   *io*.isatty → true or false

Returns true if *io* is associated with a terminal device (tty), and returns false otherwise.

```
File.new("testfile").isatty   →   false
File.new("/dev/tty").isatty   →   true
```

lineno   *io*.lineno → *int*

Returns the current line number in *io*. The stream must be opened for reading. lineno
counts the number of times gets is called, rather than the number of newlines encountered. The two values will differ if gets is called with a separator other than newline.
See also the $. variable.

```
f = File.new("testfile")
f.lineno   →   0
f.gets     →   "This is line one\n"
f.lineno   →   1
f.gets     →   "This is line two\n"
f.lineno   →   2
```

lineno=   *io*.lineno = *int* → *int*

Manually sets the current line number to the given value. `$.` is updated only on the next read.

```
f = File.new("testfile")
f.gets                     →    "This is line one\n"
$.                         →    1
f.lineno = 1000
f.lineno                   →    1000
$. # lineno of last read   →    1
f.gets                     →    "This is line two\n"
$. # lineno of last read   →    1001
```

pid   *io*.pid → *int*

Returns the process ID of a child process associated with *io*. This will be set by `IO.popen`.

```
pipe = IO.popen("-")
if pipe
  STDERR.puts "In parent, child pid is #{pipe.pid}"
else
  STDERR.puts "In child, pid is #{$$}"
end
```

produces:

```
In child, pid is 26884
In parent, child pid is 26884
```

pos   *io*.pos → *int*

Returns the current offset (in bytes) of *io*.

```
f = File.new("testfile")
f.pos    →   0
f.gets   →   "This is line one\n"
f.pos    →   17
```

pos=   *io*.pos = *int* → 0

Seeks to the given position (in bytes) in *io*.

```
f = File.new("testfile")
f.pos = 17
f.gets   →   "This is line two\n"
```

print   *io*.print(⟨ *obj*=$_ ⟩*) → nil

Writes the given object(s) to *io*. The stream must be opened for writing. If the output record separator (`$\`) is not `nil`, it will be appended to the output. If no arguments are given, prints `$_`. Objects that aren't strings will be converted by calling their `to_s` method. Returns `nil`.

```
STDOUT.print("This is ", 100, " percent.\n")
```

produces:

```
This is 100 percent.
```

printf

io.printf(*format* ⟨ , *obj* ⟩*) → nil

Formats and writes to *io*, converting parameters under control of the format string. See Kernel#sprintf on page 529 for details.

putc

io.putc(*obj*) → *obj*

Writes the given character (taken from a String or a Fixnum) on *io*.

```
STDOUT.putc "A"
STDOUT.putc 65
```

produces:

```
AA
```

puts

io.puts(⟨ *obj* ⟩*) → nil

Writes the given objects to *io* as with IO#print. Writes a newline after any that do not already end with a newline sequence. If called with an array argument, writes each element on a new line. If called without arguments, outputs a single newline.

```
STDOUT.puts("this", "is", "a", "test")
```

produces:

```
this
is
a
test
```

read

io.read(⟨ *int* ⟨ , *buffer* ⟩ ⟩) → *string* or nil

Reads at most *int* bytes from the I/O stream or to the end of file if *int* is omitted. Returns nil if called at end of file. If *buffer* (a String) is provided, it is resized accordingly and input is read directly into it.

1.8

```
f = File.new("testfile")
f.read(16)       →   "This is line one"
str = "cat"
f.read(10, str)  →   "\nThis is l"
str              →   "\nThis is l"
```

readchar

io.readchar → *int*

Reads a character as with IO#getc, but raises an EOFError on end of file.

readline

io.readline(*separator*=$/) → *string*

Reads a line as with IO#gets, but raises an EOFError on end of file.

readlines

io.readlines(*separator=$/*) → *array*

Reads all of the lines in *io*, and returns them in *array*. Lines are separated by the optional *separator*. The stream must be opened for reading or an IOerror will be raised.

```
f = File.new("testfile")
f.readlines  →  ["This is line one\n", "This is line two\n", "This
                 is line three\n", "And so on...\n"]
```

reopen

io.reopen(*other_io*) → *io*
io.reopen(*path, modestring*) → *io*

Reassociates *io* with the I/O stream given in *other_io* or to a new stream opened on *path*. This may dynamically change the actual class of this stream.

```
f1 = File.new("testfile")
f2 = File.new("testfile")
f2.readlines[0]   →   "This is line one\n"
f2.reopen(f1)     →   #<File:testfile>
f2.readlines[0]   →   "This is line one\n"
```

rewind

io.rewind → 0

Positions *io* to the beginning of input, resetting lineno to zero.

```
f = File.new("testfile")
f.readline  →  "This is line one\n"
f.rewind    →  0
f.lineno    →  0
f.readline  →  "This is line one\n"
```

seek

io.seek(*int, whence=SEEK_SET*) → 0

Seeks to a given offset *int* in the stream according to the value of *whence*.

IO::SEEK_CUR	Seeks to *int* plus current position.
IO::SEEK_END	Seeks to *int* plus end of stream (you probably want a negative value for *int*).
IO::SEEK_SET	Seeks to the absolute location given by *int*.

```
f = File.new("testfile")
f.seek(-13, IO::SEEK_END)  →  0
f.readline                 →  "And so on...\n"
```

stat

io.stat → *stat*

Returns status information for *io* as an object of type File::Stat.

```
f = File.new("testfile")
s = f.stat
"%o" % s.mode      →   "100644"
s.blksize          →   4096
s.atime            →   Thu Aug 26 22:37:41 CDT 2004
```

sync   *io*.sync → true or false

Returns the current "sync mode" of *io*. When sync mode is true, all output is immediately flushed to the underlying operating system and is not buffered by Ruby internally. See also IO#fsync.

```
f = File.new("testfile")
f.sync   →   false
```

sync=   *io*.sync = *bool* → true or false

Sets the "sync mode" to true or false. When sync mode is true, all output is immediately flushed to the underlying operating system and is not buffered internally. Returns the new state. See also IO#fsync.

```
f = File.new("testfile")
f.sync = true
```

sysread   *io*.sysread(*int* ⟨ , *buffer* ⟩) → *string*

Reads *int* bytes from *io* using a low-level read and returns them as a string. If *buffer* (a String) is provided, input is read directly in to it. Do not mix with other methods that read from *io*, or you may get unpredictable results. Raises SystemCallError on error and EOFError at end of file.

```
f = File.new("testfile")
f.sysread(16)          →   "This is line one"
str = "cat"
f.sysread(10, str)     →   "\nThis is l"
str                    →   "\nThis is l"
```

sysseek   *io*.sysseek(*offset*, *whence*=SEEK_SET) → *int*

Seeks to a given *offset* in the stream according to the value of *whence* (see IO#seek for values of *whence*). Returns the new offset into the file.

```
f = File.new("testfile")
f.sysseek(-13, IO::SEEK_END)    →   53
f.sysread(10)                   →   "And so on."
```

syswrite   *io*.syswrite(*string*) → *int*

Writes the given string to *io* using a low-level write. Returns the number of bytes written. Do not mix with other methods that write to *io*, or you may get unpredictable results. Raises SystemCallError on error.

```
f = File.new("out", "w")
f.syswrite("ABCDEF")   →   6
```

---

tell   *io*.tell → *int*

Synonym for IO#pos.

---

to_i   *io*.to_i → *int*

Synonym for IO#fileno.

---

to_io   *io*.to_io → *io*

Returns *io*.

---

tty?   *io*.tty? → true or false

Synonym for IO#isatty.

---

ungetc   *io*.ungetc(*int*) → nil

Pushes back one character onto *io*, such that a subsequent buffered read will return it.
Only one character may be pushed back before a subsequent read operation (that is,
you will be able to read only the last of several characters that have been pushed back).
Has no effect with unbuffered reads (such as IO#sysread).

```
f = File.new("testfile")   →   #<File:testfile>
c = f.getc                  →   84
f.ungetc(c)                 →   nil
f.getc                      →   84
```

---

write   *io*.write(*string*) → *int*

Writes the given string to *io*. The stream must be opened for writing. If the argument
is not a string, it will be converted to a string using to_s. Returns the number of bytes
written.

```
count = STDOUT.write( "This is a test\n" )
puts "That was #{count} bytes of data"
```

produces:

```
This is a test
That was 15 bytes of data
```

Module	
Kernel	

The Kernel module is included by class Object, so its methods are available in every Ruby object. The Kernel instance methods are documented in class Object beginning on page 567. This section documents the module methods. These methods are called without a receiver and thus can be called in functional form.

Module methods

Array   Array(*arg*) → *array*

Returns *arg* as an Array. First tries to call *arg*.to_ary, then *arg*.to_a. If both fail, creates a single element array containing *arg* (unless *arg* is nil).

```
Array(1..5)   →   [1, 2, 3, 4, 5]
```

Float   Float(*arg*) → *float*

Returns *arg* converted to a float. Numeric types are converted directly, the rest are converted using *arg*.to_f. As of Ruby 1.8, converting nil generates a TypeError.

```
Float(1)          →   1.0
Float("123.456")  →   123.456
```

Integer   Integer(*arg*) → *int*

Converts *arg* to a Fixnum or Bignum. Numeric types are converted directly (floating-point numbers are truncated). If *arg* is a String, leading radix indicators (0, 0b, and 0x) are honored. Others are converted using to_int and to_i. This behavior is different from that of String#to_i.

```
Integer(123.999)   →   123
Integer("0x1a")    →   26
Integer(Time.new)  →   1116425264
Integer(nil)       →   0
```

String   String(*arg*) → *string*

Converts *arg* to a String by calling its to_s method.

```
String(self)        →   "main"
String(self.class)  →   "Object"
String(123456)      →   "123456"
```

**` (backquote)**                                               `*cmd*` → *string*

Returns the standard output of running *cmd* in a subshell. The built-in syntax %x{...} described on page 89 uses this method. Sets $? to the process status.

```
`date`                    →    "Thu Aug 26 22:38:08 CDT 2004\n"
`ls testdir`.split[1]     →    "main.rb"
`echo oops && exit 99`    →    "oops\n"
$?.exitstatus             →    99
```

---

abort
abort
abort(msg)

1.8   Terminates execution immediately with an exit code of 1. The optional `String` parameter is written to standard error before the program terminates.

---

at_exit
at_exit { block } → proc

Converts *block* to a `Proc` object (and therefore binds it at the point of call), and registers it for execution when the program exits. If multiple handlers are registered, they are executed in reverse order of registration.

```
def do_at_exit(str1)
  at_exit { print str1 }
end
at_exit { puts "cruel world" }
do_at_exit("goodbye ")
exit
```

produces:

```
goodbye cruel world
```

---

autoload
autoload(name, file_name) → nil

Registers *file_name* to be loaded (using `Kernel.require`) the first time that the module *name* (which may be a `String` or a symbol) is accessed.

```
autoload(:MyModule, "/usr/local/lib/modules/my_module.rb")
```

1.8   Prior to Ruby 1.8, the *name* parameter was assumed to be in the top-level namespace. In Ruby 1.8, the new method `Module.autoload` lets you define namespace-specific autoload hooks. In the following code, Ruby 1.6 will load xxx.rb on references to `::XXX` whereas Ruby 1.8 will autoload on references to `X::XXX`.

```
module X
 autoload :XXX, "xxx.rb"
end
```

Note that xxx.rb should define a class in the correct namespace. That is, in this example xxx.rb should contain

```
class X::XXX
  # ...
end
```

Kernel

autoload?

autoload?(*name*) → *file_name* or nil

Returns the name of the file that will be autoloaded when the string or symbol *name* is referenced in the top-level context, or returns nil if there is no associated autoload.

```
autoload(:Fred, "module_fred")   →   nil
autoload?(:Fred)                 →   "module_fred"
autoload?(:Wilma)                →   nil
```

binding

binding → *a_binding*

Returns a Binding object, describing the variable and method bindings at the point of call. This object can be used when calling eval to execute the evaluated command in this environment. Also see the description of class Binding beginning on page 444.

```
def get_binding(param)
  return binding
end
b = get_binding("hello")
eval("param", b)   →   "hello"
```

block_given?

block_given? → true or false

Returns true if yield would execute a block in the current context.

```
def try
  if block_given?
    yield
  else
    "no block"
  end
end
try                   →   "no block"
try { "hello" }       →   "hello"
try do "hello" end    →   "hello"
```

callcc

callcc {| *cont* | *block* } → *obj*

Generates a Continuation object, which it passes to the associated block. Performing a *cont*.call will cause the callcc to return (as will falling through the end of the block). The value returned by the callcc is the value of the block or the value passed to *cont*.call. See Continuation on page 448 for more details. Also see Kernel.throw for an alternative mechanism for unwinding a call stack.

caller

caller(⟨ *int* ⟩) → *array*

Returns the current execution stack—an array containing strings in the form *file:line* or *file:line: in 'method'*. The optional *int* parameter determines the number of initial stack entries to omit from the result.

```
def a(skip)
  caller(skip)
end
def b(skip)
  a(skip)
end
def c(skip)
  b(skip)
end
c(0)  →  ["prog:2:in `a'", "prog:5:in `b'", "prog:8:in `c'",
          "prog:10"]
c(1)  →  ["prog:5:in `b'", "prog:8:in `c'", "prog:11"]
c(2)  →  ["prog:8:in `c'", "prog:12"]
c(3)  →  ["prog:13"]
```

catch

catch(*symbol*) { *block* } → obj

catch executes its block. If a throw is encountered, Ruby searches up its stack for a catch block with a tag corresponding to the throw's *symbol*. If found, that block is terminated, and catch returns the value given to throw. If throw is not called, the block terminates normally, and the value of catch is the value of the last expression evaluated. catch expressions may be nested, and the throw call need not be in lexical scope.

```
def routine(n)
  puts n
  throw :done if n <= 0
  routine(n-1)
end
catch(:done) { routine(4) }
```

produces:

```
4
3
2
1
0
```

chomp

chomp(⟨ *rs* ⟩) → $_ or *string*

Equivalent to $_ = $_.chomp(*rs*), except no assignment is made if chomp doesn't change $_. See String#chomp on page 610.

```
$_ = "now\n"
chomp         →    "now"
chomp "ow"    →    "n"
chomp "xxx"   →    "n"
$_            →    "n"
```

chomp!

chomp!(⟨ *rs* ⟩) → $_ or nil

Equivalent to $_.chomp!(*rs*). See String#chomp!

```
$_ = "now\n"
chomp!           →    "now"
$_               →    "now"
chomp! "x"       →    nil
$_               →    "now"
```

---

chop   chop → *string*

(Almost) equivalent to (`$_.dup).chop!`, except that if chop would perform no action,
`$_` is unchanged and `nil` is not returned. See `String#chop!` on page 610.

```
$_ = a = "now\r\n"
chop    →    "now"
$_      →    "now"
chop    →    "no"
chop    →    "n"
chop    →    ""
a       →    "now\r\n"
```

---

chop!   chop! → $_ or nil

Equivalent to `$_.chop!`.

```
$_  = a  = "now\r\n"
chop!    →    "now"
chop!    →    "no"
chop!    →    "n"
chop!    →    ""
chop!    →    nil
$_       →    ""
a        →    ""
```

---

eval   eval(*string* ⟨ , *binding* ⟨ , *file* ⟨ , *line* ⟩ ⟩ ⟩) → *obj*

Evaluates the Ruby expression(s) in *string*. If *binding* is given, the evaluation is performed in its context. The binding may be a `Binding` object or a `Proc` object. If the
optional *file* and *line* parameters are present, they will be used when reporting syntax
errors.

```
def get_binding(str)
  return binding
end
str = "hello"
eval "str + ' Fred'"                         →    "hello Fred"
eval "str + ' Fred'", get_binding("bye")     →    "bye Fred"
```

As of Ruby 1.8, local variables assigned within an `eval` are available after the `eval`
only if they were defined at the outer scope before the `eval` executed. In this way `eval`
has the same scoping rules as blocks.

```
a = 1
eval "a = 98; b = 99"
puts a
puts b
```

produces:

```
98
prog.rb:4: undefined local variable or method `b' for
 main:Object (NameError)
```

---

exec   exec(*command* ⟨ , *args* ⟩)

Replaces the current process by running the given external command. If exec is given a single argument, that argument is taken as a line that is subject to shell expansion before being executed. If *command* contains a newline or any of the characters *?{}[]<>()~\&|\$;'`", or under Windows if *command* looks like a shell-internal command (for example dir), *command* is run under a shell. On Unix system, Ruby does this by prepending sh -c. Under Windows, it uses the name of a shell in either RUBYSHELL or COMSPEC.

If multiple arguments are given, the second and subsequent arguments are passed as parameters to *command* with no shell expansion. If the first argument is a two-element array, the first element is the command to be executed, and the second argument is used as the argv[0] value, which may show up in process listings. In MSDOS environments, the command is executed in a subshell; otherwise, one of the exec(2) system calls is used, so the running command may inherit some of the environment of the original program (including open file descriptors). Raises SystemCallError if the *command* couldn't execute (typically Errno::ENOENT).

```
exec "echo *"       # echoes list of files in current directory
# never get here
exec "echo", "*"    # echoes an asterisk
# never get here
```

---

exit   exit(true | false | *status*=1)

1.8,   Initiates the termination of the Ruby script. If called in the scope of an exception handler, raises a SystemExit exception. This exception may be caught. Otherwise exits the process using exit(2). The optional parameter is used to return a status code to the invoking environment. With an argument of true, exits with a status of zero. With an argument that is false (or no argument), exits with a status of 1, otherwise exits with
1.8,   the given status. Note that the default exit value has changed from −1 to +1 in Ruby 1.8.

```
fork { exit 99 }
Process.wait
puts "Child exits with status: #{$?.exitstatus}"
 begin
   exit
   puts "never get here"
 rescue SystemExit
   puts "rescued a SystemExit exception"
 end
puts "after begin block"
```

produces:

```
Child exits with status: 99
rescued a SystemExit exception
after begin block
```

Just prior to termination, Ruby executes any `at_exit` functions and runs any object finalizers (see `ObjectSpace` beginning on page 578).

```
at_exit { puts "at_exit function" }
ObjectSpace.define_finalizer("string",  lambda { puts "in finalizer" })
exit
```

produces:

```
at_exit function
in finalizer
```

---

exit!   exit!(true | false | *status*=1)

1.8   Similar to `Kernel.exit`, but exception handling, `at_exit` functions, and finalizers are bypassed.

---

fail   fail
                                                                          fail(*message*)
                                                   fail(*exception* ⟨ , *message* ⟨ , *array* ⟩ ⟩)

Synonym for `Kernel.raise`.

---

fork   fork ⟨ { *block* } ⟩ → *int* or nil

Creates a subprocess. If a block is specified, that block is run in the subprocess, and the subprocess terminates with a status of zero. Otherwise, the `fork` call returns twice, once in the parent, returning the process ID of the child, and once in the child, returning nil. The child process can exit using `Kernel.exit!` to avoid running any `at_exit` functions. The parent process should use `Process.wait` to collect the termination statuses of its children or use `Process.detach` to register disinterest in their status; otherwise, the operating system may accumulate zombie processes.

```
fork do
  3.times {|i| puts "Child: #{i}" }
end
3.times {|i| puts "Parent: #{i}" }
Process.wait
```

produces:

```
Child: 0
Parent: 0
Child: 1
Parent: 1
Child: 2
Parent: 2
```

format

format(*format_string* ⟨ , *arg* ⟩*) → *string*

Synonym for `Kernel.sprintf`.

gets

gets(*separator*=$/) → *string* or nil

Returns (and assigns to $_) the next line from the list of files in ARGV (or $*) or from standard input if no files are present on the command line. Returns nil at end of file. The optional argument specifies the record separator. The separator is included with the contents of each record. A separator of nil reads the entire contents, and a zero-length separator reads the input one paragraph at a time, where paragraphs are divided by two consecutive newlines. If multiple filenames are present in ARGV, gets(nil) will read the contents one file at a time.

```
ARGV << "testfile"
print while gets
```

produces:

```
This is line one
This is line two
This is line three
And so on...
```

The style of programming using $_ as an implicit parameter is gradually losing favor in the Ruby community.

global_variables

global_variables → *array*

Returns an array of the names of global variables.

```
global_variables.grep /std/   →   ["$stdout", "$stdin", "$stderr"]
```

gsub

gsub(*pattern*, *replacement*) → *string*
gsub(*pattern*) { *block* } → *string*

Equivalent to $_.gsub(...), except that $_ will be updated if substitution occurs.

```
$_ = "quick brown fox"
gsub /[aeiou]/, '*'   →   "q**ck br*wn f*x"
$_                    →   "q**ck br*wn f*x"
```

gsub!

gsub!(*pattern*, *replacement*) → *string* or nil
gsub!(*pattern*) { *block* } → *string* or nil

Equivalent to $_.gsub!(...).

```
$_ = "quick brown fox"
gsub! /cat/, '*'   →   nil
$_                 →   "quick brown fox"
```

iterator?   iterator? → true or false

Deprecated synonym for Kernel.block_given?.

---

lambda   lambda { *block* } → *proc*

Creates a new procedure object from the given block. See page 357 for an explanation of the difference between procedure objects created using lambda and those created using Proc.new. Note that lambda is now preferred over proc.

```
prc = lambda { "hello" }
prc.call   →   "hello"
```

---

load   load(*file_name*, *wrap*=false) → true

Loads and executes the Ruby program in the file *file_name*. If the filename does not resolve to an absolute path, the file is searched for in the library directories listed in $:. If the optional *wrap* parameter is true, the loaded script will be executed under an anonymous module, protecting the calling program's global namespace. In no circumstance will any local variables in the loaded file be propagated to the loading environment.

---

local_variables   local_variables → *array*

Returns the names of the current local variables.

```
fred = 1
for i in 1..10
  # ...
end
local_variables   →   ["fred", "i"]
```

Note that local variables are associated with bindings.

```
def fred
  a = 1
  b = 2
  binding
end
freds_binding = fred
eval("local_variables", freds_binding)   →   ["a", "b"]
```

---

loop   loop { *block* }

Repeatedly executes the block.

```
loop do
  print "Input: "
  break if (line = gets).nil?  or (line =~ /^[qQ]/)
  # ...
end
```

open   open(*name* ⟨ , *modestring* ⟨ , *permission* ⟩ ⟩) → *io* or `nil`
                          open(*name* ⟨ , *modestring* ⟨ , *permission* ⟩ ⟩) {| *io* | *block* } → *obj*

Creates an IO object connected to the given stream, file, or subprocess.

If *name* does not start with a pipe character (|), treat it as the name of a file to open using the specified mode defaulting to `"r"` (see the table of valid modes on page 504). If a file is being created, its initial permissions may be set using the integer third parameter. If this third parameter is present, the file will be opened using the low-level open(2) rather than fopen(3) call.

If a block is specified, it will be invoked with the IO object as a parameter, which will be automatically closed when the block terminates. The call returns the value of the block in this case.

If *name* starts with a pipe character, a subprocess is created, connected to the caller by a pair of pipes. The returned IO object may be used to write to the standard input and read from the standard output of this subprocess. If the command following the | is a single minus sign, Ruby forks, and this subprocess is connected to the parent. In the subprocess, the open call returns `nil`. If the command is not `"-"`, the subprocess runs the command. If a block is associated with an open("|-") call, that block will be run twice—once in the parent and once in the child. The block parameter will be an IO object in the parent and `nil` in the child. The parent's IO object will be connected to the child's STDIN and STDOUT. The subprocess will be terminated at the end of the block.

```
open("testfile") do |f|
  print f.gets
end
```

produces:

```
This is line one
```

Open a subprocess and read its output.

```
cmd = open("|date")
print cmd.gets
cmd.close
```

produces:

```
Thu Aug 26 22:38:10 CDT 2004
```

Open a subprocess running the same Ruby program.

```
f = open("|-", "w+")
if f.nil?
  puts "in Child"
  exit
else
  puts "Got: #{f.gets}"
end
```

produces:

```
Got: in Child
```

Open a subprocess using a block to receive the I/O object.

```
open("|-") do |f|
  if f.nil?
    puts "in Child"
  else
    puts "Got: #{f.gets}"
  end
end
```

produces:

```
Got: in Child
```

---

p   p(⟨ *obj* ⟩⁺) → nil

For each object, writes *obj*.inspect followed by the current output record separator to the program's standard output. Also see the PrettyPrint library on page 716.

```
S = Struct.new(:name, :state)
s = S['dave', 'TX']
p s
```

produces:

```
#<struct S name="dave", state="TX">
```

---

print   print(⟨ *obj* ⟩*) → nil

1.8   Prints each object in turn to STDOUT. If the output field separator ($,) is not nil, its contents will appear between each field. If the output record separator ($\) is not nil, it will be appended to the output. If no arguments are given, prints $_. Objects that aren't strings will be converted by calling their to_s method.

```
print "cat", [1,2,3], 99, "\n"
$, = ", "
$\ = "\n"
print "cat", [1,2,3], 99
```

produces:

```
cat12399
cat, 1, 2, 3, 99
```

---

printf   printf(*io*, *format* ⟨ , *obj* ⟩*) → nil
                                         printf(*format* ⟨ , *obj* ⟩*) → nil

Equivalent to

>   *io*.write sprintf(*format*, *obj* ...)

or

>   STDOUT.write sprintf(*format*, *obj* ...)

proc

proc { *block* } → *a_proc*

1.8

Creates a new procedure object from the given block. Mildly deprecated in favor of `Kernel#lambda`.

```
prc = proc {|name| "Goodbye, #{name}" }
prc.call('Dave')   →   "Goodbye, Dave"
```

putc

putc(*int*) → *int*

Equivalent to `STDOUT.putc(int)`.

puts

puts(⟨ *arg* ⟩*) → `nil`

Equivalent to `STDOUT.puts(arg...)`.

raise

raise
raise(*message*)
raise(*exception* ⟨ , *message* ⟨ , *array* ⟩ ⟩)

With no arguments, raises the exception in `$!` or raises a `RuntimeError` if `$!` is `nil`. With a single `String` argument, raises a `RuntimeError` with the string as a message. Otherwise, the first parameter should be the name of an `Exception` class (or an object that returns an `Exception` when sent `exception`). The optional second parameter sets the message associated with the exception, and the third parameter is an array of callback information. Exceptions are caught by the `rescue` clause of `begin...end` blocks.

```
raise "Failed to create socket"
raise ArgumentError, "No parameters", caller
```

rand

rand(*max=0*) → *number*

Converts *max* to an integer using $max_1 = max.\texttt{to\_i.abs}$. If the result is zero, returns a pseudorandom floating-point number greater than or equal to 0.0 and less than 1.0. Otherwise, returns a pseudorandom integer greater than or equal to zero and less than max_1. `Kernel.srand` may be used to ensure repeatable sequences of random numbers between different runs of the program. Ruby currently uses a modified Mersenne Twister with a period of $2^{19937} - 1$.

```
srand 1234                →   0
[ rand,  rand ]           →   [0.191519450163469, 0.49766366626136]
[ rand(10), rand(1000) ]  →   [6, 817]
srand 1234                →   1234
[ rand,  rand ]           →   [0.191519450163469, 0.49766366626136]
```

readline

readline(⟨ *separator=$/* ⟩) → *string*

Equivalent to `Kernel.gets`, except `readline` raises `EOFError` at end of file.

---

readlines   readlines(⟨ *separator=$/* ⟩) → *array*

Returns an array containing the lines returned by calling Kernel.gets(*separator*) until the end of file.

---

require   require(*library_name*) → true or false

Ruby tries to load *library_name*, returning true if successful. If the filename does not resolve to an absolute path, it will be searched for in the directories listed in $:. If the file has the extension .rb, it is loaded as a source file; if the extension is .so, .o, or .dll,[1] Ruby loads the shared library as a Ruby extension. Otherwise, Ruby tries adding .rb, .so, and so on to the name. The name of the loaded feature is added to the array in $". A feature will not be loaded if its name already appears in $".[2] require returns true if the feature was successfully loaded.

```
require 'my-library.rb'
require 'db-driver'
```

1.8 The SCRIPT_LINES__ constant can be used to capture the source of code read using require.

```
SCRIPT_LINES__ = {}
require 'code/scriptlines'
puts "Files: #{SCRIPT_LINES__.keys.join(', ')}"
SCRIPT_LINES__['./code/scriptlines.rb'].each do |line|
  puts "Source: #{line}"
end
```

produces:

```
3/8
Files: ./code/scriptlines.rb, /Users/dave/ruby1.8/lib/ruby/1.8/rational.rb
Source: require 'rational'
Source:
Source: puts Rational(1,2)*Rational(3,4)
```

---

scan   scan(*pattern*) → *array*
                                          scan(*pattern*) { *block* } → $_

Equivalent to calling $_.scan. See String#scan on page 617.

---

select select(*read_array* ⟨ , *write_array* ⟨ , *error_array* ⟨ , *timeout* ⟩ ⟩ ⟩) → *array* or nil

Performs a low-level select call, which waits for data to become available from input/output devices. The first three parameters are arrays of IO objects or nil. The last is a timeout in seconds, which should be an Integer or a Float. The call waits

---

1. Or whatever the default shared library extension is on the current platform.

2. Although this name is not converted to an absolute path, so that require 'a';require './a' will load a.rb twice. This is arguably a bug.

for data to become available for any of the IO objects in *read_array*, for buffers to have cleared sufficiently to enable writing to any of the devices in *write_array*, or for an error to occur on the devices in *error_array*. If one or more of these conditions are met, the call returns a three-element array containing arrays of the IO objects that were ready. Otherwise, if there is no change in status for *timeout* seconds, the call returns nil. If all parameters are nil, the current thread sleeps forever.

```
select( [STDIN], nil, nil, 1.5 )  →  [[#<IO:0x1cfaac>], [], []]
```

---

set_trace_func   set_trace_func(*proc*) → *proc*
                                                       set_trace_func(nil) → nil

---

Establishes *proc* as the handler for tracing, or disables tracing if the parameter is nil. *proc* takes up to six parameters: an event name, a filename, a line number, an object ID, a binding, and the name of a class. *proc* is invoked whenever an event occurs. Events are c-call (call a C-language routine), c-return (return from a C-language routine), call (call a Ruby method), class (start a class or module definition), end (finish a class or module definition), line (execute code on a new line), raise (raise an exception), and return (return from a Ruby method). Tracing is disabled within the context of *proc*.

See the example starting on page 412 for more information.

---

sleep   sleep(*numeric=0*) → *fixnum*

Suspends the current thread for *numeric* seconds (which may be a Float with fractional seconds). Returns the actual number of seconds slept (rounded), which may be less than that asked for if the thread was interrupted by a SIGALRM or if another thread calls Thread#run. An argument of zero causes sleep to sleep forever.

```
Time.now   →   Thu Aug 26 22:38:10 CDT 2004
sleep 1.9  →   2
Time.now   →   Thu Aug 26 22:38:12 CDT 2004
```

---

split   split(⟨ *pattern* ⟨ , *limit* ⟩ ⟩) → *array*

Equivalent to $_.split(*pattern*, *limit*). See String#split on page 619.

---

sprintf   sprintf(*format_string* ⟨ , *arguments* ⟩*) → *string*

Returns the string resulting from applying *format_string* to any additional arguments. Within the format string, any characters other than format sequences are copied to the result.

A format sequence consists of a percent sign, followed by optional flags, width, and precision indicators, and then terminated with a field type character. The field type controls how the corresponding sprintf argument is to be interpreted, and the flags modify that interpretation. The flag characters are shown in Table 27.7 on the facing page, and the field type characters are listed in Table 27.8.

The field width is an optional integer, followed optionally by a period and a precision. The width specifies the minimum number of characters that will be written to the result for this field. For numeric fields, the precision controls the number of decimal places displayed. For string fields, the precision determines the maximum number of characters to be copied from the string. (Thus, the format sequence %10.10s will always contribute exactly ten characters to the result.)

```
sprintf("%d %04x", 123, 123)          →   "123_007b"
sprintf("%08b '%4s'", 123, 123)       →   "01111011_'_123'"
sprintf("%1$*2$s %2$d %1$s", "hello", 8)  →   "___hello_8_hello"
sprintf("%1$*2$s %2$d", "hello", -8)  →   "hello____-8"
sprintf("%+g:% g:%-g", 1.23, 1.23, 1.23)  →   "+1.23:_1.23:1.23"
```

K ernel

srand

srand(⟨ *number* ⟩) → *old_seed*

Seeds the pseudorandom number generator to the value of *number*.to_i.abs. If *number* is omitted or zero, seeds the generator using a combination of the time, the process ID, and a sequence number. (This is also the behavior if Kernel.rand is called without previously calling srand, but without the sequence.) By setting the seed to a known value, scripts that use rand can be made deterministic during testing. The previous seed value is returned. Also see Kernel.rand on page 527.

sub

sub(*pattern*, *replacement*) → $_
sub(*pattern*) { *block* } → $_

Equivalent to $_.sub(*args*), except that $_ will be updated if substitution occurs.

sub!

sub!(*pattern*, *replacement*) → $_ or nil
sub!(*pattern*) { *block* } → $_ or nil

Equivalent to $_.sub!(*args*).

syscall

syscall(*fixnum* ⟨ , *args* ⟩*) → *int*

Calls the operating system function identified by *fixnum*. The arguments must be either String objects or Integer objects that fit within a native long. Up to nine parameters may be passed. The function identified by *fixnum* is system dependent. On some Unix systems, the numbers may be obtained from a header file called syscall.h.

```
syscall 4, 1, "hello\n", 6   # '4' is write(2) on our system
```

produces:

```
hello
```

system

system(*command* ⟨ , *args* ⟩*) → true or false

Executes *command* in a subshell, returning true if the command was found and ran

Table 27.7. sprintf flag characters

Flag	Applies to	Meaning
␣ (space)	bdEefGgiouXx	Leave a space at the start of positive numbers.
digit$	all	Specify the absolute argument number for this field. Absolute and relative argument numbers cannot both be used in a sprintf string.
#	beEfgGoxX	Use an alternative format. For the conversions b, o, X, and x, prefix the result with b, 0, 0X, 0x, respectively. For E, e, f, G, and g, force a decimal point to be added, even if no digits follow. For G and g, do not remove trailing zeros.
+	bdEefGgiouXx	Add a leading plus sign to positive numbers.
−	all	Left-justify the result of this conversion.
0 (zero)	bdEefGgiouXx	Pad with zeros, not spaces.
*	all	Use the next argument as the field width. If negative, left-justify the result. If the asterisk is followed by a number and a dollar sign, use the indicated argument as the width.

successfully, false otherwise. An error status is available in $?. The arguments are processed in the same way as for Kernel.exec on page 521. Raises SystemCallError if the *command* couldn't execute (typically Errno::ENOENT).

```
system("echo *")
system("echo", "*")
```

produces:

```
config.h main.rb
*
```

---

test   test(*cmd, file1* ⟨ *, file2* ⟩) → *obj*

Uses the integer *cmd* to perform various tests on *file1* (Table 27.9 on page 533) or on *file1* and *file2* (Table 27.10).

---

throw   throw(*symbol* ⟨ *, obj* ⟩)

Transfers control to the end of the active catch block waiting for *symbol*. Raises NameError if there is no catch block for the symbol. The optional second parameter supplies a return value for the catch block, which otherwise defaults to nil. For examples, see Kernel.catch on page 519.

Table 27.8. `sprintf` field types

Field	Conversion
b	Convert argument as a binary number.
c	Argument is the numeric code for a single character.
d	Convert argument as a decimal number.
E	Equivalent to e, but uses an uppercase *E* to indicate the exponent.
e	Convert floating point-argument into exponential notation with one digit before the decimal point. The precision determines the number of fractional digits (defaulting to six).
f	Convert floating-point argument as [␣-]ddd.ddd, where the precision determines the number of digits after the decimal point.
G	Equivalent to g, but use an uppercase *E* in exponent form.
g	Convert a floating-point number using exponential form if the exponent is less than −4 or greater than or equal to the precision, or in d.dddd form otherwise.
i	Identical to d.
o	Convert argument as an octal number.
p	The value of *argument.inspect*.
s	Argument is a string to be substituted. If the format sequence contains a precision, at most that many characters will be copied.
u	Treat argument as an unsigned decimal number.
X	Convert argument as a hexadecimal number using uppercase letters. Negative numbers will be displayed with two leading periods (representing an infinite string of leading FFs).
x	Convert argument as a hexadecimal number. Negative numbers will be displayed with two leading periods (representing an infinite string of leading FFs.)

---

trace_var
trace_var(*symbol, cmd*) → nil
trace_var(*symbol*) {| *val* | *block* } → nil

Controls tracing of assignments to global variables. The parameter *symbol* identifies the variable (as either a string name or a symbol identifier). *cmd* (which may be a string or a Proc object) or the block is executed whenever the variable is assigned, and receives the variable's new value as a parameter. Only explicit assignments are traced. Also see `Kernel.untrace_var`.

```
trace_var :$_, lambda {|v| puts "$_ is now '#{v}'" }
$_ = "hello"
sub(/ello/, "i")
$_ += " Dave"
```

produces:

```
$_ is now 'hello'
$_ is now 'hi Dave'
```

Table 27.9. File tests with a single argument

Flag	Description	Returns
?A	Last access time for *file1*	Time
?b	True if *file1* is a block device	true or false
?c	True if *file1* is a character device	true or false
?C	Last change time for *file1*	Time
?d	True if *file1* exists and is a directory	true or false
?e	True if *file1* exists	true or false
?f	True if *file1* exists and is a regular file	true or false
?g	True if *file1* has the setgid bit set (false under NT)	true or false
?G	True if *file1* exists and has a group ownership equal to the caller's group	true or false
?k	True if *file1* exists and has the sticky bit set	true or false
?l	True if *file1* exists and is a symbolic link	true or false
?M	Last modification time for *file1*	Time
?o	True if *file1* exists and is owned by the caller's effective UID	true or false
?O	True if *file1* exists and is owned by the caller's real UID	true or false
?p	True if *file1* exists and is a fifo	true or false
?r	True if *file1* is readable by the effective UID/GID of the caller	true or false
?R	True if *file1* is readable by the real UID/GID of the caller	true or false
?s	If *file1* has nonzero size, return the size, otherwise return nil	Integer or nil
?S	True if *file1* exists and is a socket	true or false
?u	True if *file1* has the setuid bit set	true or false
?w	True if *file1* exists and is writable by the effective UID/ GID	true or false
?W	True if *file1* exists and is writable by the real UID/GID	true or false
?x	True if *file1* exists and is executable by the effective UID/GID	true or false
?X	True if *file1* exists and is executable by the real UID/GID	true or false
?z	True if *file1* exists and has a zero length	true or false

Table 27.10. File tests with two arguments

Flag	Description
?-	True if *file1* is a hard link to *file2*
?=	True if the modification times of *file1* and *file2* are equal
?<	True if the modification time of *file1* is prior to that of *file2*
?>	True if the modification time of *file1* is after that of *file2*

trap   trap(*signal, proc*) → *obj*
                                                       trap(*signal*) { *block* } → *obj*

See the Signal module on page 604.

untrace_var   untrace_var(*symbol* ⟨ , *cmd* ⟩) → *array* or nil

Removes tracing for the specified command on the given global variable and returns
nil. If no command is specified, removes all tracing for that variable and returns an
array containing the commands actually removed.

warn   warn *msg*

1.8   Writes the given message to STDERR (unless $VERBOSE is nil, perhaps because the -W0
command-line option was given).

warn "Danger, Will Robinson!"

produces:

Danger, Will Robinson!

Marshal

The marshaling library converts collections of Ruby objects into a byte stream, allowing them to be stored outside the currently active script. This data may subsequently be read and the original objects reconstituted. Marshaling is described starting on page 414. Also see the YAML library on page 758.

Marshaled data has major and minor version numbers stored along with the object information. In normal use, marshaling can load only data written with the same major version number and an equal or lower minor version number. If Ruby's "verbose" flag is set (normally using -d, -v, -w, or --verbose), the major and minor numbers must match exactly. Marshal versioning is independent of Ruby's version numbers. You can extract the version by reading the first two bytes of marshaled data.

```
str = Marshal.dump("thing")
RUBY_VERSION    →    "1.8.2"
str[0]          →    4
str[1]          →    8
```

Some objects cannot be dumped: if the objects to be dumped include bindings, procedure or method objects, instances of class IO, or singleton objects, or if you try to dump anonymous classes or modules, a TypeError will be raised.

If your class has special serialization needs (for example, if you want to serialize in some specific format), or if it contains objects that would otherwise not be serializable, you can implement your own serialization strategy. Prior to Ruby 1.8, you defined the methods _dump and _load.

Ruby 1.8 includes a more flexible interface to custom serialization using the instance methods marshal_dump and marshal_load: If an object to be marshaled responds to marshal_dump, that method is called instead of _dump. marshal_dump can return an object of any class (not just a String). A class that implements marshal_dump must also implement marshal_load, which is called as an instance method of a newly allocated object and passed the object originally created by marshal_dump.

The following code uses this new framework to store a Time object in the serialized version of an object. When loaded, this object is passed to marshal_load, which converts this time to a printable form, storing the result in an instance variable.

```
class TimedDump
  attr_reader :when_dumped
  def marshal_dump
    Time.now
  end
  def marshal_load(when_dumped)
    @when_dumped = when_dumped.strftime("%I:%M%p")
  end
end
```

```
t = TimedDump.new
t.when_dumped      →    nil

str = Marshal.dump(t)

newt = Marshal.load(str)
newt.when_dumped   →    "10:38PM"
```

Module constants

MAJOR_VERSION   Major part of marshal format version number.
MINOR_VERSION   Minor part of marshal format version number.

Module methods

dump   dump(*obj* ⟨ , *io* ⟩ , *limit*=–1) → *io*

Serializes *obj* and all descendent objects. If *io* is specified, the serialized data will be written to it; otherwise the data will be returned as a `String`. If *limit* is specified, the traversal of subobjects will be limited to that depth. If *limit* is negative, no checking of depth will be performed.

```
class Klass
  def initialize(str)
    @str = str
  end
  def say_hello
    @str
  end
end
o = Klass.new("hello\n")
data = Marshal.dump(o)
obj = Marshal.load(data)
obj.say_hello   →   "hello\n"
```

load   load(*from* ⟨ , *proc* ⟩) → *obj*

Returns the result of converting the serialized data in *from* into a Ruby object (possibly with associated subordinate objects). *from* may be either an instance of IO or an object that responds to `to_str`. If *proc* is specified, it will be passed each object as it is deserialized.

restore   restore(*from* ⟨ , *proc* ⟩) → *obj*

A synonym for `Marshal.load`.

Class	**MatchData** < Object

All pattern matches set the special variable $~ to a MatchData containing information about the match. The methods Regexp#match and Regexp#last_match also return a MatchData object. The object encapsulates all the results of a pattern match, results normally accessed through the special variables $&, $', $`, $1, $2, and so on (see the list on page 334). Class Matchdata is also known as MatchingData.

Instance methods

[ ]

match[*i*] → *obj*
match[*start, length*] → *array*
match[*range*] → *array*

Match Reference—MatchData acts as an array, and may be accessed using the normal array indexing techniques. *match*[0] is equivalent to the special variable $& and returns the entire matched string. *match*[1], *match*[2], and so on, return the values of the matched back references (portions of the pattern between parentheses). See also
1.8   MatchData#select and MatchData#values_at.

```
m = /(.)(.)(\d+)(\d)/.match("THX1138.")
m[0]      →    "HX1138"
m[1, 2]   →    ["H", "X"]
m[1..3]   →    ["H", "X", "113"]
m[-3, 2]  →    ["X", "113"]
```

begin

match.begin(*n*) → *int*

Returns the offset of the start of the *n*th element of the match array in the string.

```
m = /(.)(.)(\d+)(\d)/.match("THX1138.")
m.begin(0)   →   1
m.begin(2)   →   2
```

captures

match.captures → *array*

1.8   Returns the array of all the matching groups. Compare to MatchData#to_a, which returns both the complete matched string and all the matching groups.

```
m = /(.)(.)(\d+)(\d)/.match("THX1138.")
m.captures   →   ["H", "X", "113", "8"]
```

captures is useful when extracting parts of a match in an assignment.

```
f1, f2, f3 = /(.)(.)(\d+)(\d)/.match("THX1138.").captures
f1   →   "H"
f2   →   "X"
f3   →   "113"
```

---

end   *match*.end(*n*) → *int*

Returns the offset of the character immediately following the end of the *n*th element of the match array in the string.

```
m = /(.)(.)( \d+)(\d)/.match("THX1138.")
m.end(0)   →   7
m.end(2)   →   3
```

---

length   *match*.length → *int*

Returns the number of elements in the match array.

```
m = /(.)(.)( \d+)(\d)/.match("THX1138.")
m.length   →   5
m.size     →   5
```

---

offset   *match*.offset(*n*) → *array*

Returns a two-element array containing the beginning and ending offsets of the *n*th match.

```
m = /(.)(.)( \d+)(\d)/.match("THX1138.")
m.offset(0)   →   [1, 7]
m.offset(4)   →   [6, 7]
```

---

post_match   *match*.post_match → *string*

Returns the portion of the original string after the current match. Equivalent to the special variable $'.

```
m = /(.)(.)( \d+)(\d)/.match("THX1138: The Movie")
m.post_match   →   ": The Movie"
```

---

pre_match   *match*.pre_match → *string*

Returns the portion of the original string before the current match. Equivalent to the special variable $`.

```
m = /(.)(.)( \d+)(\d)/.match("THX1138.")
m.pre_match   →   "T"
```

---

select   *match*.select {| *val* | *block* } → *array*

1.8   Returns an array containing all elements of *match* for which *block* is true.

```
m = /(.)(.)( \d+)(\d)/.match("THX1138: The Movie")
m.to_a                     →   ["HX1138", "H", "X", "113", "8"]
m.select {|v| v =~ /\d\d/ }   →   ["HX1138", "113"]
```

---

size   *match*.size → *int*

A synonym for MatchData#length.

string
match.string → string

Returns a frozen copy of the string passed in to `match`.

```
m = /(.)(.)(\d+)(\d)/.match("THX1138.")
m.string   →   "THX1138."
```

to_a
match.to_a → array

Returns the array of matches. Unlike `MatchData#captures`, returns the full string matched.

```
m = /(.)(.)(\d+)(\d)/.match("THX1138.")
m.to_a   →   ["HX1138", "H", "X", "113", "8"]
```

to_s
match.to_s → string

Returns the entire matched string.

```
m = /(.)(.)(\d+)(\d)/.match("THX1138.")
m.to_s   →   "HX1138"
```

values_at
match.values_at(⟨ index ⟩*) → array

1.8, Uses each *index* to access the matching values, returning an array of the corresponding matches.

```
m = /(.)(.)(\d+)(\d)/.match("THX1138: The Movie")
m.to_a                →   ["HX1138", "H", "X", "113", "8"]
m.values_at(0, 2, -2) →   ["HX1138", "X", "113"]
```

Module **Math**

The Math module contains module methods for basic trigonometric and transcendental functions. See class `Float` on page 487 for a list of constants that define Ruby's floating-point accuracy.

Module constants

E Value of e (base of natural logarithms)
PI Value of π

Module methods

acos   Math.acos(x) → *float*

1.8 Computes the arc cosine of x. Returns $0..\pi$.

acosh   Math.acosh(x) → *float*

1.8 Computes the inverse hyperbolic cosine of x.

asin   Math.asin(x) → *float*

1.8 Computes the arc sine of x. Returns $0..\pi$.

asinh   Math.asinh(x) → *float*

1.8 Computes the inverse hyperbolic sine of x.

atan   Math.atan(x) → *float*

1.8 Computes the arc tangent of x. Returns $-\frac{\pi}{2}..\frac{\pi}{2}$.

atanh   Math.atanh(x) → *float*

1.8 Computes the inverse hyperbolic tangent of x.

atan2   Math.atan2(y, x) → *float*

Computes the arc tangent given y and x. Returns $-\pi..\pi$.

cos   Math.cos(x) → *float*

Computes the cosine of x (expressed in radians). Returns $-1..1$.

cosh   Math.cosh(x) → *float*

1.8 Computes the hyperbolic cosine of x (expressed in radians).

erf
Math.erf(*x*) → *float*

1.8   Returns the error function of *x*.

$$erf(x) = \frac{2}{\sqrt{\pi}} \int_0^x e^{-t^2} dt$$

---

erfc
Math.erfc(*x*) → *float*

1.8   Returns the complementary error function of *x*.

$$erfc(x) = 1 - \frac{2}{\sqrt{\pi}} \int_0^x e^{-t^2} dt$$

---

exp
Math.exp(*x*) → *float*

Returns e^x.

---

frexp
Math.frexp(*numeric*) → [*fraction, exponent*]

Returns a two-element array containing the normalized fraction (a `Float`) and exponent (a `Fixnum`) of *numeric*.

```
fraction, exponent = Math.frexp(1234)    →    [0.6025390625, 11]
fraction * 2**exponent                   →    1234.0
```

---

hypot
Math.hypot(*x, y*) → *float*

1.8   Returns $\sqrt{x^2 + y^2}$, the hypotenuse of a right-angled triangle with sides *x* and *y*.

```
Math.hypot(3, 4)    →    5.0
```

---

ldexp
Math.ldexp(*float, integer*) → *float*

Returns the value of *float* $\times 2^{integer}$.

```
fraction, exponent = Math.frexp(1234)
Math.ldexp(fraction, exponent)    →    1234.0
```

---

log
Math.log(*numeric*) → *float*

Returns the natural logarithm of *numeric*.

---

log10
Math.log10(*numeric*) → *float*

Returns the base 10 logarithm of *numeric*.

---

sin
Math.sin(*numeric*) → *float*

Computes the sine of *numeric* (expressed in radians). Returns −1..1.

---

sinh   Math.sinh(*numeric*) → *float*

1.8   Computes the hyperbolic sine of *numeric* (expressed in radians).

---

sqrt   Math.sqrt(*numeric*) → *float*

Returns the non-negative square root of *numeric*. Raises `ArgError` if *numeric* is less than zero.

---

tan   Math.tan(*numeric*) → *float*

Returns the tangent of *numeric* (expressed in radians).

---

tanh   Math.tanh(*numeric*) → *float*

1.8   Computes the hyperbolic tangent of *numeric* (expressed in radians).

Math

Class **Method** < Object

Method objects are created by `Object#method`. They are associated with a particular object (not just with a class). They may be used to invoke the method within the object and as a block associated with an iterator. They may also be unbound from one object (creating an `UnboundMethod`) and bound to another.

```
def square(n)
  n*n
end
meth  = self.method(:square)

meth.call(9)                →   81
[ 1, 2, 3 ].collect(&meth)  →   [1, 4, 9]
```

Instance methods

[ ]
meth[⟨ *args* ⟩*] → *object*

Synonym for `Method.call`.

==
meth== *other* → true or false

1.8 Returns true if *meth* is the same method as *other*.

```
def fred()
  puts "Hello"
end

alias bert fred    →    nil

m1 = method(:fred)
m2 = method(:bert)
m1 == m2           →    true
```

arity
meth.arity → *fixnum*

Returns an indication of the number of arguments accepted by a method. See Figure 27.2 on the next page.

call
meth.call(⟨ *args* ⟩*) → *object*

Invokes the *meth* with the specified arguments, returning the method's return value.

```
m = 12.method("+")
m.call(3)    →    15
m.call(20)   →    32
```

eql?
meth.eql?(*other*) → true or false

1.8 Returns true if *meth* is the same method as *other*.

Figure 27.2. `Method#arity` in action

`Method#arity` returns a non-negative integer for methods that take a fixed number of arguments. For Ruby methods that take a variable number of arguments, returns $-n - 1$, where n is the number of required arguments. For methods written in C, returns -1 if the call takes a variable number of arguments.

```
class C
  def one;      end
  def two(a); end
  def three(*a);  end
  def four(a, b); end
  def five(a, b, *c);    end
  def six(a, b, *c, &d); end
end
c = C.new
c.method(:one).arity    →    0
c.method(:two).arity    →    1
c.method(:three).arity  →    -1
c.method(:four).arity   →    2
c.method(:five).arity   →    -3
c.method(:six).arity    →    -3

"cat".method(:size).arity     →    0
"cat".method(:replace).arity  →    1
"cat".method(:squeeze).arity  →    -1
"cat".method(:count).arity    →    -1
```

```
def fred()
  puts "Hello"
end

alias bert fred   →    nil

m1 = method(:fred)
m2 = method(:bert)
m1.eql?(m2)       →    false
```

---

to_proc   *meth*.to_proc → *prc*

1.8 Returns a `Proc` object corresponding to this method. Because `to_proc` is called by the interpreter when passing block arguments, method objects may be used following an ampersand to pass a block to another method call. See the `Thing` example at the start of this section.

---

unbind   *meth*.unbind → unbound_method

1.8 Dissociates *meth* from its current receiver. The resulting `UnboundMethod` can subsequently be bound to a new object of the same class (see `UnboundMethod` on page 651).

<table>
</table>

| Class | Module | < | Object |

Subclasses: Class

A `Module` is a collection of methods and constants. The methods in a module may be instance methods or module methods. Instance methods appear as methods in a class when the module is included; module methods do not. Conversely, module methods may be called without creating an encapsulating object, and instance methods may not. See also `Module#module_function` on page 558.

In the descriptions that follow, the parameter *symbol* refers to a symbol, which is either a quoted string or a `Symbol` (such as `:name`).

```
module Mod
  include Math
  CONST = 1
  def meth
    #  ...
  end
end
Mod.class              →   Module
Mod.constants          →   ["E", "CONST", "PI"]
Mod.instance_methods   →   ["meth"]
```

Class methods

constants   Module.constants → *array*

Returns an array of the names of all constants defined in the system. This list includes the names of all modules and classes.

```
p Module.constants.sort[1..5]
```

produces:

```
["ARGV", "ArgumentError", "Array", "Bignum", "Binding"]
```

nesting   Module.nesting → *array*

Returns the list of `Module`s nested at the point of call.

```
module M1
  module M2
    $a = Module.nesting
  end
end
$a              →   [M1::M2, M1]
$a[0].name      →   "M1::M2"
```

new
$$\text{Module.new} \rightarrow mod$$
$$\text{Module.new} \ \{\ |\ mod\ |\ block\ \} \ \rightarrow mod$$

1.8 Creates a new anonymous module. If a block is given, it is passed the module object, and the block is evaluated in the context of this module using `module_eval`.

```
Fred = Module.new do
  def meth1
    "hello"
  end
  def meth2
    "bye"
  end
end
a = "my string"
a.extend(Fred)   →   "my string"
a.meth1          →   "hello"
a.meth2          →   "bye"
```

Instance methods

<, <=, >, >=
$$mod \ relop \ module \rightarrow \texttt{true} \ \text{or} \ \texttt{false}$$

Hierarchy Query—One module is considered *greater than* another if it is included in (or is a parent class of) the other module. The other operators are defined accordingly. If there is no relationship between the modules, all operators return `false`.

```
module Mixin
end

module Parent
  include Mixin
end

module Unrelated
end

Parent > Mixin       →   false
Parent < Mixin       →   true
Parent <= Parent     →   true
Parent < Unrelated   →   nil
Parent > Unrelated   →   nil
```

<=>
$$mod <=> other\_mod \rightarrow -1, 0, +1$$

Comparison—Returns -1 if *mod* includes *other_mod*, 0 if *mod* is the same module as *other_mod*, and $+1$ if *mod* is included by *other_mod* or if *mod* has no relationship with *other_mod*.

===
$$mod === obj \rightarrow \texttt{true} \ \text{or} \ \texttt{false}$$

Case Equality—Returns `true` if *obj* is an instance of *mod* or one of *mod*'s descendents. Of limited use for modules, but can be used in `case` statements to test objects by class.

ancestors

mod.ancestors → *array*

Returns a list of modules included in *mod* (including *mod* itself).

```
module Mod
  include Math
  include Comparable
end
```

```
Mod.ancestors    →    [Mod, Comparable, Math]
Math.ancestors   →    [Math]
```

autoload

mod.autoload(*name*, *file_name*) → nil

1.8 Registers *file_name* to be loaded (using Kernel.require) the first time that module *name* (which may be a String or a Symbol) is accessed in the namespace of *mod*. Note that the autoloaded file is evaluated in the top-level context. In this example, module_b.rb contains

```
module A::B    # in module_b.rb
  def doit
    puts "In Module A::B"
  end
  module_function :doit
end
```

Other code can then include this module automatically.

```
module A
  autoload(:B, "module_b")
end
```

```
A::B.doit          # autoloads "module_b"
```

produces:

```
In Module A::B
```

autoload?

mod.autoload?(*name*) → *file_name* or nil

1.8 Returns the name of the file that will be autoloaded when the string or symbol *name* is referenced in the context of *mod*, or returns nil if there is no associated autoload.

```
module A
  autoload(:B, "module_b")
end
A.autoload?(:B)   →    "module_b"
A.autoload?(:C)   →    nil
```

class_eval

mod.class_eval(*string* ⟨ , *file_name* ⟨ , *line_number* ⟩ ⟩) → *obj*
mod.class_eval { *block* } → *obj*

Synonym for Module.module_eval.

class_variables   *mod*.class_variables → *array*

Returns an array of the names of class variables in *mod* and the ancestors of *mod*.

```
class One
  @@var1 = 1
end
class Two < One
  @@var2 = 2
end
One.class_variables   →   ["@@var1"]
Two.class_variables   →   ["@@var2", "@@var1"]
```

clone   *mod*.clone → *other_mod*

Creates a new copy of a module.

```
m = Math.clone   →   #<Module:0x1c9760>
m.constants      →   ["E", "PI"]
m == Math        →   false
```

const_defined?   *mod*.const_defined?(*symbol*) → true or false

Returns true if a constant with the given name is defined by *mod*.

```
Math.const_defined? "PI"   →   true
```

const_get   *mod*.const_get(*symbol*) → *obj*

Returns the value of the named constant in *mod*.

```
Math.const_get :PI   →   3.14159265358979
```

const_missing   const_missing(*symbol*) → *obj*

1.8   Invoked when a reference is made to an undefined constant in *mod*. It is passed a symbol for the undefined constant and returns a value to be used for that constant. The following code is very poor style. If a reference is made to an undefined constant, it attempts to load a file whose name is the lowercase version of the constant (thus, class Fred is assumed to be in file fred.rb). If found, it returns the value of the loaded class. It therefore implements a perverse kind of autoload facility.

```
def Object.const_missing(name)
  @looked_for ||= {}
  str_name = name.to_s
  raise "Class not found: #{name}" if @looked_for[str_name]
  @looked_for[str_name] = 1
  file = str_name.downcase
  require file
  klass = const_get(name)
  return klass if klass
  raise "Class not found: #{name}"
end
```

---

const_set
mod.const_set(*symbol, obj*) → *obj*

Sets the named constant to the given object, returning that object. Creates a new constant if no constant with the given name previously existed.

```
Math.const_set("HIGH_SCHOOL_PI", 22.0/7.0)   →   3.14285714285714
Math::HIGH_SCHOOL_PI - Math::PI              →   0.00126448926734968
```

constants
mod.constants → *array*

Returns an array of the names of the constants accessible in *mod*. This includes the names of constants in any included modules (example at start of section).

include?
mod.include?(*other_mod*) → true or false

1.8 Returns true if *other_mod* is included in *mod* or one of *mod*'s ancestors.

```
module A
end

class B
  include A
end

class C < B
end

B.include?(A)   →   true
C.include?(A)   →   true
A.include?(A)   →   false
```

included_modules
mod.included_modules → *array*

Returns the list of modules included in *mod*.

```
module Mixin
end

module Outer
  include Mixin
end

Mixin.included_modules   →   []
Outer.included_modules   →   [Mixin]
```

instance_method
mod.instance_method(*symbol*) → *unbound_method*

1.8 Returns an UnboundMethod representing the given instance method in *mod*.

```
class Interpreter
  def do_a() print "there, "; end
  def do_d() print "Hello ";  end
  def do_e() print "!\n";     end
  def do_v() print "Dave";    end
```

```
  Dispatcher = {
    ?a => instance_method(:do_a),
    ?d => instance_method(:do_d),
    ?e => instance_method(:do_e),
    ?v => instance_method(:do_v)
  }

  def interpret(string)
    string.each_byte {|b| Dispatcher[b].bind(self).call }
  end
end

interpreter = Interpreter.new
interpreter.interpret('dave')
```

produces:

```
Hello there, Dave!
```

---

instance_methods

mod.instance_methods(*inc_super*=true) → *array*

Returns an array containing the names of public instance methods in the receiver. For a module, these are the public methods; for a class, they are the instance (not singleton) methods. With no argument, or with an argument that is true, the methods in *mod* and *mod*'s superclasses are returned. When called with a module as a receiver or with a parameter that is false, the instance methods in *mod* are returned. (The parameter defaults to false in versions of Ruby prior to January 2004.)

```
module A
  def method1()
  end
end

class B
  def method2()
  end
end

class C < B
  def method3()
  end
end

A.instance_methods
B.instance_methods(false)
C.instance_methods(false)
C.instance_methods(true).length
```

---

method_defined?

mod.method_defined?(*symbol*) → true or false

Returns true if the named method is defined by *mod* (or its included modules and, if *mod* is a class, its ancestors). Public and protected methods are matched.

```
module A
  def method1()  end
end
class B
  def method2()  end
end
class C < B
  include A
  def method3()  end
end

A.method_defined? :method1    →   true
C.method_defined? "method1"   →   true
C.method_defined? "method2"   →   true
C.method_defined? "method3"   →   true
C.method_defined? "method4"   →   false
```

---

module_eval   *mod*.class_eval(*string* ⟨ , *file_name* ⟨ , *line_number* ⟩ ⟩) → *obj*
                                            mod.module_eval { *block* } → *obj*

Evaluates the string or block in the context of *mod*. This can be used to add methods to a class. module_eval returns the result of evaluating its argument. The optional *file_name* and *line_number* parameters set the text for error messages.

```
class Thing
end
a = %q{def hello() "Hello there!" end}
Thing.module_eval(a)
puts Thing.new.hello()
Thing.module_eval("invalid code", "dummy", 123)
```

produces:

```
Hello there!
dummy:123:in `module_eval': undefined local variable
    or method `code' for Thing:Class
```

---

name   *mod*.name → *string*

Returns the name of the module *mod*.

---

private_class_method   *mod*.private_class_method(⟨ *symbol* ⟩$^+$) → nil

Makes existing class methods private. Often used to hide the default constructor new.

```
class SimpleSingleton  # Not thread safe
  private_class_method :new
  def SimpleSingleton.create(*args, &block)
    @me = new(*args, &block) if ! @me
    @me
  end
end
```

private_instance_methods

mod.private_instance_methods(*inc_super*=true) → *array*

1.8 Returns a list of the private instance methods defined in *mod*. If the optional parameter is true, the methods of any ancestors are included. (The parameter defaults to false in versions of Ruby prior to January 2004.)

```
module Mod
  def method1()  end
  private :method1
  def method2()  end
end
Mod.instance_methods          →    ["method2"]
Mod.private_instance_methods  →    ["method1"]
```

private_method_defined?

mod.private_method_defined?(*symbol*) → true or false

1.8 Returns true if the named private method is defined by *mod* (or its included modules and, if *mod* is a class, its ancestors).

```
module A
  def method1()  end
end
class B
  private
  def method2()  end
end
class C < B
  include A
  def method3()  end
end

A.method_defined? :method1            →    true
C.private_method_defined? "method1"   →    false
C.private_method_defined? "method2"   →    true
C.method_defined? "method2"           →    false
```

protected_instance_methods

mod.protected_instance_methods(*inc_super*=true) → *array*

1.8 Returns a list of the protected instance methods defined in *mod*. If the optional parameter is true, the methods of any ancestors are included. (The parameter defaults to false in versions of Ruby prior to January 2004.)

protected_method_defined? *mod*.protected_method_defined?(*symbol*) → true or false

1.8 Returns true if the named protected method is defined by *mod* (or its included modules and, if *mod* is a class, its ancestors).

```
module A
  def method1()  end
end
class B
  protected
  def method2()  end
end
class C < B
  include A
  def method3()  end
end
```

A.method_defined? :method1	→	true
C.protected_method_defined? "method1"	→	false
C.protected_method_defined? "method2"	→	true
C.method_defined? "method2"	→	true

---

public_class_method   *mod*.public_class_method(⟨ *symbol* ⟩⁺) → nil

Makes a list of existing class methods public.

---

public_instance_methods

mod.public_instance_methods(*inc_super*=true) → *array*

1.8 Returns a list of the public instance methods defined in *mod*. If the optional parameter is true, the methods of any ancestors are included. (The parameter defaults to false in versions of Ruby prior to January 2004.)

---

public_method_defined?   *mod*.public_method_defined?(*symbol*) → true or false

1.8 Returns true if the named public method is defined by *mod* (or its included modules and, if *mod* is a class, its ancestors).

```
module A
  def method1()  end
end
class B
  protected
  def method2()  end
end
class C < B
  include A
  def method3()  end
end
```

A.method_defined? :method1	→	true
C.public_method_defined? "method1"	→	true
C.public_method_defined? "method2"	→	false
C.method_defined? "method2"	→	true

Private instance methods

alias_method alias_method(*new_id, old_id*) → *mod*

Makes *new_id* a new copy of the method *old_id*. This can be used to retain access to methods that are overridden.

```
module Mod
  alias_method :orig_exit, :exit
  def exit(code=0)
    puts "Exiting with code #{code}"
    orig_exit(code)
  end
end
include Mod
exit(99)
```

produces:

```
Exiting with code 99
```

append_features append_features(*other_mod*) → *mod*

When this module is included in another, Ruby calls `append_features` in this module, passing it the receiving module in *other_mod*. Ruby's default implementation is to add the constants, methods, and module variables of this module to *other_mod* if this module has not already been added to *other_mod* or one of its ancestors. Prior to Ruby 1.8, user code often redefined `append_features`, added its own functionality, and then invoked `super` to handle the real include. In Ruby 1.8, you should instead implement the method `Module#included`. See also `Module#include` on page 556.

attr attr(*symbol, writable*=false) → nil

Defines a named attribute for this module, where the name is *symbol*.id2name, creating an instance variable (@name) and a corresponding access method to read it. If the optional *writable* argument is true, also creates a method called name= to set the attribute.

```
module Mod
  attr  :size, true
end
```

is equivalent to:

```
module Mod
  def size
    @size
  end
  def size=(val)
    @size = val
  end
end
```

attr_accessor
attr_accessor(⟨ symbol ⟩⁺) → nil

Equivalent to calling "attr symbol, true" on each symbol in turn.

```
module Mod
  attr_accessor(:one, :two)
end
Mod.instance_methods.sort   →   ["one", "one=", "two", "two="]
```

attr_reader
attr_reader(⟨ symbol ⟩⁺) → nil

Creates instance variables and corresponding methods that return the value of each instance variable. Equivalent to calling attr :name on each name in turn.

attr_writer
attr_writer(⟨ symbol ⟩⁺) → nil

Creates an accessor method to allow assignment to the attribute symbol.id2name.

define_method
define_method(symbol, method) → method
define_method(symbol) { block } → proc

_{1.8} Defines an instance method in the receiver. The method parameter can be a Proc or Method object. If a block is specified, it is used as the method body. This block is evaluated using instance_eval. This is tricky to demonstrate because define_method is private. (This is why we resort to the send hack in this example.)

```
class A
  def fred
    puts "In Fred"
  end
  def create_method(name, &block)
    self.class.send(:define_method, name, &block)
  end
  define_method(:wilma) { puts "Charge it!" }
end
class B < A
  define_method(:barney, instance_method(:fred))
end
b = B.new
b.barney
b.wilma
b.create_method(:betty) { p self }
b.betty
```

produces:

```
In Fred
Charge it!
#<B:0x1c9134>
```

extend_object   extend_object(*obj*) → *obj*

Extends the specified object by adding this module's constants and methods (which are added as singleton methods). This is the callback method used by Object#extend.

```
module Picky
  def Picky.extend_object(o)
    if String === o
      puts "Can't add Picky to a String"
    else
      puts "Picky added to #{o.class}"
      super
    end
  end
end
(s = Array.new).extend Picky  # Call Object.extend
(s = "quick brown fox").extend Picky
```

produces:

```
Picky added to Array
Can't add Picky to a String
```

extended   extended(*other_mod*)

1.8, Callback invoked whenever the receiver is used to extend an object. The object is passed as a parameter. This should be used in preference to Module#extend_object if your code wants to perform some action when a module is used to extend an object.

```
module A
  def A.extended(obj)
    puts "#{self} extending '#{obj}'"
  end
end
"cat".extend(A)
```

produces:

```
A extending 'cat'
```

include   include(〈 *other_mod* 〉+) → *mod*

Invokes Module.append_features (documented on page 554) on each parameter (in reverse order). Equivalent to the following code.

```
def include(*modules)
  modules.reverse_each do |mod|
    mod.append_features(self)
    mod.included(self)
  end
end
```

included   included(*other_mod*)

1.8, Callback invoked whenever the receiver is included in another module or class. This should be used in preference to `Module#append_features` if your code wants to perform some action when a module is included in another.

```
module A
  def A.included(mod)
    puts "#{self} included in #{mod}"
  end
end
module Enumerable
  include A
end
```

produces:

```
A included in Enumerable
```

---

method_added   method_added(*symbol*)

Invoked as a callback whenever a method is added to the receiver.

```
module Chatty
  def Chatty.method_added(id)
    puts "Adding #{id.id2name}"
  end
  def one()   end
end
module Chatty
  def two()   end
end
```

produces:

```
Adding one
Adding two
```

---

method_removed   method_removed(*symbol*)

1.8 Invoked as a callback whenever a method is removed from the receiver.

```
module Chatty
  def Chatty.method_removed(id)
    puts "Removing #{id.id2name}"
  end
  def one()   end
end
module Chatty
  remove_method(:one)
end
```

produces:

```
Removing one
```

---

method_undefined   method_undefined(*symbol*)

1.8 Invoked as a callback whenever a method is undefined in the receiver.

```
module Chatty
  def Chatty.method_undefined(id)
    puts "Undefining #{id.id2name}"
  end
  def one()   end
end
module Chatty
  undef_method(:one)
end
```

produces:

```
Undefining one
```

---

module_function   module_function(⟨ *symbol* ⟩*) → *mod*

Creates module functions for the named methods. These functions may be called with the module as a receiver and are available as instance methods to classes that mix in the module. Module functions are copies of the original and so may be changed independently. The instance-method versions are made private. If used with no arguments, subsequently defined methods become module functions.

```
module Mod
  def one
    "This is one"
  end
  module_function :one
end
class Cls
  include Mod
  def call_one
    one
  end
end
Mod.one      →   "This is one"
c = Cls.new
c.call_one   →   "This is one"
module Mod
  def one
    "This is the new one"
  end
end
Mod.one      →   "This is one"
c.call_one   →   "This is the new one"
```

---

private   private(⟨ *symbol* ⟩*) → *mod*

With no arguments, sets the default visibility for subsequently defined methods to private. With arguments, sets the named methods to have private visibility. See "Access Control" starting on page 356.

```
module Mod
  def a()  end
  def b()  end
  private
  def c()  end
  private :a
end
Mod.private_instance_methods   →   ["c", "a"]
```

protected   protected(⟨ *symbol* ⟩*) → *mod*

With no arguments, sets the default visibility for subsequently defined methods to protected. With arguments, sets the named methods to have protected visibility. See "Access Control" starting on page 356.

public   public(⟨ *symbol* ⟩*) → *mod*

With no arguments, sets the default visibility for subsequently defined methods to public. With arguments, sets the named methods to have public visibility. See "Access Control" starting on page 356.

remove_class_variable   remove_class_variable(*symbol*) → *obj*

1.8   Removes the definition of the *symbol*, returning that constant's value.

```
class Dummy
  @@var = 99
  puts @@var
  remove_class_variable(:@@var)
  puts(defined? @@var)
end
```

produces:

```
99
nil
```

remove_const   remove_const(*symbol*) → *obj*

Removes the definition of the given constant, returning that constant's value. Predefined classes and singleton objects (such as *true*) cannot be removed.

remove_method   remove_method(*symbol*) → *mod*

Removes the method identified by *symbol* from the current class. For an example, see `Module.undef_method`.

undef_method   undef_method(⟨ *symbol* ⟩+) → *mod*

Prevents the current class from responding to calls to the named method(s). Contrast this with `remove_method`, which deletes the method from the particular class; Ruby will still search superclasses and mixed-in modules for a possible receiver.

```
class Parent
  def hello
    puts "In parent"
  end
end
class Child < Parent
  def hello
    puts "In child"
  end
end
c = Child.new
c.hello

class Child
  remove_method :hello   # remove from child, still in parent
end
c.hello

class Child
  undef_method :hello    # prevent any calls to 'hello'
end
c.hello
```

produces:

```
In child
In parent
prog.rb:23: undefined method `hello' for #<Child:0x1c92ec> (NoMethodError)
```

| Class | **NilClass** < Object |

The class of the singleton object `nil`.

Instance methods

&   nil & *obj* → false

And—Returns `false`. As *obj* is an argument to a method call, it is always evaluated; there is no short-circuit evaluation in this case.

```
nil && puts("logical and")
nil &  puts("and")
```

produces:

```
and
```

^   nil ^ *obj* → true or false

Exclusive Or—Returns `false` if *obj* is `nil` or `false`, and returns `true` otherwise.

| nil | *obj* → true or false

Or—Returns `false` if *obj* is `nil` or `false`, and returns `true` otherwise.

```
nil | false   →   false
nil | 99      →   true
```

nil?   nil.nil? → true

Always returns `true`.

to_a   nil.to_a → []

Always returns an empty array.

```
nil.to_a   →   []
```

to_f   nil.to_f → 0.0

Always returns zero.

```
nil.to_f   →   0.0
```

to_i   nil.to_i → 0

Always returns zero.

```
nil.to_i   →   0
```

to_s   nil.to_s → ""

Always returns the empty string.

```
nil.to_s   →   ""
```

Class	**Numeric** < Object

Subclasses: Float, Integer

Numeric is the fundamental base type for the abstract class Integer and the concrete number classes Float, Fixnum, and Bignum. Many methods in Numeric are overridden in child classes, and Numeric takes some liberties by calling methods in these child classes. A complete list of the methods defined in all five classes is shown in Table 27.11 on page 564.

Mixes in

Comparable:
    <, <=, ==, >=, >, between?

Instance methods

+@   *+num → num*

Unary Plus—Returns the receiver's value.

-@   *−num → numeric*

Unary Minus—Returns the receiver's value, negated.

<=>   *num <=> other → 0 or nil*

Returns zero if *num* equals *other*, and returns nil otherwise.

abs   *num.abs → numeric*

Returns the absolute value of *num*.

```
12.abs        →   12
(-34.56).abs  →   34.56
-34.56.abs    →   34.56
```

ceil   *num.ceil → int*

Returns the smallest Integer greater than or equal to *num*. Class Numeric achieves this by converting itself to a Float and then invoking Float#ceil.

```
1.ceil        →   1
1.2.ceil      →   2
(-1.2).ceil   →   -1
(-1.0).ceil   →   -1
```

coerce   *num.coerce(numeric) → array*

coerce is both an instance method of Numeric and part of a type conversion protocol. When a number is asked to perform an operation and it is passed a parameter of a class different to its own, it must first coerce both itself and that parameter into a common class so that the operation makes sense. For example, in the expression $1 + 2.5$, the Fixnum 1 must be converted to a Float to make it compatible with 2.5. This conversion is performed by coerce. For all numeric objects, coerce is straightforward: if *numeric* is the same type as *num*, returns an array containing *numeric* and *num*. Otherwise, returns an array with both *numeric* and *num* represented as Float objects.

```
1.coerce(2.5)    →    [2.5, 1.0]
1.2.coerce(3)    →    [3.0, 1.2]
1.coerce(2)      →    [2, 1]
```

If a numeric object is asked to operate on a non-numeric, it tries to invoke coerce on that other object. For example, if you write

```
1 + "2"
```

Ruby will effectively execute the code as

```
n1, n2 = "2".coerce(1)
n2 + n1
```

In the more general case, this won't work, as most non-numerics don't define a coerce method. However, you can use this (if you feel so inclined) to implement part of Perl's automatic conversion of strings to numbers in expressions.

```
class String
  def coerce(other)
    case other
    when Integer
      begin
        return other, Integer(self)
      rescue
        return Float(other), Float(self)
      end
    when Float
      return other, Float(self)
    else super
    end
  end
end
```

```
1   + "2"     →    3
1   - "2.3"   →    -1.3
1.2 + "2.3"   →    3.5
1.5 - "2"     →    -0.5
```

coerce is discussed further on page 374.

---

div   *num*.div(*numeric*) → *int*

1.8   Uses / to perform division, and then converts the result to an integer. Numeric does not define the / operator; this is left to subclasses.

Numeric

	Numeric	Integer	Fixnum	Bignum	Float
%	–	–	✓	✓	✓
&	–	–	✓	✓	–
*	–	–	✓	✓	✓
**	–	–	✓	✓	✓
+	–	–	✓	✓	✓
+@	✓	–	–	–	–
-	–	–	✓	✓	✓
-@	✓	–	✓	✓	✓
/	–	–	✓	✓	✓
<	–	–	✓	–	✓
<<	–	–	✓	✓	–
<=	–	–	✓	–	✓
<=>	✓	–	✓	✓	✓
==	–	–	✓	✓	✓
>	–	–	✓	–	✓
>=	–	–	✓	–	✓
>>	–	–	✓	✓	–
[]	–	–	✓	✓	–
^	–	–	✓	✓	–
abs	✓	–	✓	✓	✓
ceil	✓	✓	–	–	✓
chr	–	✓	–	–	–
coerce	✓	–	–	✓	✓
div	✓	–	✓	✓	–
divmod	✓	–	✓	✓	✓
downto	–	✓	–	✓	–
eql?	✓	–	–	✓	✓
finite?	–	–	–	–	✓
floor	✓	✓	–	–	✓
hash	–	–	–	✓	✓
id2name	–	–	✓	–	–
infinite?	–	–	–	–	✓
integer?	✓	✓	–	–	–
modulo	✓	–	✓	✓	✓
nan?	–	–	–	–	✓
next	–	✓	–	–	–
nonzero?	✓	–	–	–	–
quo	✓	–	✓	✓	–
remainder	✓	–	–	✓	–
round	✓	✓	–	–	✓
size	–	–	✓	✓	–
step	✓	–	–	–	–
succ	–	✓	–	–	–
times	–	✓	–	–	–
to_f	–	–	✓	✓	✓
to_i	–	✓	–	–	✓
to_int	✓	✓	–	–	✓
to_s	–	–	✓	✓	✓
to_sym	–	–	✓	–	–
truncate	✓	✓	–	–	✓
upto	–	✓	–	–	–
zero?	✓	–	✓	–	✓
|	–	–	✓	✓	–
~	–	–	✓	✓	–

Table 27.11: Methods defined in class Numeric and its subclasses. A ✓ means that the method is defined in the corresponding class.

Table 27.12. Difference between modulo and remainder. The modulo operator ("%") always has the sign of the divisor whereas `remainder` has the sign of the dividend.

a	b	a.divmod(b)	a / b	a.modulo(b)	a.remainder(b)
13	4	3, 1	3	1	1
13	−4	−4, −3	−4	−3	1
−13	4	−4, 3	−4	3	−1
−13	−4	3, −1	3	−1	−1
11.5	4	2.0, 3.5	2.875	3.5	3.5
11.5	−4	−3.0, −0.5	−2.875	−0.5	3.5
−11.5	4	−3.0, 0.5	−2.875	0.5	−3.5
−11.5	−4	2.0, −3.5	2.875	−3.5	−3.5

---

divmod   *num*.divmod(*numeric*) → *array*

Returns an array containing the quotient and modulus obtained by dividing *num* by *numeric*. If `q,r = x.divmod(y)`, $q = floor(float(x)/float(y))$ and $x = q \times y + r$. The quotient is rounded toward $-\infty$. See Table 27.12 for examples.

---

eql?   *num*.eql?(*numeric*) → `true` or `false`

Returns `true` if *num* and *numeric* are the same type and have equal values.

```
1 == 1.0          →    true
1.eql?(1.0)       →    false
(1.0).eql?(1.0)   →    true
```

---

floor   *num*.floor → *int*

Returns the largest integer less than or equal to *num*. `Numeric` implements this by converting *int* to a `Float` and invoking `Float#floor`.

```
1.floor      →    1
(-1).floor   →    -1
```

---

integer?   *num*.integer? → `true` or `false`

Returns `true` if *num* is an `Integer` (including `Fixnum` and `Bignum`).

---

modulo   *num*.modulo(*numeric*) → *numeric*

Equivalent to *num*.divmod(*numeric*)[1].

---

nonzero?   *num*.nonzero? → *num* or `nil`

Returns *num* if *num* is not zero, and returns `nil` otherwise. This behavior is useful when chaining comparisons.

```
a = %w( z Bb bB bb BB a aA Aa AA A )
b = a.sort {|a,b| (a.downcase <=> b.downcase).nonzero? || a <=> b }
b  →  ["A", "a", "AA", "Aa", "aA", "BB", "Bb", "bB", "bb", "z"]
```

---

quo   *num*.quo(*numeric*) → *numeric*

1.8,   Equivalent to `Numeric#/`, but overridden in subclasses. The intent of quo is to return the most accurate result of division (in context). Thus `1.quo(2)` will equal 0.5, and 1/2 equals 0.

---

remainder   *num*.remainder(*numeric*) → *numeric*

If *num* and *numeric* have different signs, returns *mod−numeric*; otherwise, returns *mod*. In both cases *mod* is the value *num*.modulo(*numeric*). The differences between remainder and modulo (%) are shown in Table 27.12 on the preceding page.

---

round   *num*.round → *int*

Rounds *num* to the nearest integer. Numeric implements this by converting *int* to a Float and invoking `Float#round`.

---

step   *num*.step(*end_num*, *step*) {| i | *block* } → *num*

1.8,   Invokes *block* with the sequence of numbers starting at *num*, incremented by *step* on each call. The loop finishes when the value to be passed to the block is greater than *end_num* (if *step* is positive) or less than *end_num* (if *step* is negative). If all the arguments are integers, the loop operates using an integer counter. If any of the arguments are floating-point numbers, all are converted to floats, and the loop is executed $\lfloor n + n * \epsilon \rfloor + 1$ times, where $n = (end\_num - num)/step$. Otherwise, the loop starts at *num*, uses either the < or > operator to compare the counter against *end_num*, and increments itself using the + operator.

```
1.step(10, 2) {|i| print i, " " }
Math::E.step(Math::PI, 0.2) {|f| print f, " " }
```

produces:

```
1 3 5 7 9
2.71828182845905 2.91828182845905 3.11828182845905
```

---

to_int   *num*.to_int → *int*

Invokes the child class's `to_i` method to convert *num* to an integer.

---

truncate   *num*.truncate → *int*

Returns *num* truncated to an integer. Numeric implements this by converting its value to a float and invoking `Float#truncate`.

---

zero?   *num*.zero? → true or false

Returns `true` if *num* has a zero value.

Class Object

Subclasses: Array, Binding, Continuation, Data (used internally by the interpreter), Dir, Exception, FalseClass, File::Stat, Hash, IO, MatchData, Method, Module, NilClass, Numeric, Proc, Process::Status, Range, Regexp, String, Struct, Symbol, Thread, ThreadGroup, Time, TrueClass, UnboundMethod

Object is the parent class of all classes in Ruby. Its methods are therefore available to all objects unless explicitly overridden.

Object mixes in the Kernel module, making the built-in kernel functions globally accessible. Although the instance methods of Object are defined by the Kernel module, we have chosen to document them here for clarity.

In the descriptions that follow, the parameter *symbol* refers to a symbol, which is either a quoted string or a Symbol (such as :name).

Instance methods

== $obj == other\_obj \rightarrow$ `true` or `false`

Equality—At the Object level, == returns `true` only if *obj* and *other_obj* are the same object. Typically, this method is overridden in descendent classes to provide class-specific meaning.

=== $obj === other\_obj \rightarrow$ `true` or `false`

Case Equality—A synonym for Object#==, but typically overridden by descendents to provide meaningful semantics in `case` statements.

=~ $obj =\sim other\_obj \rightarrow$ `false`

Pattern Match—Overridden by descendents (notably Regexp and String) to provide meaningful pattern-match semantics.

__id__ $obj.\_\_id\_\_ \rightarrow$ *fixnum*

Synonym for Object#object_id.

__send__ $obj.\_\_send\_\_(symbol \langle , args \rangle^+ \langle , \&block \rangle) \rightarrow$ *other_obj*

Synonym for Object#send.

class $obj.class \rightarrow$ *klass*

Returns the class of *obj*, now preferred over Object#type, as an object's type in Ruby is only loosely tied to that object's class. This method must always be called with an explicit receiver, as class is also a reserved word in Ruby.

```
1.class      →   Fixnum
self.class   →   Object
```

clone   *obj*.clone → *other_obj*

Produces a shallow copy of *obj*—the instance variables of *obj* are copied, but not the objects they reference. Copies the frozen and tainted state of *obj*. See also the discussion under Object#dup.

```
class Klass
    attr_accessor :str
end
s1 = Klass.new        →    #<Klass:0x1c9170>
s1.str = "Hello"      →    "Hello"
s2 = s1.clone         →    #<Klass:0x1c90d0 @str="Hello">
s2.str[1,4] = "i"     →    "i"
s1.inspect            →    "#<Klass:0x1c9170 @str=\"Hi\">"
s2.inspect            →    "#<Klass:0x1c90d0 @str=\"Hi\">"
```

display   *obj*.display(*port*=$>) → nil

Prints *obj* on the given port (default $>). Equivalent to

```
def display(port=$>)
  port.write self
end
```

For example:

```
1.display
"cat".display
[ 4, 5, 6 ].display
puts
```

produces:

```
1cat456
```

dup   *obj*.dup → *other_obj*

Produces a shallow copy of *obj*—the instance variables of *obj* are copied, but not the objects they reference. dup copies the tainted state of *obj*. See also the discussion under Object#clone. In general, clone and dup may have different semantics in descendent classes. While clone is used to duplicate an object, including its internal state, dup typically uses the class of the descendent object to create the new instance.

eql?   *obj*.eql?(*other_obj*) → true or false

Returns true if *obj* and *other_obj* have the same value. Used by Hash to test members for equality. For objects of class Object, eql? is synonymous with ==. Subclasses normally continue this tradition, but there are exceptions. Numeric types, for example, perform type conversion across ==, but not across eql?, so

```
1 == 1.0      →    true
1.eql? 1.0    →    false
```

equal?

obj.equal?(other_obj) → <code>true</code> or <code>false</code>

Returns `true` if *obj* and *other_obj* have the same object ID. This method should not be overridden by subclasses.

```
a = [ 'cat', 'dog' ]
b = [ 'cat', 'dog' ]
a == b                    →    true
a.object_id == b.object_id →   false
a.eql?(b)                 →    true
a.equal?(b)               →    false
```

extend

obj.extend(⟨ mod ⟩⁺) → obj

Adds to *obj* the instance methods from each module given as a parameter. See also `Module#extend_object`.

```
module Mod
  def hello
    "Hello from Mod.\n"
  end
end

class Klass
  def hello
    "Hello from Klass.\n"
  end
end

k = Klass.new
k.hello        →    "Hello from Klass.\n"
k.extend(Mod)  →    #<Klass:0x1ce300>
k.hello        →    "Hello from Mod.\n"
```

Writing *obj*.extend(Mod) is basically the same as the following.

```
class <<obj
  include Mod
end
```

freeze

obj.freeze → obj

Prevents further modifications to *obj*. A TypeError will be raised if modification is attempted. You cannot unfreeze a frozen object. See also `Object#frozen?`.

```
a = [ "a", "b", "c" ]
a.freeze
a << "z"
```

produces:

```
prog.rb:3:in `<<': can't modify frozen array (TypeError)
	from prog.rb:3
```

frozen?   *obj*.frozen? → true or false

Returns the freeze status of *obj*.

```
a = [ "a", "b", "c" ]
a.freeze    →    ["a", "b", "c"]
a.frozen?   →    true
```

hash   *obj*.hash → *fixnum*

Generates a Fixnum hash value for this object. This function must have the property that a.eql?(b) implies a.hash == b.hash. The hash value is used by class Hash. Any hash value that exceeds the capacity of a Fixnum will be truncated before being used.

id   *obj*.id → *fixnum*

1.8 Soon-to-be-deprecated version of Object#object_id.

initialize_copy   *obj*.initialize_copy(*other*) → *other_obj* or *obj*

1.8 Part of the protocol used by Object#dup and Object#clone, initialize_copy is invoked as a callback which should copy across any state information that dup and clone cannot copy themselves. Typically this is useful only when writing C extensions. Think of initialize_copy as a kind of copy constructor.

inspect   *obj*.inspect → *string*

Returns a string containing a human-readable representation of *obj*. If not overridden, uses the to_s method to generate the string.

```
[ 1, 2, 3..4, 'five' ].inspect    →    "[1, 2, 3..4, \"five\"]"
Time.new.inspect                  →    "Thu Aug 26 22:37:49 CDT 2004"
```

instance_eval   *obj*.instance_eval(*string* ⟨ , *file* ⟨ , *line* ⟩ ⟩) → *other_obj*
                          obj.instance_eval { *block* } → *other_obj*

Evaluates a string containing Ruby source code, or the given block, within the context of the receiver (*obj*). To set the context, the variable self is set to *obj* while the code is executing, giving the code access to *obj*'s instance variables. In the version of instance_eval that takes a String, the optional second and third parameters supply a filename and starting line number that are used when reporting compilation errors.

```
class Klass
  def initialize
    @secret = 99
  end
end
k = Klass.new
k.instance_eval { @secret }   →    99
```

instance_of?

obj.instance_of?(*klass*) → `true` or `false`

Returns `true` if *obj* is an instance of the given class. See also `Object#kind_of?`.

instance_variable_get

obj.instance_variable_get(*symbol*) → *other_obj*

1.8 Returns the value of the given instance variable (or throws a `NameError` exception). The @ part of the variable name should be included for regular instance variables.

```
class Fred
  def initialize(p1, p2)
    @a, @b = p1, p2
  end
end
fred = Fred.new('cat', 99)
fred.instance_variable_get(:@a)    →    "cat"
fred.instance_variable_get("@b")   →    99
```

instance_variable_set

obj.instance_variable_set(*symbol, other_obj*) → *other_obj*

1.8 Sets the instance variable names by *symbol* to *other_obj*, thereby frustrating the efforts of the class's author to attempt to provide proper encapsulation.

```
class Fred
  def initialize(p1, p2)
    @a, @b = p1, p2
  end
end
fred = Fred.new('cat', 99)
fred.instance_variable_set(:@a, 'dog')   →    "dog"
fred.inspect                             →    "#<Fred:0x1ce4e0 @b=99,
                                              @a=\"dog\">"
```

instance_variables

obj.instance_variables → *array*

Returns an array of instance variable names for the receiver. Note that simply defining an accessor does not create the corresponding instance variable.

```
class Fred
  attr_accessor :a1
  def initialize
    @iv = 3
  end
end
Fred.new.instance_variables   →    ["@iv"]
```

is_a?

obj.is_a?(*klass*) → `true` or `false`

Synonym for `Object#kind_of?`.

kind_of?   *obj*.kind_of?(*klass*) → `true` or `false`

Returns `true` if *klass* is the class of *obj*, or if *klass* is one of the superclasses of *obj* or modules included in *obj*.

```
module M;    end
class A
  include M
end
class B < A; end
class C < B; end
b = B.new
b.instance_of? A   →    false
b.instance_of? B   →    true
b.instance_of? C   →    false
b.instance_of? M   →    false
b.kind_of? A       →    true
b.kind_of? B       →    true
b.kind_of? C       →    false
b.kind_of? M       →    true
```

method   *obj*.method(*symbol*) → *meth*

Looks up the named method in *obj*, returning a `Method` object (or raising `NameError`). The `Method` object acts as a closure in *obj*'s object instance, so instance variables and the value of `self` remain available.

```
class Demo
  def initialize(n)
    @iv = n
  end
  def hello()
    "Hello, @iv = #{@iv}"
  end
end

k = Demo.new(99)
m = k.method(:hello)
m.call   →    "Hello, @iv = 99"

l = Demo.new('Fred')
m = l.method("hello")
m.call   →    "Hello, @iv = Fred"
```

method_missing   *obj*.method_missing(*symbol* ⟨ , **args* ⟩) → *other_obj*

Invoked by Ruby when *obj* is sent a message it cannot handle. *symbol* is the symbol for the method called, and *args* are any arguments that were passed to it. The example below creates a class Roman, which responds to methods with names consisting of roman numerals, returning the corresponding integer values. A more typical use of `method_missing` is to implement proxies, delegators, and forwarders.

```
class Roman
  def roman_to_int(str)
    # ...
  end
  def method_missing(method_id)
    str = method_id.id2name
    roman_to_int(str)
  end
end

r = Roman.new
r.iv      →    4
r.xxiii   →    23
r.mm      →    2000
```

---

methods
obj.methods($regular$=true) → $array$

1.8 If $regular$ is true, returns a list of the names of methods publicly accessible in obj and obj's ancestors. Otherwise return a list of obj's singleton methods.

```
class Klass
  def my_method()
  end
end
k = Klass.new
def k.single
end
k.methods[0..9]     →    ["dup", "hash", "single", "private_methods",
                          "nil?", "tainted?", "class", "my_method",
                          "singleton_methods", "=~"]
k.methods.length    →    42
k.methods(false)    →    ["single"]
```

---

nil?
obj.nil? → true or false

All objects except nil return false.

---

object_id
obj.object_id → $fixnum$

1.8 Returns an integer identifier for obj. The same number will be returned on all calls to object_id for a given object, and no two active objects will share an ID. Object#object_id is a different concept from the :name notation, which returns the symbol ID of name. Replaces the deprecated Object#id.

---

private_methods
obj.private_methods → $array$

Returns a list of private methods accessible within obj. This will include the private methods in obj's ancestors, along with any mixed-in module functions.

---

protected_methods
obj.protected_methods → $array$

Returns the list of protected methods accessible to obj.

public_methods   *obj*.public_methods → *array*

Synonym for Object#methods.

respond_to?   *obj*.respond_to?(*symbol*, *include_priv*=false) → true or false

Returns true if *obj* responds to the given method. Private methods are included in the search only if the optional second parameter evaluates to true.

send   *obj*.send(*symbol* ⟨ , *args* ⟩* ⟨ , &*block* ⟩) → *other_obj*

Invokes the method identified by *symbol*, passing it any arguments and block. You can use __send__ if the name send clashes with an existing method in *obj*.

```
class Klass
  def hello(*args)
    "Hello " + args.join(' ')
  end
end
k = Klass.new
k.send :hello, "gentle", "readers"   →   "Hello gentle readers"
```

singleton_methods   *obj*.singleton_methods(*all*=true) → *array*

Returns an array of the names of singleton methods for *obj*. If the optional *all* parameter is true, the list will include methods in modules included in *obj*. (The parameter defaults to false in versions of Ruby prior to January 2004.)

```
module Other
  def three() end
end

class Single
  def Single.four() end
end

a = Single.new

def a.one() end

class << a
  include Other
  def two() end
end

Single.singleton_methods      →   ["four"]
a.singleton_methods(false)    →   ["two", "one"]
a.singleton_methods(true)     →   ["two", "one", "three"]
a.singleton_methods           →   ["two", "one", "three"]
```

taint   *obj*.taint → *obj*

Marks *obj* as tainted. If the $SAFE level is greater than zero, some objects will be tainted on creation. See Chapter 25, which begins on page 397.

tainted?   *obj*.tainted? → true or false

Returns true if the object is tainted.

```
a = "cat"
a.tainted?   →    false
a.taint      →    "cat"
a.tainted?   →    true
a.untaint    →    "cat"
a.tainted?   →    false
```

to_a   *obj*.to_a → *array*

Returns an array representation of *obj*. For objects of class Object and others that don't explicitly override the method, the return value is an array containing self. As of Ruby 1.9 to_a will no longer be implemented by class Object—it is up to individual subclasses to provide their own implementations.

1.8

```
self.to_a        →    -:1: warning: default `to_a' will be
                      obsolete\n[main]
"hello".to_a     →    ["hello"]
Time.new.to a    →    [50, 37, 22, 26, 8, 2004, 4, 239, true, "CDT"]
```

to_s   *obj*.to_s → *string*

Returns a string representing *obj*. The default to_s prints the object's class and an encoding of the object ID. As a special case, the top-level object that is the initial execution context of Ruby programs returns "main."

type   *obj*.type → *klass*

1.8   Deprecated synonym for Object#class.

untaint   *obj*.untaint → *obj*

Removes the taint from *obj*.

Private instance methods

initialize   initialize(⟨ *arg* ⟩⁺)

Called as the third and final step in object construction, initialize is responsible for setting up the initial state of the new object. You use the initialize method the same way you'd use constructors in other languages. If you subclass classes other than Object, you will probably want to call super to invoke the parent's initializer.

```
class A
  def initialize(p1)
    puts "Initializing A: p1 = #{p1}"
    @var1 = p1
  end
end
class B < A
  attr_reader :var1, :var2
  def initialize(p1, p2)
    super(p1)
    puts "Initializing B: p2 = #{p2}"
    @var2 = p2
  end
end
b = B.new("cat", "dog")
puts b.inspect
```

produces:

```
Initializing A: p1 = cat
Initializing B: p2 = dog
#<B:0x1c9224 @var2="dog", @var1="cat">
```

---

remove_instance_variable   remove_instance_variable(*symbol*) → *other_obj*

1.8   Removes the named instance variable from *obj*, returning that variable's value.

```
class Dummy
  attr_reader :var
  def initialize
    @var = 99
  end
  def remove
    remove_instance_variable(:@var)
  end
end
d = Dummy.new
d.var       →   99
d.remove    →   99
d.var       →   nil
```

---

singleton_method_added   singleton_method_added(*symbol*)

1.8   Invoked as a callback whenever a singleton method is added to the receiver.

```
module Chatty
  def Chatty.singleton_method_added(id)
    puts "Adding #{id.id2name} to #{self.name}"
  end
  def self.one()    end
  def two()         end
end
def Chatty.three() end
```

```
obj = "cat"
def obj.singleton_method_added(id)
  puts "Adding #{id.id2name} to #{self}"
end
def obj.speak
  puts "meow"
end
```

produces:

```
Adding singleton_method_added to Chatty
Adding one to Chatty
Adding three to Chatty
Adding singleton_method_added to cat
Adding speak to cat
```

singleton_method_removed   singleton_method_removed(*symbol*)

1.8   Invoked as a callback whenever a singleton method is removed from the receiver.

```
module Chatty
  def Chatty.singleton_method_removed(id)
    puts "Removing #{id.id2name}"
  end
  def self.one()    end
  def two()         end
  def Chatty.three() end
  class <<self
    remove_method :three
    remove_method :one
  end
end
```

produces:

```
Removing three
Removing one
```

singleton_method_undefined   singleton_method_undefined(*symbol*)

1.8   Invoked as a callback whenever a singleton method is undefined in the receiver.

```
module Chatty
  def Chatty.singleton_method_undefined(id)
    puts "Undefining #{id.id2name}"
  end
  def Chatty.one()   end
  class << self
     undef_method(:one)
  end
end
```

produces:

```
Undefining one
```

Object

Module **ObjectSpace**

The ObjectSpace module contains a number of routines that interact with the garbage collection facility and allow you to traverse all living objects with an iterator.

ObjectSpace also provides support for object finalizers. These are procs that will be called when a specific object is about to be destroyed by garbage collection.

```
include ObjectSpace
a, b, c = "A", "B", "C"
puts "a's id is #{a.object_id}"
puts "b's id is #{b.object_id}"
puts "c's id is #{c.object_id}"
define_finalizer(a, lambda {|id| puts "Finalizer one on #{id}" })
define_finalizer(b, lambda {|id| puts "Finalizer two on #{id}" })
define_finalizer(c, lambda {|id| puts "Finalizer three on #{id}" })
```

produces:

```
a's id is 936150
b's id is 936140
c's id is 936130
Finalizer three on 936130
Finalizer two on 936140
Finalizer one on 936150
```

Module methods

_id2ref   ObjectSpace._id2ref(*object_id*) → *obj*

Converts an object ID to a reference to the object. May not be called on an object ID passed as a parameter to a finalizer.

```
s = "I am a string"          →    "I am a string"
oid = s.object_id            →    936550
r = ObjectSpace._id2ref(oid) →    "I am a string"
r                            →    "I am a string"
r.equal?(s)                  →    true
```

define_finalizer   ObjectSpace.define_finalizer(*obj*, *a_proc*=proc())

Adds *a_proc* as a finalizer, called when *obj* is about to be destroyed.

each_object   ObjectSpace.each_object(⟨ *class_or_mod* ⟩) {| *obj* | *block* } → *fixnum*

Calls the block once for each living, nonimmediate object in this Ruby process. If *class_or_mod* is specified, calls the block for only those classes or modules that match (or are a subclass of) *class_or_mod*. Returns the number of objects found. Immediate objects (Fixnums, Symbols true, false, and nil) are never returned. In the example below, each_object returns both the numbers we defined and several constants defined in the Math module.

```
a = 102.7
b = 95       # Fixnum: won't be returned
c = 12345678987654321
count = ObjectSpace.each_object(Numeric) {|x| p x }
puts "Total count: #{count}"
```

produces:

```
12345678987654321
102.7
2.71828182845905
3.14159265358979
2.22044604925031e-16
1.79769313486232e+308
2.2250738585072e-308
Total count: 7
```

---

garbage_collect   ObjectSpace.garbage_collect → `nil`

Initiates garbage collection (see module GC on page 491).

---

undefine_finalizer   ObjectSpace.undefine_finalizer(*obj*)

Removes all finalizers for *obj*.

ObjectSpace

Class	
Proc	< Object

Proc objects are blocks of code that have been bound to a set of local variables. Once bound, the code may be called in different contexts and still access those variables.

```
def gen_times(factor)
  return Proc.new {|n| n*factor }
end

times3 = gen_times(3)
times5 = gen_times(5)

times3.call(12)               →    36
times5.call(5)                →    25
times3.call(times5.call(4))   →    60
```

Class methods

new　　　　　　　　　　　　　　　　　Proc.new { *block* } → *a_proc*
　　　　　　　　　　　　　　　　　　　　　　Proc.new → *a_proc*

Creates a new Proc object, bound to the current context. Proc.new may be called without a block only within a method with an attached block, in which case that block is converted to the Proc object.

```
def proc_from
  Proc.new
end
proc = proc_from { "hello" }
proc.call   →   "hello"
```

Instance methods

[ ]　　　　　　　　　　　　　　　　　*prc*[⟨ *params* ⟩*] → *obj*

Synonym for Proc.call.

==　　　　　　　　　　　　　　　　*prc*== *other* → true or false

1.8　　Returns true if *prc* is the same as *other*.

arity　　　　　　　　　　　　　　　　　　*prc*.arity → *integer*

1.8　　Returns the number of arguments required by the block. If the block is declared to take no arguments, returns 0. If the block is known to take exactly n arguments, returns n. If the block has optional arguments, return $-(n+1)$, where n is the number of mandatory arguments. A proc with no argument declarations also returns -1, as it can accept (and ignore) an arbitrary number of parameters.

```
Proc.new {}.arity          →  -1
Proc.new {||}.arity        →  0
Proc.new {|a|}.arity       →  1
Proc.new {|a,b|}.arity     →  2
Proc.new {|a,b,c|}.arity   →  3
Proc.new {|*a|}.arity      →  -1
Proc.new {|a,*b|}.arity    →  -2
```

1.8, In Ruby 1.9, arity is defined as the number of parameters that would not be ignored. In 1.8, `Proc.new{}.arity` returns -1, and in 1.9 it returns 0.

binding
prc.binding → binding

1.8, Returns the binding associated with *prc*. Note that Kernel#eval accepts either a Proc or a Binding object as its second parameter.

```
def fred(param)
  lambda {}
end

b = fred(99)
eval("param", b.binding)  →  99
eval("param", b)          →  99
```

call
prc.call(⟨ params ⟩*) → obj

Invokes the block, setting the block's parameters to the values in *params* using something close to method-calling semantics. Returns the value of the last expression evaluated in the block.

```
a_proc = Proc.new {|a, *b| b.collect {|i| i*a }}
a_proc.call(9, 1, 2, 3)   →   [9, 18, 27]
a_proc[9, 1, 2, 3]        →   [9, 18, 27]
```

1.8, If the block being called explicitly accepts a single parameter, call issues a warning unless it has been given exactly one parameter. Otherwise it happily accepts what it is given, ignoring surplus passed parameters and setting unset block parameters to nil.

```
a_proc = Proc.new {|a| a}
a_proc.call(1,2,3)
```

produces:

```
prog.rb:1: warning: multiple values for a block parameter (3 for 1)
from prog.rb:2
```

If you want a block to receive an arbitrary number of arguments, define it to accept *args.

```
a_proc = Proc.new {|*a| a}
a_proc.call(1,2,3)   →   [1, 2, 3]
```

Blocks created using Kernel.lambda check that they are called with exactly the right number of parameters.

```
p_proc = Proc.new {|a,b| puts "Sum is: #{a + b}" }
p_proc.call(1,2,3)
p_proc = lambda {|a,b| puts "Sum is: #{a + b}" }
p_proc.call(1,2,3)
```

produces:

```
Sum is: 3
prog.rb:3: wrong number of arguments (3 for 2) (ArgumentError)
from prog.rb:3:in `call'
from prog.rb:4
```

---

to_proc   *prc*.to_proc → *prc*

1.8 Part of the protocol for converting objects to Proc objects. Instances of class Proc simply return themselves.

---

to_s   *prc*.to_s → *string*

Returns a description of *prc*, including information on where it was defined.

```
def create_proc
  Proc.new
end

my_proc = create_proc { "hello" }
my_proc.to_s    →    "#<Proc:0x001c7abc@prog.rb:5>"
```

Module Process

The Process module is a collection of methods used to manipulate processes. Programs that want to manipulate real and effective user and group IDs should also look at the Process::GID, and Process::UID modules. Much of the functionality here is duplicated in the Process::Sys module.

Module constants

PRIO_PGRP	Process group priority.
PRIO_PROCESS	Process priority.
PRIO_USER	User priority.
WNOHANG	Do not block if no child has exited. Not available on all platforms.
WUNTRACED	Return stopped children as well. Not available on all platforms.

Module methods

abort
                                                                  abort
                                                            abort(*msg*)

1.8   Synonym for Kernel.abort.

detach   Process.detach(*pid*) → *thread*

1.8   Some operating systems retain the status of terminated child processes until the parent collects that status (normally using some variant of wait()). If the parent never collects this status, the child stays around as a *zombie* process. Process.detach prevents this by setting up a separate Ruby thread whose sole job is to reap the status of the process *pid* when it terminates. Use detach only when you do not intend to explicitly wait for the child to terminate. detach checks the status only periodically (currently once each second).

In this first example, we don't reap the first child process, so it appears as a zombie in the process status display.

```
pid = fork { sleep 0.1 }
sleep 1
system("ps -o pid,state p #{pid}")
```

produces:

```
  PID STAT
27836 ZN+
```

In the next example, Process.detach is used to reap the child automatically—no child processes are left running.

```
pid = fork { sleep 0.1 }
Process.detach(pid)
sleep 1
```

```
system("ps -o pid,state -p #{pid}")
```

produces:

```
  PID STAT
```

---

egid   Process.egid → *int*

Returns the effective group ID for this process.

```
Process.egid   →   502
```

---

egid=   Process.egid= *int* → *int*

Sets the effective group ID for this process.

---

euid   Process.euid → *int*

Returns the effective user ID for this process.

```
Process.euid   →   502
```

---

euid=   Process.euid= *int*

Sets the effective user ID for this process. Not available on all platforms.

---

exit   Process.exit(*int*=0)

1.8   Synonym for Kernel.exit.

---

exit!   Process.exit!(true | false | *status*=1)

1.8   Synonym for Kernel.exit!. No exit handlers are run. 0, 1, or *status* is returned to the
underlying system as the exit status.

```
Process.exit!(0)
```

---

fork   Process.fork ⟨ { *block* } ⟩ → *int* or nil

See Kernel.fork on page 522.

---

getpgid   Process.getpgid(*int*) → *int*

Returns the process group ID for the given process id. Not available on all platforms.

```
Process.getpgid(Process.ppid())   →   25122
```

---

getpgrp   Process.getpgrp → *int*

Returns the process group ID for this process. Not available on all platforms.

```
Process.getpgid(0)     →    25122
Process.getpgrp        →    25122
```

getpriority

Process.getpriority(*kind*, *int*) → *int*

Gets the scheduling priority for specified process, process group, or user. *kind* indicates the kind of entity to find: one of `Process::PRIO_PGRP`, `Process::PRIO_USER`, or `Process::PRIO_PROCESS`. *int* is an ID indicating the particular process, process group, or user (an ID of 0 means *current*). Lower priorities are more favorable for scheduling. Not available on all platforms.

```
Process.getpriority(Process::PRIO_USER, 0)      →    19
Process.getpriority(Process::PRIO_PROCESS, 0)   →    19
```

gid

Process.gid → *int*

Returns the group ID for this process.

```
Process.gid   →    502
```

gid=

Process.gid= *int* → *int*

Sets the group ID for this process.

groups

Process.groups → *groups*

1.8, Returns an array of integer supplementary group IDs. Not available on all platforms. See also `Process.maxgroups`.

```
Process.groups   →    [502, 79, 80, 81]
```

groups=

Process.groups = *array* → *groups*

1.8, Sets the supplementary group IDs from the given array, which may contain either numbers of group names (as strings). Not available on all platforms. Only available to superusers. See also `Process.maxgroups`.

initgroups

Process.initgroups(*user*, *base_group*) → *groups*

1.8, Initializes the group access list using the operating system's `initgroups` call. Not available on all platforms. May require superuser privilege.

```
Process.initgroups("dave", 500)
```

kill

Process.kill(*signal*, ⟨ *pid* ⟩+) → *int*

Sends the given signal to the specified process ID(s) or to the current process if *pid* is zero. *signal* may be an integer signal number or a POSIX signal name (either with or without a `SIG` prefix). If *signal* is negative (or starts with a - sign), kills process groups instead of processes. Not all signals are available on all platforms.

```
pid = fork do
   Signal.trap("USR1") { puts "Ouch!"; exit }
   # ... do some work ...
end
```

```
# ...
Process.kill("USR1", pid)
Process.wait
```

produces:

```
-:2: SIGUSR1 (SignalException)
from -:1:in `fork'
from -:1
```

---

maxgroups   Process.maxgroups → *count*

_{1.8} The `Process` module has a limit on the number of supplementary groups it supports
in the calls `Process.groups` and `Process.groups=`. The `maxgroups` call returns that
limit (by default 32), and the `maxgroups=` call sets it.

```
Process.maxgroups    →    32
Process.maxgroups = 64
Process.maxgroups    →    64
```

---

maxgroups=   Process.maxgroups= *limit* → *count*

_{1.8} Sets the maximum number of supplementary group IDs that can be processed by the
`groups` and `groups=` methods. If a number larger that 4096 is given, 4096 will be
used.

---

pid   Process.pid → *int*

Returns the process ID of this process. Not available on all platforms.

```
Process.pid    →    27864
```

---

ppid   Process.ppid → *int*

Returns the process ID of the parent of this process. Always returns 0 on Windows. Not
available on all platforms.

```
puts "I am #{Process.pid}"
Process.fork { puts "Dad is #{Process.ppid}" }
```

produces:

```
I am 27866
Dad is 27866
```

---

setpgid   Process.setpgid(*pid*, *int*) → 0

Sets the process group ID of *pid* (0 indicates this process) to *int*. Not available on all
platforms.

---

setpgrp   Process.setpgrp → 0

Equivalent to `setpgid(0,0)`. Not available on all platforms.

setpriority
Process.setpriority(*kind, int, int_priority*) → 0

See Process#getpriority.

```
Process.setpriority(Process::PRIO_USER, 0, 19)      →    0
Process.setpriority(Process::PRIO_PROCESS, 0, 19)   →    0
Process.getpriority(Process::PRIO_USER, 0)          →    19
Process.getpriority(Process::PRIO_PROCESS, 0)       →    19
```

setsid
Process.setsid → *int*

Establishes this process as a new session and process group leader, with no controlling tty. Returns the session ID. Not available on all platforms.

```
Process.setsid   →    27871
```

times
Process.times → *struct_tms*

1.8 Returns a Tms structure (see Struct::Tms on page 630) that contains user and system CPU times for this process.

```
t = Process.times
[ t.utime, t.stime ]   →   [0.01, 0.01]
```

uid
Process.uid → *int*

Returns the user ID of this process.

```
Process.uid   →    502
```

uid=
Process.uid= *int* → *numeric*

Sets the (integer) user ID for this process. Not available on all platforms.

wait
Process.wait → *int*

Waits for any child process to exit and returns the process ID of that child. Also sets $? to the Process::Status object containing information on that process. Raises a SystemError if there are no child processes. Not available on all platforms.

```
Process.fork { exit 99 }   →    27878
Process.wait               →    27878
$?.exitstatus              →    99
```

waitall
Process.waitall → [[*pid1,status*], …]

1.8 Waits for all children, returning an array of *pid/status* pairs (where *status* is an object of class Process::Status).

```
fork { sleep 0.2; exit 2 }  →  27881
fork { sleep 0.1; exit 1 }  →  27882
fork {            exit 0 }  →  27883
Process.waitall             →  [[27883, #<Process::Status:
                                 pid=27883,exited(0)>], [27882,
                                 #<Process::Status:
                                 pid=27882,exited(1)>], [27881,
                                 #<Process::Status:
                                 pid=27881,exited(2)>]]
```

wait2   Process.wait2 → [*pid, status*]

1.8, Waits for any child process to exit and returns an array containing the process ID and the exit status (a `Process::Status` object) of that child. Raises a `SystemError` if no child processes exist.

```
Process.fork { exit 99 }  →  27886
pid, status = Process.wait2
pid                       →  27886
status.exitstatus         →  99
```

waitpid   Process.waitpid(*pid, int=0*) → *pid*

Waits for a child process to exit depending on the value of *pid*:

   < -1 Any child whose progress group ID equals the absolute value of *pid*.
   -1 Any child (equivalent to `wait`).
   0   Any child whose process group ID equals that of the current process.
   > 0 The child with the given PID.

int may be a logical or of the flag values `Process::WNOHANG` (do not block if no child available) or `Process::WUNTRACED` (return stopped children that haven't been reported). Not all flags are available on all platforms, but a flag value of zero will work on all platforms.

```
include Process
pid = fork { sleep 3 }          →  27889
Time.now                        →  Thu Aug 26 22:38:17 CDT 2004
waitpid(pid; Process::WNOHANG)  →  nil
Time.now                        →  Thu Aug 26 22:38:17 CDT 2004
waitpid(pid, 0)                 →  27889
Time.now                        →  Thu Aug 26 22:38:20 CDT 2004
```

waitpid2   Process.waitpid2(*pid, int=0*) → [*pid, status*]

Waits for the given child process to exit, returning that child's process ID and exit status (a `Process::Status` object). *int* may be a logical or of the values `Process::WNOHANG` (do not block if no child available) or `Process::WUNTRACED` (return stopped children that haven't been reported). Not all flags are available on all platforms, but a flag value of zero will work on all platforms.

Module Process::GID

Provides a higher-level (and more portable) interface to the underlying operating system's concepts of real, effective, and saved group IDs. Discussing of the semantics of these IDs is well beyond the scope of this book: readers who want to know more should consult POSIX documentation or read the intro(2) man pages on a recent Unix platform. All these methods throw NotImplementedError if the host operating does not support a sufficient set of calls. The descriptions that follow are based on notes in ruby-talk:76218 by Hidetoshi Nagai.

Module methods

change_privilege   Process::GID.change_privilege(*gid*) → *gid*

1.8 Sets the real, effective, and saved group IDs to *gid*, raising an exception on failure (in which case the state of the IDs is not known).

This method is not compatible with Process.gid=.

eid   Process::GID.eid → *egid*

1.8 Returns the effective group ID for this process. Synonym for Process.egid.

eid=   Process::GID.eid = *egid*

1.8 Synonym for Process::GID.grant_privilege.

grant_privilege   Process::GID.grant_privilege(*egid*) → *egid*

1.8 Sets the effective group ID to *egid*, raising an exception on failure. One some environments this may also change the saved group ID (see re_exchangeable?).

re_exchange   Process::GID.re_exchange → *egid*

1.8 Exchange the real and effective group IDs, setting the saved group ID to the new effective group ID. Returns the new effective group ID.

re_exchangeable?   Process::GID.re_exchangeable → true or false

1.8 Returns true if real and effective group IDs can be exchanged on the host operating system, and returns false otherwise.

rid   Process::GID.rid → *gid*

1.8 Returns the real group ID for this process. Synonym for Process.gid.

sid_available?   Process::GID.sid_available? → true or false

1.8 Returns true if the underlying platform supports saved group IDs, and returns false otherwise. Currently, Ruby assumes support if the operating system has `setresgid(2)` or `setegid(2)` calls or if the configuration includes the `POSIX_SAVED_IDS` flag.

---

switch   Process::GID.switch → *egid*
                   Process::GID.switch { *block* } → *obj*

1.8   Handles the toggling of group privilege. In the block form, automatically toggles the IDs back when the block terminates (but only if the block doesn't use other calls into Process::GID calls which would interfere). Without a block, returns the original effective group ID.

Class Process::Status < Object

Process::Status encapsulates the information on the status of a running or terminated system process. The built-in variable $? is either nil or a Process::Status object.

```
fork { exit 99 }       →    27186
Process.wait           →    27186
$?.class               →    Process::Status
$?.to_i                →    25344
$? >> 8                →    99
$?.stopped?            →    false
$?.exited?             →    true
$?.exitstatus          →    99
```

POSIX systems record information on processes using a 16-bit integer. The lower bits recorded the process status (stopped, exited, signaled), and the upper bits possibly contain additional information (for example, the program's return code in the case of exited processes). Before Ruby 1.8, these bits were exposed directly to the Ruby program. Ruby now encapsulates these in a Process::Status object. To maximize compatibility, however, these objects retain a bit-oriented interface. In the descriptions that follow, when we talk about the integer value of *stat*, we're referring to this 16-bit value.

Instance methods

==   *stat* == *other* → true or false

Returns true if the integer value of *stat* equals *other*.

&   *stat* & *num* → *fixnum*

Logical AND of the bits in *stat* with *num*.

```
fork { exit 0x37 }
Process.wait
sprintf('%04x', $?.to_i)          →    "3700"
sprintf('%04x', $? & 0x1e00)      →    "1600"
```

>>   *stat* >> *num* → *fixnum*

Shift the bits in *stat* right *num* places.

```
fork { exit 99 }       →    27192
Process.wait           →    27192
$?.to_i                →    25344
$? >> 8                →    99
```

coredump?   *stat*.coredump → true or false

Returns true if *stat* generated a coredump when it terminated. Not available on all platforms.

exited?   *stat*.exited? → `true` or `false`

Returns `true` if *stat* exited normally (for example using an `exit` call or finishing the program).

---

exitstatus   *stat*.exitstatus → *fixnum* or `nil`

Returns the least significant 8 bits of the return code of *stat*. Only available if `exited?` is `true`.

```
fork { }           →    27195
Process.wait       →    27195
$?.exited?         →    true
$?.exitstatus      →    0

fork { exit 99 }   →    27196
Process.wait       →    27196
$?.exited?         →    true
$?.exitstatus      →    99
```

---

pid   *stat*.pid → *fixnum*

Returns the ID of the process associated with this status object.

```
fork { exit }    →    27199
Process.wait     →    27199
$?.pid           →    27199
```

---

signaled?   *stat*.signaled? → `true` or `false`

Returns `true` if *stat* terminated because of an uncaught signal.

```
pid = fork { sleep 100 }
Process.kill(9, pid)   →    1
Process.wait           →    27202
$?.signaled?           →    true
```

---

stopped?   *stat*.stopped? → `true` or `false`

Returns `true` if this process is stopped. This is returned only if the corresponding `wait` call had the `WUNTRACED` flag set.

---

success?   *stat*.success? → `nil`, or `true` or `false`

Returns `true` if *stat* refers to a process that exited successfully, returns `false` if it exited with a failure, and returns `nil` if *stat* does not refer to a process that has exited.

---

stopsig   *stat*.stopsig → *fixnum* or `nil`

Returns the number of the signal that caused *stat* to stop (or `nil` if self is not stopped).

---

termsig *stat*.termsig → *fixnum* or `nil`

Returns the number of the signal that caused *stat* to terminate (or `nil` if self was not terminated by an uncaught signal).

---

to_i *stat*.to_i → *fixnum*

Returns the bits in *stat* as a `Fixnum`. Poking around in these bits is platform dependent.

```
fork { exit 0xab }        →    27205
Process.wait              →    27205
sprintf('%04x', $?.to_i)  →    "ab00"
```

---

to_int *stat*.to_int → *fixnum*

Synonym for `Process::Status#to_i`.

---

to_s *stat*.to_s → *string*

Equivalent to *stat*`.to_i.to_s`.

Module Process::Sys

`Process::Sys` provides system call–level access to the process user and group environment. Many of the calls are aliases of those in the `Process` module and are packaged here for completeness. See also `Process::GID` and `Process::UID` for a higher-level (and more portable) interface.

Module methods

getegid   Process::Sys.getegid → *gid*

1.8 Returns the effective group ID for this process. Synonym for `Process.egid`.

geteuid   Process::Sys.getugid → *uid*

1.8 Returns the effective user ID for this process. Synonym for `Process.euid`.

getgid   Process::Sys.getgid → *gid*

1.8 Returns the group ID for this process. Synonym for `Process.gid`.

getuid   Process::Sys.getuid → *uid*

1.8 Returns the user ID for this process. Synonym for `Process.uid`.

issetugid   Process::Sys.issetugid → `true` or `false`

1.8 Returns `true` if this process was made setuid or setgid as a result of the last `execve()` system call, and returns `false` if not. On systems that don't support `issetugid(2)`, throws `NotImplementedError`.

setegid   Process::Sys.setegid(*gid*)

1.8 Set the effective group ID to *gid*, failing if the underlying system call fails. On systems that don't support `setegid(2)`, throws `NotImplementedError`.

seteuid   Process::Sys.seteuid(*uid*)

1.8 Set the effective user ID to *uid*, failing if the underlying system call fails. On systems that don't support `seteuid(2)`, throws `NotImplementedError`.

setgid   Process::Sys.setgid(*gid*)

1.8 Set the group ID to *gid*, failing if the underlying system call fails. On systems that don't support `setgid(2)`, throws `NotImplementedError`.

setregid   Process::Sys.setregid(*rgid*, *egid*)

1.8 Set the real and effective group IDs to *rgid* and *egid*, failing if the underlying system call fails. On systems that don't support `setregid(2)`, throws `NotImplementedError`.

setresgid   Process::Sys.setresgid(*rgid*, *egid*, *sgid*)

1.8   Set the real, effective, and saved group IDs to *rgid*, *egid*, and *sgid*, failing if the underlying system call fails. On systems that don't support `setresgid(2)`, throws `NotImplementedError`.

setresuid   Process::Sys.setresuid(*ruid*, *euid*, *suid*)

1.8   Set the real, effective, and saved user IDs to *ruid*, *euid*, and *suid*, failing if the underlying system call fails. On systems that don't support `setresuid(2)`, throws `NotImplementedError`.

setreuid   Process::Sys.setreuid(*ruid*, *euid*)

1.8   Set the real and effective user IDs to *ruid* and *euid*, failing if the underlying system call fails. On systems that don't support `setreuid(2)`, throws `NotImplementedError`.

setrgid   Process::Sys.setrgid(*rgid*)

1.8   Set the real group ID to *rgid*, failing if the underlying system call fails. On systems that don't support `setrgid(2)`, throws `NotImplementedError`.

setruid   Process::Sys.setruid(*ruid*)

1.8   Set the real user ID to *ruid*, failing if the underlying system call fails. On systems that don't support `setruid(2)`, throws `NotImplementedError`.

setuid   Process::Sys.setuid(*uid*)

1.8   Set the user ID to *uid*, failing if the underlying system call fails. On systems that don't support `setuid(2)`, throws `NotImplementedError`.

Module Process::UID

Provides a higher-level (and more portable) interface to the underlying operating system's concepts of real, effective, and saved user IDs. For more information, see the introduction to `Process::GID` on page 589.

Module methods

change_privilege   Process::UID.change_privilege(*uid*) → *uid*

1.8 Sets the real, effective, and saved user IDs to *uid*, raising an exception on failure (in which case the state of the IDs is not known). Not compatible with `Process.uid=`.

eid   Process::UID.eid → *euid*

1.8 Returns the effective user ID for this process. Synonym for `Process.euid`.

eid=   Process::UID.eid = *euid*

1.8 Synonym for `Process::UID.grant_privilege`.

grant_privilege   Process::UID.grant_privilege(*euid*) → *euid*

1.8 Sets the effective user ID to *euid*, raising an exception on failure. One some environments this may also change the saved user ID.

re_exchange   Process::UID.re_exchange → *euid*

1.8 Exchange the real and effective user IDs, setting the saved user ID to the new effective user ID. Returns the new effective user ID.

re_exchangeable?   Process::UID.re_exchangeable → `true` or `false`

1.8 Returns `true` if real and effective user IDs can be exchanged on the host operating system, and returns `false` otherwise.

rid   Process::UID.rid → *uid*

1.8 Returns the real user ID for this process. Synonym for `Process.uid`.

sid_available?   Process::UID.sid_available? → `true` or `false`

1.8 Returns `true` if the underlying platform supports saved user IDs, and returns `false` otherwise. Currently, Ruby assumes support if the operating system has `setresuid(2)` or `seteuid(2)` calls, or if the configuration includes the `POSIX_SAVED_IDS` flag.

switch   Process::UID.switch → *euid*
                                              Process::UID.switch { *block* } → *obj*

1.8 Handles the toggling of user privilege. In the block form, automatically toggles the IDs back when the block terminates (as long as the block doesn't use other Process::UID calls to interfere). Without a block, returns the original effective user ID.

Class **Range** < Object

A Range represents an interval—a set of values with a start and an end. Ranges may be constructed using the *s..e* and *s...e* literals or using Range.new. Ranges constructed using .. run from the start to the end inclusively. Those created using ... exclude the end value. When used as an iterator, ranges return each value in the sequence.

```
(-1..-5).to_a      →   []
(-5..-1).to_a      →   [-5, -4, -3, -2, -1]
('a'..'e').to_a    →   ["a", "b", "c", "d", "e"]
('a'...'e').to_a   →   ["a", "b", "c", "d"]
```

Ranges can be constructed using objects of any type, as long as the objects can be compared using their <=> operator and they support the succ method to return the next object in sequence.

```
class Xs                    # represent a string of 'x's
  include Comparable
  attr :length
  def initialize(n)
    @length = n
  end
  def succ
    Xs.new(@length + 1)
  end
  def <=>(other)
    @length <=> other.length
  end
  def to_s
    sprintf "%2d #{inspect}", @length
  end
  def inspect
    'x' * @length
  end
end
```

```
r = Xs.new(3)..Xs.new(6)  →   xxx..xxxxxx
r.to_a                    →   [xxx, xxxx, xxxxx, xxxxxx]
r.member?(Xs.new(5))      →   true
```

In the previous code example, class Xs includes the Comparable module. This is because Enumerable#member? checks for equality using ==. Including Comparable ensures that the == method is defined in terms of the <=> method implemented in Xs.

Mixes in

Enumerable:

> all?, any?, collect, detect, each_with_index, entries, find, find_all, grep, include?, inject, map, max, member?, min, partition, reject, select, sort, sort_by, to_a, zip

Class methods

new   Range.new(*start, end, exclusive*=false) → *rng*

Constructs a range using the given *start* and *end*. If the third parameter is omitted or is false, the range will include the end object; otherwise, it will be excluded.

Instance methods

==   *rng* == *obj* → true or false

Returns true if *obj* is a range whose beginning and end are the same as those in *rng* (compared using ==) and whose *exclusive* flag is the same as *rng*.

===   *rng* === *val* → true or false

If *rng* excludes its end, returns $rng.start \leq val < rng.end$. If *rng* is inclusive returns $rng.start \leq val \leq rng.end$. Note that this implies that *val* need not be a member of the range itself (for example a float could fall between the start and end values of a range of integers). Conveniently, the === operator is used by case statements.

```
case 74.95
when  1...50  then   puts "low"
when 50...75  then   puts "medium"
when 75...100 then   puts "high"
end
```

produces:

```
medium
```

begin   *rng*.begin → *obj*

Returns the first object of *rng*.

each   *rng*.each {| i | *block* } → *rng*

Iterates over the elements *rng*, passing each in turn to the block. Successive elements are generated using the succ method.

```
(10..15).each do |n|
   print n, ' '
end
```

produces:

```
10 11 12 13 14 15
```

end   *rng*.end → *obj*

Returns the object that defines the end of *rng*.

```
(1..10).end    →    10
(1...10).end   →    10
```

eql?

$$rng.eql?(obj) \rightarrow true \text{ or } false$$

Returns true if *obj* is a range whose beginning and end are the same as those in *rng* (compared using eql?) and whose *exclusive* flag is the same as *rng*.

exclude_end?

$$rng.exclude\_end? \rightarrow true \text{ or } false$$

Returns true if *rng* excludes its end value.

first

$$rng.first \rightarrow obj$$

Synonym for Range#begin.

include?

$$rng.include?(val) \rightarrow true \text{ or } false$$

Synonym for Range#===.

last

$$rng.last \rightarrow obj$$

Synonym for Range#end.

member?

$$rng.member?(val) \rightarrow true \text{ or } false$$

Return true if *val* is one of the values in *rng* (that is if Range#each would return *val* at some point).

```
r = 1..10
r.include?(5)      →    true
r.member?(5)       →    true
r.include?(5.5)    →    true
r.member?(5.5)     →    false
```

step

$$rng.step(n=1) \{ | obj | block \} \rightarrow rng$$

1.8 Iterates over *rng*, passing each nth element to the block. If the range contains numbers, addition by one is used to generate successive elements. Otherwise step invokes succ to iterate through range elements. The following code uses class Xs defined at the start of this section.

```
range = Xs.new(1)..Xs.new(10)
range.step(2) {|x| puts x}
range.step(3) {|x| puts x}
```

produces:

```
 1 x
 3 xxx
 5 xxxxx
 7 xxxxxxx
 9 xxxxxxxxx
 1 x
 4 xxxx
 7 xxxxxxx
10 xxxxxxxxxx
```

Regexp < Object

A Regexp holds a regular expression, used to match a pattern against strings. Regexps are created using the /.../ and %r... literals and using the Regexp.new constructor. This section documents Ruby 1.8 regular expressions. Versions 1.9 and later use a different regular expression engine.

Class constants

EXTENDED	Ignore spaces and newlines in regexp.
IGNORECASE	Matches are case insensitive.
MULTILINE	Newlines treated as any other character.

Class methods

compile
Regexp.compile(*pattern* ⟨ , *options* ⟨ , *lang* ⟩ ⟩) → *rxp*

Synonym for Regexp.new.

escape
Regexp.escape(*string*) → *escaped_string*

Escapes any characters that would have special meaning in a regular expression. For any string, Regexp.new(Regexp.escape(*str*))=~*str* will be true.

```
Regexp.escape('\\[]*?{}.')    →    \\\[\]\*\?\{\}\.
```

last_match
Regexp.last_match → *match*
Regexp.last_match(*int*) → *string*

1.8 The first form returns the MatchData object generated by the last successful pattern match. This is equivalent to reading the global variable $~. MatchData is described on page 537. The second form returns the nth field in this MatchData object.

```
/c(.)t/ =~ 'cat'         →    0
Regexp.last_match        →    #<MatchData:0x1ce468>
Regexp.last_match(0)     →    "cat"
Regexp.last_match(1)     →    "a"
Regexp.last_match(2)     →    nil
```

new
Regexp.new(*string* ⟨ , *options* ⟨ , *lang* ⟩ ⟩) → *rxp*
Regexp.new(*regexp*) → *new_regexp*

1.8 Constructs a new regular expression from the *string* or the *regexp*. In the latter case that regexp's options are propagated, and new options may not be specified (a change as of Ruby 1.8). If *options* is a Fixnum, it should be one or more of Regexp::EXTENDED, Regexp::IGNORECASE, and Regexp::MULTILINE, *or*-ed together. Otherwise, if the *options* parameter is not nil, the regexp will be case insensitive. The *lang* parameter enables multibyte support for the regexp: n, N, or nil = none, e, E = EUC, s, S = SJIS, u, U = UTF-8.

```
r1 = Regexp.new('^[a-z]+:\\s+\w+')        →    /^[a-z]+:\s+\w+/
r2 = Regexp.new('cat', true)              →    /cat/i
r3 = Regexp.new('dog', Regexp::EXTENDED)  →    /dog/x
r4 = Regexp.new(r2)                       →    /cat/i
```

---

quote   Regexp.quote(*string*) → *escaped_string*

Synonym for Regexp.escape.

Instance methods

==   *rxp* == *other_regexp* → true or false

Equality—Two regexps are equal if their patterns are identical, they have the same character set code, and their casefold? values are the same.

```
/abc/   == /abc/x   →    false
/abc/   == /abc/i   →    false
/abc/u == /abc/n   →    false
```

===   *rxp* === *string* → true or false

Case Equality—Synonym for Regexp#=~ used in case statements.

```
a = "HELLO"
case a
when /^[a-z]*$/; print "Lower case\n"
when /^[A-Z]*$/; print "Upper case\n"
else             print "Mixed case\n"
end
```

produces:

```
Upper case
```

=~   *rxp* =~ *string* → *int* or nil

Match—Matches *rxp* against *string*, returning the offset of the start of the match or nil if the match failed. Sets $~ to the corresponding MatchData or nil.

```
/SIT/   =~ "insensitive"   →    nil
/SIT/i =~ "insensitive"   →    5
```

~   ~ *rxp* → *int* or nil

Match—Matches *rxp* against the contents of $_. Equivalent to *rxp* =~ $_.

```
$_ = "input data"
~ /at/   →    7
```

casefold?   *rxp*.casefold? → `true` or `false`

Returns the value of the case-insensitive flag.

---

inspect   *rxp*.inspect → *string*

Returns a readable version of *rxp*.

```
/cat/mi.inspect   →   "/cat/mi"
/cat/mi.to_s      →   "(?mi-x:cat)"
```

---

kcode   *rxp*.kcode → *string*

Returns the character set code for the regexp.

```
/cat/.kcode    →   nil
/cat/s.kcode   →   "sjis"
```

---

match   *rxp*.match(*string*) → *match* or `nil`

Returns a `MatchData` object (see page 537) describing the match, or `nil` if there was no match. This is equivalent to retrieving the value of the special variable `$~` following a normal match.

```
/(.)(.)(.)/.match("abc")[2]   →   "b"
```

---

options   *rxp*.options → *int*

1.8 Returns the set of bits corresponding to the options used when creating this Regexp (see `Regexp.new` for details). Note that additional bits may be set in the returned options: these are used internally by the regular expression code. These extra bits are ignored if the options are passed to `Regexp.new`.

```
# Let's see what the values are...
Regexp::IGNORECASE                →   1
Regexp::EXTENDED                  →   2
Regexp::MULTILINE                 →   4

/cat/.options                     →   0
/cat/ix.options                   →   3
Regexp.new('cat', true).options   →   1
Regexp.new('cat', 0, 's').options →   48

r = /cat/ix
Regexp.new(r.source, r.options)   →   /cat/ix
```

---

source   *rxp*.source → *string*

Returns the original string of the pattern.

```
/ab+c/ix.source   →   "ab+c"
```

Regexp

to_s

Returns a string containing the regular expression and its options (using the (?xx:yyy) notation). This string can be fed back in to Regexp.new to a regular expression with the same semantics as the original. (However, Regexp#== may not return true when comparing the two, as the source of the regular expression itself may differ, as the example shows.) Regexp#inspect produces a generally more readable version of *rxp*.

```
r1 = /ab+c/ix          →   /ab+c/ix
s1 = r1.to_s           →   "(?ix-m:ab+c)"
r2 = Regexp.new(s1)    →   /(?ix-m:ab+c)/
r1 == r2               →   false
r1.source              →   "ab+c"
r2.source              →   "(?ix-m:ab+c)"
```

Regexp

Signal

Many operating systems allow signals to be sent to running processes. Some signals have a defined effect on the process, and others may be trapped at the code level and acted upon. For example, your process may trap the USR1 signal and use it to toggle debugging, and it may use TERM to initiate a controlled shutdown.

```
pid = fork do
  Signal.trap("USR1") do
    $debug = !$debug
    puts "Debug now: #$debug"
  end
  Signal.trap("TERM") do
    puts "Terminating..."
    shutdown()
  end
  # . . . do some work . . .
end
Process.detach(pid)

# Controlling program:
Process.kill("USR1", pid)
# ...
Process.kill("USR1", pid)
# ...
Process.kill("TERM", pid)
```

produces:

```
Debug now: true
Debug now: false
Terminating...
```

The list of available signal names and their interpretation is system dependent. Signal delivery semantics may also vary between systems; in particular signal delivery may not always be reliable.

Module methods

list

Signal.list → *hash*

Returns a list of signal names mapped to the corresponding underlying signal numbers.

```
Signal.list  →  {"ABRT"=>6, "ALRM"=>14, "BUS"=>10, "CHLD"=>20,
                 "CLD"=>20, "CONT"=>19, "EMT"=>7, "FPE"=>8, "HUP"=>1,
                 "ILL"=>4, "INFO"=>29, "INT"=>2, "IO"=>23, "IOT"=>6,
                 "KILL"=>9, "PIPE"=>13, "PROF"=>27, "QUIT"=>3,
                 "SEGV"=>11, "STOP"=>17, "SYS"=>12, "TERM"=>15,
                 "TRAP"=>5, "TSTP"=>18, "TTIN"=>21, "TTOU"=>22,
                 "URG"=>16, "USR1"=>30, "USR2"=>31, "VTALRM"=>26,
                 "WINCH"=>28, "XCPU"=>24, "XFSZ"=>25}
```

trap

Signal.trap(*signal, proc*) → *obj*
Signal.trap(*signal*) { *block* } → *obj*

Specifies the handling of signals. The first parameter is a signal name (a string such as SIGALRM, SIGUSR1, and so on) or a signal number. The characters SIG may be omitted from the signal name. The command or block specifies code to be run when the signal is raised. If the command is the string IGNORE or SIG_IGN, the signal will be ignored. If the command is DEFAULT or SIG_DFL, the operating system's default handler will be invoked. If the command is EXIT, the script will be terminated by the signal. Otherwise, the given command or block will be run.

The special signal name EXIT or signal number zero will be invoked just prior to program termination.

trap returns the previous handler for the given signal.

```
Signal.trap(0, lambda { puts "Terminating: #{$$}" })
Signal.trap("CLD")  { puts "Child died" }
fork && Process.wait
```

produces:

```
Terminating: 27913
Child died
Terminating: 27912
```

Class	
String	< Object

A `String` object holds and manipulates a sequence of bytes, typically representing characters. String objects may be created using `String.new` or as literals (see page 320).

Because of aliasing issues, users of strings should be aware of the methods that modify the contents of a `String` object. Typically, methods with names ending in ! modify their receiver, while those without a ! return a new `String`. However, exceptions exist, such as `String#[]=`.

Mixes in

Comparable:

    <, <=, ==, >=, >, between?

Enumerable:

    all?, any?, collect, detect, each_with_index, entries, find, find_all,
    grep, include?, inject, map, max, member?, min, partition, reject,
    select, sort, sort_by, to_a, zip

Class methods

new   String.new(*val=""*) → *str*

1.8   Returns a new string object containing a copy of *val* (which should be a `String` or implement `to_str`).

```
str1 = "wibble"
str2 = String.new(str1)
str1.object_id    →    946790
str2.object_id    →    946780
str1[1] = "o"
str1              →    "wobble"
str2              →    "wibble"
```

Instance methods

%   *str* % *arg* → *string*

Format—Uses *str* as a format specification, and returns the result of applying it to *arg*. If the format specification contains more than one substitution, then *arg* must be an `Array` containing the values to be substituted. See `Kernel.sprintf` on page 529 for details of the format string.

```
"%05d" % 123                          →    "00123"
"%-5s: %08x" % [ "ID", self.object_id ]   →    "ID␣␣␣:␣000eecdc"
```

---

*

str * int → string

Copies—Returns a new `String` containing *int* copies of the receiver.

```
"Ho! " * 3   →   "Ho! Ho! Ho! "
```

+

str + string → string

Concatenation—Returns a new `String` containing *string* concatenated to *str*.

```
"Hello from " + self.to_s   →   "Hello from main"
```

<<

str << fixnum → str
str << obj → str

Append—Concatenates the given object to *str*. If the object is a `Fixnum` between 0 and 255, it is converted to a character before concatenation.

```
a = "hello "
a << "world"   →   "hello world"
a << 33        →   "hello world!"
```

<=>

str <=> other_string → −1, 0, +1

Comparison—Returns −1 if *str* is less than, 0 if *str* is equal to, and +1 if *str* is greater than *other_string*. If the strings are of different lengths, and the strings are equal when compared up to the shortest length, then the longer string is considered greater than the shorter one. If the variable $= is `false`, the comparison is based on comparing the binary values of each character in the string. In older versions of Ruby, setting $= allowed case-insensitive comparisons; this is now deprecated in favor of using `String#casecmp`.

1.8

<=> is the basis for the methods <, <=, >, >=, and between?, included from module `Comparable`. The method `String#==` does not use `Comparable#==`.

```
"abcdef" <=> "abcde"    →   1
"abcdef" <=> "abcdef"   →   0
"abcdef" <=> "abcdefg"  →   -1
"abcdef" <=> "ABCDEF"   →   1
```

==

str == obj → true or false

1.8

Equality—If *obj* is a `String`, returns `true` if *str* <=> *obj* equals zero; returns `false` otherwise. If *obj* is not a `String` but responds to `to_str`, return *obj* == *str*; otherwise returns false.

```
"abcdef" == "abcde"    →   false
"abcdef" == "abcdef"   →   true
```

===

str === obj → true or false

Case Equality—Synonym for `String#==`.

=~

$$str =\sim regexp \rightarrow int \text{ or } \texttt{nil}$$

Match—Equivalent to *regexp* =~ *str*. Prior versions of Ruby permitted an arbitrary operand to =~; this is now deprecated. Returns the position the match starts, or returns nil if there is no match.

```
"cat o' 9 tails" =~ /\d/    →    7
```

[ ]

$$str[\, int \,] \rightarrow int \text{ or } \texttt{nil}$$
$$str[\, int, int \,] \rightarrow string \text{ or } \texttt{nil}$$
$$str[\, range \,] \rightarrow string \text{ or } \texttt{nil}$$
$$str[\, regexp \,] \rightarrow string \text{ or } \texttt{nil}$$
$$str[\, regexp, int \,] \rightarrow string \text{ or } \texttt{nil}$$
$$str[\, string \,] \rightarrow string \text{ or } \texttt{nil}$$

Element Reference—If passed a single *int*, returns the code of the character at that position. If passed two *ints*, returns a substring starting at the offset given by the first, and a length given by the second. If given a range, a substring containing characters at offsets given by the range is returned. In all three cases, if an offset is negative, it is counted from the end of *str*. Returns nil if the initial offset falls outside the string and the length is not given, the length is negative, or the beginning of the range is greater than the end.

If *regexp* is supplied, the matching portion of *str* is returned. If a numeric parameter follows the regular expression, that component of the MatchData is returned instead. If a String is given, that string is returned if it occurs in *str*. In both cases, nil is returned if there is no match.

```
a = "hello there"
a[1]                     →    101
a[1,3]                   →    "ell"
a[1..3]                  →    "ell"
a[1...3]                 →    "el"
a[-3,2]                  →    "er"
a[-4..-2]                →    "her"
a[-2..-4]                →    ""
a[/[aeiou](.)\1/]        →    "ell"
a[/[aeiou](.)\1/, 0]     →    "ell"
a[/[aeiou](.)\1/, 1]     →    "l"
a[/[aeiou](.)\1/, 2]     →    nil
a[/(..)e/]               →    "the"
a[/(..)e/, 1]            →    "th"
a["lo"]                  →    "lo"
a["bye"]                 →    nil
```

[ ]=

$$str[\ int\ ] = int$$
$$str[\ int\ ] = string$$
$$str[\ int, int\ ] = string$$
$$str[\ range\ ] = string$$
$$str[\ regexp\ ] = string$$
$$str[\ regexp, int\ ] = string$$
$$str[\ string\ ] = string$$

Element Assignment—Replaces some or all of the content of *str*. The portion of the string affected is determined using the same criteria as String#[ ]. If the replacement string is not the same length as the text it is replacing, the string will be adjusted accordingly. If the regular expression or string is used as the index doesn't match a position in the string, IndexError is raised. If the regular expression form is used, the optional second *int* allows you to specify which portion of the match to replace (effectively using the MatchData indexing rules). The forms that take a Fixnum will raise an IndexError if the value is out of range; the Range form will raise a RangeError, and the Regexp and String forms will silently ignore the assignment.

```
a = "hello"
a[2] = 96                          (a → "he`lo")
a[2, 4] = "xyz"                    (a → "hexyz")
a[-4, 2] = "xyz"                   (a → "hxyzlo")
a[2..4] = "xyz"                    (a → "hexyz")
a[-4..-2] = "xyz"                  (a → "hxyzo")
a[/[aeiou](.)\1(.)/] = "xyz"       (a → "hxyz")
a[/[aeiou](.)\1(.)/, 1] = "xyz"    (a → "hexyzlo")
a[/[aeiou](.)\1(.)/, 2] = "xyz"    (a → "hellxyz")
a["l"] = "xyz"                     (a → "hexyzlo")
a["ll"] = "xyz"                    (a → "hexyzo")
a[2, 0] = "xyz"                    (a → "hexyzllo")
```

~

$$\sim str \rightarrow int \text{ or } nil$$

Equivalent to $_ =~ *str*.

capitalize

$$str.capitalize \rightarrow string$$

Returns a copy of *str* with the first character converted to uppercase and the remainder to lowercase.

```
"hello".capitalize     →    "Hello"
"HELLO".capitalize     →    "Hello"
"123ABC".capitalize    →    "123abc"
```

capitalize!

$$str.capitalize! \rightarrow str \text{ or } nil$$

Modifies *str* by converting the first character to uppercase and the remainder to lowercase. Returns nil if no changes are made.

```
a = "hello"
a.capitalize!  →  "Hello"
a              →  "Hello"
a.capitalize!  →  nil
```

casecmp   *str*.casecmp(*string*) → −1, 0, +1

1.8   Case-insensitive version of `String#<=>`.

```
"abcdef".casecmp("abcde")    →   1
"abcdef".casecmp("abcdef")   →   0
"aBcDeF".casecmp("abcdef")   →   0
"abcdef".casecmp("abcdefg")  →  -1
"abcdef".casecmp("ABCDEF")   →   0
```

center   *str*.center(*int, pad=" "*) → *string*

If *int* is greater than the length of *str*, returns a new `String` of length *int* with *str* centered between the given padding (defaults to spaces); otherwise, returns *str*.

```
"hello".center(4)           →   "hello"
"hello".center(20)          →   "⎵⎵⎵⎵⎵⎵⎵hello⎵⎵⎵⎵⎵⎵⎵⎵"
"hello".center(4,  "_-^-")  →   "hello"
"hello".center(20, "_-^-")  →   "_-^-_-^hello_-^-_-^-"
"hello".center(20, "-")     →   "-------hello--------"
```

chomp   *str*.chomp(*rs=$/*) → *string*

Returns a new `String` with the given record separator removed from the end of *str* (if present). If `$/` has not been changed from the default Ruby record separator, then
1.8   chomp also removes carriage return characters (that is it will remove \n, \r, and \r\n).

```
"hello".chomp          →   "hello"
"hello\n".chomp        →   "hello"
"hello\r\n".chomp      →   "hello"
"hello\n\r".chomp      →   "hello\n"
"hello\r".chomp        →   "hello"
"hello \n there".chomp →   "hello \n there"
"hello".chomp("llo")   →   "he"
```

chomp!   *str*.chomp!(*rs=$/*) → *str* or nil

Modifies *str* in place as described for `String#chomp`, returning *str*, or returning `nil` if no modifications were made.

chop   *str*.chop → *string*

Returns a new `String` with the last character removed. If the string ends with \r\n, both characters are removed. Applying chop to an empty string returns an empty string. `String#chomp` is often a safer alternative, as it leaves the string unchanged if it doesn't end in a record separator.

```
"string\r\n".chop    →    "string"
"string\n\r".chop    →    "string\n"
"string\n".chop      →    "string"
"string".chop        →    "strin"
"x".chop.chop        →    ""
```

chop!

str.chop! → str or nil

Processes *str* as for String#chop, returning *str*, or returning nil if *str* is the empty string. See also String#chomp!.

concat

str.concat(int) → str
str.concat(obj) → str

Synonym for String#<<.

count

str.count(⟨ string ⟩⁺) → int

Each *string* parameter defines a set of characters to count. The intersection of these sets defines the characters to count in *str*. Any parameter that starts with a caret (^) is negated. The sequence c_1–c_2 means all characters between c_1 and c_2.

```
a = "hello world"
a.count "lo"              →    5
a.count "lo", "o"         →    2
a.count "hello", "^l"     →    4
a.count "ej-m"            →    4
```

crypt

str.crypt(settings) → string

Applies a one-way cryptographic hash to *str* by invoking the standard library function crypt. The argument is to some extent system dependent. On traditional Unix boxes, it is often a two-character *salt* string. On more modern boxes, it may also control things such as DES encryption parameters. See the man page for crypt(3) for details.

```
# standard salt
"secret".crypt("sh")          →    "shRK3aVg8FsI2"
# On OSX: DES, 2 interactions, 24-bit salt
"secret".crypt("_...0abcd")   →    "_...0abcdROn65JNDj12"
```

delete

str.delete(⟨ string ⟩⁺) → new_string

Returns a copy of *str* with all characters in the intersection of its arguments deleted. Uses the same rules for building the set of characters as String#count.

```
"hello".delete("l","lo")      →    "heo"
"hello".delete("lo")          →    "he"
"hello".delete("aeiou", "^e") →    "hell"
"hello".delete("ej-m")        →    "ho"
```

String

delete!   *str*.delete!(⟨ *string* ⟩$^+$) → *str* or `nil`

Performs a `delete` operation in place, returning *str*, or returning `nil` if *str* was not modified.

```
a = "hello"
a.delete!("l","lo")   →   "heo"
a                     →   "heo"
a.delete!("l")        →   nil
```

downcase   *str*.downcase → *string*

Returns a copy of *str* with all uppercase letters replaced with their lowercase counterparts. The operation is locale insensitive—only characters *A* to *Z* are affected. Multibyte characters are skipped.

```
"hEllO".downcase   →   "hello"
```

downcase!   *str*.downcase! → *str* or `nil`

Replace uppercase letters in *str* with their lowercase counterparts, returning `nil` if no changes were made.

dump   *str*.dump → *string*

Produces a version of *str* with all nonprinting characters replaced by `\nnn` notation and all special characters escaped.

each   *str*.each(*sep=$/*) {| *substr* | *block* } → *str*

Splits *str* using the supplied parameter as the record separator (`$/` by default), passing each substring in turn to the supplied block. If a zero-length record separator is supplied, the string is split into paragraphs, each terminated by multiple `\n` characters.

```
print "Example one\n"
"hello\nworld".each {|s| p s}
print "Example two\n"
"hello\nworld".each('l') {|s| p s}
print "Example three\n"
"hello\n\n\nworld".each('') {|s| p s}
```

produces:

```
Example one
"hello\n"
"world"
Example two
"hel"
"l"
"o\nworl"
"d"
Example three
"hello\n\n\n"
"world"
```

each_byte

str.each_byte { | *int* | *block* } → *str*

Passes each byte in *str* to the given block.

```
"hello".each_byte {|c| print c, ' ' }
```

produces:

```
104 101 108 108 111
```

each_line

str.each_line(*sep=$/*) { | *substr* | *block* } → *str*

Synonym for String#each.

empty?

str.empty? → true or false

Returns true if *str* has a length of zero.

```
"hello".empty?   →    false
"".empty?        →    true
```

eql?

str.eql?(*obj*) → true or false

Returns true if *obj* is a String with identical contents to *str*.

```
"cat".eql?("cat")   →    true
```

gsub

str.gsub(*pattern*, *replacement*) → *string*
str.gsub(*pattern*) { | *match* | *block* } → *string*

Returns a copy of *str* with *all* occurrences of *pattern* replaced with either *replacement* or the value of the block. The *pattern* will typically be a Regexp; if it is a String then no regular expression metacharacters will be interpreted (that is /\d/ will match a digit, but '\d' will match a backslash followed by a *d*).

If a string is used as the replacement, special variables from the match (such as $& and $1) cannot be substituted into it, as substitution into the string occurs before the pattern match starts. However, the sequences \1, \2, and so on may be used to interpolate successive groups in the match. These sequences are shown in Table 27.13 on the following page.

In the block form, the current match is passed in as a parameter, and variables such as $1, $2, $`, $&, and $' will be set appropriately. The value returned by the block will be substituted for the match on each call.

The result inherits any tainting in the original string or any supplied replacement string.

```
"hello".gsub(/[aeiou]/, '*')              →    "h*ll*"
"hello".gsub(/([aeiou])/, '<\1>')         →    "h<e>ll<o>"
"hello".gsub(/./) {|s| s[0].to_s + ' '}   →    "104 101 108 108 111 "
```

S tring

Table 27.13. Backslash sequences in substitution strings

Sequence	Text That Is Substituted
\1, \2, ... \9	The value matched by the *n*th grouped subexpression
\&	The last match
\`	The part of the string before the match
\'	The part of the string after the match
\+	The highest-numbered group matched

---

gsub!

$$str.\text{gsub!}(\ pattern,\ replacement\ ) \rightarrow str \text{ or } \texttt{nil}$$
$$str.\text{gsub!}(\ pattern\ )\ \{\,|\,match\,|\ block\ \}\ \rightarrow str \text{ or } \texttt{nil}$$

Performs the substitutions of `String#gsub` in place, returning *str*, or returning `nil` if no substitutions were performed.

---

hex

$$str.\text{hex} \rightarrow int$$

Treats leading characters from *str* as a string of hexadecimal digits (with an optional sign and an optional 0x), and returns the corresponding number. Zero is returned on error.

```
"0x0a".hex      →    10
"-1234".hex     →    -4660
"0".hex         →    0
"wombat".hex    →    0
```

---

include?

$$str.\text{include?}(\ string\ ) \rightarrow \texttt{true} \text{ or } \texttt{false}$$
$$str.\text{include?}(\ int\ ) \rightarrow \texttt{true} \text{ or } \texttt{false}$$

Returns `true` if *str* contains the given string or character.

```
"hello".include? "lo"    →    true
"hello".include? "ol"    →    false
"hello".include? ?h      →    true
```

---

index

$$str.\text{index}(\ string\ \langle\,,offset\,\rangle\ ) \rightarrow int \text{ or } \texttt{nil}$$
$$str.\text{index}(\ int\ \langle\,,offset\,\rangle\ ) \rightarrow int \text{ or } \texttt{nil}$$
$$str.\text{index}(\ regexp\ \langle\,,offset\,\rangle\ ) \rightarrow int \text{ or } \texttt{nil}$$

Returns the index of the first occurrence of the given substring, character, or pattern in *str*. Returns `nil` if not found. If the second parameter is present, it specifies the position in the string to begin the search.

```
"hello".index('e')           →    1
"hello".index('lo')          →    3
"hello".index('a')           →    nil
"hello".index(101)           →    1
"hello".index(/[aeiou]/, -3) →    4
```

String

insert

str.insert(*index, string*) → *str*

1.8

Inserts *string* before the character at the given *index*, modifying *str*. Negative indices count from the end of the string and insert *after* the given character. After the insertion, *str* will contain *string* starting at *index*.

```
"abcd".insert(0, 'X')    →    "Xabcd"
"abcd".insert(3, 'X')    →    "abcXd"
"abcd".insert(4, 'X')    →    "abcdX"
"abcd".insert(-3, 'X')   →    "abXcd"
"abcd".insert(-1, 'X')   →    "abcdX"
```

intern

str.intern → *symbol*

1.8

Returns the Symbol corresponding to *str*, creating the symbol if it did not previously exist. Can intern any string, not just identifiers. See Symbol#id2name on page 631.

```
"Koala".intern   →   :Koala
sym = "$1.50 for a soda!?!?".intern
sym.to_s         →   "$1.50 for a soda!?!?"
```

length

str.length → *int*

Returns the length of *str*.

ljust

str.ljust(*width, padding*=" ") → *string*

1.8

If *width* is greater than the length of *str*, returns a new String of length *width* with *str* left justified and padded with copies of *padding*; otherwise, returns a copy of *str*.

```
"hello".ljust(4)            →    "hello"
"hello".ljust(20)           →    "hello⎵⎵⎵⎵⎵⎵⎵⎵⎵⎵⎵⎵⎵⎵⎵"
"hello".ljust(20, "*")      →    "hello***************"
"hello".ljust(20, " dolly") →    "hello⎵dolly⎵dolly⎵do"
```

lstrip

str.lstrip → *string*

1.8

Returns a copy of *str* with leading whitespace characters removed. Also see the methods String#rstrip and String#strip.

```
"  hello  ".lstrip    →    "hello⎵⎵"
"\000 hello  ".lstrip →    "\000⎵hello⎵⎵"
"hello".lstrip        →    "hello"
```

lstrip!

str.lstrip! →
self or nil

1.8

Removes leading whitespace characters from *str*, returning nil if no change was made. See also String#rstrip! and String#strip!.

```
"  hello  ".lstrip!   →    "hello⎵⎵"
"hello".lstrip!       →    nil
```

match   *str*.match(*pattern*) → *match_data* or `nil`

1.8 Converts *pattern* to a Regexp (if it isn't already one), and then invokes its `match` method on *str*.

```
'hello'.match('(.)\1')      →   #<MatchData:0x1c9468>
'hello'.match('(.)\1')[0]   →   "ll"
'hello'.match(/(.)\1/)[0]   →   "ll"
'hello'.match('xx')         →   nil
```

next   *str*.next → *string*

Synonym for `String#succ`.

next!   *str*.next! → *str*

Synonym for `String#succ!`.

oct   *str*.oct → *int*

Treats leading characters of *str* as a string of octal digits (with an optional sign), and returns the corresponding number. Returns 0 if the conversion fails.

```
"123".oct       →   83
"-377".oct      →   -255
"bad".oct       →   0
"0377bad".oct   →   255
```

replace   *str*.replace(*string*) → *str*

Replaces the contents and taintedness of *str* with the corresponding values in *string*.

```
s = "hello"         →   "hello"
s.replace "world"   →   "world"
```

reverse   *str*.reverse → *string*

Returns a new string with the characters from *str* in reverse order.

```
# Every problem contains its own solution...
"stressed".reverse   →   "desserts"
```

reverse!   *str*.reverse! → *str*

Reverses *str* in place.

rindex   *str*.rindex(*string* ⟨ , *int* ⟩) → *int* or `nil`
str.rindex(*int* ⟨ , *int* ⟩) → *int* or `nil`
str.rindex(*regexp* ⟨ , *int* ⟩) → *int* or `nil`

Returns the index of the last occurrence of the given substring, character, or pattern in *str*. Returns `nil` if not found. If the second parameter is present, it specifies the position in the string to end the search—characters beyond this point will not be considered.

```
"hello".rindex('e')         →   1
"hello".rindex('l')         →   3
"hello".rindex('a')         →   nil
"hello".rindex(101)         →   1
"hello".rindex(/[aeiou]/, -2)  →   1
```

---

rjust

str.rjust(width, padding=" ") → string

1.8

If *width* is greater than the length of *str*, returns a new `String` of length *width* with *str* right justified and padded with copies of *padding*; otherwise, returns a copy of *str*.

```
"hello".rjust(4)           →   "hello"
"hello".rjust(20)          →   "⎵⎵⎵⎵⎵⎵⎵⎵⎵⎵⎵⎵⎵⎵⎵hello"
"hello".rjust(20, "-")     →   "---------------hello"
"hello".rjust(20, "padding") →  "paddingpaddingphello"
```

---

rstrip

str.rstrip → string

1.8

Returns a copy of *str*, stripping first trailing NUL characters and then stripping trailing whitespace characters. See also `String#lstrip` and `String#strip`.

```
"  hello  ".rstrip     →   "⎵⎵hello"
"  hello \000 ".rstrip →   "⎵⎵hello⎵\000"
"  hello \000".rstrip  →   "⎵⎵hello"
"hello".rstrip         →   "hello"
```

---

rstrip!

str.rstrip! →
self or nil

1.8

Removes trailing NUL characters and then removes trailing whitespace characters from *str*. Returns nil if no change was made. See also `String#lstrip!` and `#strip!`.

```
"  hello  ".rstrip!    →   "⎵⎵hello"
"hello".rstrip!        →   nil
```

---

scan

str.scan(pattern) → array
str.scan(pattern) {| match, ... | block } → str

Both forms iterate through *str*, matching the pattern (which may be a `Regexp` or a `String`). For each match, a result is generated and either added to the result array or passed to the block. If the pattern contains no groups, each individual result consists of the matched string, $&. If the pattern contains groups, each individual result is itself an array containing one entry per group. If the pattern is a `String`, it is interpreted literally (i.e., it is not taken to be a regular expression pattern).

```
a = "cruel world"
a.scan(/\w+/)       →   ["cruel", "world"]
a.scan(/.../)       →   ["cru", "el ", "wor"]
a.scan(/(...)/)     →   [["cru"], ["el "], ["wor"]]
a.scan(/(..)(..)/)  →   [["cr", "ue"], ["l ", "wo"]]
```

And the block form

```
a.scan(/\w+/) {|w| print "<<#{w}>> " }
puts
a.scan(/(.)(.)/) {|a,b| print b, a }
puts
```

produces:

```
<<cruel>> <<world>>
rceu lowlr
```

---

size   *str*.size → *int*

Synonym for `String#length`.

---

slice   *str*.slice(*int*) → *int* or nil
                                            str.slice(*int, int*) → *string* or nil
                                            str.slice(*range*) → *string* or nil
                                            str.slice(*regexp*) → *string* or nil
                                   str.slice(*match_string*) → *string* or nil

Synonym for `String#[ ]`.

```
a = "hello there"
a.slice(1)         →   101
a.slice(1,3)       →   "ell"
a.slice(1..3)      →   "ell"
a.slice(-3,2)      →   "er"
a.slice(-4..-2)    →   "her"

a.slice(-2..-4)       →   ""
a.slice(/th[aeiou]/)  →   "the"
a.slice("lo")         →   "lo"
a.slice("bye")        →   nil
```

---

slice!   *str*.slice!(*int*) → *int* or nil
                                            str.slice!(*int, int*) → *string* or nil
                                            str.slice!(*range*) → *string* or nil
                                            str.slice!(*regexp*) → *string* or nil
                                   str.slice!(*match_string*) → *string* or nil

Deletes the specified portion from *str*, and returns the portion deleted. The forms that take a Fixnum will raise an IndexError if the value is out of range; the Range form will raise a RangeError, and the Regexp and String forms will silently not change the string.

```
string = "this is a string"
string.slice!(2)       →   105
string.slice!(3..6)    →   " is "
string.slice!(/s.*t/)  →   "sa st"
string.slice!("r")     →   "r"
string                 →   "thing"
```

split   str.split(*pattern*=$;, ⟨ *limit* ⟩) → *array*

Divides *str* into substrings based on a delimiter, returning an array of these substrings.

If *pattern* is a String, then its contents are used as the delimiter when splitting *str*. If *pattern* is a single space, *str* is split on whitespace, with leading whitespace and runs of contiguous whitespace characters ignored.

If *pattern* is a Regexp, *str* is divided where the pattern matches. Whenever the pattern matches a zero-length string, *str* is split into individual characters. If pattern includes groups, these groups will be included in the returned values.

If *pattern* is omitted, the value of $; is used. If $; is nil (which is the default), *str* is split on whitespace as if "␣" were specified.

If the *limit* parameter is omitted, trailing empty fields are suppressed. If *limit* is a positive number, at most that number of fields will be returned (if *limit* is 1, the entire string is returned as the only entry in an array). If negative, there is no limit to the number of fields returned, and trailing null fields are not suppressed.

```
" now's   the time".split        →  ["now's", "the", "time"]
" now's   the time".split(' ')   →  ["now's", "the", "time"]
" now's   the time".split(/ /)   →  ["", "now's", "", "", "the",
                                      "time"]
"a@1bb@2ccc".split(/@\d/)        →  ["a", "bb", "ccc"]
"a@1bb@2ccc".split(/@(\d)/)      →  ["a", "1", "bb", "2", "ccc"]
"1, 2.34,56, 7".split(/,\s*/)    →  ["1", "2.34", "56", "7"]
"hello".split(//)                →  ["h", "e", "l", "l", "o"]
"hello".split(//, 3)             →  ["h", "e", "llo"]
"hi mom".split(/\s*/)            →  ["h", "i", "m", "o", "m"]

"".split                         →  []

"mellow yellow".split("ello")    →  ["m", "w y", "w"]
"1,2,,3,4,,".split(',')          →  ["1", "2", "", "3", "4"]
"1,2,,3,4,,".split(',', 4)       →  ["1", "2", "", "3,4,,"]
"1,2,,3,4,,".split(',', -4)      →  ["1", "2", "", "3", "4", "", ""]
```

squeeze   str.squeeze(⟨ *string* ⟩*) → *squeezed_tring*

Builds a set of characters from the *string* parameter(s) using the procedure described for String#count on page 611. Returns a new string where runs of the same character that occur in this set are replaced by a single character. If no arguments are given, all runs of identical characters are replaced by a single character.

```
"yellow moon".squeeze              →   "yelow mon"
"  now   is  the".squeeze(" ")     →   " now is the"
"putters putt balls".squeeze("m-z") →  "puters put balls"
```

squeeze!   *str*.squeeze!(⟨ *string* ⟩*) → *str* or `nil`

Squeezes *str* in place, returning *str*. Returns `nil` if no changes were made.

---

strip   *str*.strip → *string*

1.8   Returns a copy of *str* with leading whitespace and trailing NUL and whitespace characters removed.

```
"    hello   ".strip     →    "hello"
"\tgoodbye\r\n".strip    →    "goodbye"
"goodbye \000".strip     →    "goodbye"
"goodbye \000 ".strip    →    "goodbye \000"
```

---

strip!   *str*.strip! → *str* or `nil`

1.8   Removes leading whitespace and trailing NUL and whitespace characters removed from *str*. Returns `nil` if *str* was not altered.

---

sub   *str*.sub(*pattern, replacement*) → *string*
                                               str.sub(*pattern*) {| *match* | *block* } → *string*

Returns a copy of *str* with the *first* occurrence of *pattern* replaced with either *replacement* or the value of the block. The *pattern* will typically be a `Regexp`; if it is a `String` then no regular expression metacharacters will be interpreted (that is /\d/ will match a digit, but '\d' will match a backslash followed by a *d*).

If the method call specifies *replacement*, special variables such as $& will not be useful, as substitution into the string occurs before the pattern match starts. However, the sequences \1, \2, listed in Table 27.13 on page 614 may be used.

In the block form, the current match is passed in as a parameter, and variables such as $1, $2, $`, $&, and $' will be set appropriately. The value returned by the block will be substituted for the match on each call.

```
"hello".sub(/[aeiou]/, '*')           →    "h*llo"
"hello".sub(/([aeiou])/, '<\1>')      →    "h<e>llo"
"hello".sub(/./) {|s| s[0].to_s + ' ' }   →    "104 ello"
```

---

sub!   *str*.sub!(*pattern, replacement*) → *str* or `nil`
                                               str.sub!(*pattern*) {| *match* | *block* } → *str* or `nil`

Performs the substitutions of `String#sub` in place, returning *str*. Returns `nil` if no substitutions were performed.

---

succ   *str*.succ → *string*

Returns the successor to *str*. The successor is calculated by incrementing characters starting from the rightmost alphanumeric (or the rightmost character if there are no alphanumerics) in the string. Incrementing a digit always results in another digit, and incrementing a letter results in another letter of the same case. Incrementing nonalpha-numerics uses the underlying character set's collating sequence.

If the increment generates a "carry," the character to the left of it is incremented. This process repeats until there is no carry, adding an additional character if necessary.

```
"abcd".succ      →    "abce"
"THX1138".succ   →    "THX1139"
"<<koala>>".succ →    "<<koalb>>"
"1999zzz".succ   →    "2000aaa"
"ZZZ9999".succ   →    "AAAA0000"
"***".succ       →    "**+"
```

succ!

str.succ! → str

Equivalent to String#succ, but modifies the receiver in place.

sum

str.sum(n=16) → int

1.8 Returns a basic n-bit checksum of the characters in str, where n is the optional parameter, defaulting to 16. The result is simply the sum of the binary value of each character in str modulo $2^n - 1$. This is not a particularly good checksum—see the digest libraries on page 668 for better alternatives.

```
"now is the time".sum    →    1408
"now is the time".sum(8) →    128
```

swapcase

str.swapcase → string

Returns a copy of str with uppercase alphabetic characters converted to lowercase and lowercase characters converted to uppercase.

```
"Hello".swapcase         →    "hELLO"
"cYbEr_PuNk11".swapcase  →    "CyBeR_pUnK11"
```

swapcase!

str.swapcase! → str or nil

Equivalent to String#swapcase, but modifies str in place, returning str. Returns nil if no changes were made.

to_f

str.to_f → float

Returns the result of interpreting leading characters in str as a floating-point number. Extraneous characters past the end of a valid number are ignored. If there is not a valid number at the start of str, 0.0 is returned. The method never raises an exception (use Kernel.Float to validate numbers).

```
"123.45e1".to_f      →    1234.5
"45.67 degrees".to_f →    45.67
"thx1138".to_f       →    0.0
```

to_i   *str*.to_i(*base*=10) → *int*

1.8
Returns the result of interpreting leading characters in *str* as an integer base *base* (2 to 36). Given a base of zero, to_i looks for leading 0, 0b, 0o, 0d, or 0x and sets the base accordingly. Leading spaces are ignored, and leading plus or minus signs are honored. Extraneous characters past the end of a valid number are ignored. If there is not a valid number at the start of *str*, 0 is returned. The method never raises an exception.

```
"12345".to_i              →   12345
"99 red balloons".to_i    →   99
"0a".to_i                 →   0
"0a".to_i(16)             →   10
"0x10".to_i               →   0
"0x10".to_i(0)            →   16
"-0x10".to_i(0)           →   -16
"hello".to_i              →   0
"hello".to_i(30)          →   14167554
"1100101".to_i(2)         →   101
"1100101".to_i(8)         →   294977
"1100101".to_i(10)        →   1100101
"1100101".to_i(16)        →   17826049
"1100101".to_i(24)        →   199066177
```

to_s   *str*.to_s → *str*

Returns the receiver.

to_str   *str*.to_str → *str*

Synonym for String#to_s. to_str is used by methods such as String#concat to convert their arguments to a string. Unlike to_s, which is supported by almost all classes, to_str is normally implemented only by those classes that act like strings. Of the built-in classes, only Exception and String implement to_str.

to_sym   *str*.to_s → *symbol*

Returns the symbol for *str*. This can create symbols that cannot be represented using the :xxx notation. A synonym for String#intern.

```
s = 'cat'.to_sym          →   :cat
s == :cat                 →   true
'cat and dog'.to_sym      →   :"cat and dog"
s == :'cat and dog'       →   false
```

tr   *str*.tr(*from_string*, *to_string*) → *string*

Returns a copy of *str* with the characters in *from_string* replaced by the corresponding characters in *to_string*. If *to_string* is shorter than *from_string*, it is padded with its last character. Both strings may use the c_1–c_2 notation to denote ranges of characters, and *from_string* may start with a ^, which denotes all characters except those listed.

```
"hello".tr('aeiou', '*')    →    "h*ll*"
"hello".tr('^aeiou', '*')   →    "*e**o"
"hello".tr('el', 'ip')      →    "hippo"
"hello".tr('a-y', 'b-z')    →    "ifmmp"
```

---

tr!   *str*.tr!(*from_string*, *to_string*) → *str* or nil

Translates *str* in place, using the same rules as String#tr. Returns *str*, or returns nil if no changes were made.

---

tr_s   *str*.tr_s(*from_string*, *to_string*) → *string*

Processes a copy of *str* as described under String#tr, and then removes duplicate characters in regions that were affected by the translation.

```
"hello".tr_s('l', 'r')    →    "hero"
"hello".tr_s('el', '*')   →    "h*o"
"hello".tr_s('el', 'hx')  →    "hhxo"
```

---

tr_s!   *str*.tr_s!(*from_string*, *to_string*) → *str* or nil

Performs String#tr_s processing on *str* in place, returning *str*. Returns nil if no changes were made.

---

unpack   *str*.unpack(*format*) → *array*

Decodes *str* (which may contain binary data) according to the format string, returning an array of the extracted values. The format string consists of a sequence of single-character directives, summarized in Table 27.14 on the next page. Each directive may be followed by a number, indicating the number of times to repeat this directive. An asterisk (*) will use up all remaining elements. The directives sSiIlL may each be followed by an underscore (_) to use the underlying platform's native size for the specified type; otherwise, it uses a platform-independent consistent size. Spaces are ignored in the format string. Comments starting with # to the next newline or end of string are also ignored. See also Array#pack on page 436.

```
"abc \0\0abc \0\0".unpack('A6Z6')    →    ["abc", "abc "]
"abc \0\0".unpack('a3a3')            →    ["abc", " \000\000"]
"aa".unpack('b8B8')                  →    ["10000110", "01100001"]
"aaa".unpack('h2H2c')                →    ["16", "61", 97]
"\xfe\xff\xfe\xff".unpack('sS')      →    [-257, 65279]
"now=20is".unpack('M*')              →    ["now is"]
"whole".unpack('xax2aX2aX1aX2a')     →    ["h", "e", "l", "l", "o"]
```

---

upcase   *str*.upcase → *string*

Returns a copy of *str* with all lowercase letters replaced with their uppercase counterparts. The operation is locale insensitive—only characters *a* to *z* are affected.

```
"hEllO".upcase    →    "HELLO"
```

Table 27.14. Directives for `String#unpack`

Format	Function	Returns
A	String with trailing NULs and spaces removed.	String
a	String.	String
B	Extract bits from each character (MSB first).	String
b	Extract bits from each character (LSB first).	String
C	Extract a character as an unsigned integer.	Fixnum
c	Extract a character as an integer.	Fixnum
d,D	Treat *sizeof(double)* characters as a native double.	Float
E	Treat *sizeof(double)* characters as a double in little-endian byte order.	Float
e	Treat *sizeof(float)* characters as a float in little-endian byte order.	Float
f,F	Treat *sizeof(float)* characters as a native float.	Float
G	Treat *sizeof(double)* characters as a double in network byte order.	Float
g	Treat *sizeof(float)* characters as a float in network byte order.	Float
H	Extract hex nibbles from each character (most significant first).	String
h	Extract hex nibbles from each character (least significant first).	String
I	Treat *sizeof(int)*[1] successive characters as an unsigned native integer.	Integer
i	Treat *sizeof(int)*[1] successive characters as a signed native integer.	Integer
L	Treat four[1] successive characters as an unsigned native long integer.	Integer
l	Treat four[1] successive characters as a signed native long integer.	Integer
M	Extract a quoted-printable string.	String
m	Extract a Base64 encoded string.	String
N	Treat four characters as an unsigned long in network byte order.	Fixnum
n	Treat two characters as an unsigned short in network byte order.	Fixnum
P	Treat *sizeof(char *)* characters as a pointer, and return *len* characters from the referenced location.	String
p	Treat *sizeof(char *)* characters as a pointer to a null-terminated string.	String
Q	Treat eight characters as an unsigned quad word (64 bits).	Integer
q	Treat eight characters as a signed quad word (64 bits).	Integer
S	Treat two[1] successive characters as an unsigned short in native byte order.	Fixnum
s	Treat two[1] successive characters as a signed short in native byte order.	Fixnum
U	Extract UTF-8 characters as unsigned integers.	Integer
u	Extract a UU-encoded string.	String
V	Treat four characters as an unsigned long in little-endian byte order.	Fixnum
v	Treat two characters as an unsigned short in little-endian byte order.	Fixnum
w	BER-compressed integer (see `Array#pack` for more information).	Integer
X	Skip backward one character.	—
x	Skip forward one character.	—
Z	String with trailing NULs removed.	String
@	Skip to the offset given by the length argument.	—

[1] May be modified by appending "_" to the directive.

---

upcase!   *str*.upcase! → *str* or nil

Upcases the contents of *str*, returning nil if no changes were made.

---

upto   *str*.upto(*string*) {| *s* | *block* } → *str*

Itcrates through successive values, starting at *str* and ending at *string* inclusive, passing each value in turn to the block. The String#succ method is used to generate each value.

```
"a8".upto("b6") {|s| print s, ' ' }
for s in "a8".."b6"
  print s, ' '
end
```

produces:

```
a8 a9 b0 b1 b2 b3 b4 b5 b6
a8 a9 b0 b1 b2 b3 b4 b5 b6
```

Struct < Object

Subclasses: Struct::Tms

A Struct is a convenient way to bundle a number of attributes together, using accessor methods, without having to write an explicit class.

The Struct class is a generator of specific classes, each one of which is defined to hold a set of variables and their accessors. In these examples, we'll call the generated class *Customer*, and we'll show an example instance of that class as *joe*.

Also see OpenStruct on page 710.

In the descriptions that follow, the parameter *symbol* refers to a symbol, which is either a quoted string or a Symbol (such as :name).

Mixes in

Enumerable:
all?, any?, collect, detect, each_with_index, entries, find, find_all, grep, include?, inject, map, max, member?, min, partition, reject, select, sort, sort_by, to_a, zip

Class methods

new

$$\text{Struct.new(} \langle \text{ string } \rangle \text{ } \langle \text{ , symbol } \rangle^+ \text{)} \rightarrow \textit{Customer}$$
$$_{[1.9]}\text{ Struct.new(} \langle \text{ string } \rangle \text{ } \langle \text{ , symbol } \rangle^+ \text{) \{ \textit{block} \} } \rightarrow \textit{Customer}$$

Creates a new class, named by *string*, containing accessor methods for the given symbols. If the name *string* is omitted, an anonymous structure class will be created. Otherwise, the name of this struct will appear as a constant in class Struct, so it must be unique for all Structs in the system and should start with a capital letter. Assigning a structure class to a constant effectively gives the class the name of the constant.

Struct.new returns a new Class object, which can then be used to create specific instances of the new structure. The remaining methods listed below (class and instance) are defined for this generated class. See the description that follows for an example.

Ruby 1.9 and later allow you to pass a block to a Struct's constructor. This block is evaluated in the context of the new struct's class and hence allows you conveniently to add instance methods to the new struct.

```
# Create a structure with a name in Struct
Struct.new("Customer", :name, :address)    →    Struct::Customer
Struct::Customer.new("Dave", "123 Main")   →    #<struct
                                                 Struct::Customer
                                                 name="Dave",
                                                 address="123 Main">
```

```
# Create a structure named by its constant
Customer = Struct.new(:name, :address)   →   Customer
Customer.new("Dave", "123 Main")         →   #<struct Customer
                                             name="Dave", address="123
                                             Main">
```

new
Customer.new(⟨ *obj* ⟩⁺) → *joe*

Creates a new instance of a structure (the class created by Struct.new). The number of actual parameters must be less than or equal to the number of attributes defined for this class; unset parameters default to nil. Passing too many parameters will raise an ArgumentError.

```
Customer = Struct.new(:name, :address, :zip)

joe = Customer.new("Joe Smith", "123 Maple, Anytown NC", 12345)
joe.name   →   "Joe Smith"
joe.zip    →   12345
```

[ ]
Customer[⟨ *obj* ⟩⁺] → *joe*

Synonym for new (for the generated structure).

```
Customer = Struct.new(:name, :address, :zip)

joe = Customer["Joe Smith", "123 Maple, Anytown NC", 12345]
joe.name   →   "Joe Smith"
joe.zip    →   12345
```

members
Customer.members → *array*

Returns an array of strings representing the names of the instance variables.

```
Customer = Struct.new("Customer", :name, :address, :zip)
Customer.members   →   ["name", "address", "zip"]
```

Instance methods

==
joe == *other_struct* → true or false

Equality—Returns true if *other_struct* is equal to this one: they must be of the same class as generated by Struct.new, and the values of all instance variables must be equal (according to Object#==).

```
Customer = Struct.new(:name, :address, :zip)

joe   = Customer.new("Joe Smith", "123 Maple, Anytown NC", 12345)
joejr = Customer.new("Joe Smith", "123 Maple, Anytown NC", 12345)
jane  = Customer.new("Jane Doe", "456 Elm, Anytown NC", 12345)

joe == joejr   →   true
joe == jane    →   false
```

[ ]

joe[*symbol*] → *obj*
joe[*integer*] → *obj*

Attribute Reference—Returns the value of the instance variable named by *symbol* or indexed (0..*length* − 1) by *int*. Raises NameError if the named variable does not exist, or raises IndexError if the index is out of range.

```
Customer = Struct.new(:name, :address, :zip)
joe = Customer.new("Joe Smith", "123 Maple, Anytown NC", 12345)
joe["name"]   →   "Joe Smith"
joe[:name]    →   "Joe Smith"
joe[0]        →   "Joe Smith"
```

[ ]=

joe[*symbol*] = *obj* → *obj*
joe[*int*] = *obj* → *obj*

Attribute Assignment—Assigns to the instance variable named by *symbol* or *int* the value *obj* and returns it. Raises a NameError if the named variable does not exist, or raises an IndexError if the index is out of range.

```
Customer = Struct.new(:name, :address, :zip)
joe = Customer.new("Joe Smith", "123 Maple, Anytown NC", 12345)
joe["name"] = "Luke"
joe[:zip]   = "90210"
joe.name   →   "Luke"
joe.zip    →   "90210"
```

---

each

joe.each { | *obj* | *block* } → *joe*

Calls *block* once for each instance variable, passing the value as a parameter.

```
Customer = Struct.new(:name, :address, :zip)
joe = Customer.new("Joe Smith", "123 Maple, Anytown NC", 12345)
joe.each {|x| puts(x) }
```

produces:

```
Joe Smith
123 Maple, Anytown NC
12345
```

---

each_pair

joe.each_pair { | *symbol, obj* | *block* } → *joe*

1.8

Calls *block* once for each instance variable, passing the name (as a symbol) and the value as parameters.

```
Customer = Struct.new(:name, :address, :zip)
joe = Customer.new("Joe Smith", "123 Maple, Anytown NC", 12345)
joe.each_pair {|name, value| puts("#{name} => #{value}") }
```

produces:

```
name => Joe Smith
address => 123 Maple, Anytown NC
zip => 12345
```

length
joe.length → *int*

Returns the number of instance variables.

```
Customer = Struct.new(:name, :address, :zip)
joe = Customer.new("Joe Smith", "123 Maple, Anytown NC", 12345)
joe.length   →   3
```

members
joe.members → *array*

Returns an array of strings representing the names of the instance variables.

```
Customer = Struct.new(:name, :address, :zip)
joe = Customer.new("Joe Smith", "123 Maple, Anytown NC", 12345)
joe.members   →   ["name", "address", "zip"]
```

size
joe.size → *int*

Synonym for Struct#length.

to_a
joe.to_a → *array*

Returns the values for this instance as an array.

```
Customer = Struct.new(:name, :address, :zip)
joe = Customer.new("Joe Smith", "123 Maple, Anytown NC", 12345)
joe.to_a[1]   →   "123 Maple, Anytown NC"
```

values
joe.values → *array*

Synonym for to_a.

values_at
joe.values_at(⟨ *selector* ⟩*) → *array*

1.8

Returns an array containing the elements in *joe* corresponding to the given indices. The selectors may be integer indices or ranges.

```
Lots = Struct.new(:a, :b, :c, :d, :e, :f)
l = Lots.new(11, 22, 33, 44, 55, 66)
l.values_at(1, 3, 5)     →   [22, 44, 66]
l.values_at(0, 2, 4)     →   [11, 33, 55]
l.values_at(-1, -3, -5)  →   [66, 44, 22]
```

Struct

Class **Struct::Tms** < Struct

This structure is returned by `Process.times`. It holds information on process times on those platforms that support it. Not all values are valid on all platforms. This structure contains the following instance variables and the corresponding accessors:

utime	Amount of user CPU time, in seconds
stime	Amount of system CPU time, in seconds
cutime	Total of completed child processes' user CPU time, in seconds (always 0 on Windows)
cstime	Total of completed child processes' system CPU time, in seconds (always 0 on Windows)

See also `Struct` on page 626 and `Process.times` on page 587.

```
def eat_cpu
  100_000.times { Math.sin(0.321) }
end
3.times { fork { eat_cpu } }
eat_cpu
Process.waitall
t = Process::times
[ t.utime, t.stime]      →   [0.28, 0.03]
[ t.cutime, t.cstime ]   →   [0.74, 0.01]
```

Class **Symbol** < Object

Symbol objects represent names inside the Ruby interpreter. They are generated using the :name literal syntax and by using the various to_sym methods. The same Symbol object will be created for a given name string for the duration of a program's execution, regardless of the context or meaning of that name. Thus, if Fred is a constant in one context, a method in another, and a class in a third, the Symbol :Fred will be the same object in all three contexts.

```
module One
  class Fred
  end
  $f1 = :Fred
end
module Two
  Fred = 1
  $f2 = :Fred
end
def Fred()
end
$f3 = :Fred
$f1.object_id   →   2526478
$f2.object_id   →   2526478
$f3.object_id   →   2526478
```

Class methods

all_symbols   Symbol.all_symbols → *array*

1.8   Returns an array of all the symbols currently in Ruby's symbol table.

```
Symbol.all_symbols.size    →   913
Symbol.all_symbols[1,20]   →   [:floor, :ARGV, :Binding, :symlink,
                               :chown, :EOFError, :$;, :String,
                               :LOCK_SH, :"setuid?", :$<,
                               :default_proc, :compact, :extend, :Tms,
                               :getwd, :$=, :ThreadGroup, :"success?",
                               :wait2]
```

Instance methods

id2name   *sym*.id2name → *string*

1.8   Returns the string representation of *sym*. Prior to Ruby 1.8, symbols typically represented names; now they can be arbitrary strings.

```
:fred.id2name              →   "fred"
:"99 red balloons!".id2name   →   "99 red balloons!"
```

---

inspect   *sym*.inspect → *string*

Returns the representation of *sym* as a symbol literal.

```
:fred.inspect              →    :fred
:"99 red balloons!".inspect   →    :"99 red balloons!"
```

---

to_i   *sym*.to_i → *fixnum*

Returns an integer that is unique for each symbol within a particular execution of a program.

```
:fred.to_i           →    9857
"fred".to_sym.to_i   →    9857
```

---

to_int   *sym*.to_int → *fixnum*

Synonym for `Symbol#to_i`. Allows symbols to have integer-like behavior.

---

to_s   *sym*.to_s → *string*

Synonym for `Symbol#id2name`.

---

to_sym   *sym*.to_sym → *sym*

Symbols are symbol-like!

Symbol

Thread < Object

Thread encapsulates the behavior of a thread of execution, including the main thread of the Ruby script. See the tutorial in Chapter 11, beginning on page 135.

In the descriptions that follow, the parameter *symbol* refers to a symbol, which is either a quoted string or a Symbol (such as :name).

Class methods

---

abort_on_exception   Thread.abort_on_exception → true or false

Returns the status of the global "abort on exception" condition. The default is false. When set to true, or if the global $DEBUG flag is true (perhaps because the command line option –d was specified) all threads will abort (the process will exit(0)) if an exception is raised in any thread. See also Thread.abort_on_exception=.

---

abort_on_exception=   Thread.abort_on_exception= *bool*→ true or false

When set to true, all threads will abort if an exception is raised. Returns the new state.

```
Thread.abort_on_exception = true
t1 = Thread.new do
  puts  "In new thread"
  raise "Exception from thread"
end
sleep(1)
puts "not reached"
```

produces:

```
In new thread
prog.rb:4: Exception from thread (RuntimeError)
from prog.rb:2:in `initialize'
from prog.rb:2:in `new'
from prog.rb:2
```

---

critical   Thread.critical → true or false

Returns the status of the global "thread critical" condition.

---

critical=   Thread.critical= *bool* → true or false

Sets the status of the global "thread critical" condition and returns it. When set to true, prohibits scheduling of any existing thread. Does not block new threads from being created and run. Certain thread operations (such as stopping or killing a thread, sleeping in the current thread, and raising an exception) may cause a thread to be scheduled even when in a critical section. Thread.critical is not intended for daily use: it is primarily there to support folks writing threading libraries.

T hread

---

current   Thread.current → *thread*

Returns the currently executing thread.

```
Thread.current   →   #<Thread:0x1d5790 run>
```

---

exit   Thread.exit

Terminates the currently running thread and schedules another thread to be run. If this thread is already marked to be killed, `exit` returns the Thread. If this is the main thread, or the last thread, exit the process.

---

fork   Thread.fork { *block* } → *thread*

Synonym for `Thread.start`.

---

kill   Thread.kill(*thread*)

Causes the given thread to exit (see `Thread.exit`).

```
count = 0
a = Thread.new { loop { count += 1 } }
sleep(0.1)       →   0
Thread.kill(a)   →   #<Thread:0x1c947c dead>
count            →   39410
a.alive?         →   false
```

---

list   Thread.list → *array*

Returns an array of Thread objects for all threads that are either runnable or stopped.

```
Thread.new { sleep(200) }
Thread.new { 1000000.times {|i| i*i } }
Thread.new { Thread.stop }
Thread.list.each {|thr| p thr }
```

produces:

```
#<Thread:0x1c960c sleep>
#<Thread:0x1c9698 run>
#<Thread:0x1c96fc sleep>
#<Thread:0x1d5790 run>
```

---

main   Thread.main → *thread*

Returns the main thread for the process.

```
Thread.main   →   #<Thread:0x1d5790 run>
```

---

new   Thread.new(⟨ *arg* ⟩*) {| *args* | *block* } → *thread*

Creates and runs a new thread to execute the instructions given in *block*. Any arguments passed to `Thread.new` are passed into the block.

```
x = Thread.new { sleep 0.1; print "x"; print "y"; print "z" }
a = Thread.new { print "a"; print "b"; sleep 0.2; print "c" }
x.join; a.join # wait for threads to finish
```

produces:

abxyzc

---

pass   Thread.pass

Invokes the thread scheduler to pass execution to another thread.

```
a = Thread.new { print "a"; Thread.pass; print "b" }
b = Thread.new { print "x"; Thread.pass; print "y" }
a.join; b.join
```

produces:

axby

---

start   Thread.start(⟨ *args* ⟩*) {| *args* | *block* } → *thread*

Basically the same as Thread.new. However, if class Thread is subclassed, then calling start in that subclass will not invoke the subclass's initialize method.

---

stop   Thread.stop

Stops execution of the current thread, putting it into a "sleep" state, and schedules execution of another thread. Resets the "critical" condition to false.

```
a = Thread.new { print "a"; Thread.stop; print "c" }
Thread.pass
print "b"
a.run
a.join
```

produces:

abc

Instance methods

[ ]   *thr*[*symbol*] → *obj* or nil

Attribute Reference—Returns the value of a thread-local variable, using either a symbol or a string name. If the specified variable does not exist, returns nil.

```
a = Thread.new { Thread.current["name"] = "A"; Thread.stop }
b = Thread.new { Thread.current[:name]  = "B"; Thread.stop }
c = Thread.new { Thread.current["name"] = "C"; Thread.stop }
Thread.list.each {|x| puts "#{x.inspect}: #{x[:name]}" }
```

produces:

```
#<Thread:0x1c92b0 sleep>: C
#<Thread:0x1c9328 sleep>: B
#<Thread:0x1c93b4 sleep>: A
#<Thread:0x1d5790 run>:
```

[ ]=   *thr*[*symbol*] = *obj*→ *obj*

Attribute Assignment—Sets or creates the value of a thread-local variable, using either a symbol or a string. See also Thread#[ ].

---

abort_on_exception   *thr*.abort_on_exception → true or false

---

Returns the status of the thread-local "abort on exception" condition for *thr*. The default is false. See also Thread.abort_on_exception=.

---

abort_on_exception=   *thr*.abort_on_exception= true or false→ true or false

---

When set to true, causes all threads (including the main program) to abort if an exception is raised in *thr*. The process will effectively exit(0).

---

alive?   *thr*.alive? → true or false

Returns true if *thr* is running or sleeping.

```
thr = Thread.new { }
thr.join              →    #<Thread:0x1c96fc dead>
Thread.current.alive? →    true
thr.alive?            →    false
```

---

exit   *thr*.exit → *thr* or nil

Terminates *thr* and schedules another thread to be run. If this thread is already marked to be killed, exit returns the Thread. If this is the main thread, or the last thread, exits the process.

---

group   *thr*.group → *thread_group*

_1.8_ Returns the ThreadGroup owning *thr*, or nil.

```
thread = Thread.new { sleep 99 }
Thread.current.group.list   →   [#<Thread:0x1c9418 sleep>,
                                 #<Thread:0x1d5790 run>]
new_group = ThreadGroup.new
thread.group.list           →   [#<Thread:0x1c9418 sleep>,
                                 #<Thread:0x1d5790 run>]
new_group.add(thread)
thread.group.list           →   [#<Thread:0x1c9418 sleep>]
Thread.current.group.list   →   [#<Thread:0x1d5790 run>]
```

---

join   *thr*.join → *thr*
                                                       thr.join(*limit*) → *thr*

_1.8_ The calling thread will suspend execution and run *thr*. Does not return until *thr* exits or until *limit* seconds have passed. If the time limit expires, nil will be returned; otherwise *thr* is returned.

Any threads not joined will be killed when the main program exits. If *thr* had previously raised an exception and the `abort_on_exception` and `$DEBUG` flags are not set (so the exception has not yet been processed), it will be processed at this time.

```
a = Thread.new { print "a"; sleep(10); print "b"; print "c" }
x = Thread.new { print "x"; Thread.pass; print "y"; print "z" }
x.join # Let x thread finish, a will be killed on exit.
```

produces:

```
axyz
```

The following example illustrates the *limit* parameter.

```
y = Thread.new { 4.times { sleep 0.1; print "tick...\n" }}
print "Waiting\n" until y.join(0.15)
```

produces:

```
tick...
Waiting
tick...
Waiting
tick...
tick...
```

keys   *thr*.keys → *array*

1.8   Returns an array of the names of the thread-local variables (as symbols).

```
thr = Thread.new do
  Thread.current[:cat] = 'meow'
  Thread.current["dog"] = 'woof'
end
thr.join   →   #<Thread:0x1c965c dead>
thr.keys   →   [:dog, :cat]
```

key?   *thr*.key?(*symbol*) → true or false

Returns `true` if the given string (or symbol) exists as a thread-local variable.

```
me = Thread.current
me[:oliver] = "a"
me.key?(:oliver)   →   true
me.key?(:stanley)  →   false
```

kill   *thr*.kill

Synonym for `Thread#exit`.

priority   *thr*.priority → *int*

Returns the priority of *thr*. Default is zero; higher-priority threads will run before lower-priority threads.

```
Thread.current.priority   →   0
```

priority=   *thr*.priority= *int* → *thr*

Sets the priority of *thr* to *integer*. Higher-priority threads will run before lower-priority threads.

```
count1 = count2 = 0
a = Thread.new do
      loop { count1 += 1 }
    end
a.priority = -1

b = Thread.new do
      loop { count2 += 1 }
    end
b.priority = -2
sleep 1
Thread.critical = 1
count1   →   451372
count2   →   4514
```

raise   *thr*.raise
thr.raise(*message*)
thr.raise(*exception* ⟨ , *message* ⟨ , *array* ⟩ ⟩)

1.8   Raises an exception (see `Kernel.raise` on page 527 for details) from *thr*. The caller does not have to be *thr*.

```
Thread.abort_on_exception = true
a = Thread.new { sleep(200) }
a.raise("Gotcha")
```

produces:

```
prog.rb:3: Gotcha (RuntimeError)
from prog.rb:2:in `initialize'
from prog.rb:2:in `new'
from prog.rb:2
```

run   *thr*.run → *thr*

Wakes up *thr*, making it eligible for scheduling. If not in a critical section, then invokes the scheduler.

```
a = Thread.new { puts "a"; Thread.stop; puts "c" }
Thread.pass
puts "Got here"
a.run
a.join
```

produces:

```
a
Got here
c
```

safe_level
thr.safe_level → *int*

Returns the safe level in effect for *thr*. Setting thread-local safe levels can help when implementing sandboxes that run insecure code.

```
thr = Thread.new { $SAFE = 3; sleep }
Thread.current.safe_level   →   0
thr.safe_level              →   3
```

status
thr.status → *string*, false or nil

Returns the status of *thr*: sleep if *thr* is sleeping or waiting on I/O, run if *thr* is executing, aborting if *thr* is aborting, false if *thr* terminated normally, and nil if *thr* terminated with an exception.

```
a = Thread.new { raise("die now") }
b = Thread.new { Thread.stop }
c = Thread.new { Thread.exit }
d = Thread.new { sleep }
Thread.critical = true
d.kill                  →   #<Thread:0x1c8e00 aborting>
a.status                →   nil
b.status                →   "sleep"
c.status                →   false
d.status                →   "aborting"
Thread.current.status   →   "run"
```

stop?
thr.stop? → true or false

Returns true if *thr* is dead or sleeping.

```
a = Thread.new { Thread.stop }
b = Thread.current
a.stop?   →   true
b.stop?   →   false
```

terminate
thr.terminate

Synonym for Thread#exit.

value
thr.value → *obj*

Waits for *thr* to complete (via Thread#join) and returns its value.

```
a = Thread.new { 2 + 2 }
a.value   →   4
```

wakeup
thr.wakeup → *thr*

Marks *thr* as eligible for scheduling (it may still remain blocked on I/O, however). Does not invoke the scheduler (see Thread#run).

Class **ThreadGroup** < Object

A ThreadGroup keeps track of a number of threads. A Thread can belong to only one ThreadGroup at a time; adding a thread to a group will remove it from the its current group. Newly created threads belong to the group of the thread that created them.

ThreadGroup constants

Default   Default thread group.

Class methods

new   ThreadGroup.new → *thgrp*

Returns a newly created ThreadGroup. The group is initially empty.

Instance methods

add   *thgrp*.add(*thread*) → *thgrp*

Adds the given thread to this group, removing it from any other group to which it may have previously belonged.

```
puts "Default group is #{ThreadGroup::Default.list}"
tg = ThreadGroup.new
t1 = Thread.new { sleep }
t2 = Thread.new { sleep }
puts "t1 is #{t1}, t2 is #{t2}"
tg.add(t1)
puts "Default group now #{ThreadGroup::Default.list}"
puts "tg group now #{tg.list}"
```

produces:

```
Default group is #<Thread:0x1d6790>
t1 is #<Thread:0x1ca24c>, t2 is #<Thread:0x1ca1e8>
Default group now #<Thread:0x1ca1e8>#<Thread:0x1d6790>
tg group now #<Thread:0x1ca24c>
```

enclose   *thgrp*.enclose → *thgrp*

1.8 Prevents threads being added to and removed from *thgrp*. New threads may still be started.

```
thread = Thread.new { sleep 99 }
group = ThreadGroup.new
group.add(thread)
group.enclose
ThreadGroup::Default.add(thread)
```

produces:

```
prog.rb:5:in `add': can't move from the enclosed thread group (ThreadError)
        from prog.rb:5
```

enclosed?   *thgrp*.enclose → true or false

1.8 Returns true if this thread group has been enclosed.

freeze   *thgrp*.freeze

Stops new threads being added to or removed from *thgrp*. New threads may not be started.

list   *thgrp*.list → *array*

Returns an array of all existing Thread objects that belong to this group.

```
ThreadGroup::Default.list   →   [#<Thread:0x1d6790 run>]
```

Class   Time   <   Object

Time is an abstraction of dates and times. Time is stored internally as the number of seconds and microseconds since the *epoch*, January 1, 1970 00:00 UTC. On some operating systems, this offset is allowed to be negative. Also see the library modules Date and ParseDate, described on pages 665 and 713, respectively.

The Time class treats GMT (Greenwich Mean Time) and UTC (Coordinated Universal Time)[3] as equivalent. GMT is the older way of referring to these baseline times but persists in the names of calls on POSIX systems.

All times are stored with some number of microseconds. Be aware of this fact when comparing times with each other—times that are apparently equal when displayed may be different when compared.

Mixes in

Comparable:
   <, <=, ==, >=, >, between?

Class methods

at

$$\text{Time.at}(\ time\ ) \rightarrow time$$
$$\text{Time.at}(\ seconds\ \langle\,,\ microseconds\ \rangle\ ) \rightarrow time$$

1.8

Creates a new time object with the value given by *time*, or the given number of *seconds* (and optional *microseconds*) from epoch. A nonportable feature allows the offset to be negative on some systems.

```
Time.at(0)          →    Wed Dec 31 18:00:00 CST 1969
Time.at(946702800)  →    Fri Dec 31 23:00:00 CST 1999
Time.at(-284061600) →    Sat Dec 31 00:00:00 CST 1960
```

gm

$$\text{Time.gm}(\ year\ \langle\,,\ month,\ day,\ hour,\ min,\ sec,\ usec\ \rangle\ ) \rightarrow time$$
$$\text{Time.gm}(\ sec,\ min,\ hour,\ day,\ month,\ year,\ wday,\ yday,\ isdst,\ tz\ ) \rightarrow time$$

Creates a time based on given values, interpreted as UTC (GMT). The year must be specified. Other values default to the minimum value for that field (and may be nil or omitted). Months may be specified by numbers from 1 to 12 or by the three-letter English month names. Hours are specified on a 24-hour clock (0..23). Raises an ArgumentError if any values are out of range. Will also accept ten arguments in the order output by Time#to_a.

```
Time.gm(2000,"jan",1,20,15,1)   →   Sat Jan 01 20:15:01 UTC 2000
```

---

3.   Yes, UTC really does stand for Coordinated Universal Time. There was a committee involved.

local

Time.local(*year* ⟨ *, month, day, hour, min, sec, usec* ⟩) → *time*
Time.local(*sec, min, hour, day, month, year, wday, yday, isdst, tz*) → *time*

Same as `Time.gm`, but interprets the values in the local time zone. The first form can be used to construct a `Time` object given the result of a call to `ParseDate#parsedate` (described on page 713).

```
require 'parsedate'
Time.local(2000,"jan",1,20,15,1)    →   Sat Jan 01 20:15:01 CST 2000

res = ParseDate.parsedate("2000-01-01 20:15:01")
Time.local(*res)                    →   Sat Jan 01 20:15:01 CST 2000
```

mktime

Time.mktime(*year, month, day, hour, min, sec, usec*) → *time*

Synonym for `Time.local`.

new

Time.new → *time*

Returns a `Time` object initialized to the current system time. **Note:** The object created will be created using the resolution available on your system clock and so may include fractional seconds.

```
a = Time.new       →   Thu Aug 26 22:38:02 CDT 2004
b = Time.new       →   Thu Aug 26 22:38:02 CDT 2004
a == b             →   false
"%.6f" % a.to_f    →   "1093577882.292375"
"%.6f" % b.to_f    →   "1093577882.293183"
```

now

Time.now → *time*

Synonym for `Time.new`.

times

Time.times → *struct_tms*

1.8   Deprecated in favor of `Process.times`, documented on page 587.

utc

Time.utc(*year* ⟨ *, month, day, hour, min, sec, usec* ⟩) → *time*
Time.utc(*sec, min, hour, day, month, year, wday, yday, isdst, tz*) → *time*

Synonym for `Time.gm`.

```
Time.utc(2000,"jan",1,20,15,1)    →   Sat Jan 01 20:15:01 UTC 2000
```

Instance methods

+   *time + numeric → time*

Addition—Adds some number of seconds (possibly fractional) to *time* and returns that value as a new time.

```
t = Time.now          →    Thu Aug 26 22:38:02 CDT 2004
t + (60 * 60 * 24)    →    Fri Aug 27 22:38:02 CDT 2004
```

−   *time − time → float*
                                                       time − numeric → time

Difference—Returns a new time that represents the difference between two times, or subtracts the given number of seconds in *numeric* from *time*.

```
t = Time.now          →    Thu Aug 26 22:38:02 CDT 2004
t2 = t + 2592000      →    Sat Sep 25 22:38:02 CDT 2004
t2 - t                →    2592000.0
t2 - 2592000          →    Thu Aug 26 22:38:02 CDT 2004
```

<=>   *time <=> other_time → −1, 0, +1*
                                                 time <=> numeric → −1, 0, +1

Comparison—Compares *time* with *other_time* or with *numeric*, which is the number of seconds (possibly fractional) since epoch.

```
t = Time.now          →    Thu Aug 26 22:38:02 CDT 2004
t2 = t + 2592000      →    Sat Sep 25 22:38:02 CDT 2004
t <=> t2              →    -1
t2 <=> t              →    1
t <=> t               →    0
```

asctime   *time.asctime → string*

Returns a canonical string representation of *time*.

```
Time.now.asctime   →    "Thu Aug 26 22:38:02 2004"
```

ctime   *time.ctime → string*

Synonym for Time#asctime.

day   *time.day → int*

Returns the day of the month ($1..n$) for *time*.

```
t = Time.now    →    Thu Aug 26 22:38:02 CDT 2004
t.day           →    26
```

dst?   *time.*dst? → true or false

1.8 Synonym for Time#isdst.

```
Time.local(2000, 7, 1).dst?   →   true
Time.local(2000, 1, 1).dst?   →   false
```

---

getgm

1.8   Returns a new Time object representing *time* in UTC.

```
t = Time.local(2000,1,1,20,15,1)   →   Sat Jan 01 20:15:01 CST 2000
t.gmt?                             →   false
y = t.getgm                        →   Sun Jan 02 02:15:01 UTC 2000
y.gmt?                             →   true
t == y                            →   true
```

---

getlocal

1.8   Returns a new Time object representing *time* in local time (using the local time zone in effect for this process).

```
t = Time.gm(2000,1,1,20,15,1)   →   Sat Jan 01 20:15:01 UTC 2000
t.gmt?                          →   true
l = t.getlocal                  →   Sat Jan 01 14:15:01 CST 2000
l.gmt?                          →   false
t == l                         →   true
```

---

getutc

1.8   Synonym for Time#getgm.

---

gmt?

Returns true if *time* represents a time in UTC (GMT).

```
t = Time.now                    →   Thu Aug 26 22:38:02 CDT 2004
t.gmt?                          →   false
t = Time.gm(2000,1,1,20,15,1)   →   Sat Jan 01 20:15:01 UTC 2000
t.gmt?                          →   true
```

---

gmtime

Converts *time* to UTC (GMT), modifying the receiver.

```
t = Time.now   →   Thu Aug 26 22:38:02 CDT 2004
t.gmt?         →   false
t.gmtime       →   Fri Aug 27 03:38:02 UTC 2004
t.gmt?         →   true
```

---

gmt_offset

1.8   Returns the offset in seconds between the timezone of *time* and UTC.

```
t = Time.gm(2000,1,1,20,15,1)   →   Sat Jan 01 20:15:01 UTC 2000
t.gmt_offset                    →   0
l = t.getlocal                  →   Sat Jan 01 14:15:01 CST 2000
l.gmt_offset                    →   -21600
```

---

gmtoff   *time*.gmtoff → *int*

_{1.8} Synonym for `Time#gmt_offset`.

---

hour   *time*.hour → *int*

Returns the hour of the day (0..23) for *time*.

```
t = Time.now    →    Thu Aug 26 22:38:02 CDT 2004
t.hour          →    22
```

---

isdst   *time*.isdst → `true` or `false`

Returns `true` if *time* occurs during Daylight Saving Time in its time zone.

```
Time.local(2000, 7, 1).isdst    →    true
Time.local(2000, 1, 1).isdst    →    false
```

---

localtime   *time*.localtime → *time*

Converts *time* to local time (using the local time zone in effect for this process) modifying the receiver.

```
t = Time.gm(2000, "jan", 1, 20, 15, 1)
t.gmt?          →    true
t.localtime     →    Sat Jan 01 14:15:01 CST 2000
t.gmt?          →    false
```

---

mday   *time*.mday → *int*

Synonym for `Time#day`.

---

min   *time*.min → *int*

Returns the minute of the hour (0..59) for *time*.

```
t = Time.now    →    Thu Aug 26 22:38:03 CDT 2004
t.min           →    38
```

---

mon   *time*.mon → *int*

Returns the month of the year (1..12) for *time*.

```
t = Time.now    →    Thu Aug 26 22:38:03 CDT 2004
t.mon           →    8
```

---

month   *time*.month → *int*

Synonym for `Time#mon`.

---

sec $\qquad\qquad\qquad\qquad\qquad\qquad\qquad\qquad\qquad$ *time*.sec → *int*

Returns the second of the minute $(0..60)$[4] for *time*.

```
t = Time.now    →    Thu Aug 26 22:38:03 CDT 2004
t.sec           →    3
```

---

strftime $\qquad\qquad\qquad\qquad\qquad\qquad\qquad$ *time*.strftime(*format*) → *string*

Formats *time* according to the directives in the given format string. See Table 27.15 on the following page for the available values. Any text not listed as a directive will be passed through to the output string.

```
t = Time.now
t.strftime("Printed on %m/%d/%Y")    →    "Printed on 08/26/2004"
t.strftime("at %I:%M%p")             →    "at 10:38PM"
```

---

to_a $\qquad\qquad\qquad\qquad\qquad\qquad\qquad\qquad\qquad$ *time*.to_a → *array*

Returns a ten-element *array* of values for *time*: [sec, min, hour, day, month, year, wday, yday, isdst, zone]. See the individual methods for an explanation of the valid ranges of each value. The ten elements can be passed directly to the methods Time.utc or Time.local to create a new Time.

```
now = Time.now    →    Thu Aug 26 22:38:03 CDT 2004
t = now.to_a      →    [3, 38, 22, 26, 8, 2004, 4, 239, true, "CDT"]
```

---

to_f $\qquad\qquad\qquad\qquad\qquad\qquad\qquad\qquad\qquad$ *time*.to_f → *float*

Returns the value of *time* as a floating-point number of seconds since epoch.

```
t = Time.now
"%10.5f" % t.to_f    →    "1093577883.33171"
t.to_i               →    1093577883
```

---

to_i $\qquad\qquad\qquad\qquad\qquad\qquad\qquad\qquad\qquad$ *time*.to_i → *int*

Returns the value of *time* as an integer number of seconds since epoch.

```
t = Time.now
"%10.5f" % t.to_f    →    "1093577883.37052"
t.to_i               →    1093577883
```

---

to_s $\qquad\qquad\qquad\qquad\qquad\qquad\qquad\qquad\qquad$ *time*.to_s → *string*

Returns a string representing *time*. Equivalent to calling Time#strftime with a format string of %a %b %d %H:%M:%S %Z %Y.

```
Time.now.to_s    →    "Thu Aug 26 22:38:03 CDT 2004"
```

---

4.   Yes, seconds really can range from zero to 60. This allows the system to inject leap seconds every now and then to correct for the fact that years are not really a convenient number of hours long.

Table 27.15. Time#strftime directives

Format	Meaning
%a	The abbreviated weekday name ("Sun")
%A	The full weekday name ("Sunday")
%b	The abbreviated month name ("Jan")
%B	The full month name ("January")
%c	The preferred local date and time representation
%d	Day of the month (01..31)
%H	Hour of the day, 24-hour clock (00..23)
%I	Hour of the day, 12-hour clock (01..12)
%j	Day of the year (001..366)
%m	Month of the year (01..12)
%M	Minute of the hour (00..59)
%p	Meridian indicator ("AM" or "PM")
%S	Second of the minute (00..60)
%U	Week number of the current year, starting with the first Sunday as the first day of the first week (00..53)
%W	Week number of the current year, starting with the first Monday as the first day of the first week (00..53)
%w	Day of the week (Sunday is 0, 0..6)
%x	Preferred representation for the date alone, no time
%X	Preferred representation for the time alone, no date
%y	Year without a century (00..99)
%Y	Year with century
%Z	Time zone name
%%	Literal % character

---

tv_sec   *time*.tv_sec → *int*

Synonym for Time#to_i.

---

tv_usec   *time*.tv_usec → *int*

Synonym for Time#usec.

---

usec   *time*.usec → *int*

Returns just the number of microseconds for *time*.

```
t = Time.now          →   Thu Aug 26 22:38:03 CDT 2004
"%10.6f" % t.to_f     →   "1093577883.448204"
t.usec                →   448204
```

utc
time.utc → *time*

Synonym for Time#gmtime.

```
t = Time.now    →    Thu Aug 26 22:38:03 CDT 2004
t.utc?          →    false
t.utc           →    Fri Aug 27 03:38:03 UTC 2004
t.utc?          →    true
```

utc?
time.utc? → true or false

Returns true if *time* represents a time in UTC (GMT).

```
t = Time.now                            →    Thu Aug 26 22:38:03 CDT 2004
t.utc?                                  →    false
t = Time.gm(2000,"jan",1,20,15,1)       →    Sat Jan 01 20:15:01 UTC 2000
t.utc?                                  →    true
```

utc_offset
time.utc_offset → *int*

1.8 Synonym for Time#gmt_offset.

wday
time.wday → *int*

Returns an integer representing the day of the week, 0..6, with Sunday == 0.

```
t = Time.now    →    Thu Aug 26 22:38:03 CDT 2004
t.wday          →    4
```

yday
time.yday → *int*

Returns an integer representing the day of the year, 1..366.

```
t = Time.now    →    Thu Aug 26 22:38:03 CDT 2004
t.yday          →    239
```

year
time.year → *int*

Returns the year for *time* (including the century).

```
t = Time.now    →    Thu Aug 26 22:38:03 CDT 2004
t.year          →    2004
```

zone
time.zone → *string*

1.8 Returns the name of the time zone used for *time*. As of Ruby 1.8, returns "UTC" rather than "GMT" for UTC times.

```
t = Time.gm(2000, "jan", 1, 20, 15, 1)
t.zone    →    "UTC"
t = Time.local(2000, "jan", 1, 20, 15, 1)
t.zone    →    "CST"
```

| Class | **TrueClass** | < | Object |

The global value `true` is the only instance of class `TrueClass` and represents a logically true value in boolean expressions. The class provides operators allowing `true` to be used in logical expressions.

Instance methods

| **&** | true & *obj* → true or false |

And—Returns `false` if *obj* is `nil` or `false`, and returns `true` otherwise.

| **^** | true ^ *obj* → true or false |

Exclusive Or—Returns `true` if *obj* is `nil` or `false`, and returns `false` otherwise.

| **|** | true | *obj* → true |

Or—Returns `true`. As *obj* is an argument to a method call, it is always evaluated; short-circuit evaluation is not performed in this case.

```
true |  puts("or")
true || puts("logical or")
```

produces:

```
or
```

UnboundMethod < Object

1.8 Ruby supports two forms of objectified methods. Class Method is used to represent methods that are associated with a particular object: these method objects are bound to that object. Bound method objects for an object can be created using Object#method.

Ruby also supports unbound methods, which are methods objects that are not associated with a particular object. These can be created either by calling unbind on a bound method object or by calling Module#instance_method.

Unbound methods can be called only after they are bound to an object. That object must be a *kind_of?* the method's original class.

```
class Square
  def area
    @side * @side
  end
  def initialize(side)
    @side = side
  end
end

area_unbound = Square.instance_method(:area)

s = Square.new(12)
area = area_unbound.bind(s)
area.call    →    144
```

Unbound methods are a reference to the method at the time it was objectified: subsequent changes to the underlying class will not affect the unbound method.

```
class Test
  def test
    :original
  end
end
um = Test.instance_method(:test)
class Test
  def test
    :modified
  end
end
t = Test.new
t.test             →    :modified
um.bind(t).call    →    :original
```

UnboundMethod

Instance methods

---

arity   *umeth*.arity → *fixnum*

See Method#arity on page 543.

---

bind   *umeth*.bind(*obj*) → *method*

1.8   Bind *umeth* to *obj*. If Klass was the class from which *umeth* was originally obtained, obj.kind_of?(Klass) must be true.

```
class A
  def test
    puts "In test, class = #{self.class}"
  end
end
class B < A
end
class C < B
end
um = B.instance_method(:test)
bm = um.bind(C.new)
bm.call
bm = um.bind(B.new)
bm.call
bm = um.bind(A.new)
bm.call
```

produces:

```
In test, class = C
In test, class = B
prog.rb:16:in `bind': bind argument must be an instance of B (TypeError)
from prog.rb:16
```

UnboundMethod

Chapter 28

Standard Library

The Ruby interpreter comes with a large number of classes, modules, and methods built in—they are available as part of the running program. When you need a facility that isn't part of the built-in repertoire, you'll often find it in a library that you can `require` into your program.

A large number of Ruby libraries are available on the Internet. Sites such as the Ruby Application Archive[1] and RubyForge[2] have great indices and a lot of code.

However, Ruby also ships as standard with a large number of libraries. Some of these are written in pure Ruby and will be available on all Ruby platforms. Others are Ruby extensions, and some of these will be present only if your system supports the resources that they need. All can be included into your Ruby program using `require`. And, unlike libraries you may find on the Internet, you can pretty much guarantee that all Ruby users will have these libraries already installed on their machines.

In this chapter, we present the standard libraries in a new *smorgasbord* format. Rather than go into depth on a few libraries, this chapter presents the entire contents of the standard library, one entry per page. For each library we give some introductory notes and typically give an example or two of use. You won't find detailed method descriptions here: for that consult the library's own documentation.

It's all very well suggesting that you "consult the library's own documentation," but where can you find it? The answer is "it depends." Some libraries have already been documented using RDoc (see Chapter 16). That means you can use the ri command to get their documentation. For example, from a command line, you may be able to see the following documentation on the `decode64` method in the `Base64` standard library member.

---

1. `http://raa.ruby-lang.org`

2. `http://rubyforge.org`

```
% ri Base64.decode64
---------------------------------------------------- Base64#decode64
     decode64(str)
------------------------------------------------------------------------

     Returns the Base64-decoded version of str.

        require 'base64'
        str = 'VGhpcyBpcyBsaW5lIG9uZQpUaGlzIG' +
              'lzIGxpbmUgdHdvClRoaXMgaXMgbGlu' +
              'ZSBOaHJlZQpBbmQgc28gb24uLi4K'
        puts Base64.decode64(str)

     Generates:

        This is line one
        This is line two
        This is line three
        And so on...
```

If there's no RDoc documentation available, the next place to look is the library itself. If you have a source distribution of Ruby, these are in the ext/ and lib/ subdirectories. If instead you have a binary-only installation, you can still find the source of pure-Ruby library modules (normally in the lib/ruby/1.8/ directory under your Ruby installation). Often, library source directories contain documentation that the author has not yet converted to RDoc format.

If you still can't find documentation, turn to Google. Many of the Ruby standard libraries are also hosted as external projects. The authors develop them stand-alone and then periodically integrate the code into the standard Ruby distribution. For example, if you want detailed information on the API for the YAML library, Googling "yaml ruby" may lead you to http://yaml4r.sourceforge.net. After admiring *why the lucky stiff's* artwork, a click will take you to his 40+ page reference manual.

The next port of call is the ruby-talk mailing list. Ask a (polite) question there, and chances are that you'll get a knowledgeable response within hours. See page 784 for pointers on how to subscribe.

And if you *still* can't find documentation, you can always follow Obi Wan's advice and do what we did when documenting Ruby—use the source. You'd be surprised at how easy it is to read the actual source of Ruby libraries and work out the details of usage.

| Library **Abbrev** | Generate Sets of Unique Abbreviations |

Given a set of strings, calculate the set of unambiguous abbreviations for those strings, and return a hash where the keys are all the possible abbreviations and the values are the full strings. Thus, given input of "car" and "cone," the keys pointing to "car" would be "ca" and "car," and those pointing to "cone" would be "co," "con," and "cone."

An optional pattern or a string may be specified—only those input strings matching the pattern, or beginning with the string, are considered for inclusion in the output hash.

Including the Abbrev library also adds an abbrev method to class Array.

- Show the abbreviation set of some words.

```ruby
require 'abbrev'

Abbrev::abbrev(['ruby', 'rules'])    →    {"rules"=>"rules",
                                           "ruby"=>"ruby",
                                           "rul"=>"rules",
                                           "rub"=>"ruby",
                                           "rule"=>"rules"}

%w{ car cone }.abbrev                →    {"co"=>"cone",
                                           "con"=>"cone",
                                           "cone"=>"cone",
                                           "ca"=>"car", "car"=>"car"}

%w{ car cone }.abbrev("ca")          →    {"ca"=>"car",
                                           "car"=>"car"}
```

- A trivial command loop using abbreviations.

```ruby
require 'abbrev'
COMMANDS = %w{ sample send start status stop }.abbrev
while line = gets
  line = line.chomp
  case COMMANDS[line]
  when "sample":  # ...
  when "send":    # ...
  # ...
  else
    STDERR.puts "Unknown command: #{line}"
  end
end
```

B ase64

Base64

Base64 Conversion Functions

Perform encoding and decoding of binary data using a Base64 representation. This allows you to represent any binary data in purely printable characters. The encoding is specified in RFC 2045 (http://www.faqs.org/rfcs/rfc2045.html).

1.8 Prior to Ruby 1.8.2, these methods were added to the global namespace. This is now deprecated; the methods should instead be accessed as members of the Base64 module.

- Decode an encoded string.

```
require 'base64'
str = 'VGhpcyBpcyBsaW5lIG9uZQpUaGlzIG' +
      'lzIGxpbmUgdHdvClRoaXMgaXMgbGlu' +
      'ZSBOaHJlZQpBbmQgc28gb24uLi4K'
puts Base64.decode64(str)
```

produces:

```
This is line one
This is line two
This is line three
And so on...
```

- Convert and return a string.

```
require 'base64'
puts Base64.encode64("Now is the time\nto learn Ruby")
```

produces:

```
Tm93IGlzIHRoZSB0aW1lCnRvIGxlYXJuIFJ1Ynk=
```

- Convert a string into Base64 and print it to STDOUT.

```
require 'base64'
Base64.b64encode("Now is the time\nto learn Ruby")
```

produces:

```
Tm93IGlzIHRoZSB0aW1lCnRvIGxlYXJuIFJ1Ynk=
```

Library **Benchmark** — Time Code Execution

Allows code execution to be timed and the results tabulated. The Benchmark module is easier to use if you include it in your top-level environment.

See also: Profile (page 717)

- Compare the costs of three kinds of method dispatch.

```ruby
require 'benchmark'
include Benchmark
string = "Stormy Weather"
m = string.method(:length)
bm(6) do |x|
  x.report("call") { 10_000.times { m.call } }
  x.report("send") { 10_000.times { string.send(:length) } }
  x.report("eval") { 10_000.times { eval "string.length" } }
end
```

produces:

```
            user       system      total        real
call    0.020000    0.000000    0.020000 (  0.045998)
send    0.040000    0.000000    0.040000 (  0.051318)
eval    0.130000    0.000000    0.130000 (  0.177950)
```

- Which is better: reading all of a dictionary and splitting it, or splitting it line by line? Use bmbm to run a rehearsal before doing the timing.

```ruby
require 'benchmark'
include Benchmark
bmbm(6) do |x|
  x.report("all") do
    str = File.read("/usr/share/dict/words")
    words = str.scan(/[-\w']+/)
  end
  x.report("lines") do
    words = []
    File.foreach("/usr/share/dict/words") do |line|
      words << line.chomp
    end
  end
end
```

produces:

```
Rehearsal -----------------------------------------
all     0.980000    0.070000    1.050000 (  1.256552)
lines   2.310000    0.120000    2.430000 (  2.720674)
------------------------------- total: 3.480000sec

            user       system      total        real
all     0.870000    0.030000    0.900000 (  0.949623)
lines   1.720000    0.030000    1.750000 (  1.926910)
```

| Library **BigDecimal** | Large-Precision Decimal Numbers |

Ruby's standard `Bignum` class supports integers with large numbers of digits. The `BigDecimal` class supports decimal numbers with large numbers of decimal places. The standard library supports all the normal arithmetic operations. `BigDecimal` also comes with some extension libraries.

bigdecimal/ludcmp
> Performs an LU decomposition of a matrix.

bigdecimal/math
> Provides the transcendental functions *sqrt*, *sin*, *cos*, *atan*, *exp*, and *log*, along with functions for computing *PI* and *E*. All functions take an arbitrary precision argument.

bigdecimal/jacobian
> Constructs the Jacobian (a matrix enumerating the partial derivatives) of a given function. Not dependent on `BigDecimal`.

bigdecimal/newton
> Solves the roots of nonlinear function using Newton's method. Not dependent on `BigDecimal`.

bigdecimal/nlsolve
> Wraps the `bigdecimal/newton` library for equations of `BigDecimals`.

You can find English-language documentation in the Ruby source distribution in the file `ext/bigdecimal/bigdecimal_en.html`.

```
require 'bigdecimal'
require 'bigdecimal/math'
include BigMath

pi = BigMath::PI(20)     # 20 is the number of decimal digits

radius = BigDecimal("2.14156987652974674392")

area = pi * radius**2

area.to_s             →     "0.14408354044685604417672003380667956168
                             85998464104450325832158247587804055458 61
                             780909930190528E2"

# The same with regular floats

radius = 2.14156987652974674392

Math::PI * radius**2  →     14.4083540446856
```

The CGI class provides support for programs used as CGI (Common Gateway Interface) scripts in a Web server. CGI objects are initialized with data from the environment and from the HTTP request, and they provide convenient accessors to form data and cookies. They can also manage sessions using a variety of storage mechanisms. Class CGI also provides basic facilities for HTML generation and class methods to escape and unescape requests and HTML.

1.8 **Note:** The 1.8 implementation of CGI introduces a change in the way form data is accessed. See the `ri` documentation of `CGI#[]` and `CGI#params` for details.

See also: `CGI::Session` (page 661)

- Escape and unescape special characters in URLs and HTML. If the `$KCODE` variable is set to "u" (for UTF8), the library will convert from HTML's Unicode to internal UTF8.

```
require 'cgi'
CGI.escape('c:\My Files')              →   c%3A%5CMy+Files
CGI.unescape('c%3a%5cMy+Files')       →   c:\My Files
CGI::escapeHTML('"a"<b & c')           →   &quot;a&quot;&lt;b &amp; c

$KCODE = "u"   # Use UTF8
CGI.unescapeHTML('&quot;a&quot;&lt;=&gt;b')   →   "a"<=>b
CGI.unescapeHTML('&#65;&#x41;')               →   AA
CGI.unescapeHTML('&#x3c0;r&#178;')            →   πr²
```

- Access information from the incoming request.

```
require 'cgi'
c = CGI.new
c.auth_type    →   "basic"
c.user_agent   →   "Mozscape Explorari V5.6"
```

- Access form fields from an incoming request. Assume the following script is installed as `test.cgi` and the user linked to it using `http://mydomain.com/test.cgi?fred=10&barney=cat`.

```
require 'cgi'
c = CGI.new
c['fred']   →   "10"
c.keys      →   ["barney", "fred"]
c.params    →   {"barney"=>["cat"], "fred"=>["10"]}
```

- If a form contains multiple fields with the same name, the corresponding values will be returned to the script as an array. The [ ] accessor returns just the first of these—index the result of the `params` method to get them all. In this example, assume the form has three fields called "name."

```
require 'cgi'
c = CGI.new
c['name']              →    "fred"
c.params['name']       →    ["fred", "wilma", "barney"]
c.keys                 →    ["name"]
c.params               →    {"name"=>["fred", "wilma", "barney"]}
```

- Send a response to the browser. (Not many folks use this form of HTML generation. Consider one of the templating libraries—see page 239.)

```
require 'cgi'
cgi = CGI.new("html4Tr")
cgi.header("type" => "text/html", "expires" => Time.now + 30)
cgi.out do
  cgi.html do
    cgi.head{ cgi.title{"Hello World!"} } +
    cgi.body do
      cgi.pre do
        CGI::escapeHTML(
          "params: " + cgi.params.inspect + "\n" +
          "cookies: " + cgi.cookies.inspect + "\n")
      end
    end
  end
end
```

- Store a cookie in the client browser.

```
require 'cgi'
cgi = CGI.new("html4")
cookie = CGI::Cookie.new('name' => 'mycookie',
                         'value' => 'chocolate chip',
                         'expires' => Time.now + 3600)
cgi.out('cookie' => cookie) do
  cgi.head + cgi.body { "Cookie stored" }
end
```

- Retrieve a previously stored cookie.

```
require 'cgi'
cgi = CGI.new("html4")
cookie = cgi.cookies['mycookie']
cgi.out('cookie' => cookie) do
  cgi.head + cgi.body { "Flavor: " + cookie[0] }
end
```

Library **CGI::Session** CGI Sessions

A CGI::Session maintains a persistent state for Web users in a CGI environment. Sessions may be memory resident or may be stored on disk. See the discussion on page 246 for details.

See also: CGI (page 659)

```ruby
require 'cgi'
require 'cgi/session'
cgi = CGI.new("html3")
sess = CGI::Session.new(cgi,
                        "session_key" => "rubyweb",
                        "prefix" => "web-session."
                        )
if sess['lastaccess']
  msg = "You were last here #{sess['lastaccess']}."
else
  msg = "Looks like you haven't been here for a while"
end
count = (sess["accesscount"] || 0).to_i
count += 1
msg << "<p>Number of visits: #{count}"
sess["accesscount"] = count
sess["lastaccess"]  = Time.now.to_s
sess.close
cgi.out {
  cgi.html {
    cgi.body {
      msg
    }
  }
}
```

C omplex

| Library | **Complex** | Complex Numbers |

Class `Complex` represents complex numbers. As well as the methods here, including class `Complex` in your program alters class `Numeric` (and subclasses) in order to give the illusion that *all* numbers are complex (by giving them the methods `real`, `image`, `arg`, `polar`, `conjugate`, and `power`!).

```
require 'complex'
include Math

v1 = Complex(2,3)      →   Complex(2, 3)
v2 = 2.im              →   Complex(0, 2)
v1 + v2                →   Complex(2, 5)
v1 * v2                →   Complex(-6, 4)
v2**2                  →   Complex(-4, 0)
cos(v1)                →   Complex(-4.18962569096881, -9.10922789375534)
v1 < v2                →   false
v2**2 == -4            →   true

# Euler's theorem
E**(PI*Complex::I)     →   Complex(-1.0, 1.22464679914735e-16)
```

| Library | **CSV** | Comma-Separated Values |

C SV

Comma-separated data files are often used to transfer tabular information (and are a *lingua franca* for importing and exporting spreadsheet and database information).

Ruby's CSV library deals with arrays (corresponding to the rows in the CSV file) and strings (corresponding to the elements in a row). If an element in a row is missing, it will be represented as a `nil` in Ruby.

The files used in the following examples are:

csvfile:
```
12,eggs,2.89,
2,"shirt, blue",21.45,special
1,"""Hello Kitty"" bag",13.99
```

csvfile_hdr:
```
Count, Description, Price
12,eggs,2.89,
2,"shirt, blue",21.45,special
1,"""Hello Kitty"" bag",13.99
```

- Read a file containing CSV data and process line-by-line.

```ruby
require 'csv'
CSV.open("csvfile", "r") do |row|
  qty = row[0].to_i
  price = row[2].to_f
  printf "%20s: $%5.2f %s\n", row[1], qty*price, row[3] || "  ---"
end
```

produces:

```
            eggs: $34.68   ---
     shirt, blue: $42.90 special
"Hello Kitty" bag: $13.99   ---
```

- Some CSV files have a header line. Read it, and then process the rest of the file.

```ruby
require 'csv'
reader = CSV.open("csvfile_hdr", "r")
header = reader.shift
reader.each {|row| process(header, row) }
```

- Write CSV data to an existing open stream (STDOUT in this case). Use | as the column separator.

```ruby
require 'csv'
CSV::Writer.generate(STDOUT, '|') do |csv|
  csv << [ 1, "line 1", 27 ]
  csv << [ 2, nil, 123 ]
  csv << [ 3, "|bar|", 32.5]
end
```

produces:

```
1|line 1|27
2||123
3|"|bar|"|32.5
```

Library

Curses   CRT Screen Handling

Only if: curses or ncurses installed in target environment

The Curses library is a fairly thin wrapper around the C curses or ncurses libraries, allowing applications a device-independent way of drawing on consoles and other terminal-like devices. As a nod toward object-orientation, curses windows and mouse events are represented as Ruby objects. Otherwise, the standard curses calls and constants are simply defined in the Curses module.

```ruby
# Draw the paddle of a simple game of 'pong'. It moves
# in response to the up and down keys
require 'curses'
include Curses
class Paddle
  HEIGHT = 4
  PADDLE = " \n" + "|\n"*HEIGHT + " "
  def initialize
    @top = (Curses::lines - HEIGHT)/2
    draw
  end
  def up
    @top -= 1 if @top > 1
  end
  def down
    @top += 1 if (@top + HEIGHT + 1) < lines
  end
  def draw
    setpos(@top-1, 0)
    addstr(PADDLE)
    refresh
  end
end
init_screen
begin
  crmode
  noecho
  stdscr.keypad(true)
  paddle = Paddle.new
  loop do
    case getch
    when ?Q, ?q    :  break
    when Key::UP   :  paddle.up
    when Key::DOWN :  paddle.down
    else beep
    end
    paddle.draw
  end
ensure
  close_screen
end
```

Library **Date/DateTime**   Date and Time Manipulation

The `date` library implements classes `Date` and `DateTime`, which provide a comprehensive set of facilities for storing, manipulating, and converting dates with or without time components. The classes can represent and manipulate civil, ordinal, commercial, Julian, and standard dates, starting January 1, 4713 BCE. The `DateTime` class extends `Date` with hours, minutes, seconds, and fractional seconds, and it provides some support for time zones. The classes also provide support for parsing and formatting date and datetime strings. The classes have a rich interface—consult the `ri` documentation for details. The introductory notes in the file `lib/date.rb` are also well worth reading.

See also: `ParseDate` (page 713)

- Experiment with various representations

```
require 'date'

d = Date.new(2000, 3, 31)                 →   #<Date:
                                              4903269/2,0,2299161>
[d.year, d.yday, d.wday]                   →   [2000, 91, 5]
[d.month, d.mday]                          →   [3, 31]
[d.cwyear, d.cweek, d.cwday]               →   [2000, 13, 5]
[d.jd, d.mjd]                              →   [2451635, 51634]
d1 = Date.commercial(2000, 13, 7)          →   #<Date:
                                              4903273/2,0,2299161>
d1.to_s                                    →   "2000-04-02"
[d1.cwday, d1.wday]                        →   [7, 0]
```

- Essential information about Christmas.

```
require 'date'
now = DateTime.now
year = now.year
year += 1 if now.month -- 12 && now.day > 25
xmas = DateTime.new(year, 12, 25)

diff = xmas - now

puts "It's #{diff.to_i} days to Christmas"
h,m,s,frac = Date.day_fraction_to_time(diff)
s += frac.to_f
puts "That's #{h} hours, #{m} minutes, #{s} seconds"
puts "Christmas falls on a #{xmas.strftime('%A')}"
```

produces:

```
It's 119 days to Christmas
That's 2876 hours, 21 minutes, 28.0000094433912 seconds
Christmas falls on a Saturday
```

| Library **DBM** | Interface to DBM Databases |

DBM files implement simple, hashlike persistent stores. Many DBM implementations exist—the Ruby library can be configured to use one of the DBM libraries db, dbm (ndbm), gdbm, and qdbm. The interface to DBM files is similar to class Hash, except that DBM keys and values will be strings. This can cause confusion, as the conversion to a string is performed silently when the data is written. The DBM library is a wrapper around the lower-level access method. For true low-level access, see also the GDBM and SDBM libraries.

Only if: a DBM library is installed in target environment

See also: gdbm (page 682), sdbm (page 730)

- Create a simple DBM file, then re-open it read-only and read some data. Note the conversion of a date object to its string form.

```
require 'dbm'
require 'date'
DBM.open("data.dbm") do |dbm|
  dbm['name'] = "Walter Wombat"
  dbm['dob']  = Date.new(1997, 12,25)
end
DBM.open("data.dbm", nil, DBM::READER) do |dbm|
  p dbm.keys
  p dbm['dob']
  p dbm['dob'].class
end
```

produces:

```
["name", "dob"]
"1997-12-25"
String
```

- Read from the system's *aliases* file. Note the trailing null bytes on all strings.

```
require 'dbm'
DBM.open("/etc/aliases", nil) do |dbm|
  p dbm.keys
  p dbm["postfix\000"]
end
```

produces:

```
["postmaster\000", "daemon\000", "ftp-bugs\000",
 "operator\000", "abuse\000", "decode\000", "@\000",
 "mailer-daemon\000", "bin\000", "named\000", "nobody\
000", "uucp\000", "www\000", "postfix\000", "manager\
000", "dumper\000"]
"root\000"
```

Library **Delegator**   Delegate Calls to Other Object

Object delegation is a way of *composing* objects—extending an object with the capabilities of another—at runtime. The Ruby `Delegator` class implements a simple but powerful delegation scheme, where requests are automatically forwarded from a master class to delegates or their ancestors and where the delegate can be changed at runtime with a single method call.

See also: Forwardable (page 680)

- For simple cases where the class of the delegate is fixed, make the master class a subclass of `DelegateClass`, passing the name of the class to be delegated as a parameter. In the master class's `initialize` method, pass the object to be delegated to the superclass.

```
require 'delegate'

class Words < DelegateClass(Array)
  def initialize(list = "/usr/share/dict/words")
    words = File.read(list).split
    super(words)
  end
end


words = Words.new
words[9999]             →    "anticritique"
words.size              →    234937
words.grep(/matz/)      →    ["matzo", "matzoon", "matzos", "matzoth"]
```

- Use `SimpleDelegator` to delegate to a particular object (which can be changed).

```
require 'delegate'

words = File.read("/usr/share/dict/words").split
names = File.read("/usr/share/dict/propernames").split

stats = SimpleDelegator.new(words)
stats.size    →   234937
stats[226]    →   "abidingly"
stats.__setobj__(names)
stats.size    →   1323
stats[226]    →   "Dave"
```

Library **Digest** MD5, RIPEMD-160 SHA1, and SHA2 Digests

The Digest module is the home for a number of classes that implement secure digest algorithms: MD5, RIPEMD-160, SHA1, and SHA2 (256, 384, and 512 bit). The interface to all these classes is identical.

- You can create a binary or hex digest for a given string by calling the class method digest or hexdigest.

- You can also create an object (optionally passing in an initial string) and determine the object's hash by calling the digest or hexdigest instance methods. In this case you can then append to the string using the update method and then recover an updated hash value.

- Calculate some MD5 and SHA1 hashes.

```
require 'digest/md5'
require 'digest/sha1'

for hash_class in [ Digest::MD5, Digest::SHA1 ]
  puts "Using #{hash_class.name}"

  # Calculate directly
  puts hash_class.hexdigest("hello world")

  # Or by accumulating
  digest = hash_class.new
  digest << "hello"
  digest << " "
  digest << "world"
  puts digest.hexdigest
  puts
end
```

produces:

```
Using Digest::MD5
5eb63bbbe01eeed093cb22bb8f5acdc3
5eb63bbbe01eeed093cb22bb8f5acdc3

Using Digest::SHA1
2aae6c35c94fcfb415dbe95f408b9ce91ee846ed
2aae6c35c94fcfb415dbe95f408b9ce91ee846ed
```

The DL module interfaces to the underlying operating system's dynamic loading capabilities. On Windows boxes, it can be used to interface with functions in DLLs (replacing the Win32API class—see dl/win32 for a compatible wrapper library). Under Unix it can load shared libraries. Because Ruby does not have typed method parameters or return values, you must define the types expected by the methods you call by specifying their signatures. This can be done using a C-like syntax (if you use the high-level methods in dl/import) or using explicit type specifiers in the lower-level DL module. Good documentation is provided in the source tree's ext/dl/doc/ directory.

See also: Win32API (page 755)

- Here's a trivial C program that we'll build as a shared library.

```
#include <stdio.h>
int print_msg(text, number) {
  return printf("Text: %s (%d)\n", text, number);
}
```

- Generate a proxy to access the print_msg method in the shared library. The way this book is built, the shared library ends up in the subdirectory code/dl; this explains the name in the dlopen call.

```
require 'dl'
Message = DL.dlopen("code/dl/lib.so")
print_msg = Message[ "print_msg", "ISI" ]
msg_size, args = print_msg.call("Answer", 42)
puts "Just wrote #{msg_size} bytes"
```

produces:

```
Text: Answer (42)
Just wrote 18 bytes
```

- We can also wrap the method in a module. Here we use an environment variable to set the path to the shared object. This is operating system specific.

```
ENV['DYLD_LIBRARY_PATH'] = ":code/dl"  # Mac OS X
require 'dl/import'
module Message
  extend DL::Importable
  dlload "lib.so"
  extern "int print_msg(char *, int)"
end
msg_size = Message.print_msg("Answer", 42)
puts "Just wrote #{msg_size} bytes"
```

produces:

```
Text: Answer (42)
Just wrote 18 bytes
```

Library	**dRuby**	Distributed Ruby Objects (drb)

dRuby allows Ruby objects to be distributed across a network connection. Although expressed in terms of clients and servers, once the initial connection is established, the protocol is effectively symmetrical: either side can invoke methods in objects on the other side. Normally, objects passed and returned by remote calls are passed by value; including the DRbUndumped module in an object forces it to be passed by reference (useful when implementing callbacks).

See also: Rinda (page 727), XMLRPC (page 757)

- This server program is *observable*—it notifies all registered listeners of changes to a count value.

```ruby
require 'drb'
require 'drb/observer'
class Counter
  include DRb::DRbObservable
  def run
    5.times do |count|
      changed
      notify_observers(count)
    end
  end
end
counter = Counter.new
DRb.start_service('druby://localhost:9001', counter)
DRb.thread.join
```

- This client program interacts with the server, registering a listener object to receive callbacks before invoking the server's run method.

```ruby
require 'drb'
class Listener
  include DRbUndumped
  def update(value)
    puts value
  end
end
DRb.start_service
counter = DRbObject.new(nil, "druby://localhost:9001")
listener = Listener.new
counter.add_observer(listener)
counter.run
```

Library **English** — English Names For Global Symbols

Include the English library file in a Ruby script, and you can reference the global variables such as $_ using less-cryptic names, listed in the following table.

$*	$ARGV	$"	$LOADED_FEATURES
$?	$CHILD_STATUS	$&	$MATCH
$<	$DEFAULT_INPUT	$.	$NR
$>	$DEFAULT_OUTPUT	$,	$OFS
$!	$ERROR_INFO	$\	$ORS
$@	$ERROR_POSITION	$,	$OUTPUT_FIELD_SEPARATOR
$;	$FIELD_SEPARATOR	$\	$OUTPUT_RECORD_SEPARATOR
$;	$FS	$$	$PID
$=	$IGNORECASE	$'	$POSTMATCH
$.	$INPUT_LINE_NUMBER	$`	$PREMATCH
$/	$INPUT_RECORD_SEPARATOR	$$	$PROCESS_ID
$~	$LAST_MATCH_INFO	$0	$PROGRAM_NAME
$+	$LAST_PAREN_MATCH	$/	$RS
$_	$LAST_READ_LINE		

```ruby
require 'English'
$OUTPUT_FIELD_SEPARATOR = ' -- '
"waterbuffalo" =~ /buff/
print $LOADED_FEATURES, $POSTMATCH, $PID, "\n"
print $", $', $$, "\n"
```

produces:

```
English.rb -- alo -- 28035 --
English.rb -- alo -- 28035 --
```

Library	**Enumerator**	Define External Iterators

The Ruby convention is that enumerable objects should define a method called each that returns the contents one item at a time. This each method is used as the basis of the Enumerable module, as well as the built-in for loop. Even if a class defines multiple enumeration methods, Enumerable can only use each.

The Enumerator module creates a new iterable object based on an existing object, mapping the each method in the new object to an arbitrary method in the original. This allows you to use standard Ruby enumeration techniques on arbitrary methods.

See also: Enumerable (page 454), Generator (page 683)

- Define an external iterator that returns all the keys in a hash.

```
require 'enumerator'
hash = { "cow" => "bovine", "cat" => "feline", "dog" => "canine" }
key_iter = Enumerable::Enumerator.new(hash, :each_key)
puts "Max key is #{key_iter.max}"
for key in key_iter
  puts "Key is #{key}"
end
```

produces:

```
Max key is dog
Key is cat
Key is cow
Key is dog
```

- Methods to_enum and enum_for also create Enumerator objects.

```
require 'enumerator'
hash = { "cow" => "bovine", "cat" => "feline", "dog" => "canine" }
key_iter = hash.enum_for(:each_key)
key_iter.min   →   "cat"
key_iter.max   →   "dog"
```

- Methods each_slice and each_cons return elements from an enumeration *n* elements at a time. each_slice returns disjoint sets, and each_cons returns a moving window over the collection.

```
require 'enumerator'
(1..7).each_slice(3) {|slice| print slice.inspect, " " }
puts
(1..7).each_cons(3)  {|cons|  print cons.inspect, " " }
```

produces:

```
[1, 2, 3] [4, 5, 6] [7]
[1, 2, 3] [2, 3, 4] [3, 4, 5] [4, 5, 6] [5, 6, 7]
```

ERB is a lightweight templating system, allowing you to intermix Ruby code and plain text. This is sometimes a convenient way to create HTML documents but also is usable in other plain-text situations. For other templating solutions, see 239.

ERB breaks its input text into checks of regular text and program fragments. It then builds a Ruby program that, when run, outputs the result text and executes the program fragments. Program fragments are enclosed between <% and %> markers. The exact interpretation of these fragments depends on the character following the opening <%, as shown in Table 28.1 on the next page.

```
require 'erb'
input = %{\
<% high.downto(low) do |n|   # set high, low externally %>
  <%= n %> green bottles, hanging on the wall
  <%= n %> green bottles, hanging on the wall
  And if one green bottle should accidentally fall
  There'd be <%= n-1 %> green bottles, hanging on the wall
<% end %>
}
high,low = 10, 8
erb = ERB.new(input)
erb.run
```

produces:

```
10 green bottles, hanging on the wall
10 green bottles, hanging on the wall
And if one green bottle should accidentally fall
There'd be 9 green bottles, hanging on the wall
      . . .
```

An optional second parameter to ERB.new sets the safe level for evaluating expressions. If nil, expressions are evaluated in the current thread; otherwise a new thread is created, and its $SAFE level is set to the parameter value.

The optional third parameter to ERB.new allows some control of the interpretation of the input and of the way whitespace is added to the output. If the third parameter is a string, and that string contains a percent sign, then ERB treats lines starting with a percent sign specially. Lines starting with a single percent sign are treated as if they were enclosed in <%...%>. Lines starting with a double percent sign are copied to the output with a single leading percent sign.

```
str = %{\
% 2.times do |i|
  This is line <%= i %>
%end
%% done}
ERB.new(str, 0, '%').run
```

produces:

⇒
```
  This is line 0
  This is line 1
% done
```

E rb

Table 28.1. Directives for ERB

Sequence	Action
<% *ruby code* %>	Insert the given Ruby code at this point in the generated program. If it outputs anything, include this output in the result.
<%= *ruby expression* %>	Evaluate expression and insert its value in the output of the generated program.
<%# ... %>	Comment (ignored).
<%% and %%>	Replaced in the output by <% and%> respectively.

If the third parameter contains the string <> then a newline will not be written if an input line starts with an ERB directive and ends with %>. If the trim parameter contains >, then a newline will not be written if an input line ends %>.

```
str1 = %{\
* <%= "cat" %>
<%= "dog" %>
}
ERB.new(str1, 0, ">").run
ERB.new(str1, 0, "<>").run
```

produces:

```
* catdog* cat
dog
```

The erb library also defines the helper module ERB::Util that contains two methods: html_escape (aliased as h) and url_encode (aliased as u). These are equivalent to the CGI methods escapeHTML and escape, respectively (except escape encodes spaces as plus signs, and url_encode uses %20).

```
include ERB::Util
str1 = %{\
h(a) = <%= h(a) %>
u(a) = <%= u(a) %>
}
a = "< a & b >"
ERB.new(str1).run
```

produces:

```
h(a) = &lt; a &amp; b &gt;
u(a) = %3C%20a%20%26%20b%20%3E
```

You may find the command-line utility erb is supplied with your Ruby distribution. This allows you to run erb substitutions on an input file; see erb --help for details.

Etc
Access User and Group Information in /etc/passwd

Only if: Unix or Cygwin

The Etc module provides a number of methods for querying the passwd and group facilities on Unix systems.

- Find out information about the currently logged-in user.

```
require 'etc'

name = Etc.getlogin
info = Etc.getpwnam(name)
info.name   →   "dave"
info.uid    →   502
info.dir    →   "/Users/dave"
info.shell  →   "/bin/bash"

group = Etc.getgrgid(info.gid)
group.name  →   "dave"
```

- Return the names of all users and groups on the system used to create this book.

```
require 'etc'

users = []
Etc.passwd {|passwd| users << passwd.name }
users.join(", ")   →   "nobody, root, daemon, unknown, smmsp, lp,
                        postfix, www, eppc, mysql, sshd, qtss,
                        cyrus, mailman, appserver, dave, testuser"

groups = []
Etc.group {|group| groups << group.name }
groups.join(", ")  →   "nobody, nogroup, wheel, daemon, kmem,
                        sys, tty, operator, mail, bin, staff,
                        smmsp, lp, postfix, postdrop, guest, utmp,
                        uucp, dialer, network, www, mysql, sshd,
                        qtss, mailman, appserverusr, admin,
                        appserveradm, unknown, dave, testuser"
```

Library		
expect		Expect Method for IO Objects

The expect library adds the method expect to all IO objects. This allows you to write code that waits for a particular string or pattern to be available from the I/O stream. The expect method is particularly useful with pty objects (see page 720) and with network connections to remote servers, where it can be used to coordinate the use of external interactive processes.

If the global variable $expect_verbose is true, the expect method writes all characters read from the I/O stream to STDOUT.

See also: pty (page 720)

- Connect to the local FTP server, log in, and print out the name of the user's directory. (Note that it would be a lot easier to do this using the library.)

```
# This code might be specific to the particular
# ftp daemon.
require 'expect'
require 'socket'
$expect_verbose = true
socket = TCPSocket.new('localhost', 'ftp')
socket.expect("ready")
socket.puts("user testuser")
socket.expect("Password required for testuser")
socket.puts("pass secret")
socket.expect("logged in.\r\n")
socket.puts("pwd")
puts(socket.gets)
socket.puts "quit"
```

produces:

```
220 localhost FTP server (lukemftpd 1.1) ready.
331 Password required for testuser.
230-
    Welcome to Darwin!
230 User testuser logged in.
257 "/Users/testuser" is the current directory.
```

The Fcntl module provides symbolic names for each of the host system's available fcntl constants (defined in fcntl.h). That is, if the host system has a constant named F_GETLK defined in fcntl.h, then the Fcntl module will have a corresponding constant Fcntl::F_GETLK with the same value as the header file's #define.

- Different operating system will have different Fcntl constants available. The value associated with a constant of a given name may also differ across platforms. Here are the values on my Mac OS X system.

```
require 'fcntl'
Fcntl.constants.sort.each do |name|
  printf "%10s: %04x\n", name, Fcntl.const_get(name)
end
```

produces:

```
FD_CLOEXEC: 0001
   F_DUPFD: 0000
   F_GETFD: 0001
   F_GETFL: 0003
   F_GETLK: 0007
   F_RDLCK: 0001
   F_SETFD: 0002
   F_SETFL: 0004
   F_SETLK: 0008
  F_SETLKW: 0009
   F_UNLCK: 0002
   F_WRLCK: 0003
 O_ACCMODE: 0003
  O_APPEND: 0008
   O_CREAT: 0200
    O_EXCL: 0800
  O_NDELAY: 0004
  O_NOCTTY: 0000
O_NONBLOCK: 0004
  O_RDONLY: 0000
    O_RDWR: 0002
   O_TRUNC: 0400
  O_WRONLY: 0001
```

Library **FileUtils**   File and Directory Manipulation

FileUtils is a collection of methods for manipulating files and directories. Although generally applicable, the model is particularly useful when writing installation scripts.

Many methods take a *src* and a *dest* parameter. If *dest* is a directory, then *src* may be a single filename or an array of filenames. For example, the following copies the files a, b, and c to /tmp.

```
cp( %w{ a b c }, "/tmp")
```

Most functions take a set of options. These may be zero or more of

Option	Meaning
:verbose	Trace execution of each function (by default to STDERR, although this can be overridden by setting the class variable @fileutils_output).
:noop	Do not perform the action of the function (useful for testing scripts).
:force	Override some default conservative behavior of the method (for example overwriting an existing file).
:preserve	Attempt to preserve atime, mtime, and mode information from *src* in *dest*. (Setuid and setgid flags are always cleared.)

For maximum portability, use forward slashes to separate the directory components of filenames, even on Windows.

FileUtils contains three submodules which duplicate the top-level methods but with different default options: module FileUtils::Verbose sets the verbose option, module FileUtils::NoWrite sets noop, and FileUtils::DryRun sets verbose and noop.

See also: un (page 751)

```
require 'fileutils'
include FileUtils::Verbose
cd("/tmp") do
  cp("/etc/passwd", "tmp_passwd")
  chmod(0666, "tmp_passwd")
  cp_r("/usr/include/net/", "headers")
  rm("tmp_passwd")        # Tidy up
  rm_rf("headers")
end
```

produces:

```
cd /tmp
cp /etc/passwd tmp_passwd
chmod 666 tmp_passwd
cp -r /usr/include/net/ headers
rm tmp_passwd
rm -rf headers
cd -
```

| Library | **Find** | Traverse Directory Trees |

The Find module supports the top-down traversal of a set of file paths, given as arguments to the find method. If an argument is a file, its name is passed to the block. If it's a directory, then its name and the name of all its files and subdirectories will be passed in.

Within the block, the method prune may be called, which skips the current file or directory, restarting the loop with the next directory. If the current file is a directory, that directory will not be recursively entered.

```
require 'find'
Find.find("/etc/passwd", "code/cdjukebox") do |f|
  type = case
         when File.file?(f): "F"
         when File.directory?(f): "D"
         else "?"
         end
  puts "#{type}: #{f}"
  Find.prune if f =~ /CVS/
end
```

produces:

```
F: /etc/passwd
D: code/cdjukebox
F: code/cdjukebox/Makefile
F: code/cdjukebox/libcdjukebox.a
D: code/cdjukebox/CVS
F: code/cdjukebox/cdjukebox.o
F: code/cdjukebox/cdjukebox.h
F: code/cdjukebox/cdjukebox.c
```

| Library | **Forwardable** | Object Delegation |

Forwardable provides a mechanism to allow classes to delegate named method calls to other objects.

See also: `Delegator` (page 667)

- This simple symbol table uses a hash, exposing a subset of the hash's methods.

```
require 'forwardable'

class SymbolTable
  extend Forwardable
  def_delegator(:@hash, :[],  :lookup)
  def_delegator(:@hash, :[]=, :add)
  def_delegators(:@hash, :size, :has_key?)
  def initialize
    @hash = Hash.new
  end
end

st = SymbolTable.new
st.add('cat', 'feline animal')   →    "feline animal"
st.add('dog', 'canine animal')   →    "canine animal"
st.add('cow', 'bovine animal')   →    "bovine animal"

st.has_key?('cow')               →    true
st.lookup('dog')                 →    "canine animal"
```

- Forwards can also be defined for individual objects by extending them with the `SingleForwardable` module. It's hard to think of a good reason to use this feature, so here's a silly one....

```
require 'forwardable'
TRICKS = [ "roll over", "play dead" ]
dog = "rover"
dog.extend SingleForwardable
dog.def_delegator(:TRICKS, :each, :can)
dog.can do |trick|
  puts trick
end
```

produces:

```
roll over
play dead
```

Library ftools   Extra Tools for Class File

The ftools library adds methods to class File, primarily aimed at programs that move and copy files, such as installers. The FileUtils library is now recommended over ftools.

See also: fileutils (page 678)

- Install the file testfile into the /tmp directory. Don't bother copying the file if the target already exists and is the same as the original.

```
require 'ftools'
def install_if_different(source, dest)
  if File.exist?(dest) && File.compare(source, dest)
    puts "#{dest} is up to date"
  else
    File.copy(source, dest)
    puts "#{source} copied to #{dest}"
  end
end
install_if_different('testfile', '/tmp/testfile')
puts "Second time..."
install_if_different('testfile', '/tmp/testfile')
puts "Done"
```

produces:

```
testfile copied to /tmp/testfile
Second time...
/tmp/testfile is up to date
Done
```

- Do the same (with slightly different logging) using FTool's install method.

```
require 'ftools'
File.install('testfile', '/tmp', 0644, true)
puts "Second time..."
File.install('testfile', '/tmp', 0644, true)
puts "Done"
```

produces:

```
testfile -> /tmp/testfile
chmod 0644 /tmp/testfile
Second time...
Done
```

DBM

G DBM

| Library GDBM | Interface to GDBM Database |

Interfaces to the gdbm database library.[3] Although the DBM library provides generic access to gdbm databases, it doesn't expose some features of the full gdbm interface. The GDBM library gives you access to underlying gdbm features such as the cache size, synchronization mode, reorganization, and locking. Only one process may have a GDBM database open for writing (unless locking is disabled).

Only if: gdbm library available

See also: DBM (page 666), SDBM (page 730)

- Store some values into a database, and then read them back. The second parameter to the open method specifies the file mode, and the next parameter uses two flags which (1) create the database if it doesn't exist, and (2) force all writes to be synced to disk. Create on open is the default Ruby gdbm behavior.

```
require 'gdbm'
GDBM.open("data.dbm", 0644, GDBM::WRCREAT | GDBM::SYNC) do |dbm|
  dbm['name'] = "Walter Wombat"
  dbm['dob']  = "1969-12-25"
  dbm['uses'] = "Ruby"
end
GDBM.open("data.dbm") do |dbm|
  p dbm.keys
  p dbm['dob']
  dbm.delete('dob')
  p dbm.keys
end
```

produces:

```
["uses", "dob", "name"]
"1969-12-25"
["uses", "name"]
```

- Open a database read-only. Note that the attempt to delete a key fails.

```
require 'gdbm'
GDBM.open("data.dbm", 0, GDBM::READER) do |dbm|
  p dbm.keys
  dbm.delete('name')
end
```

produces:

```
["uses", "name"]
prog.rb:4:in `delete': Reader can't delete (GDBMError)
from prog.rb:4
from prog.rb:2:in `open'
```

---

3.   http://www.gnu.org/software/gdbm/gdbm.html

| Library | **Generator** | External Iterators |

The generator library implements external iterators (as in Java and C++) based either on Enumerable objects or on a block that yields values. The Generator class is a simple iterator. The library also include SyncEnumerator, which creates an Enumerable object that iterates over several collections at once.

See also: Enumerable (page 454), Enumerator (page 672)

- Iterate over an Enumerable object.

```
require 'generator'
gen = Generator.new(1..4)
while gen.next?
  print gen.next, "--"
end
```

produces:

```
1--2--3--4--
```

- Iterate over a block.

```
require 'generator'
gen = Generator.new do |result|
  result.yield "Start"
  3.times {|i| result.yield i}
  result.yield "done"
end
while gen.next?
  print gen.next, "--"
end
```

produces:

```
Start--0--1--2--done--
```

- Iterate over two collections at once.

```
require 'generator'
gen = SyncEnumerator.new(1..3, "a".."c")
gen.each {|num, char| print num, "(", char, ") " }
```

produces:

```
1(a) 2(b) 3(c)
```

GetoptLong — Parse Command-Line Options

Library

Class `GetoptLong` supports GNU-style command-line option parsing. Options may be a minus sign (–) followed by a single character, or two minus signs (- -) followed by a name (a long option). Long options may be abbreviated to their shortest unambiguous lengths.

A single internal option may have multiple external representations. For example, the option to control verbose output could be any of –v, --verbose, or --details. Some options may also take an associated value.

Each internal option is passed to `GetoptLong` as an array, containing strings representing the option's external forms and a flag. The flag specifies how `GetoptLong` is to associate an argument with the option (NO_ARGUMENT, REQUIRED_ARGUMENT, or OPTIONAL_ARGUMENT).

If the environment variable POSIXLY_CORRECT is set, all options must precede non-options on the command line. Otherwise, the default behavior of `GetoptLong` is to reorganize the command line to put the options at the front. This behavior may be changed by setting `GetoptLong#ordering=` to one of the constants PERMUTE, REQUIRE_ORDER, or RETURN_IN_ORDER. POSIXLY_CORRECT may not be overridden.

See also: `OptionParser` (page 711)

```
# Call using "ruby example.rb --size 10k -v -q a.txt b.doc"
require 'getoptlong'
# specify the options we accept and initialize
# the option parser
opts = GetoptLong.new(
  [ "--size",    "-s",              GetoptLong::REQUIRED_ARGUMENT ],
  [ "--verbose", "-v",              GetoptLong::NO_ARGUMENT ],
  [ "--query",   "-q",              GetoptLong::NO_ARGUMENT ],
  [ "--check",   "--valid", "-c",   GetoptLong::NO_ARGUMENT ]
)
# process the parsed options
opts.each do |opt, arg|
  puts "Option: #{opt}, arg #{arg.inspect}"
end
puts "Remaining args: #{ARGV.join(', ')}"
```

produces:

```
Option: --size, arg "10k"
Option: --verbose, arg ""
Option: --query, arg ""
Remaining args: a.txt, b.doc
```

| Library | **GServer** | Generic TCP Server |

Simple framework for writing TCP servers. Subclass the GServer class, set the port (and potentially other parameters) in the constructor, and then implement a serve method to handle incoming requests.

GServer manages a thread pool for incoming connections, so your serve method may be running in multiple threads in parallel.

You can run multiple GServer copies on different ports in the same application.

- When a connection is made on port 2000, respond with the current time as a string. Terminate after handling three requests.

```ruby
require 'gserver'
class TimeServer < GServer
  def initialize
    super(2000)
    @count = 3
  end
  def serve(client)
    client.puts Time.now.to_s
    @count -= 1
    stop if @count.zero?
  end
end

server = TimeServer.new
server.audit = true    # enable logging
server.start
server.join
```

- You can test this server by telnetting into *localhost* on port 2000.

```
% telnet localhost 2000
```

produces:

```
Trying 127.0.0.1...
Connected to localhost.
Escape character is '^]'.
Thu Aug 26 22:38:41 CDT 2004
Connection closed by foreign host.
```

Iconv Character Encoding Conversion

The Iconv class is an interface to the Open Group's iconv library, which supports the translation of strings between character encodings. For a list of the supported encodings on your platform, see the iconv_open man pages for your system.

Only if: libiconv installed

An Iconv object encapsulates a conversion descriptor, which contains the information needed to convert from one encoding to another. The converter can be used multiple times, until closed.

The conversion method iconv can be called multiple times to convert input strings. At the end, it should be called with a nil argument to flush out any remaining output.

- Convert from ISO-8859-1 to UTF-16.

```
require 'iconv'

conv = Iconv.new("UTF-16", "ISO-8859-1")
result = conv.iconv("hello")
result << conv.iconv(nil)
result    →    "\376\377\000h\000e\0001\0001\000o"
```

- Do the same conversion using a class method. Not we use Iconv.conv, which returns a single string, as opposed to Iconv.iconv, which returns an array of strings.

```
require 'iconv'
result = Iconv.conv("UTF-16", "ISO-8859-1", "hello")
result    →    "\376\377\000h\000e\0001\0001\000o"
```

- Convert *olé* from UTF-8 to ISO-8859-1.

```
require 'iconv'
result = Iconv.conv("ISO-8859-1", "UTF-8", "ol\303\251")
result    →    "ol\351"
```

- Convert *olé* from UTF-8 to ASCII. This throws an exception, as ASCII doesn't have an *é* character.

```
require 'iconv'
result = Iconv.conv("ASCII", "UTF-8", "ol\303\251")
```

produces:

```
prog.rb:2:in `conv': "\303\251" (Iconv::IllegalSequence)
from prog.rb:2
```

- This time, convert to ASCII with transliteration, which shows approximations of missing characters.

```
require 'iconv'
result = Iconv.iconv("ASCII//TRANSLIT", "UTF-8", "ol\303\251")
result    →    ["ol'e"]
```

| Library | **IO/Wait** | Check for Pending Data to Be Read |

Only if:
FIONREAD feature
in ioctl(2)

Including the library io/wait adds the methods IO#ready? and IO#wait to the standard IO class. These allow an IO object opened on a stream (not a file) to be queried to see if data is available to be read without reading it and to wait for a given number of bytes to become available.

- Set up a pipe between two processes, and write ten bytes at a time into it. Periodically see how much data is available.

```ruby
require 'io/wait'
reader, writer = IO.pipe
if (pid = fork)
  writer.close
  8.times do
    sleep 0.03
    len = reader.ready?
    puts "Ready? = #{len.inspect}"
    puts(reader.sysread(len)) if len
  end
  Process.waitpid(pid)
else
  reader.close
  5.times do |n|
    sleep 0.04
    writer.write n.to_s * 10
  end
  writer.close
end
```

produces:

```
Ready? = 10
0000000000
Ready? = nil
Ready? = 10
1111111111
Ready? = 10
2222222222
Ready? = 10
3333333333
Ready? = nil
Ready? = 10
4444444444
Ready? = nil
```

| Library | **IPAddr** | Represent and Manipulate IP Addresses |

Class `IPAddr` holds and manipulates Internet Protocol (IP) addresses. Each address contains three parts: an address, a mask, and an address family. The family will typically be `AF_INET` for IPv4 and IPv6 addresses. The class contains methods for extracting parts of an address, checking for IPv4 compatible addresses (and IPv4 mapped IPv6 addresses), testing whether an address falls within a subnet and many other functions. It is also interesting in that it contains as data its own unit tests.

```
require 'ipaddr'

v4 = IPAddr.new('192.168.23.0/24')
v4              →    #<IPAddr: IPv4:192.168.23.0/ 255.255.255.0>
v4.mask(16)     →    #<IPAddr: IPv4:192.168.0.0/ 255.255.0.0>
v4.reverse      →    "0.23.168.192.in-addr.arpa"
v6 = IPAddr.new('3ffe:505:2::1')
v6              →    #<IPAddr:
                     IPv6:3ffe:0505:0002:0000:0000:0000:0000:0001/
                     ffff:ffff:ffff:ffff:ffff:ffff:ffff:ffff>
v6.mask(48)     →    #<IPAddr:
                     IPv6:3ffe:0505:0002:0000:0000:0000:0000:0000/
                     ffff:ffff:ffff:0000:0000:0000:0000:0000>

# the value for 'family' is OS dependent. This
# value is for OS X
v6.family       →    30

other = IPAddr.new("192.168.23.56")
v4.include?(other)   →    true
```

Library jcode   Encoding Support for Strings

Requiring the jcode library augments the built-in String class with additional support for EUC and SJIS Japanese encodings and UTF8. This is effective only if $KCODE is one of EUC, SJIS, or UTF8. The following methods are updated: chop!, chop, delete!, delete, squeeze!, squeeze, succ!, succ, tr!, tr, tr_s!, and tr_s.

For example, the string "\342\210\202x/\342\210\202y" contains nine 8-bit characters. However, the sequence \343\210\202 could also be interpreted as a single UTF-8 character (a math delta symbol, making the string $\delta x/\delta y$). If we don't tell Ruby about the encoding, it treats each byte in the string as a separate character:

- Without encoding support, the string contains bytes.

```
$KCODE = "NONE"
require 'jcode'

str = "\342\210\202x/\342\210\202y"
str.length           →  9
str.jlength          →  9
str.jcount("\210")   →  2
str.chop!            →  "\342\210\202x/\342\210\202"
str.chop!            →  "\342\210\202x/\342\210"

str.each_char {|ch| print ch.inspect, " "}
```
produces:
```
"\342" "\210" "\202" "x" "/" "\342" "\210" "\202" "y"
```

- However, tell Ruby that it is dealing with UTF8 strings and the result changes.

```
$KCODE = 'UTF8'
require 'jcode'

str = "\342\210\202x/\342\210\202y"
str.length           →  9
str.jlength          →  5
str.jcount("\210")   →  0
str.chop!            →  "δx/δ"
str.chop!            →  "δx/"

str = "\342\210\202x/\342\210\202y"
str.each_char {|ch| print ch.inspect, "  "}
```
produces:
```
"δ"  "x"  "/"  "δ"  "y"
```

Logger

Application Logging

Writes log messages to a file or stream. Supports automatic time- or size-based rolling of log files. Messages can be assigned severities, and only those messages at or above the logger's current reporting level will be logged.

- During development, you may want to see all messages.

```
require 'logger'
log = Logger.new(STDOUT)
log.level = Logger::DEBUG
log.datetime_format = "%H:%M:%S"
log.info("Application starting")
3.times do |i|
  log.debug("Executing loop, i = #{i}")
  temperature = some_calculation(i)  # defined externally
  if temperature > 50
    log.warn("Possible overheat. i = #{i}")
  end
end
log.info("Application terminating")
```

produces:

```
I, [09:08:05#11118]  INFO -- : Application starting
D, [09:08:05#11118] DEBUG -- : Executing loop, i = 0
D, [09:08:05#11118] DEBUG -- : Executing loop, i = 1
D, [09:08:05#11118] DEBUG -- : Executing loop, i = 2
W, [09:08:05#11118]  WARN -- : Possible overheat. i = 2
I, [09:08:05#11118]  INFO -- : Application terminating
```

- In deployment, you can turn off anything below INFO.

```
require 'logger'
log = Logger.new(STDOUT)
log.level = Logger::INFO
log.datetime_format = "%H:%M:%S"
# as above...
```

produces:

```
I, [09:08:05#11120]  INFO -- : Application starting
W, [09:08:05#11120]  WARN -- : Possible overheat. i = 2
I, [09:08:05#11120]  INFO -- : Application terminating
```

- Log to a file, which is rotated when it gets to about 10k bytes. Keep up to five old files.

```
require 'logger'
log = Logger.new("application.log", 5, 10*1024)
log.info("Application starting")
# ...
```

Class `Mail` provides basic parsing for e-mail messages. It can read an individual message from a named file, or it can be called repeatedly to read messages from a stream on an opened mbox format file. Each `Mail` object represents a single e-mail message, which is split into a header and a body. The body is an array of lines, and the header is a hash indexed by the header name. `Mail` correctly joins multiline headers.

- Read a single e-mail from a file.

```
require 'mailread'

MAILBOX = "/Users/dave/Library/Mail/Mailboxes/Ruby/Talk.mbox/mbox"
msg = Mail.new(MAILBOX)
msg.header.keys    →    ["Status", "List-software", "Message-id",
                         "Subject", "Received",
                         "X-spambayes-classification",
                         "List-unsubscribe", "Posted",
                         "X-spam-level", "Content-type", "From",
                         "X-virus-scanned", "List-post",
                         "X-spam-status",
                         "Content-transfer-encoding", "X-mlserver",
                         "To", "In-reply-to", "X-ml-info",
                         "X-mail-count", "Date", "List-owner",
                         "X-ml-name", "References", "Reply-to",
                         "Delivered-to", "List-help", "Lines",
                         "Mime-version", "X-spam-checker-version",
                         "List-id", "Precedence"]
msg.body[0]        →    "On Sat, 14 Aug 2004 03:02:42 +0900, Curt
                         Hibbs <curt@hibbs.com> wrote:\n"
msg.body[1]        →    "> We've change the name of the project from
                         \"Ruby Installer for Windows\" to\n"
msg.body[2]        →    "> the \"One-Click Ruby Installer\" because
                         we are branching out more platforms\n"
```

- Read successive messages from an mbox format file.

```
require 'mailread'

MAILBOX = "/Users/dave/Library/Mail/Mailboxes/Ruby/Talk.mbox/mbox"
mbox = File.open(MAILBOX)
count = 0
lines = 0
while !mbox.eof?
  msg = Mail.new(mbox)
  count += 1
  lines += msg.header['Lines'].to_i
end

count   →   180
lines   →   5927
```

Library **mathn**   Unified Numbers

The mathn library attempts to bring some unity to numbers under Ruby, making classes Bignum, Complex, Fixnum, Integer, and Rational work and play better together.

- Types will tend to convert between themselves in a more natural way (so, for example, Complex::I squared will evaluate to −1, rather than Complex[-1,0]).

- Division will tend to produce more accurate results. The conventional division operator (/) is redefined to use quo, which doesn't round (quo is documented on page 566).

- Related to the previous point, rational numbers will be used in preference to floats when possible. Dividing one by two results in the rational number $\frac{1}{2}$, rather than 0.5 (or 0, the result of normal integer division).

See also: Matrix (page 694), Rational (page 721), Complex (page 662)

- Without mathn

```
require 'matrix'
require 'complex'
```

```
36/16                        →    2
Math.sqrt(36/16)             →    1.4142135623731

Complex::I * Complex::I      →    Complex(-1, 0)

m = Matrix[[1,2],[3,4]]
i = m.inv
```

$$i*m \quad \rightarrow \quad \begin{pmatrix} 1 & 0 \\ -2 & -2 \end{pmatrix}$$

```
(36/16)**-2                  →    0.25
(36.0/16.0)**-2              →    0.197530864197531
(-36/16)**-2                 →    0.111111111111111

(36/16)**(1/2)               →    1
(-36/16)**(1/2)              →    1

(36/16)**(-1/2)              →    0.5
(-36/16)**(-1/2)             →    -0.333333333333333
```

$$\text{Matrix.diagonal(6,7,8)/3} \quad \rightarrow \quad \begin{pmatrix} 2 & 0 & 0 \\ 0 & 2 & 0 \\ 0 & 0 & 2 \end{pmatrix}$$

- With mathn:

```
require 'mathn'
require 'matrix'
require 'complex'

36/16                      →    9/4
Math.sqrt(36/16)           →    3/2

Complex::I * Complex::I    →    -1

m = Matrix[[1,2],[3,4]]
i = m.inv
```

$$i*m \quad\rightarrow\quad \begin{pmatrix} 1 & 0 \\ 0 & 1 \end{pmatrix}$$

```
(36/16)**-2                →    16/81
(36.0/16.0)**-2            →    0.197530864197531
(-36/16)**-2               →    16/81

(36/16)**(1/2)             →    3/2
(-36/16)**(1/2)            →    Complex(9.18485099360515e-17, 1.5)

(36/16)**(-1/2)            →    2/3
(-36/16)**(-1/2)           →    Complex(4.08215599715784e-17,
                                -0.666666666666667)
```

$$Matrix.diagonal(6,7,8)/3 \quad\rightarrow\quad \begin{pmatrix} 2 & 0 & 0 \\ 0 & 7/3 & 0 \\ 0 & 0 & 8/3 \end{pmatrix}$$

- The mathn library also extends the number classes to include new functionality and adds a new class Prime.

```
require 'mathn'
primes = Prime.new
3.times { puts primes.succ }
primes.each {|p| puts p; break if p > 20 }
```

produces:

```
2
3
5
7
11
13
17
19
23
```

Matrix   Matrix and Vector Manipulation

The matrix library defines classes Matrix and Vector, representing rectangular matrices and vectors. As well as the normal arithmetic operations, they provide methods for matrix-specific functions (such as rank, inverse, and determinants) and a number of constructor methods (for creating special-case matrices—zero, identity, diagonal, singular, and vector).

Because by default integer arithmetic truncates, the determinant of integer matrices may be incorrectly calculated unless you also require the mathn library.

See also: mathn (page 692), Rational (page 721)

```
require 'matrix'
require 'mathn'
```

m1 = Matrix[[2, 1], [-1, 1]] $\rightarrow$ $\begin{pmatrix} 2 & 1 \\ -1 & 1 \end{pmatrix}$

m1[0,1] $\rightarrow$ 1

m1.inv $\rightarrow$ $\begin{pmatrix} 1/3 & -1/3 \\ 1/3 & 2/3 \end{pmatrix}$

m1 * m1.inv $\rightarrow$ $\begin{pmatrix} 1 & 0 \\ 0 & 1 \end{pmatrix}$

m1.determinant $\rightarrow$ 3

m1.singular? $\rightarrow$ false

m2 = Matrix[[1,2,3], [4,5,6], [7,8,9]] $\rightarrow$ $\begin{pmatrix} 1 & 2 & 3 \\ 4 & 5 & 6 \\ 7 & 8 & 9 \end{pmatrix}$

m2.minor(1, 2, 1, 2) $\rightarrow$ $\begin{pmatrix} 5 & 6 \\ 8 & 9 \end{pmatrix}$

m2.rank $\rightarrow$ 2

v1 = Vector[3, 4] $\rightarrow$ Vector[3, 4]

v1.covector $\rightarrow$ $\begin{pmatrix} 3 & 4 \end{pmatrix}$

m1 * v1 $\rightarrow$ Vector[10, 1]

Monitor   Monitor-Based Synchronization

Monitors are a form of mutual-exclusion mechanism first proposed back in 1974. They allow separate threads to define shared resources which will be accessed exclusively, and they provide a mechanism for a thread to wait for resources to become available in a controlled way.

The monitor library actually defines three separate ways of using monitors: as a parent class, as a mixin, and as a extension to a particular object. Examples of all three (and other code showing monitors in action) starts on page 142. In this section we document the module form of Monitor. The class form is effectively identical. In both the class form and when including MonitorMixin in an existing class it is essential to invoke super in the class's initialize method.

See also: Mutex (page 696), Sync (page 738), Thread (page 633)

```ruby
require 'monitor'
require 'mathn'
numbers = []
numbers.extend(MonitorMixin)
number_added = numbers.new_cond
# Reporter thread
Thread.new do
  loop do
    numbers.synchronize do
      number_added.wait_while { numbers.empty? }
      puts numbers.shift
    end
  end
end
# Prime number generator thread
generator = Thread.new do
  p = Prime.new
  5.times do
    numbers.synchronize do
      numbers << p.succ
      number_added.signal
    end
  end
end
generator.join
```

produces:

```
2
3
5
7
11
```

M onitor

| Library | **Mutex** | Thread Synchronization Support |

The `Mutex` class allows threads to gain exclusive access to some shared resource. That is, only one thread may hold the lock at any given time. Other threads may choose to wait for the lock to become available or may choose to get an immediate error indicating that the lock is not available. The library also implements condition variables, allowing a thread to give up control while holding a mutex and regain the lock when the resource becomes available, and queues, allowing threads to pass messages safely. We describe threading in Chapter 11 on page 135, and discuss *monitors*, an alternative synchronization mechanism, starting on page 142.

See also: Monitor (page 695), Sync (page 738), Queue (page 743), Thread (page 633)

```
require 'thread'
class Resource
  attr_reader :left, :times_had_to_wait
  def initialize(count)
    @left = count
    @times_had_to_wait = 0
    @mutex = Mutex.new
    @empty = ConditionVariable.new
  end
  def use
    @mutex.synchronize do
      while @left <= 0
        @times_had_to_wait += 1
        @empty.wait(@mutex)
      end
      @left -= 1
    end
  end
  def release
    @mutex.synchronize do
      @left += 1
      @empty.signal if @left == 1
    end
  end
end

def do_something_with(resource)
  resource.use
  sleep 0.001 # to simulate doing something that takes time
  resource.release
end

resource = Resource.new(2)
user1 = Thread.new { 100.times { do_something_with(resource) } }
user2 = Thread.new { 100.times { do_something_with(resource) } }
user3 = Thread.new { 100.times { do_something_with(resource) } }
user1.join; user2.join; user3.join

resource.times_had_to_wait   →   152
```

Library **Mutex_m** — Mutex Mix-In

mutex_m is a variant of class Mutex (contained in the thread library documented on the facing page) that allows mutex facilities to be mixed into any object.

The Mutex_m module defines methods that correspond to those in Mutex but with the prefix mu_ (so that lock is defined as mu_lock and so on). It then aliases these to the original Mutex names.

See also: Mutex (page 696), Sync (page 738), Thread (page 633)

```
require 'mutex_m'

class Counter
  include Mutex_m
  attr_reader :count
  def initialize
    @count = 0
    super
  end
  def tick
    lock
    @count += 1
    unlock
  end
end

c = Counter.new

t1 = Thread.new { 10000.times {  c.tick } }
t2 = Thread.new { 10000.times {  c.tick } }

t1.join
t2.join

c.count    →    20000
```

| Library | **Net::FTP** | FTP Client |

The net/ftp library implements a File Transfer Protocol (FTP) client. As well as data transfer commands (getbinaryfile, gettextfile, list, putbinaryfile, and puttextfile), the library supports the full complement of server commands (acct, chdir, delete, mdtm, mkdir, nlst, rename, rmdir, pwd, size, status, and system). Anonymous and password-authenticated sessions are supported. Connections may be active or passive.

See also: open-uri (page 707)

```
require 'net/ftp'
ftp = Net::FTP.new('ftp.netlab.co.jp')
ftp.login
ftp.chdir('pub/lang/ruby/contrib')
files = ftp.list('n*')
ftp.getbinaryfile('nif.rb-0.91.gz', 'nif.gz', 1024)
ftp.close
```

Net::FTP

| Library | **Net::HTTP** | HTTP Client |

The net/http library provides a simple client to fetch headers and Web page contents using the HTTP protocol.

The interface to the get, post, and head methods has changed between Ruby 1.6 and 1.8. Now, a single response object is returned, with the content of the response accessible through the response's body method. In addition, these methods no longer raise exceptions on recoverable errors.

See also: OpenSSL (page 709), open-uri (page 707), URI (page 752)

- Open a connection and fetch a page, displaying the response code and message, header information, and some of the body.

```
require 'net/http'
Net::HTTP.start('www.pragmaticprogrammer.com') do |http|
  response = http.get('/index.html')
  puts "Code = #{response.code}"
  puts "Message = #{response.message}"
  response.each {|key, val| printf "%-14s = %-40.40s\n", key, val }
  p response.body[400, 55]
end
```

produces:

```
Code = 200
Message = OK
last-modified  = Fri, 27 Aug 2004 02:25:48 GMT
content-type   = text/html
etag           = "b00d226-35b4-412e9bac"
date           = Fri, 27 Aug 2004 03:38:47 GMT
server         = Rapidsite/Apa/1.3.31 (Unix) FrontPage/5.
content-length = 13748
accept-ranges  = bytes
"-selling book 'The Pragmatic Programmer' and The\n        "
```

- Fetch a single page, displaying the response code and message, header information, and some of the body.

```
require 'net/http'
response = Net::HTTP.get_response('www.pragmaticprogrammer.com',
                                  '/index.html')
puts "Code = #{response.code}"
puts "Message = #{response.message}"
response.each {|key, val| printf "%-14s = %-40.40s\n", key, val }
p response.body[400, 55]
```

produces:

```
Code = 200
Message = OK
last-modified  = Fri, 27 Aug 2004 02:25:48 GMT
```

```
content-type    = text/html; charset=iso-8859-1
etag            = "b00d226-608b-43cbbebf"
date            = Tue, 17 Jan 2006 03:47:51 GMT
server          = Rapidsite/Apa/1.3.31 (Unix) FrontPage/5.
content-length = 24715
accept-ranges  = bytes
"lling book 'The Pragmatic Programmer' and The\n          "
```

- Follow redirections (the open-uri library does this automatically). This code comes from the RDoc documentation.

```ruby
require 'net/http'
require 'uri'
def fetch(uri_str, limit=10)
  fail 'http redirect too deep' if limit.zero?
  puts "Trying: #{uri_str}"
  response = Net::HTTP.get_response(URI.parse(uri_str))
  case response
  when Net::HTTPSuccess
    response
  when Net::HTTPRedirection
    fetch(response['location'], limit-1)
  else
    response.error!
  end
end
response = fetch('http://www.ruby-lang.org')
p response.body[500, 50]
```

produces:

```
Trying: http://www.ruby-lang.org
Trying: http://www.ruby-lang.org/en/
"rg\">\n\t<link rel=\"start\" title=\"Top\" href=\"./\">\n\t\n\t"
```

- Search Dave's blog by posting form data and reading back the response (doesn't work with my new blog, though...).

```ruby
require 'net/http'
Net::HTTP.start('blogs.pragprog.com') do |query|
  response = query.post("/pragdave", "terms=jolt&handler=searching")
  response.body.scan(%r{<span class="itemtitle">(.*?)</span>}m) do
  |title|
    puts title
  end
end
```

produces:

```
We're Jolt Finalists
We Got a Jolt Award!
```

| Library | **Net::IMAP** | Access an IMAP Mail Server |

The Internet Mail Access Protocol (IMAP) is used to allow mail clients to access mail servers. It supports plain text login and the IMAP login and CRAM-MD5 authentication mechanisms. Once connected, the library supports threading, so multiple interactions with the server may take place at the same time.

The examples that follow are taken with minor modifications from the RDoc documentation in the library source file.

See also: Net::POP (page 702)

- List senders and subjects of messages to "dave" in the INBOX.

```
require 'net/imap'
imap = Net::IMAP.new('my.mailserver.com')
imap.authenticate('LOGIN', 'dave', 'secret')
imap.examine('INBOX')
puts "Message count: #{ imap.responses["EXISTS"]}"
imap.search(["TO", "dave"]).each do |message_id|
  envelope = imap.fetch(message_id, "ENVELOPE")[0].attr["ENVELOPE"]
    puts "#{envelope.from[0].name}: \t#{envelope.subject}"
end
```

- Move all messages with a date in April 2003 from the folder Mail/sent-mail to Mail/sent-apr03.

```
require 'net/imap'
imap = Net::IMAP.new('my.mailserver.com')
imap.authenticate('LOGIN', 'dave', 'secret')
imap.select('Mail/sent-mail')
if not imap.list('Mail/', 'sent-apr03')
  imap.create('Mail/sent-apr03')
end
imap.search(["BEFORE", "01-May-2003",
             "SINCE",  "1-Apr-2003"]).each do |message_id|
  imap.copy(message_id, "Mail/sent-apr03")
  imap.store(message_id, "+FLAGS", [:Deleted])
end
imap.expunge
```

| Library | Net::POP | Access a POP Mail Server |

The net/pop library provides a simple client to fetch and delete mail on a Post Office Protocol (POP) server.

The class Net::POP3 is used to access a POP server, returning a list of Net::POPMail objects, one per message stored on the server. These POPMail objects are then used to fetch and/or delete individual messages.

The library also provides class APOP, an alternative to the POP3 class that performs authentication.

```
require 'net/pop'
pop = Net::POP3.new('server.ruby-stuff.com')
pop.start('joe', 'secret') do |server|
  msg = server.mails[0]
  # Print the 'From:' header line
  from = msg.header.split("\r\n").grep(/^From: /)[0]
  puts from
  puts
  puts "Full message:"
  text = msg.pop
  puts text
end
```

produces:

```
From: dave@facet.ruby-stuff.com (Dave Thomas)

Full message:
Return-Path: <dave@facet.ruby-stuff.com>
Received: from facet.ruby-stuff.com (facet.ruby-stuff.com [10.96.0.122])
        by pragprog.com (8.11.6/8.11.6) with ESMTP id i2PJMW701809
        for <joe@carat.ruby-stuff.com>; Thu, 25 Mar 2004 13:22:32 -0600
Received: by facet.ruby-stuff.com (Postfix, from userid 502)
        id 4AF228B1BD; Thu, 25 Mar 2004 13:22:36 -0600 (CST)
To: joe@carat.ruby-stuff.com
Subject: Try out the new features!
Message-Id: <20040325192236.4AF228B1BD@facet.ruby-stuff.com>
Date: Thu, 25 Mar 2004 13:22:36 -0600 (CST)
From: dave@facet.ruby-stuff.com (Dave Thomas)
Status: RO

Ruby 1.8 has a boatload of new features, both in
the core language and in the supplied libraries.

Try it out!
```

| Library | **Net::SMTP** | Simple SMTP Client |

The net/smtp library provides a simple client to send electronic mail using the Simple Mail Transfer Protocol (SMTP). It does not assist in the creation of the message payload—it simply delivers messages once an RFC822 message has been constructed.

- Send an e-mail from a string.

```
require 'net/smtp'
msg = "Subject: Test\n\nNow is the time\n"
Net::SMTP.start('pragprog.com') do |smtp|
  smtp.send_message(msg, 'dave@pragprog.com', ['dave'])
end
```

- Send an e-mail using an SMTP object and an adapter.

```
require 'net/smtp'
Net::SMTP::start('pragprog.com', 25, "pragprog.com") do |smtp|
  smtp.open_message_stream('dave@pragprog.com', # from
                           [ 'dave' ]           # to
                          ) do |stream|
    stream.puts "Subject: Test1"
    stream.puts
    stream.puts "And so is this"
  end
end
```

- Send an e-mail to a server requiring CRAM-MD5 authentication.

```
require 'net/smtp'
msg = "Subject: Test\n\nNow is the time\n"
Net::SMTP.start('pragprog.com', 25, 'pragprog.com',
                'user', 'password', :cram_md5) do |smtp|
  smtp.send_message(msg, 'dave@pragprog.com', ['dave'])
end
```

Net::SMTP

| Library | **Net::Telnet** | Telnet Client |

The net/telnet library provides a complete implementation of a telnet client and includes features that make it a convenient mechanism for interacting with nontelnet services.

Class Net::Telnet delegates to class Socket. As a result, the methods of Socket and its parent, class IO, are available through Net::Telnet objects.

- Connect to a localhost, run the date command, and disconnect.

```
require 'net/telnet'
tn = Net::Telnet.new({})
tn.login "guest", "secret"
tn.cmd "date"    →    "date\nThu Aug 26 22:38:56 CDT 2004\n% "
tn.close         →    nil
```

- The methods new, cmd, login, and waitfor take an optional block. If present, the block is passed output from the server as it is received by the routine. This can be used to provide realtime output, rather than waiting (for example) for a login to complete before displaying the server's response.

```
require 'net/telnet'
tn = Net::Telnet.new({})       {|str| print str }
tn.login("guest", "secret")  {|str| print str }
tn.cmd("date")               {|str| print str }
tn.close
```

produces:

```
Connected to localhost.
Darwin/BSD (wireless_2.local.thomases.com) (ttyp1)
login: guest
Password:Last login: Thu Aug 26 22:38:56 from localhost
Welcome to Darwin!
% date
Thu Aug 26 22:38:57 CDT 2004
%
```

- Get the time from an NTP server.

```
require 'net/telnet'
tn = Net::Telnet.new('Host'       => 'time.nonexistent.org',
                     'Port'       => 'time',
                     'Timeout'    => 60,
                     'Telnetmode' => false)
atomic_time = tn.recv(4).unpack('N')[0]
puts "Atomic time: " + Time.at(atomic_time - 2208988800).to_s
puts "Local time:  " + Time.now.to_s
```

produces:

```
Atomic time: Thu Aug 26 22:38:56 CDT 2004
Local time:  Thu Aug 26 22:38:59 CDT 2004
```

Library **NKF**   Interface to Network Kanji Filter

The NKF module is a wrapper around Itaru Ichikawa's Network Kanji Filter (NKF) library (version 1.7). It provides functions to guess at the encoding of JIS, EUC, and SJIS streams, and to convert from one encoding to another.

- Unlike the interpreter, which uses strings to represent the encodings, NKF uses integer constants.

```
require 'nkf'
NKF::AUTO   →   0
NKF::JIS    →   1
NKF::EUC    →   2
NKF::SJIS   →   3
```

- Guess at the encoding of a string. (Thanks to Nobu Nakada for the examples on this page.)

```
require 'nkf'

NKF.guess("Yukihiro Matsumoto")                                                              →   5
NKF.guess("\e$B$^$D$b$H$f$ -$R$m\e(B")                                                        →   1
NKF.guess("\244\336\244\304\244\342\244\310\244\346\244\255\244\322\244\355")                 →   2
NKF.guess("\202\334\202\302\202\340\202\306\202\344\202\253\202\320\202\353")                 →   3
```

- The NKF.nfk method takes two parameters. The first is a set of options, passed on to the NKF library. The second is the string to translate. The following examples assume that your console is set up to accomdate Japanese characters. The text at the end of the three ruby commands is Yukihiro Matsumoto.

```
$ ruby -e 'p *ARGV'  まつもと ゆきひろ

"\244\336\244\304\244\342\244\310\244\346\244\255\244\322\244\355"

$ ruby -rnkf -e 'p NKF.nkf(*ARGV)' - -Es  まつもと ゆきひろ

"\202\334\202\302\202\340\202\306\202\344\202\253\202\320\202\353"

$ ruby -rnkf -e 'p NKF.nkf(*ARGV)' - -Ej  まつもと ゆきひろ

"\e$B$^$D$b$H$f$-$R$m\e(B"
```

NKF

Observable
The Observer Pattern

The Observer pattern, also known as Publish/Subscribe, provides a simple mechanism for one object (the source) to inform a set of interested third-party objects when its state changes (see *Design Patterns* [GHJV95]). In the Ruby implementation, the notifying class mixes in the module Observable, which provides the methods for managing the associated observer objects. The observers must implement the update method to receive notifications.

```ruby
require 'observer'
class CheckWaterTemperature # Periodically check the water
  include Observable

  def run
    last_temp = nil
    loop do
      temp = Temperature.fetch   # external class...
      puts "Current temperature: #{temp}"
      if temp != last_temp
        changed                  # notify observers
        notify_observers(Time.now, temp)
        last_temp = temp
      end
    end
  end
end
class Warner
  def initialize(&limit)
    @limit = limit
  end
  def update(time, temp)         # callback for observer
    if @limit.call(temp)
      puts "--- #{time.to_s}: Temperature outside range: #{temp}"
    end
  end
end
checker = CheckWaterTemperature.new
checker.add_observer(Warner.new {|t| t < 80})
checker.add_observer(Warner.new {|t| t > 120})
checker.run
```

produces:

```
Current temperature: 83
Current temperature: 75
--- Thu Aug 26 22:38:59 CDT 2004: Temperature outside range: 75
Current temperature: 90
Current temperature: 134
--- Thu Aug 26 22:38:59 CDT 2004: Temperature outside range: 134
Current temperature: 134
Current temperature: 112
Current temperature: 79
--- Thu Aug 26 22:38:59 CDT 2004: Temperature outside range: 79
```

| Library | **open-uri** | Treat FTP and HTTP Resources as Files |

The open-uri library extends `Kernel#open`, allowing it to accept URIs for FTP and HTTP as well as local filenames. Once opened, these resources can be treated as if they were local files, accessed using conventional IO methods. The URI passed to open is either a string containing an HTTP or FTP URL, or a URI object (described on page 752). When opening an HTTP resource, the method automatically handles redirection and proxies. When using an FTP resource, the method logs in as an anonymous user.

The IO object returned by open in these cases is extended to support methods that return meta-information from the request: `content_type`, `charset`, `content_encoding`, `last_modified`, `status`, `base_uri`, `meta`.

See also: URI (page 752)

```
require 'open-uri'
require 'pp'
open('http://localhost/index.html') do |f|
  puts "URI: #{f.base_uri}"
  puts "Content-type: #{f.content_type}, charset: #{f.charset}"
  puts "Encoding: #{f.content_encoding}"
  puts "Last modified: #{f.last_modified}"
  puts "Status: #{f.status.inspect}"
  pp f.meta
  puts "----"
  3.times {|i| puts "#{i}: #{f.gets}" }
end
```

produces:

```
URI: http://localhost/index.html
Content-type: text/html, charset: iso-8859-1
Encoding:
Last modified: Wed Jul 18 23:44:21 UTC 2001
Status: ["200", "OK"]
{"vary"=>"negotiate,accept-language,accept-charset",
 "last-modified"=>"Wed, 18 Jul 2001 23:44:21 GMT",
 "content-location"=>"index.html.en",
 "date"=>"Fri, 27 Aug 2004 03:38:59 GMT",
 "etag"=>"\"6657-5b0-3b561f55;411edab5\"",
 "content-type"=>"text/html",
 "content-language"=>"en",
 "server"=>"Apache/1.3.29 (Darwin)",
 "content-length"=>"1456",
 "tcn"=>"choice",
 "accept-ranges"=>"bytes"}
----
0: <!DOCTYPE html PUBLIC "-//W3C//DTD XHTML 1.0 Transitional//EN"
1:     "http://www.w3.org/TR/xhtml1/DTD/xhtml1-transitional.dtd">
2: <html xmlns="http://www.w3.org/1999/xhtml">
```

O | pen-uri

Open3   Run Subprocess and Connect to All Streams

Runs a command in a subprocess. Data written to *stdin* can be read by the subprocess, and data written to standard output and standard error in the subprocess will be available on the *stdout* and *stderr* streams. The subprocess is actually run as a grandchild, and as a result Process#waitall cannot be used to wait for its termination (hence the sleep in the following example).

```
require 'open3'
Open3.popen3('bc') do | stdin, stdout, stderr |
  Thread.new { loop { puts "Err stream:    #{stderr.gets}" } }
  Thread.new { loop { puts "Output stream: #{stdout.gets}" } }
  stdin.puts "3 * 4"
  stdin.puts "1 / 0"
  stdin.puts "2 ^ 5"
  sleep 0.1
end
```

produces:

```
Output stream: 12
Err stream:    Runtime error (func=(main), adr=3): Divide by zero
Output stream: 32
Err stream:
```

Only if: OpenSSL
library available
(http://www.
openssl.org)

Library		
OpenSSL		SSL Library

The Ruby OpenSSL extension wraps the freely available OpenSSL library. It provides Secure Sockets Layer and Transport Layer Security (SSL and TLS) protocols, allowing for secure communications over networks. The library provides functions for certificate creation and management, message signing, and encryption/decryption. It also provides wrappers to simplify access to https servers, along with secure FTP. The interface to the library is large (roughly 330 methods), but the average Ruby user will probably only use a small subset of the library's capabilities.

See also: Net::FTP (page 698), Net::HTTP (page 699), Socket (page 735)

- Access a secure Web site using HTTPS. Note that SSL is used to tunnel to the site, but the requested page also requires standard HTTP basic authorization.

```ruby
require 'net/https'
USER = "xxx"
PW   = "yyy"
site = Net::HTTP.new("www.securestuff.com", 443)
site.use_ssl = true
response = site.get2("/cgi-bin/cokerecipe.cgi",
                     'Authorization' => 'Basic ' +
                     ["#{USER}:#{PW}"].pack('m').strip)
```

- Create a socket that uses SSL. This isn't a good example of accessing a Web site. However, it illustrates how a socket can be encrypted.

```ruby
require 'socket'
require 'openssl'
socket = TCPSocket.new("www.secure-stuff.com", 443)
ssl_context = OpenSSL::SSL::SSLContext.new()
unless ssl_context.verify_mode
  warn "warning: peer certificate won't be verified this session."
  ssl_context.verify_mode = OpenSSL::SSL::VERIFY_NONE
end
sslsocket = OpenSSL::SSL::SSLSocket.new(socket, ssl_context)
sslsocket.sync_close = true
sslsocket.connect
sslsocket.puts("GET /secret-info.shtml")
while line =  sslsocket.gets
  p line
end
```

| Library | OpenStruct | Open (dynamic) Structure |

An open structure is an object whose attributes are created dynamically when first assigned. In other words, if *obj* is an instance of an OpenStruct, then the statement obj.abc=1 will create the attribute *abc* in *obj*, and then assign the value 1 to it.

```
require 'ostruct'

os = OpenStruct.new( "f1" => "one", :f2 => "two" )
os.f3 = "cat"
os.f4 = 99
os.f1    →    "one"
os.f2    →    "two"
os.f3    →    "cat"
os.f4    →    99
```

OpenStruct

OptionParser is a flexible and extensible way to parse command-line arguments. It has a particularly rich abstraction of the concept of an option.

- An option can have multiple short names (options preceded by a single hyphen) and multiple long names (options preceded by two hyphens). Thus, an option that displays help may be available as -h, -?, --help, and --about. Users may abbreviate long option names to the shortest nonambiguous prefix.

- An option may be specified as having no argument, an optional argument, or a required argument. Arguments can be validated against patterns or lists of valid values.

- Arguments may be returned as objects of any type (not just strings). The argument type system is extensible (we add Date handling in the example).

- Arguments can have one or more lines of descriptive text, used when generating usage information.

Options are specified using the on and def methods. These methods take a variable number of arguments that cumulatively build a definition of each option. The arguments accepted by these methods are listed in Table 28.2 on the following page.

See also: GetoptLong (page 684)

```
require 'optparse'
require 'date'
# Add Dates as a new option type
OptionParser.accept(Date, /(\d+)-(\d+)-(\d+)/) do |d, mon, day, year|
  Date.new(year.to_i, mon.to_i, day.to_i)
end
opts = OptionParser.new
opts.on("-x")                          {|val| puts "-x seen" }
opts.on("-s", "--size VAL", Integer) {|val| puts "-s #{val}" }
opts.on("-a", "--at DATE",  Date)    {|val| puts "-a #{val}" }
my_argv = [ "--size", "1234", "-x", "-a", "12-25-2003", "fred", "wilma" ]
rest = opts.parse(*my_argv)
puts "Remainder = #{rest.join(', ')}"
puts opts.to_s
```

produces:

```
-s 1234
-x seen
-a 2003-12-25
Remainder = fred, wilma
Usage: myprog [options]
    -x
    -s, --size VAL
    -a, --at DATE
```

Table 28.2. Option definition arguments

"-x" "-xARG" "-x=ARG" "-x[OPT]" "-x[=OPT]" "-x PLACE"

Option has short name x. First form has no argument, next two have mandatory argument, next two have optional argument, last specifies argument follows option. The short names may also be specified as a range (such as "-[a-c]").

"--*switch*" "--*switch*=ARG" "--*switch*=[OPT]" "--*switch* PLACE"

Option has long name switch. First form has no argument, next has a mandatory argument, the next has an optional argument, and the last specifies the argument follows the switch.

"--no-*switch*"

Defines a option whose default value is false.

"=ARG" "=[OPT]"

Argument for this option is mandatory or optional. For example, the following code says there's an option known by the aliases –x, –y, and –z that takes a mandatory argument, shown in the usage as N.

opt.on("-x", "-y", "-z", "=N")

"description"

Any string that doesn't start – or = is used as a description for this option in the summary. Multiple descriptions may be given; they'll be shown on additional lines.

/pattern/

Any argument must match the given pattern.

array

Argument must be one of the values from array.

proc or method

Argument type conversion is performed by the given proc or method (rather than using the block associated with the on or def method call).

ClassName

Argument must match that defined for ClassName, which may be predefined or added using OptionParser.accept. Built-in argument classes are

Object: Any string. No conversion. This is the default.

String: Any nonempty string. No conversion.

Integer: Ruby/C-like integer with optional sign (0ddd is octal, 0bddd binary, 0xddd hexadecimal). Converts to Integer.

Float: Float number format. Converts to Float.

Numeric: Generic numeric format. Converts to Integer for integers, Float for floats.

Array: Argument must be of list of strings separated by a comma.

OptionParser::DecimalInteger: Decimal integer. Converted to Integer.

OptionParser::OctalInteger: Ruby/C-like octal/hexadecimal/binary integer.

OptionParser::DecimalNumeric: Decimal integer/float number. Integers converted to Integer, floats to Float.

TrueClass, FalseClass: Boolean switch.

ParseDate Parse a Date String

The `ParseDate` module defines a single method, `ParseDate.parsedate`, which converts a date and/or time string into an array of Fixnum values representing the date and/or time's constituents (year, month, day, hour, minute, second, time zone, and weekday). `nil` is returned for fields that cannot be parsed from the string. If the result contains a year that is less than 100 and the *guess* parameter is true, `parsedate` will return a year value equal to *year* plus 2000 if *year* is less than 69, and will return *year* plus 1900 otherwise.

See also: Date (page 665)

string	guess	ParseDate::parsedate(string, guess)							
		yy	mm	dd	hh	min	sec	zone	wd
1999-09-05 23:55:21+0900	F	1999	9	5	23	55	21	+0900	–
1983-12-25	F	1983	12	25	–	–	–	–	–
1965-11-10 T13:45	F	1965	11	10	13	45	–	–	–
10/9/75 1:30pm	F	75	10	9	13	30	–	–	–
10/9/75 1:30pm	T	1975	10	9	13	30	–	–	–
Wed Feb 2 17:15:49 CST 2000	F	2000	2	2	17	15	49	CST	3
Tue, 02-Mar-99 11:20:32 GMT	F	99	3	2	11	20	32	GMT	2
Tue, 02-Mar-99 11:20:32 GMT	T	1999	3	2	11	20	32	GMT	2
12-January-1990, 04:00 WET	F	1990	1	12	4	0	–	WET	–
4/3/99	F	99	4	3	–	–	–	–
4/3/99	T	1999	4	3	–	–	–	–	–
10th February, 1976	F	1976	2	10	–	–	–	–	–
March 1st, 84	T	1984	3	1	–	–	–	–	–
Friday	F	–	–	–	–	–	–	–	5

Pathname   Representation of File Paths

A `Pathname` represents the absolute or relative name of a file. It has two distinct uses. First, it allows manipulation of the parts of a file path (extracting components, building new paths, and so on). Second (and somewhat confusingly), it acts as a façade for some methods in classes `Dir`, `File`, and module `FileTest`, forwarding on calls for the file named by the `Pathname` object.

See also: File (page 465)

- Path name manipulation:

```
require 'pathname'

p1 = Pathname.new("/usr/bin")    →    #<Pathname:/usr/bin>
p2 = Pathname.new("ruby")        →    #<Pathname:ruby>
p3 = p1 + p2                     →    #<Pathname:/usr/bin/ruby>
p4 = p2 + p1                     →    #<Pathname:/usr/bin>
p3.parent                       →    #<Pathname:/usr/bin>
p3.parent.parent                →    #<Pathname:/usr>
p1.absolute?                    →    true
p2.absolute?                    →    false
p3.split                        →    [#<Pathname:/usr/bin>,
                                      #<Pathname:ruby>]

p5 = Pathname.new("testdir")     →    #<Pathname:testdir>

p5.realpath   →   #<Pathname:/Users/dave/Work/rubybook/testdir>
p5.children   →   [#<Pathname:testdir/config.h>,
                   #<Pathname:testdir/main.rb>]
```

- Pathname as proxy for file and directory status requests.

```
require 'pathname'

p1 = Pathname.new("/usr/bin/ruby")
p1.file?                         →    true
p1.directory?                    →    false
p1.executable?                   →    true
p1.size                          →    1913444

p2 = Pathname.new("testfile")    →    #<Pathname:testfile>

p2.read                          →    "This is line one\nThis is
                                      line two\nThis is line
                                      three\nAnd so on...\n"
p2.readlines                     →    ["This is line one\n", "This
                                      is line two\n", "This is line
                                      three\n", "And so on...\n"]
```

PP uses the `PrettyPrint` library to format the results of inspecting Ruby objects. As well as the methods in the class, it defines a global function, `pp`, which works like the existing `p` method but which formats its output.

PP has a default layout for all Ruby objects. However, you can override the way it handles a class by defining the method `pretty_print`, which takes a PP object as a parameter. It should use that PP object's methods `text`, `breakable`, `nest`, `group`, and `pp` to format its output (see `PrettyPrint` for details).

See also: `PrettyPrint` (page 716), `YAML` (page 758)

- Compare "p" and "pp."

```
require 'pp'
Customer = Struct.new(:name, :sex, :dob, :country)
cust = Customer.new("Walter Wall", "Male", "12/25/1960", "Niue")
puts "Regular print"
p cust
puts "\nPretty print"
pp cust
```

produces:

```
Regular print
#<struct Customer name="Walter Wall", sex="Male", dob="12/25/1960",
 country="Niue">

Pretty print
#<struct Customer
 name="Walter Wall",
 sex="Male",
 dob="12/25/1960",
 country="Niue">
```

- You can tell PP not to display an object if it has already displayed it.

```
require 'pp'
a = "string"
b = [ a ]
c = [ b, b ]
PP.sharing_detection = false
pp c
PP.sharing_detection = true
pp c
```

produces:

```
[["string"], ["string"]]
[["string"], [...]]
```

Library **PrettyPrint**   General Pretty Printer

PrettyPrint implements a pretty printer for structured text. It handles details of wrapping, grouping, and indentation. The PP library uses PrettyPrint to generate more legible dumps of Ruby objects.

See also: PP (page 715)

- The following program prints a chart of Ruby's classes, showing subclasses as a bracketed list following the parent. To save some space, we show just the classes in the Numeric branch of the tree.

```ruby
require 'prettyprint'
require 'complex'
require 'rational'
@children = Hash.new { |h,k| h[k] = Array.new }
ObjectSpace.each_object(Class) do |cls|
  @children[cls.superclass] << cls if cls <= Numeric
end
def print_children_of(printer, cls)
  printer.text(cls.name)
  kids = @children[cls].sort_by {|k| k.name}
  unless kids.empty?
    printer.group(0, " [", "]") do
      printer.nest(3) do
        printer.breakable
        kids.each_with_index do |k, i|
          printer.breakable unless i.zero?
          print_children_of(printer, k)
        end
      end
      printer.breakable
    end
  end
end
printer = PrettyPrint.new($stdout, 30)
print_children_of(printer, Object)
printer.flush
```

produces:

```
Object [
   Numeric [
      Complex
      Float
      Integer [
         Bignum
         Fixnum
      ]
      Rational
   ]
]
```

Profile
Profile Execution of a Ruby Program

The `profile` library is a trivial wrapper around the `Profiler` module, making it easy to profile the execution of an entire program. Profiling can be enabled from the command line using the `-rprofile` option or from within a source program by requiring the `profile` module.

See also: Benchmark (page 657), Profiler__ (page 718)

```
require 'profile'
def ackerman(m, n)
  if m == 0 then  n+1
  elsif n == 0 and m > 0 then ackerman(m-1, 1)
  else ackerman(m-1, ackerman(m, n-1))
  end
end
ackerman(3, 3)
```

produces:

% time	cumulative seconds	self seconds	calls	self ms/call	total ms/call	name
75.14	2.75	2.75	2432	1.13	46.92	Object#ackerman
13.39	3.24	0.49	3676	0.13	0.13	Fixnum#-=
7.65	3.52	0.28	2431	0.12	0.12	Fixnum#-
3.83	3.66	0.14	1188	0.12	0.12	Fixnum#+
0.55	3.68	0.02	1	20.00	20.00	Profiler__.start_profile
0.00	3.68	0.00	1	0.00	0.00	Kernel.puts
0.00	3.68	0.00	1	0.00	0.00	Module#method_added
0.00	3.68	0.00	2	0.00	0.00	IO#write
0.00	3.68	0.00	57	0.00	0.00	Fixnum#>
0.00	3.68	0.00	1	0.00	3660.00	#toplevel

Profile

Profiler__
Control Execution Profiling

The Profiler__ module can be used to collect a summary of the number of calls to, and the time spent in, methods in a Ruby program. The output is sorted by the total time spent in each method. The profile library is a convenience wrapper than profiles an entire program.

See also: Benchmark (page 657), profile (page 717)

```ruby
require 'profiler'
# Omit definition of connection and fetching methods
def calc_discount(qty, price)
  case qty
  when 0..10 then 0.0
  when 11..99 then price * 0.05
  else price * 0.1
  end
end
def calc_sales_totals(rows)
    total_qty =  total_price = total_disc = 0
    rows.each do |row|
      total_qty   += row.qty
      total_price += row.price
      total_disc  += calc_discount(row.qty, row.price)
    end
end

connect_to_database

rows = read_sales_data

Profiler__::start_profile
calc_sales_totals(rows)
Profiler__::stop_profile
Profiler__::print_profile($stdout)
```

produces:

% time	cumulative seconds	self seconds	calls	self ms/call	total ms/call	name
31.19	0.34	0.34	1	340.00	1090.00	Array#each
20.18	0.56	0.22	648	0.34	0.80	Range#===
15.60	0.73	0.17	648	0.26	0.39	Fixnum#<=>
10.09	0.84	0.11	324	0.34	2.01	Object#calc_discount
6.42	0.91	0.07	648	0.11	0.11	Float#coerce
5.50	0.97	0.06	1296	0.05	0.05	Float#<=>
3.67	1.01	0.04	969	0.04	0.04	Float#+
2.75	1.04	0.03	648	0.05	0.05	S#price
2.75	1.07	0.03	648	0.05	0.05	S#qty
1.83	1.09	0.02	324	0.06	0.06	Float#*
0.92	1.10	0.01	1	10.00	10.00	Profiler__.start_profile
0.00	1.10	0.00	1	0.00	1090.00	#toplevel
0.00	1.10	0.00	1	0.00	1090.00	Object#calc_sales_totals
0.00	1.10	0.00	3	0.00	0.00	Fixnum#+

The PStore class provides transactional, file-based, persistent storage of Ruby objects. Each PStore can store several object hierarchies. Each hierarchy has a root, identified by a key (often a string). At the start of a PStore transaction, these hierarchies are read from a disk file and made available to the Ruby program. At the end of the transaction, the hierarchies are written back to the file. Any changes made to objects in these hierarchies are therefore saved on disk, to be read at the start of the next transaction that uses that file.

In normal use, a PStore object is created and then is used one or more times to control a transaction. Within the body of the transaction, any object hierarchies that had previously been saved are made available, and any changes to object hierarchies, and any new hierarchies, are written back to the file at the end.

- The following example stores two hierarchies in a PStore. The first, identified by the key "names", is an array of strings. The second, identified by "tree", is a simple binary tree.

```
require 'pstore'
require 'pp'
class T
  def initialize(val, left=nil, right=nil)
    @val, @left, @right = val, left, right
  end
  def to_a
    [ @val, @left.to_a, @right.to_a ]
  end
end

store = PStore.new("/tmp/store")
store.transaction do
  store['names'] = [ 'Douglas', 'Barenberg', 'Meyer' ]
  store['tree']  = T.new('top',
                    T.new('A', T.new('B')),
                    T.new('C', T.new('D', nil, T.new('E'))))
end
# now read it back in
store.transaction do
  puts "Roots: #{store.roots.join(', ')}"
  puts store['names'].join(', ')
  pp store['tree'].to_a
end
```

produces:

```
Roots: names, tree
Douglas, Barenberg, Meyer
["top",
 ["A", ["B", [], []], []],
 ["C", ["D", [], ["E", [], []]], []]]
```

PTY   Pseudo-Terminal Interface: Interact with External Processes

Only if: Unix with
pty support

Many Unix platforms support a *pseudo-terminal*—a device pair where one end emulates a process running on a conventional terminal, and the other end can read and write that terminal as if it were a user looking at a screen and typing on a keyboard.

The PTY library provides the method spawn, which starts the given command (by default a shell), connecting it to one end of a pseudo-terminal. It then returns the reader and writer streams connected to that terminal, allowing your process to interact with the running process.

Working with pseudo-terminals can be tricky. See IO#expect on page 676 for a convenience method that makes life easier. You might also want to track down Ara T. Howard's Session module for an even simpler approach to driving subprocesses.[4]

See also: expect (page 676)

- Run irb in a subshell and ask it to convert the string "cat" to uppercase.

```
require 'pty'
require 'expect'
$expect_verbose = true
PTY.spawn("ruby /usr/local/bin/irb") do |reader, writer, pid|
  reader.expect(/irb.*:0> /)
  writer.puts "'cat'.upcase"
  reader.expect("=> ")
  answer = reader.gets
  puts "Answer = #{answer}"
end
```

produces:

```
irb(main):001:0> 'cat'.upcase
=> Answer = "CAT"
```

---

4.   Currently found at http://www.codeforpeople.com/lib/ruby/session/.

Library **Rational**   Rational Numbers

Rational numbers are expressed as the ratio of two integers. When the denominator exactly divides the numerator, a rational number is effectively an integer. Rationals allow exact representation of fractional numbers, but some real values cannot be expressed exactly and so cannot be represented as rationals.

Class `Rational` is normally relatively independent of the other numeric classes, in that the result of dividing two integers will normally be a (truncated) integer. However, if the `mathn` library is loaded into a program, integer division may generate a `Rational` result.

See also: `mathn` (page 692), `Matrix` (page 694), `Complex` (page 662)

- Rational as a free-standing class.

```
require 'rational'
r1 = Rational(3, 4)    →    Rational(3, 4)
r2 = Rational(2, 3)    →    Rational(2, 3)
r1 * 2                 →    Rational(3, 2)
r1 * 8                 →    Rational(6, 1)
r1 / 6                 →    Rational(1, 8)
r1 * r2                →    Rational(1, 2)
r1 + r2                →    Rational(17, 12)
r1 ** r2               →    0.825481812223657
```

- Rational integrated with integers using `mathn`. Notice how `mathn` also changes the string representation of numbers.

```
require 'rational'
require 'mathn'
r1 = Rational(3, 4)    →    3/4
r2 = Rational(2, 3)    →    2/3
r1 * 2                 →    3/2
r1 * 8                 →    6
5/3                    →    5/3
5/3 * 6                →    10
5/3 * 6/15             →    2/3
Math::sin(r1)          →    0.681638760023334
```

Rational

Adds the method `readbytes` to class IO. This method will guarantee to read exactly the requested number of bytes from a stream, throwing either an EOFError at end of file or a TruncatedDataError if fewer than the requested number of bytes remain in the stream.

- Normally, `readbytes` would be used with a network connection. Here we illustrate its use with a regular file.

```ruby
require 'readbytes'
File.open("testfile") do |f|
  begin
    loop do
      data = f.readbytes(10)
      p data
    end
  rescue EOFError
    puts "End of File"
  rescue TruncatedDataError => td
    puts "Truncated data: read '#{td.data.inspect}'"
  end
end
```

produces:

```
"This is li"
"ne one\nThi"
"s is line "
"two\nThis i"
"s line thr"
"ee\nAnd so "
Truncated data: read '"on...\n"'
```

| Library | **Readline** | Interface to GNU Readline Library |

Only if: GNU
readline present

The Readline module allows programs to prompt for and receive lines of user input. The module allows lines to be edited during entry, and command history allows previous commands to be recalled and edited. The history can be searched, allowing the user to (for example) recall a previous command containing the text *ruby*. Command completion allows context-sensitive shortcuts: tokens can be expanded in the command line under control of the invoking application. In typical GNU fashion, the underlying readline library supports more options than any user could need and emulates both vi and emacs key bindings.

- This meaningless program implements a trivial interpreter that can increment and decrement a value. It uses the Abbrev module (described on page 655) to expand abbreviated commands when the tab key is pressed.

```ruby
require 'readline'
include Readline
require 'abbrev'
COMMANDS = %w{ exit inc dec }
ABBREV = COMMANDS.abbrev
Readline.completion_proc = proc do |string|
  ABBREV[string]
end
value = 0
loop do
  cmd = readline("wibble [#{value}]: ", true)
  break if cmd.nil?
  case cmd.strip
  when "exit"
    break
  when "inc"
    value += 1
  when "dec"
    value -= 1
  else
    puts "Invalid command #{cmd}"
  end
end
```

```
% ruby code/readline.rb
wibble [0]: inc
wibble [1]: <up-arrow>      => inc
wibble [2]: d<tab>          => dec
wibble [1]: ^r i            => inc
wibble [2]: exit
%
```

Readline

Resolv DNS Client Library

The resolv library is a pure-Ruby implementation of a DNS client—it can be used to convert domain names into corresponding IP addresses. It also supports reverse lookups and the resolution of names in the local hosts file.

The resolv library exists to overcome a problem with the interaction of the standard operating system DNS lookup and the Ruby threading mechanism. On most operating systems, name resolution is synchronous: you issue the call to look up a name, and the call returns when an address has been fetched. Because this lookup often involves network traffic, and because DNS servers can be slow, this call may take a (relatively) long time. During this time, the thread that issued the call is effectively suspended. Because Ruby does not use operating system threads, this means that the interpreter is effectively suspended while a DNS request is being executed from any running Ruby thread. This is sometimes unacceptable. Enter the resolv library. Because it is written in Ruby, it automatically participates in Ruby threading, and hence other Ruby threads can run while a DNS lookup is in progress in one thread.

Loading the additional library resolv-replace insinuates the resolv library into Ruby's socket library (see page 735).

- Use the standard socket library to look up a name. A counter running in a separate thread is suspended while this takes place.

```
require 'socket'

count = 0
Thread.critical = true
thread = Thread.new { Thread.pass; loop {   count += 1;  } }
IPSocket.getaddress("www.ruby-lang.org")   →   "210.163.138.100"
count                                      →   0
```

- Repeat the experiment, but use the resolv library to allow Ruby's threading to work in parallel.

```
require 'socket'
require 'resolv-replace'

count = 0
Thread.critical = true
thread = Thread.new { Thread.pass; loop {   count += 1;  } }
IPSocket.getaddress("www.ruby-lang.org")   →   "210.163.138.100"
count                                      →   370141
```

REXML   XML Processing Library

REXML is a pure-Ruby XML processing library, including DTD-compliant document parsing, XPath querying, and document generation. It supports both tree-based and stream-based document processing. As it is written in Ruby, it is available on all platforms supporting Ruby. REXML has a full and complex interface—this section contains a few small examples.

- Assume the file demo.xml contains

```
<classes language="ruby">
  <class name="Numeric">
    Numeric represents all numbers.
    <class name="Float">
      Floating point numbers have a fraction and a mantissa.
    </class>
    <class name="Integer">
      Integers contain exact integral values.
      <class name="Fixnum">
        Fixnums are stored as machine ints.
      </class>
      <class name="Bignum">
        Bignums store arbitraty-sized integers.
      </class>
    </class>
  </class>
</classes>
```

- Read and process the XML.

```
require 'rexml/document'
xml = REXML::Document.new(File.open("demo.xml"))

puts "Root element: #{xml.root.name}"
puts "\nThe names of all classes"
xml.elements.each("//class") {|c| puts c.attributes["name"] }
puts "\nThe description of Fixnum"
p xml.elements["//class[@name='Fixnum']"].text
```

produces:

```
Root element: classes

The names of all classes
Numeric
Float
Integer
Fixnum
Bignum

The description of Fixnum
"\n      Fixnums are stored as machine ints.\n      "
```

R EXML

- Read in a document, add and delete elements, and manipulate attributes before writing it back out.

```
require 'rexml/document'
include REXML

xml = Document.new(File.open("demo.xml"))

cls = Element.new("class")
cls.attributes["name"] = "Rational"
cls.text = "Represents complex numbers"

# Remove Integer's children, and add our new node as
# the one after Integer
int = xml.elements["//class[@name='Integer']"]

int.delete_at(1)
int.delete_at(2)

int.next_sibling = cls

# Change all the 'name' attributes to class_name
xml.elements.each("//class") do |c|
  c.attributes['class_name'] = c.attributes['name']
  c.attributes.delete('name')
end

# and write it out with a XML declaration at the front
xml << XMLDecl.new
xml.write(STDOUT, 0)
```

produces:

```
<?xml version='1.0'?>
<classes language='ruby'>
  <class class_name='Numeric'>
    Numeric represents all numbers.
    <class class_name='Float'>
      Floating point numbers have a fraction and a mantissa.
    </class>
    <class class_name='Integer'>
      Integers contain exact integral values.


    </class>
    <class class_name='Rational'>Represents complex numbers</class>
  </class>
</classes>
```

| Library | **Rinda** | Tuplespace Implementation |

Tuplespaces are a distributed blackboard system. Processes may add tuples to the blackboard, and other processes may remove tuples from the blackboard that match a certain pattern. Originally presented by David Gelernter, tuplespaces offer an interesting scheme for distributed cooperation among heterogeneous processes.

Rinda, the Ruby implementation of tuplespaces, offers some interesting additions to the concept. In particular, the Rinda implementation uses the === operator to match tuples. This means that tuples may be matched using regular expressions, the classes of their elements, as well as the element values.

See also: DRb (page 670)

- The blackboard is a DRb server that offers a shared tuplespace.

```
require 'drb/drb'
require 'rinda/tuplespace'
require 'my_uri'      # Defines the constant MY_URI
DRb.start_service(MY_URI, Rinda::TupleSpace.new)
DRb.thread.join
```

- The arithmetic agent accepts messages containing an arithmetic operator and two numbers. It stores the result back on the blackboard.

```
require 'drb/drb'
require 'rinda/rinda'
require 'my_uri'
DRb.start_service
ts = Rinda::TupleSpaceProxy.new(DRbObject.new(nil, MY_URI))
loop do
  op, v1, v2 = ts.take([ %r{^[-+/*]$}, Numeric, Numeric])
  ts.write(["result", v1.send(op, v2)])
end
```

- The client places a sequence of tuples on the blackboard and reads back the result of each.

```
require 'drb/drb'
require 'rinda/rinda'
require 'my_uri'
DRb.start_service
ts = Rinda::TupleSpaceProxy.new(DRbObject.new(nil, MY_URI))
queries = [[ "+", 1, 2 ], [ "*", 3, 4 ], [ "/", 8, 2 ]]
queries.each do |q|
  ts.write(q)
  ans = ts.take(["result", nil])
  puts "#{q[1]} #{q[0]} #{q[2]} = #{ans[1]}"
end
```

Rich (or RDF) Site Summary, Really Simple Syndication, take your pick. RSS is the
protocol of choice for disseminating news on the Internet. The Ruby RSS library supports creating and parsing streams compliant with the RSS 0.9, RSS 1.0, and RSS 2.0
specifications.

• Read and summarize the latest stories from http://ruby-lang.org.

```
require 'rss/1.0'
require 'open-uri'
open('http://ruby-lang.org/en/index.rdf') do |http|
  response = http.read
  result = RSS::Parser.parse(response, false)
  puts "Channel: " + result.channel.title
  result.items.each_with_index do |item, i|
    puts "#{i+1}. #{item.title}" if i < 4
  end
end
```

produces:

```
Channel: Ruby Home Page
1. Brad Cox to keynote RubyConf 2004
2. Download Ruby
3. RubyConf 2004 registration now open
4. ruby 1.8.2 preview1 released
```

• Generate some RSS information.

```
require 'rss/0.9'
rss = RSS::Rss.new("0.9")
chan = RSS::Rss::Channel.new
chan.description = "Dave's Feed"
chan.link = "http://pragprog.com/pragdave"
rss.channel = chan

image = RSS::Rss::Channel::Image.new
image.url = "http://pragprog.com/pragdave.gif"
image.title = "PragDave"
image.link = chan.link
chan.image = image

3.times do |i|
  item = RSS::Rss::Channel::Item.new
  item.title = "My News Number #{i}"
  item.link = "http://pragprog.com/pragdave/story_#{i}"
  item.description = "This is a story about number #{i}"
  chan.items << item
end

puts rss.to_s
```

Scanf   Input Format Conversion

Implements a version of the C library `scanf` function, which extracts values from a string under the control of a format specifier.

The Ruby version of the library adds a `scanf` method to both class `IO` and class `String`. The version in `IO` applies the format string to the next line read from the receiver. The version in `String` applies the format string to the receiver. The library also adds the global method `Kernel.scanf`, which uses as its source the next line of standard input.

Scanf has one main advantage over using regular expressions to break apart a string: a regular expression extracts strings whereas `scanf` will return objects converted to the correct type.

- Split a date string into its constituents.

```
require 'scanf'

date = "2004-12-15"
year, month, day = date.scanf("%4d-%2d-%2d")
year            →    2004
month           →    12
day             →    15
year.class      →    Fixnum
```

- The block form of `scanf` applies the format multiple times to the input string, returning each set of results to the block.

```
require 'scanf'
data = "cat:7 dog:9 cow:17 walrus:31"
data.scanf("%[^:]:%d ") do |animal, value|
  puts "A #{animal.strip} has #{value*1.4}"
end
```

produces:

```
A cat has 9.8
A dog has 12.6
A cow has 23.8
A walrus has 43.4
```

- Extract hex numbers.

```
require 'scanf'

data = "decaf bad"
data.scanf("%3x%2x%x")    →    [3564, 175, 2989]
```

SDBM
Interface to SDBM Database

The SDBM database implements a simple key/value persistence mechanism. Because the underlying SDBM library itself is provided with Ruby, there are no external dependencies, and SDBM should be available on all platforms supported by Ruby. SDBM database keys and values must be strings. SDBM databases are effectively hashlike.

See also: DBM (page 666), GDBM (page 682)

- Store a record in a new database, and then fetch it back. Unlike the DBM library, all values to SDBM must be strings (or implement to_str).

```
require 'sdbm'
require 'date'
SDBM.open("data.dbm") do |dbm|
  dbm['name'] = "Walter Wombat"
  dbm['dob']  = Date.new(1997, 12,25).to_s
  dbm['uses'] = "Ruby"
end
SDBM.open("data.dbm", nil) do |dbm|
  p dbm.keys
  p dbm['dob']
  p dbm['dob'].class
end
```

produces:

```
["name", "dob", "uses"]
"1997-12-25"
String
```

Set

Implement Various Forms of Set

A Set is a collection of unique values (where uniqueness is determined using eql? and hash). Convenience methods let you build sets from enumerable objects.

- Basic set operations.

```
require 'set'

set1 = Set.new([:bear, :cat, :deer])

set1.include?(:bat)   →   false
set1.add(:fox)        →   #<Set: {:cat, :deer, :fox, :bear}>

partition = set1.classify {|element| element.to_s.length }

partition    →    {3=>#<Set: {:cat, :fox}>, 4=>#<Set: {:deer,
                   :bear}>}

set2 = [ :cat, :dog, :cow ].to_set
set1 | set2   →   #<Set: {:cat, :dog, :deer, :cow, :fox, :bear}>
set1 & set2   →   #<Set: {:cat}>
set1 - set2   →   #<Set: {:deer, :fox, :bear}>
set1 ^ set2   →   #<Set: {:dog, :deer, :cow, :fox, :bear}>
```

- Partition the users in our /etc/passwd file into subsets where members of each subset have adjacent user IDs.

```
require 'etc'
require 'set'
users = []
Etc.passwd {|u| users << u }
related_users = users.to_set.divide do |u1, u2|
  (u1.uid - u2.uid).abs <= 1
end
related_users.each do |relatives|
  relatives.each {|u| print "#{u.uid}/#{u.name} " }
  puts
end
```

produces:

```
75/sshd 79/appserver 78/mailman 77/cyrus 76/qtss 74/mysql
503/testuser 502/dave
27/postfix 25/smmsp 26/lp
70/www 71/eppc
99/unknown
-2/nobody
1/daemon 0/root
```

Shellwords   Split Line into Words Using POSIX Semantics

Given a string representative of a shell command line, split it into word tokens according to POSIX semantics.

- Spaces between double or single quotes are treated as part of a word.

- Double quotes may be escaped using a backslash.

- Spaces escaped by a backslash are not used to separate words.

- Otherwise tokens separated by whitespace are treated as words.

```
require 'shellwords'
include Shellwords

line = %{Code Ruby, Be Happy!}
shellwords(line)   →   ["Code", "Ruby,", "Be", "Happy!"]

line = %{"Code Ruby", 'Be Happy'!}
shellwords(line)   →   ["Code Ruby,", "Be Happy!"]

line = %q{Code\ Ruby, \"Be Happy\"!}
shellwords(line)   →   ["Code Ruby,", "\"Be", "Happy\"!"]
```

Singleton   The Singleton Pattern

The Singleton design pattern ensures that only one instance of a particular class may be created for the lifetime of a program (see *Design Patterns* [GHJV95]).

The `singleton` library makes this simple to implement. Mix the `Singleton` module into each class that is to be a singleton, and that class's new method will be made private. In its place, users of the class call the method `instance`, which returns a singleton instance of that class.

In this example, the two instances of `MyClass` are the same object.

```
require 'singleton'

class MyClass

  attr_accessor :data
  include Singleton
end

a = MyClass.instance    →    #<MyClass:0x1c20dc>
b = MyClass.instance    →    #<MyClass:0x1c20dc>

a.data = 123            →    123
b.data                  →    123
```

The SOAP library implements both the client and server sides of the SOAP protocol, including support for WSDL, the Web Services Description Language.

A fuller discussion of the SOAP library, including some examples of accessing the Google search API, starts on page 249.

- Create a simple SOAP service that returns the current local time as a string.

```
require 'soap/rpc/standaloneServer'
module TimeServant
  def TimeServant.now
    Time.now.to_s
  end
end
class Server < SOAP::RPC::StandaloneServer
  def on_init
    servant = TimeServant
    add_method(servant, 'now')
  end
end
if __FILE__ == $0
  svr = Server.new('Server',
                   'http://pragprog.com/TimeServer',
                   '0.0.0.0',
                   12321)
  trap('INT') { svr.shutdown }
  svr.start
end
```

- Query the server using a simple SOAP client.

```
require 'soap/rpc/driver'
proxy = SOAP::RPC::Driver.new("http://localhost:12321",
                              "http://pragprog.com/TimeServer")

proxy.add_method("now")
p proxy.now
```

produces:

```
"Thu Aug 26 22:39:14 CDT 2004"
```

The socket extension defines nine classes for accessing the socket-level communications of the underlying system. All of these classes are (indirect) subclasses of class IO, meaning that IO's methods can be used with socket connections.

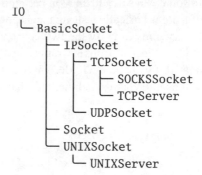

```
IO
 └─ BasicSocket
     ├─ IPSocket
     │   ├─ TCPSocket
     │   │   ├─ SOCKSSocket
     │   │   └─ TCPServer
     │   └─ UDPSocket
     ├─ Socket
     └─ UNIXSocket
         └─ UNIXServer
```

The hierarchy of socket classes reflects the reality of network programming and hence is somewhat confusing. The BasicSocket class largely contains methods common to data transfer for all socket-based connections. It is subclassed to provide protocol-specific implementations: IPSocket, UNIXSocket (for domain sockets), and (indirectly) TCPSocket, UDPSocket, and SOCKSSocket.

BasicSocket is also subclassed by class Socket, which is a more generic interface to socket-oriented networking. While classes such as TCPSocket are specific to a protocol, Socket objects can, with some work, be used regardless of protocol.

TCPSocket, SOCKSSocket, and UNIXSocket are each connection oriented. Each has a corresponding *xxxx*Server class, which implements the server end of a connection.

The socket libraries are something that you may never use directly. However, if you do use them, you'll need to know the details. For that reason, we've included a reference section covering the socket library methods in Appendix A on page 763.

The following code shows a trivial UDP server and client. For more examples see Appendix A.

```ruby
# Simple logger prints messages
# received on UDP port 12121
require 'socket'
socket = UDPSocket.new
socket.bind("127.0.0.1", 12121)
loop do
  msg, sender = socket.recvfrom(100)
  host = sender[3]
  puts "#{Time.now}: #{host} '#{msg}'"
end
```

```ruby
# Exercise the logger
require 'socket'
log = UDPSocket.new
log.connect("127.0.0.1", 12121)
log.print "Up and Running!"
# process ... process ..
log.print "Done!"
```

This produces:

```
Wed Jun 30 17:30:24 CDT 2004: 127.0.0.1 'Up and Running!'
Wed Jun 30 17:30:24 CDT 2004: 127.0.0.1 'Done!'
```

Socket

StringIO   Treat Strings as IO Objects

In some ways the distinction between strings and file contents is artificial: the contents of a file is basically a string that happens to live on disk, not in memory. The `StringIO` library aims to unify the two concepts, making strings act as if they were opened IO objects. Once a string is wrapped in a `StringIO` object, it can be read from and written to as if it were an open file. This can make unit testing a lot easier. It also lets you pass strings into classes and methods that were originally written to work with files.

- Read and write from a string.

```
require 'stringio'

sio = StringIO.new("time flies like an arrow")

sio.read(5)              →   "time "
sio.read(5)              →   "flies"
sio.pos = 18
sio.read(5)              →   " arro"
sio.rewind               →   0
sio.write("fruit")       →   5
sio.pos = 16
sio.write("a banana")    →   8
sio.rewind               →   0
sio.read                 →   "fruitflies like a banana"
```

- Use `StringIO` as a testing aid.

```
require 'stringio'
require 'csv'
require 'test/unit'
class TestCSV < Test::Unit::TestCase
  def test_simple
    StringIO.open do |op|
      CSV::Writer.generate(op) do |csv|
        csv << [ 1, "line 1", 27 ]
        csv << [ 2, nil, 123 ]
      end
      assert_equal("1,line 1,27\n2,,123\n", op.string)
    end
  end
end
```

produces:

```
Loaded suite -
Started
.
Finished in 0.001857 seconds.

1 tests, 1 assertions, 0 failures, 0 errors
```

| Library | **StringScanner** | Basic String Tokenizer |

`StringScanner` objects progress through a string, matching (and optionally returning) tokens that match a given pattern. Unlike the built-in scan methods, `StringScanner` objects maintain a current position pointer in the string being examined, so each call resumes from the position in the string where the previous call left off. Pattern matches are anchored to this previous point.

- Implement a simple language.

```
require 'strscan'
# Handle the language:
#    set <var> = <value>
#    get <var>
values = {}
loop do
  line = gets or break
  scanner = StringScanner.new(line.chomp)
  scanner.scan(/(get|set)\s+/) or fail "Missing command"
  cmd = scanner[1]
  var_name = scanner.scan(/\w+/) or fail "Missing variable"
  case cmd
  when "get"
    puts "#{var_name} => #{values[var_name].inspect}"
  when "set"
    scanner.skip(/\s*=\s+/) or fail "Missing '='"
    value = scanner.rest
    values[var_name] = value
  else
    fail cmd
  end
end
```

produces:

```
% ruby code/strscan.rb
set a = dave
set b = hello
get b
b => "hello"
get a
a => "dave"
```

Sync   Thread Synchronization with Shared Regions

The sync library synchronizes the access to shared data across multiple, concurrent threads. Unlike Monitor, the sync library supports both exclusive access to data and shared (read-only) access.

See also: Monitor (page 695), Mutex (page 696), Thread (page 633)

- Without synchronization, the following code has a race condition: the inc method can be interrupted between fetching the count and storing the incremented value back, resulting in updates being lost.

```
require 'thwait'

class Counter
  attr_reader :total_count
  def initialize
    @total_count = 0
  end
  def inc
    @total_count += 1
  end
end


count = Counter.new
waiter = ThreadsWait.new([])

# create 10 threads that each inc() 10,000 times
10.times do
  waiter.join_nowait(Thread.new { 10000.times { count.inc } })
end

waiter.all_waits
count.total_count   →   62449
```

- Add exclusive synchronization to ensure the count is correct.

```
require 'thwait'
require 'sync'
class Counter
  attr_reader :total_count
  def initialize
    @total_count = 0
    @sync = Sync.new
  end
  def inc
    @sync.synchronize(:EX) do
      @total_count += 1
    end
  end
end
```

```
count = Counter.new
waiter = ThreadsWait.new([])

# create 10 threads that each inc() 10,000 times
10.times do
  waiter.join_nowait(Thread.new { 10000.times { count.inc } })
end

waiter.all_waits    →    nil
count.total_count   →    100000
```

• Add shared region to ensure that readers get consistent picture.

```
require 'thwait'
require 'sync'

class Counter
  attr_reader :total_count
  def initialize
    @total_count = 0
    @count_down = 0
    @sync = Sync.new
  end
  def inc
    @sync.synchronize(:EX) do
      @total_count += 1
      @count_down -= 1
    end
  end
  def test_consistent
    @sync.synchronize(:SH) do
      fail "Bad counts" unless @total_count + @count_down == 0
    end
  end
end

count = Counter.new
waiter = ThreadsWait.new([])

# create 10 threads that each inc() 10,000 times
10.times do
  waiter.join_nowait(Thread.new { 10000.times do
    count.inc
    count.test_consistent
  end })
end

waiter.all_waits    →    nil
count.total_count   →    100000
```

Library **Syslog**   Interface to Unix System Logging

Only if: Unix
system with syslog

The Syslog class is a simple wrapper around the Unix syslog(3) library. It allows messages to be written at various severity levels to the logging daemon, where they are disseminated according to the configuration in syslog.conf. The following examples assume the log file is /var/log/system.log.

- Add to our local system log. We'll log all the levels configured for the user facility for our system (which is every level except debug messages).

```
require 'syslog'
log = Syslog.open("test")   # "test" is the app name
log.debug("Warm and fuzzy greetings from your program")
log.info("Program starting")
log.notice("I said 'Hello!'")
log.warning("If you don't respond soon, I'm quitting")
log.err("You haven't responded after %d milliseconds", 7)
log.alert("I'm telling your mother...")
log.emerg("I'm feeling totally crushed")
log.crit("Aarrgh....")

system("tail -7 /var/log/system.log")
```

produces:

```
Aug 26 22:39:38 wireless_2 test[28505]: Program starting
Aug 26 22:39:38 wireless_2 test[28505]: I said 'Hello!'
Aug 26 22:39:38 wireless_2 test[28505]: If you don't respond soon, I'm quitting
Aug 26 22:39:38 wireless_2 test[28505]: You haven't responded after 7 milliseconds
Aug 26 22:39:38 wireless_2 test[28505]: I'm telling your mother...
Aug 26 22:39:38 wireless_2 test[28505]: I'm feeling totally crushed
Aug 26 22:39:38 wireless_2 test[28505]: Aarrgh....
```

- Only log errors and above.

```
require 'syslog'
log = Syslog.open("test")
log.mask = Syslog::LOG_UPTO(Syslog::LOG_ERR)
log.debug("Warm and fuzzy greetings from your program")
log.info("Program starting")
log.notice("I said 'Hello!'")
log.warning("If you don't respond soon, I'm quitting")
log.err("You haven't responded after %d milliseconds", 7)
log.alert("I'm telling your mother...")
log.emerg("I'm feeling totally crushed")
log.crit("Aarrgh....")

system("tail -7 /var/log/system.log")
```

produces:

```
Aug 26 22:39:38 wireless_2 test[28510]: You haven't responded after 7 milliseconds
Aug 26 22:39:38 wireless_2 test[28510]: I'm telling your mother...
Aug 26 22:39:38 wireless_2 test[28510]: I'm feeling totally crushed
Aug 26 22:39:38 wireless_2 test[28510]: Aarrgh....
```

Tempfile   Temporary File Support

Class `Tempfile` creates managed temporary files. Although they behave the same as any other IO objects, temporary files are automatically deleted when the Ruby program terminates. Once a `Tempfile` object has been created, the underlying file may be opened and closed a number of times in succession.

`Tempfile` does not directly inherit from IO. Instead, it delegates calls to a `File` object. From the programmer's perspective, apart from the unusual new, `open`, and `close` semantics, a `Tempfile` object behaves as if it were an IO object.

If you don't specify a directory to hold temporary files when you create them, the `tmpdir` library will be used to find a system-dependent location.

See also: tmpdir (page 748)

```
require 'tempfile'
```

```
tf = Tempfile.new("afile")
tf.path                    →    "/tmp/afile28519.0"
tf.puts("Cosi Fan Tutte")  →    nil
tf.close                   →    nil
tf.open                    →    #<File:/tmp/afile28519.0>
tf.gets                    →    "Cosi Fan Tutte\n"
tf.close(true)             →    #<File:/tmp/afile28519.0 (closed)>
```

Test::Unit   Unit Testing Framework

Test::Unit is a unit testing framework based on the original SUnit Smalltalk framework. It provides a structure in which unit tests may be organized, selected, and run. Tests can be run from the command line or using one of several GUI-based interfaces.

Chapter 12 on page 151 contains a tutorial on Test::Unit.

We could have a simple playlist class, designed to store and retrieve songs.

```ruby
require 'code/testunit/song.rb'
require 'forwardable'
class Playlist
  extend Forwardable
  def_delegator(:@list, :<<, :add_song)
  def_delegator(:@list, :size)
  def initialize
    @list = []
  end
  def find(title)
    @list.find {|song| song.title == title}
  end
end
```

We can write unit tests to exercise this class. The Test::Unit framework is smart enough to run the tests in a test class if no main program is supplied.

```ruby
require 'test/unit'
require 'code/testunit/playlist.rb'
class TestPlaylist < Test::Unit::TestCase
  def test_adding
    pl = Playlist.new
    assert_equal(0, pl.size)
    assert_nil(pl.find("My Way"))
    pl.add_song(Song.new("My Way", "Sinatra"))
    assert_equal(1, pl.size)
    s = pl.find("My Way")
    assert_not_nil(s)
    assert_equal("Sinatra", s.artist)
    assert_nil(pl.find("Chicago"))
    # .. and so on
  end
end
```

produces:

```
Loaded suite -
Started
.
Finished in 0.002046 seconds.

1 tests, 6 assertions, 0 failures, 0 errors
```

| Library | **thread** | Utility Functionality for Threading |

The `thread` library adds some utility functions and classes for supporting threads. Much of this has been superseded by the `Monitor` class, but it contains two classes, `Queue` and `SizedQueue`, that are still useful. Both classes implement a thread-safe queue that can be used to pass objects between producers and consumers in multiple threads. The `Queue` object implements a unbounded queue. A `SizedQueue` is told its capacity; any producer who tries to add an object when the queue is at that capacity will block until a consumer has removed an object.

- The following example was provided by Robert Kellner. It has three consumers taking objects from an unsized queue. Those objects are provided by two producers, which each add three items.

```ruby
require 'thread'
queue = Queue.new
consumers = (1..3).map do |i|
  Thread.new("consumer #{i}") do |name|
    begin
      obj = queue.deq
      print "#{name}: consumed #{obj.inspect}\n"
      sleep(rand(0.05))
    end until obj == :END_OF_WORK
  end
end
producers = (1..2).map do |i|
  Thread.new("producer #{i}") do |name|
    3.times do |j|
      sleep(0.1)
      queue.enq("Item #{j} from #{name}")
    end
  end
end
producers.each {|th| th.join}
consumers.size.times { queue.enq(:END_OF_WORK) }
consumers.each {|th| th.join}
```

produces:

```
consumer 1: consumed "Item 0 from producer 1"
consumer 2: consumed "Item 0 from producer 2"
consumer 3: consumed "Item 1 from producer 1"
consumer 3: consumed "Item 1 from producer 2"
consumer 3: consumed "Item 2 from producer 2"
consumer 2: consumed "Item 2 from producer 1"
consumer 3: consumed :END_OF_WORK
consumer 2: consumed :END_OF_WORK
consumer 1: consumed :END_OF_WORK
```

Library ThreadsWait   Wait for Multiple Threads to Terminate

Class ThreadsWait handles the termination of a group of thread objects. It provides methods to allow you to check for termination of any managed thread and to wait for all managed threads to terminate.

The following example kicks off a number of threads that each wait for a slightly shorter length of time before terminating and returning their thread number. Using ThreadsWait, we can capture these threads as they terminate, either individually or as a group.

```
require 'thwait'

group = ThreadsWait.new

# construct 10 threads that wait for 1 second, .9 second, etc.
# add each to the group

9.times do |i|
  thread = Thread.new(i) {|index| sleep 1.0 - index/10.0; index }
  group.join_nowait(thread)
end

# any threads finished?
group.finished?              →   false

# wait for one to finish
group.next_wait.value        →   8

# wait for 5 more to finish
5.times { group.next_wait }  →   5

# wait for next one to finish
group.next_wait.value        →   2

# and then wait for all the rest
group.all_waits              →   nil
```

Library **Time**	Extended Functionality for Class Time

The time library adds functionality to the built-in class Time, supporting date and/or time formats used by RFC 2822 (e-mail), RFC 2616 (HTTP), and ISO 8601 (the subset used by XML schema).

```
require 'time'
Time.rfc2822("Thu, 1 Apr 2004 16:32:45 CST")
                          → Thu Apr 01 16:32:45 CST 2004

Time.rfc2822("Thu, 1 Apr 2004 16:32:45 -0600")
                          → Thu Apr 01 16:32:45 CST 2004

Time.now.rfc2822          → Wed, 18 May 2005 09:08:37 -0500

Time.httpdate("Thu, 01 Apr 2004 16:32:45 GMT")
                          → Thu Apr 01 16:32:45 UTC 2004

Time.httpdate("Thursday, 01-Apr-04 16:32:45 GMT")
                          → Thu Apr 01 16:32:45 UTC 2004

Time.httpdate("Thu Apr 1 16:32:45 2004")
                          → Thu Apr 01 16:32:45 UTC 2004

Time.now.httpdate         → Wed, 18 May 2005 14:08:37 GMT

Time.xmlschema("2004-04-01T16:32:45")
                          → Thu Apr 01 16:32:45 CST 2004

Time.xmlschema("2004-04-01T16:32:45.12-06:00")
                          → Thu Apr 01 22:32:45 UTC 2004

Time.now.xmlschema        → 2005-05-18T09:08:37-05:00
```

Timeout   Run a Block with Timeout

The `Timeout.timeout` method takes a parameter representing a timeout period in seconds, an optional exception parameter, and a block. The block is executed, and a timer is run concurrently. If the block terminates before the timeout, `timeout` returns the value of the block. Otherwise, the exception (default `Timeout::Error`) is raised.

```
require 'timeout'
for snooze in 1..2
  puts "About to sleep for #{snooze}"
  begin
    Timeout::timeout(1.5) do |timeout_length|
      puts "Timeout period is #{timeout_length}"
      sleep(snooze)
      puts "That was refreshing"
    end
  rescue Timeout::Error
    puts "Woken up early!!"
  end
end
```

produces:

```
About to sleep for 1
Timeout period is 1.5
That was refreshing
About to sleep for 2
Timeout period is 1.5
Woken up early!!
```

Library		Wrapper for Tcl/Tk
Tk		

Only if: Tk library installed

Of all the Ruby options for creating GUIs, the Tk library is probably the most widely supported, running on Windows, Linux, Mac OS X, and other Unix-like platforms.[5] Although it doesn't produce the prettiest interfaces, Tk is functional and relatively simple to program. The Tk extension is documented more fully in Chapter 19 on page 255.

```ruby
require 'tk'
include Math

TkRoot.new do |root|
  title "Curves"
  geometry "400x400"

 TkCanvas.new(root) do |canvas|
  width 400
  height 400
  pack('side'=>'top', 'fill'=>'both', 'expand'=>'yes')
    points = [ ]
    10.upto(30) do |scale|
      (0.0).step(2*PI,0.1) do |i|
        new_x = 5*scale*sin(i) + 200  +  scale*sin(i*2)
        new_y = 5*scale*cos(i) + 200  +  scale*cos(i*6)
        points << [ new_x, new_y ]
        f = scale/5.0
        r = (Math.sin(f)+1)*127.0
        g = (Math.cos(2*f)+1)*127.0
        b = (Math.sin(3*f)+1)*127.0
        col = sprintf("#%02x%02x%02x", r.to_i, g.to_i, b.to_i)
        if points.size == 3
          TkcLine.new(canvas,
                      points[0][0], points[0][1],
                      points[1][0], points[1][1],
                      points[2][0], points[2][1],
                      'smooth'=>'on',
                      'width'=> 7,
                      'fill'      => col,
                      'capstyle' => 'round')
          points.shift
        end
      end
    end
  end
end
Tk.mainloop
```

5.   Although all these environments require that the Tcl/Tk libraries are installed before the Ruby Tk extension can be used.

Library **tmpdir** System-Independent Temporary Directory Location

The tmpdir library adds the tmpdir method to class Dir. This method returns the path to a temporary directory that *should* be writable by the current process. (This will not be true if none of the well-known temporary directories is writable, and if the current working directory is also not writable.) Candidate directories include those referenced by the environment variables TMPDIR, TMP, TEMP, and USERPROFILE, the directory /tmp, and (on Windows boxes) the temp subdirectory of the Windows or System directory.

```
require 'tmpdir'

Dir.tmpdir   →   "/tmp"

ENV['TMPDIR'] = "/wibble"    # doesn't exist
ENV['TMP']    = "/sbin"      # not writable
ENV['TEMP']   = "/Users/dave/tmp" # just right

Dir.tmpdir   →   "/Users/dave/tmp"
```

Tracer Trace Program Execution

The `tracer` library uses `Kernel.set_trace_func` to trace all or part of a Ruby program's execution. The traced lines show the thread number, file, line number, class, event, and source line. The events shown are "-" for a change of line, ">" for a call, "<" for a return, "C" for a class definition, and "E" for the end of a definition.

- You can trace an entire program by including the `tracer` library from the command line.

```ruby
class Account
  def initialize(balance)
    @balance = balance
  end
  def debit(amt)
    if @balance < amt
      fail "Insufficient funds"
    else
      @balance -= amt
    end
  end
end
acct = Account.new(100)
acct.debit(40)
```

```
% ruby -r tracer account.rb
#0:account.rb:1::-: class Account
#0:account.rb:1:Class:>: class Account
#0:account.rb:1:Class:<: class Account
#0:account.rb:1::C: class Account
#0:account.rb:2::-:   def initialize(balance)
#0:account.rb:2:Module:>:   def initialize(balance)
#0:account.rb:2:Module:<:   def initialize(balance)
#0:account.rb:5::-:   def debit(amt)
#0:account.rb:5:Module:>:   def debit(amt)
#0:account.rb:5:Module:<:   def debit(amt)
#0:account.rb:1::E: class Account
#0:account.rb:13::-: acct = Account.new(100)
#0:account.rb:13:Class:>: acct = Account.new(100)
#0:account.rb:2:Account:>:   def initialize(balance)
#0:account.rb:3:Account:-:     @balance = balance
#0:account.rb:13:Account:<: acct = Account.new(100)
#0:account.rb:13:Class:<: acct = Account.new(100)
#0:account.rb:14::-: acct.debit(40)
#0:account.rb:5:Account:>:   def debit(amt)
#0:account.rb:6:Account:-:     if @balance < amt
#0:account.rb:6:Account:-:     if @balance < amt
#0:account.rb:6:Fixnum:>:     if @balance < amt
#0:account.rb:6:Fixnum:<:     if @balance < amt
#0:account.rb:9:Account:-:       @balance -= amt
#0:account.rb:9:Fixnum:>:       @balance -= amt
#0:account.rb:9:Fixnum:<:       @balance -= amt
#0:account.rb:9:Account:<:       @balance -= amt
```

- You can also use tracer objects to trace just a portion of your code and use filters to select what to trace.

```ruby
require 'tracer'

class Account
  def initialize(balance)
    @balance = balance
  end
  def debit(amt)
    if @balance < amt
      fail "Insufficient funds"
    else
      @balance -= amt
    end
  end
end

tracer = Tracer.new
tracer.add_filter lambda {|event, *rest| event == "line" }
acct = Account.new(100)
tracer.on do
  acct.debit(40)
end
```

```
#0:account.rb:20::-:   acct.debit(40)
#0:account.rb:8:Account:-:     if @balance < amt
#0:account.rb:8:Account:-:     if @balance < amt
#0:account.rb:11:Account:-:       @balance -= amt
```

Given a set of dependencies between nodes (where each node depends on zero or more other nodes, and there are no cycles in the graph of dependencies), a topological sort will return a list of the nodes ordered such that no node follows a node that depends on it. One use for this is scheduling tasks, where the order means that you will complete the dependencies before you start any task that depends on them. The make program uses a topological sort to order its execution.

In this library's implementation, you mix in the TSort module and define two methods: tsort_each_node, which yields each node in turn, and tsort_each_child, which, given a node, yields each of that nodes dependencies.

- Given the set of dependencies among the steps for making a piña colada, what is the optimum order for undertaking the steps?

```
require 'tsort'
class Tasks
  include TSort
  def initialize
    @dependencies = {}
  end
  def add_dependency(task, *relies_on)
    @dependencies[task] = relies_on
  end
  def tsort_each_node(&block)
    @dependencies.each_key(&block)
  end
  def tsort_each_child(node, &block)
    deps = @dependencies[node]
    deps.each(&block) if deps
  end
end
tasks = Tasks.new
tasks.add_dependency(:add_rum,       :open_blender)
tasks.add_dependency(:add_pc_mix,    :open_blender)
tasks.add_dependency(:add_ice,       :open_blender)
tasks.add_dependency(:close_blender, :add_rum, :add_pc_mix, :add_ice)
tasks.add_dependency(:blend_mix,     :close_blender)
tasks.add_dependency(:pour_drink,    :blend_mix)
tasks.add_dependency(:pour_drink,    :open_blender)
puts tasks.tsort
```

produces:

```
open_blender
add_pc_mix
add_ice
add_rum
close_blender
blend_mix
pour_drink
```

Library un — Command-Line Interface to FileUtils

Why un? Because when you invoke it from the command line with the −r option to Ruby, it spells −run. This pun gives a hint as to the intent of the library: it lets you run commands (in this case, a subset of the methods in FileUtils) from the command line. In theory this gives you an operating system–independent set of file manipulation commands, possibly useful when writing portable Makefiles.

See also: FileUtils (page 678)

- The available commands are

```
% ruby -run -e cp -- <options> source dest
% ruby -run -e ln -- <options> target linkname
% ruby -run -e mv -- <options> source dest
% ruby -run -e rm -- <options> file
% ruby -run -e mkdir -- <options> dirs
% ruby -run -e rmdir -- <options> dirs
% ruby -run -e install -- <options> source dest
% ruby -run -e chmod -- <options> octal_mode file
% ruby -run -e touch -- <options> file
```

Note the use of −− to tell the Ruby interpreter that options to the program follow.

You can get a list of all available commands with

```
% ruby -run -e help
```

For help on a particular command, append the command's name.

```
% ruby -run -e help mkdir
```

Library URI — RFC 2396 Uniform Resource Identifier (URI) Support

URI encapsulates the concept of a Uniform Resource Identifier (URI), a way of specifying some kind of (potentially networked) resource. URIs are a superset of URLs: URLs (such as the addresses of Web pages) allow specification of addresses by location, and URIs also allow specification by name.

URIs consist of a scheme (such as `http`, `mailto`, `ftp`, and so on), followed by structured data identifying the resource within the scheme.

URI has factory methods that take a URI string and return a subclass of URI specific to the scheme. The library explicitly supports the `ftp`, `http`, `https`, `ldap`, and `mailto` schemes; others will be treated as generic URIs. The module also has convenience methods to escape and unescape URIs. The class `Net::HTTP` accepts URI objects where a URL parameter is expected.

See also: open-uri (page 707), Net::HTTP (page 699)

```
require 'uri'

uri = URI.parse("http://pragprog.com:1234/mypage.cgi?q=ruby")
uri.class      →    URI::HTTP
uri.scheme     →    "http"
uri.host       →    "pragprog.com"
uri.port       →    1234
uri.path       →    "/mypage.cgi"
uri.query      →    "q=ruby"

uri = URI.parse("mailto:ruby@pragprog.com?Subject=help&body=info")
uri.class      →    URI::MailTo
uri.scheme     →    "mailto"
uri.to         →    "ruby@pragprog.com"
uri.headers    →    [["Subject", "help"], ["body", "info"]]

uri = URI.parse("ftp://dave@anon.com:/pub/ruby;type=i")
uri.class      →    URI::FTP
uri.scheme     →    "ftp"
uri.host       →    "anon.com"
uri.port       →    21
uri.path       →    "/pub/ruby"
uri.typecode   →    "i"
```

URI

In Ruby, objects are not eligible for garbage collection if references still exist to them. Normally, this is a Good Thing—it would be disconcerting to have an object simply evaporate while you were using it. However, sometimes you may need more flexibility. For example, you might want to implement an in-memory cache of commonly used file contents. As you read more files, the cache grows. At some point, you may run low on memory. The garbage collector will be invoked, but the objects in the cache are all referenced by the cache data structures and so will not be deleted.

A weak reference behaves exactly as any normal object reference with one important exception—the referenced object may be garbage collected, even while references to it exist. In the cache example, if the cached files were accessed using weak references, once memory runs low they will be garbage collected, freeing memory for the rest of the application.

- Weak references introduce a slight complexity. As the object referenced can be deleted by garbage collection at any time, code that accesses these objects must take care to ensure that the references are valid. Two techniques can be used. First, the code can reference the objects normally. Any attempt to reference an object that has been garbage collected will raise a WeakRef::RefError exception.

```
require 'weakref'
ref = "fol de rol"
puts "Initial object is #{ref}"
ref = WeakRef.new(ref)
puts "Weak reference is #{ref}"
ObjectSpace.garbage_collect
puts "But then it is #{ref}"
```

produces:

```
Initial object is fol de rol
Weak reference is fol de rol
prog.rb:8: Illegal Reference - probably recycled (WeakRef::RefError)
```

- Alternatively, use the WeakRef#weakref_alive? method to check that a reference is valid before using it. Garbage collection must be disabled during the test and subsequent reference to the object. In a single-threaded program, you could use something like

```
ref = WeakRef.new(some_object)
# .. some time later
gc_was_disabled = GC.disable
if ref.weakref_alive?
  # do stuff with 'ref'
end
GC.enable unless gc_was_disabled
```

WeakRef

WEBrick   Web Server Toolkit

WEBrick is a pure-Ruby framework for implementing HTTP-based servers. The standard library includes WEBrick services that implement a standard Web server (serving files and directory listings), and servlets supporting CGI, erb, file download, and the mounting of Ruby lambdas.

More examples of WEBrick start on page 247.

- The following code mounts two Ruby procs on a Web server. Requests to the URI `http://localhost:2000/hello` run one proc, and requests to `http://localhost:2000/bye` run the other.

```ruby
#!/usr/bin/ruby
require 'webrick'
include WEBrick
hello_proc = lambda do |req, resp|
  resp['Content-Type'] = "text/html"
  resp.body = %{
      <html><body>
        Hello. You're calling from a #{req['User-Agent']}
       <p>
        I see parameters: #{req.query.keys.join(', ')}
      </body></html>
  }
end
bye_proc = lambda do |req, resp|
  resp['Content-Type'] = "text/html"
  resp.body = %{
      <html><body>
        <h3>Goodbye!</h3>
      </body></html>
  }
end

hello =  HTTPServlet::ProcHandler.new(hello_proc)
bye   =  HTTPServlet::ProcHandler.new(bye_proc)
s = HTTPServer.new(:Port => 2000)
s.mount("/hello", hello)
s.mount("/bye",    bye)
trap("INT"){ s.shutdown }
s.start
```

WEBrick

| Library | **Win32API** | Access Entry Points in Windows DLLs |

Only if: Windows
The Win32API module allows access to any arbitrary Windows 32 function. Many of these functions take or return a Pointer data type—a region of memory corresponding to a C string or structure type.

In Ruby, these pointers are represented using class String, which contains a sequence of 8-bit bytes. It is up to you to pack and unpack the bits in the String. See the reference section for unpack on page 623 and pack on page 436 for details.

Parameters 3 and 4 of the new call specify the parameter and return types of the method to be called. The type specifiers are n and l for numbers, i for integers, p for pointers to data stored in a string, and v for the void type (used for export parameters only). These strings are case-insensitive. Method parameters are specified as an array of strings, and the return type is a single string.

The functionality of Win32API is also provided using the dl/win32 library. As the DL library is newer, this may be a sign that the original Win32API may be phased out over time.

See also: DL (page 669)

- This example is from the Ruby distribution, in ext/Win32API.

```
require 'Win32API'
get_cursor_pos = Win32API.new("user32", "GetCursorPos", ['P'], 'V')
lpPoint = " " * 8 # store two LONGs
get_cursor_pos.Call(lpPoint)
x, y = lpPoint.unpack("LL") # get the actual values
print "x: ", x, "\n"
print "y: ", y, "\n"
ods = Win32API.new("kernel32", "OutputDebugString", ['P'], 'V')
ods.Call("Hello, World\n")

GetDesktopWindow = Win32API.new("user32", "GetDesktopWindow", [], 'L')
GetActiveWindow = Win32API.new("user32", "GetActiveWindow", [], 'L')
SendMessage = Win32API.new("user32", "SendMessage", ['L'] * 4, 'L')
SendMessage.Call(GetDesktopWindow.Call, 274, 0xf140, 0)
```

WIN32OLE Windows Automation

Interface to Windows automation, allowing Ruby code to interact with Windows applications. The Ruby interface to Windows is discussed in more detail in Chapter 20 on page 267.

Only if: Windows

See also: Win32API (page 755)

- Open Internet Explorer, and ask it to display our home page.

```
ie = WIN32OLE.new('InternetExplorer.Application')
ie.visible = true
ie.navigate("http://www.pragmaticprogrammer.com")
```

- Create a new chart in Microsoft Excel, and then rotate it.

```
require 'win32ole'
#   -4100 is the value for the Excel constant xl3DColumn.
ChartTypeVal = -4100;
excel = WIN32OLE.new("excel.application")
# Create and rotate the chart
excel['Visible'] = TRUE
excel.Workbooks.Add()
excel.Range("a1")['Value'] = 3
excel.Range("a2")['Value'] = 2
excel.Range("a3")['Value'] = 1
excel.Range("a1:a3").Select()
excelchart = excel.Charts.Add()
excelchart['Type'] = ChartTypeVal
30.step(180, 5) do |rot|
  excelchart.rotation = rot
  sleep(0.1)
end
excel.ActiveWorkbook.Close(0)
excel.Quit()
```

Library **XMLRPC**   Remote Procedure Calls using XML-RPC

XMLRPC allows clients to invoke methods on networked servers using the XML-RPC protocol. Communications take place over HTTP. The server may run in the context of a Web server, in which case ports 80 or 443 (for SSL) will typically be used. The server may also be run stand-alone. The Ruby XML-RPC server implementation supports operation as a CGI script, as a mod_ruby script, as a WEBrick handler, and as a stand-alone server. Basic authentification is supported, and clients can communicate with servers via proxies. Servers may throw FaultException errors—these generate the corresponding exception on the client (or optionally may be flagged as a status return to the call).

See also: SOAP (page 249), dRuby (page 670), WEBrick (page 754)

- The following simple server accepts a temperature in Celsius and converts it to Fahrenheit. It runs within the context of the WEBrick Web server.

```
require 'webrick'
require 'xmlrpc/server'
xml_servlet = XMLRPC::WEBrickServlet.new
xml_servlet.add_handler("convert_celcius") do |celcius|
  celcius*1.8 + 32
end
xml_servlet.add_multicall # Add support for multicall
server = WEBrick::HTTPServer.new(:Port => 2000)
server.mount("/RPC2", xml_servlet)
trap("INT"){ server.shutdown }
server.start
```

- This client makes calls to the temperature conversion server. Note that in the output we show both the server's logging and the client program's output.

```
require 'xmlrpc/client'
server = XMLRPC::Client.new("localhost", "/RPC2", 2000)
puts server.call("convert_celcius", 0)
puts server.call("convert_celcius", 100)
puts server.multicall(['convert_celcius', -10],
                      ['convert_celcius', 200])
```

produces:

```
[2004-04-16 00:5/:02] INFO  WEBrick 1.3.1
[2004-04-16 06:57:02] INFO  WEBrick::HTTPServer#start: pid=11956 port=2000
localhost - - [16/Apr/2004:06:57:13 PDT] "POST /RPC2 HTTP/1.1" 200 124 - -> /RPC2
32.0
localhost - - [16/Apr/2004:06:57:13 PDT] "POST /RPC2 HTTP/1.1" 200 125 - -> /RPC2
212.0
localhost - - [16/Apr/2004:06:57:14 PDT] "POST /RPC2 HTTP/1.1" 200 290 - -> /RPC2
14.0
392.0
```

X MLRPC

YAML   Object Serialization/Deserialization

The YAML library (also described in the tutorial starting on page 416) serializes and deserializes Ruby object trees to and from an external, readable, plain-text format. YAML can be used as a portable object marshaling scheme, allowing objects to be passed in plain text between separate Ruby processes. In some cases, objects may also be exchanged between Ruby programs and programs in other languages that also have YAML support.

• YAML can be used to store an object tree in a flat file.

```
require 'yaml'
tree = { :name => 'ruby',
         :uses => [ 'scripting', 'web', 'testing', 'etc' ]
       }
File.open("tree.yaml", "w") {|f| YAML.dump(tree, f)}
```

• Once stored, it can be read by another program.

```
require 'yaml'
tree = YAML.load_file("tree.yaml")
tree[:uses][1]    →    "web"
```

• The YAML format is also a convenient way to store configuration information for programs. Because it is readable, it can be maintained by hand using a normal editor, and then read as objects by programs. For example, a configuration file may contain

```
---
username: dave
prefs:
  background: dark
  foreground: cyan
  timeout: 30
```

We can use this in a program:

```
require 'yaml'

config = YAML.load_file("code/config.yaml")
config["username"]                →    "dave"
config["prefs"]["timeout"] * 10   →    300
```

Library Zlib — Read and Write Compressed Files

Only if: zlib library available

The Zlib module is home to a number of classes for compressing and decompressing streams, and for working with gzip-format compressed files. They also calculate zip checksums.

• Compress /etc/passwd as a gzip file, and then read the result back.

```
require 'zlib'
# These methods can take a filename
Zlib::GzipWriter.open("passwd.gz") do |gz|
  gz.write(File.read("/etc/passwd"))
end
system("ls -l /etc/passwd passwd.gz")
# or a stream
File.open("passwd.gz") do |f|
  gzip = Zlib::GzipReader.new(f)
  data = gzip.read.split(/\n/)
  puts data[15,3]
end
```

produces:

```
-rw-r--r--  1 root   wheel  1374  8 Dec  2003 /etc/passwd
-rw-r--r--  1 dave   dave    635 18 May 09:08 passwd.gz

daemon:*:1:1:System Services:/var/root:/usr/bin/false
smmsp:*:25:25:Sendmail User:/private/etc/mail:/usr/bin/false
lp:*:26:26:Printing Services:/var/spool/cups:/usr/bin/false
```

• Compress data sent between two processes.

```
require 'zlib'
rd, wr = IO.pipe
if fork
  rd.close
  zipper = Zlib::Deflate.new
  zipper << "This is a string "
  data = zipper.deflate("to compress", Zlib::FINISH)
  wr.write(data)
  wr.close
  Process.wait
else
  wr.close
  unzipper = Zlib::Inflate.new
  unzipper << rd.read
  puts "We got: #{unzipper.inflate(nil)}"
end
```

produces:

```
We got: This is a string to compress
```

Part V

Appendixes

Appendix A

Socket Library

Because the socket and network libraries are such important parts of integrating Ruby applications with the 'net, we've decided to document them in more detail than the other standard libraries.

The hierarchy of socket classes is shown in the diagram below.

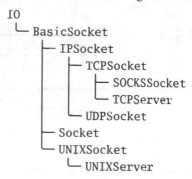

Class **BasicSocket** < IO

BasicSocket is an abstract base class for all other socket classes.

This class and its subclasses often manipulate addresses using something called a struct sockaddr, which is effectively an opaque binary string.[1]

Class methods

do_not_reverse_lookup   BasicSocket.do_not_reverse_lookup → true or false

Returns the value of the global reverse lookup flag.

do_not_reverse_lookup=   BasicSocket.do_not_reverse_lookup = true or false

Sets the global reverse lookup flag. If set to true, queries on remote addresses will return the numeric address but not the host name.

By default the socket library performs this reverse lookup on connections. If for some reason this lookup is slow or times out, connecting to a host can take a long time. Set this option to false to fix this.

for_fd   BasicSocket.for_fd(*fd*) → *sock*

Wraps an already open file descriptor into a socket object.

lookup_order=   BasicSocket.lookup_order = *int*

Sets the global address lookup order.

Instance methods

close_read   *sock*.close_read → nil

Closes the readable connection on this socket.

close_write   *sock*.close_write → nil

Closes the writable connection on this socket.

getpeername   *sock*.getpeername → *string*

Returns the struct sockaddr structure associated with the other end of this socket connection.

getsockname   *sock*.getsockname → *string*

Returns the struct sockaddr structure associated with *sock*.

---

1.   In reality, it maps onto the underlying C-language struct sockaddr set of structures, documented in the man pages and in the books by Stevens.

getsockopt
sock.getsockopt(*level*, *optname*) → *string*

Returns the value of the specified option.

recv
sock.recv(*len*, ⟨ , *flags* ⟩) → *string*

Receives up to *len* bytes from *sock*.

send
sock.send(*string*, *flags*, ⟨ , *to* ⟩) → *int*

Sends *string* over *sock*. If specified, *to* is a `struct sockaddr` specifying the recipient address. *flags* are the sum of one or more of the `MSG_` options (listed on the following page). Returns the number of characters sent.

setsockopt
sock.setsockopt(*level*, *optname*, *optval*) → 0

Sets a socket option. *level* is one of the socket-level options (listed on the next page). *optname* and *optval* are protocol specific—see your system documentation for details.

shutdown
sock.shutdown(*how=2*) → 0

Shuts down the receive (*how* == 0), sender (*how* == 1), or both (*how* == 2), parts of this socket.

Class **Socket** < BasicSocket

Class Socket provides access to the underlying operating system socket implementation. It can be used to provide more operating system–specific functionality than the protocol-specific socket classes but at the expense of greater complexity. In particular, the class handles addresses using struct sockaddr structures packed into Ruby strings, which can be a joy to manipulate.

Class constants

Class Socket defines constants for use throughout the socket library. Individual constants are available only on architectures that support the related facility.

Types:
SOCK_DGRAM, SOCK_PACKET, SOCK_RAW, SOCK_RDM, SOCK_SEQPACKET, SOCK_STREAM

Protocol families:
PF_APPLETALK, PF_AX25, PF_INET6, PF_INET, PF_IPX, PF_UNIX, PF_UNSPEC

Address families:
AF_APPLETALK, AF_AX25, AF_INET6, AF_INET, AF_IPX, AF_UNIX, AF_UNSPEC

Lookup-order options:
LOOKUP_INET6, LOOKUP_INET, LOOKUP_UNSPEC

Send/receive options:
MSG_DONTROUTE, MSG_OOB, MSG_PEEK

Socket-level options:
SOL_ATALK, SOL_AX25, SOL_IPX, SOL_IP, SOL_SOCKET, SOL_TCP, SOL_UDP

Socket options:
SO_BROADCAST, SO_DEBUG, SO_DONTROUTE, SO_ERROR, SO_KEEPALIVE, SO_LINGER, SO_NO_CHECK, SO_OOBINLINE, SO_PRIORITY, SO_RCVBUF, SO_REUSEADDR, SO_SNDBUF, SO_TYPE

QOS options:
SOPRI_BACKGROUND, SOPRI_INTERACTIVE, SOPRI_NORMAL

Multicast options:
IP_ADD_MEMBERSHIP, IP_DEFAULT_MULTICAST_LOOP, IP_DEFAULT_MULTICAST_TTL, IP_MAX_MEMBERSHIPS, IP_MULTICAST_IF, IP_MULTICAST_LOOP, IP_MULTICAST_TTL

TCP options:
TCP_MAXSEG, TCP_NODELAY

getaddrinfo error codes:

EAI_ADDRFAMILY, EAI_AGAIN, EAI_BADFLAGS, EAI_BADHINTS, EAI_FAIL, EAI_FAMILY, EAI_MAX, EAI_MEMORY, EAI_NODATA, EAI_NONAME, EAI_PROTOCOL, EAI_SERVICE, EAI_SOCKTYPE, EAI_SYSTEM

ai_flags values:

AI_ALL, AI_CANONNAME, AI_MASK, AI_NUMERICHOST, AI_PASSIVE, AI_V4MAPPED_CFG

Class methods

getaddrinfo   Socket.getaddrinfo(*hostname, port,*
⟨ *family* ⟨ *, socktype* ⟨ *, protocol* ⟨ *, flags* ⟩ ⟩ ⟩ ⟩) → *array*

Returns an array of arrays describing the given host and port (optionally qualified as shown). Each subarray contains the address family, port number, host name, host IP address, protocol family, socket type, and protocol.

```
for line in Socket.getaddrinfo('www.microsoft.com', 'http')
  puts line.join(", ")
end
```

produces:

```
AF_INET, 80, 207.46.134.221, 207.46.134.221, 2, 2, 17
AF_INET, 80, 207.46.134.221, 207.46.134.221, 2, 1, 6
AF_INET, 80, origin2.microsoft.com, 207.46.144.188, 2, 2, 17
AF_INET, 80, origin2.microsoft.com, 207.46.144.188, 2, 1, 6
AF_INET, 80, microsoft.com, 207.46.230.219, 2, 1, 6
AF_INET, 80, microsoft.net, 207.46.130.14, 2, 1, 6
```

gethostbyaddr   Socket.gethostbyaddr(*addr, type*=AF_INET) → *array*

Returns the host name, address family, and sockaddr component for the given address.

```
a = Socket.gethostbyname("161.58.146.238")
res = Socket.gethostbyaddr(a[3], a[2])
res.join(', ')  →  "www.pragmaticprogrammer.com, , 2, \241:\222\356"
```

gethostbyname   Socket.gethostbyname(*hostname*) → *array*

Returns a four-element array containing the canonical host name, a subarray of host aliases, the address family, and the address portion of the sockaddr structure.

```
a = Socket.gethostbyname("63.68.129.130")
a.join(', ')  →  "63.68.129.130, , 2, ?D\201\202"
```

gethostname   *sock*.gethostname → *string*

Returns the name of the current host.

```
Socket.gethostname  →  "wireless_2.local.thomases.com"
```

---

getnameinfo   Socket.getnameinfo(*addr* ⟨ , *flags* ⟩) → *array*

Looks up the given address, which may be either a string containing a `sockaddr` or a three- or four-element array. If *addr* is an array, it should contain the string address family, the port (or nil), and the host name or IP address. If a fourth element is present and not `nil`, it will be used as the host name. Returns a canonical host name (or address) and port number as an array.

```
Socket.getnameinfo(["AF_INET", '23', 'www.ruby-lang.org'])
```

---

getservbyname   Socket.getservbyname(*service*, *proto*=`'tcp'`) → *int*

Returns the port corresponding to the given service and protocol.

```
Socket.getservbyname("telnet")   →   23
```

---

new   Socket.new(*domain*, *type*, *protocol*) → *sock*

Creates a socket using the given parameters.

---

open   Socket.open(*domain*, *type*, *protocol*) → *sock*

Synonym for `Socket.new`.

---

pack_sockaddr_in   Socket.pack_sockaddr_in(port, host) → *str_address*

1.8 Given a port and a host, return the (system dependent) `sockaddr` structure as a string of bytes.

```
require 'socket'
addr = Socket.pack_sockaddr_in(80, "pragprog.com")
# Pragprog.com is 216.87.136.211
addr.unpack("CCnC4")   →   [16, 2, 80, 216, 87, 136, 211]
```

---

pack_sockaddr_un   Socket.pack_sockaddr_in(path) → *str_address*

1.8 Given a path to a Unix socket, return the (system dependent) `sock_addr_un` structure as a string of bytes. Only available on boxes supporting the Unix address family.

```
require 'socket'
addr = Socket.pack_sockaddr_un("/tmp/sample")
addr[0,20]   →   "\000\001/tmp/sample\000\000\000\000\000\000\000"
```

---

pair   Socket.pair(*domain*, *type*, *protocol*) → *array*

Returns an array containing a pair of connected, anonymous Socket objects with the given domain, type, and protocol.

---

socketpair   Socket.socketpair(*domain*, *type*, *protocol*) → *array*

Synonym for `Socket.pair`.

unpack_sockaddr_in
`Socket.pack_sockaddr_in(string_address)` → [*port, host*]

_{1.8,} Given a string containing a binary `addrinfo` structure, return the port and host.

```
require 'socket'
addr = Socket.pack_sockaddr_in(80, "pragprog.com")
Socket.unpack_sockaddr_in(addr)   →   [80, "216.87.136.211"]
```

unpack_sockaddr_un
`Socket.pack_sockaddr_in(string_address)` → [*port, host*]

_{1.8,} Given a string containing a binary `sock_addr_un` structure, returns the path to the Unix socket. Only available on boxes supporting the Unix address family.

```
require 'socket'
addr = Socket.pack_sockaddr_in(80, "pragprog.com")
Socket.unpack_sockaddr_in(addr)   →   [80, "216.87.136.211"]
```

Instance methods

accept
`sock.accept` → [*socket, address*]

Accepts an incoming connection returning an array containing a new `Socket` object and a string holding the `struct sockaddr` information about the caller.

bind
`sock.bind( sockaddr )` → 0

Binds to the given `struct sockaddr`, contained in a string.

connect
`sock.connect( sockaddr )` → 0

Connects to the given `struct sockaddr`, contained in a string.

listen
`sock.listen( int )` → 0

Listens for connections, using the specified *int* as the backlog.

recvfrom
`sock.recvfrom( len ⟨ , flags ⟩ )` → [*data, sender*]

Receives up to *len* bytes from *sock. flags* is zero or more of the MSG_ options. The first element of the result is the data received. The second element contains protocol-specific information on the sender.

sysaccept
`sock.sysaccept` → [*socket_fd, address*]

_{1.8,} Accepts an incoming connection. Returns an array containing the (integer) file descriptor of the incoming connection and a string holding the `struct sockaddr` information about the caller.

IPSocket < BasicSocket

Class IPSocket is a base class for sockets using IP as their transport. TCPSocket and UDPSocket are based on this class.

Class methods

getaddress   IPSocket.getaddress(*hostname*) → *string*

Returns the dotted-quad IP address of *hostname*.

```
a = IPSocket.getaddress('www.ruby-lang.org')
a   →   "210.251.121.210"
```

Instance methods

addr   *sock*.addr → *array*

Returns the domain, port, name, and IP address of *sock* as a four-element array. The name will be returned as an address if the do_not_reverse_lookup flag is true.

```
u = UDPSocket.new
u.bind('localhost', 8765)
u.addr   →   ["AF_INET", 8765, "localhost", "127.0.0.1"]
BasicSocket.do_not_reverse_lookup = true
u.addr   →   ["AF_INET", 8765, "127.0.0.1", "127.0.0.1"]
```

peeraddr   *sock*.peeraddr → *array*

Returns the domain, port, name, and IP address of the peer.

recvfrom   *sock*.recvfrom(*len* ⟨ ,*flags* ⟩) → [*data*, *sender*]

Receives up to *len* bytes on the connection. *flags* is zero or more of the MSG_ options (listed on page 766). Returns a two-element array. The first element is the received data, and the second is an array containing information about the peer. On systems such as my Mac OS X box where the native recvfrom() method does not return peer information for TCP connections, the second element of the array is nil.

```
require 'socket'
t = TCPSocket.new('localhost', 'ftp')
data = t.recvfrom(40)
data    →   ["220 localhost FTP server (lukemftpd 1.1)", nil]
t.close   →   nil
```

Class **TCPSocket** < IPSocket

```
t = TCPSocket.new('localhost', 'ftp')
t.gets    →    "220 localhost FTP server (lukemftpd 1.1) ready.\r\n"
t.close   →    nil
```

Class methods

gethostbyname   TCPSocket.gethostbyname(*hostname*) → *array*

Looks up *hostname* and returns its canonical name, an array containing any aliases, the address type (AF_INET), and the dotted-quad IP address.

```
a = TCPSocket.gethostbyname('ns.pragprog.com')
a    →    ["pragprog.com", [], 2, "216.87.136.211"]
```

---

new   TCPSocket.new(*hostname*, *port*) → *sock*

Opens a TCP connection to *hostname* on the *port*.

---

open   TCPSocket.open(*hostname*, *port*) → *sock*

Synonym for TCPSocket.new.

Class **SOCKSSocket** < TCPSocket

Class SOCKSSocket supports connections based on the SOCKS protocol.

Class methods

new   SOCKSSocket.new(*hostname*, *port*) → *sock*

Opens a SOCKS connection to *port* on *hostname*.

---

open   SOCKSSocket.open(*hostname*, *port*) → *sock*

Synonym for SOCKSSocket.new.

Instance methods

close   *sock*.close → `nil`

Closes this SOCKS connection.

Class **TCPServer** < TCPSocket

A TCPServer accepts incoming TCP connections. Here is a Web server that listens on a given port and returns the time.

```
require 'socket'
port = (ARGV[0] || 80).to_i
server = TCPServer.new('localhost', port)
while (session = server.accept)
  puts "Request: #{session.gets}"
  session.print "HTTP/1.1 200/OK\r\nContent-type: text/html\r\n\r\n"
  session.print "<html><body><h1>#{Time.now}</h1></body></html>\r\n"
  session.close
end
```

Class methods

new   TCPServer.new(⟨ *hostname,* ⟩ *port*) → *sock*

Creates a new socket on the given interface (identified by *hostname* and port). If *hostname* is omitted, the server will listen on all interfaces on the current host (equivalent to an address of 0.0.0.0).

open   TCPServer.open(⟨ *hostname,* ⟩ *port*) → *sock*

Synonym for TCPServer.new.

Instance methods

accept   *sock*.accept → *tcp_socket*

Waits for a connection on *sock*, and returns a new tcp_socket connected to the caller. See the example on the current page.

Class UDPSocket < IPSocket

UDP sockets send and receive datagrams. To receive data, a socket must be bound to a particular port. You have two choices when sending data: you can connect to a remote UDP socket and thereafter send datagrams to that port, or you can specify a host and port for use with every packet you send. This example is a UDP server that prints the message it receives. It is called by both connectionless and connection-based clients.

```
require 'socket'
$port = 4321
server_thread = Thread.start do      # run server in a thread
  server = UDPSocket.open
  server.bind(nil, $port)
  2.times { p server.recvfrom(64) }
end
# Ad-hoc client
UDPSocket.open.send("ad hoc", 0, 'localhost', $port)

# Connection based client
sock = UDPSocket.open
sock.connect('localhost', $port)
sock.send("connection-based", 0)
server_thread.join
```

produces:

```
["ad hoc", ["AF_INET", 55668, "localhost", "127.0.0.1"]]
["connection-based", ["AF_INET", 55669, "localhost", "127.0.0.1"]]
```

Class methods

new
UDPSocket.new(*family* = AF_INET) → *sock*

Creates a UDP endpoint, optionally specifying an address family.

open
UDPSocket.open(*family* = AF_INET) → *sock*

Synonym for UDPSocket.new.

Instance methods

bind
sock.bind(*hostname, port*) → 0

Associates the local end of the UDP connection with a given *hostname* and *port*. As well as a host name, the first parameter may to "<broadcast>" or "" (the empty string) to bind to INADDR_BROADCAST and INADDR_ANY respectively. Must be used by servers to establish an accessible endpoint.

connect
sock.connect(*hostname, port*) → 0

Creates a connection to the given *hostname* and *port*. Subsequent UDPSocket#send requests that don't override the recipient will use this connection. Multiple connect requests may be issued on *sock*: the most recent will be used by send. As well as a host name, the first parameter may to "<broadcast>" or "" (the empty string) to bind to INADDR_BROADCAST and INADDR_ANY respectively.

---

recvfrom   *sock*.recvfrom(*len* ⟨ , *flags* ⟩) → [*data, sender*]

Receives up to *len* bytes from *sock*. *flags* is zero or more of the MSG_ options (listed on page 766). The result is a two-element array containing the received data and information on the sender. See the example on the preceding page.

---

send   *sock*.send(*string, flags*) → *int*
                                                    sock.send(*string, flags, hostname, port*) → *int*

The two-parameter form sends *string* on an existing connection. The four-parameter form sends *string* to *port* on *hostname*.

Class   UNIXSocket   <   BasicSocket

Class UNIXSocket supports interprocess communications using the Unix domain protocol. Although the underlying protocol supports both datagram and stream connections, the Ruby library provides only a stream-based connection.

```
require 'socket'
SOCKET = "/tmp/sample"
server_thread = Thread.start do      # run server in a thread
  sock = UNIXServer.open(SOCKET)
  s1 = sock.accept
  p s1.recvfrom(124)
end
client = UNIXSocket.open(SOCKET)
client.send("hello", 0)
client.close
server_thread.join
```
produces:
```
["hello", ["AF_UNIX", "q\240"]]
```

Class methods

new   UNIXSocket.new(*path*) → *sock*

Opens a new domain socket on *path*, which must be a pathname.

open   UNIXSocket.open(*path*) → *sock*

Synonym for UNIXSocket.new.

Instance methods

addr   *sock*.addr → *array*

Returns the address family and path of this socket.

path   *sock*.path → *string*

Returns the path of this domain socket.

peeraddr   *sock*.peeraddr → *array*

Returns the address family and path of the server end of the connection.

recvfrom   *sock*.recvfrom(*len* ⟨ , *flags* ⟩) → *array*

Receives up to *len* bytes from *sock*. *flags* is zero or more of the MSG_ options (listed on page 766). The first element of the returned array is the received data, and the second contains (minimal) information on the sender.

| Class | **UNIXServer** < UNIXSocket |

Class UNIXServer provides a simple Unix domain socket server. See UNIXSocket for example code.

Class methods

new   UNIXServer.new(*path*) → *sock*

Creates a server on the given *path*. The corresponding file must not exist at the time of the call.

open   UNIXServer.open(*path*) → *sock*

Synonym for UNIXServer.new.

Instance methods

accept   *sock*.accept → *unix_socket*

Waits for a connection on the server socket and returns a new socket object for that connection. See the example for UNIXSocket on the preceding page.

MKMF Reference

The mkmf library is used by Ruby extension modules to help create Makefiles. Chapter 21, which starts on page 275, describes how these extensions are created and built. This appendix describes the details of the mkmf library.

Module	**mkmf**	require	**"mkmf"**

When writing an extension, you create a program named extconf.rb, which may be as simple as

```
require 'mkmf'
create_makefile("Test")
```

When run, this script will produce a Makefile suited to the target platform. It also produces a log file, mkmf.log, which may help in diagnosing build problems.

mkmf contains several methods you can use to find libraries and include files and to set compiler flags.

mkmf takes configuration information from a variety of sources

- The configuration used when Ruby was built.

- The environment variable CONFIGURE_ARGS, a list of *key=value* pairs.

- Command line arguments of the form key=value or --key=value.

You can examine the configuration by dumping the variable $configure_args.

```
% export CONFIGURE_ARGS="ruby=ruby18 --enable-extras"
% ruby -rmkmf -rpp -e 'pp $configure_args'  -- --with-cflags=-O3
{"--topsrcdir"=>".",
 "--topdir"=>"/Users/dave/Work/rubybook/tmp",
 "--enable-extras"=>true,
 "--with-cflags"=>"-O3",
 "--ruby"=>"ruby18"}
```

The following configuration options are recognized.

CFLAGS

Flags passed to the C compiler (overridden by `--with-cflags`).

CPPFLAGS

Flags passed to the C++ compiler (overridden by `--with-cppflags`).

curdir

Sets the global $curdir, which may be used inside the `extconf.rb` script. Otherwise has no effect.

disable-xxx

Disables extension-specific option *xxx*.

enable-xxx

Enables extension-specific option *xxx*.

LDFLAGS

Flags passed to the linker (overridden by `--with-ldlags`).

ruby

Sets the name and/or path of the Ruby interpreter used in the Makefile.

srcdir

Sets the path to the source directory in the Makefile.

with-cflags

Flags passed to the C compiler. Overrides the `CFLAGS` environment variable.

with-cppflags

Flags passed to the C++ compiler. Overrides the `CPPFLAGS` environment variable.

with-ldflags

Flags passed to the linker compiler. Overrides the `LDFLAGS` environment variable.

with-make-prog

Sets the name of the make program. If running on Windows, the choice of make program affects the syntax of the generated Makefile (`nmake` vs. Borland `make`).

with-xxx-{dir|include|lib}

Controls where the `dir_config` method looks.

Instance methods

create_makefile   create_makefile(*target*, *srcprefix*=nil)

Creates a Makefile for an extension named *target*. The *srcprefix* can override the default source directory. If this method is not called, no Makefile is created.

dir_config   dir_config(*name*)

Looks for directory configuration options for *name* given as arguments to this program or to the original build of Ruby. These arguments may be one of

```
--with-name-dir=directory
--with-name-include=directory
--with-name-lib=directory
```

The given directories will be added to the appropriate search paths (include or link) in the Makefile.

enable_config   enable_config(*name*, *default*=nil) → true or false or *default*

Tests for the presence of an --enable-*name* or --disable-*name* option. Returns true if the enable option is given, false if the disable option is given, and the default value otherwise.

find_library   find_library(*name*, *function*, ⟨ *path* ⟩+) → true or false

Same as have_library, but will also search in the given directory paths.

have_func   have_func(*function*) → true or false

If the named function exists in the standard compile environment, adds the directive -D HAVE_*FUNCTION* to the compile command in the Makefile and returns true.

have_header   have_header(*header*) → true or false

If the given header file can be found in the standard search path, adds the directive -D HAVE_*HEADER* to the compile command in the Makefile and returns true.

have_library   have_library(*library*, *function*) → true or false

If the given function exists in the named library, which must exist in the standard search path or in a directory added with dir_config, adds the library to the link command in the Makefile and returns true.

Support

One of the major features of open source projects is the technical support. Articles in the mass media often criticize open source efforts for not having the same tech support that a commercial product has. And boy is that a good thing! Instead of dialing up some overworked and understaffed help desk and being treated to Music On Hold for an hour or so *without* ever getting the answer you need, we have a better solution: the Ruby community. The author of Ruby, the authors of this book, and many other Ruby users are willing and able to lend you a hand, should you need it.

The syntax of Ruby remains fairly stable, but as with all evolving software, new features are added every now and again. As a result, both printed books and the online documentation can fall behind. All software has bugs, and Ruby is no exception. There aren't many, but they do crop up.

If you experience a problem with Ruby, feel free to ask in the mailing lists or on the newsgroup (more on those in just a minute). Generally you'll get timely answers from Matz himself, the author of the language, from other gurus, and from those who've solved problems similar to your own.

You may be able to find similar questions in the mailing lists or on the newsgroup, and it is good "netiquette" to read through recent postings before asking. If you can't find the answer you need, ask, and a correct answer will usually show up with remarkable speed and precision.

Web Sites

Because the Web changes too fast, we've kept this list short. Visit one of the sites here, and you'll find a wealth of links to other online Ruby resources.

The official Ruby home page is http://www.ruby-lang.org.

You'll find a number of Ruby libraries and applications on RubyForge (`http://www.rubyforge.org`).

RubyForge hosts open-source projects for Ruby developers. Each project has a CVS repository, space to store releases, bug and feature request tracking, a WikiWiki web and mailing lists. Anyone can apply to have a project hosted on this site. RubyForge is also the repository for downloadable RubyGems.

The Ruby Production Archive (RPA) at `http://www.rubyarchive.org` hosts a number of prepackaged Ruby libraries and applications. The site is intended to offer a service similar to that provided by Debian or FreeBSD to their respective communities but for Ruby users. The site had only just become available as this book went to press, and we have no direct experience using it.

Rubygarden hosts both a portal (`http://www.rubygarden.org`) and a WikiWiki site (`http://www.rubygarden.org/ruby`), both full of useful Ruby information.

`http://www.ruby-doc.org` is a portal to various sources of Ruby documentation.

While you're surfing, drop in on `http://www.pragmaticprogrammer.com` and see what we're up to.

Download Sites

You can download the latest version of Ruby from

    http://www.ruby-lang.org/en/

A precompiled Windows distribution is available from

    http://rubyinstaller.rubyforge.org/

This project is also planning to release a Mac OS X One-Click Installer, but this was not ready at the time this book went to press.

Usenet Newsgroup

Ruby has its own newsgroup, `comp.lang.ruby`. Traffic on this group is archived and mirrored to the `ruby-talk` mailing list.

Mailing Lists

You'll find many mailing lists talking about Ruby. The first three below are in English, and the remainder are mostly Japanese, but with some English language posts.

`ruby-talk@ruby-lang.org`	English language discussion of Ruby (mirrored to `comp.lang.ruby`)
`ruby-doc@ruby-lang.org`	Documentation standards and tools
`ruby-cvs@ruby-lang.org`	Notifications of CVS commits to Ruby source
`ruby-core@ruby-lang.org`	Mixed English/Japanese discussion of core implementation topics
`ruby-list@ruby-lang.org`	Japanese language discussion of Ruby
`ruby-dev@ruby-lang.org`	List for Ruby developers
`ruby-ext@ruby-lang.org`	List for people writing extensions for or with Ruby
`ruby-math@ruby-lang.org`	Ruby in mathematics

See the "Mailing Lists" topic under `http://www.ruby-lang.org/` for details on joining a mailing list.

The mailing lists are archived and can be searched using

    `http://blade.nagaokaut.ac.jp/ruby/ruby-talk/index.shtml`,

or using

    `http://www.ruby-talk.org`.

Appendix D

Bibliography

[FJN02]   Robert Feldt, Lyle Johnson, and Micheal Neuman. *The Ruby Developer's Guide*. Syngress Publishing, Inc, Rockland, MA, 2002.

[Fri02]   Jeffrey E. F. Friedl. *Mastering Regular Expressions: Powerful Techniques for Perl and Other Tools*. O'Reilly & Associates, Inc., Sebastopol, CA, second edition, 2002.

[Ful01]   Hal Fulton. *The Ruby Way*. Sams Publishing, 2001.

[GHJV95]   Erich Gamma, Richard Helm, Ralph Johnson, and John Vlissides. *Design Patterns: Elements of Reusable Object-Oriented Software*. Addison-Wesley, Reading, MA, 1995.

[Lid98]   Stephen Lidie. *Perl/Tk Pocket Reference*. O'Reilly & Associates, Inc., Sebastopol, CA, 1998.

[Mcy97]   Bertrand Meyer. *Object-Oriented Software Construction*. Prentice Hall, Englewood Cliffs, NJ, second edition, 1997.

[Wal99]   Nancy Walsh. *Learning Perl/Tk: Graphical User Interfaces with Perl*. O'Reilly & Associates, Inc., Sebastopol, CA, 1999.

Index

Order

!
"
#
$
%
&
'
(
)
*
+
,
-
.
/
:
;
<
=
>
?
@
[
\
]
^
_
`
{
|
}
~

Every built-in and library method described in this book is indexed at least twice, once under the method's name and again under the name of the class or module that contains it. These entries have the method and class/module names in typewriter font and have the word method, class, or module appended. If you want to know what methods class String contains, you can look up "String class" in the index. If instead you want to know which classes and modules support a method called index, look under "index method." A bold page number for these method listings shows the reference section entry.

When a class or method name corresponds with a broader concept (such as String), we've indexed the class separately from the concept.

Symbols are sorted using ASCII collation. The table on the right may help those who haven't yet memorized the positions of the punctuation characters (shame on you all).

Symbols

! (logical not) 94, 341
!= (not equal) 95, 341
!~ (does not match) 69, 95, 341
(comment) 317
#! (shebang) 7
#{...}
   substitute in pattern 70, 326
   substitute in string 61, 321
$ (global variable prefix) 328
$ (in pattern) 70, 324
$ variables
   $! 108, 334, 360, 362
   $" 124, 335
   $$ 335
   $& 69, 334, 537
   $* 335, 523
   $+ 334
   $, 334, 436, 526
   $-0 334
   $-F 335
   $-I 336

$-K 336
$-a 335
$-d 336
$-i 336
$-l 336
$-p 336
$-v 336
$-w 336
$. 334, 510
$/ 178, 179, 334, 610
$: 124, 160, 178, 183, 304, 335
$; 178, 334
$< 335
$= 324, 334
$> 335
$? 89, 148, 150, 335, 338, 516, 531, 587, 591
$@ 334
$\ 179, 334, 511, 526
$_ 24, 95, 101, 178, 335, 342, 510, 523
$` 69, 334, 538

$~ 69, 77, 334, 537, 600–602
$1 to $9 334
$1...$9 69, 74, 326
$0 180, 335, 337
$configure_args 779
$DEBUG 178, 336, 633, 637
$deferr 335
$defout 335
$expect_verbose 676
$F 178, 336
$FILENAME 336
$KCODE 324, 659, 689
$LOAD_PATH 160, 178, 186, 221–223, 225, 228, 336
$SAFE 179, 313, 336, 398, 575, 673
$stderr 335
$stdin 335
$stdout 335
$' 69, 334, 538
$VERBOSE 178, 179, 336, 534
English names 333, 671

% method
   class Bignum **441**
   class Fixnum **484**
   class Float **487**
   class String **606**
%W{...} (array of words) 322
%q{...}, %Q{...} (string
     literal) 62, 320
%r{...} (regexp) 69, 324
%w{...} (array of words) 16,
   322
%x{...} (command expansion)
   89, 338, 516
%{...} (string literal) 62, 320
& (block parameter to method)
   56, 81, 349
& method
   class Array **428**
   class Bignum **441**
   class FalseClass **464**
   class Fixnum **484**
   class NilClass **561**
   class Process::Status **591**
   class TrueClass **650**
&& (logical and) 94, 341
(...) (in pattern) 73, 326
(?...) (regexp extensions)
   326
* (array argument) 347
* (in pattern) 72, 325
* method
   class Array **428**
   class Bignum **441**
   class Fixnum **484**
   class Float **487**
   class String **607**
** method
   class Bignum **441**
   class Fixnum **484**
   class Float **487**
+ (in pattern) 72, 325
+ method
   class Array **428**
   class Bignum **441**
   class Fixnum **484**
   class Float **487**
   class String **607**
   class Time **644**
+@ method
   class Numeric **562**
- method
   class Array **428**
   class Bignum **441**
   class Fixnum **484**

   class Float **487**
   class Time **644**
-@ method
   class Bignum **441**
   class Fixnum **484**
   class Float **487**
   class Numeric **562**
. (in pattern) 325
.. and ... (range) 66, 342
/ method
   class Bignum **441**
   class Fixnum **484**
   class Float **487**
/.../ (regexp) 69, 324
: (symbol creation) 323, 338
: (then replacement) 97, 99
:: (scope resolution) 330, 338,
   352, 354
   vs. "." 349
; (line separator) 317
< (superclass) 352
< method
   module Comparable 447
<, <=, >, >= method
   class Module **546**
<= method
   module Comparable 447
<=> (comparison operator) 67,
   95, 447, 454
<=> method
   class Array **429**
   class Bignum **441**
   class File::Stat **477**
   class Fixnum **484**
   class Float **487**
   class Module **546**
   class Numeric **562**
   class String **607**
   class Time **644**
<<
   here document 62, 321
   singleton object 352, 382
<< method
   class Array **428**
   class Bignum **441**
   class Fixnum **484**
   class IO 132, **507**
   class String **607**
= (assignment) 90, 338
== (equals) 95
== method
   class Array **429**
   class Bignum **441**
   class Float **488**

   class Hash **493**
   class Method **543**
   class Object **567**
   class Process::Status **591**
   class Proc **580**
   class Range **598**
   class Regexp **601**
   class String **607**
   class Struct **627**
   module Comparable 447
=== (case equals) 95, 99, 110,
   343
=== method
   class Module **546**
   class Object **567**
   class Range **598**
   class Regexp **601**
   class String **607**
=>
   hash creation 46, 322
   in argument list 85, 348
   rescue clause 110, 361
=begin...=end 318
   embedded documentation
   202
=~ (match) 69, 95
=~ method
   class Object **567**
   class Regexp **601**
   class String **608**
> method
   module Comparable 447
>= method
   module Comparable 447
>> method
   class Bignum **441**
   class Fixnum **484**
   class Process::Status **591**
? (in pattern) 72, 325
? (ternary operator) 97
@ (instance variable prefix) 328
@@ (class variable prefix) 328
[ ] method
   class Array 44, **427**, **429**
   class Bignum **442**
   class Dir **449**
   class Fixnum **485**
   class Hash **492**, **493**
   class MatchData **537**
   class Method **543**
   class Proc **580**
   class String **608**
   class Struct **627**, **628**
   class Thread **635**

[ ]= method
   class Array 44, **430**
   class Hash **493**
   class String **609**
   class Struct **628**
   class Thread **636**
[...]
   array literal 16, 322
   bracket expression 325
   character class 71
$\ variable 179, 334, 511, 526
\ (line continuation) 317
\& (in substitution) 75
\' (in substitution) 75
\+ (in substitution) 75
\1...\9
   in pattern 74, 326
   in substitution 75
\A (in pattern) 324
\B (in pattern) 325
\D (in pattern) 325
\G (in pattern) 325, 326
\S (in pattern) 325
\W (in pattern) 325
\Z (in pattern) 325
\' (in substitution) 75
\b (in pattern) 325
\d (in pattern) 325
\n (newline) 14, 321
\s (in pattern) 325
\w (in pattern) 325
\z (in pattern) 325
^ (in pattern) 70, 71, 324
^ method
   class Bignum **441**
   class FalseClass **464**
   class Fixnum **484**
   class NilClass **561**
   class TrueClass **650**
__id__ method
   class Object **567**
__send__ method
   class Object **567**
_id2ref method
   module ObjectSpace **578**
$` variable 69, 334, 538
` (backquote) method
   module Kernel 89, 148, **516**
{...}
   hash literal 17, 322
   in pattern 72, 325
   see also Block
--verbose (Ruby option) 535
|

in file name 149
in pattern 73, 325
| method
   class Array **430**
   class Bignum **441**
   class FalseClass **464**
   class Fixnum **484**
   class NilClass **561**
   class TrueClass **650**
|| (logical or) 94, 341
$~ variable 69, 77, 334, 537, 600–602
~ method
   class Bignum **441**
   class Fixnum **484**
   class Regexp **601**
   class String **609**
-0[*octal*] (Ruby option) 178

A

-a (Ruby option) 178, 335, 336
$-a variable 335
Abbrev module 655, 723
Abbreviations, calculating 655
Abort *see* Exception
abort method
   module Kernel **517**
   module Process **583**
abort_on_exception method
   class Thread 138, **633**, **636**
abort_on_exception= method
   class Thread **633**, **636**
abs method
   class Bignum **442**
   class Fixnum **485**
   class Float **488**
   class Numeric **562**
accept method
   class Socket **769**
   class TCPServer **773**
   class UNIXServer **777**
Access control 37, 356
   method 551, 553, 558, 559
   overriding in subclass 393
   see also File, permission
Accessor method 29, 92
acos method
   module Math **540**
acosh method
   module Math **540**
ActiveX *see* Microsoft
   Windows, automation
Ad hoc testing 151

add method
   class ThreadGroup **640**
add_observer method
   module Observable 706
addr method
   class IPSocket **770**
   class UNIXSocket **776**
AF_INET class 688
Alias 40, 169, 330
alias 351
alias_method method
   class Module **554**
   module Kernel 410
alive? method
   class Thread **636**
all? method
   module Enumerable **454**
all_symbols method
   class Symbol **631**
ALLOC 293
ALLOC_N 293
ALLOCA_N 294
allocate method
   class Class **446**
Allocation 287
Amrita
   templates 241
Ancestor 27
ancestors method
   class Module 382, 405, **547**
and (logical and) 94, 341
Anonymous class 382, 445
any? method
   module Enumerable **454**
Aoki, Minero 112
Aoyama, Wakou 76
Apache Web server 243
   mod_ruby 247
API
   Microsoft Windows 268, 755
   Ruby *see* Extend Ruby
APOP authentification 702
append_features method
   class Module **554**
ARGF constant 180
ARGF variable 24, 336
Argument, command-line *see*
   Command line
Argument, method 79, 80
ARGV variable 178–180, 336,
   523, 684, 711
Arithmetic 692, 721
Arithmetic operations
   method

class Bignum **441**
class Fixnum **484**
class Float **487**
arity method
class Method **543**
class Proc **580**
class UnboundMethod **652**
Array
associative *see* Hash
creating 43
expanding as method
parameter 83, 348
indexing 44
literal 16, 322
method argument 347
Array class 373, 427
& **428**
* **428**
+ **428**
- **428**
<=> **429**
<< **428**
== **429**
[ ] 44, **427**, **429**
[ ]= 44, **430**
| **430**
assoc **430**
at **430**
clear **431**
collect! **431**
compact **431**
compact! **431**
concat **431**
delete **431**
delete_at **432**
delete_if **432**
each **432**
each_index **432**
empty? **432**
eql? **432**
fetch **433**
fill **433**
first **433**
flatten **433**
flatten! **434**
include? **434**
index **434**
indexes **434**
indices **434**
insert **434**
join **436**
last **436**
length **436**
map! **436**

new **427**
nitems **436**
pack 131, 435, **436**
pop **437**
push **437**
rassoc **437**
reject! **437**
replace **437**
reverse **437**
reverse! **437**
reverse_each **438**
rindex **438**
scanf 729
shift **438**
size **438**
slice **438**
slice! **439**
sort **439**
sort! **439**
to_a **439**
to_ary **439**
to_s **440**
transpose **440**
uniq **440**
uniq! **440**
unshift **440**
values_at **440**
Array method
module Kernel **516**
ASCII 317
character literal 60, 320
convert integer to 501
asctime method
class Time **644**
asin method
module Math **540**
asinh method
module Math **540**
ASP *see* eruby
assert_equal method 152
assert_not_nil method 156
Assertions *see* Test::Unit,
assertions
Assignment 90, 338
attribute 350
parallel 91, 340
assoc method
class Array **430**
Associative array *see* Hash
Asynchronous I/O 687
at method
class Array **430**
class Time **642**
at_exit method

module Kernel **517**
atan method
module Math **540**
atan2 method
module Math **540**
atanh method
module Math **540**
atime method
class File::Stat **477**
class File **465**, **475**
Atom *see* Symbol
attr method 354
class Module **554**
attr_accessor method 354
class Module **555**
attr_reader method 30, 354,
388
class Module **555**
attr_writer method 354
class Module **555**
Attribute 29
assignment 167, 350
virtual 32
writable 31
see also Class attribute
autoload method
class Module **547**
module Kernel **517**
autoload? method
class Module **547**
module Kernel **518**
Automation, Windows 269, 756
Autosplit mode 178

B

Backquote character *see*
`(backquote)
Backreferences (in regular
expressions) 73–75, 326,
351
Backtrace *see* $@, caller
backtrace method
class Exception **461**
Backup files, creating 178
Base
number 443, 486, 622
Base (numeric) *see* to_s
methods,
Kernel.Integer,
String#to_i
Base64 module 656
base_uri method 707
basename method

class File **465**
BasicSocket class 127, 735,
    764
    close_read **764**
    close_write **764**
    do_not_reverse_lookup
        764
    do_not_reverse_lookup=
        764
    for_fd **764**
    getpeername **764**
    getsockname **764**
    getsockopt **764**
    lookup_order= **764**
    recv **765**
    send **765**
    setsockopt **765**
    shutdown **765**
BEGIN {...} 318
begin method
    class MatchData **537**
    class Range **598**
=begin...=end 318
begin...end 101, 108, 340,
    361
Benchmark module 170, 409,
    657
Berger, Daniel 273
between? method
    module Comparable **447**
BigDecimal class 658
BigMath module 658
Bignum class 59, 441, 484, 658,
    692
    % **441**
    & **441**
    * **441**
    ** **441**
    + **441**
    - **441**
    -@ **441**
    / **441**
    <=> **441**
    << **441**
    == **441**
    >> **441**
    [ ] **442**
    ^ **441**
    | **441**
    ~ **441**
    abs **442**
Arithmetic operations
    441
Bit operations **441**

div **442**
divmod **442**
eql? **442**
literal 59, 319
modulo **442**
quo **442**
remainder **443**
size **443**
to_f **443**
to_s **443**
Binary data 131, 321, 436, 623
Binary notation 59, 319
bind method
    class Socket **769**
    class UDPSocket **774**
    class UnboundMethod **652**
Binding
    in block 333
    GUI events 260
Binding class 337, 444
binding method
    class Proc **581**
    module Kernel 409, 444,
        518
binmode method
    class IO **507**
Bit operations method
    class Bignum **441**
    class Fixnum **484**
blksize method
    class File::Stat **477**
Block 21, 49, 356
    break and next 357
    as closure 55
    and files 128
    for busy cursor 263
    fork, popen, and subprocess
        150, 506, 525, 708
    with method 408
    as parameter to method 80,
        348, 349
    parameters 21, 51
    return from 359
    as transaction 53
    variable scope 105, 136, 333
    see also Iterator
block_given? method
    module Kernel 54, 349, **518**
blockdev? method
    class File::Stat **477**
    class File **466**
blocks method
    class File::Stat **478**
BlueCloth 218

Boolean expressions 341
    see also FalseClass,
        TrueClass
Bottlenecks 170
break 104, 345, 357
Breakpoint 163
Buffering problems 169
Bug see Testing
Build environment see Config
    module
Busy cursor 263

C

-c (Ruby option) 178
-C directory (Ruby option)
    178
C language see Extend Ruby
C language API
    ALLOC 293
    ALLOC_N 293
    ALLOCA_N 294
    Data_Get_Struct 285
    Data_Make_Struct 285
    Data_Wrap_Struct 285
    OBJ_FREEZE 312
    OBJ_FROZEN 313
    OBJ_TAINT 312
    OBJ_TAINTED 312
    rb_apply 309
    rb_ary_entry 314
    rb_ary_new 313
    rb_ary_new2 313
    rb_ary_new3 313
    rb_ary_new4 313
    rb_ary_pop 313
    rb_ary_push 313
    rb_ary_shift 313
    rb_ary_store 313
    rb_ary_unshift 314
    rb_block_given_p 311
    rb_bug 310
    rb_call_super 309
    rb_catch 311
    rb_create_new_instance
        309
    rb_cv_get 312
    rb_cv_set 312
    rb_cvar_defined 312
    rb_cvar_get 312
    rb_cvar_set 312
    rb_define_alias 307
    rb_define_alloc_func
        307

rb_define_attr 309
rb_define_class 305
rb_define_class_under
    305
rb_define_class_
    variable
    308
rb_define_const 308
rb_define_global_const
    308
rb_define_global_
    function
    307
rb_define_hooked_
    variable
    308
rb_define_method 307
rb_define_module 305
rb_define_module_
    function
    307
rb_define_module_under
    306
rb_define_readonly_
    variable
    308
rb_define_singleton_
    method
    307
rb_define_variable 308
rb_define_virtual_
    variable
    308
rb_each 311
rb_ensure 310
rb_exit 310
rb_extend_object 306
rb_fatal 310
rb_funcall 309
rb_funcall2 309
rb_funcall3 309
rb_global_variable 309
rb_gv_get 312
rb_gv_set 312
rb_hash_aref 314
rb_hash_aset 314
rb_hash_new 314
rb_id2name 309
rb_include_module 306
rb_intern 309
rb_iter_break 311
rb_iterate 311
rb_iv_get 311
rb_iv_set 312

rb_ivar_get 312
rb_ivar_set 312
rb_load_file 304
rb_notimplement 310
rb_obj_is_instance_of
    314
rb_obj_is_kind_of 314
rb_protect 310
rb_raise 310
rb_require 306
rb_rescue 310
rb_respond_to 314
rb_safe_level 313
rb_scan_args 307
rb_secure 313
rb_set_safe_level 313
rb_str_cat 314
rb_str_concat 314
rb_str_dup 314
rb_str_new 314
rb_str_new2 314
rb_str_split 314
rb_struct_aref 306
rb_struct_aset 306
rb_struct_define 306
rb_struct_new 306
rb_sys_fail 310
rb_thread_create 314
rb_throw 311
rb_undef_method 307
rb_warn 311
rb_warning 311
rb_yield 311
REALLOC_N 294
ruby_finalize 304
ruby_init 304
ruby_init_loadpath 304
ruby_options 304
ruby_run 304
ruby_script 304
SafeStringValue 313
call method
    class Continuation 448
    class Method 408, 543
    class Proc 581
:call-seq: (RDoc) 206, 209
Callback
    from GUI widget 257
    Ruby runtime 411
    see also Block, closure
callcc method
    module Kernel 448, 518
caller method

module Kernel 113, 412,
    413, 518
CamelCase 328
capitalize method
    class String 609
capitalize! method
    class String 609
captures method
    class MatchData 537
case expression 98, 343
Case insensitive
    string comparison 610
Case insensitive (regexp) 324
casecmp method
    class String 610
casefold? method
    class Regexp 602
catch method
    module Kernel 105, 114,
        362, 519
ceil method
    class Float 488
    class Integer 501
    class Numeric 562
center method
    class String 610
CFLAGS (mkmf) 780
CGI class 236, 659
    cookies 244
    has_key? 238
    params 237
CGI programming 235–253
    cookies 244
    embedding Ruby (eruby)
        242
    forms 237
    generate HTML 238
    mod_ruby 247
    query parameters 237
    quoting 236
    session 246
    WEBrick 247
    see also Network protocols,
        Templates
CGI::Session class 661
CGIKit, Web framework 253
change_privilege method
    module Process::GID 589
    module Process::UID 596
changed method
    module Observable 706
changed? method
    module Observable 706
Character

convert integer to 501
 literal 60, 320
Character class 71
chardev? method
 class File::Stat **478**
 class File **466**
charset method 707
chdir method
 class Dir 182, **449**
Checksum 621, 668
Child process *see* Process
chmod method
 class File **466, 475**
chomp method
 class String 63, **610**
 module Kernel **519**
chomp! method
 class String **610**
 module Kernel **519**
chop method
 class String **610**, 689
 module Kernel **520**
chop! method
 class String **611**, 689
 module Kernel **520**
chown method
 class File **466, 475**
chr method
 class Integer **501**
chroot method
 class Dir **450**
Class
 anonymous 382, 445
 attribute 29, 354
 defining 352, 387
 extending 26
 generator 626
 hierarchy 546
 instance 12, 353
 listing hierarchy 405
 metaclass 380
 method 34, 385
 mixing in module 355
 naming 16, 392
 object specific 382
 vs type 366
 variable 33
 virtual 381, 382
Class class 379, 445
 allocate **446**
 inherited 411, **445**
 new 353, **445, 446**
 superclass 405, **446**
class method

class Object 370, **567**
class_eval method
 class Module **547**
class_variables method
 class Module **548**
Classes
 list of methods 424
 AF_INET 688
 Array 373, 427
 BasicSocket 127, 735, 764
 BigDecimal 658
 Bignum 59, 441, 484, 658, 692
 Binding 337, 444
 CGI 236, 659
 CGI::Session 661
 Class 379, 445
 Complex 662, 692
 Continuation 448, 518
 CSV 663
 CSV::Row 663
 Date 665
 DateTime 665
 DBM 666
 Delegator 667
 Dir 449, 714
 DRb 670
 ERB 673
 Exception 107, 360, 461
 FalseClass 464
 File 127, 465, 483, 681, 714
 File::Stat 477
 Fixnum 59, 484, 692
 Float 60, 487
 GDBM 682
 Generator 683
 GetoptLong 684
 GServer 685
 Hash 373, 492
 Iconv 686
 Integer 373, 501, 692
 IO 127, 373, 503, 676, 729, 735, 736
 IPAddr 688
 IPSocket 735, 770
 Logger 690
 Mail 691
 MatchData 69, 77, 537, 600, 602, 608
 MatchingData 537
 Matrix 694
 Method 408, 543, 555
 Module 545

Monitor 142, 144, 738, 743
Mutex 696, 697
Net::FTP 698
Net::HTTP 699, 752
Net::IMAP 701
Net::POP3 702
Net::SMTP 703
Net::Telnet 704
NilClass 561
Numeric 562, 662
Object 29, 393, 567
OpenStruct 626, 710
OptionParser 711
Pathname 714
PP 715
PrettyPrint 526, 715, 716
Proc 56, 81, 357, 359, 373, 544, 555, 580
Process::Status 150, 587, 588, 591
PStore 719
Queue 141, 145, 743
Range 67, 322, 597
Rational 692, 721
Regexp 76, 600
SDBM 730
Set 428, 430, 731
SimpleDelegator 667
SizedQueue 743
Socket 735, 766
SOCKSSocket 735, 772
String 61, 320, 374, 606, 689, 729
StringIO 132, 736
StringScanner 737
Struct 626
Struct::Tms 630
Symbol 31, 338, 374, 615, 631
Sync 738
SyncEnumerator 683
Syslog 740
TCPServer 773
TCPSocket 735, 771
Tempfile 741
Test::Unit 742
Thread 633
ThreadGroup 636, 640
ThreadsWait 744
Time 465, 642, 745
Tk 747
TrueClass 650
UDPSocket 735, 774

UnboundMethod 408, 543, 544, 549, 651
UNIXServer 777
UNIXSocket 735, 776
URI 752
Vector 694
WeakRef 753
Win32API 669, 755
WIN32OLE 756
clear method
    class Array **431**
    class Hash **493**
Client/Server 417, 670, 685, 734
clone method
    class IO **507**
    class Module **548**
    class Object 288, **568**
close method
    class Dir **452**
    class IO **507**
    class SOCKSSocket **772**
close_read method
    class BasicSocket **764**
    class IO **507**
close_write method
    class BasicSocket **764**
    class IO **508**
closed? method
    class IO **508**
Closure 55, *see* Block
Code profiler 171
Coding system (ASCII, EUC, SJIS, UTF-8) 179, 317n, 321n, 686, 689, 705
coerce method 374
    class Numeric 374, **562**
Coercion 374
Coffee coaster
    attractive xxxii
collect method
    module Enumerable 52, 431, **454**
collect! method
    class Array **431**
COM *see* Microsoft Windows, automation
Comma-separated data 663
Command (type of method) 82n
Command expansion 89
    see also ` (backquote)
Command line 129, 177
    options 178–180
    parsing 684, 711

see also ARGV
Command line, parsing 732
Command, editing with readline 723
Comment 317
    for RDoc 199
    regular expression 326
Common Gateway Interface
    see CGI programming
compact method
    class Array **431**
compact! method
    class Array **431**
Comparable module 119, 447
    < 447
    <= 447
    == 447
    > 447
    >= 447
    between? **447**
    Comparisons **447**
Comparison operators 341
    see also <=>
Comparisons method
    module Comparable **447**
compile method
    class Regexp **600**
Completion, trb 187
Complex class 662, 692
Compression, gzip and zip 759
COMSPEC 182, 521
concat method
    class Array **431**
    class String **611**
Condition variable *see* Thread, condition variable (and Thread, synchronization)
Conditional expression 97, 343
    see also Range
Config module 183
CONFIGURE_ARGS 779
$configure_args variable 779
connect method
    class Socket **769**
    class UDPSocket **774**
const_defined? method
    class Module **548**
const_get method
    class Module **548**
const_missing method
    class Module **548**
const_set method
    class Module **549**
Constant 330

class name 392
    listing in module 406
    scope 330
Constants
    ARGF 180
    DATA 318, 337
    Errno 110
    FALSE 337
    false 93, 336, 341
    __FILE__ 337
    NIL 337
    nil 16, 93, 336, 341
    RUBY_PLATFORM 337
    RUBY_RELEASE_DATE 337
    RUBY_VERSION 337
    SCRIPT_LINES__ 337, 414, 528
    STDERR 337, 534
    STDIN 337, 525
    STDOUT 337, 525, 526
    TOPLEVEL_BINDING 337
    TRUE 337
    true 93, 337, 341
constants method
    class Module **545, 549**
Constructor 12, 25
    initialize method 575
    private 35
Contact, authors' e-mail xxvii
Containers *see* Array and Hash
content_encoding method 707
content_type method 707
Continuation class 448, 518
    call **448**
Control character
    \n etc. 60, 320, 321
Conventions, typographic xxix
Conversion protocols 372
Cookies *see* CGI programming, cookies
cookies method
    class CGI 244
Cookies, HTTP 244
Coordinated Universal Time 642
--copyright (Ruby option) 178
CORBA *see* Distributed Ruby
coredump? method
    class Process::Status **591**
cos method
    module Math **540**
cosh method

module Math **540**
count method
  class String **611**
count_observers method
  module Observable 706
CPPFLAGS (mkmf) 780
CPU times 630
CRAM-MD5 authentication
  701
create_makefile method
  module mkmf 296, **781**
Critical section *see* Thread,
  synchronization
critical method
  class Thread **633**
critical= method
  class Thread 141, **633**
crypt method
  class String **611**
Cryptographic Hashes 668
CSV class 663
CSV::Row class 663
ctime method
  class File::Stat **478**
  class File **466**, **475**
  class Time **644**
curdir (mkmf) 780
Current directory 450
current method
  class Thread **634**
Curses module 664
CVS access to Ruby 6
CVSup 6
cygwin32 267

D

-d (Ruby option) 138, 336, 535
-d, --debug (Ruby option)
  178
$-d variable 336
DATA constant 318, 337
Data_Get_Struct 285
Data_Make_Struct 285
Data_Wrap_Struct 285
Database *see* dbm, gdbm,
  qdbm, sdbm
Datagram *see* Network
  protocols, UDP
Date class 665
  parsing 713
  see also Time class
Date module 642
DateTime class 665

day method
  class Time **644**
DBM class 666
dbm 666
DCOM *see* Microsoft
  Windows, automation
Deadlock *see* Thread
Debian installation 4
$DEBUG variable 178, 336, 633,
  637
Debug mode 138, 178
Debugger 163
  commands 173f
Decimal notation 59, 319
Decoupling 28
Decoux, Guy 289
def (method definition) 79
Default (ThreadGroup
  constant) 640
Default parameters 79, 347
default method
  class Hash **494**
default= method
  class Hash **494**
default_proc method
  class Hash **494**
$deferr variable 335
define_finalizer method
  module ObjectSpace **578**
define_method method
  class Module **555**
  module Module 360
defined? operator 94, 341
$defout variable 335
Delegation 667, 680
Delegator class 667
delete method
  class Array **431**
  class Dir **450**
  class File **466**
  class Hash **494**
  class String **611**, 689
delete! method
  class String **612**, 689
delete_at method
  class Array **432**
delete_if method
  class Array **432**
  class Hash **495**
delete_observer method
  module Observable 706
delete_observers method
  module Observable 706
Delimited string 318

Dependency, RubyGems 215
Design Pattern *see* Patterns
detach method
  module Process **583**
detect method
  module Enumerable **454**
Determinant, matrix 694
dev method
  class File::Stat **478**
dev_major method
  class File::Stat **478**
dev_minor method
  class File::Stat **478**
Dictionary *see* Hash
DIG (Float constant) 487
Digest module 668
Dir
  match modes 468f
Dir class 449, 714
  [ ] **449**
  chdir 182, **449**
  chroot **450**
  close **452**
  delete **450**
  each **452**
  entries **450**
  foreach **450**
  getwd **450**
  glob **451**
  mkdir **451**
  new **451**
  open **452**
  path **452**
  pos **452**
  pos= **453**
  pwd **452**
  read **453**
  rewind **453**
  rmdir **452**
  seek **453**
  tell **453**
  tmpdir 246, 748
  unlink **452**
  see also Find module
dir_config method
  module mkmf 297, **781**
Directories
  include and library for
    extensions 297
  lib/ 296
  pathname 714
  search path 298
  searched 183
  temporary 748

working 178
directory? method
    class File::Stat **478**
    class File **467**
dirname method
    class File **467**
disable method
    module GC **491**
disable-xxx (mkmf) 780
Dispatch table 407
display method
    class Object **568**
Distributed Ruby 417, 670, 727,
    757
Distribution *see* RubyGems
div method
    class Bignum **442**
    class Fixnum **485**
    class Numeric **563**
Division, accuracy 692, 721
divmod method
    class Bignum **442**
    class Fixnum **485**
    class Float **488**
    class Numeric **565**
DL module 669
DL library 273
DLL, accessing API 268, 669,
    755
DLN_LIBRARY_PATH 182
DNS 724
do (in loops) 344
do...end *see* Block
do_not_reverse_lookup
    method
    class BasicSocket **764**
do_not_reverse_lookup=
    method
    class BasicSocket **764**
:doc: (RDoc) 206
Document Type Definition 725
Document-class: (RDoc) 209
Document-method: (RDoc)
    209
Documentation
    doc string example 389
    embedded 199, 318
    modifiers 205
    see also RDoc
doGoogleSearch method 251
Domain Name System 724
Dotted quad *see* Network
    protocols
Double dispatch 375

Double-quoted string 61, 320
downcase method
    class String **612**
downcase! method
    class String **612**
Download
    Ruby 3
    source from book 5
Download Ruby
    sites 784
downto method
    class Integer 102, **501**
dpkg installation 4
DRb
    see also Distributed Ruby
DRb class 670
DRbUndumped module 670
dst? method
    class Time **644**
DTD 725
Duck typing 294, 365–377
_dump 415, 535
dump method
    class String **612**
    module Marshal 414, **536**
dup method
    class Object 288, **568**
Dynamic
    compilation 520
    definitions 387
    linking 301, 669
    method invocation 407
    see also Reflection

E

E (Math constant) 540
-e '*command*' (Ruby option)
    178
E-mail
    date/time formats 745
each method 672
    class Array **432**
    class Dir **452**
    class Hash **495**
    class IO **508**
    class Range **598**
    class String **612**
    class Struct **628**
    module Enumerable 52, 454
each_byte method
    class IO 130, **508**
    class String **613**
each_cons method 672

each_index method
    class Array **432**
each_key method
    class Hash **495**
each_line method
    class IO 130, **509**
    class String **613**
each_object method
    module ObjectSpace 382,
    404, 406, **578**
each_pair method
    class Hash **495**
    class Struct **628**
each_slice method 672
each_value method
    class Hash **495**
each_with_index method
    module Enumerable **455**
Editor
    run Ruby in 165
egid method
    module Process **584**
egid= method
    module Process **584**
eid method
    module Process::GID **589**
    module Process::UID **596**
eid= method
    module Process::GID **589**
    module Process::UID **596**
Eiffel
    once modifier 391
Element reference ([ ]) 351
else (exceptions) 111, 362
    see also if, case
elsif 343
Emacs 165
    tag file 196
Emacs key binding 723
E-mail
    address for feedback xxvii
    fetching with IMAP 701
    fetching with POP 702
    parsing 691
    sending with SMTP 703
Embed Ruby
    in HTML etc. *see* eruby
    interpreter in application 301
Embedded documentation 199,
    318
empty? method
    class Array **432**
    class Hash **495**
    class String **613**

enable method
    module GC **491**
enable-xxx (mkmf) 780
enable_config method
    module mkmf **781**
enclose method
    class ThreadGroup **640**
enclosed? method
    class ThreadGroup **641**
Encodings, character 686, 689,
    705
Encryption 611
__END__ 318, 337
END {...} 318
End of line 130
end method
    class MatchData **538**
    class Range **598**
:enddoc: (RDoc) 207
English library 671
English names for $ variables
    333, 671
ensure (exceptions) 111, 362
entries method
    class Dir **450**
    module Enumerable **455**
enum_for method 672
Enumerable class
    Enumerator 672
Enumerable module 52, 120,
    454, 672, 683
    all? **454**
    any? **454**
    collect 52, 431, **454**
    convert to Set 731
    detect **454**
    each 52, 454
    each_with_index **455**
    entries **455**
    find **455**
    find_all **455**
    grep **455**
    include? **455**
    inject 52, 120, **456**
    map **456**
    max **456**
    member? **456**
    min **456**
    partition **457**
    reject 437, **457**
    select **457**
    sort **457**
    sort_by **457**
    to_a **459**

    zip **459**
Enumerator module 672
ENV variable 181, 336
Environment variables 181
    COMSPEC 182, 521
    DLN_LIBRARY_PATH 182
    HOME 182, 449, 467
    LOGDIR 182, 449
    OPENSSL_CONF 182
    PATH 179
    POSIXLY_CORRECT 684
    RI 9, 214
    RUBY_TCL_DLL 182
    RUBY_TK_DLL 182
    RUBYLIB 182, 183, 401
    RUBYLIB_PREFIX 182
    RUBYOPT 182, 401
    RUBYPATH 179, 182
    RUBYSHELL 182, 521
    SHELL 182
    see also ENV variable
eof method
    class IO **509**
eof? method
    class IO **509**
Epoch 642
EPSILON (Float constant) 487
eql? method 95
    class Array **432**
    class Bignum **442**
    class Float **488**
    class Method **543**
    class Numeric **565**
    class Object **568**
    class Range **599**
    class String **613**
equal? method 95
    class Object **569**
ERB class 673
erb 242, 673
ERB::Util module 674
erf method
    module Math **541**
erfc method
    module Math **541**
Errno constant 110
Errno module 110, 460, 461
Error handling *see* Exception
Errors in book, reporting xxvii
eruby 242–244
    in Apache 243
    see also CGI programming
escape method
    class Regexp **600**

Escaping characters *see*
    Quoting
Etc module 675
EUC 317, 324, 686, 689, 705
euid method
    module Process **584**
euid= method
    module Process **584**
eval method
    module Kernel 408, 444,
    520
Event binding *see* GUI
    programming
Example code, download 5
Example printer 197
Exception 107–115, 360
    ClassCastException 366
    EOFError 722
    in extensions 310
    FaultException 757
    handling 108
    hierarchy 109f
    IndexError 433, 609
    LoadError 222
    LocalJumpError 359
    NameError 333, 363
    raising 112, 527
    RuntimeError 113, 360
    SecurityError 397
    StandardError 108, 110,
    361
    stored in $! 334
    SystemCallError 110, 460,
    521, 531
    SystemExit 180, 462, 463,
    521
    testing 155
    in thread 138, 633
    ThreadError 359
    Timeout::Error 746
    TruncatedDataError 722
    TypeError 40, 280, 415,
    516
Exception class 107, 360, 461
    backtrace **461**
    exception **461**
    message **462**
    new **461**
    set_backtrace **462**
    status **462**
    success? **463**
    to_s **463**
    to_str **463**
exception method

class Exception **461**
exclude_end? method
  class Range **599**
exec method
  module Kernel 149, 506,
    521
executable? method
  class File::Stat **479**
  class File **467**
executable_real? method
  class File::Stat **479**
  class File **467**
Execution
  environment 393
  profiler 171
  tracing 412
exist? method
  class File **467**
exists? method
  class File **467**
Exit status *see* $?
exit method
  class Thread **634**, **636**
  module Kernel 180, 462,
    521
  module Process **584**
exit! method
  module Kernel **522**
  module Process **584**
exited? method
  class Process::Status **592**
exitstatus method
  class Process::Status **592**
exp method
  module Math **541**
expand_path method
  class File **467**
expect library 676
expect method
  class IO 676, 720
$expect_verbose variable 676
Expression 87–106, 338–345
  boolean 93, 341
  case 98, 343
  if 96, 343
  range as boolean 95
  substitution in string 321
  ternary 97, 343
  unless *see* if
extconf.rb 277, 296
  see also mkmf module
Extend Ruby 275–315, 779
  allocation 287
  building extensions 296

    see also mkmf module
call method API 309
clone and dup 288
create object 276, 287
data type conversion API
  280
data type wrapping API 285
define classes API 305
define methods API 306
define structures API 306
documentation (RDoc) 207
embedded Ruby API 304
embedding 301
example code 290
exception API 310
garbage collection 285
initialize 276
internal types 278
iterator API 311
linking 301
memory allocation API 293
object status API 312
strings 280
variable API 308, 311
variables 283
extend method
  class Object 383, 385, **569**
extend_object method
  class Module 411, **556**
EXTENDED (Regexp constant)
  600
Extended mode (regexp) 324
extended method
  class Module **556**
Extending classes 26
External iterator 53, 683
extname method
  class File **467**

F

$F variable 178, 336
-F *pattern* (Ruby option)
  178, 334
$-F variable 335
Factory method 36
fail method
  module Kernel 112, **522**
FALSE constant 337
false constant 93, 336, 341
FalseClass class 464
  & **464**
  ^ **464**
  | **464**

Fcntl module 509, 677
fcntl method
  class IO **509**
FD (file descriptor) 507
Feedback, e-mail address xxvii
fetch method
  class Array **433**
  class Hash **496**
Fibonacci series (fib_up_to)
  50
Field separator *see* $;
__FILE__ constant 337
File
  associations under Windows
    268
  and blocks 128
  descriptor 507
  directory operations *see* Dir
    class
  directory traversal 679
  expanding names 467, 468
  FNM_NOESCAPE 468
  including source 124, 178,
    182
  lock modes 476f
  match modes 468f
  modes 504f
  open modes 472f
  opening 128
  owner 466, 475, 479, 481,
    482
  pathname 470f, 503, 714
  permission 465, 474
  reading 129
  temporary 741
  tests 531
  writing 131
File class 127, 465, 483, 681,
  714
  atime **465**, **475**
  basename **465**
  blockdev? **466**
  chardev? **466**
  chmod **466**, **475**
  chown **466**, **475**
  ctime **466**, **475**
  delete **466**
  directory? **467**
  dirname **467**
  executable? **467**
  executable_real? **467**
  exist? **467**
  exists? **467**
  expand_path **467**

extname 467
file? 468
flock 475
fnmatch 451, 468
fnmatch? 469
ftools extension 681
ftype 469
grpowned? 469
join 469
lchmod 469, 475
lchown 470, 475
link 470
lstat 470, 476
mtime 470, 476
new 128, 470
open 54, 128, 471
owned? 471
path 476
pipe? 471
readable? 471
readable_real? 471
readlink 471
rename 472
setgid? 472
setuid? 472
size 472
size? 472
socket? 473
split 473
stat 473
sticky? 473
symlink 473
symlink? 473
truncate 473, 476
umask 474
unlink 474
utime 474
writable? 474
writable_real? 474
zero? 474
File Transfer Protocol *see*
    Network protocols, FTP
File, reading 722
File::Stat class 477
    <=> 477
    atime 477
    blksize 477
    blockdev? 477
    blocks 478
    chardev? 478
    ctime 478
    dev 478
    dev_major 478
    dev_minor 478

directory? 478
executable? 479
executable_real? 479
file? 479
ftype 479
gid 479
grpowned? 479
ino 479
mode 479
mtime 480
nlink 480
owned? 480
pipe? 480
rdev 480
rdev_major 480
rdev_minor 480
readable? 480
readable_real? 481
setgid? 481
setuid? 481
size 481
size? 481
socket? 481
sticky? 481
symlink? 482
uid 482
writable? 482
writable_real? 482
zero? 482
file? method
    class File::Stat 479
    class File 468
$FILENAME variable 336
fileno method
    class IO 509
FileTest module 483, 714
FileUtils module 678, 751
fill method
    class Array 433
Find module 679
find method
    module Enumerable 455
find_all method
    module Enumerable 455
find_library method
    module mkmf 299, 781
Finger client 133
finite? method
    class Float 488
first method
    class Array 433
    class Range 599
Fixnum class 59, 484, 692
    % 484

& 484
* 484
** 484
+ 484
- 484
-@ 484
/ 484
<=> 484
<< 484
>> 484
[ ] 485
^ 484
| 484
~ 484
abs 485
Arithmetic operations
    484
Bit operations 484
div 485
divmod 485
id2name 485
literal 59, 319
modulo 485
quo 485
range of 59
size 486
to_f 486
to_s 486
to_sym 486
zero? 486
flatten method
    class Array 433
flatten! method
    class Array 434
Float class 60, 487
    % 487
    * 487
    ** 487
    + 487
    - 487
    -@ 487
    / 487
    <=> 487
    == 488
    abs 488
    Arithmetic operations
        487
    ceil 488
    divmod 488
    eql? 488
    finite? 488
    floor 488
    infinite? 489
    literal 60, 320

modulo **489**
nan? **489**
round **489**
to_f **489**
to_i **489**
to_int **489**
to_s **490**
truncate **490**
zero? **490**
Float method
    module Kernel **516**, 621
flock method
    class File **475**
floor method
    class Float **488**
    class Integer **501**
    class Numeric **565**
flush method
    class IO **509**
FNM_*xxx*
    filename match constants
        468
fnmatch method
    class File 451, **468**
fnmatch? method
    class File **469**
for...in loop 103, 344, 672
for_fd method
    class BasicSocket **764**
    class IO **504**
foreach method
    class Dir **450**
    class IO 131, **504**
Fork *see* Process
fork method
    class Thread **634**
    module Kernel 149, 150,
        522
    module Process **584**
format method
    module Kernel **523**
Forms *see* CGI programming,
    forms
Forms (Web) 237
Fortran, documentation 199n
Forwardable module **680**
Forwarding 667, 680
Fowler, Chad xxviii, 215
freeze method
    class Object 170, 394, **569**
    class ThreadGroup **641**
frexp method
    module Math **541**
frozen? method

class Object **570**
fsync method
    class IO **509**
ftools library 681
FTP *see* Network protocols,
    FTP
FTP site for Ruby 3
ftype method
    class File::Stat **479**
    class File **469**
Funaba, Tadayoshi 390
Function *see* Method
Function pointer 408

G

Garbage collection 369, 491,
    578, 753
    internals 285
garbage_collect method
    module GC **491**
    module ObjectSpace **579**
GC module 491
    disable **491**
    enable **491**
    garbage_collect **491**
    start **491**
GDBM class **682**
gdbm 666, 682
Gelernter, David 727
Gem *see* RubyGems
gem_server 220
gemspec 224–226
General delimited string 318
Generator class **683**
Generator library 53
Geometry management 260
get method 699
getaddress method
    class IPSocket **770**
getaddrinfo method
    class Socket **767**
getc method
    class IO **510**
getegid method
    module Process::Sys **594**
geteuid method
    module Process::Sys **594**
getgid method
    module Process::Sys **594**
getgm method
    class Time **645**
gethostbyaddr method
    class Socket **767**

gethostbyname method
    class Socket **767**
    class TCPSocket **771**
gethostname method
    class Socket **767**
getlocal method
    class Time **645**
getnameinfo method
    class Socket **768**
GetoptLong class **684**
getpeername method
    class BasicSocket **764**
getpgid method
    module Process **584**
getpgrp method
    module Process **584**
getpriority method
    module Process **585**
gets method
    class IO **510**
    module Kernel 335, **523**
getservbyname method
    class Socket **768**
getsockname method
    class BasicSocket **764**
getsockopt method
    class BasicSocket **764**
Getter method 29
getuid method
    module Process::Sys **594**
getutc method
    class Time **645**
getwd method
    class Dir **450**
gid method
    class File::Stat **479**
    module Process **585**
gid= method
    module Process **585**
GIF 260, 264
Glob *see* File, expanding names
glob method
    class Dir **451**
Global variables *see* Variables
global_variables method
    module Kernel **523**
gm method
    class Time **642**
GMT 642
gmt? method
    class Time **645**
gmt_offset method
    class Time **645**
gmtime method

class Time **645**
gmtoff method
  class Time **646**
GNU readline 723
Google
  developer key 251
  Web API 251
  WSDL 252
Granger, Michael 218
grant_privilege method
  module Process::GID **589**
  module Process::UID **596**
Graphic User Interface *see* GUI
  programming
Greedy patterns 73
Greenwich Mean Time 642
grep method
  module Enumerable **455**
group method
  class Thread **636**
Grouping (regular expression)
  73
groups method
  module Process **585**, 586
groups= method
  module Process **585**, 586
grpowned? method
  class File::Stat **479**
  class File **469**
GServer class 685
gsub method
  class String 74, 326, **613**
  module Kernel **523**
gsub! method
  class String 326, **614**
  module Kernel **523**
GUI programming 255–266,
  747
  callback from widget 257
  events 260
  geometry management 260
  scrolling 263
  widgets 256–259
GZip compression 759

H

-h, --help (Ruby option) 178
has_key? method
  class CGI 238
  class Hash **496**
has_value? method
  class Hash **496**
Hash 45

creating 46
default value 18
indexing 46
key requirements 323
literal 17, 322
as method parameter 84, 348
Hash class 373, 492
  == **493**
  [ ] **492, 493**
  [ ]= **493**
  => 46
  clear **493**
  default **494**
  default= **494**
  default_proc **494**
  delete **494**
  delete_if **495**
  each **495**
  each_key **495**
  each_pair **495**
  each_value **495**
  empty? **495**
  fetch **496**
  has_key? **496**
  has_value? **496**
  include? **496**
  index **496**
  indexes **497**
  indices **497**
  invert **497**
  key? **497**
  keys **497**
  length **497**
  member? **497**
  merge **497**
  merge! **498**
  new **492**
  rehash 323, **498**
  reject **498**
  reject! **498**
  replace 373, **498**
  select **499**
  shift **499**
  size **499**
  sort **499**
  store **499**
  to_a **499**
  to_hash **499**
  to_s **499**
  update **500**
  value? **500**
  values **500**
  values_at **500**
Hash functions 668

hash method
  class Object **570**
have_func method
  module mkmf 300, **781**
have_header method
  module mkmf 299, **781**
have_library method
  module mkmf 299, **781**
head method 699
Heading, RDoc 205
Here document 62, 321
Hex notation 59, 319
hex method
  class String **614**
Hintze, Clemens 329
HOME 182, 449, 467
Hook 410
hour method
  class Time **646**
Howard, Ara T. 720
HTML *see* CGI programming
HTML, documentation 199
HTTP *see* Network protocols,
  HTTP
HTTPS protocol 709
Hyperlink in documentation
  204
hypot method
  module Math **541**

I

/i regexp option 324
-i [*extension*] (Ruby option)
  178, 336
-I *directories* (Ruby option)
  178, 335
$-I variable 336
$-i variable 336
Ichikawa, Itaru 705
Iconv class 686
id method
  class Object **570**
id2name method
  class Fixnum **485**
  class Symbol **631**
Identifier
  object ID 12, 405
  see also Variable
IEEE floating point 487
-I*directories* (Ruby option)
  183
if expression 96, 343
  as modifier 97, 343

IGNORECASE (Regexp constant) 600

Igpay atinlay *see* Pig latin

in (for loop) 344

In-place edit mode 178

:include: (RDoc) 206

include method 119
   class Module 355, **556**

include? method
   class Array **434**
   class Hash **496**
   class Module **549**
   class Range **599**
   class String **614**
   module Enumerable **455**

included method
   class Module **556**

included_modules method
   class Module **549**

Including source files *see* File, including source

Incremental development 170

Indentation 14

index method
   class Array **434**
   class Hash **496**
   class String 326, **614**

indexes method
   class Array **434**
   class Hash **497**

Indexing
   array 44
   hash 46

indices method
   class Array **434**
   class Hash **497**

infinite? method
   class Float **489**

Inheritance 27, 352
   and access control 393
   method lookup 349, 380
   single *versus* multiple 30
   see also Delegation; Module, mixin

inherited method
   class Class 411, **445**

initgroups method
   module Process **585**

initialize method 25, 37, 353
   class Object **575**

initialize_copy method
   class Object 289, **570**

inject method 52

module Enumerable 52, 120, **456**

ino method
   class File::Stat **479**

Input/Output *see* I/O

insert method
   class Array **434**
   class String **615**

inspect method
   class Object **570**, 715
   class Regexp **602**
   class Symbol **632**

Installation script 678, 751

Installing Ruby 3

Instance
   class instance method *see* Object
   method method *see* Method
   variable *see* Variable

instance_eval method
   class Object **570**

instance_method method
   class Module **549**, 651

instance_methods method
   class Module **550**

instance_of? method
   class Object **571**

instance_variable_get method
   class Object **571**

instance_variable_set method
   class Object **571**

instance_variables method
   class Object **571**

Integer class 373, 501, 692
   ceil **501**
   chr **501**
   downto 102, **501**
   floor **501**
   integer? **501**
   next **501**
   round **501**
   succ **502**
   times 102, **502**
   to_i **502**
   to_int **502**
   truncate **502**
   upto 102, **502**
   see also Fixnum, Bignum

Integer method
   module Kernel 373, **516**

integer? method
   class Integer **501**

class Numeric **565**

Interactive Ruby *see* irb

Intern *see* Symbol

intern method
   class String **615**

Internal iterator 53

Internet *see* Network protocols

Internet Mail Access Protocol (IMAP) *see* Network protocols, IMAP

Interval *see* Range

Introspection *see* Reflection

Inverse, matrix 694

invert method
   class Hash **497**

Invoking *see* Method, calling

IO class 127, 373, 503, 676, 729, 735, 736
   << 132, **507**
   binmode **507**
   clone **507**
   close **507**
   close_read **507**
   close_write **508**
   closed? **508**
   each **508**
   each_byte 130, **508**
   each_line 130, **509**
   eof **509**
   eof? **509**
   expect 676, 720
   fcntl **509**
   fileno **509**
   flush **509**
   for_fd **504**
   foreach 131, **504**
   fsync **509**
   getc **510**
   gets **510**
   ioctl **510**
   isatty **510**
   lineno **510**
   lineno= **511**
   new **504**
   open **505**
   pid **511**
   pipe 149, **505**
   popen 148, **505**
   pos **511**
   pos= **511**
   print **511**
   printf **512**
   putc **512**
   puts **512**

read 506, 512
readbytes 722
readchar 512
readline 512
readlines 506, 513
ready? 687
reopen 373, 513
rewind 513
seek 513
select 373, 507
stat 513
StringIO 736
sync 514
sync= 514
sysopen 507
sysread 514
sysseek 514
syswrite 514
tell 515
to_i 515
to_io 515
tty? 515
ungetc 515
wait 687
write 515
I/O 127–134
  binary data 131
  buffering problems 169
  see also classes File, IO,
    and Network Protocols
io/wait library 687
ioctl method
  class IO 510
Iowa, Web framework 239
IP address representation 688
IP, IPv4, IPv6 see Network
  protocols
IPAddr class 688
IPSocket class 735, 770
  addr 770
  getaddress 770
  peeraddr 770
  recvfrom 770
irb 6, 164, 185–196
  commands 194
  configuration 190
  extending 191
  load files into 187
  options 186f
  prompt 190, 195
  adding ri 191
  subsession 188
  tab completion 187

.irbrc, _irbrc, irb.rc,
  $irbrc 190
is_a? method
  class Object 571
isatty method
  class IO 510
isdst method
  class Time 646
ISO 8601 date 713, 745
issetugid method
  module Process::Sys 594
Iterator 21, 49, 101
  on arbitrary method 672
  in extension 311
  external, internal 53, 683
  for reading files 130
  see also Block
iterator? method
  module Kernel 524

J
JavaSpaces see Distributed
  Ruby
jcode library 689
JINI see Distributed Ruby
JIS 317, 686, 689, 705
join method
  class Array 436
  class File 469
  class Thread 137, 636
JSP see eruby
Jukebox example 25–34, 55–57,
  284–293

K
-K kcode (Ruby option) 179,
  336
$-K variable 336
Kanji 705
$KCODE variable 324, 659, 689
kcode method
  class Regexp 602
Kellner, Robert 743
Kernel module 516
  ` (backquote) 89, 148,
    516
  abort 517
  alias_method 410
  Array 516
  at_exit 517
  autoload 517
  autoload? 518
  binding 409, 444, 518

block_given? 54, 349, 518
callcc 448, 518
caller 113, 412, 413, 518
catch 105, 114, 362, 519
chomp 519
chomp! 519
chop 520
chop! 520
eval 408, 444, 520
exec 149, 506, 521
exit 180, 462, 521
exit! 522
fail 112, 522
Float 516, 621
fork 149, 150, 522
format 523
gets 335, 523
global_variables 523
gsub 523
gsub! 523
Integer 373, 516
iterator? 524
lambda 56, 358, 360, 524,
  581
load 182, 335, 398, 524
local_variables 524
loop 102, 524
method_missing 349, 379
open 134, 525, 707
p 526
pp 715
print 335, 526
printf 335, 526
proc 358, 360, 527
putc 527
puts 527
raise 112, 360, 527
rand 527
readline 335, 527
readlines 528
require 182, 335, 528, 547
scan 528
scanf 729
select 528
set_trace_func 412, 444,
  529, 749
singleton_method_added
  411
singleton_method_
  removed
  411
singleton_method_
  undefineded
  411

sleep **529**
split 178, **529**
sprintf **529**
srand **530**
String **516**
sub **530**
sub! **530**
syscall **530**
system 148, **530**
test **531**
throw 114, 362, **531**
trace_var **532**
trap 150, **534**
untrace_var **534**
warn 179, 336, **534**
   see also Object class
key? method
  class Hash **497**
  class Thread **637**
keys method
  class Hash **497**
  class Thread **637**
Keyword argument 84
Keywords 329
kill method
  class Thread **634**, **637**
  module Process **585**
kind_of? method
  class Object **572**

L

-l (Ruby option) 179, 336
$-l variable 336
lambda method
  module Kernel 56, 358,
    360, **524**, 581
last method
  class Array **436**
  class Range **599**
last_match method
  class Regexp **600**
last_modified method 707
Latent types *see* Duck typing
Layout, source code 317
lchmod method
  class File **469**, **475**
lchown method
  class File **470**, **475**
ldexp method
  module Math **541**
LDFLAGS (mkmf) 780
Leap seconds 647n
Leap year 98

length method
  class Array **436**
  class Hash **497**
  class MatchData **538**
  class String **615**
  class Struct **629**
Library
  Abbrev 655
  Base64 656
  Benchmark 657
  BigDecimal 658
  BigMath 658
  CGI 659
  CGI::Session 661
  Complex 662
  CSV 663
  CSV::Row 663
  Curses 664
  Date 665
  DateTime 665
  DBM 666
  Delegator 667
  Digest 668
  DL 273, 669
  DRb 670
  English 671
  Enumerator 672
  ERB 673
  expect 676
  Fcntl 677
  FileUtils 678
  Find 679
  Forwardable 680
  ftools 681
  GDBM 682
  Generator 53, 683
  GetoptLong 684
  GServer 685
  Iconv 686
  io/wait 687
  IPAddr 688
  jcode 689
  Logger 690
  Mail 691
  mathn 193, 692, 721
  Matrix 694
  mkmf 779
  Monitor 695
  monitor 142
  MonitorMixin 695
  Mutex 696
  Mutex_m 697
  net/http 136
  Net::FTP 698

  Net::HTTP 699
  Net::IMAP 701
  Net::POP3 702
  Net::SMTP 703
  Net::Telnet 704
  NKF 705
  Observable 706
  open-uri 134, 707
  Open3 708
  OpenSSL 709
  OpenStruct 710
  OptionParser 711
  ParseDate 713
  Pathname 714
  PP 715
  PrettyPrint 716
  profile 171, 717
  Profiler__ 718
  PStore 719
  PTY 720
  Queue 743
  Rational 721
  readbytes 722
  Readline 723
  readline 163, 187, 193
  resolv 724
  resolv-replace 724
  REXML 725
  Rinda 727
  RSS 728
  scanf 729
  SDBM 730
  Set 731
  Shellwords 732
  SimpleDelegator 667
  Singleton 733
  SizedQueue 743
  SOAP 734
  Socket 735
  standard 653–759
  StringIO 736
  StringScanner 737
  Sync 738
  SyncEnumerator 683
  Syslog 740
  Tempfile 741
  Test::Unit 742
  thread 141, 145
  ThreadsWait 744
  time 745
  Timeout 746
  Tk 747
  tmpdir 741, 748
  tracer 749

TSort 750
un 751
URI 752
Vector 694
WeakRef 753
WEBrick 754
Win32API 268, 755
WIN32OLE 269, 756
XMLRPC 757
YAML 416, 535, 654, 758
Zlib 759
    see also RubyGems
lib/ directory 296
Linda *see* Distributed Ruby,
    Rinda
Line continuation 317
Line separator *see* End of line
lineno method
    class IO **510**
lineno= method
    class IO **511**
link method
    class File **470**
List *see* Array
    RDoc 204
list method
    class ThreadGroup **641**
    class Thread **634**
    module Signal **604**
listen method
    class Socket **769**
Listener *see* Observer
Literal
    array 322
    ASCII 60, 320
    Bignum 59, 319
    Fixnum 59, 319
    Float 60, 320
    hash 322
    range 66, 322
    regular expression 68, 324
    String 61, 320
    symbol 323
ljust method
    class String **615**
_load 415, 535
load method 119, 124
    module Kernel 182, 335,
        398, **524**
    module Marshal 414, 415,
        536
$LOAD_PATH variable 160, 178,
    186, 221–223, 225, 228,
    336

Local variable *see* Variable
local method
    class Time **643**
local_variables method
    module Kernel **524**
localtime method
    class Time **646**
Locking *see* File class, flock
Locking (file) 475
log method
    module Math **541**
log10 method
    module Math **541**
LOGDIR 182, 449
Logger
    system 740
Logger class 690
lookup_order= method
    class BasicSocket **764**
Loop 501, 502, 566
    see also Iterator
loop method 102, 344
    module Kernel 102, **524**
lstat method
    class File **470**, **476**
lstrip method
    class String **615**
lstrip! method
    class String **615**
Lvalue 90, 338

M

/m regexp option 324
Macdonald, Ian 253
Maeda, Shugo 242
Mail class 691
Mailing lists 784
:main: (RDoc) 207
Main program 393
main method
    class Thread **634**
MAJOR_VERSION (Marshal
    constant) 536
MANIFEST file 301
MANT_DIG (Float constant) 487
map method
    module Enumerable **456**
map! method
    class Array **436**
Marshal module 414–416,
    535–536
    dump 414, **536**
    limitations 535

load 414, 415, **536**
restore **536**
    see also YAML
marshal_dump method 415,
    535
marshal_load method 535
match method
    class Regexp 69, 77, **602**
    class String **616**
MatchData class 69, 77, 537,
    600, 602, 608
    [ ] **537**
    begin **537**
    captures **537**
    end **538**
    length **538**
    offset **538**
    post_match **538**
    pre_match **538**
    select **538**
    size **538**
    string **539**
    to_a **539**
    to_s **539**
    values_at **539**
    see also $~
MatchingData class 537
Math module 540
    acos **540**
    acosh **540**
    asin **540**
    asinh **540**
    atan **540**
    atan2 **540**
    atanh **540**
    cos **540**
    cosh **540**
    erf **541**
    erfc **541**
    exp **541**
    frexp **541**
    hypot **541**
    ldexp **541**
    log **541**
    log10 **541**
    sin **541**
    sinh **542**
    sqrt **542**
    tan **542**
    tanh **542**
mathn library 193, 692, 721
Matrix class 694
Matsumoto, Yukihiro xxii, xxiii,
    xxviii, 76

Matz *see* Matsumoto, Yukihiro
MAX (Float constant) 487
max method
    module Enumerable **456**
MAX_10_EXP (Float constant)
    487
MAX_EXP (Float constant) 487
maxgroups method
    module Process **586**
maxgroups= method
    module Process **586**
mbox (e-mail file) 691
MD5 hash 668
mday method
    class Time **646**
member? method
    class Hash **497**
    class Range **599**
    module Enumerable **456**
members method
    class Struct **627**, **629**
merge method
    class Hash **497**
merge! method
    class Hash **498**
Message
    receiver 13
    sending 12, 28
Message box, Windows 273
message method
    class Exception **462**
Meta character 60, 320
meta method 707
Metaclass 380, 382
Metaprogramming *see*
    Reflection
Method 85
    access control 37, 551, 553,
        558, 559
    aliasing 351
    ambiguity 123
    arguments 347
    array parameter 83
    block as parameter 80
    call, in extension 309
    calling 81, 348
    calling dynamically 407
    class 34, 385
    defining 79, 80, 345
    in extension 306
    getter 29
    instance 12
    with iterator 408
    keyword argument 84

module 118
    naming 16, 79, 346
    nested definition 80
    nested method definition 346
    object 408, 572
    as operator 88
    parameters 79, 80
    private 81
    renaming 410
    return value 80, 82, 350
    setter 31, 92
    vs. variable name 329
    variable-length arguments 80
Method class 408, 543, 555
    == **543**
    [ ] **543**
    arity **543**
    call 408, **543**
    eql? **543**
    to_proc **544**
    unbind **544**
Method module 651
method method
    class Object 543, **572**
method_added method
    class Module 411, **557**
method_defined? method
    class Module **550**
method_missing method
    class Object **572**
    module Kernel 349, 379
method_removed method
    class Module 411, **557**
method_undefined method
    class Module 411, **557**
methods method
    class Object 405, **573**
Meyer, Bertrand 32
Microsoft Windows 267–274
    accessing API 268, 755
    automation 269, 756
    file associations 268
    installing Ruby 4, 784
    message box 273
    printing under 268
    running Ruby 268
    scripting *see* automation
        (above)
MIN (Float constant) 487
min method
    class Time **646**
    module Enumerable **456**
MIN_10_EXP (Float constant)
    487

MIN_EXP (Float constant) 487
MINOR_VERSION (Marshal
    constant) 536
Mirroring, using CVSup 6
MixedCase 16, 328
Mixin *see* Module
mkdir method
    class Dir **451**
mkmf module 779
    building extensions with 296
    create_makefile 296, **781**
    dir_config 297, **781**
    enable_config **781**
    find_library 299, **781**
    have_func 300, **781**
    have_header 299, **781**
    have_library 299, **781**
mkmf library 779
mktime method
    class Time **643**
mod_ruby 247
    safe level 398
mode method
    class File::Stat **479**
Module 117–125
    constant 118
    creating extension *see*
        Extend Ruby
    defining 354
    function 355
    include 119
    instance variable 122
    load 119
    as mixin 118, 355, 383
    as namespace 117
    naming 16
    require 119
    wrap 398
Module class 545
    <, <=, >, >= **546**
    <=> **546**
    === **546**
    alias_method **554**
    ancestors 382, 405, **547**
    append_features **554**
    attr **554**
    attr_accessor **555**
    attr_reader **555**
    attr_writer **555**
    autoload **547**
    autoload? **547**
    class_eval **547**
    class_variables **548**
    clone **548**

const_defined? **548**
const_get **548**
const_missing **548**
const_set **549**
constants 545, **549**
define_method **555**
extend_object 411, **556**
extended **556**
include 355, **556**
include? **549**
included **556**
included_modules **549**
instance_method **549**, 651
instance_methods **550**
method_added 411, **557**
method_defined? **550**
method_removed 411, **557**
method_undefined 411, **557**
module_eval **551**
module_function 355, **558**
name **551**
nesting 545
new **546**
private **558**
private_class_method 35, **551**
private_instance_ methods **552**
private_method_defined? **552**
protected **559**
protected_instance_ methods **552**
protected_method_ defined? **552**
public **559**
public_class_method **553**
public_instance_methods **553**
public_method_defined? **553**
remove_class_variable **559**
remove_const **559**
remove_method **559**
undef_method **559**
Module module
define_method 360
module_eval method
class Module **551**

module_function method
class Module 355, **558**
Modules
list of methods 426
Abbrev 655, 723
Base64 656
Benchmark 170, 409, 657
BigMath 658
Comparable 119, 447
Config 183
Curses 664
Date 642
Digest 668
DL 669
DRbUndumped 670
Enumerable 52, 120, 454, 672, 683
Enumerator 672
ERB::Util 674
Errno 110, 460, 461
Etc 675
Fcntl 509, 677
FileTest 483, 714
FileUtils 678, 751
Find 679
Forwardable 680
GC 491
Kernel 516
Marshal 535
Math 540
Method 651
mkmf 779
Monitor 695
MonitorMixin 144, 695
Mutex_m 141, 697
NKF 705
ObjectSpace 578
Observable 706
Open3 506, 708
ParseDate 642, 713
Process 150, 583, 594
Process::GID 589, 594
Process::Sys 594
Process::UID 594, 596
Profiler 717
Profiler__ 718
PTY 720
Readline 723
REXML 725
Rinda 727
RSS 728
Session 720
Shellwords 732
Signal 534, 604

SingleForwardable 680
Singleton 733
SOAP 734
Sync 141
Timeout 746
TSort 750
WEBrick 754
XMLRPC 757
Zlib 759
modulo method
class Bignum **442**
class Fixnum **485**
class Float **489**
class Numeric **565**
mon method
class Time **646**
Monitor class 142, 144, 738, 743
Monitor module 695
monitor library 142
MonitorMixin module 144, 695
month method
class Time **646**
mswin32 267
mtime method
class File::Stat **480**
class File **470**, **476**
MULTILINE (Regexp constant) 600
Multiline mode (regexp) 324
Multiple inheritance 30
see also Module, mixin
Multithreading *see* Thread
Music on hold 783
Mutex class 696, 697
Mutex_m module 141, 697
Mutual exclusion *see* Thread, synchronization
"My Way" 27

N

-n (Ruby option) 179
Nagai, Hidetoshi 589
Nakada, Nobuyoshi 705
name method
class Module **551**
Namespace *see* Module
Naming conventions 16, 328
file pathnames 503
method names 79
Test::Unit 161
nan? method

class Float **489**
Native thread *see* Thread
ncurses *see* Curses
ndbm 666
Nested assignment 92
nesting method
   class Module **545**
net/http library 136
Net::FTP class 698
Net::HTTP class 699, 752
Net::IMAP class 701
Net::POP3 class 702
Net::SMTP class 703
Net::Telnet class 704
Network protocols
   DNS 724
   domain socket 776
   finger 133
   ftp 698, 707, 752
      secure 709
   generic server for 685
   HTTP 699, 707, 752
   HTTPS 709, 752
   IMAP 701
   IP 770
   IP address representation
      688
   IPv4/IPv6 688
   LDAP 752
   POP 702
   server 773, 777
   SMTP 703
   socket 133, 735, 764, 766
   SOCKS 772
   TCP 771
   telnet 704
   UDP 774
new method
    see also Constructor
new method
   class Array **427**
   class Class 353, **445, 446**
   class Dir **451**
   class Exception **461**
   class File 128, **470**
   class Hash **492**
   class IO **504**
   class Module **546**
   class Proc 524, **580**
   class Range **598**
   class Regexp **600**
   class Socket **768**
   class SOCKSSocket **772**
   class String **606**

class Struct **626, 627**
class TCPServer **773**
class TCPSocket **771**
class ThreadGroup **640**
class Thread 136, **634**
class Time **643**
class UDPSocket **774**
class UNIXServer **777**
class UNIXSocket **776**
Newline (\n) 14, 321
Newsgroup 784
next 104, 345, 357
next method
   class Integer **501**
   class String **616**
next! method
   class String **616**
nfk method
   module NKF 705
NIL constant 337
nil constant 16, 93, 336, 341
nil? method
   class NilClass **561**
   class Object **573**
NilClass class 561
   & **561**
   ^ **561**
   | **561**
   nil? **561**
   to_a **561**
   to_f **561**
   to_i **561**
   to_s **561**
nitems method
   class Array **436**
NKF module 705
   nfk 705
nlink method
   class File::Stat **480**
No-wait mode I/O 687
:nodoc: (RDoc) 206
nonzero? method
   class Numeric **565**
not (logical not) 94, 341
Notation xxix
   binary, decimal, hex, octal
     59, 319
notify_observers method
   module Observable 706
:notnew: (RDoc) 206
now method
   class Time **643**
NTP (Network Time Protocol)
   704

Numbers, unifying 692
Numeric class 562, 662
   +@ **562**
   -@ **562**
   <=> **562**
   abs **562**
   ceil **562**
   coerce 374, **562**
   div **563**
   divmod **565**
   eql? **565**
   floor **565**
   integer? **565**
   mathn 692
   modulo **565**
   nonzero? **565**
   quo **566**
   Rational 721
   remainder **566**
   round **566**
   step 102, **566**
   to_int **566**
   truncate **566**
   zero? **566**

O

/o regexp option 324
OBJ_FREEZE 312
OBJ_FROZEN 313
OBJ_TAINT 312
OBJ_TAINTED 312
Object 12
   aliasing 40, 169, 330
   allocation 287
   creation 25, 353, 410
   extending 382, 385
   finalizer 578
   freezing 394
   ID 12, 405
   immediate 279, 404, 484
   listing active 404
   listing methods in 405
   object_id 578
   persistence 719
   tainting 399
Object class 29, 393, 567
   == **567**
   === **567**
   =~ **567**
   __id__ **567**
   __send__ **567**
   class 370, **567**
   clone 288, **568**

display **568**
dup 288, **568**
eql? **568**
equal? **569**
extend 383, 385, **569**
freeze 170, 394, **569**
frozen? **570**
hash **570**
id **570**
initialize **575**
initialize_copy 289, **570**
inspect **570**, 715
instance_eval **570**
instance_of? **571**
instance_variable_get
    571
instance_variable_set
    571
instance_variables **571**
is_a? **571**
kind_of? **572**
method 543, **572**
method_missing **572**
methods 405, **573**
nil? **573**
object_id **573**
private_methods **573**
protected_methods **573**
public_methods **574**
remove_instance_
    variable
    576
respond_to? 405, **574**
send **574**
singleton_method_added
    576
singleton_method_
    removed
    577
singleton_method_
    undefined
    577
singleton_methods **574**
taint **575**
tainted? **575**
to_a **575**
to_s 26, **575**
to_str 280
type 370, **575**
untaint **575**
    see also Kernel module
Object-oriented terminology 11
object_id method
    class Object **573**

ObjectSpace module 578
    _id2ref **578**
    define_finalizer **578**
    each_object 382, 404, 406,
        578
    garbage_collect **579**
    undefine_finalizer **579**
Observable module 706
    add_observer 706
    changed 706
    changed? 706
    count_observers 706
    delete_observer 706
    delete_observers 706
    notify_observers 706
Observer pattern 706
oct method
    class String **616**
Octal notation 59, 319
offset method
    class MatchData **538**
OLE *see* Microsoft Windows,
    automation
olegen.rb 272
once example 391
Once option (regexp) 324
One-Click Installer 4, 267, 784
OO *see* Object-oriented
open method
    class Dir **452**
    class File 54, 128, **471**
    class IO **505**
    class Socket **768**
    class SOCKSSocket **772**
    class TCPServer **773**
    class TCPSocket **771**
    class UDPSocket **774**
    class UNIXServer **777**
    class UNIXSocket **776**
    module Kernel 134, **525**,
        707
open-uri library 134, 707
Open3 module 506, 708
OpenSSL library 709
OPENSSL_CONF 182
OpenStruct class 626, 710
Operating system errors 460
Operator
    as method call 88, 350
    precedence 339
Optimizing *see* Performance
Option, command line *see*
    Command line
OptionParser class 711

options method
    class Regexp **602**
or (logical or) 94, 341
owned? method
    class File::Stat **480**
    class File **471**
Ownership, file *see* File, owner

P

-p (Ruby option) 179, 336
p method
    module Kernel **526**
$-p variable 336
pack method
    class Array 131, 435, **436**
pack_sockaddr_in method
    class Socket **768**
pack_sockaddr_un method
    class Socket **768**
Packaging *see* RubyGems
pair method
    class Socket **768**
Paragraph mode 178
Parallel assignment 91, 340
Parameter
    default 79
    to block 21
params method
    class CGI 237
Parent-child 27
Parse error 167
ParseDate module 642, 713
    parsedate 643
        see also Time class and
        library
parsedate method
    module ParseDate 643
partition method
    module Enumerable **457**
pass method
    class Thread **635**
PATH 179
path method
    class Dir **452**
    class File **476**
    class UNIXSocket **776**
Pathname *see* File, pathname
Pathname class 714
Pattern *see* Regular expression
Patterns
    factory 36
    observer 706
    singleton 35, 733

peeraddr method
  class IPSocket **770**
  class UNIXSocket **776**
Performance 170, 369, 657
  caching method values 390
  CGI 247
  dynamic method invocation
    409
  profiling 171, 717, 718
  windows automation 272
Perl/Tk *see* GUI programming
Perlisms 24, 76, 100
Permission *see* File, permission
Persistent object storage 719
PHP *see* eruby
PI (Math constant) 540
pid method
  class IO **511**
  class Process::Status **592**
  module Process **586**
Pig latin 148, 259
Pipe *see* IO.pipe, IO.popen
pipe method
  class IO 149, **505**
pipe? method
  class File::Stat **480**
  class File **471**
pop method
  class Array **437**
popen method
  class IO 148, **505**
pos method
  class Dir **452**
  class IO **511**
pos= method
  class Dir **453**
  class IO **511**
POSIX
  character classes 71
  error codes 110
POSIXLY_CORRECT 684
Post Office Protocol (POP) *see*
  Network protocols, POP
post method 699
post_match method
  class MatchData **538**
PP class 715
pp method
  module Kernel 715
ppid method
  module Process **586**
Pragmatic Programmer
  e-mail address xxvii

Pre-defined variables *see*
  Variables
pre_match method
  class MatchData **538**
Precedence
  do...end *vs* {} 168, 356
  of operators 339
Pretty printing 715, 716
pretty_print method 715
PrettyPrint class 526, 715,
  716
Print
  under Windows 268
print method
  class IO **511**
  module Kernel 335, **526**
printf method
  class IO **512**
  module Kernel 335, **526**
PRIO_PGRP (Process constant)
  583
PRIO_PROCESS (Process
  constant) 583
PRIO_USER (Process constant)
  583
priority method
  class Thread **637**
priority= method
  class Thread **638**
Private *see* Access control
private method 38
  class Module **558**
private_class_method
  method
  class Module 35, **551**
private_instance_methods
  method
  class Module **552**
private_method_defined?
  method
  class Module **552**
private_methods method
  class Object **573**
Proc class 56, 81, 357, 359,
  373, 544, 555, 580
  == **580**
  [ ] **580**
  arity **580**
  binding **581**
  call **581**
  new 524, **580**
  to_proc **582**
  to_s **582**
proc method

module Kernel 358, 360,
  527
  return from 360
  and safe level 399
Process 147–150
  block 150
  creating 147, 503, 506, 525,
    708
  exec 521
  ID (*see also* $$) 511
  priority 585, 587
  Ruby subprocess 149, 150,
    503, 506, 708
  setting name 335
  termination 150, 180, 517,
    522, 584, 587
  times 630
Process module 150, 583, 594
  abort **583**
  detach **583**
  egid **584**
  egid= **584**
  euid **584**
  euid= **584**
  exit **584**
  exit! **584**
  fork **584**
  getpgid **584**
  getpgrp **584**
  getpriority **585**
  gid **585**
  gid= **585**
  groups **585**, 586
  groups= **585**, 586
  initgroups **585**
  kill **585**
  maxgroups **586**
  maxgroups= **586**
  pid **586**
  ppid **586**
  setpgid **586**
  setpgrp **586**
  setpriority **587**
  setsid **587**
  times **587**, 630
  uid **587**
  uid= **587**
  wait 149, **587**
  wait2 **588**
  waitall **587**
  waitpid **588**
  waitpid2 **588**
Process::GID module 589,
  594

change_privilege **589**
eid **589**
eid= **589**
grant_privilege **589**
re_exchange **589**
re_exchangeable? **589**
rid **589**
sid_available? **589**
switch **590**
Process::Status class 150,
    587, 588, 591
& **591**
== **591**
>> **591**
coredump? **591**
exited? **592**
exitstatus **592**
pid **592**
signaled? **592**
stopped? **592**
stopsig **592**
success? **592**
termsig **593**
to_i **593**
to_int **593**
to_s **593**
Process::Sys module 594
getegid **594**
geteuid **594**
getgid **594**
getuid **594**
issetugid **594**
setegid **594**
seteuid **594**
setgid **594**
setregid **594**
setresgid **595**
setresuid **595**
setreuid **595**
setrgid **595**
setruid **595**
setuid **595**
Process::UID module 594,
    596
change_privilege **596**
eid **596**
eid= **596**
grant_privilege **596**
re_exchange **596**
re_exchangeable? **596**
rid **596**
sid_available? **596**
switch **596**
profile library 171, 717

Profiler 171
Profiler module 717
Profiler__ module 718
Program *see* Process
Protected *see* Access control
protected method 38
    class Module **559**
protected_instance_
        methods
        method
    class Module **552**
protected_method_defined?
        method
    class Module **552**
protected_methods method
    class Object **573**
Protocols 372
Pseudo terminal 720
PStore class 719
PTY module 720
Public *see* Access control
public method 38
    class Module **559**
public_class_method method
    class Module **553**
public_instance_methods
        method
    class Module **553**
public_method_defined?
        method
    class Module **553**
public_methods method
    class Object **574**
Publish/subscribe 706
push method
    class Array **437**
putc method
    class IO **512**
    module Kernel **527**
puts method
    class IO **512**
    module Kernel **527**
pwd method
    class Dir **452**

Q
qdbm 666
Queue class 141, 145, 743
quo method
    class Bignum **442**
    class Fixnum **485**
    class Numeric **566**
quote method

class Regexp **601**
Quoting
    characters in regexp 70, 600
    URLs and HTML 236

R
-r (Ruby option) 751
-r *library* (Ruby option)
    179
Race condition 137
RADIX (Float constant) 487
Radix *see* to_s methods,
    Kernel.Integer,
    String#to_i
Rails, Web framework 253
raise method
    class Thread **638**
    module Kernel 112, 360,
    527
Rake 229
Rake (build tool) 216
rand method
    module Kernel **527**
Range 66
    as condition 68, 95, 100, 342
    as interval 68
    literal 66, 322
    as sequence 66
Range class 67, 322, 597
    == **598**
    === **598**
    begin **598**
    each **598**
    end **598**
    eql? **599**
    exclude_end? **599**
    first **599**
    include? **599**
    last **599**
    member? **599**
    new **598**
    step **599**
Rank, matrix 694
rassoc method
    class Array **437**
Rational class 692, 721
rb_apply 309
rb_ary_entry 314
rb_ary_new 313
rb_ary_new2 313
rb_ary_new3 313
rb_ary_new4 313
rb_ary_pop 313
rb_ary_push 313

rb_ary_shift 313
rb_ary_store 313
rb_ary_unshift 314
rb_block_given_p 311
rb_bug 310
rb_call_super 309
rb_catch 311
rb_create_new_instance
    309
rb_cv_get 312
rb_cv_set 312
rb_cvar_defined 312
rb_cvar_get 312
rb_cvar_set 312
rb_define_alias 307
rb_define_alloc_func 307
rb_define_attr 309
rb_define_class 305
rb_define_class_under 305
rb_define_class_variable
    308
rb_define_const 308
rb_define_global_const
    308
rb_define_global_function
    307
rb_define_hooked_variable
    308
rb_define_method 307
rb_define_module 305
rb_define_module_function
    307
rb_define_module_under
    306
rb_define_readonly_
    variable
    308
rb_define_singleton_
    method
    307
rb_define_variable 308
rb_define_virtual_
    variable
    308
rb_each 311
rb_ensure 310
rb_exit 310
rb_extend_object 306
rb_fatal 310
rb_funcall 309
rb_funcall2 309
rb_funcall3 309
rb_global_variable 309
rb_gv_get 312

rb_gv_set 312
rb_hash_aref 314
rb_hash_aset 314
rb_hash_new 314
rb_id2name 309
rb_include_module 306
rb_intern 309
rb_iter_break 311
rb_iterate 311
rb_iv_get 311
rb_iv_set 312
rb_ivar_get 312
rb_ivar_set 312
rb_load_file 304
rb_notimplement 310
rb_obj_is_instance_of 314
rb_obj_is_kind_of 314
rb_protect 310
rb_raise 310
rb_require 306
rb_rescue 310
rb_respond_to 314
rb_safe_level 313
rb_scan_args 307
rb_secure 313
rb_set_safe_level 313
rb_str_cat 314
rb_str_concat 314
rb_str_dup 314
rb_str_new 314
rb_str_new2 314
rb_str_split 314
rb_struct_aref 306
rb_struct_aset 306
rb_struct_define 306
rb_struct_new 306
rb_sys_fail 310
rb_thread_create 314
rb_throw 311
rb_undef_method 307
rb_warn 311
rb_warning 311
rb_yield 311
rbconfig.rb 183
rbconfig.rb *see* Config
    module
rdev method
    class File::Stat **480**
rdev_major method
    class File::Stat **480**
rdev_minor method
    class File::Stat **480**
RDoc 8, 199–212
    C extensions 207

:call-seq: 206, 209
comment format 199–205
:doc: 206
Document-class: 209
Document-method: 209
documentation modifiers
    205
embedding in Ruby 199
:enddoc: 207
heading 205
hyperlink 204
:include: 206
lists 204
:main: 207
:nodoc: 206
:notnew: 206
including README 211
generate ri documentation
    212
for RubyGems 219
rules 205
running 211
:startdoc: 207
:stopdoc: 207
templates 240
:title: 207
yield parameters 205
:yields: 206
RDoc::usage method 213
RDoc::usage_no_exit method
    213
rdtool 318
re_exchange method
    module Process::GID **589**
    module Process::UID **596**
re_exchangeable? method
    module Process::GID **589**
    module Process::UID **596**
read method
    class Dir **453**
    class IO **506**, **512**
readable? method
    class File::Stat **480**
    class File **471**
readable_real? method
    class File::Stat **481**
    class File **471**
readbytes library 722
readbytes method
    class IO 722
readchar method
    class IO **512**
Readline module 723
readline library 163, 187, 193

readline method
　　class IO **512**
　　module Kernel 335, **527**
readlines method
　　class IO **506**, **513**
　　module Kernel **528**
readlink method
　　class File **471**
README 211
ready? method
　　class IO 687
REALLOC_N 294
Really Simple Syndication 728
Receiver 13, 81, 349, 379
Record separator *see* $/
recv method
　　class BasicSocket **765**
recvfrom method
　　class IPSocket **770**
　　class Socket **769**
　　class UDPSocket **775**
　　class UNIXSocket **776**
redo 104, 345
Reference
　　to object 39
　　weak 753
Reflection 403–414
　　callbacks 411
Regexp class 76, 600
　　== **601**
　　=== **601**
　　=~ **601**
　　~ **601**
　　casefold? **602**
　　compile **600**
　　escape **600**
　　inspect **602**
　　kcode **602**
　　last_match **600**
　　match 69, 77, **602**
　　new **600**
　　options **602**
　　quote **601**
　　source **602**
　　to_s **603**
Regular expression 68–77,
　　324–328
　　alternation 73
　　anchor 70
　　character class 71
　　as condition 342
　　extensions 326
　　greedy 73
　　grouping 73

literal 68, 324
　　nested 327
object-oriented 76
options 324, 327, 600
pattern match variables 334
quoting within 70
repetition 72
substitution 74, 614
rehash method
　　class Hash 323, **498**
reject method
　　class Hash **498**
　　module Enumerable 437,
　　457
reject! method
　　class Array **437**
　　class Hash **498**
remainder method
　　class Bignum **443**
　　class Numeric **566**
Remote Procedure Call *see*
　　Distributed Ruby, SOAP,
　　XMLRPC
remove_class_variable
　　method
　　class Module **559**
remove_const method
　　class Module **559**
remove_instance_variable
　　method
　　class Object **576**
remove_method method
　　class Module **559**
rename method
　　class File **472**
reopen method
　　class IO 373, **513**
replace method
　　class Array **437**
　　class Hash 373, **498**
　　class String **616**
require method 119, 124
　　loading extensions 278
　　module Kernel 182, 335,
　　528, 547
require_gem 220
rescue 108, 361, 460
Reserved words 329
resolv library 724
resolv-replace library 724
respond_to? method
　　class Object 405, **574**
restore method
　　module Marshal **536**

retry
　　in exceptions 112, 113, 362
　　in loops 105, 345
return
　　from block 359
　　from lambda/proc 360
　　from Proc 359
　　see also Method, return
　　value
reverse method
　　class Array **437**
　　class String **616**
reverse! method
　　class Array **437**
　　class String **616**
reverse_each method
　　class Array **438**
rewind method
　　class Dir **453**
　　class IO **513**
REXML module 725
RFC 2045 (base 64) 656
RFC 2396 (URI) 752
RFC 2616 (HTTP) 745
RFC 2882 (e-mail) 745
.rhtml (eruby) 243
RI 9, 214
ri 8, 199–212
　　add to irb 191
　　directories 212
　　sample output 203
　　see also RDoc
Rich Site Summary 728
rid method
　　module Process::GID **589**
　　module Process::UID **596**
Rinda module 727
rinda *see* Distributed Ruby
rindex method
　　class Array **438**
　　class String **616**
RIPEMD-160 hash 668
rjust method
　　class String **617**
rmdir method
　　class Dir **452**
RMI *see* Distributed Ruby
Roll, log files 690
Roman numerals 151
　　example 372
round method
　　class Float **489**
　　class Integer **501**
　　class Numeric **566**

ROUNDS (Float constant) 487
RPM installation 3
RSS module 728
RSTRING macro 280
rstrip method
   class String **617**
rstrip! method
   class String **617**
rtags 196
Ruby
   debugger 163
   distributed 417–418
   download 784
   embed in application 301
   installing 3, 298
   language reference 317–363
   and Perl 24, 76, 100
   versions xxv
   Web sites xxvii, 783
   ports to Windows 267
ruby (mkmf) 780
Ruby Documentation Project 9,
   784
Ruby mode (emacs) 165
Ruby On Rails 253
Ruby Production Archive (RPA)
   784
ruby-doc.org 9
ruby-mode.el 165
ruby.exe and rubyw.exe 268
ruby_finalize 304
ruby_init 304
ruby_init_loadpath 304
ruby_options 304
ruby_run 304
ruby_script 304
RUBY_TCL_DLL 182
RUBY_TK_DLL 182
RUBY_PLATFORM constant 337
RUBY_PLATFORM variable 228
RUBY_RELEASE_DATE constant
   337
RUBY_VERSION constant 337
RubyForge 229, 784
RubyGarden 784
RubyGems 215–233
   creating 223
   documentation 219
   extensions 227
   gem_server 220
   gemspec 224–226
   installing applications 216
   installing library 218
   installing RubyGems 216

   package layout 223
   repository 784
   require_gem 220
   stub 222
   test on install 217
   versioning 217, 218f, 221
RUBYLIB 182, 183, 401
RUBYLIB_PREFIX 182
RUBYOPT 182, 401
RUBYPATH 179, 182
RUBYSHELL 182, 521
Rule, RDoc 205
run method
   class Thread **638**
Runtime Type Information
   (RTTI) *see* Reflection
Rvalue 90, 338

S

−S (Ruby option) 179
−s (Ruby option) 179
$SAFE variable 179, 313, 336,
   398, 575, 673
Safe level 397–400
   in extensions 312
   list of constraints 401f
   and proc 399
   setting using −T 179
   and tainting 399
safe_level method
   class Thread **639**
SafeStringValue 313
SafeStringValue method 281
Sandbox 398, 399, *see* Safe
   level
   chroot 450
scan method
   class String 64, 65, 326,
   617, 737
   module Kernel **528**
scanf library 729
scanf method
   class Array 729
   class String 729
   module Kernel 729
Scheduler, thread 140
Schneiker, Conrad 83n
Schwartz, Randal 458
Schwartzian transform 458
Scope of variables 105, 330
Screen output *see* Curses
SCRIPT_LINES__ constant 337,
   414, 528

SDBM class 730
sdbm 730
Search path 183, 298
sec method
   class Time **647**
seek method
   class Dir **453**
   class IO **513**
Seki, Masatoshi 417
select method
   class Hash **499**
   class IO 373, **507**
   class MatchData **538**
   module Enumerable **457**
   module Kernel **528**
self variable 81, 122, 337,
   349, 379
   in class definition 387
Semaphore *see* Thread,
   synchronization
Send message 12, 28
send method
   class BasicSocket **765**
   class Object **574**
   class UDPSocket **775**
Sequence *see* Range
Serialization *see* Marshal
Server 685
Session *see* CGI programming,
   session
Session module 720
Session leader 587
Session, HTTP 246
Set class 428, 430, 731
Set operations *see* Array class
set_backtrace method
   class Exception **462**
set_trace_func method
   module Kernel 412, 444,
   529, 749
setegid method
   module Process::Sys **594**
seteuid method
   module Process::Sys **594**
setgid, setuid 398
setgid method
   module Process::Sys **594**
setgid? method
   class File::Stat **481**
   class File **472**
setpgid method
   module Process **586**
setpgrp method
   module Process **586**

setpriority method
    module Process **587**
setregid method
    module Process::Sys **594**
setresgid method
    module Process::Sys **595**
setresuid method
    module Process::Sys **595**
setreuid method
    module Process::Sys **595**
setrgid method
    module Process::Sys **595**
setruid method
    module Process::Sys **595**
setsid method
    module Process **587**
setsockopt method
    class BasicSocket **765**
Setter method *see* Method,
    setter
setuid method
    module Process::Sys **595**
setuid? method
    class File::Stat **481**
    class File **472**
setup method 158
SHA1/2 hash 668
Shallow copy 568
Shared library, accessing 669
Shebang (#!) 7
SHELL 182
Shell glob *see* File, expanding
    names
Shellwords module 732
shift method
    class Array **438**
    class Hash **499**
shutdown method
    class BasicSocket **765**
sid_available? method
    module Process::GID **589**
    module Process::UID **596**
SIGALRM 529
SIGCLD 150
Signal
    handling 150
    sending 585
    see also trap method
Signal module 534, 604
    list **604**
    trap **605**
signaled? method
    class Process::Status **592**

Simple Mail Transfer Protocol
    see Network protocols,
    SMTP
Simple Object Access protocol
    see SOAP
SimpleDelegator class 667
sin method
    module Math **541**
Sinatra, Frank 27
Single inheritance 30
Single-quoted string 61, 320
SingleForwardable module
    680
Singleton module 733
Singleton class 382
Singleton pattern 35, 733
singleton_method_added
    method
    class Object **576**
    module Kernel 411
singleton_method_removed
    method
    class Object **577**
    module Kernel 411
singleton_method_
    undefined
    method
    class Object **577**
singleton_method_
    undefineded
    method
    module Kernel 411
singleton_methods method
    class Object **574**
sinh method
    module Math **542**
site_ruby directory 183
size method
    class Array **438**
    class Bignum **443**
    class File::Stat **481**
    class File **472**
    class Fixnum **486**
    class Hash **499**
    class MatchData **538**
    class String **618**
    class Struct **629**
size? method
    class File::Stat **481**
    class File **472**
SizedQueue class 743
SJIS 317, 324, 689
sleep method
    module Kernel **529**

slice method
    class Array **438**
    class String **618**
slice! method
    class Array **439**
    class String **618**
Smalltalk 12n, 382
SMTP *see* Network protocols,
    SMTP
SOAP 249, 418, 734
SOAP module 734
Socket *see* Network protocols
Socket class 735, 766
    accept **769**
    bind **769**
    connect **769**
    getaddrinfo **767**
    gethostbyaddr **767**
    gethostbyname **767**
    gethostname **767**
    getnameinfo **768**
    getservbyname **768**
    listen **769**
    new **768**
    open **768**
    pack_sockaddr_in **768**
    pack_sockaddr_un **768**
    pair **768**
    recvfrom **769**
    socketpair **768**
    sysaccept **769**
    unpack_sockaddr_in **769**
    unpack_sockaddr_un **769**
socket? method
    class File::Stat **481**
    class File **473**
socketpair method
    class Socket **768**
SOCKS *see* Network protocols
SOCKSSocket class 735, 772
    close **772**
    new **772**
    open **772**
Sort
    topological 750
sort method
    class Array **439**
    class Hash **499**
    module Enumerable **457**
    Schwartzian transform 458
sort! method
    class Array **439**
sort_by method
    module Enumerable **457**

Source code
  layout 317
  reflecting on 413
Source code from book 5
source method
  class Regexp **602**
Spaceship *see* <=>
Spawn *see* Process, creating
spawn method 720
split method
  class File **473**
  class String 63, **619**
  module Kernel 178, **529**
sprintf method
  field types 532
  flag characters 531
  module Kernel **529**
sqrt method
  module Math **542**
squeeze method
  class String 64, **619**, 689
squeeze! method
  class String **620**, 689
srand method
  module Kernel **530**
srcdir (mkmf) 780
Stack
  execution *see* caller
    method
  operations *see* Array class
  unwinding 110, 114, 361
Stack frame 163
Standard Library 653–759
start method
  class Thread **635**
  module GC **491**
:startdoc: (RDoc) 207
stat method
  class File **473**
  class IO **513**
Statement modifier
  if/unless 97, 343
  while/until 100, 345
Static linking 301
Static method *see* Class, method
Static typing *see* Duck typing
status method 707
  class Exception **462**
  class Thread **639**
STDERR constant 337, 534
$stderr variable 335
STDIN constant 337, 525
$stdin variable 335
STDOUT constant 337, 525, 526

$stdout variable 335
step method
  class Numeric 102, **566**
  class Range **599**
Stephenson, Neal 177n
sticky? method
  class File::Stat **481**
  class File **473**
stiff, why the lucky 654
stop method
  class Thread **635**
stop? method
  class Thread **639**
:stopdoc: (RDoc) 207
stopped? method
  class Process::Status **592**
stopsig method
  class Process::Status **592**
store method
  class Hash **499**
strftime method
  class Time **647**
String 61
  #{...} 61
  %... delimiters 318
  control characters \n etc.
    321
  conversion for output 131,
    526
  expression interpolation 15
  here document 62, 321
  literal 14, 61, 320
    concatenation 321
String class 61, 320, 374, 606,
  689, 729
  % **606**
  * **607**
  + **607**
  <=> **607**
  << **607**
  == **607**
  === **607**
  =~ **608**
  [ ] **608**
  [ ]= **609**
  ~ **609**
  capitalize **609**
  capitalize! **609**
  casecmp **610**
  center **610**
  chomp 63, **610**
  chomp! **610**
  chop **610**, 689
  chop! **611**, 689

concat **611**
count **611**
crypt **611**
delete **611**, 689
delete! **612**, 689
downcase **612**
downcase! **612**
dump **612**
each **612**
each_byte **613**
each_line **613**
empty? **613**
eql? **613**
gsub 74, 326, **613**
gsub! 326, **614**
hex **614**
include? **614**
index 326, **614**
insert **615**
intern **615**
length **615**
ljust **615**
lstrip **615**
lstrip! **615**
match **616**
new **606**
next **616**
next! **616**
oct **616**
replace **616**
reverse **616**
reverse! **616**
rindex **616**
rjust **617**
rstrip **617**
rstrip! **617**
scan 64, 65, 326, **617**, 737
scanf 729
size **618**
slice **618**
slice! **618**
split 63, **619**
squeeze 64, **619**, 689
squeeze! **620**, 689
strip **620**
strip! **620**
sub 74, **620**
sub! **620**
succ **620**, 689
succ! **621**, 689
sum **621**
swapcase **621**
swapcase! **621**
to_f **621**

to_i **622**
to_s **622**
to_str **622**
to_sym **622**
tr **622**, 689
tr! **623**, 689
tr_s **623**, 689
tr_s! **623**, 689
unpack **623**
upcase **623**
upcase! **625**
upto **625**
String method
    module Kernel **516**
string method
    class MatchData **539**
StringIO class 132, 736
StringScanner class 737
StringValue method 280
StringValuePtr method 281
strip method
    class String **620**
strip! method
    class String **620**
Struct class 626
    == **627**
    [ ] **627, 628**
    [ ]= **628**
    each **628**
    each_pair **628**
    length **629**
    members **627, 629**
    new **626, 627**
    OpenStruct 710
    size **629**
    to_a **629**
    values **629**
    values_at **629**
struct sockaddr 764
Struct::Tms class 630
Stub
    RubyGems 222
    WIN32OLE 272
sub method
    class String 74, **620**
    module Kernel **530**
sub! method
    class String **620**
    module Kernel **530**
Subclass 27
Subnet, testing address in 688
Subprocess *see* Process
Subroutine *see* Method

Substitution *see* Regular
    expression
succ method
    class Integer **502**
    class String **620**, 689
    for generating sequences 67
succ! method
    class String **621**, 689
success? method
    class Exception **463**
    class Process::Status **592**
Suites, test 160
Suketa, Masaki 269
sum method
    class String **621**
super 29, 350, 575
Superclass 27, 379, 405
    see also Module, mixin
superclass method
    class Class 405, **446**
swapcase method
    class String **621**
swapcase! method
    class String **621**
SWIG 301
switch method
    module Process::GID **590**
    module Process::UID **596**
Symbol
    literal 323
Symbol class 31, 338, 374, 615, 631
    all_symbols **631**
    id2name **631**
    inspect **632**
    to_i **632**
    to_int **632**
    to_s **632**
    to_sym **632**
symlink method
    class File **473**
symlink? method
    class File::Stat **482**
    class File **473**
Sync class 738
Sync module 141
sync method
    class IO **514**
sync= method
    class IO **514**
SyncEnumerator class 683
Synchronization *see* Thread,
    synchronization
sysaccept method

class Socket **769**
syscall.h 530
syscall method
    module Kernel **530**
Syslog class 740
sysopen method
    class IO **507**
sysread method
    class IO **514**
sysseek method
    class IO **514**
system method
    module Kernel 148, **530**
syswrite method
    class IO **514**

T

-T[*level*] (Ruby option) 179
Tab completion
    irb 187
Tag file 196
taint method
    class Object **575**
Tainted objects 281, 399, 575
    see also Safe level
tainted? method
    class Object **575**
Talbott, Nathaniel 151, 161
tan method
    module Math **542**
tanh method
    module Math **542**
Tcl/Tk *see* GUI programming
TCP *see* Network protocols
TCPServer class 773
    accept **773**
    new **773**
    open **773**
TCPSocket class 735, 771
    gethostbyname **771**
    new **771**
    open **771**
teardown method 158
Technical support 783
tell method
    class Dir **453**
    class IO **515**
Telnet *see* Network protocols,
    telnet
Tempfile class 741
Templates 239–244
    Amrita 241
    BlueCloth 218

eruby 242, 673
    RDoc 240
Temporary directory 748
Temporary file 741
Terminal
    pseudo 720
terminate method
    class Thread 639
termsig method
    class Process::Status 593
Ternary operator 97, 343
Test case 156
Test suites 160
test method
    module Kernel 531
Test::Unit 152–161
    exceptions 155
    assertions 152, 162f
    cases 156
    naming conventions 161
    setup 158
    suites 160
    teardown 158
    see also Testing
Test::Unit class 742
Testing 151–161
    ad hoc 151
    assertions 152
    exceptions 155
    gem 217
    Roman numerals 151
    using StringIO 736
    structuring tests 156
    what is a unit test? 152
    where to put files 159
$' variable 69, 334, 538
then 343
Thread 135–147
    condition variable 145
    creating 135
    exception 138
    group 640
    queue 743
    race condition 137
    scheduling 140
    synchronization 141–147,
        695–697, 738, 743
    variable 137
    variable scope 136
    waiting for multiple 744
Thread class 633
    [ ] 635
    [ ]= 636

abort_on_exception 138,
    633, 636
abort_on_exception= 633,
    636
alive? 636
critical 633
critical= 141, 633
current 634
exit 634, 636
fork 634
group 636
join 137, 636
key? 637
keys 637
kill 634, 637
list 634
main 634
new 136, 634
pass 635
priority 637
priority= 638
Queue 743
raise 638
run 638
safe_level 639
SizedQueue 743
start 635
status 639
stop 635
stop? 639
terminate 639
value 137, 639
wakeup 639
thread library 141, 145
ThreadGroup class 636, 640
    add 640
    enclose 640
    enclosed? 641
    freeze 641
    list 641
    new 640
ThreadsWait class 744
throw method
    module Kernel 114, 362,
        531
Time class 465, 642, 745
    + 644
    - 644
    <=> 644
    asctime 644
    at 642
    ctime 644
    day 644
    dst? 644

extensions to 745
getgm 645
getlocal 645
getutc 645
gm 642
gmt? 645
gmt_offset 645
gmtime 645
gmtoff 646
hour 646
isdst 646
local 643
localtime 646
mday 646
min 646
mktime 643
mon 646
month 646
new 643
now 643
sec 647
strftime 647
times 643
to_a 647
to_f 647
to_i 647
to_s 647
tv_sec 648
tv_usec 648
usec 648
utc 643, 649
utc? 649
utc_offset 649
wday 649
yday 649
year 649
zone 649
time library 745
Timeout module 746
times method
    class Integer 102, 502
    class Time 643
    module Process 587, 630
:title: (RDoc) 207
Tk see GUI programming
Tk class 747
tmpdir library 741, 748
tmpdir method
    class Dir 246, 748
to_a method
    class Array 439
    class Hash 499
    class MatchData 539
    class NilClass 561

class Object **575**
class Struct **629**
class Time **647**
module Enumerable **459**
to_ary method 340, 373, 429, 439
class Array **439**
to_enum method 672
to_f method
class Bignum **443**
class Fixnum **486**
class Float **489**
class NilClass **561**
class String **621**
class Time **647**
to_hash method 373, 493
class Hash **499**
to_i method
class Float **489**
class Integer **502**
class IO **515**
class NilClass **561**
class Process::Status **593**
class String **622**
class Symbol **632**
class Time **647**
to_int method 372, 373
class Float **489**
class Integer **502**
class Numeric **566**
class Process::Status **593**
class Symbol **632**
to_io method 373
class IO **515**
to_proc method 373
class Method **544**
class Proc **582**
to_s method 372
class Array **440**
class Bignum **443**
class Exception **463**
class Fixnum **486**
class Float **490**
class Hash **499**
class MatchData **539**
class NilClass **561**
class Object 26, **575**
class Process::Status **593**
class Proc **582**
class Regexp **603**
class String **622**
class Symbol **632**
class Time **647**
and print 131, 526

to_str method 372, 374, 606
class Exception **463**
class Object 280
class String **622**
to_sym method 374
class Fixnum **486**
class String **622**
class Symbol **632**
to_yaml_properties method 416
Top-level environment 393
TOPLEVEL_BINDING constant 337
Topological sort 750
tr method
class String **622**, 689
tr! method
class String **623**, 689
tr_s method
class String **623**, 689
tr_s! method
class String **623**, 689
trace_var method
module Kernel **532**
tracer library 749
Tracing 412, *see* Logger
Transactions 53
Transcendental functions 540
Transparent language 53, 59
transpose method
class Array **440**
trap method
module Kernel 150, **534**
module Signal **605**
Trigonometric functions 540
Troubleshooting 167
TRUE constant 337
true constant 93, 337, 341
TrueClass class 650
& **650**
^ **650**
| **650**
truncate method
class File **473**, **476**
class Float **490**
class Integer **502**
class Numeric **566**
TSort module 750
tsort_each_child method 750
tsort_each_node method 750
tty? method
class IO **515**
Tuning *see* Performance

Tuplespace *see* Distributed Ruby, Rinda
tv_sec method
class Time **648**
tv_usec method
class Time **648**
type method
class Object 370, **575**
Types *see* Duck typing
Typographic conventions xxix

U

UDP *see* Network protocols
UDPSocket class 735, 774
bind **774**
connect **774**
new **774**
open **774**
recvfrom **775**
send **775**
uid method
class File::Stat **482**
module Process **587**
uid= method
module Process **587**
umask method
class File **474**
un library 751
Unary minus, unary plus 562
unbind method
class Method **544**
UnboundMethod class 408, 543, 544, 549, 651
arity **652**
bind **652**
undef_method method
class Module **559**
undefine_finalizer method
module ObjectSpace **579**
ungetc method
class IO **515**
Unicode 317
Uniform Access Principle 32
uniq method
class Array **440**
uniq! method
class Array **440**
Unit test *see* Testing
UNIXServer class 777
accept **777**
new **777**
open **777**
UNIXSocket class 735, 776

addr **776**
new **776**
open **776**
path **776**
peeraddr **776**
recvfrom **776**
unless　*see* if expression
unlink method
　class Dir **452**
　class File **474**
unpack method
　class String **623**
unpack_sockaddr_in method
　class Socket **769**
unpack_sockaddr_un method
　class Socket **769**
unshift method
　class Array **440**
untaint method
　class Object **575**
until　*see* while loop
untrace_var method
　module Kernel **534**
upcase method
　class String **623**
upcase! method
　class String **625**
update
　Observable callback **706**
update method
　class Hash **500**
upto method
　class Integer 102, **502**
　class String **625**
URI class **752**
URI, opening as file **707**
Usage, message **213**
usec method
　class Time **648**
Usenet **784**
UTC **642**
utc method
　class Time **643**, **649**
utc? method
　class Time **649**
utc_offset method
　class Time **649**
UTF **317**
UTF8 **324, 689**
utime method
　class File **474**

V

-v (Ruby option) **535**

-v, --verbose (Ruby option) **179, 336**
$-v variable **336**
VALUE (C extension) **278**
value method
　class Thread 137, **639**
value? method
　class Hash **500**
values method
　class Hash **500**
　class Struct **629**
values_at method
　class Array **440**
　class Hash **500**
　class MatchData **539**
　class Struct **629**
Variable
　class **33**
　in extension **308, 311**
　instance 12, 26, 122, **406**
　vs. method name **329**
　naming 16, **328**
　predefined **333**
　as reference 39, **330**
　scope 105, 124, 136, **330**
　thread **137**
　weak reference **753**
Variable-length argument list **80**
Variables
　$! 108, 334, 360, 362
　$" 124, 335
　$$ 335
　$& 69, 334, 537
　$* 335, 523
　$+ 334
　$, 334, 436, 526
　$-0 334
　$-F 335
　$-I 336
　$-K 336
　$-a 335
　$-d 336
　$-i 336
　$-l 336
　$-p 336
　$-v 336
　$-w 336
　$. 334, 510
　$/ 178, 179, 334, 610
　$0 180, 335, 337
　$1 to $9 334
　$1...$9 69, 74, 326
　$: 124, 160, 178, 183, 304,
　　335

　$; 178, 334
　$< 335
　$= 324, 334
　$> 335
　$? 89, 148, 150, 335, 338,
　　516, 531, 587, 591
　$@ 334
　$DEBUG 178, 336, 633, 637
　$F 178, 336
　$FILENAME 336
　$KCODE 324, 659, 689
　$LOAD_PATH 160, 178, 186,
　　221–223, 225, 228, 336
　$SAFE 179, 313, 336, 398,
　　575, 673
　$VERBOSE 178, 179, 336,
　　534
　$\ 179, 334, 511, 526
　$_ 24, 95, 101, 178, 335,
　　342, 510, 523
　$` 69, 334, 538
　$configure_args 779
　$deferr 335
　$defout 335
　$expect_verbose 676
　$stderr 335
　$stdin 335
　$stdout 335
　$' 69, 334, 538
　$~ 69, 77, 334, 537, 600–602
　@fileutils_output 678
　__FILE__ 413
　ARGF 24, 336
　ARGV 178–180, 336, 523,
　　684, 711
　ENV 181, 336
　environment *see*
　　Environment variables
　__FILE__ 336
　__LINE__ 336
　predefined 333
　　English names 333,
　　671
　RUBY_PLATFORM 228
　self 81, 122, 337, 349, 379
Vector class **694**
$VERBOSE variable 178, 179,
　336, 534
--version (Ruby option) **179**
Versions of Ruby **xxv**
vi and vim **165**
　tag file **196**
vi key binding **723**
Virtual

class 381
Virtual attribute 32

W

-w (Ruby option) 179, 336, 535
-W *level* (Ruby option) 179, 534
$-w variable 336
wait method
  class IO 687
  module Process 149, **587**
wait2 method
  module Process **588**
waitall method
  module Process **587**
waitpid method
  module Process **588**
waitpid2 method
  module Process **588**
wakeup method
  class Thread **639**
Walk directory tree 679
warn method
  module Kernel 179, 336, **534**
Warnings 179
  ARGV[0] is not $0 180
  be careful with tainted data 397
  C functions must return VALUE 277
  strings aren't numbers 60, 169
wday method
  class Time **649**
Weak reference 753
WeakRef class 753
  weakref_alive? 753
weakref_alive? method
  class WeakRef 753
Web *see* CGI programming
Web framework
  CGIKit 253
  Iowa 239
  Rails 253

Web server
  trivial 773
  WEBrick 247, 754
  see also Apache
Web services 249
  description language 252
  Google 251
Web sites for Ruby xxvii, 783
Webcoder, Walter 397
WEBrick 247
WEBrick module 754
Weirich, Jim 216
when (in case) 343
while loop 100, 344
  as modifier 100, 345
why the lucky stiff 654
Widget *see* GUI programming
Wildcard *see* fnmatch and glob
Win32API class 669, 755
Win32API library 268
WIN32OLE class 756
WIN32OLE library 269
Windows *see* Microsoft Windows, GUI programming
with-cflags (mkmf) 780
with-cppflags (mkmf) 780
with-ldflags (mkmf) 780
with-make-prog (mkmf) 780
WNOHANG (Process constant) 583
Words
  array of 16, 322
Working directory 178, 450
Wrap *see* Module, wrap
writable? method
  class File::Stat **482**
  class File **474**
writable_real? method
  class File::Stat **482**
  class File **474**
write method
  class IO **515**
WSDL 252, 734

Google interface 252
WUNTRACED (Process constant) 583
Wyss, Clemens 398

X

/x regexp option 324
-x [*directory*] (Ruby option) 180
-X *directory* (Ruby option) 180
XML 725, 757
XMLRPC module 757
xmp 197

Y

-y, --yydebug (Ruby option) 180
YAML library 416, 535, 654, 758
yday method
  class Time **649**
year method
  class Time **649**
yield 50, 357
  arguments 21, 51
  and RDoc 205
:yields: (RDoc) 206
Yukihiro, Matsumoto 382

Z

zero? method
  class File::Stat **482**
  class File **474**
  class Fixnum **486**
  class Float **490**
  class Numeric **566**
Zip compression 759
zip method
  module Enumerable **459**
Zlib module 759
zone method
  class Time **649**

Template characters for `Array#pack`

Directive	Meaning
@	Moves to absolute position
A	ASCII string (space padded, count is width)
a	ASCII string (null padded, count is width)
B	Bit string (descending bit order)
b	Bit string (ascending bit order)
C	Unsigned char
c	Char
D, d	Double-precision float, native format
E	Double-precision float, little-endian byte order
e	Single-precision float, little-endian byte order
F, f	Single-precision float, native format
G	Double-precision float, network (big-endian) byte order
g	Single-precision float, network (big-endian) byte order
H	Hex string (high nibble first)
h	Hex string (low nibble first)
I	Unsigned integer
i	Integer
L	Unsigned long
l	Long
M	Quoted printable, MIME encoding (see RFC2045)
m	Base64 encoded string
N	Long, network (big-endian) byte order
n	Short, network (big-endian) byte order
P	Pointer to a structure (fixed-length string)
p	Pointer to a null-terminated string
Q, q	64-bit number
S	Unsigned short
s	Short
U	UTF-8
u	UU-encoded string
V	Long, little-endian byte order
v	Short, little-endian byte order
w	BER-compressed integer[1]
X	Back up a byte
x	Null byte
Z	Same as A

1.8 (Q, q)

1.8 (w)

[1] The octets of a BER-compressed integer represent an unsigned integer in base 128, most significant digit first, with as few digits as possible. Bit eight (the high bit) is set on each byte except the last (*Self-Describing Binary Data Representation*, MacLeod)

Template characters for `String#unpack`

Format	Function	Returns
A	String with trailing NULs and spaces removed.	String
a	String.	String
B	Extract bits from each character (MSB first).	String
b	Extract bits from each character (LSB first).	String
C	Extract a character as an unsigned integer.	Fixnum
c	Extract a character as an integer.	Fixnum
d,D	Treat *sizeof(double)* characters as a native double.	Float
E	Treat *sizeof(double)* characters as a double in little-endian byte order.	Float
e	Treat *sizeof(float)* characters as a float in little-endian byte order.	Float
f,F	Treat *sizeof(float)* characters as a native float.	Float
G	Treat *sizeof(double)* characters as a double in network byte order.	Float
g	Treat *sizeof(float)* characters as a float in network byte order.	Float
H	Extract hex nibbles from each character (most significant first).	String
h	Extract hex nibbles from each character (least significant first).	String
I	Treat *sizeof(int)*[1] successive characters as an unsigned native integer.	Integer
i	Treat *sizeof(int)*[1] successive characters as a signed native integer.	Integer
L	Treat four[1] successive characters as an unsigned native long integer.	Integer
l	Treat four[1] successive characters as a signed native long integer.	Integer
M	Extract a quoted-printable string.	String
m	Extract a Base64 encoded string.	String
N	Treat four characters as an unsigned long in network byte order.	Fixnum
n	Treat two characters as an unsigned short in network byte order.	Fixnum
P	Treat *sizeof(char *)* characters as a pointer, and return *len* characters from the referenced location.	String
p	Treat *sizeof(char *)* characters as a pointer to a null-terminated string.	String
Q	Treat eight characters as an unsigned quad word (64 bits).	Integer
q	Treat eight characters as a signed quad word (64 bits).	Integer
S	Treat two[1] successive characters as an unsigned short in native byte order.	Fixnum
s	Treat two[1] successive characters as a signed short in native byte order.	Fixnum
U	Extract UTF-8 characters as unsigned integers.	Integer
u	Extract a UU-encoded string.	String
V	Treat four characters as an unsigned long in little-endian byte order.	Fixnum
v	Treat two characters as an unsigned short in little-endian byte order.	Fixnum
w	BER-compressed integer (see `Array#pack` for more information).	Integer
X	Skip backward one character.	—
x	Skip forward one character.	—
Z	String with trailing NULs removed.	String
@	Skip to the offset given by the length argument.	—

[1] May be modified by appending "_" to the directive.

Character class abbreviations

Sequence	As [...]	Meaning
\d	[0-9]	Digit character
\D	[^0-9]	Any character except a digit
\s	[\s\t\r\n\f]	Whitespace character
\S	[^\s\t\r\n\f]	Any character except whitespace
\w	[A-Za-z0-9_]	Word character
\W	[^A-Za-z0-9_]	Any character except a word character

POSIX Character Classes

[:alnum:]	Alphanumeric
[:alpha:]	Uppercase or lowercase letter
[:blank:]	Blank and tab
[:cntrl:]	Control characters (at least 0x00–0x1f, 0x7f)
[:digit:]	Digit
[:graph:]	Printable character excluding space
[:lower:]	Lowercase letter
[:print:]	Any printable character (including space)
[:punct:]	Printable character excluding space and alphanumeric
[:space:]	Whitespace (same as \s)
[:upper:]	Uppercase letter
[:xdigit:]	Hex digit (0–9, a–f, A–F)

sprintf flag characters

Flag	Applies to	Meaning
␣ (space)	bdEefGgiouXx	Leave a space at the start of positive numbers.
digit$	all	Specify the absolute argument number for this field. Absolute and relative argument numbers cannot both be used in a sprintf string.
#	beEfgGoxX	Use an alternative format. For the conversions b, o, X, and x, prefix the result with b, 0, 0X, 0x, respectively. For E, e, f, G, and g, force a decimal point to be added, even if no digits follow. For G and g, do not remove trailing zeros.
+	bdEefGgiouXx	Add a leading plus sign to positive numbers.
–	all	Left-justify the result of this conversion.
0 (zero)	bdEefGgiouXx	Pad with zeros, not spaces.
*	all	Use the next argument as the field width. If negative, left-justify the result. If the asterisk is followed by a number and a dollar sign, use the indicated argument as the width.

`sprintf` field types

Field	Conversion
b	Convert argument as a binary number.
c	Argument is the numeric code for a single character.
d	Convert argument as a decimal number.
E	Equivalent to e, but uses an uppercase E to indicate the exponent.
e	Convert floating point-argument into exponential notation with one digit before the decimal point. The precision determines the number of fractional digits (defaulting to six).
f	Convert floating-point argument as [␣-]ddd.ddd, where the precision determines the number of digits after the decimal point.
G	Equivalent to g, but use an uppercase E in exponent form.
g	Convert a floating-point number using exponential form if the exponent is less than −4 or greater than or equal to the precision, or in d.dddd form otherwise.
i	Identical to d.
o	Convert argument as an octal number.
p	The value of *argument.inspect*.
s	Argument is a string to be substituted. If the format sequence contains a precision, at most that many characters will be copied.
u	Treat argument as an unsigned decimal number.
X	Convert argument as a hexadecimal number using uppercase letters. Negative numbers will be displayed with two leading periods (representing an infinite string of leading FFs).
x	Convert argument as a hexadecimal number. Negative numbers will be displayed with two leading periods (representing an infinite string of leading FFs.)

1.8

File tests with a single argument

Flag	Description	Returns
?A	Last access time for *file1*	Time
?b	True if *file1* is a block device	true or false
?c	True if *file1* is a character device	true or false
?C	Last change time for *file1*	Time
?d	True if *file1* exists and is a directory	true or false
?e	True if *file1* exists	true or false
?f	True if *file1* exists and is a regular file	true or false
?g	True if *file1* has the setgid bit set (false under NT)	true or false
?G	True if *file1* exists and has a group ownership equal to the caller's group	true or false
?k	True if *file1* exists and has the sticky bit set	true or false
?l	True if *file1* exists and is a symbolic link	true or false
?M	Last modification time for *file1*	Time
?o	True if *file1* exists and is owned by the caller's effective UID	true or false
?O	True if *file1* exists and is owned by the caller's real UID	true or false
?p	True if *file1* exists and is a fifo	true or false
?r	True if *file1* is readable by the effective UID/GID of the caller	true or false
?R	True if *file1* is readable by the real UID/GID of the caller	true or false
?s	If *file1* has nonzero size, return the size, otherwise return nil	Integer or nil
?S	True if *file1* exists and is a socket	true or false
?u	True if *file1* has the setuid bit set	true or false
?w	True if *file1* exists and is writable by the effective UID/ GID	true or false
?W	True if *file1* exists and is writable by the real UID/GID	true or false
?x	True if *file1* exists and is executable by the effective UID/GID	true or false
?X	True if *file1* exists and is executable by the real UID/GID	true or false
?z	True if *file1* exists and has a zero length	true or false

File tests with two arguments

Flag	Description
?-	True if *file1* is a hard link to *file2*
?=	True if the modification times of *file1* and *file2* are equal
?<	True if the modification time of *file1* is prior to that of *file2*
?>	True if the modification time of *file1* is after that of *file2*

Time#strftime directives

Format	Meaning
%a	The abbreviated weekday name ("Sun")
%A	The full weekday name ("Sunday")
%b	The abbreviated month name ("Jan")
%B	The full month name ("January")
%c	The preferred local date and time representation
%d	Day of the month (01..31)
%H	Hour of the day, 24-hour clock (00..23)
%I	Hour of the day, 12-hour clock (01..12)
%j	Day of the year (001..366)
%m	Month of the year (01..12)
%M	Minute of the hour (00..59)
%p	Meridian indicator ("AM" or "PM")
%S	Second of the minute (00..60)
%U	Week number of the current year, starting with the first Sunday as the first day of the first week (00..53)
%W	Week number of the current year, starting with the first Monday as the first day of the first week (00..53)
%w	Day of the week (Sunday is 0, 0..6)
%x	Preferred representation for the date alone, no time
%X	Preferred representation for the time alone, no date
%y	Year without a century (00..99)
%Y	Year with century
%Z	Time zone name
%%	Literal % character